PEARSON CUSTOM BUSINESS RESOURCES

Compiled by

Management Information Systems:

Managing the Digital Firm, 10/e

Kenneth C. Laudon & Jane P. Laudon

Prepared for

Keller Graduate School of Management

Pearson Custom Publishing

New York   Boston   San Francisco
London   Toronto   Sydney   Tokyo   Singapore   Madrid
Mexico City   Munich   Paris   Cape Town   Hong Kong   Montreal

Senior Vice President, Editorial and Marketing: Patrick F. Boles
Senior Sponsoring Editor: Robin J. Lazrus
Development Editor: Abbey Lee Briggs
Marketing Manager: Jack Cooney
Associate Editor: Ana Díaz-Caneja
Operations Manager: Eric M. Kenney
Database Product Manager: Jennifer Berry
Art Director: Renée Sartell
Cover Designer: Renée Sartell

Cover Art: Courtesy of EyeWire/Getty Images and PhotoDisc/Getty Images. Photodisc, "Globe surrounded by business people on computer monitors," courtesy of Photodisc/Getty Images. Dave Cutler (Artist), "Man Dropping Coins Into Glass Jar," courtesy of David Cutler/Images.com. Dave Cutler (Artist), "Three Coins in Glass Jar," courtesy of David Cutler/Images.com.

This special edition published in cooperation with Pearson Custom Publishing.

Printed in the United States of America.

Please visit our web site at *www.pearsoncustom.com.*

Attention bookstores: For permission to return any unsold stock, contact us at *pe-uscustomreturns@pearson.com.*

**Pearson
Custom Publishing**
is a division of

www.pearsonhighered.com

ISBN 10: 0558210422
ISBN 13: 9780558210427

Editorial Advisory Board

Contents

Information Systems in Global Business Today

Information Systems in Global Business Today

SMART SYSTEMS AND SMART WAYS OF WORKING HELP TOYOTA BECOME NUMBER ONE

Toyota Motor Corporation is about to surpass GM as the world's largest auto maker, selling over 9 million vehicles in 2006. It is also considered the world's best auto maker. The quality and reliability of Toyota vehicles are the gold standard of the industry, even among its lower-priced models. Customer loyalty is so high that Toyota can make sales without heavy discounting.

Toyota stands head and shoulders above fierce competition because it has been so skillful at combining quality with efficiency. One key to Toyota's success is its vaunted Toyota Production System, which is based on lean production—eliminating waste while optimizing value. Toyota has based its business processes and information systems on the principles of just-in-time delivery, quality, and continuous improvement.

By organizing its business processes and information systems around these principles, Toyota delivers value to the customer at a competitive price. As Ludo Vandervelden, vice president of Finance and Accounting, Information Systems, and Vehicle Logistics for Toyota Motor Europe points out, "you can achieve cost reductions and, at the same time, make your customers happy through implementation of smarter business processes."

Toyota Motor Europe and other Toyota divisions around the world use information systems to support these business processes. Vehicle production is based on actual customer orders rather than "best guesses" of what to stock in dealer showrooms, so the company only builds cars that customers want, when they want them, without additional delays or quality problems.

Toyota Motor Europe uses a vehicle orders management system based on Oracle E-Business Suite software to reduce the time it takes between placing a customer order and delivering the vehicle to the customer. The software integrates easily with the company's existing systems and also with those of Toyota's independent dealerships and national marketing and sales companies, which run their own separate information systems based on a variety of technologies.

This system encompasses several business processes. It starts with the customer selecting a car and various options, such as tinted windows or a navigation system. The dealer uses the system to configure a car with all of the selected options in front of the customer and then locates the best available car and options in the Toyota supply chain, including vehicles scheduled for production in the future. The dealer then uses the system to place the order through national distributors, who consolidate the order with those of their other retailers and place an order through Toyota Motors Europe. Toyota Motor Europe consolidates orders from the national distributors and places an order with Toyota's factories. Each car is then shipped and invoiced from the factory to headquarters to national distributors to retailers, triggering all related accounting processes at each step. National distributors can use the system to monitor their orders and those of different dealers and even "swap" cars with various retailers.

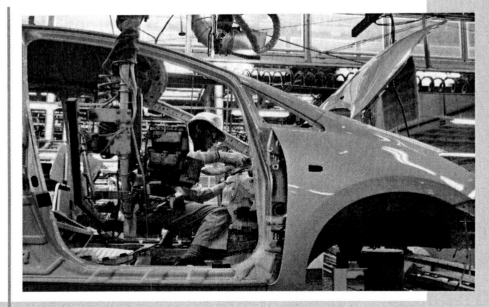

Photo courtesy of The Image Works

The vehicle order management system has helped Toyota reduce production time and the cost of maintaining materials and finished cars in inventory, while increasing customer service and satisfaction. According to Vandervelden, "with improved information transparency, we would be able to better readjust...our allocation of available product to markets that would be in high demand...and to reduce stock."

Sources: Katheryn Potterf, "Ready to Roll," *Profit Magazine,* May 26; Ian Rowley, "No Traffic Ahead for Toyota," *Business Week,* February 6, 2006; and "Triumphs & Trip-Ups in 2004," *Baseline Magazine,* December 20, 2004.

Toyota has flourished in a highly competitive environment because it has created a set of finely tuned business processes and information systems that simultaneously promote agility, efficiency, and quality. It can respond instantly to customers and changes in the marketplace as events unfold, while working closely with suppliers and retailers. The experience of Toyota and other companies described in this text will help you learn how to make your own business more competitive, efficient, and profitable.

The chapter-opening diagram highlights important points raised by this case and this chapter. As part of its ongoing effort to monitor quality, efficiency and costs, Toyota management saw there was an opportunity to use information systems to improve business performance. Technology alone would not have provided a solution. Toyota had to carefully revise its business processes to support a build-to-order production model that based vehicle production on actual customer orders rather than "best guesses" of customer demand. Once that was accomplished, Oracle E-Business software was useful for coordinating the flow of information among disparate internal production, ordering, and invoicing systems within the company and with systems of retailers and suppliers.

By helping Toyota build only the cars customers have ordered, its vehicle order management system reduces inventory costs, because the company and its dealers do not have to pay for making and storing vehicles customers did not want. The system also increases customer satisfaction by making it easier for customers to buy exactly the model, make, and option they desire. Information provided by the system helps management monitor trends and forecast demand and production requirements more accurately.

HEADS UP

This chapter introduces you to the roles that information systems and technologies play in business firms. All firms today, large and small, local and global, use information systems to achieve important business objectives, such as operational efficiency, customer and supplier intimacy, better decision making, and new products and services. You will need to know how to use information systems and technologies to help your firm solve problems and overcome challenges.

- If your career is in finance or accounting, you will need information systems to summarize transactions, organize data, and perform financial analysis.
- If your career is in human resources or management, you will need information systems to communicate with employees, maintain employee records, and coordinate work activities.
- If your career is in information systems, you will be working with management and other business professionals to develop and support new systems that serve the needs of the business.
- If your career is in manufacturing, production, or operations management, you will need information systems for planning, forecasting, and monitoring production and services.
- If your career is in sales and marketing, you will need information systems for branding, promotions, processing orders, and providing customer service.

1 THE ROLE OF INFORMATION SYSTEMS IN BUSINESS TODAY

It's not business as usual in America anymore, or the rest of the global economy. In 2006, American businesses will spend $1.8 trillion on information systems hardware, software, and telecommunications equipment. In addition, they will spend another $1.7 trillion on business and management consulting and services, much of which involves redesigning firms' business operations to take advantage of these new technologies. Figure 1 shows that between 1980 and 2004, private business investment in information technology consisting of hardware, software, and communications equipment grew from 34 percent to 50 percent of all invested capital.

As managers, most of you will work for firms that are intensively using information systems and making large investments in information technology. You will certainly want to know how to invest this money wisely. If you make wise choices, your firm can outperform competitors. If you make poor choices, you will be wasting valuable capital. This text is dedicated to helping you make wise decisions about information technology and information systems.

HOW INFORMATION SYSTEMS ARE TRANSFORMING BUSINESS

You can see the results of the massive spending on information technology and systems around you everyday by observing how people conduct business. More wireless cell phone accounts were opened in 2005 than telephone land lines installed. Cell phones, BlackBerrys, handhelds, e-mail, online conferencing,

FIGURE 1   **INFORMATION TECHNOLOGY CAPITAL INVESTMENT**

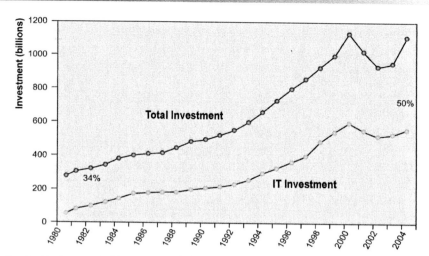

Information technology capital investment, defined as hardware, software, and communications equipment, grew from 34% to 50% between 1980 and 2004.

Source: Based on data in U.S. Department of Commerce, Bureau of Economic Analysis, *National Income and Product Accounts,* 2006.

and international teleconferencing over the Internet have all become essential tools of business. In 2005, more than 40 million businesses had dot-com Internet sites registered. Five million Americans purchase something every day on the Internet and another 19 million research a product.

In 2005, FedEx moved nearly 100 million packages in the United States, mostly overnight, and the United Parcel Service (UPS) moved more than 380 million packages as businesses sought to sense and respond to rapidly changing customer demand, reduce inventories to the lowest possible levels, and achieve higher levels of operational efficiency, especially in their supply chains. The responsiveness of this new "FedEx" economy has led many experts to believe the era of massive recessions and booms of the typical business cycle is over, replaced by much smaller contractions and expansions, and strong long-term growth.

There's been a massive shift in media markets. As newspaper readership continues to decline, more than 35 million people receive their news online. Thirty-two million Americans now read blogs, and eight million write blogs, creating an explosion of new writers and new forms of customer feedback that did not exist five years ago (Pew, 2005).

E-commerce and Internet advertising are booming: Google's online ad revenues surpassed $6 billion in 2005, and Internet advertising continues to grow at more than 30 percent a year, reaching more than $11 billion in revenues in 2005.

New federal security and accounting laws, requiring many businesses to keep e-mail messages for five years, coupled with existing occupational and health laws requiring firms to store employee chemical exposure data for up to 60 years, are spurring the growth of digital information now estimated to be 5 exabytes annually, equivalent to 37,000 new Libraries of Congress.

GLOBALIZATION OPPORTUNITIES

A growing percentage of the American economy—and other advanced industrial economies in Europe and Asia—depend on imports and exports. Foreign trade, both exports and imports, accounts for more than 25 percent of the goods and services produced in the United States, and even more in countries such as Japan and Germany.

The emergence of the Internet into a full-blown international communications system has drastically reduced the costs of operating on a global scale. Customers now can shop in a worldwide marketplace, obtaining price and quality information reliably 24 hours a day. Firms can achieve extraordinary cost reductions by finding low-cost suppliers and managing production facilities in other countries. Digital content firms that produce Hollywood movies are able to sell millions more copies of DVDs of popular films by using foreign markets. Internet service firms, such as Google and eBay, are able to replicate their business models and services in multiple countries without having to redesign their expensive fixed-cost information systems infrastructure.

THE EMERGING DIGITAL FIRM

All of the changes we have just described, coupled with equally significant organizational redesign, have created the conditions for a fully **digital firm**. A digital firm can be defined along several dimensions. A digital firm is one in which nearly all of the organization's *significant business relationships* with customers, suppliers, and employees are digitally enabled and mediated. *Core business processes* are accomplished through digital networks spanning the entire organization or linking multiple organizations.

Business processes refer to the set of logically related tasks and behaviors that organizations develop over time to produce specific business results and the unique manner in which these activities are organized and coordinated. Developing a new product, generating and fulfilling an order, creating a marketing plan, and hiring an employee are examples of business processes, and the ways organizations accomplish their business processes can be a source of competitive strength.

Key corporate assets—intellectual property, core competencies, and financial and *human assets*—are managed through digital means. In a digital firm, any piece of information required to support key business decisions is available at any time and anywhere in the firm.

Digital firms sense and respond to their environments far more rapidly than traditional firms, giving them more flexibility to survive in turbulent times. Digital firms offer extraordinary opportunities for more flexible global organization and management. In digital firms, both *time shifting* and *space shifting* are the norm. Time shifting refers to business being conducted continuously, 24x7, rather than in narrow "work day" time bands of 9 a.m. to 5 p.m. Space shifting means that work takes place in a global workshop, as well as within national boundaries. Work is accomplished physically wherever in the world it is best accomplished.

Toyota Motor Company, described in the chapter-opening case, illustrates some of these features. Electronically integrating key business processes in vehicle ordering and inventory management has made this company much more agile and adaptive to customer demands and changes in its supplier and dealer network. A few firms, such as Cisco Systems or Dell Computers, are close to becoming digital firms, using the Internet to drive every aspect of their business. Most other companies are not fully digital, but they are moving toward close digital integration with suppliers, customers, and employees.

The Interactive Session on Organizations describes another example. Accenture is a global consulting services and outsourcing firm with over 129,000 employees serving clients in 48 different countries. It has no operational headquarters and no formal branches, encouraging its employees to work on site with its clients. Managers use e-mail, phones, the Web, and other information technologies to manage virtually, often while they are traveling themselves. As you read this case, try to identify the problems facing this company, how information systems are helping it solve them, and the management, organization, and technology issues it must address.

STRATEGIC BUSINESS OBJECTIVES OF INFORMATION SYSTEMS

What makes information systems so essential today? Why are businesses investing so much in information systems and technologies? In the United States, more than 23 million managers and 113 million workers in the labor force rely on information systems to conduct business. Information systems are essential for conducting day-to-day business in the United States and most other advanced countries, as well as achieving strategic business objectives.

Entire sectors of the economy are nearly inconceivable without substantial investments in information systems. E-commerce firms such as Amazon, eBay, Google, and E*Trade simply would not exist. Today's service industries—finance, insurance, and real estate, as well as personal services such as travel, medicine, and education—could not operate without information systems. Similarly, retail firms such as Wal-Mart and Sears and manufacturing firms such as General Motors and General Electric require information systems to survive and prosper. Just like offices, telephones, filing cabinets, and efficient tall buildings with elevators were once the foundations of business in the twentieth century, information technology is a foundation for business in the twenty-first century.

There is a growing interdependence between a firm's ability to use information technology and its ability to implement corporate strategies and achieve corporate goals (see Figure 2). What a business would like to do in five years often depends on what its systems will be able to do. Increasing market share, becoming the high-quality or low-cost producer, developing new products, and increasing employee productivity depend more and more on the kinds and quality of information systems in the organization. The more you understand about this relationship, the more valuable you will be as a manager.

Specifically, business firms invest heavily in information systems to achieve six strategic business objectives: operational excellence; new products, services, and business models; customer and supplier intimacy; improved decision making; competitive advantage; and survival.

Operational Excellence
Businesses continuously seek to improve the efficiency of their operations in order to achieve higher profitability. Information systems and technologies are some of the most important tools available to managers for achieving higher levels of efficiency and productivity in business operations, especially when coupled with changes in business practices and management behavior.

Wal-Mart, the largest retailer on Earth, exemplifies the power of information systems coupled with brilliant business practices and supportive management to

INTERACTIVE SESSION: ORGANIZATIONS

VIRTUAL MANAGEMENT AT ACCENTURE

Accenture is a global management consulting, technology services, and outsourcing company, with over 129,000 employees in 48 countries. It specializes in helping businesses and governments improve their performance. Its information systems and business processes are designed so that consultants can work from virtually any location.

Accenture has no operational headquarters and no formal branches. Its chief financial officer lives in Silicon Valley, California, while the head of human resources is in Chicago and its chief technology officer is based in Germany. Accenture's thousands of management and technology consultants are constantly on the move, on site with clients or working temporarily in offices that the company leases in more than 100 locations around the world.

When a new consultant is hired, Accenture's system automatically sets up an e-mail account and instructions on where to pick up a laptop. Managers rely heavily on telephone and e-mail to keep up with their staff, and many of them are constantly in motion.

Every day, Accenture employees log on to the company's internal Web site, which they can access from anywhere in the world. They use this system to record where they are working, and to access e-mail, phone messages, and their files. The system enables them to share documents and other data with Accenture colleagues and to conduct videoconferences when more face-to-face interaction is needed. If a consultant or manager is about to travel to London, Chicago, or Beijing, he or she uses the system to find a cubicle with a desk in that location. Clients who call a manager whose home base is Los Angeles are automatically routed to his or her current working location, even if it is several time zones away.

To print a document, a person uses the Accenture internal Web site to click on the country where he or she is currently working. This action brings up a list of offices. After selecting an office, the employee selects a floor, which brings up a floor plan of the building and displays all of the available printers. When the employee clicks on a printer, it automatically prints the employee's documents.

Employees can't pop into co-workers' offices for informal meetings. Participants in a specific project may be working from many different locations and time zones around the world, so scheduling phone conferences may require a few to give up some sleep. For global phone conferences, the best time appears to be around 1 P.M. London time, which is 9 P.M. in Beijing, midnight in Australia, and 5 A.M. in California.

For executives who are constantly on the go, jet lag adds to the problem.

Accenture outsources about 82 percent of the information technology it uses. It hires other companies to manage its network, computer centers, and help desk, as well as technologies used at specific locations. External vendors provide the support for Accenture's PCs and conference call technology.

Accenture also outsources other parts of its business, such as the management of employee travel. Its travel vendors are able to track employee movements. When a major client in Copenhagen asked to see Accenture's chief operating officer Steve Rohleder in person, Accenture was able to locate Rohleder just as his plane was landing in Nice, France, en route from New York to India. Rohleder was able to change planes and head directly to Copenhagen.

Some problems, however, require Accenture managers and clients to "be there in person." When London-based Adrian Lajtha, who heads Accenture's financial services group, learned that a project team in the United States felt bogged down, he made an impromptu visit to their work site and staged a three-hour meeting. Personal contact is especially useful when sensitive personnel matters must be addressed or when employees need extra motivation and encouragement during hard times. That means more travel and conferences around the clock for Accenture virtual executives. During the last economic slowdown, for example, Lajtha held 280 meetings in 18 months with groups of the 12,000 employees he oversees.

Despite these challenges, Accenture believes virtual management works. The company doesn't have to maintain overhead costs for large headquarters, which it believes would amount to much more than its extensive travel expenses. Managers see many benefits to spending time in the field where clients are located. Managers meeting with lower-level employees who work with the clients obtain information that would not be available if they remained at headquarters. And their presence helps cement client relationships. Almost 85 percent of Accenture's one hundred largest accounts have been its clients for 10 years or more.

Sources: Carol Hymowitz, "Have Advice, Will Travel," *Wall Street Journal,* June 5, 2006; Rachel Rosmarin, "Accenture CIO Frank Modruson," *Forbes,* June 2, 2006; and www.accenture.com, accessed June 15, 2006.

CASE STUDY QUESTIONS

MIS IN ACTION

1. What are the advantages of working in a virtual environment like the one created by Accenture? What are the disadvantages?

2. Would you like to work in a company like Accenture? Why or why not? Explain your answer.

3. What kinds of companies could benefit from being run virtually like Accenture? Could all companies be run virtually like Accenture?

1. Go to the Accenture.com Web site. On the home page, Accenture promises to help its clients achieve "high performance." According to Accenture, how does information technology help create high-performance organizations? Hint: Click on the word "Technology" on the home page. Or, enter "information technology" into the search box on the home page, and read one of the articles linking IT with high-performance businesses. Write several paragraphs on Accenture's definition of a "high-performance" organization and the role of information systems in enabling such organizations.

2. OK, it's time to look for a job. What kinds of business and information system skills is Accenture looking for in recent college graduates? Hint: Click on the Careers tab and review the desired skills for "Consulting Analysts" in the United States. Make a list of these skills in electronic presentation software for your class.

FIGURE 2   **THE INTERDEPENDENCE BETWEEN ORGANIZATIONS AND INFORMATION SYSTEMS**

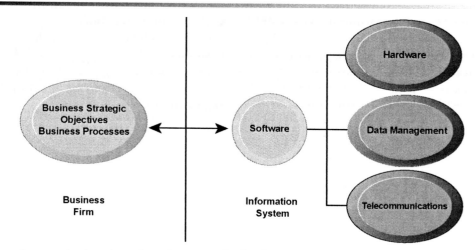

There is a growing interdependence between a firm's information systems and its business capabilities. Changes in strategy, rules, and business processes increasingly require changes in hardware, software, databases, and telecommunications. Often, what the organization would like to do depends on what its systems will permit it to do.

achieve world-class operational efficiency. In 2005, Wal-Mart attained more than $285 billion in sales—nearly one-tenth of retail sales in the United States—in large part because of its RetailLink system, which digitally links its suppliers to every one of Wal-Mart's 5,289 stores worldwide. As soon as a customer purchases an item, the supplier monitoring the item knows to ship a replacement to the shelf. Wal-Mart is the most efficient retail store in the industry, achieving sales of more than $28 per square foot, compared to its closest competitor, Target, at $23 a square foot, with other retail firms producing less than $12 a square foot.

New Products, Services, and Business Models

Information systems and technologies are a major enabling tool for firms to create new products and services, as well as entirely new business models. A **business model** describes how a company produces, delivers, and sells a product or service to create wealth.

For example, today's music industry is vastly different from the industry in 2000. Apple Inc. transformed an old business model of music distribution based on vinyl records, tapes, and CDs into an online, legal distribution model based on its own iPod technology platform. Apple has prospered from a continuing stream of iPod innovations, including the original iPod, to the iPod nano, the iTunes music service, and the iPod video player.

Likewise, Netflix transformed the video rental business with a new Internet-enabled business model which makes over 60,000 DVD titles (just about the entire population of DVD titles) available by postal mail to millions of users in the United States. A typical Blockbuster video store, in contrast, stocks about 1200 titles.

Customer and Supplier Intimacy

When a business really knows its customers and serves them well, the way they want to be served, the customers generally respond by returning and purchasing more. This raises revenues and profits. Likewise with suppliers: the more a business engages its suppliers, the better the suppliers can provide vital inputs. This lowers costs. How to really know your customers, or suppliers, is a central problem for businesses with millions of offline and online customers.

The Mandarin Oriental in Manhattan and other high-end hotels exemplify the use of information systems and technologies to achieve customer intimacy. These hotels use computers to keep track of guests' preferences, such as their preferred room temperature, check-in time, frequently dialed telephone numbers, and television programs, and store this data in a giant data repository. Individual rooms in the hotels are networked to a central network server computer so that they can be remotely monitored or controlled. When a customer arrives at one of these hotels, the system automatically changes the

Apple's iPod, iPod nano, and iPod video player are popular new products based on information technology that are transforming the music and entertainment industries.

Photo courtesy of AP Wide World Photos

room conditions, such as dimming the lights, setting the room temperature, or selecting appropriate music, based on the customer's digital profile. The hotels also analyze their customer data to identify their best customers and to develop individualized marketing campaigns based on customers' preferences.

JCPenney demonstrates the benefits of information systems-enabled supplier intimacy. Every time a dress shirt is bought at a JCPenney store in the United States, the record of the sale appears immediately on computers in Hong Kong at its supplier, TAL Apparel Ltd., a large contract manufacturer that produces one in eight dress shirts sold in the United States. TAL runs the numbers through a computer model it developed and then decides how many replacement shirts to make, and in what styles, colors, and sizes. TAL then sends the shirts to each JCPenney store, bypassing completely the retailer's warehouses. In other words, JCPenney's shirt inventory is near zero, as is the cost of storing it.

Improved Decision Making

Many business managers operate in an information fog bank, never really having the right information at the right time to make an informed decision. Instead, managers rely on forecasts, best guesses, and luck. The result is over-production or underproduction of goods and services, misallocation of resources, and poor response times. These poor outcomes raise costs and lose customers. In the past 10 years, information systems and technologies have made it possible for managers to use real-time data from the marketplace when making decisions.

For instance, Verizon Corporation, one of the largest regional Bell operating companies in the United States, uses a Web-based digital dashboard to provide managers with precise real-time information on customer complaints, network performance for each locality served, and line outages or storm-damaged lines. Using this information, managers can immediately allocate repair resources to affected areas, inform consumers of repair efforts, and restore service fast.

Competitive Advantage

When firms achieve one or more of these business objectives—operational excellence; new products, services, and business models; customer/supplier intimacy; and improved decision making—chances are they have already

Business Objects' digital dashboard delivers comprehensive and accurate information for decision making. The graphical overview of key performance indicators helps managers quickly spot areas that need attention.

Photo courtesy of Business Objects Americas

achieved a competitive advantage. Doing things better than your competitors, charging less for superior products, and responding to customers and suppliers in real time all add up to higher sales and higher profits that your competitors cannot match.

Perhaps no other U.S. company exemplifies all of these attributes leading to competitive advantage more than Dell Computer. In a period when PC prices have been falling at 25 percent a year, forcing most manufacturers into losses, Dell Computer has shown consistent profitability during its life span of 25 years. Although recently its margins have fallen as competitors improve their own business processes, Dell remains the most efficient producer of PCs in the world. A large part of Dell's operational efficiency results from "mass customization," staying close to the customer by using a Web-based order entry model that can build and ship a customized PC to any of its millions of consumers in only a few days, even overnight if the customer is really in a hurry. Dell has used its commanding position to introduce many new products and services, especially to corporate customers, such as a custom Dell Web page for corporate accounts.

Survival

Business firms also invest in information systems and technologies because they are necessities of doing business. Sometimes these "necessities" are driven by industry-level changes. For instance, after Citibank introduced the first automatic teller machines (ATMs) in the New York region in 1977 to attract customers through higher service levels, its competitors rushed to provide ATMs to their customers to keep up with Citibank. Today, virtually all banks in the United States have regional ATMs and link to national and international ATM networks, such as CIRRUS. Providing ATM services to retail banking customers is simply a requirement of being in and surviving in the retail banking business.

There are many federal and state statutes and regulations that create a legal duty for companies and their employees to retain records, including digital records. For instance, the Toxic Substances Control Act (1976), which regulates the exposure of U.S. workers to more than 75,000 toxic chemicals, requires firms to retain records on employee exposure for 30 years. The Sarbanes-Oxley Act (2002), which was intended to improve the accountability of public firms and their auditors, requires certified public accounting firms that audit public companies to retain audit working papers and records, including all e-mails, for five years. Many other pieces of federal and state legislation in healthcare, financial services, education, and privacy protection impose significant information retention and reporting requirements on U.S. businesses. Firms turn to information systems and technologies to provide the capability to respond to these requirements.

2   PERSPECTIVES ON INFORMATION SYSTEMS

So far we've used *information systems* and *technologies* informally without defining the terms. **Information technology (IT)** consists of all the hardware and software that a firm needs to use in order to achieve its business objectives. This includes not only computers, printers, handheld personal digital assistants, and, yes, even iPods (where they are used for a business purpose) but also software, such as the Windows or Linux operating systems, the Microsoft Office desktop productivity suite, and the many thousands of computer programs that can be found in a typical large firm. "Information systems" are more complex and can be best understood by looking at them from both a technology and a business perspective.

WHAT IS AN INFORMATION SYSTEM?

An **information system** can be defined technically as a set of interrelated components that collect (or retrieve), process, store, and distribute information to support decision making and control in an organization. In addition to supporting decision making, coordination, and control, information systems may also help managers and workers analyze problems, visualize complex subjects, and create new products.

Information systems contain information about significant people, places, and things within the organization or in the environment surrounding it. By **information** we mean data that have been shaped into a form that is meaningful and useful to human beings. **Data**, in contrast, are streams of raw facts representing events occurring in organizations or the physical environment before they have been organized and arranged into a form that people can effectively understand and use.

A brief example contrasting information and data illustrates the difference between them. Supermarket checkout counters scan millions of pieces of data, such as bar codes, that describe the product. Such pieces of data can be totaled and analyzed to provide meaningful information, such as the total number of bottles of dish detergent sold at a particular store, which brands of dish detergent were selling the most rapidly at that store or sales territory, or the total amount spent on that brand of dish detergent at that store or sales region (see Figure 3).

Three activities in an information system produce the information that organizations need to make decisions, control operations, analyze problems, and create new products or services. These activities are input, processing, and

FIGURE 3   **DATA AND INFORMATION**

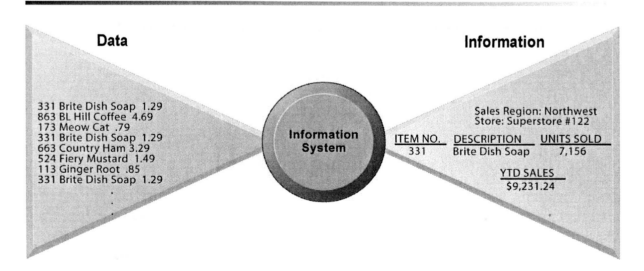

Raw data from a supermarket checkout counter can be processed and organized to produce meaningful information, such as the total unit sales of dish detergent or the total sales revenue from dish detergent for a specific store or sales territory.

FIGURE 4   FUNCTIONS OF AN INFORMATION SYSTEM

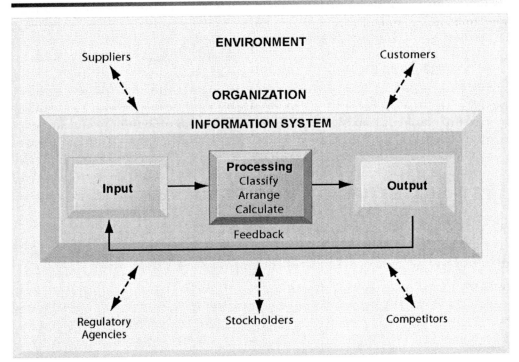

An information system contains information about an organization and its surrounding environment. Three basic activities—input, processing, and output—produce the information organizations need. Feedback is output returned to appropriate people or activities in the organization to evaluate and refine the input. Environmental actors, such as customers, suppliers, competitors, stockholders, and regulatory agencies, interact with the organization and its information systems.

output (see Figure 4). **Input** captures or collects raw data from within the organization or from its external environment. **Processing** converts this raw input into a meaningful form. **Output** transfers the processed information to the people who will use it or to the activities for which it will be used. Information systems also require **feedback**, which is output that is returned to appropriate members of the organization to help them evaluate or correct the input stage.

In Toyota's vehicle orders management system, the raw input consists of customer order data including the dealer identification number, model, color, and optional features of each car ordered. Toyota's computers store this data and process it to locate the models with options specified by the customer that are either in inventory or under production, to place orders to national distributors, to consolidate the orders, and then to transmit them to factories. Toyota's production systems then tell its factories how many vehicles to manufacture for each model, color, and option package, how much to bill for each vehicle, and where to ship the vehicles. The output consists of shipping instructions, invoices, and production reports. The system provides meaningful information, such as which models, colors, and options are selling in which locations, the most popular models and colors, and which dealers sell the most cars.

Although computer-based information systems use computer technology to process raw data into meaningful information, there is a sharp distinction between a computer and a computer program on the one hand, and an information system on the other. Electronic computers and related software programs are the technical foundation, the tools and materials, of modern information systems. Computers provide the equipment for storing and processing information. Computer programs, or software, are sets of operating instructions that direct and control computer processing. Knowing how computers and computer programs work is important in designing solutions to organizational problems, but computers are only part of an information system.

A house is an appropriate analogy. Houses are built with hammers, nails, and wood, but these do not make a house. The architecture, design, setting, landscaping, and all of the decisions that lead to the creation of these features are part of the house and are crucial for solving the problem of putting a roof over one's head. Computers and programs are the hammer, nails, and lumber of computer-based information systems, but alone they cannot produce the information a particular organization needs. To understand information systems, you must understand the problems they are designed to solve, their architectural and design elements, and the organizational processes that lead to these solutions.

DIMENSIONS OF INFORMATION SYSTEMS

To fully understand information systems, you must understand the broader organization, management, and information technology dimensions of systems (see Figure 5) and their power to provide solutions to challenges and problems in the business environment. We refer to this broader understanding of information systems, which encompasses an understanding of the management and organizational dimensions of systems as well as the technical dimensions of systems, as **information systems literacy**. Information systems literacy includes a behavioral as well as a technical approach to studying information systems. **Computer literacy**, in contrast, focuses primarily on knowledge of information technology.

The field of **management information systems (MIS)** tries to achieve this broader information systems literacy. MIS deals with behavioral issues as well

FIGURE 5   INFORMATION SYSTEMS ARE MORE THAN COMPUTERS

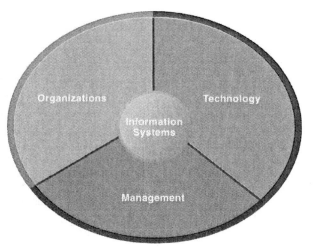

Using information systems effectively requires an understanding of the organization, management, and information technology shaping the systems. An information system creates value for the firm as an organizational and management solution to challenges posed by the environment.

FIGURE 6   **LEVELS IN A FIRM**

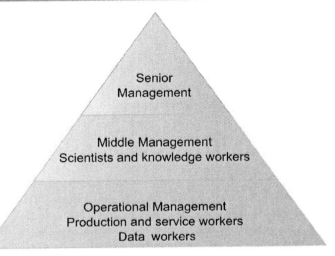

Business organizations are hierarchies consisting of three principal levels: senior management, middle management, and operational management. Information systems serve each of these levels. Scientists and knowledge workers often work with middle management.

as technical issues surrounding the development, use, and impact of information systems used by managers and employees in the firm.

Let's examine each of the dimensions of information systems—organizations, management, and information technology.

Organizations

Information systems are an integral part of organizations. Indeed, for some companies, such as credit reporting firms, without an information system, there would be no business. The key elements of an organization are its people, structure, business processes, politics, and culture.

Organizations have a structure that is composed of different levels and specialties. Their structures reveal a clear-cut division of labor. Authority and responsibility in a business firm is organized as a hierarchy, or a pyramid structure, of rising authority and responsibility. The upper levels of the hierarchy consist of managerial, professional, and technical employees, whereas the lower levels consist of operational personnel.

Senior management makes long-range strategic decisions about products and services as well as ensures financial performance of the firm. **Middle management** carries out the programs and plans of senior management and **operational management** is responsible for monitoring the daily activities of the business. **Knowledge workers**, such as engineers, scientists, or architects, design products or services and create new knowledge for the firm, whereas **data workers**, such as secretaries or clerks, assist with paperwork at all levels of the firm. **Production** or **service workers** actually produce the product and deliver the service (see Figure 6).

Experts are employed and trained for different business functions. The major **business functions**, or specialized tasks performed by business organizations, consist of sales and marketing, manufacturing and production, finance and accounting, and human resources (see Table 1).

TABLE 1   MAJOR BUSINESS FUNCTIONS

FUNCTION	PURPOSE
Sales and marketing	Selling the organization's products and services
Manufacturing and production	Producing products and services
Finance and accounting	Managing the organization's financial assets and maintaining the organization's financial records
Human resources	Attracting, developing, and maintaining the organization's labor force; maintaining employee records

An organization coordinates work through its hierarchy and through its business processes, which we defined earlier in this chapter. Most organizations' business processes include formal rules that have been developed over a long time for accomplishing tasks. These rules guide employees in a variety of procedures, from writing an invoice to responding to customer complaints. Some of these business processes have been written down, but others are informal work practices, such as a requirement to return telephone calls from co-workers or customers, that are not formally documented. Information systems automate many business processes. For instance, how a customer receives credit or how a customer is billed is often determined by an information system that incorporates a set of formal business processes.

Each organization has a unique **culture**, or fundamental set of assumptions, values, and ways of doing things, that has been accepted by most of its members. You can see organizational culture at work by looking around your university or college. Some bedrock assumptions of university life are that professors know more than students, the reasons students attend college is to learn, and that classes follow a regular schedule.

Parts of an organization's culture can always be found embedded in its information systems. For instance, UPS's concern with placing service to the customer first is an aspect of its organizational culture that can be found in the company's package tracking systems, which we describe later in this section.

Different levels and specialties in an organization create different interests and points of view. These views often conflict over how the company should be run and how resources and rewards should be distributed. Conflict is the basis for organizational politics. Information systems come out of this cauldron of differing perspectives, conflicts, compromises, and agreements that are a natural part of all organizations.

Management

Management's job is to make sense out of the many situations faced by organizations, make decisions, and formulate action plans to solve organizational problems. Managers perceive business challenges in the environment; they set the organizational strategy for responding to those challenges; and they allocate the human and financial resources to coordinate the work and achieve success. Throughout, they must exercise responsible leadership. The business information systems described in this text reflect the hopes, dreams, and realities of real-world managers.

But managers must do more than manage what already exists. They must also create new products and services and even re-create the organization from time to time. A substantial part of management responsibility is creative work driven by new knowledge and information. Information technology can play a powerful role in helping managers design and deliver new products and services and redirecting and redesigning their organizations.

Technology

Information technology is one of many tools managers use to cope with change. **Computer hardware** is the physical equipment used for input, processing, and output activities in an information system. It consists of the following: computers of various sizes and shapes; various input, output, and storage devices; and telecommunications devices that link computers together.

Computer software consists of the detailed, preprogrammed instructions that control and coordinate the computer hardware components in an information system.

Data management technology consists of the software governing the organization of data on physical storage media.

Networking and telecommunications technology, consisting of both physical devices and software, links the various pieces of hardware and transfers data from one physical location to another. Computers and communications equipment can be connected in networks for sharing voice, data, images, sound, and video. A **network** links two or more computers to share data or resources, such as a printer.

The world's largest and most widely used network is the **Internet**. The Internet is a global "network of networks" that uses universal standards to connect millions of different networks with more than 350 million host computers in over 200 countries around the world.

The Internet has created a new "universal" technology platform on which to build new products, services, strategies, and business models. This same technology platform has internal uses, providing the connectivity to link different systems and networks within the firm. Internal corporate networks based on Internet technology are called **intranets**. Private intranets extended to authorized users outside the organization are called **extranets**, and firms use such networks to coordinate their activities with other firms for making purchases, collaborating on design, and other interorganizational work. For most business firms today, using Internet technology is both a business necessity and a competitive advantage.

The **World Wide Web** is a service provided by the Internet that uses universally accepted standards for storing, retrieving, formatting, and displaying information in a page format on the Internet. Web pages contain text, graphics, animations, sound, and video and are linked to other Web pages. By clicking on highlighted words or buttons on a Web page, you can link to related pages to find additional information and links to other locations on the Web. The Web can serve as the foundation for new kinds of information systems such as UPS's Web-based package tracking system described in the following Interactive Session.

All of these technologies, along with the people required to run and manage them, represent resources that can be shared throughout the organization and

INTERACTIVE SESSION: TECHNOLOGY

UPS COMPETES GLOBALLY WITH INFORMATION TECHNOLOGY

United Parcel Service (UPS), is the world's largest air and ground package-distribution company. It started out in 1907 in a closet-sized basement office. Jim Casey and Claude Ryan—two teenagers from Seattle with two bicycles and one phone—promised the "best service and lowest rates." UPS has used this formula successfully for more than 90 years.

Today UPS delivers more than 14.1 million parcels and documents each day in the United States and more than 200 other countries and territories. The firm has been able to maintain leadership in small-package delivery services despite stiff competition from FedEx and Airborne Express by investing heavily in advanced information technology. During the past decade, UPS has poured billions of dollars into technology and systems to boost customer service while keeping costs low and streamlining its overall operations.

Using a handheld computer called a Delivery Information Acquisition Device (DIAD), a UPS driver can automatically capture customers' signatures along with pickup, delivery, and time-card information. The driver then places the DIAD into the UPS truck's vehicle adapter, an information-transmitting device that is connected to the cellular telephone network. Package tracking information is then transmitted to UPS's computer network for storage and processing by UPS's main computers in Mahwah, New Jersey, and Alpharetta, Georgia. From there, the information can be accessed worldwide to provide proof of delivery to customers or to respond to customer queries.

Through its automated package tracking system, UPS can monitor packages throughout the delivery process. At various points along the route from sender to receiver, bar code devices scan shipping information on the package label; the information is then fed into the central computer. Customer service representatives can check the status of any package from desktop computers linked to the central computers and are able to respond immediately to inquiries from customers. UPS customers can also access this information from the company's Web site using their own computers or wireless devices, such as pagers and cell phones.

Anyone with a package to ship can access the UPS Web site to track packages, check delivery routes, calculate shipping rates, determine time in transit, and schedule a pickup. Businesses can use the Web site to arrange UPS shipments and bill the shipments to the company's UPS account number or to a credit card. The data collected at the UPS Web site are transmitted to the UPS central computer and then back to the customer after processing. UPS also provides tools that enable customers, such Cisco Systems, to embed UPS functions, such as tracking and cost calculations, into their own Web sites so that they can track shipments without visiting the UPS site.

Information technology has helped UPS reinvent itself and keep growing. UPS implemented a suite of custom-built software that uses operations research and mapping technology to optimize the way packages are loaded and delivered. Because UPS delivers 14 million small packages each day, the resulting information is cutting the distance that delivery trucks travel by more than 100 million miles each year.

UPS is now leveraging its decades of expertise managing its own global delivery network to manage logistics and supply-chain management for other companies. It created a UPS Supply Chain Solutions division that provides a complete bundle of standardized services to subscribing companies at a fraction of what it would cost to build their own systems and infrastructure. These services include supply-chain design and management, freight forwarding, customs brokerage, mail services, multimodal transportation, and financial services, in addition to logistics services.

Adidas America, based in Portland, Oregon, is one of many companies benefiting from these services. Every three months the company introduces as many as 10,000 new apparel items and 4,000 new footwear items. It must handle orders for many thousands of retailers for these orders, and many of these orders are priority requests that must be fulfilled within one or two days. UPS Supply Chain Solutions consolidated what was previously handled by multiple third-party logistics providers into a single streamlined network outfitted with automated inventory and order fulfillment systems. By having UPS coordinate and manage distribution, Adidas America increased its order accuracy rate, boosted on-time deliveries, and improved customer service.

Sources: "Adidas Goes for the Gold in Customer Service," www.ups.com, accessed June 14, 2006; United Parcel Service, *Round UPS*, Winter 2006; and Dave Barnes, "Delivering Corporate Citizenship," *Optimize*, September 2005.

CASE STUDY QUESTIONS

1. What are the inputs, processing, and outputs of UPS's package tracking system?
2. What technologies are used by UPS? How are these technologies related to UPS's business strategy?
3. What problems do UPS's information systems solve? What would happen if these systems were not available?

Explore the UPS Web site (www.ups.com) and answer the following questions:

MIS IN ACTION

1. What kinds of information and services does the Web site provide for individuals, small businesses, and large businesses? List these services and write several paragraphs describing one of them, such as UPS Trade Direct or Automated Shipment Processing. Explain how you or your business would benefit from the service.
2. Explain how the Web site helps UPS achieve some or all of the strategic business objectives we described earlier in this chapter. What would be the impact on UPS's business if this Web site were not available?

Using a handheld computer called a Delivery Information Acquisition Device (DIAD), UPS drivers automatically capture customers' signatures along with pickup, delivery, and time-card information. UPS information systems use these data to track packages while they are being transported.

Photo courtesy of David Frazier/ The Image Works

constitute the firm's **information technology (IT) infrastructure**. The IT infrastructure provides the foundation, or *platform*, on which the firm can build its specific information systems. Each organization must carefully design and manage its information technology infrastructure so that it has the set of technology services it needs for the work it wants to accomplish with information systems.

The Interactive Session on Technology describes some of the typical technologies used in computer-based information systems today. UPS invests heavily in information systems technology to make its business more efficient and customer oriented. It uses an array of information technologies including bar code scanning systems, wireless networks, large mainframe computers, handheld computers, the Internet, and many different pieces of software for tracking packages, calculating fees, maintaining customer accounts, and managing logistics.

Let's identify the organization, management, and technology elements in the UPS package tracking system we have just described. The organization element anchors the package tracking system in UPS's sales and production functions (the main product of UPS is a service—package delivery). It specifies the required procedures for identifying packages with both sender and recipient information, taking inventory, tracking the packages en route, and providing package status reports for UPS customers and customer service representatives.

The system must also provide information to satisfy the needs of managers and workers. UPS drivers need to be trained in both package pickup and delivery procedures and in how to use the package tracking system so that they can work efficiently and effectively. UPS customers may need some training to use UPS in-house package tracking software or the UPS Web site.

UPS's management is responsible for monitoring service levels and costs and for promoting the company's strategy of combining low-cost and superior service. Management decided to use automation to increase the ease of sending a package using UPS and checking its delivery status, thereby reducing delivery costs and increasing sales revenues.

The technology supporting this system consists of handheld computers, bar code scanners, wired and wireless communications networks, desktop computers, UPS's central computer, storage technology for the package delivery data, UPS in-house package tracking software, and software to access the Internet. The result is an information system solution to the business challenge of providing a high level of service with low prices in the face of mounting competition.

IT ISN'T JUST TECHNOLOGY: A BUSINESS PERSPECTIVE ON INFORMATION SYSTEMS

Managers and business firms invest in information technology and systems because they provide real economic value to the business. The decision to build or maintain an information system assumes that the returns on this investment will be superior to other investments in buildings, machines, or other assets. These superior returns will be expressed as increases in productivity, increases in revenues (which will increase the firm's stock market value), or perhaps superior long-term strategic positioning of the firm in certain markets (which produces superior revenues in the future).

We can see that from a business perspective, an information system is an important instrument for creating value for the firm. Information systems enable the firm to increase its revenue or decrease its costs by providing information that helps managers make better decisions or that improves the execution of business processes. For example, the information system for analyzing supermarket checkout data illustrated in Figure 3 can increase firm profitability by helping managers make better decisions on which products to stock and promote in retail supermarkets and as a result increase business value.

Every business has an information value chain, illustrated in Figure 7, in which raw data is systematically acquired and then transformed through various stages that add value to that information. The value of an information

FIGURE 7   **THE BUSINESS INFORMATION VALUE CHAIN**

From a business perspective, information systems are part of a series of value-adding activities for acquiring, transforming, and distributing information that managers can use to improve decision making, enhance organizational performance, and, ultimately, increase firm profitability.

system to a business, as well as the decision to invest in any new information system, is, in large part, determined by the extent to which the system will lead to better management decisions, more efficient business processes, and higher firm profitability. Although there are other reasons why systems are built, their primary purpose is to contribute to corporate value.

The business perspective calls attention to the organizational and managerial nature of information systems. An information system represents an organizational and management solution, based on information technology, to a challenge or problem posed by the environment.

Review the diagram at the beginning of the chapter that reflects this expanded definition of an information system. The diagram shows how Toyota's vehicle orders management system solves the business challenge presented by fierce competition and rapidly changing consumer preferences. The system creates value for Toyota by making its ordering and production processes more efficient and effective. The diagram also illustrates how management, technology, and organizational elements work together to create the system.

**FIGURE 8   VARIATION IN RETURNS ON INFORMATION TECHNOLOGY
INVESTMENT**

IT Capital Stock (relative to industry average)

Although, on average, investments in information technology produce returns far above those
returned by other investments, there is considerable variation across firms.

Source: Erik Brynjolfsson and Lorin M. Hitt, "Beyond Computation: Information Technology, Organizational Transformation and
Business Performance," *Journal of Economic Perspectives* 14, no. 4 (Fall 2000).

COMPLEMENTARY ASSETS: ORGANIZATIONAL CAPITAL AND THE RIGHT BUSINESS MODEL

Awareness of the organizational and managerial dimensions of information
systems can help us understand why some firms achieve better results from
their information systems than others. Studies of returns from information
technology investments show that there is considerable variation in the returns
firms receive (see Figure 8). Some firms invest a great deal and receive a great
deal (quadrant 2); others invest an equal amount and receive few returns
(quadrant 4). Still other firms invest little and receive much (quadrant 1),
whereas others invest little and receive little (quadrant 3). This suggests that
investing in information technology does not by itself guarantee good returns.
What accounts for this variation among firms?

Some firms fail to adopt the right business model that suits the new
technology, or seek to preserve an old business model that is doomed by new
technology. For instance, recording label companies refused to change their old
business model, which was based on physical music stores for distribution
rather than adopt a new online distribution model. As a result, online legal
music sales are dominated not by record companies but by Apple Computer, a
technology company.

In another example, Blockbuster has invested millions in new Internet sites
and technologies to compete with Netflix, the mail-order video champion. But
Blockbuster has refused to give up its physical distribution business model and
maintains thousands of stores around the country. Blockbuster's share price
has fallen with its earnings, while Netflix continues to set revenue records.

Complementary assets are those assets required to derive value from a
primary investment (Teece, 1988). For instance, to realize value from automobiles requires substantial complementary investments in highways, roads,

gasoline stations, repair facilities, and a legal regulatory structure to set standards and control drivers.

Recent research on business information technology investment indicates that firms that support their technology investments with investments in complementary assets, such as new business models, new business processes, management behavior, organizational culture, or training, receive superior returns, whereas those firms failing to make these complementary investments receive less or no returns on their information technology investments (Brynjolfsson, 2003; Brynjolfsson and Hitt, 2000; Davern and Kauffman, 2000; Laudon, 1974). These investments in organization and management are also known as **organizational and management capital**.

Table 2 lists the major complementary investments that firms need to make to realize value from their information technology investments. Some of this investment involves tangible assets, such as buildings, machinery, and tools. However, the value of investments in information technology depends to a large extent on complementary investments in management and organization.

Key organizational complementary investments are a supportive business culture that values efficiency and effectiveness, an appropriate business model, efficient business processes, decentralization of authority, highly distributed decision rights, and a strong information system (IS) development team.

Important managerial complementary assets are strong senior management support for change, incentive systems that monitor and reward individual innovation, an emphasis on teamwork and collaboration, training programs, and a management culture that values flexibility and knowledge.

Important social investments (not made by the firm but by the society at large, other firms, governments, and other key market actors) are the Internet and the supporting Internet culture, educational systems, network and computing standards, regulations and laws, and the presence of technology and service firms.

TABLE 2 COMPLEMENTARY SOCIAL, MANAGERIAL, AND ORGANIZATIONAL ASSETS REQUIRED TO OPTIMIZE RETURNS FROM INFORMATION TECHNOLOGY INVESTMENTS

Organizational assets	Supportive organizational culture that values efficiency and effectiveness
	Appropriate business model
	Efficient business processes
	Decentralized authority
	Distributed decision-making rights
	Strong IS development team
Managerial assets	Strong senior management support for technology investment and change
	Incentives for management innovation
	Teamwork and collaborative work environments
	Training programs to enhance management decision skills
	Management culture that values flexibility and knowledge-based decision making
Social assets	The Internet and telecommunications infrastructure
	IT-enriched educational programs raising labor force computer literacy
	Standards (both government and private sector)
	Laws and regulations creating fair, stable market environments
	Technology and service firms in adjacent markets to assist implementation

Managers need to consider the broader organization and management dimensions of information systems to understand current problems, as well as to derive substantial above-average returns from their information technology investments. Firms that can address these related dimensions of the IT investment are, on average, richly rewarded.

3 CONTEMPORARY APPROACHES TO INFORMATION SYSTEMS

The study of information systems is a multidisciplinary field. No single theory or perspective dominates. Figure 9 illustrates the major disciplines that contribute problems, issues, and solutions in the study of information systems. In general, the field can be divided into technical and behavioral approaches. Information systems are sociotechnical systems. Though they are composed of machines, devices, and "hard" physical technology, they require substantial social, organizational, and intellectual investments to make them work properly.

TECHNICAL APPROACH

The technical approach to information systems emphasizes mathematically based models to study information systems, as well as the physical technology and formal capabilities of these systems. The disciplines that contribute to the technical approach are computer science, management science, and operations research.

FIGURE 9   CONTEMPORARY APPROACHES TO INFORMATION SYSTEMS

The study of information systems deals with issues and insights contributed from technical and behavioral disciplines.

Computer science is concerned with establishing theories of computability, methods of computation, and methods of efficient data storage and access. Management science emphasizes the development of models for decision-making and management practices. Operations research focuses on mathematical techniques for optimizing selected parameters of organizations, such as transportation, inventory control, and transaction costs.

BEHAVIORAL APPROACH

An important part of the information systems field is concerned with behavioral issues that arise in the development and long-term maintenance of information systems. Issues such as strategic business integration, design, implementation, utilization, and management cannot be explored usefully with the models used in the technical approach. Other behavioral disciplines contribute important concepts and methods.

For instance, sociologists study information systems with an eye toward how groups and organizations shape the development of systems and also how systems affect individuals, groups, and organizations. Psychologists study information systems with an interest in how human decision makers perceive and use formal information. Economists study information systems with an interest in understanding the production of digital goods, the dynamics of digital markets, and understanding how new information systems change the control and cost structures within the firm.

The behavioral approach does not ignore technology. Indeed, information systems technology is often the stimulus for a behavioral problem or issue. But the focus of this approach is generally not on technical solutions. Instead, it concentrates on changes in attitudes, management and organizational policy, and behavior.

APPROACH OF THIS TEXT: SOCIOTECHNICAL SYSTEMS

Throughout this text you may find a rich story with four main actors: suppliers of hardware and software (the technologists); business firms making investments and seeking to obtain value from the technology; managers and employees seeking to achieve business value (and other goals); and the contemporary legal, social, and cultural context (the firm's environment). Together these actors produce what we call *management information systems*.

The study of management information systems (MIS) arose in the 1970s to focus on the use of computer-based information systems in business firms and government agencies (Laudon, 1974; Davis and Olson, 1985). MIS combines the work of computer science, management science, and operations research with a practical orientation toward developing system solutions to real-world problems and managing information technology resources. It is also concerned with behavioral issues surrounding the development, use, and impact of information systems, which are typically discussed in the fields of sociology, economics, and psychology.

Our experience as academics and practitioners leads us to believe that no single approach effectively captures the reality of information systems. The successes and failures of information are rarely all technical or all behavioral. Our best advice to students is to understand the perspectives of many disciplines. Indeed, the challenge and excitement of the information systems field is that it requires an appreciation and tolerance of many different approaches.

FIGURE 10   **A SOCIOTECHNICAL PERSPECTIVE ON INFORMATION SYSTEMS**

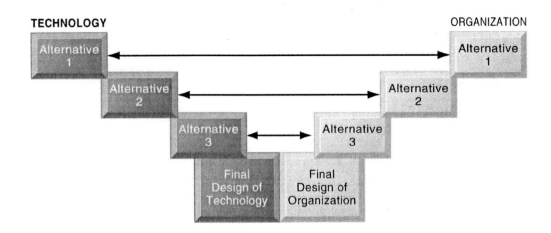

In a sociotechnical perspective, the performance of a system is optimized when both the technology and the organization mutually adjust to one another until a satisfactory fit is obtained.

The view we adopt in this text is best characterized as the **sociotechnical view** of systems. In this view, optimal organizational performance is achieved by jointly optimizing both the social and technical systems used in production.

Adopting a sociotechnical systems perspective helps to avoid a purely technological approach to information systems. For instance, the fact that information technology is rapidly declining in cost and growing in power does not necessarily or easily translate into productivity enhancement or bottom-line profits. The fact that a firm has recently installed an enterprise-wide financial reporting system does not necessarily mean that it will be used, or used effectively. Likewise, the fact that a firm has recently introduced new business procedures and processes does not necessarily mean employees will be more productive in the absence of investments in new information systems to enable those processes.

In this text, we stress the need to optimize the firm's performance as a whole. Both the technical and behavioral components need attention. This means that technology must be changed and designed in such a way as to fit organizational and individual needs. Sometimes, the technology may have to be "de-optimized" to accomplish this fit. For instance, mobile phone users adapt this technology to their personal needs, and as a result manufacturers quickly seek to adjust the technology to conform with user expectations (Lee, 2003; Sawyer and Allen, 2003; Bautsch, 2001). Organizations and individuals must also be changed through training, learning, and planned organizational change to allow the technology to operate and prosper (Lamb et al., 2004; Orlikowski and Baroudi, 1991; Orlikowski, 1992). Figure 10 illustrates this process of mutual adjustment in a sociotechnical system.

4   HANDS-ON MIS

The projects in this section give you hands-on experience in analyzing a real-world company's information systems needs based on an understanding of its business, using a database to improve management decision making and using Internet software to improve operational efficiency.

Understanding Information System Requirements

Software skills: Presentation software
Business skills: Management analysis and information system
            recommendations

How do you know what information systems are really needed by a business and which are the most important? How should a company's structure or culture affect the building and use of information systems?

The Dirt Bikes case describes a real-world company that makes dirt bikes—a kind of motorcycle that is used off-road and often raced in competition. This case appears in every chapter with different assignments linked to the chapter contents. There is a complete description of the company, including its organizational structure, culture, management, and goals at the Laudon Web site for this text. The case contains spreadsheets and databases that complete the description of the company. Below is an illustration of the company's organization chart, showing how the company is organized.

Dirt Bikes's management has asked you to prepare a management analysis of the company to help it assess the firm's current situation and future plans. Review Dirt Bikes's company history, organization chart, products and services, and sales and marketing in the Introduction to Dirt Bikes. Then prepare a report that addresses these questions:

- What are the company's goals and culture?
- What products and services does Dirt Bikes USA provide? How many types of products and services are available to customers? How does Dirt Bikes sell its products?
- How many employees are managers, production workers, or knowledge or information workers? Are there levels of management?
- What kinds of information systems and technologies would be the most important for a company such as Dirt Bikes?
- (Optional) Use electronic presentation software to summarize for management your analysis of Dirt Bikes's performance.

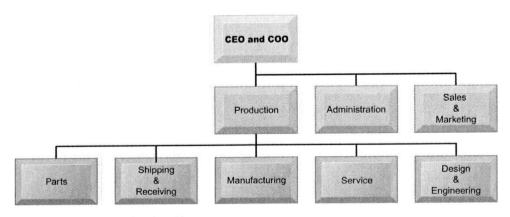

Dirt Bikes USA Organization Chart

Improving Decision Making: Using Databases to Analyze Sales Trends

Software skills: Database querying and reporting
Business skills: Sales trend analysis

You can find out how information systems improve management decision making in this exercise. Rather than guessing or relying on estimates and experience, managers today rely on information stored in databases. In this project, you will start out with raw transactional sales data and use Microsoft Access database software to develop queries and reports that help managers make better decisions about product pricing, sales promotions, and inventory replenishment.

At the Laudon Web site for this chapter, you can find a Store and Regional Sales Database developed in Microsoft Access. A part of the database is shown below. The database contains raw data on weekly store sales of computer equipment in various sales regions. You'll be using Access to manage the data and turn it into useful business information.

The database includes fields for record number, store identification number, sales region, item number, item description, unit price, units sold, and the weekly sales period when the sales were made.

Develop some reports and queries to make this information more useful for running the business. Sales and production managers want answers to the following questions:

- Which products should be restocked?
- Which stores and sales regions would benefit from a promotional campaign and additional marketing?
- When (what time of year) should products be offered at full price, and when should discounts be used?

You can easily modify the database table to find and report your answers. Print your reports and results of queries.

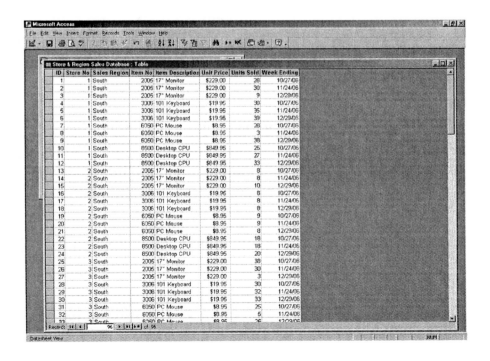

Achieving Operational Excellence: Using Internet Software to Budget for Shipping Costs

Software skills: Internet-based software
Business skills: Information-driven decision making and cost management

The Internet provides some marvelous tools for driving down business costs both because of the powerful Internet software tools that are available, and because vendors compete with one another in a transparent electronic marketplace. The result is lower costs to businesses that use these services.

In this exercise, you will use the same online software tools that businesses use to calculate and budget for shipping costs. Using these tools, you will choose the "best" shipper for your business. "Best" does not necessarily mean lowest cost but includes a consideration of other factors, such as scheduling, ease of use, and compatibility with your business schedule.

Assume you are the shipping clerk of a small firm that prints, binds, and ships popular books for a midlevel publisher. Your production facilities are located in Albany, New York (ZIP code 12250). Your customers' warehouses are located in Rye, New York (10580); Irving, Texas (75015); Charlotte, North Carolina (28201); Sioux Falls, South Dakota (57117); and Tustin, California (92680). The production facility operates 250 days per year. Your books are usually shipped in one of two package sizes:

- 9 inches tall by 13 inches long by 17 inches wide, weighing 45 pounds
- 10 inches tall by 6 inches long by 12 inches wide, weighing 16 pounds

The company ships about four of the A boxes to each of the warehouses on an average day and about eight B boxes daily.

What's the best shipper for your company? Go on the Web and compare three shippers, such as Federal Express (www.fedex.com), UPS (www.ups.com), and the United States Postal Service (www.usps.gov). Consider not only costs but also such issues as delivery speed, pickup schedules, drop-off locations, tracking ability, and ease of use of the Web site. Which service did you select? Explain why in a slide presentation.

5   LEARNING TRACK MODULE

How Much Does IT Matter? In May 2003 Nicholas Carr, an editor at *Harvard Business Review*, wrote an article titled "IT Doesn't Matter." This and subsequent articles with a similar theme created a vigorous debate about the potential and actual role of information technology and systems in creating business strategic advantage. If you would like to participate in this debate and learn more, you will find a Learning Track module on this topic at the Laudon Web site for this chapter and on the Student CD-ROM. You can also find more information about the current state of this debate on the Web. Just Google "IT doesn't matter" and read several rebuttals, one of the best being an article by Robert M. Metcalfe, inventor of Ethernet, called "Why I.T. Matters," *MIT Technology Review*, January 2004. It's free at Technologyreview.com on the Internet. IT really does matter!

Summary

1. *Explain why information systems are so essential in business today.*

   Information systems are a foundation for conducting business today. In many industries, survival and even existence is difficult without extensive use of information technology. Information systems have become essential for helping organizations operate in a global economy. Organizations are trying to become more competitive and efficient by transforming themselves into digital firms where nearly all core business processes and relationships with customers, suppliers, and employees are digitally enabled. Businesses today use information systems to achieve six major objectives: operational excellence; new products, services, and business models; customer/supplier intimacy; improved decision making; competitive advantage; and day-to-day survival.

2. *Define an information system from both a technical and a business perspective.*

   From a technical perspective, an information system collects, stores, and disseminates information from an organization's environment and internal operations to support organizational functions and decision making, communication, coordination, control, analysis, and visualization. Information systems transform raw data into useful information through three basic activities: input, processing, and output. From a business perspective, an information system provides a solution to a problem or challenge facing a firm and provides real economic value to the business.

3. *Identify and describe the three dimensions of information systems.*

   An information system represents a combination of management, organization, and technology elements. The management dimension of information systems involves leadership, strategy, and management behavior. The technology dimension consists of computer hardware, software, data management technology, and networking/telecommunications technology (including the Internet). The organization dimension of information systems involves the organization's hierarchy, functional specialties, business processes, culture, and political interest groups.

4. *Assess the complementary assets required for information technology to provide value to a business.*

   An information system is part of a series of value-adding activities for acquiring, transforming, and distributing information to improve management decision making, enhance organizational performance, and, ultimately, increase firm profitability. Information technology cannot provide this value unless it is accompanied by supportive changes in organization and management called complementary assets. These complementary assets include new business models, new business processes, a supportive organizational culture, incentives for management support and innovation, training, and social assets such as standards, laws and regulations, and telecommunications infrastructure. Firms that make appropriate investments in these complementary assets, also known as organizational and management capital, receive superior returns on their information technology investments.

5. *Identify and describe contemporary approaches to the study of information systems and distinguish between computer literacy and information systems literacy.*

   The study of information systems deals with issues and insights contributed from technical and behavioral disciplines. The disciplines that contribute to the technical approach are computer science, management science, and operations research. The disciplines contributing to the behavioral approach are psychology, sociology, and economics.

   Information systems literacy requires an understanding of the organizational and management dimensions of information systems, as well as the technical dimensions addressed by computer literacy. Information systems literacy draws on both technical and behavioral approaches to studying information systems. The field of MIS promotes information systems literacy by combining all of these disciplines with a practical orientation toward developing system solutions to real-world problems and managing information technology resources.

Key Terms

Business functions
Business model
Business processes
Complementary assets
Computer hardware
Computer literacy
Computer software
Culture
Data
Data management technology
Data workers
Digital firm
Extranets
Feedback
Information
Information system
Information systems literacy
Information technology (IT)

Information technology (IT) infrastructure
Input
Internet
Intranets
Knowledge workers
Management information systems (MIS)
Middle management
Network
Networking and telecommunications technology
Operational management
Organizational and management capital
Output
Processing
Production or service workers
Senior management
Sociotechnical view
World Wide Web

Review Questions

1. Describe three ways in which information systems are transforming business.
2. Describe the qualities of a digital firm. Why are digital firms so powerful?
3. List and describe six reasons why information systems are so important for business today.
4. What is an information system? What activities does it perform?
5. What is the difference between data and information?
6. What is information systems literacy? How does it differ from computer literacy?
7. List and describe the organizational, management, and technology dimensions of information systems.

8. What are the Internet and the World Wide Web? How have they changed the role played by information systems in organizations?
9. What is the purpose of an information system from a business perspective? What role does it play in the business information value chain?
10. Why do some firms obtain greater value from their information systems than others? What role do complementary assets and organizational and management capital play?
11. Distinguish between a behavioral and a technical approach to information systems in terms of the questions asked and the answers provided. What major disciplines contribute to an understanding of information systems?

Discussion Questions

1. Information systems are too important to be left to computer specialists. Do you agree? Why or why not?
2. It has been said that Toyota's most valuable asset is "The Toyota Way." Discuss the implications of this statement for the role of information systems in that company.

Video Case

You will find a video case illustrating some of the concepts in this chapter on the Laudon Web site and Student CD-ROM along with questions to help you analyze the case.

Teamwork: Analyzing a Business System

In a group with three or four classmates, find a description in a computer or business magazine of an information system used by an organization. Look for information about the company on the Web to gain further insight into the company, and prepare a brief description of the business. Describe the system you have selected in terms of its inputs, processes, and outputs and in terms of its organization, management, and technology features and the importance of the system to the company. If possible, use electronic presentation software to present your analysis to the class.

REFERENCES

Avison, David. "Information Systems in the MBA Curriculum: An International Perspective." *Communications of the AIS* 11, Article 6 (January 2003)

Baskerville, Richard L. and Michael D. Myers. "Information Systems as a Reference Discipline." *MIS Quarterly* 26, no. 1 (March 2002).

Bautsch, Holly et. al. "An Investigation of Mobile Phone Use: A Sociotechnical Approach. Department of Industrial Engineering, University of Wisconsin, Madison (2001).

Bebasat, Izak and Robert W. Zmud. "The Identity Crisis Within the is Discipline: Defining and Communicating the Discipline's Core Properties." *MIS Quarterly* 27, no. 2 (June 2003).

Brynjolffson, Erik. "The IT Productivity Gap." *Optimize Magazine* 21 (July 2003).

Brynjolfsson, Erik and Lorin M. Hitt. "Beyond Computation: Information Technology, Organizational Transformation, and Business Performance." *Journal of Economic Perspectives* 14 no. 4 (2000).

Carr, Nicholas. "IT Doesn't Matter." *Harvard Business Review* (May 2003).

Dedrick, Jason, Vijay Gurbaxani, and Kenneth L. Kraemer. "Information Technology and Economic Performance: A Critical Review of the Empirical Evidence," Center for Research on Information Technology and Organizations, University of California, Irvine (December 2001).

Galliers, Robert D. and Maureen Meadows. "A Discipline Divided: Globalization and Parochialism in Information Systems Research". *Communications of the AIS* 11, Article 5 (January 2003)

Greenspan Alan. "The Revolution in Information Technology." Boston College Conference on the New Economy (March 6, 2000).

Hacki, Remo and Julian Lighton, "The Future of the Networked Company," *McKinsey Quarerly* 3 (2001).

Jorgenson, Dale W. "Information Technology and Economic Performance: A Critical Review of Empirical Evidence." Center for Research on Information Technology and Organizations, University of California, Irvine (December, 2001).

Lamb, Roberta; Steve Sawyer, and Rob Kling. "A Social Informatics Perspective on Socio-Technical Networks." http://lamb.cba.hawaii.edu/pubs (2004).

Laudon, Kenneth C. *Computers and Bureaucratic Reform*. New York: John Wiley and Sons (1974).

Lee, H. "Broadband and Mobile Opportunities: A Socio-technical Perspective." Journal of Information Technology 18 (2003).

Lev, Baruch. *Intangibles: Management, Measurement and Reporting*. The Brookings Institution Press, (2001).

Marchand, Donald A. "Extracting the Business Value of IT: IT Is Usage, Not Just Deployment that Counts!" The Copco Institute Journal of Financial Transformation (2004).

Mumford, Enid. "Socio Technical Design: An Unfulfilled Promise or a Future Opportunity." in R. Baskerville, et. al. The Social and Organizational Perspective on Research and Practice in Information Technology. London: Chapman-Hall (2000).

Orlikowski, Wanda J. and Stephen R. Bailey. "Technology and Institutions: What Can Research on Information Technology and Research on Organizations Learn from Each Other?" *MIS Quarterly* 25, no. 2 (June 2001).

Pew Research Center. "Trends 2005; Chapter 4: Internet: Mainstreaming of Online Life." (January 25, 2005).

Quinn, Francis J. "eBusiness Evangelist; An Interview with Erik Brynjolfsson." *Supply Chain Management Review* (May/June 2006).

Ross, Jeanne W. and Peter Weill. "Six IT Decisions Your IT People Shouldn't Make." *Harvard Business Review* (November 2002).

Sawyer, S., and J. P. Allen. "Broadband and Mobile Opportunities: A Socio-technical Perspective." Journal of Information Technology 18 (June 2003).

Stiroh, Kevin. "The Economic Impact of Information Technology." Federal Reserve Bank of New York, (2001).

Teece, David. Economic Performance and Theory of the Firm: The Selected Papers of David Teece. London: Edward Elgar Publishing (1998).

Triplett, Jack E. and Barry P. Bosworth. "Productivity in Services Industries: Trends and Measurement Issues". The Brookings Institution, Washington D.C.: (2003).

Morgan Stanley is a global financial services firm with more than 600 offices in 30 countries and over 53,000 employees. It was founded in 1935 and is headquartered in New York City. The firm operates in four segments: Institutional Securities, Asset Management, Retail Brokerage, and Discover (which provides Discover Card services.) The firm acquired the Discover Card business as a result of its merger with retail brokerage Dean Witter Discover and Co.in 1997.

The unification of Morgan Stanley and Dean Witter created a digital, cultural, and philosophical divide, which was extremely difficult to overcome. One of the business sectors to suffer the most under this arrangement has been Retail Brokerage, which manages $616 billion in client assets. Retail Brokerage provides comprehensive brokerage, investment, and financial services to individual investors globally, with 9,526 worldwide representatives in more than 500 retail locations, including 485 in the United States.

Despite the merger, the Retail Brokerage group was never accepted as an equal partner by the rest of Morgan Stanley. Former Dean Witter employees have claimed they felt like disrespected outsiders after the merger. The feeling persisted and many retail brokers viewed their job security as tenuous at best.

Moreover, Retail Brokerage was not well-integrated with the rest of the company. It ran on a different systems platform than the institutional brokerage side, and its employee systems were not integrated. Retail Brokerage systems were also much more antiquated than those at other parts of the company. Brokers had to visit their offices on weekends to print portfolio summaries in advance of client meetings, because the outdated computer systems could not handle the task during normal business hours. Even on those off-hours, desktop PCs, which hadn't been upgraded in years, would often crash and printers clogged if they were being used by more than two people. Brokers did their work without benefit of an application that provided both real-time stock quotes and transaction histories. Some of the firm's technology problems couldn't be hidden from clients, who routinely complained about the customer Web site and sparsely detailed year-end tax reports they received.

Top brokers started to leave, taking with them the portfolios of numerous important clients. Profits specifically from Retail Brokerage dropped precipitously and margins lagged behind those of comparable brokerage firms. During this time, nearly 1,500 brokers left the company. Bill Doyle, an analyst with Forrester Research Inc., pointed out that the business was ailing partially as a result of a lack of investment in technology.

When the stock market crashed in 2001, CEO Philip Purcell believed that the market's comeback would happen slowly. He therefore focused his business strategy on maximizing profits instead of generating revenue. The implementation of this strategy involved cutting costs. Each of Morgan Stanley's divisions received less funding for their operations, jobs were eliminated, and investing in technology was obviously a low priority. Purcell, of course, had miscalculated. The market rebounded within a few years, and Morgan Stanley was not positioned to compete in retail. While his firm was watching its margins, Merrill Lynch was spending $1 billion on new systems for its brokers. The turmoil in the inner sanctum of Morgan Stanley's leadership also contributed to the company's woes.

Purcell locked horns with investors, executives, and former executives over a number of issues, one of which was selling the underperforming Discover credit card division. Some investors even wanted Purcell to spin off the entire Dean Witter part of the company. In March 2005, eight former executives appealed to Morgan Stanley's board of directors to remove Purcell as CEO for his mismanagement of Discover and Retail Brokerage. The board determined that the best interest of the firm was served by keeping Purcell and divesting itself of its struggling divisions. The board also approved Purcell's appointments of two executives who were considered loyal to him and to the board.

Protesting Purcell's leadership, two leading executives in the investment banking division resigned. More departures followed. Purcell's critics now had even more ammunition with which to bring him down: in addition to mismanaging the struggling areas of the business, his actions had threatened the performance of the firm's strength, investment banking. Purcell finally resigned in June 2005, unable to shake the claims that his solutions to problems were lightweight rather than dramatic and far-reaching, and that his decisions were based on protecting his job rather than improving the firm. He was succeeded by John Mack, a former Morgan Stanley president who had left the company in 2001 as a result of a power struggle with Purcell.

With new leadership in place, Morgan Stanley has finally begun to address the issue of technology in its Retail Brokerage division, which has been renamed the Global Wealth Management Group. In October 2005, the firm hired Eileen Murray as its head of Global Operations and Technology. She works directly under Chief Executive John Mack, with whom she has a strong professional history. Murray has committed to boosting Morgan Stanley's investment in technology for retail, saying, "We expect to make substantial improvements" that "will ultimately help our financial advisors better serve our clients, while also helping our clients better manage their relationship with us." As proof, the technology and operations budget for the Global Wealth Management Group for 2006 exceeded $500 million. Mack also brought in a new boss for the group. It is now under the leadership of James Gorman, who performed a successful parallel makeover at Merrill Lynch's brokerage division.

Mack has been under some pressure to sell the retail division, a choice he has been reluctant to make. He subscribes to the view that ownership of a retail brokerage business is an investment in the firm because, in addition to providing revenue from individual investors, it gives Morgan Stanley a direct channel for selling its own investment banking products. Mack's goal is to increase the profit margin of the Global Wealth Management Group retail brokerage, which ranges from 11 percent to 20 percent, which would make it as profitable as rivals' businesses.

Mack has stated both publicly and privately that some of Morgan Stanley's businesses had not received the technology they needed, and he intends to make the necessary investments. In the firm's 2005 annual report, Mack said, "We are committed to addressing underinvestment," and "We're going to upgrade our technology platforms and provide our financial advisors and investment representatives with a tool kit that is as competitive as that of our leading peers."

Some of the overwhelmed broker desktop workstations have been replaced. The new systems are better integrated with backend systems so that brokers have a better view of client portfolios. The company plans further improvements in this area so that brokers will have access to all relevant client data at once, including transaction history, contact history, and portfolio performance. Consolidating all of these features will require several years of work. The company also rolled out a new tax-reporting application that automatically reconciles gains and losses and allows users to download information from its client Web site into popular tax programs. Before that time, customers had to wade through a confusing maze of figures to add up gains and losses on their year-end tax reports.

In response to customer demands, Morgan Stanley scheduled an upgrade of its Web site for May 2006, which analyst Doyle described as a particularly weak area for the firm. The services available online to Morgan Stanley customers dated back to pre-2000 technology. Doyle sees the Web presence as a major challenge because Morgan Stanley has been focusing more on its wealthiest clients than on the rank-and-file small investors. The firm had previously assumed that these top clients weren't interested in online services because they get the direct attention of brokers (whereas investors with portfolios under $100,000 must deal with call centers). Research by Forrester has shown the opposite to be true: wealthy customers actually want more hands-on control of their portfolios, and therefore want more tools and services available online. These customers prefer to approach their brokers with their own ideas. Gorman, as head of retail brokerage, must not lose sight of the significance that online technology holds for his division.

Mack and Gorman must also take measures to repair the schism that developed after the merger with Dean Witter. Mack has been addressing the issue of a "one-firm culture." The firm is trying to stem the loss of productive brokers. Increasing salaries and expense accounts are not enough. The top brokers still feel they can fulfill their earning potential better and hold jobs longer at other firms. It's not just that their print queue gets jammed; it's that they question how much the company values them if it's not willing to support them in such a way that they can best perform their jobs.

By the spring of 2006, signs of progress were evident. In June 2006, Morgan Stanley generated second-quarter net income of $1.96 billion. The retail brokerage division posted $157 million in pretax profit, the largest profit since the first quarter of 2005.

Sources: Edward Cone, "Morgan Stanley: Trading Sideways," "Return on Noninvestment," and "Follow the Money," *CIO Insight*, April 4, 2006; "Morgan Stanley's Mack Attack," *Business Week*, June 22, 2006; George Stein and Gregory Cresci, "Morgan Stanley Soars as Mack Delivers in 2nd Quarter (Update2)," Bloomberg.com, June 21, 2006; and www.morganstanley.com, accessed June 21, 2006.

CASE STUDY QUESTIONS

1. Why did Morgan Stanley underinvest in information technology?

2. Why was the merger with Dean Witter disruptive for the company?

3. Why was Dean Witter and Retail Brokerage a good place to increase spending on information systems? (Review the six strategic objectives of information systems discussed in section 1 of the chapter "Information Systems in Global Business Today.")

4. If you were James Gorman, the new head of Global Wealth Management Group, what information systems would you invest in? Why? Do you think Morgan Stanley's plans for an integrated client information system are worthwhile? [Hint: Think of the services you would like to receive from your banker or stock broker.]

5. Aside from new systems, what changes in management and organization are required to restore revenue and profit growth at the Global Wealth Management Group?

Global E-Business: How Businesses Use Information Systems

LEARNING OBJECTIVES

After reading this chapter, you will be able to:

1. Define and describe business processes and their relationship to information systems.

2. Describe the information systems supporting the major business functions: sales and marketing, manufacturing and production, finance and accounting, and human resources.

3. Evaluate the role played by systems serving the various levels of management in a business and their relationship to each other.

4. Explain how enterprise applications and intranets promote business process integration and improve organizational performance.

5. Assess the role of the information systems function in a business.

Interactive Sessions:

Information Systems Help Kia Solve Its Quality Problems

Managing Travel Expenses: New Tools, New Savings

CHAPTER OUTLINE

INFORMATION SYSTEMS JOIN THE TUPPERWARE PARTY

E arl Tupper patented the airtight Tupper seal for food storage containers in 1947, but it wasn't catching on in retail stores. He turned to an engaging single mother, Brownie Wise, to help him sell his Tupperware through home demonstration parties. The strategy worked: Tupperware grew into a $1.3 billion company that sells through home parties using an independent sales force of one million members. A Tupperware party begins every two seconds somewhere in the world.

In 2005, Tupperware faced another challenge. The company changed its U.S. operations from a distributorship model to a multilevel compensation structure. Tupperware's U.S. sales force mushroomed from three levels of compensation (sales consultant, manager, and distributor) to a dozen levels. Sales consultants are paid a commission for their own sales plus a smaller commission based on sales of consultants that they recruited to the business.

As a sales consultant became successful and recruited more people to the business, that person was also responsible for her paperwork, plus paperwork from the people she had recruited to her downline sales team. There was not enough time left for the really important job of selling and recruiting. Tupperware's order entry system was not able to handle peak demand during sales promotions and busy times of the year. To support growth and improve business processes for both the sales force and corporate staff, Tupperware needed a system that could handle an additional 5,000 users each month, send e-mail messages to 50,000 recipients at a time, and allow restricted access to documents based on an employee's job position in the company.

In 2004, Tupperware began implementing an integrated Web-based order management system called My.Tupperware.com that relieves distributors from the task of entering the orders from everyone they recruited. Now each sales consultant enters his or her own orders.

The Web-based system serves as a portal that integrates with Tupperware's existing systems so that authorized users can access information from related systems with a single sign-on. Different groups in the company, such as sales promotion, training, and Web support, have tools to publish and retire Web content for specific audiences in the company on their own without requiring help from the company's information systems staff. The system also streamlines communications among corporate managers, support staff and sales consultants, and provides better support to sales consultants in promoting product sales, recruiting new sales consultants, and managing downline sales teams.

The portal provides four levels of access. There is a home page accessible to consumers, which provides information on Tupperware products and increases brand awareness. A second level gives all sales consultants access to order entry, e-mail, a calendar, training

Photo courtesy of Peter Arnold, Inc.

41

materials, and list functions. A third level offers sales consultants, who wish to pay a fee, additional marketing and promotional features and tools to create their own e-commerce Web sites linked to My.Tupperware.com. The highest level lets users perform additional promotional activities and links to higher compensation opportunities. Any sales consultant can choose any level of accessibility she wishes.

Tupperware chose Oracle Collaboration Suite and Oracle Portal software as the platform for the system because they enabled the company to integrate functions for data management, financial systems, calendar, and e-mail into a single secure environment that could scale up to meet future growth in Tupperware sales and sales consultants. The company had also been using other Oracle software for a decade, so it felt comfortable with Oracle products.

Tupperware finished rolling out My.Tupperware.com to 50,000 North American users in the final months of 2004. Reaction to the system has been very positive. Tupperware is now enhancing the system to provide online Web conferencing and voice and text messaging.

Sources: Molly Rose Teuke, "Sealing Success," *Profit Magazine*, February 2006, and www.tupperware.com, accessed June 21, 2006.

Tupperware's experience illustrates how much companies today rely on information systems to run their businesses and drive growth and profitability. Tupperware has a unique business model based on selling food storage and preparation products at home parties using a large independent sales force. But its information systems were inadequate for supporting its new multilevel compensation structure and continuing growth.

The chapter-opening diagram calls attention to important points raised by this case and this chapter. Tupperware's old business model was outdated. When it changed its business model, moving toward a multilevel compensation structure, its sales agents were overwhelmed with paperwork. Tupperware management identified an opportunity to use information systems to solve this challenge and greatly improve business performance. Tupperware needed to change its technology, management, and organizational processes. The Oracle software made it possible to support additional levels of Tupperware consul-

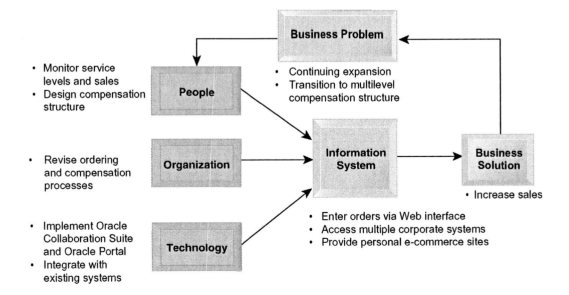

tants and gave individual consultants tools to process their own orders and set up personal e-commerce sites. To make the system effective, Tupperware had to revise its business processes for placing orders and compensating consultants. Tupperware's new ordering and compensation systems have increased employee productivity and provided a new channel for reaching customers on the Web.

HEADS UP

This chapter provides you with a quick overview of the significant role of information systems in a business. You'll learn about the different types of information systems used by businesses, including systems based on the Internet, and how these systems support the firm's core business processes.

• If your career is in finance and accounting, you will be working with systems that keep track of your company's assets, fund flows, and overall financial performance.

• If your career is in human resources, information systems will help you develop staffing requirements; identify potential new employees; maintain employee records; track employee training, skills, and job performance; and design appropriate plans for employee compensation and career development.

• If your career is in information systems, you'll be responsible for supplying and overseeing the hardware, software and other technologies used by the various types of systems in organizations.

• If your career is in manufacturing and production, information systems will help you solve problems related to the planning, development, and delivery of products and services and control the flow of production.

• If your career is in sales and marketing, information systems will help you promote products, contact customers, track sales, identify profitable customers, provide ongoing service and support, and analyze the performance of the firm's sales staff.

---

1 BUSINESS PROCESSES AND INFORMATION SYSTEMS

I n order to operate, businesses must deal with many different pieces of information about suppliers, customers, employees, invoices and payments, and of course their products and services. They must organize work activities that use this information to operate efficiently and enhance the overall performance of the firm. Information systems make it possible for firms to manage all their information, make better decisions, and improve the execution of their business processes.

BUSINESS PROCESSES

Information systems are all about improving business processes which lie at the very heart of a business. So it's important to understand just what is meant by "business processes."

Business processes refer to the manner in which work is organized, coordinated, and focused to produce a valuable product or service. Business processes are workflows of material, information, and knowledge—sets of activities. Business processes also refer to the unique ways in which organizations coordinate work, information, and knowledge, and the ways in which management chooses to coordinate work. Every business can be seen as a collection of business processes. Some of these processes are part of larger encompassing processes.

For example, almost every business has a way to hire employees. The process of hiring employees is a business process in the sense that it is a set of activities that a firm uses to hire new employees. The business process of hiring can be broken down into a number of different steps such as place advertisements, contact employment agencies, collect resumes, review resumes, interview candidates, rank candidates, make employment decision, and enroll employee in employment systems such as payroll, health, and pension. In some businesses this process can be slow and inefficient, whereas in others, it can be swift and highly efficient. One of the major purposes of information systems is to enable highly efficient business processes.

To a large extent, the performance of a business firm depends on how well its business processes are designed and coordinated. A company's business processes can be a source of competitive strength if they enable the company to innovate or to execute better than its rivals. Business processes can also be liabilities if they are based on outdated ways of working that impede organizational responsiveness and efficiency.

Many business processes are tied to a specific functional area. For example, the sales and marketing function would be responsible for identifying customers, and the human resources function would be responsible for hiring employees. Table 1 describes some typical business processes for each of the functional areas of business.

Other business processes cross many different functional areas and require coordination across departments. For instance, consider the seemingly simple business process of fulfilling a customer order (see Figure 1). Initially, the sales department would receive a sales order. The order will pass first to accounting to ensure the customer can pay for the order either by a credit verification or

TABLE 1   EXAMPLES OF FUNCTIONAL BUSINESS PROCESSES

FUNCTIONAL AREA	BUSINESS PROCESS
Manufacturing and production	Assembling the product
	Checking for quality
	Producing bills of materials
Sales and marketing	Identifying customers
	Making customers aware of the product
	Selling the product
Finance and accounting	Paying creditors
	Creating financial statements
	Managing cash accounts
Human resources	Hiring employees
	Evaluating employees' job performance
	Enrolling employees in benefits plans

FIGURE 1   THE ORDER FULFILLMENT PROCESS

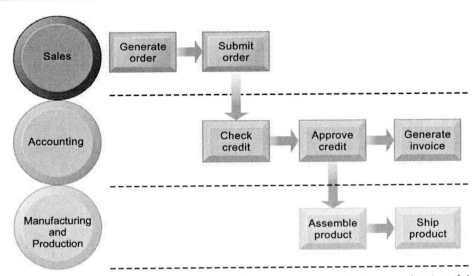

Fulfilling a customer order involves a complex set of steps that requires the close coordination of the sales, accounting, and manufacturing functions.

request for immediate payment prior to shipping. Once the customer credit is established, the production department has to pull the product from inventory or produce the product. Then the product will need to be shipped (and this may require working with a logistics firm, such as UPS or FedEx). A bill or invoice will then have to be generated by the accounting department, and a notice will be sent to the customer indicating that the product has shipped. Sales will have to be notified of the shipment and prepare to support the customer by answering calls or fulfilling warranty claims.

While at first appearing to be a simple process, fulfilling an order turns out to be a very complicated series of business processes that require the close coordination of major functional groups in a firm. Moreover, to efficiently perform all these steps in the order fulfillment process requires a great deal of information. The required information must flow rapidly within the firm; with business partners, such as delivery firms; and with the customer. Information systems make this possible.

HOW INFORMATION TECHNOLOGY ENHANCES BUSINESS PROCESSES: EFFICIENCY AND TRANSFORMATION

Exactly how do information systems enhance business processes? Primarily in two ways: increasing the efficiency of existing processes and enabling entirely new processes that are capable of transforming the business. Information systems automate many steps in business processes that were formerly performed manually, such as checking a client's credit, or generating an invoice and shipping order. But today, information technology can do much more. New technology can actually change the flow of information, making it possible for many more people to access and share information, replacing sequential steps with tasks that can be performed simultaneously in

45

parallel, and eliminating delays in decision making. In other words, information can enable entirely new business processes. It can even transform the way the business works and drive entirely new business models. Ordering a book online from Amazon.com or downloading a music track from iTunes are entirely new business processes based on new business models that would be inconceivable without information technology. Both iTunes and Amazon represent business transformations.

That's why it's so important to pay close attention to business processes, both in your information systems course and in your future career. By analyzing business processes in your firm, you can achieve a very clear understanding of how your business actually works. For instance, by analyzing the customer service process, you will learn how long it takes to answer a customer request for service, how many steps are involved, how many people are involved, and how much it costs. Moreover, by conducting a business process analysis, you will also begin to understand how to change the business to make it more efficient or effective.

2 | TYPES OF BUSINESS INFORMATION SYSTEMS

Now that you understand business processes, it's time to look more closely at the many types of information systems that support the business processes of the firm. Because a business may have tens or even hundreds of different business processes, and because there are different people, specialties, and levels in an organization, there are different kinds of systems. No single system can provide all the information an organization needs. In fact, large- and medium-size firms have thousands of computer programs and hundreds of different systems. Even small firms have a collection of different systems: a system for conducting e-mail campaigns to customers, a system for monitoring advertisements placed on Google, a system for keeping track of basic sales transactions, a system for keeping track of vendors, and so forth. At first glance, it can be difficult to comprehend all the different systems in a business, and even more difficult to understand how they relate to one another.

We attempt to describe this complex situation by looking at all these different systems from two different perspectives: a functional perspective identifying systems by their major business function, and a constituency perspective that identifies systems in terms of the major organizational groups that they serve.

SYSTEMS FROM A FUNCTIONAL PERSPECTIVE

We will start by describing systems using a functional perspective, because this is how you will likely first encounter systems in a business. For instance, if you are a marketing major and take a job in marketing, you will be working on the job first with marketing information systems. If you are an accounting major, you will be working with accounting and financial systems first. From a historical perspective, functional systems were the first kinds of systems developed by business firms. These systems were located in specific departments, such as accounting, marketing and sales, production, and human resources. Let's take a close look at systems from this functional perspective.

TABLE 2   EXAMPLES OF SALES AND MARKETING INFORMATION SYSTEMS

SYSTEM	DESCRIPTION	GROUPS SERVED
Order processing	Enter, process, and track orders	Operational management and employees
Pricing analysis	Determine prices for products and services	Middle management
Sales trend forecasting	Prepare five-year sales forecasts	Senior management

Sales and Marketing Systems

The sales and marketing function is responsible for selling the organization's products or services. Marketing is concerned with identifying the customers for the firm's products or services, determining what customers need or want, planning and developing products and services to meet their needs, and advertising and promoting these products and services. Sales is concerned with contacting customers, selling the products and services, taking orders, and following up on sales. These activities can be thought of as business processes. **Sales and marketing information systems** support these business processes.

Table 2 shows that information systems are used in sales and marketing in a number of ways. Sales and marketing systems help senior management monitor trends affecting new products and sales opportunities, support planning for new products and services, and monitor the performance of competitors. Sales and marketing systems aid middle management by supporting market research and by analyzing advertising and promotional campaigns, pricing decisions, and sales performance. Sales and marketing systems assist operational management and employees in locating and contacting prospective customers, tracking sales, processing orders, and providing customer service support.

Figure 2 illustrates a sales information system used by retailers, such as The Gap or Target. Point-of-sale devices (usually handheld scanners at the checkout counter) capture data about each item sold, which update the sales system's figures about sales and send data about items sold to related systems dealing with items remaining in inventory and with production. These businesses use this information to track which items have been sold, to determine sales revenue, and to identify hot-selling items and other sales trends.

Manufacturing and Production Systems

The manufacturing and production function is responsible for actually producing the firm's goods and services. Manufacturing and production systems deal with the planning, development, and maintenance of production facilities; the establishment of production goals; the acquisition, storage, and availability of production materials; and the scheduling of equipment, facilities, materials, and labor required to fashion finished products. **Manufacturing and production information systems** support these activities.

Table 3 shows some typical manufacturing and production information systems for each major organizational group. Senior management uses manufacturing and production systems that deal with the firm's long-term manufacturing goals, such as where to locate new plants or whether to invest in new manufacturing technology. Manufacturing and production systems

INTERACTIVE SESSION: ORGANIZATIONS

INFORMATION SYSTEMS HELP KIA SOLVE ITS QUALITY PROBLEMS

A decade ago, few Americans had heard of Korean car maker Kia Motors. The company only started selling cars in the United States in 1994, promising high-quality vehicles at prices well below the competition. That year, Kia sold 12,163 vehicles. By 2004, Kia had sold 270,000 cars and expects to sell 500,000 annually in the U.S. market by 2010. Kias are 10 to 15 percent cheaper than comparable vehicles by competitors.

From a marketing and sales standpoint, Kia has been a phenomenal success. But until 2002, Kia ranked at the bottom of J.D. Power and Associates' annual initial-quality survey of new vehicle owners. In 1997, when the average North American car had 1.1 defects per vehicle, Kia had 2.75. In 2002, Kia had improved to 2.12 defects per vehicle, but the industry average was 1.33. Kia had a long way to go, and this was affecting its ability to sell cars, retain customers, and keep operational costs down.

Kia has tried to keep customers happy despite its quality problems by offering a 10 Year/100,000 Mile Warranty Program, which provides coverage until either the yearly or total mileage figure is reached, whichever occurs first. That means that Kia must pay for repairs on all warrantied items in its vehicles for many more years than its competitors are willing to do for their products, which raises operating costs and eats into profits.

Like all manufacturers of vehicles sold in North America, Kia had to create a system by December 1, 2003, to report any defects, accidents, or injuries involving its vehicles to the U.S. National Highway Traffic Safety Administration (NHTSA). This was a major challenge for the company. The information Kia had to report was stored in at least seven different systems run by Kia's warranty, parts, consumer, and legal affairs departments.

Fragmentation of this information in different systems prevented Kia from getting a complete picture of defects. Parts sales are the first indicator of a defect, warranty claims the second, and consumer complaints the third. Looking at parts sales alone won't provide an answer. A sudden increase in brake pad orders from Kia dealers making repairs indicates there might be a problem with a particular pad. By examining warranty claims, Kia might discover that brake pads were only being ordered for four-wheel drive models of one of its vehicles and

not for two-wheel drive models. This additional information might show that the problem was actually a result of excess vibration caused by the vehicle's design rather than the brake pads.

Kia could have created a series of stopgap software programs to extract the required information out of these various computer systems and collate it manually. But this would have been time-consuming and would not provide any other benefits to the company. So Kia's management decided instead to create a defect early warning system that could identify potential problems, such as faulty brake parts, by combining warranty claims, parts orders, field reports, and consumer complaints.

Kia enlisted Infogain, a Los Gatos, California, software consulting firm to help it design a new system solution. Infogain created a software "engine" that examines six Kia systems for warranty claims, parts sales, vehicle identification number master storage files, and vehicle inventories and stores the essential information in a single common data repository. The system automatically breaks down and categorizes reports based on individual components, such as steering assemblies or headlights, and links to Kia's Clarify customer relationship management system, tracking consumer complaints received by phone, e-mail, or postal mail.

Once the data have been stored in a single place, Kia can use Crystal Analysis software to analyze them, highlighting events, such as spikes in warranty claims related to a particular vehicle model, unusual increases in parts orders, or high numbers of accidents resulting in serious injury or death, on an early warning dashboard. Managers are able to analyze the data by daily, weekly, or monthly reporting periods and by specific car models, model years, and components. They also can break down the data in detail to see how many complaints or warranty claims are associated with a specific item, such as a steering assembly.

Information from this system is helping Kia pinpoint the sources of defects and determine what percentage of its vehicles is likely to have problems. The company can then improve its production processes before the problems become more widespread, thus lowering costs for warranty repairs. This information also helps Kia determine the most cost-effective strategy for dealing with its quality problems. For example, should Kia recall all batteries if battery defects occur in extreme heat or limit recalls to states in the southern United States?

Kia's quality has indeed improved. In quality rankings released on May 18, 2005, J.D. Power reported that Kia had 1.40 problems per vehicle, finishing second for quality in the compact-car category behind the Toyota Prius. According to

Hirofumi Yokoi, an analyst with auto industry consulting firm CSM Worldwide, today "Kia quality is relatively comparable" with established U.S. automakers.

Sources: Craig Simons, "Kia Makes U.S. Inroads and Builds for Future Growth," Cox News Service, March 14, 2006; Mel Duvall, "Kia Motors America: Lemon Aid," *Baseline Magazine*, June 2005; and www.kia.com, accessed June 18, 2006.

CASE STUDY QUESTIONS

1. Why was it so difficult for Kia to identify sources of defects in the cars it produced?
2. What was the business impact of Kia not having an information system to track defects? What other business processes besides manufacturing and production were affected?
3. How did Kia's new defect-reporting system improve the way it ran its business?
4. What management, organization, and technology issues did Kia have to address when it adopted its new quality control system?
5. What new business processes were enabled by Kia's new quality control system?

MIS IN ACTION

1. Visit the Autobytel Web site and select a Kia model to research. Investigate the retail price, warranties, and any relevant reviews and safety data. Select a comparable model (suggested by Autobytel) from another automobile manufacturer and gather the same data for that make and model.
2. Visit the J.D. Power Web site and explore the Brand Ratings section. Examine Kia's overall quality rating and the quality ratings for overall quality-manufacturing, mechanical quality-manufacturing, and body and interior quality-manufacturing. Compare Kia's quality ratings to the quality ratings for the competing automaker you have been researching.
3. Create a table comparing the two cars you have selected on the basis of price, warranties, and quality. Would you select the Kia? Why or why not?

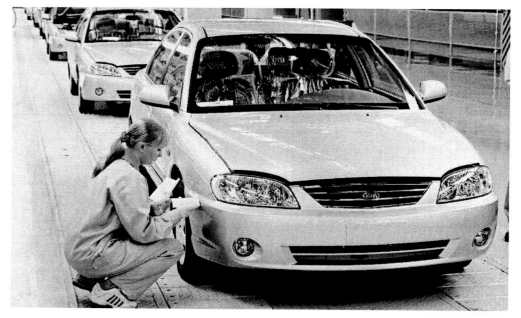

Kia uses information systems to help it identify sources of defects in cars so it can improve vehicle quality, reduce warranty repair costs, and increase customer satisfaction.

Photo courtesy of ITAR-TASS/ Udmurtsky Publishing House/NewsCom

TABLE 4 EXAMPLES OF FINANCE AND ACCOUNTING INFORMATION SYSTEMS

SYSTEM	DESCRIPTION	GROUPS SERVED
Accounts receivable	Tracks money owed the firm	Operational management
Budgeting	Prepares short-term budgets	Middle management
Profit planning	Plans long-term profits	Senior management

financial assets? What records exist for disbursements, receipts, payroll, and other fund flows?

Table 4 shows some of the typical **finance and accounting information systems** found in large organizations. Senior management uses finance and accounting systems to establish long-term investment goals for the firm and to provide long-range forecasts of the firm's financial performance. Middle management uses systems to oversee and control the firm's financial resources. Operational management uses finance and accounting systems to track the flow of funds in the firm through transactions, such as paychecks, payments to vendors, securities reports, and receipts.

Figure 4 illustrates an accounts receivable system, which keeps track of what customers who have made purchases on credit owe to a company. Every invoice generates an "account receivable"—that is, the customer owes the firm money. Some customers pay immediately in cash, but others are granted credit. The accounts receivable system records each invoice in a master file

FIGURE 4   AN ACCOUNTS RECEIVABLE SYSTEM

An accounts receivable system tracks and stores important customer data, such as payment history, credit rating, and billing history.

TABLE 5   EXAMPLES OF HUMAN RESOURCES INFORMATION SYSTEMS

SYSTEM	DESCRIPTION	GROUPS SERVED
Training and development	Tracks employee training, skills, and performance appraisals	Operational management
Compensation analysis	Monitors the range and distribution of employee wages, salaries, and benefits	Middle management
Human resources planning	Plans the long-term labor force needs of the organization	Senior management

that also contains information on each customer, including that person's credit rating. The system also keeps track of all the bills outstanding and can produce a variety of output reports, both on paper and on the computer screen, to help the business collect bills. The system also answers queries about a customer's credit rating and payment history.

Human Resources Systems

The human resources function is responsible for attracting, developing, and maintaining the firm's workforce. **Human resources information systems** support activities such as identifying potential employees, maintaining complete records on existing employees, and creating programs to develop employees' talents and skills.

Human resources systems help senior management identify the human resources requirements (skills, educational level, types of positions, number of positions, and cost) for meeting the firm's long-term business plans. Middle management uses human resources systems to monitor and analyze the recruitment, allocation, and compensation of employees. Operational management uses human resources systems to track the recruitment and placement of the firm's employees (see Table 5).

Figure 5 illustrates a typical human resources system for employee record keeping. It maintains basic employee data, such as the employee's name, age,

FIGURE 5   AN EMPLOYEE RECORD KEEPING SYSTEM

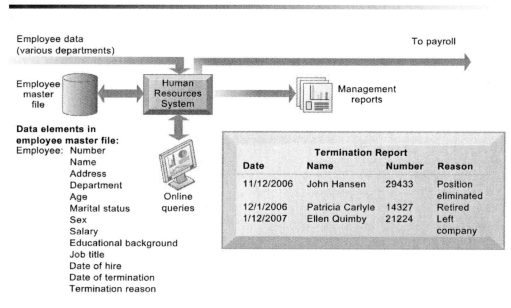

This system maintains data on the firm's employees to support the human resources function.

sex, marital status, address, educational background, salary, job title, date of hire, and date of termination. The system can produce a variety of reports, such as lists of newly hired employees, employees who are terminated or on leaves of absence, employees classified by job type or educational level, or employee job performance evaluations. Such systems are typically designed to provide data that can satisfy federal and state record keeping requirements for Equal Employment Opportunity (EEO) and other purposes.

SYSTEMS FROM A CONSTITUENCY PERSPECTIVE

Although a functional perspective is very useful for understanding how business systems serve specific functions, this perspective does not tell us how systems help managers manage the firm. Here we need a perspective that examines systems in terms of the various levels of management and types of decisions that they support.

Each of these levels has different information needs given their different responsibilities, and each can be seen as major information constituents. Senior managers need summary information that can quickly inform them about the overall performance of the firm, such as gross sales revenues, sales by product group and region, and overall profitability. Middle managers need more specific information on the results of specific functional areas and departments of the firm, such as sales contacts by the sales force, production statistics for specific factories or product lines, employment levels and costs, and sales revenues for each month or even each day. Operational managers need transaction-level information, such as the number of parts in inventory each day or the number of hours logged on Tuesday by each employee. Knowledge workers may need access to external scientific databases or internal databases with organizational knowledge. Finally, production or service workers need access to information from production machines, and service workers need access to customer records in order to take orders and answer questions from customers.

Transaction Processing Systems

Operational managers need systems that keep track of the elementary activities and transactions of the organization, such as sales, receipts, cash deposits, payroll, credit decisions, and the flow of materials in a factory. **Transaction processing systems (TPS)** provide this kind of information. A transaction processing system is a computerized system that performs and records the daily routine transactions necessary to conduct business, such as sales order entry, hotel reservations, payroll, employee record keeping, and shipping.

The principal purpose of systems at this level is to answer routine questions and to track the flow of transactions through the organization. How many parts are in inventory? What happened to Mr. Williams's payment? To answer these kinds of questions, information generally must be easily available, current, and accurate.

At the operational level, tasks, resources, and goals are predefined and highly structured. The decision to grant credit to a customer, for instance, is made by a lower-level supervisor according to predefined criteria. All that must be determined is whether the customer meets the criteria. The systems illustrated in Figures 4 and 5 are transaction processing systems.

Managers need TPS to monitor the status of internal operations and the firm's relations with the external environment. TPS are also major producers of information for the other types of systems. (For example, the accounts receivable system illustrated in Figure 5, along with other accounting TPS, sup-

FIGURE 6 **HOW MANAGEMENT INFORMATION SYSTEMS OBTAIN THEIR DATA FROM THE ORGANIZATION'S TPS**

In the system illustrated by this diagram, three TPS supply summarized transaction data to the MIS reporting system at the end of the time period. Managers gain access to the organizational data through the MIS, which provides them with the appropriate reports.

plies data to the company's general ledger system, which is responsible for maintaining records of the firm's income and expenses and for producing reports such as income statements and balance sheets.)

Transaction processing systems are often so central to a business that TPS failure for a few hours can lead to a firm's demise and perhaps that of other firms linked to it. Imagine what would happen to UPS if its package tracking system were not working! What would the airlines do without their computerized reservation systems?

Management Information Systems and Decision-Support Systems

Middle management needs systems to help with monitoring, controlling, decision-making, and administrative activities. The principal question addressed by such systems is this: Are things working well?

Management information systems can be defined as the study of information systems in business and management. The term **management information systems (MIS)** also designates a specific category of information systems serving the middle management. MIS provide middle managers with reports on the organization's current performance. This information is used to monitor and control the business and predict future performance.

MIS summarize and report on the company's basic operations using data supplied by transaction processing systems. The basic transaction data from TPS are compressed and usually presented in reports that are produced on a regular schedule. Today, many of these reports are delivered online. Figure 6 shows how a typical MIS transforms transaction-level data from inventory, production, and accounting into MIS files that are used to provide managers with reports. Figure 7 shows a sample report from this system.

MIS serve managers primarily interested in weekly, monthly, and yearly results, although some MIS enable managers to drill down to see daily or hourly

FIGURE 7   **SAMPLE MIS REPORT**

Consolidated Consumer Products Corporation Sales by Product and Sales Region: 2007

PRODUCT CODE	PRODUCT DESCRIPTION	SALES REGION	ACTUAL SALES	PLANNED	ACTUAL versus PLANNED
4469	Carpet Cleaner	Northeast	4,066,700	4,800,000	0.85
		South	3,778,112	3,750,000	1.01
		Midwest	4,867,001	4,600,000	1.06
		West	4,003,440	4,400,000	0.91
	TOTAL		16,715,253	17,550,000	0.95
5674	Room Freshener	Northeast	3,676,700	3,900,000	0.94
		South	5,608,112	4,700,000	1.19
		Midwest	4,711,001	4,200,000	1.12
		West	4,563,440	4,900,000	0.93
	TOTAL		18,559,253	17,700,000	1.05

This report, showing summarized annual sales data, was produced by the MIS in Figure 6.

data if required. MIS generally provide answers to routine questions that have been specified in advance and have a predefined procedure for answering them. For instance, MIS reports might list the total pounds of lettuce used this quarter by a fast-food chain or, as illustrated in Figure 7, compare total annual sales figures for specific products to planned targets. These systems generally are not flexible and have little analytical capability. Most MIS use simple routines, such as summaries and comparisons, as opposed to sophisticated mathematical models or statistical techniques.

The Interactive Session on Management describes an MIS that has helped companies monitor and control employee travel and entertainment expenses and reduce their operational costs. MarketStar is one of many firms using the Concur Expense Service system to automate its processes for reporting, auditing, and analyzing travel and entertainment expenses. As you read this case, try to identify the problems facing this company, how information systems are helping it solve them, and the management, organization, and technology issues it must address.

Decision-support systems (DSS) support nonroutine decision making for middle management. They focus on problems that are unique and rapidly changing, for which the procedure for arriving at a solution may not be fully predefined in advance. They try answer questions such as these: What would be the impact on production schedules if we were to double sales in the month of December? What would happen to our return on investment if a factory schedule were delayed for six months?

Although DSS use internal information from TPS and MIS, they often bring in information from external sources, such as current stock prices or product prices of competitors. These systems use a variety of models to analyze data, or they condense large amounts of data into a form in which decision makers can analyze them. DSS are designed so that users can work with them directly; these systems explicitly include user-friendly software.

An interesting, small, but powerful, DSS is the voyage-estimating system of a subsidiary of a large American metals company that exists primarily to carry

INTERACTIVE SESSION: MANAGEMENT

MANAGING TRAVEL EXPENSES: NEW TOOLS, NEW SAVINGS

Business travel and entertainment are requirements of many jobs, and often a hefty component of corporate expenses. According to American Express and Concur Technologies, travel and entertainment expenditures for U.S. companies amount to more than $200 billion each year. In 2004, IBM spent $493 million on airline tickets alone, while General Electric spent $280 million.

Processing travel and entertainment expense reports adds to the cost. According to the Aberdeen Group consulting firm in Boston, the cost to process a single expense report is $48 dollars. Aberdeen found that an employee typically takes 57 minutes to complete an expense report.

Processing travel and entertainment expenditures is especially burdensome for smaller companies whose processes tend to be paper-based. MarketStar, an Ogden, Utah-based provider of outsourced sales and marketing services to other companies was drowning in a sea of expense reports. About 650 of its 1,200 employees regularly file expense reports to its accounting department. Three full-time employees were required to manually approve, process, and audit 300 expense reports per week, most from remote locations. Expense disbursements were delayed for several weeks.

Jeff Jones, MarketStar's controller, likened this process to building "a dam when the flood waters were rising around your knees. We could never get ahead of the curve, and it was all we could do to just keep pace." In addition to processing reports, MarketStar's staff was also required to audit every single expense report to ensure that reports were accurately tabulated and all expenses were properly coded.

MarketStar decided to implement Concur Expense Service software, which automates the travel and entertainment expense-reporting process. Employees can input their expense data via a Web interface from wherever they are working with a computer, or by telephone or Palm handheld device. The system also automatically imports travel and expense data from corporate credit cards. Electronic receipt imaging uses any available fax machine to digitize and attach receipts to expense reports.

Managers approve reports with just a mouse click, cutting processing time in half while boosting accuracy and productivity. Reports produced by the system help managers keep tabs on travel spending as transactions occur.

Control and compliance tools help firms minimize fraud and maximize compliance with company policies and government regulations such as Sarbanes-Oxley. The system captures firms' business rules about corporate travel policies, such as the maximum amount allowed for airfare, hotel rooms, and meals. A built-in audit feature automatically flags expenses that are not in compliance with these policies. This feature helps companies identify employees who aren't booking airline flights with their companies' preferred vendors, those who are "padding" their expense accounts with fictitious expenses for taxis and tips, or even those who use their expense accounts for unauthorized purchases.

Corporate executives assert that instant feedback of information helps curb pervasive abuses. If, for example, the system shows a red flag on a Delta Airlines booking when a cheaper Southwest flight is available, the traveler can be alerted to rebook or pay the difference.

Concur software can be customized. MarketStar bills approximately 80 percent of its employee expenses back to its clients, who have their own expense policies. So it had to build special rules into its travel management application. MarketStar employees frequently work on a variety of projects at one time, and the software enables them to tie their expenses to a specific project as well as to a specific client.

Since implementing Concur Expense Service in early 2001, MarketStar was able to reduce staff size for travel and expense processing down to one person and reduce the time to reimburse employees to a few days. It has used information provided by the system to negotiate better rates from preferred vendors, saving over $134,000. Altogether, MarketStar has realized over $1 million in savings, representing a return on investment of 19 percent per year.

Many other companies have benefited from Concur and competing expense reporting systems. For instance, Mercer HR Consulting reduced the number of auditors required to process and audit employee expense spending by 75 percent and Dell Computer reduced the cost of processing an expense report to less than $2.

Sources: Paul Burnham Finney, "Tools Can Catch Expense-Account Padders (and Make Filing Easier)," *New York Times*, June 27, 2006, and "Corporate Expense Management Case Study: MarketStar Stays Ahead of the ROI Curve with Concur Expense,"www.concur.com, accessed June 28, 2006.

CASE STUDY QUESTIONS

1. What kinds of systems are described here? What valuable information do they provide for employees and managers? What decisions do they support?

2. What problems do automated expense reporting systems solve for companies? How do they provide value for companies that use them?

3. Compare MarketStar's manual process for travel and entertainment expense reporting with its new process based on Concur Expense Service. Diagram the two processes.

4. What management, organization, and technology issues did MarketStar have to address when adopting Concur Expense Service?

5. Are there any disadvantages to using computerized expense processing systems? Explain your answer.

MIS IN ACTION

Explore the Concur Technologies Web site (www.concur.com) and answer the following questions:

1. What kind of services does Concur Technologies provide for businesses? What kinds of businesses would benefit from using its software?

2. Compare Concur's services with those of another travel expense management vendor, such as American Express. If you were trying to manage your company's travel and entertainment expenses, which service would you prefer?

bulk cargoes of coal, oil, ores, and finished products for its parent company. The firm owns some vessels, charters others, and bids for shipping contracts in the open market to carry general cargo. A voyage-estimating system calculates financial and technical voyage details. Financial calculations include ship/time costs (fuel, labor, capital), freight rates for various types of cargo, and port expenses. Technical details include a myriad of factors, such as ship cargo capacity, speed, port distances, fuel and water consumption, and loading patterns (location of cargo for different ports).

The system can answer questions such as the following: Given a customer delivery schedule and an offered freight rate, which vessel should be assigned at what rate to maximize profits? What is the optimal speed at which a particular vessel can optimize its profit and still meet its delivery schedule? What is the optimal loading pattern for a ship bound for the U.S. West Coast from Malaysia? Figure 8 illustrates the DSS built for this company. The system operates on a powerful desktop personal computer, providing a system of menus that makes it easy for users to enter data or obtain information.

This voyage-estimating DSS draws heavily on analytical models. Other types of DSS are less model driven, focusing instead on extracting useful information to support decision making from large amounts of data.

For example, Intrawest—the largest ski operator in North America—collects and stores customer data from its Web site, call center, lodging reservations, ski schools, and ski equipment rental stores. It uses several software programs to analyze these data to determine the value, revenue potential, and loyalty of each customer so managers can make better decisions on how to target their marketing programs. The system segments customers into seven categories

FIGURE 8   VOYAGE-ESTIMATING DECISION-SUPPORT SYSTEM

This DSS operates on a powerful PC. It is used daily by managers who must develop bids on shipping contracts.

based on needs, attitudes, and behaviors, ranging from "passionate experts" to "value-minded family vacationers." The company then e-mails video clips that would appeal to each segment to encourage more visits to its resorts.

Sometimes you'll hear DSS referred to as *business intelligence systems* because they focus on helping users make better business decisions.

Executive Support Systems

Senior managers need systems that address strategic issues and long-term trends, both in the firm and in the external environment. They are concerned with questions such as these: What will employment levels be in five years? What are the long-term industry cost trends, and where does our firm fit in? How well are competitors performing? What products should we be making in five years? What new acquisitions would protect us from cyclical business swings?

Executive support systems (ESS) help senior management make these decisions. ESS address nonroutine decisions requiring judgment, evaluation, and insight because there is no agreed-on procedure for arriving at a solution. ESS provide a generalized computing and communications capacity that can be applied to a changing array of problems.

ESS are designed to incorporate data about external events, such as new tax laws or competitors, but they also draw summarized information from internal MIS and DSS. They filter, compress, and track critical data, displaying the data of greatest importance to senior managers. For example, the CEO of Leiner Health Products, the largest manufacturer of private-label vitamins and supplements in the United States, has an ESS that provides on his desktop a minute-to-minute view of the firm's financial performance as measured by working capital, accounts receivable, accounts payable, cash flow, and inventory.

FIGURE 9   MODEL OF AN EXECUTIVE SUPPORT SYSTEM

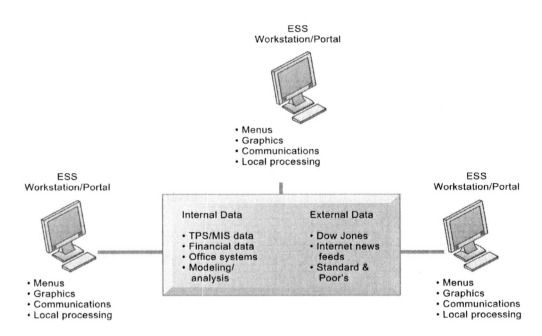

This system pools data from diverse internal and external sources and makes them available to executives in an easy-to-use form.

ESS present graphs and data from many sources through an interface that is easy for senior managers to use. Often the information is delivered to senior executives through a **portal**, which uses a Web interface to present integrated personalized business content.

Figure 9 illustrates a model of an ESS. It consists of workstations with menus, interactive graphics, and communications capabilities that can be used to access historical and competitive data from internal corporate systems and external databases such as Dow Jones News/Retrieval or the Gallup Poll.

RELATIONSHIP OF SYSTEMS TO ONE ANOTHER

Ideally, the systems we have just described are interrelated, as illustrated in Figure 10. TPS are typically a major source of data for other systems, whereas ESS are primarily a recipient of data from lower-level systems. The other types of systems may exchange data with each other as well. Data also may be exchanged among systems serving different functional areas. For example, an order captured by a sales system may be transmitted to a manufacturing system as a transaction for producing or delivering the product specified in the order or to an MIS for financial reporting. In reality, in most business firms, these systems are only loosely integrated. As in the Kia case described earlier, many firms are unable to quickly move data from one system to another, and therefore are unable to respond rapidly to challenges in the business environment. But this situation is changing

FIGURE 10   INTERRELATIONSHIPS AMONG SYSTEMS

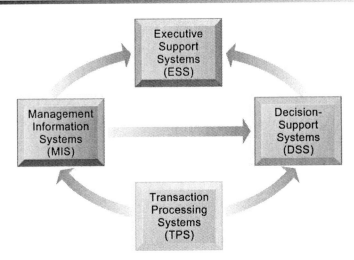

The various types of systems in the organization have interdependencies. TPS are major producers of information that is required by many other systems in the firm, which, in turn, produce information for other systems. These different types of systems are loosely coupled in most business firms, but increasingly firms are using new technologies to integrate information that resides in many different systems.

because of new networking technologies and enterprise-wide software systems described in the next section.

3   SYSTEMS THAT SPAN THE ENTERPRISE

Reviewing all the different types of systems we have just described, you might wonder how a business can manage all the information in these different systems. You might also wonder how costly it is to maintain so many different systems. And you might wonder how these different systems can share information. In fact, these are all excellent questions and challenges for businesses today.

ENTERPRISE APPLICATIONS

Getting all the different kinds of systems in a company to work together is a major challenge. Typically, corporations are put together both through normal "organic" or internal growth and through acquisition of smaller firms. After periods of acquisition, corporations end up with a collection of systems, most of them older, and face the challenge of getting them all to "talk" with one another and work together as one corporate system. There are several solutions to this problem.

One solution is to implement **enterprise applications**, which are systems that span functional areas, focus on executing business processes across the business firm, and include all levels of management. Enterprise applications help businesses become more flexible and productive by coordinating their business processes more closely and integrating groups of processes so they focus on efficient management of resources and customer service.

FIGURE 11   ENTERPRISE APPLICATION ARCHITECTURE

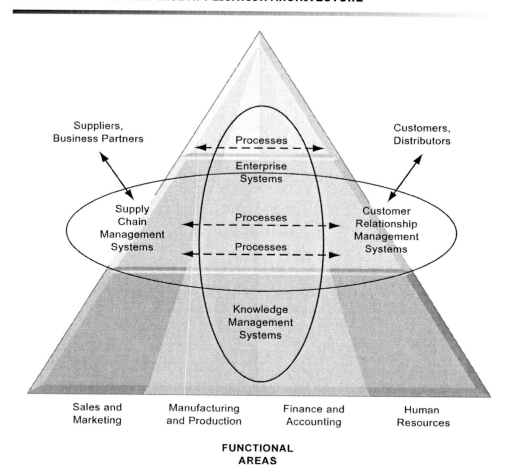

Enterprise applications automate processes that span multiple business functions and organizational levels and may extend outside the organization.

There are four major enterprise applications: enterprise systems, supply chain management systems, customer relationship management systems, and knowledge management systems. Each of these enterprise applications integrates a related set of functions and business processes to enhance the performance of the organization as a whole. Figure 11 shows that the architecture for these enterprise applications encompasses processes spanning the entire organization and, in some cases, extending beyond the organization to customers, suppliers, and other key business partners.

Enterprise Systems

A large organization typically has many different kinds of information systems built around different functions, organizational levels, and business processes that cannot automatically exchange information. Managers might have a hard time assembling the data they need for a comprehensive, overall picture of the organization's operations. For instance, sales personnel might not be able to tell at the time they place an order whether the items that were ordered are in inventory, customers cannot track their orders, and manufacturing cannot communicate easily with finance to plan for new production. This fragmentation of data in hundreds of separate systems degrades organizational efficiency and business performance.

FIGURE 12   ENTERPRISE SYSTEMS

Enterprise systems integrate the key business processes of an entire firm into a single software system that enables information to flow seamlessly throughout the organization. These systems focus primarily on internal processes but may include transactions with customers and vendors.

For example, Alcoa, the world's leading producer of aluminum and aluminum products with operations spanning 41 countries and 500 locations, had initially been organized around lines of business, each of which had its own set of information systems. Many of these systems were redundant and inefficient. Alcoa's costs for executing requisition-to-pay and financial processes were much higher and its cycle times were longer than those of other companies in its industry. (*Cycle time* refers to the total elapsed time from the beginning to the end of a process.) The company could not operate as a single worldwide entity (Oracle, 2005; Sullivan, 2005).

Enterprise systems, also known as *enterprise resource planning (ERP) systems,* solve this problem by collecting data from various key business processes in manufacturing and production, finance and accounting, sales and marketing, and human resources and storing the data in a single central data repository. This makes it possible for information that was previously fragmented in different systems to be shared across the firm and for different parts of the business to work more closely together (see Figure 12).

Enterprise systems speed communication of information throughout the company, making it easier for businesses to coordinate their daily operations. When a customer places an order, the data flow automatically to other parts of the company that are affected by them. The order transaction triggers the warehouse to pick the ordered products and schedule shipment. The warehouse informs the factory to replenish whatever has depleted. The accounting department is notified to send the customer an invoice. Customer service representatives track the progress of the order through every step to inform customers about the status of their orders.

Enterprise systems give companies the flexibility to respond rapidly to customer requests while producing and stocking inventory only with what is needed to fulfill existing orders. Their ability to increase accurate and on-time shipments, minimize costs, and increase customer satisfaction adds to firm profitability.

After implementing enterprise software from Oracle, Alcoa eliminated many redundant processes and systems. The enterprise system helped Alcoa reduce requisition-to-pay cycle time (the total elapsed time from the time a purchase requisition is generated to the time the payment for the purchase is made) by verifying receipt of goods and automatically generating receipts for payment. Alcoa's accounts payable transaction processing dropped 89 percent. Alcoa was able to centralize financial and procurement activities, which helped the company reduce nearly 20 percent of its worldwide costs. The company expects continued use of the enterprise system to reduce inventory by 25 percent, increase productivity by 15 percent, reduce materials costs by 5 percent, and improve customer service by 20 percent.

Enterprise systems provide valuable information for improving management decision making. Corporate headquarters has access to up-to-the-minute data on sales, inventory, and production and uses this information to create more accurate sales and production forecasts. Enterprise systems provide company-wide information to help managers analyze overall product profitability or cost structures. For example, Alcoa's new enterprise system includes functionality for global human resources management that shows correlations between investment in employee training and quality; measures the company-wide costs of delivering services to employees; and measures the effectiveness of employee recruitment, compensation, and training.

Supply Chain Management Systems

Supply chain management (SCM) systems help businesses manage relationships with their suppliers. These systems provide information to help suppliers, purchasing firms, distributors, and logistics companies share information about orders, production, inventory levels, and delivery of products and services so that they can source, produce, and deliver goods and services efficiently. The ultimate objective is to get the right amount of their products from their source to their point of consumption with the least amount of time and with the lowest cost.

If a company and its supply network do not have accurate information, they will most likely be saddled by excessive inventories, inaccurate manufacturing plans, and missed production schedules. Inability to move products efficiently through the supply chain raises costs while degrading customer service.

For example, until it implemented a supply chain management system from SAP, Alcan Packaging had trouble fulfilling customer orders for its packaging materials for food, pharmaceuticals, and cosmetics. It did not have the information to make good decisions about how much to produce, how to allocate personnel, or how to meet the delivery dates requested by customers. It would go from working employees overtime one month to cutting back staff the next. It could not accurately project when it would meet shipment requirements (SAP, 2005).

Table 6 describes how firms can benefit from supply chain management systems. These systems increase firm profitability by lowering the costs of moving and making products and by enabling managers to make better decisions about how to organize and schedule sourcing, production, and distribution. Alcan expects its supply chain management system to reduce overtime by 25 percent, reduce setup costs by up to 7.5 percent, and reduce carrying inventory by up to 10 percent.

TABLE 6 HOW INFORMATION SYSTEMS FACILITATE SUPPLY CHAIN MANAGEMENT

INFORMATION FROM SUPPLY CHAIN MANAGEMENT SYSTEMS HELPS FIRMS
Decide when and what to produce, store, and move
Rapidly communicate orders
Track the status of orders
Check inventory availability and monitor inventory levels
Reduce inventory, transportation, and warehousing costs
Track shipments
Plan production based on actual customer demand
Rapidly communicate changes in product design

Supply chain management systems are one type of **interorganizational system** because they automate the flow of information across organizational boundaries. You might not know it, but when you purchase a book or DVD from Amazon.com and then trace the shipping of your order at Amazon, the information is being supplied to Amazon (and you) by the shipper's tracking system through the Amazon Web site. When you book a flight at Orbitz, Travelocity, or Hotels.com, you are in fact dealing with several interorganizational systems that link reservation systems on the Web with flight and room inventory systems maintained by airlines and hotels. Interorganizational systems are increasingly common as firms combine their capabilities to offer customers an integrated online shopping experience.

Figure 13 illustrates supply chain management systems used by Haworth Incorporated, a world-leading manufacturer and designer of office furniture. Haworth's 15 North American manufacturing facilities are located in North Carolina, Arkansas, Michigan, Mississippi, Texas, Ontario, Alberta, and Quebec. These facilities supply inventory to distribution centers in Michigan, Pennsylvania, Georgia, and Arkansas.

FIGURE 13 EXAMPLE OF A SUPPLY CHAIN MANAGEMENT SYSTEM

Customer orders, shipping notifications, optimized shipping plans, and other supply chain information flow among Haworth's Warehouse Management System (WMS), Transportation Management System (TMS), and its back-end corporate systems.

Haworth's Transportation Management System (TMS) examines customer orders, factory schedules, carrier rates and availability, and shipping costs to produce optimal lowest-cost delivery plans. These plans are generated daily and updated every 15 minutes. The TMS works with Haworth's Warehouse Management System (WMS), which tracks and controls the flow of finished goods from Haworth's distribution centers to its customers. Acting on shipping plans from TMS, WMS directs the movement of goods based on immediate conditions for space, equipment, inventory, and personnel. Haworth uses special "middleware" software to link its TMS and WMS to order entry, manufacturing planning, and shipping systems. The middleware passes customer orders, shipping plans, and shipping notifications among the applications.

Customer Relationship Management Systems

Customer relationship management (CRM) systems help firms manage their relationships with customers. CRM systems provide information to coordinate all of the business processes that deal with customers in sales, marketing, and service to optimize revenue, customer satisfaction, and customer retention. This information helps firms identify, attract, and retain the most profitable customers; provide better service to existing customers; and hopefully increase sales.

In the past, a firm's processes for sales, service, and marketing were highly compartmentalized, and these departments did not share essential customer information. Some information on a specific customer might be stored and organized in terms of that person's account with the company. Other pieces of information about the same customer might be organized by products that were purchased. There was no way to consolidate all of this information to provide a unified view of a customer across the company.

For example, until recently, Saab U.S.A., which imports and distributes Saab vehicles to U.S. dealerships, had a splintered view of its customers. It had been engaging customers through three channels: its dealer network, a customer assistance center dealing with service inquiries, and a lead management center handling marketing and information requests from prospective customers. Each of these channels maintained customer data in its own systems. Fragmented customer data meant that a prospective customer might receive a direct mail offer from Saab one week and e-mail with an unrelated offer from a third-party marketing company the next week. The local dealer might not know about either of these offers, which prevented the dealer from delivering an effective pitch when the prospect visited the showroom. Lead quality was highly variable so many dealers ignored the leads and the company had no way of tracking leads faxed to dealers.

CRM systems try to solve this problem by integrating the firm's customer-related processes and consolidating customer information from multiple communication channels—telephone, e-mail, wireless devices, retail outlets, or the Web. Detailed and accurate knowledge of customers and their preferences helps firms increase the effectiveness of their marketing campaigns and provide higher-quality customer service and support.

After Saab U.S.A. implemented three CRM applications for automotive dealers from Siebel Systems, it was able to have a 360-degree view of each customer, including prior service-related questions and all the marketing communication the customer had ever received. Saab can track the status of referred leads by monitoring events, such as the salesperson's initial call to the

Illustrated here are some of t capabilities of salesforce.com, a market-leading provider of on-demand customer relationship management (CRM) software. CRM systems integrate information from sales, marketing, and customer service.

© Copyright 2007 salesforce.com, inc.

customer and the scheduling and completion of a test drive. The systems provide detailed information to measure the sales results of specific leads, and target leads are directed more precisely to the right salespeople at the right dealerships. Since the CRM applications were implemented, Saab's follow-up rate on sales leads has increased from 38 to 50 percent and customer satisfaction rose from 69 to 75 percent (Picarille, 2004; Siebel, 2005).

Knowledge Management Systems

The value of a firm's products and services is based not only on its physical resources but also on intangible knowledge assets. By some estimates, over half the stock market value of firms results from intangible assets, a large part of which is knowledge. Some firms perform better than others because they have better knowledge about how to create, produce, and deliver products and services. This firm knowledge is difficult to imitate, unique, and can be leveraged into long-term strategic benefits. **Knowledge management systems (KMS)** enable organizations to better manage processes for capturing and applying knowledge and expertise. These systems collect all relevant knowledge and experience in the firm, and make it available wherever and whenever it is needed to improve business processes and management decisions. They also link the firm to external sources of knowledge.

KMS support processes for acquiring, storing, distributing, and applying knowledge, as well as processes for creating new knowledge and integrating it into the organization. They include enterprise-wide systems for managing and distributing documents, graphics, and other digital knowledge objects;

systems for creating corporate knowledge directories of employees with special areas of expertise; office systems for distributing knowledge and information; and knowledge work systems to facilitate knowledge creation. Other knowledge management applications use intelligent techniques that codify knowledge for use by other members of the organization and tools for knowledge discovery that recognize patterns and important relationships in large pools of data.

INTRANETS AND EXTRANETS

Enterprise applications create deep-seated changes in the way a firm conducts its business, and they are often costly to implement. Companies that do not have the resources to invest in enterprise applications can still achieve some measure of information integration by using intranets and extranets.

Intranets and extranets are really more technology platforms than specific applications, but they deserve mention here as one of the tools firms use to increase integration and expedite the flow of information within the firm, and with customers and suppliers. Intranets are internal networks built with the same tools and communication standards as the Internet and are used for the internal distribution of information to employees, and as repositories of corporate policies, programs, and data. Extranets are intranets extended to authorized users outside the company.

An intranet typically presents information to users through a private portal that provides a single point of access to information from several different systems and to documents using a Web interface. Just as Yahoo!'s public portal combines information from multiple sources, and can be customized to user preferences, corporate portals can be customized to suit the information needs of specific business groups and individual users. They also typically feature e-mail, collaboration tools, and tools for searching for internal corporate systems and documents.

For example, SwissAir's corporate intranet for sales provides its salespeople with sales leads, fares, statistics, libraries of best practices, access to incentive programs, discussion groups, and collaborative workspaces. The intranet includes a Sales Ticket capability that displays bulletins about unfilled airplane seats around the world to help the sales staff work with colleagues and with travel agents who can help them fill those seats.

Companies can connect their intranets to internal company transaction systems, enabling employees to take actions central to a company's operations, such as checking the status of an order or granting a customer credit. SwissAir's intranet connects to its reservation system. GUESS Jeans has an intranet called ApparelBuy.com that links to its core order processing systems.

Extranets expedite the flow of information between the firm and its suppliers and customers. SwissAir uses an extranet to provide travel agents with fare data from its intranet electronically. GUESS Jeans allows store buyers to order merchandise electronically from ApparelBuy.com. The buyers can use this extranet to track their orders through fulfillment or delivery.

Extranets allow different firms to work collaboratively on product design, marketing, and production. Engineers at Johnson Controls and Daimler-Chrysler used an extranet design and collaboration system to design part of the Jeep Liberty interior together. Hewlett-Packard (HP) Laserjet Imaging Systems uses an extranet workgroup collaboration system to share information with its contract manufacturers, distribution centers, and resellers. The application makes parts plans from HP's internal production system available on a shared electronic workspace that can be accessed by suppliers. Suppliers then adjust their plans to coordinate their inventory with that of HP.

E-BUSINESS, E-COMMERCE, AND E-GOVERNMENT

The systems and technologies we have just described are transforming firms' relationships with customers, employees, suppliers, and logistic partners into digital relationships using networks and the Internet. So much business is now enabled by or based upon digital networks that we use the terms *electronic business* and *electronic commerce* frequently throughout this text. **Electronic business**, or **e-business**, refers to the use of digital technology and the Internet to execute the major business processes in the enterprise. E-business includes activities for the internal management of the firm and for coordination with suppliers and other business partners. It also includes **electronic commerce**, or **e-commerce**. E-commerce is the part of e-business that deals with the buying and selling of goods and services over the Internet. It also encompasses activities supporting those market transactions, such as advertising, marketing, customer support, security, delivery, and payment.

The technologies associated with e-business have also brought about similar changes in the public sector. Governments on all levels are using Internet technology to deliver information and services to citizens, employees, and businesses with which they work. **E-government** refers to the application of the Internet and networking technologies to digitally enable government and public sector agencies' relationships with citizens, businesses, and other arms of government. In addition to improving delivery of government services, e-government can make government operations more efficient and also empower citizens by giving them easier access to information and the ability to network electronically with other citizens. For example, citizens in some states can renew their driver's licenses or apply for unemployment benefits online, and the Internet has become a powerful tool for instantly mobilizing interest groups for political action and fund-raising.

4 THE INFORMATION SYSTEMS FUNCTION IN BUSINESS

We've seen that businesses need information systems to operate today and that they use many different kinds of systems. But who is responsible for running these systems? Who is responsible for making sure the hardware, software, and other technologies used by these systems are running properly and are up-to-date? End users manage their systems from a business standpoint, but managing the technology requires a special information systems function.

In all but the smallest of firms, the **information systems department** is the formal organizational unit responsible for information technology services. The information systems department is responsible for maintaining the hardware, software, data storage, and networks that comprise the firm's IT infrastructure.

THE INFORMATION SYSTEMS DEPARTMENT

The information systems department consists of specialists, such as **programmers,** systems analysts, project leaders, and information systems managers. Programmers are highly trained technical specialists who write the software instructions for computers. **Systems analysts** constitute the principal liaisons between the information systems groups and the rest of the organization. It is the systems analyst's job to translate business problems and requirements into information requirements and systems. **Information systems managers** are leaders of teams of programmers and analysts, project managers, physical facility managers, telecommunications managers, or database specialists. They are also managers of computer operations and data entry staff. Also, external specialists, such as hardware vendors and manufacturers, software firms, and consultants, frequently participate in the day-to-day operations and long-term planning of information systems.

In many companies, the information systems department is headed by a **chief information officer (CIO)**. The CIO is a senior manager who oversees the use of information technology in the firm.

End users are representatives of departments outside of the information systems group for whom applications are developed. These users are playing an increasingly large role in the design and development of information systems.

In the early years of computing, the information systems group was composed mostly of programmers who performed very highly specialized but limited technical functions. Today, a growing proportion of staff members are systems analysts and network specialists, with the information systems department acting as a powerful change agent in the organization. The information systems department suggests new business strategies and new information-based products and services, and coordinates both the development of the technology and the planned changes in the organization.

In the past, firms generally built their own software and managed their own computing facilities. Today, many firms are turning to external vendors to provide these services and are using their information systems departments to manage these service providers.

ORGANIZING THE INFORMATION SYSTEMS FUNCTION

There are many types of business firms, and there are many ways in which the IT function is organized within the firm (see Figure 14). A very small company with fewer than 100 employees will not have a formal information systems group. It will have one or two employees who are responsible for keeping its networks and applications running, or it might use consultants for these services. Larger companies will have a separate information systems department, which may be organized along several different lines, depending on the nature and interests of the firm.

Sometimes you'll see a decentralized arrangement where each functional area of the business has its own information systems department and management that typically reports to a senior manager or chief information officer. In other words, the marketing department would have its own information systems group as would manufacturing and each of the other business functions. The job of the CIO is to review information technology investments and decisions in the functional areas. The advantage of this

FIGURE 14   ORGANIZATION OF THE INFORMATION SYSTEMS FUNCTION

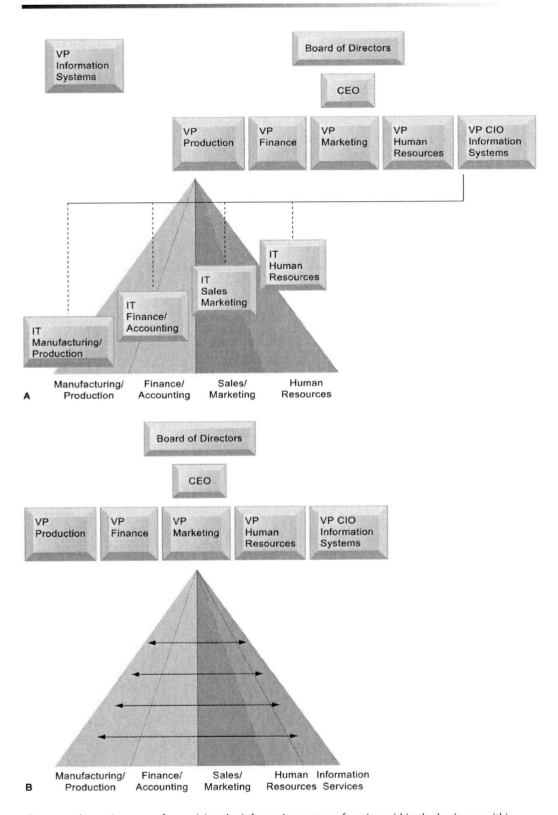

There are alternative ways of organizing the information systems function within the business: within each functional area (A), as a separate department under central control (B), or represented in each division of a large multidivisional company but under centralized control (C).

FIGURE 14   **ORGANIZATION OF THE INFORMATION SYSTEMS FUNCTION** (CONT'D)

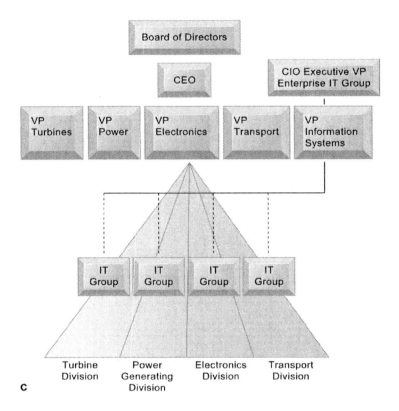

approach is that systems are built that directly address the business needs of the functional areas. However, central guidance is weak and the danger is high that many incompatible systems will be built, increasing costs as each group makes its own technology purchases.

In another arrangement, the information systems function operates as a separate department similar to the other functional departments with a large staff, a group of middle managers, and a senior management group that fights for its share of the company's resources. You'll see this approach in many large firms. This central information systems department makes technology decisions for the entire company, which is more likely to produce more compatible systems and more coherent long-term systems development plans.

Very large "Fortune 1000"-size firms with multiple divisions and product lines might allow each division (such as the Consumer Products Division or the Chemicals and Additives Division) to have its own information systems group. All of these divisional information systems groups report to a high-level central information systems group and CIO. The central IS group establishes corporate-wide standards, centralizes purchasing, and develops long-term plans for evolving the corporate computing platform. This model combines some divisional independence with some centralization.

5   HANDS-ON MIS

The projects in this section give you hands-on experience analyzing a company's financial and sales data to assess business performance and

Microsoft Excel - Sales by Model

File Edit View Insert Format Tools Data Window Help Acrobat

N31 =

Dirt Bikes Sales by Model

Model	2002	2003	2004	2005	2006
Enduro 250	1201	1663	2291	2312	2195
Enduro 550	2832	3290	3759	4078	3647
Moto 300	1755	1932	2454	2615	2627
Moto 450	463	598	661	773	823
TOTAL	6251	7483	9165	9778	9292

Amounts are in thousands of dollars

profitability, using a spreadsheet to improve decision making about suppliers, and using Internet software to plan efficient transportation routes.

Analyzing Financial Performance

Software skills: Spreadsheet charts and formulas
Business skills: Financial statement analysis

In this exercise, you will use spreadsheet software to analyze company financial statements and create graphs of important financial data.

As part of your analysis of the company for management, you have been asked to analyze data on Dirt Bikes's financial performance and prepare a report for management. Review Dirt Bikes's selected financial data in the Introduction to Dirt Bikes, which can be found at the Laudon Web site. There you will find Dirt Bikes's income statement and summary balance sheet data from 2004 to 2006, annual sales of Dirt Bikes models between 2002 and 2006, and total domestic versus international sales between 2002 and 2006.

Use your spreadsheet software to create graphs of Dirt Bikes's sales history from 2002 to 2006 and its domestic versus international sales from 2002 to 2006. Select the type of graph that is most appropriate for presenting the data you are analyzing.

Use the instructions at the Laudon Web site and your spreadsheet software to calculate the gross and net margins in Dirt Bikes's income statements from 2004 to 2006. You can also create graphs showing trends in selected pieces of Dirt Bikes's income statement and balance sheet data if you wish. (You may want to rearrange the historical ordering of the data if you decide to do this.)

Your management report should answer these questions:

- What are Dirt Bikes's best- and worst-performing products? What is the proportion of domestic to international sales? Have international sales grown relative to domestic sales?

- Are sales (revenues) growing steadily, and, if so, at what rate? What is the cost of goods sold compared to revenues? Is it increasing or decreasing? Are the firm's gross and net margins increasing or decreasing? Are the firm's operating expenses increasing or decreasing? Is the firm heavily in debt? Does it have sufficient assets to pay for operational expenses and to finance the development of new products and information systems?

- (Optional) Prepare a slide show that summarizes your analysis of Dirt Bikes's performance.

Improving Decision Making: Using a Spreadsheet to Select Suppliers

In this exercise, you will learn how to use spreadsheet software to improve management decisions about selecting suppliers. You will start with raw transactional data about suppliers organized as a large spreadsheet list. You will use Microsoft Excel software to filter the data based on several different criteria to select the best suppliers for your company.

Software skills: Spreadsheet date functions, data filtering, DAVERAGE function
Business skills: Analyzing supplier performance and pricing

You run a company that manufactures aircraft components. You have many competitors who are trying to offer lower prices and better service to customers, and you are trying to determine whether you can benefit from better supply chain management. At the Laudon Web site for this chapter, you will find a spreadsheet file that contains a list of all of the items that your firm has ordered from its suppliers during the past three months. The fields in the spreadsheet file include vendor name, vendor identification number, purchaser's order number, item identification number and item description (for

Microsoft Excel - MIS10ch02_questionfile

File Edit View Insert Format Tools Data Window Help

	B	C	D	E	F	G	H	I	J	K
2				**Orders and Suppliers**						
3										
4	Vendor No.	Order No.	Item No.	Item Description	Item Cost	Quantity	Cost per order	A/P Terms	Order Date	Arrival Date
5	2	A0111	6489	O-Ring	$ 3.00	900	$ 2,700.00	25	10/10/06	10/18/05
6	6	A0115	5319	Shielded Cable/ft.	$ 1.10	17,500	$ 19,250.00	30	08/20/06	08/31/06
7	6	A0123	4312	Bolt-nut package	$ 3.75	4,250	$ 15,937.50	30	08/25/06	09/01/06
8	6	A0204	5319	Shielded Cable/ft.	$ 1.10	16,500	$ 18,150.00	30	09/15/06	10/05/06
9	6	A0205	5677	Side Panel	$ 195.00	120	$ 23,400.00	30	11/02/06	11/13/06
10	6	A0207	4312	Bolt-nut package	$ 3.75	4,200	$ 15,750.00	30	09/01/06	09/10/06
11	5	A0223	4224	Bolt-nut package	$ 3.95	4,500	$ 17,775.00	30	10/15/06	10/20/06
12	5	A0433	5417	Control Panel	$ 255.00	500	$ 127,500.00	30	10/20/06	10/27/06
13	5	A0443	1243	Airframe fasteners	$ 4.25	10,000	$ 42,500.00	30	08/08/06	08/14/06
14	5	A0446	5417	Control Panel	$ 255.00	406	$ 103,530.00	30	09/01/06	09/10/06
15	2	A0533	9752	Gasket	$ 4.05	1,500	$ 6,075.00	25	09/20/06	09/25/06
16	2	A0555	6489	O-Ring	$ 3.00	1,100	$ 3,300.00	25	10/05/06	10/10/06
17	2	A0622	9752	Gasket	$ 4.05	1,550	$ 6,277.50	25	09/25/06	10/05/06
18	2	A0666	5125	Shielded Cable/ft.	$ 1.15	15,000	$ 17,250.00	25	10/01/06	10/05/06
19	2	A0777	6489	O-Ring	$ 3.00	1,050	$ 3,150.00	25	10/29/06	11/10/06
20	2	A1222	4111	Bolt-nut package	$ 3.55	4,200	$ 14,910.00	25	09/15/06	10/15/06
21	3	A1234	9399	Gasket	$ 3.65	1,250	$ 4,562.50	45	10/01/06	10/06/06
22	3	A1235	9399	Gasket	$ 3.65	1,450	$ 5,292.50	45	10/03/06	10/08/06
23	3	A1344	5454	Control Panel	$ 220.00	550	$ 121,000.00	45	10/09/06	10/14/06
24	3	A1345	9399	Gasket	$ 3.65	1,470	$ 5,365.50	45	10/07/06	10/12/06
25	3	A1346	9399	Gasket	$ 3.65	1,985	$ 7,245.25	45	10/05/06	10/11/06
26	2	A1444	4111	Bolt-nut package	$ 3.55	4,250	$ 15,087.50	25	09/20/06	10/10/06
27	2	A1445	4111	Bolt-nut package	$ 3.55	4,200	$ 14,910.00	25	09/25/06	10/25/06
28	2	A1449	4111	Bolt-nut package	$ 3.55	4,600	$ 16,330.00	25	10/05/06	10/19/06
29	3	A1456	5454	Control Panel	$ 220.00	500	$ 110,000.00	45	10/15/06	10/20/06

each item ordered from the vendor), cost per item, number of units of the item ordered (quantity), total cost of each order, vendor's accounts payable terms, order date, and actual arrival date for each order.

Prepare a recommendation of how you can use the data in this spreadsheet database to improve your decisions about selecting suppliers. Some criteria to consider for identifying preferred suppliers include the supplier's track record for on-time deliveries, suppliers offering the best accounts payable terms, and suppliers offering lower pricing when the same item can be provided by multiple suppliers. Prepare a report to support your recommendations.

Achieving Operational Excellence: Using Internet Software to Plan Efficient Transportation Routes

In this exercise, you will use the same online software tool that businesses use to map out their transportation routes and select the most efficient route. The MapQuest (www.mapquest.com) Web site includes interactive capabilities for planning a trip. The software on this Web site can calculate the distance between two points and provide itemized driving directions to any location.

You have just started working as a dispatcher for Cross-Country Transport, a new trucking and delivery service based in Cleveland, Ohio. Your first assignment is to plan a delivery of office equipment and furniture from Elkhart, Indiana (at the corner of E. Indiana Ave. and Prairie Street) to Hagerstown, Maryland (corner of Eastern Blvd. N. and Potomac Ave.). To guide your trucker, you need to know the most efficient route between the two cities. Use MapQuest to find the route that is the shortest distance between the two cities. Use MapQuest again to find the route that takes the least time. Compare the results. Which route should Cross-Country use? Prepare a one-page analysis of this problem and your answer.

LEARNING TRACK MODULE

Challenges of Using Business Information Systems. This Learning Track provides a brief overview of the central management issues raised by information systems and their potential solutions. This Learning Track also provides a useful introduction to IS implementation issues that are described throughout the text. You can find the Learning Track on the Laudon Web site for this chapter and on the Student CD-ROM.

Summary

1. *Define and describe business processes and their relationship to information systems.*

   A business process is a logically related set of activities that define how specific business tasks are performed, and a business can be viewed as a collection of business processes. Business processes are concrete workflows of material, information, and knowledge. They also represent unique ways in which organizations coordinate work, information, and knowledge, and the ways in which management chooses to coordinate work. Managers need to pay attention to business processes because they determine how well the organization can execute its business, and thus be a potential source of strategic success or failure. Although each of the major business functions has its own set of business processes, many other business processes are cross-functional, such as order fulfillment. Information systems can help organizations achieve great efficiencies by automating parts of these processes or by helping organizations redesign and streamline them. Firms can become more flexible and efficient by coordinating their business processes closely, and, in some cases, integrating these processes so they are focused on efficient management of resources and customer service.

2. *Describe the information systems supporting the major business functions: sales and marketing, manufacturing and production, finance and accounting, and human resources.*

   At each level of the organization, information systems support the major functional areas of the business. Sales and marketing systems help the firm identify customers for the firm's products or services, develop products and services to meet customers' needs, promote the products and services, sell the products and services, and provide ongoing customer support. Manufacturing and production systems deal with the planning, development, and production of products and services, and control the flow of production. Finance and accounting systems keep track of the firm's financial assets and fund flows. Human resources systems maintain employee records; track employee skills, job performance, and training; and support planning for employee compensation and career development.

3. *Evaluate the role played by systems serving the various levels of management in a business and their relationship to each other.*

   There are four major types of information systems in contemporary organizations serving operational, middle, and senior management. Systems serving operational management are transaction processing systems (TPS), such as payroll or order processing, that track the flow of the daily routine transactions necessary to conduct business. MIS and DSS provide middle management with reports and access to the organization's current performance and historical records. Most MIS reports condense information from TPS and are not highly analytical. DSS support management decisions when these decisions are unique, rapidly changing, and not specified easily in advance. They have more advanced analytical models and data analysis capabilities than MIS and often draw on information from external as well as internal sources. ESS support senior management by providing data of greatest importance to senior management decision makers, often in the form of graphs and charts delivered via portals. They have limited analytical capabilities but can draw on sophisticated graphics software and many sources of internal and external information.

4. *Explain how enterprise applications and intranets promote business process integration and improve organizational performance.*

   Enterprise applications, such as enterprise systems, supply chain management systems, customer relationship management systems, and knowledge management systems, are designed to support organization-wide process coordination and integration so that the organization can operate efficiently. They span multiple functions and business processes and may be tied to the business processes of other organizations. Enterprise systems integrate the key internal business processes of a firm into a single software system so that information can flow throughout the organization, improving coordination, efficiency, and decision making. Supply chain management systems help the firm manage its relationship with suppliers to optimize the planning, sourcing, manufacturing, and delivery of products and services. Customer relationship management uses information systems to coordinate all of the business processes surrounding the firm's interactions with its customers to optimize firm revenue and customer satisfaction. Knowledge management systems enable firms to optimize the creation, sharing, and distribution of knowledge to improve business processes and management decisions.

Intranets and extranets use Internet technology and standards to assemble information from various systems and present it to the user in a Web page format. Extranets make portions of private corporate intranets available to outsiders.

5. *Assess the role of the information systems function in a business.*

The information systems department is the formal organizational unit responsible for information technology services. The information systems department is responsible for maintaining the hardware, software, data storage, and networks that comprise the firm's IT infrastructure. The information systems department consists of specialists, such as programmers, systems analysts, project leaders, and information systems managers, and is often headed by a CIO.

There are alternative ways of organizing the IT function within the firm. A very small company will not have a formal information systems group. Larger companies will have a separate information systems department, which may be organized along several different lines, depending on the nature and interests of the firm. Each functional area of the business may have its own information systems department, overseen by a corporate CIO. The information systems function may be run as a separate department similar to the other functional departments. A third arrangement found in very large firms with multiple divisions and product lines is to have an information systems department for each division reporting to a high-level central information systems group and CIO.

Key Terms

Chief information officer (CIO)
Customer relationship management (CRM) systems
Decision-support systems (DSS)
Electronic business (e-business)
Electronic commerce (e-commerce)
E-government
End users
Enterprise applications
Enterprise systems
Executive support systems (ESS)
Finance and accounting information systems
Human resources information systems

Information systems department
Information systems managers
Interorganizational system
Knowledge management systems (KMS)
Management information systems (MIS)
Manufacturing and production information systems
Portal
Programmers
Sales and marketing information systems
Supply chain management (SCM) systems
Systems analysts
Transaction processing systems (TPS)

Review Questions

1. What are business processes? What role do they play in organizations? How are they enhanced by information systems?

2. List and describe the information systems serving each of the major functional areas of a business.

3. What are the characteristics of transaction processing systems? What role do they play in a business?

4. What are the characteristics of MIS? How do MIS differ from TPS? From DSS?

5. What are the characteristics of DSS? How do they differ from those of ESS?

6. Describe the relationship between TPS, MIS, DSS, and ESS.

7. Why are organizations trying to integrate their business processes? What are the four key enterprise applications?

8. What are enterprise systems? How do they benefit businesses?

9. What are supply chain management systems? How do they benefit businesses?

10. What are customer relationship management systems? How do they benefit businesses?

11. What is the role of knowledge management systems in the enterprise?

12. Describe how the information systems function supports a business. What roles are played by programmers, systems analysts, information systems managers, and the chief information officer (CIO)?

13. Describe alternative ways of organizing the information systems function in a business.

Discussion Questions

1. How could information systems be used to support the order fulfillment process illustrated in Figure 1? What are the most important pieces of information these systems should capture? Explain your answer.

2. Adopting an enterprise application is a key business decision as well as a technology decision. Do you agree? Why or why not? Who should make this decision?

Video Case

You will find a video case illustrating some of the concepts in this chapter on the Laudon Web site and Student CD-ROM along with questions to help you analyze the case.

Teamwork: Describing Management Decisions and Systems

With a group of three or four other students, find a description of a manager in a corporation in *Business Week*, *Forbes*, *Fortune*, or another business magazine. Write a description of the kinds of decisions this manager has to make and the kind of information that manager would need for those decisions. Suggest how information systems could supply this information. If possible, use presentation software to present your findings to the class.

REFERENCES

Choi, Soon-Yong, and Andrew B. Whinston. "Communities of Collaboration." *IQ Magazine*. (July/August 2001).

Ferdows, Kasra, Michael A. Lewis, and Jose A. D. Machuca. "Rapid-Fire Fulfillment." *Harvard Business Review* (November 2004).

Gruman, Galen. "Strategic HR Integration." *CIO Magazine* (August 15, 2005).

Kalakota, Ravi, and Marcia Robinson. e-Business2.0: Roadmap for *Success*. Reading, MA: Addison-Wesley (2001).

Keen, Peter G. W., and M. S. Morton. *Decision Support Systems: An Organizational Perspective*. Reading, MA: Addison-Wesley (1978).

Malone, Thomas M., Kevin Crowston, Jintae Lee, and Brian Pentland. "Tools for Inventing Organizations: Toward a Handbook of Organizational Processes." *Management Science* 45, no. 3 (March 1999).

Nolan, Richard, and F. Warren McFarland. "Information Technology and the Board of Directors." *Harvard Business Review* (October 1, 2005).

O'Leary, Daniel E. *Enterprise Resource Planning Systems: Systems Life Cycle, Electronic Commerce, and Risk*. New York: Cambridge University Press (2000).

Oracle Corporation. "Alcoa Implements Oracle Solution 20% below Projected Cost, Eliminates 43 Legacy Systems." www.oracle.com, accessed August 21, 2005.

Picarelle, Lisa. Planes, Trains, and Automobiles. *Customer Relationship Management* (February 2004).

SAP. "Alcan Packaging Implements mySAP SCM to Increase Shareholder Value." www.mysap.com, accessed August 20, 2005.

Siebel Systems. "Saab Cars USA Increases Lead Follow-Up from 38 Percent to 50 Percent with Siebel Automotive." www.siebel.com, accessed October 15, 2005.

Sprague, Ralph H., Jr., and Eric D. Carlson. *Building Effective Decision Support Systems*. Englewood Cliffs, NJ: Prentice Hall (1982)

Weill, Peter, and Jeanne Ross. "A Matrixed Approach to Designing IT Governance." *MIT Sloan Management Review* 46, no. 2 (Winter 2005).

Can Information Systems Help Prevent a Public Health Crisis?
CASE STUDY

If you turn on the television, read a newspaper, or surf the Web, you're bound to find many dire predictions about large-scale loss of life from biological or chemical attacks or an avian influenza pandemic. Computer models estimate that between 2 and 100 million people could die in the event of a flu pandemic, depending on the characteristics of the virus. Fears of a major public health crisis are greater now than ever before, and governments throughout the world are trying to improve their capabilities for identifying biochemical attacks or pandemic outbreaks more rapidly.

On May 3, 2006, the United States government issued an Implementation Plan for its National Strategy for Pandemic Influenza to improve coordination among federal, state, and local authorities and the private sector for pandemics and other public health emergencies. The implementation plan calls for improving mechanisms for real-time clinical surveillance in acute care settings such as hospital emergency rooms, intensive care units, and laboratories to provide local, state, and federal public health officials with continuous awareness of the profile of illness in communities.

One such initiative is the BioSense Real-Time Clinical Connections Program developed by the U.S. Federal Centers for Disease Control and Prevention (CDC). BioSense sits atop a hospital's existing information systems, continually gathering and analyzing their data in real time. Custom software developed by CDC monitors the facility's network traffic and captures relevant patient records, diagnoses, and prescription information. The data include patient age, sex, ZIP code of residence, ZIP code of the medical facility handling the patient, the principal medical complaint, symptoms, onset of illness, diagnoses, medical procedures, medications prescribed, and laboratory results. The software converts these data to the HL7 data messaging format, which is the standard for the health-care industry, encrypts the data, and transmits them every 15 minutes over the Web to the CDC where they are maintained in a large data repository.

The system summarizes and presents analytical results by source, day, and syndrome for each ZIP code, state, and metropolitan area using maps, graphs, and tables. Registered state and local public health agencies as well as hospitals and health care providers are allowed to access data that pertain to their jurisdiction. They access BioSense via a Web-based application over a secure data network. Information from BioSense could show early signs of a pandemic or biologic attack and alert local hospitals, health workers, and federal and state agencies to take preventive measures.

The traditional process for public health surveillance is manual and much slower. Hospitals, physicians, and laboratories would mail or fax paper reports to public health agencies, who would then call health care providers for more detailed information. This slow chain of person-to-person communication is not well-suited to a major public health emergency.

By monitoring streaming data about health events as they occur, the system helps CDC epidemiologists quickly detect early signs of a flu pandemic or bioterrorist attack and provide public health and government decision makers with the information needed to manage preparedness and response. Simultaneous access of the data by all levels of public health decreases the time needed to classify health events as serious public health problems; decreases the time to identify causes, risk factors, and appropriate interventions; and decreases the time needed to implement countermeasures and health guidance.

BioSense first became operational in 2004, when it began gathering daily data from U.S. Defense Department and Veterans Affairs (VA) hospitals and Laboratory Corporation of America (LabCorp) orders for medical tests. (LabCorp operates a large nationwide network of testing locations and service centers and is one of the largest clinical lab service providers in the United States.) Approximately 700 Defense Department and 1,110 VA facilities report data to BioSense. In late 2005, CDC started to expand the BioSense network to civilian hospitals in major metropolitan areas and anticipates sharing its analysis of local and regional influenza-like illness trends with health care and other public agencies in affected areas. The CDC expects to connect 300 hospitals to BioSense by the end of 2006.

To help civilian hospitals link to BioSense, the CDC enlisted the Consella Group health care information technology consultants. Consella explains the benefits of participating in a project that will serve their specific interests as well as those of the public at large and will put their data in standardized form.

However, many hospitals have not been anxious to jump on the bandwagon because the transition would be burdensome and time-consuming. To transmit data to BioSense, each hospital must standardize its patient and other medical data. Most hospitals use their own coding systems for symptoms, diseases, and medications. CDC's contractors would have to work with the hospital to translate its data codes into the standards used by CDC's software. According to Barry Rhodes, CDC's associate director for technology and informatics, "To standardize the data and do all the data validation steps is a huge technological challenge."

Some in the medical community question whether the BioSense network is worth the effort. "If there is a pandemic flu, we are not going to know about it from a system like this," says Dr. Susan Fernyak, director of communicable disease control and prevention at the San Franscisco Department of Public Health. According to Dr. John Rosenberg, director of the Infectious Disease Laboratory at the State of California's Department of Health Services in Richmond, California, if an epidemic broke out, "You'd know it before the data rolled in. When your emergency rooms fill up you make a phone call; this is probably a better measure."

David Groves, CDC project head at SAIC, a BioSense contractor, points out that a hospital's medical staff might not know right away that there's a serious problem when patients start showing up with symptoms. CDC scientists using the system will be in a better position to spot a major pandemic or biological or chemical attack over a wider geographic area. Having a bigger picture of what's happening will help CDC help hospitals, police, and emergency units mobilize a better response.

Although participation in BioSense is voluntary, physicians and health officials might resent the system because it enables the federal government to encroach on what has traditionally been the domain of local health care providers and organizations. They note that they and not the CDC have the responsibility for responding to and managing a pandemic. Additionally, hospitals are reluctant to sign up because of concerns about maintaining privacy and security of patient information. BioSense would let the CDC "listen in" on their treatment of patients on a real-time basis. The CDC does not use any data that would identify individual patients.

Sources: Doug Bartholomew, "Second Opinions," *Baseline Magazine*, March 2006; Wilson P. Dizard III, "CDC Weaving National Information Web," *Government Computer News*, April 3, 2006; Colleen A. Bradley, H. Rolka, D. Walker, and J. Loons, "BioSense: Implementation of a National Early Event Detection and Situational Awareness System," www.cdc.gov, accessed July 1, 2006; Homeland Security Council, "National Strategy for Pandemic Influenza Implementation Plan," May 3, 2006; and Lynn Steele, "BioSense" Using Clinical Data for Early Event Detection and Situational Awareness," Centers for Disease Control, September 7, 2005.

CASE STUDY QUESTIONS

1. Describe and diagram the existing process for reporting and identifying major public health problems, such as a flu pandemic.

2. How does BioSense improve this process? Diagram the process for reporting and identifying public health problems using BioSense.

3. Discuss the pros and cons of adopting BioSense for public health surveillance. Should all hospitals and public health agencies switch to BioSense? Why or why not?

4. Put yourself in the role of hospital director at a large urban hospital. Would you support joining up with the BioSense system? Why or why not? What factors would you want to take into account before joining?

Information Systems, Organizations, and Strategy

From *Management Information Systems: Managing the Digital Firm, 10/e.* Kenneth C. Laudon, Jane P. Laudon.
Copyright © 2007 by Pearson Prentice Hall. All rights reserved.

Information Systems, Organizations, and Strategy

LEARNING OBJECTIVES

After reading this chapter, you will be able to:

1. Identify and describe important features of organizations that managers need to know about in order to build and use information systems successfully.

2. Evaluate the impact of information systems on organizations.

3. Demonstrate how Porter's competitive forces model and the value chain model help businesses use information systems for competitive advantage.

4. Demonstrate how information systems help businesses use synergies, core competencies, and network-based strategies to achieve competitive advantage.

5. Assess the challenges posed by strategic information systems and management solutions.

Interactive Sessions:

7-Eleven Stores Ask the Customer by Asking the Data

Amazon.com: An Internet Giant Fine-Tunes Its Strategy

CHAPTER OUTLINE

1 **ORGANIZATIONS AND INFORMATION SYSTEMS**
   What Is an Organization?
   Features of Organizations

2 **HOW INFORMATION SYSTEMS IMPACT ORGANIZATIONS AND BUSINESS FIRMS**
   Economic Impacts
   Organizational and Behavioral Impacts
   The Internet and Organizations
   Implications for the Design and Understanding of Information Systems

3 **USING INFORMATION SYSTEMS TO ACHIEVE COMPETITIVE ADVANTAGE**
   Porter's Competitive Forces Model
   Information System Strategies for Dealing with Competitive Forces
   The Internet's Impact on Competitive Advantage
   The Business Value Chain Model
   Synergies, Core Competencies, and Network-Based Strategies

4 **USING SYSTEMS FOR COMPETITIVE ADVANTAGE: MANAGEMENT ISSUES**
   Sustaining Competitive Advantage
   Performing a Strategic Systems Analysis
   Managing Strategic Transitions

5 **HANDS-ON MIS**
   Analyzing Competitive Strategy: Dirt Bikes USA
   Improving Decision Making: Using a Database to Clarify Business Strategy
   Improving Decision Making: Using Web Tools to Configure and Price an Automobile

LEARNING TRACK MODULE
   The Changing Business Environment for Information Technology

WILL THE NEW US AIRWAYS BE ABLE TO FLY?

In September 2005, US Airways and America West Airlines merged to create something that may shake up the airline industry: a low-cost full-service airline. The new company, which retains the US Airways name, combines a fully developed national route network, first class seating, and customer loyalty program comparable to those offered by traditional airlines such as American and Continental with low prices competitive with budget carriers such as JetBlue, AirTran, and Southwest Airlines.

The merging companies couldn't have been more different in terms of their business strategies, organizational culture, and information systems: US Airways, which originated with the formation of All American Aviation in 1939, was a traditional hub-and-spoke carrier with an older workforce, lumbering bureaucracy, and a rigid information systems function that had been outsourced to Electronic Data Systems (EDS). America West was very different. Formed in 1981, it had a younger workforce, a more freewheeling entrepreneurial culture, and a penchant for managing its own information systems.

But by the late 1990s, both had something in common: They were considered airlines of last resort, that people flew only when there were no other alternatives. US Airways was forced to file for bankruptcy first in 2002 and again in 2004, laying off thousands of employees. America West was struggling with surging fuel costs and competition from Southwest Airlines, another low-cost carrier.

The US Airways merger was designed to create synergies between a traditional full-service airline and a newer low-cost carrier. The resulting company combines US Airways' experience and strong network on the east coast of the United States and America West's low-cost structure, information systems, and routes in the western United States.

Management believes the merger will produce $600 million in annual cost savings. To achieve these cost savings, the new US Airways will reduce the merged companies' annual IT spending of $240 million by about 40 percent by eliminating redundant information systems. The merged company adopted primarily the simple, flexible information systems and business processes of America West. It eliminated systems and business processes for carrying hazardous materials and handling unaccompanied minors on connecting flights because their costs were too high relative to the benefits they provided. The company only retained a few of the old US Airways' processes and systems, such as an application for determining where and when to purchase fuel or check-in applications to support international routes.

The new US Airways is now the fifth-largest carrier in the United States and the world's largest low-cost airline. Will it be successful? It's still too early to tell. It cost around $75 to $80 million to integrate the information system applications and business processes of the merging companies. Whether the merger will produce bene-

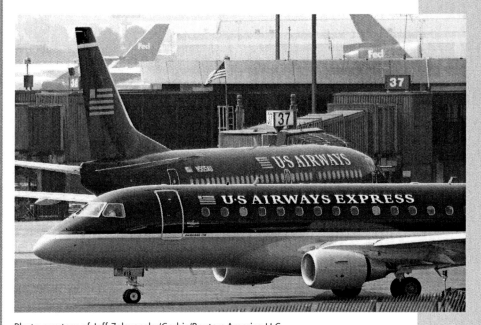

Photo courtesy of Jeff Zelevansky/Corbis/Reuters America LLC fits depends on how well the two companies' systems and business processes are integrated.

US Airways noted in regulatory filings "that the merger will result in certain synergies, business opportunities, and growth prospects" but the company "may never realize" them. "Significant challenges in consolidating functions, integrating...organizations, procedures and operations" will make the integration of the two airlines "costly, complex, and time-consuming."

If the merger is successful, the new US Airways will have a network like Continental Airlines and a cost structure similar to Southwest. The question then becomes whether the company will be able to take advantage of its new strengths. A low-cost airline with a national network might still wind up as a carrier of last resort if it merely focuses on costs and does not provide a good customer experience. But if the new US Airways is able to provide customer value and service along with low costs, it could become a highly sought-after brand.

Sources: Stephanie Overby, "How to Save an Airline," *CIO Magazine*, February 15, 2006; Tony Kontzer, "Merger on the Fly," *Information Week*, February 27, 2005; and U.S. Airways, "U.S. Airways 10-K Report for the year ending December 31, 2005," filed March 15, 2006.

The experience of US Airways illustrates the interdependence of business environments, organizational culture, business processes, business strategy, and the development of information systems. US Airways and America West merged in response to competitive pressures from their surrounding environment. The merging companies had different organizational cultures, business processes and information systems, which had to be integrated for the new company to run effectively. The new information systems—many taken over from a more modernized America West—had to be fine-tuned to support the new US Airways' business strategy. US Airways' systems effort can't succeed without a significant amount of organizational and management change.

The chapter-opening diagram calls attention to important points raised by this case and this chapter. Both US Airways and America West faced intense pressure from airline industry competitors and from rising fuel costs. Management at both companies decided their business strategy needed to change and it should focus on synergies created by merging. The new business strategy required investments in information systems, and changes in management and organization. The newly merged company provides value to customers by competing on both price and quality service. To make the merger profitable, US Airways had to revise its business processes so that two formerly separate companies could operate as a single entity, and it also had to eliminate redundant information systems. The opening case also shows that such changes are not easy to make and that it is still unclear whether the new US Airways has a successful strategy and business model.

HEADS UP

As a manager, you'll need to know about the relationship between organizations, information systems, and business strategy. This chapter first introduces the features of organizations that you will need to understand when you design, build, and operate information systems. Then it examines the problems firms face from competition and the various ways in which information systems can provide competitive advantage. Every business student and future manager should know about these strategic uses of information technology.

• If your career is in finance and accounting, you will be developing and managing strategic products and services that are largely based on information systems such as wealth management, financial advising, risk management systems, online financial services, and credit services.

• If your career is in human resources, you will be working with systems that could give your firm a strategic edge by providing information and communication capabilities that lower the cost of managing employees or by organizing jobs and work assignments to reduce operational costs.

• If your career is in information systems, you will be working with managers from all the other business areas to identify opportunities for strategic information systems and their technology requirements.

• If your career is in manufacturing and production, you will be developing production systems based on information technology and systems that help your firm compete by lowering supply chain costs, increasing quality, and enabling the firm to design and bring new products to market more rapidly.

• If your career is in sales and marketing, you will be working with information systems and technologies that create strategic advantages for your firm such as customer relationship management systems, online Web site monitoring tools, and business analytics tools that can help you understand your customers better.

---

1   ORGANIZATIONS AND INFORMATION SYSTEMS

Information systems and organizations influence one another. Information systems are built by managers to serve the interests of the business firm. At the same time, the organization must be aware of and open to the influences of information systems to benefit from new technologies.

The interaction between information technology and organizations is complex and is influenced by many mediating factors, including the organization's structure, business processes, politics, culture, surrounding environment, and management decisions (see Figure 1). You will need to understand how information systems can change social and work life in your firm. You will not be able to design new systems successfully or understand existing systems without understanding your own business organization.

FIGURE 1   **THE TWO-WAY RELATIONSHIP BETWEEN ORGANIZATIONS AND INFORMATION TECHNOLOGY**

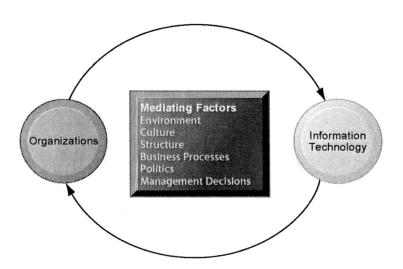

This complex two-way relationship is mediated by many factors, not the least of which are the decisions made—or not made—by managers. Other factors mediating the relationship include the organizational culture, structure, politics, business processes, and environment.

As a manager, you will be the one to decide which systems will be built, what they will do, and how they will be implemented. You may not be able to anticipate all of the consequences of these decisions. Some of the changes that occur in business firms because of new information technology (IT) investments cannot be foreseen and have results that may or may not meet your expectations. Who would have imagined ten years ago, for instance, that e-mail and instant messaging would become a dominant form of business communication and that many managers would be inundated with more than 200 e-mail messages each day (Walker, 2004)?

WHAT IS AN ORGANIZATION?

An **organization** is a stable, formal social structure that takes resources from the environment and processes them to produce outputs. This technical definition focuses on three elements of an organization. Capital and labor are primary production factors provided by the environment. The organization (the firm) transforms these inputs into products and services in a production function. The products and services are consumed by environments in return for supply inputs (see Figure 2).

An organization is more stable than an informal group (such as a group of friends that meets every Friday for lunch) in terms of longevity and routineness. Organizations are formal legal entities with internal rules and procedures that must abide by laws. Organizations are also social structures because they are a collection of social elements, much as a machine has a structure—a particular arrangement of valves, cams, shafts, and other parts.

This definition of organizations is powerful and simple, but it is not very descriptive or even predictive of real-world organizations. A more realistic behavioral definition of an organization is that it is a collection of rights,

FIGURE 2   **THE TECHNICAL MICROECONOMIC DEFINITION OF THE ORGANIZATION**

In the microeconomic definition of organizations, capital and labor (the primary production factors provided by the environment) are transformed by the firm through the production process into products and services (outputs to the environment). The products and services are consumed by the environment, which supplies additional capital and labor as inputs in the feedback loop.

privileges, obligations, and responsibilities that is delicately balanced over a period of time through conflict and conflict resolution (see Figure 3).

In this behavioral view of the firm, people who work in organizations develop customary ways of working; they gain attachments to existing relationships; and they make arrangements with subordinates and superiors about how work will be done, the amount of work that will be done, and under what conditions work will be done. Most of these arrangements and feelings are not discussed in any formal rulebook.

How do these definitions of organizations relate to information systems technology? A technical view of organizations encourages us to focus on how inputs are combined to create outputs when technology changes are introduced into the company. The firm is seen as infinitely malleable, with capital and labor substituting for each other quite easily. But the more realistic behavioral

FIGURE 3   **THE BEHAVIORAL VIEW OF ORGANIZATIONS**

The behavioral view of organizations emphasizes group relationships, values, and structures.

definition of an organization suggests that building new information systems, or rebuilding old ones, involves much more than a technical rearrangement of machines or workers—that some information systems change the organizational balance of rights, privileges, obligations, responsibilities, and feelings that have been established over a long period of time.

Changing these elements can take a long time, be very disruptive, and require more resources to support training and learning. For instance, the length of time required to implement effectively a new information system is much longer than usually anticipated simply because there is a lag between implementing a technical system and teaching employees and managers how to use the system.

Technological change requires changes in who owns and controls information; who has the right to access and update that information; and who makes decisions about whom, when, and how. This more complex view forces us to look at the way work is designed and the procedures used to achieve outputs.

The technical and behavioral definitions of organizations are not contradictory. Indeed, they complement each other: The technical definition tells us how thousands of firms in competitive markets combine capital, labor, and information technology, whereas the behavioral model takes us inside the individual firm to see how that technology affects the organization's inner workings. Section 2 describes how each of these definitions of organizations can help explain the relationships between information systems and organizations.

FEATURES OF ORGANIZATIONS

All modern organizations have certain characteristics. They are bureaucracies with clear-cut divisions of labor and specialization. Organizations arrange specialists in a hierarchy of authority in which everyone is accountable to someone and authority is limited to specific actions governed by abstract rules or procedures. These rules create a system of impartial and universal decision making. Organizations try to hire and promote employees on the basis of technical qualifications and professionalism (not personal connections). The organization is devoted to the principle of efficiency: maximizing output using limited inputs. Other features of organizations include their business processes, organizational culture, organizational politics, surrounding environments, structure, goals, constituencies, and leadership styles. All of these features affect the kinds of information systems used by organizations.

Routines and Business Processes

All organizations, including business firms, become very efficient over time because individuals in the firm develop **routines** for producing goods and services. Routines—sometimes called *standard operating procedures*—are precise rules, procedures, and practices that have been developed to cope with virtually all expected situations. As employees learn these routines, they become highly productive and efficient, and the firm is able to reduce its costs over time as efficiency increases. For instance, when you visit a doctor's office, receptionists have a well-developed set of routines for gathering basic information from you; nurses have a different set of routines for preparing you for an interview with a doctor; and the doctor has a well-developed set of routines for diagnosing you. *Business processes* are collections of such routines. A business firm in turn is a collection of business processes (Figure 4).

FIGURE 4   ROUTINES, BUSINESS PROCESSES, AND FIRMS

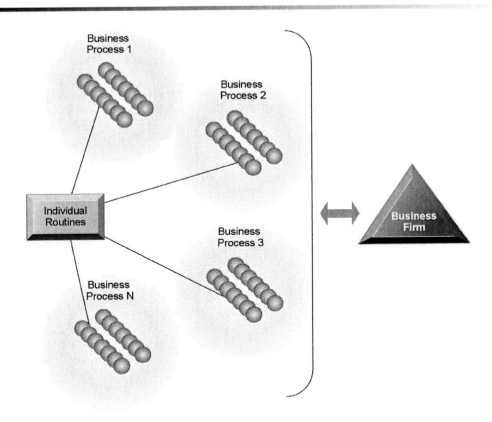

All organizations are composed of individual routines and behaviors, a collection of which make up a business process. A collection of business processes make up the business firm. New information system applications require that individual routines and business processes change to achieve high levels of organizational performance.

Organizational Politics

People in organizations occupy different positions with different specialties, concerns, and perspectives. As a result, they naturally have divergent viewpoints about how resources, rewards, and punishments should be distributed. These differences matter to both managers and employees, and they result in political struggle for resources, competition, and conflict within every organization. Political resistance is one of the great difficulties of bringing about organizational change, especially the development of new information systems. Virtually all large information systems investments by a firm that bring about significant changes in strategy, business objectives, business processes, and procedures become politically charged events. Managers that know how to work with the politics of an organization will be more successful than less-skilled managers in implementing new information systems.

Organizational Culture

All organizations have bedrock, unassailable, unquestioned (by the members) assumptions that define their goals and products. Organizational culture encompasses this set of assumptions about what products the organization

89

should produce, how it should produce them, where, and for whom. Generally, these cultural assumptions are taken totally for granted and are rarely publicly announced or spoken about. Business processes—the actual way business firms produce value—are usually ensconced in the organization's culture.

You can see organizational culture at work by looking around your university or college. Some bedrock assumptions of university life are that professors know more than students, the reason students attend college is to learn, and classes follow a regular schedule. Organizational culture is a powerful unifying force that restrains political conflict and promotes common understanding, agreement on procedures, and common practices. If we all share the same basic cultural assumptions, agreement on other matters is more likely.

At the same time, organizational culture is a powerful restraint on change, especially technological change (review the chapter-opening case). Most organizations will do almost anything to avoid making changes in basic assumptions. Any technological change that threatens commonly held cultural assumptions usually meets a great deal of resistance. However, there are times when the only sensible way for a firm to move forward is to employ a new technology that directly opposes an existing organizational culture. When this occurs, the technology is often stalled while the culture slowly adjusts.

Organizational Environments

Organizations reside in environments from which they draw resources and to which they supply goods and services. Organizations and environments have a reciprocal relationship. On the one hand, organizations are open to, and dependent on, the social and physical environment that surrounds them. Without financial and human resources—people willing to work reliably and consistently for a set wage or revenue from customers—organizations could not exist. Organizations must respond to legislative and other requirements imposed by government, as well as the actions of customers and competitors. On the other hand, organizations can influence their environments. For example, business firms form alliances with other businesses to influence the political process; they advertise to influence customer acceptance of their products.

Figure 5 illustrates the role of information systems in helping organizations perceive changes in their environments and also in helping organizations act on their environments. Information systems are key instruments for *environmental scanning*, helping managers identify external changes that might require an organizational response.

Environments generally change much faster than organizations. The main reasons for organizational failure are an inability to adapt to a rapidly changing environment and a lack of resources—particularly among young firms—to sustain even short periods of troubled times. New technologies, new products, and changing public tastes and values (many of which result in new government regulations) put strains on any organization's culture, politics, and people. Most organizations do not cope well with large environmental shifts. The inertia built into an organization's standard operating procedures, the political conflict raised by changes to the existing order, and the threat to closely held cultural values typically inhibit organizations from making significant changes. It is not surprising that only 10 percent of the Fortune 500 companies in 1919 still exist today.

Organizational Structure

Organizations all have a structure or shape. Mintzberg's classification, described in Table 1, identifies five basic kinds of organizational structure (Mintzberg, 1979).

FIGURE 5   ENVIRONMENTS AND ORGANIZATIONS HAVE A RECIPROCAL RELATIONSHIP

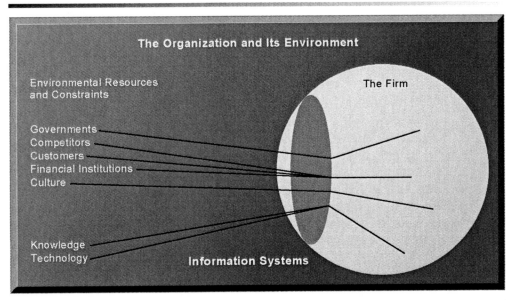

Environments shape what organizations can do, but organizations can influence their environments and decide to change environments altogether. Information technology plays a critical role in helping organizations perceive environmental change and in helping organizations act on their environment.

TABLE 1   ORGANIZATIONAL STRUCTURES

ORGANIZATIONAL TYPE	DESCRIPTION	EXAMPLES
Entrepreneurial structure	Young, small firm in a fast-changing environment. It has a simple structure and is managed by an entrepreneur serving as its single chief executive officer.	Small start-up business
Machine bureaucracy	Large bureaucracy existing in a slowly changing environment, producing standard products. It is dominated by a centralized management team and centralized decision making.	Midsize manufacturing firm
Divisionalized bureaucracy	Combination of multiple machine bureaucracies, each producing a different product or service, all topped by one central headquarters.	Fortune 500 firms, such as General Motors
Professional bureaucracy	Knowledge-based organization where goods and services depend on the expertise and knowledge of professionals. Dominated by department heads with weak centralized authority.	Law firms, school systems, hospitals
Adhocracy	Task force organization that must respond to rapidly changing environments. Consists of large groups of specialists organized into short-lived multidisciplinary teams and has weak central management.	Consulting firms, such as the Rand Corporation

The kind of information systems you find in a business firm—and the nature of problems with these systems—often reflects the type of organizational structure. For instance, in a professional bureaucracy such as a hospital, it is not unusual to find parallel patient record systems, one operated by the administration, another by doctors, and another by other professional staff such as nurses and social workers. In small entrepreneurial firms you will often find poorly designed systems developed in a rush that often outgrow their useful-

91

ness quickly. In huge multidivisional firms operating in hundreds of locations you will often find there is not a single integrating information system, but instead each locale or each division has its set of information systems.

Other Organizational Features

Organizations have goals and use different means to achieve them. Some organizations have coercive goals (e.g., prisons); others have utilitarian goals (e.g., businesses). Still others have normative goals (universities, religious groups). Organizations also serve different groups or have different constituencies, some primarily benefiting their members, others benefiting clients, stockholders, or the public. The nature of leadership differs greatly from one organization to another—some organizations may be more democratic or authoritarian than others. Another way organizations differ is by the tasks they perform and the technology they use. Some organizations perform primarily routine tasks that can be reduced to formal rules that require little judgment (such as manufacturing auto parts), whereas others (such as consulting firms) work primarily with nonroutine tasks.

HOW INFORMATION SYSTEMS IMPACT ORGANIZATIONS AND BUSINESS FIRMS

Information systems have become integral, online, interactive tools deeply involved in the minute-to-minute operations and decision making of large organizations. Over the last decade, information systems have fundamentally altered the economics of organizations and greatly increased the possibilities for organizing work. Theories and concepts from economics and sociology help us understand the changes brought about by IT.

ECONOMIC IMPACTS

From the point of view of economics, IT changes both the relative costs of capital and the costs of information. Information systems technology can be viewed as a factor of production that can be substituted for traditional capital and labor. As the cost of information technology decreases, it is substituted for labor, which historically has been a rising cost. Hence, information technology should result in a decline in the number of middle managers and clerical workers as information technology substitutes for their labor (Laudon, 1990).

As the cost of information technology decreases, it also substitutes for other forms of capital, such as buildings and machinery, which remain relatively expensive. Hence, over time we should expect managers to increase their investments in IT because of its declining cost relative to other capital investments.

IT also obviously affects the cost and quality of information and changes the economics of information. Information technology helps firms contract in size because it can reduce transaction costs—the costs incurred when a firm buys on the marketplace what it cannot make itself. According to **transaction cost theory**, firms and individuals seek to economize on transaction costs, much as they do on production costs. Using markets is expensive (Coase, 1937; Williamson, 1985) because of costs such as locating and communicating with distant suppliers, monitoring contract compliance, buying insurance, obtaining information on products, and so forth. Traditionally, firms have tried to reduce

FIGURE 6   **THE TRANSACTION COST THEORY OF THE IMPACT OF INFORMATION TECHNOLOGY ON THE ORGANIZATION**

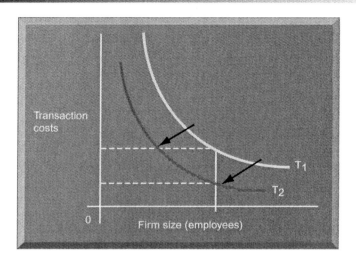

Firms traditionally grew in size to reduce transaction costs. IT potentially reduces the costs for a given size, shifting the transaction cost curve inward, opening up the possibility of revenue growth without increasing size, or even revenue growth accompanied by shrinking size.

transaction costs through vertical integration, by getting bigger, hiring more employees, and buying their own suppliers and distributors, as both General Motors and Ford used to do.

Information technology, especially the use of networks, can help firms lower the cost of market participation (transaction costs), making it worthwhile for firms to contract with external suppliers instead of using internal sources. For instance, by using computer links to external suppliers, the Chrysler Corporation can achieve economies by obtaining more than 70 percent of its parts from the outside. Information systems make it possible for companies such as Cisco Systems and Dell Computer to outsource their production to contract manufacturers such as Flextronics instead of making their products themselves.

Figure 6 shows that as transaction costs decrease, firm size (the number of employees) should shrink because it becomes easier and cheaper for the firm to contract for the purchase of goods and services in the marketplace rather than to make the product or offer the service itself. Firm size can stay constant or contract even if the company increases its revenues. For example, when Eastman Chemical Company split off from Kodak in 1994, it had $3.3 billion in revenue and 24,000 full-time employees. By 2005, it generated $7.1 billion in revenue with only 12,000 employees.

Information technology also can reduce internal management costs. According to **agency theory**, the firm is viewed as a "nexus of contracts" among self-interested individuals rather than as a unified, profit-maximizing entity (Jensen and Meckling, 1976). A principal (owner) employs "agents" (employees) to perform work on his or her behalf. However, agents need constant supervision and management; otherwise, they will tend to pursue their own interests rather than those of the owners. As firms grow in size and scope, agency costs or coordination costs rise because owners must expend more and more effort supervising and managing employees.

FIGURE 7   **THE AGENCY COST THEORY OF THE IMPACT OF INFORMATION TECHNOLOGY ON THE ORGANIZATION**

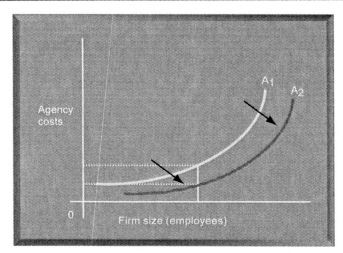

As firms grow in size and complexity, traditionally they experience rising agency costs. IT shifts the agency cost curve down and to the right, enabling firms to increase size while lowering agency costs.

Information technology, by reducing the costs of acquiring and analyzing information, permits organizations to reduce agency costs because it becomes easier for managers to oversee a greater number of employees. Figure 7 shows that by reducing overall management costs, information technology enables firms to increase revenues while shrinking the number of middle managers and clerical workers. You may have already seen examples where information technology expanded the power and scope of small organizations by enabling them to perform coordinating activities such as processing orders or keeping track of inventory with very few clerks and managers.

ORGANIZATIONAL AND BEHAVIORAL IMPACTS

Theories based on the sociology of complex organizations also provide some understanding about how and why firms change with the implementation of new IT applications.

IT Flattens Organizations
Large, bureaucratic organizations, which primarily developed before the computer age, are often inefficient, slow to change, and less competitive than newly created organizations. Some of these large organizations have down-sized, reducing the number of employees and the number of levels in their organizational hierarchies.

Behavioral researchers have theorized that information technology facilitates flattening of hierarchies by broadening the distribution of information to empower lower-level employees and increase management efficiency (see Figure 8). IT pushes decision-making rights lower in the organization because lower-level employees receive the information they need to make decisions without supervision. (This empowerment is also possible because of higher educational levels among the workforce, which give employees the capabilities to make intelligent decisions.) Because managers now receive so much more

FIGURE 8   FLATTENING ORGANIZATIONS

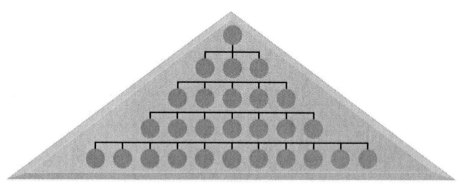

A traditional hierarchical organization with many levels of management

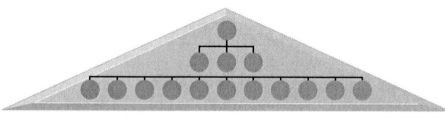

An organization that has been "flattened" by removing layers of management

Information systems can reduce the number of levels in an organization by providing managers with information to supervise larger numbers of workers and by giving lower-level employees more decision-making authority.

accurate information on time, they become much faster at making decisions, so fewer managers are required. Management costs decline as a percentage of revenues, and the hierarchy becomes much more efficient.

These changes mean that the management span of control has also been broadened, enabling high-level managers to manage and control more workers spread over greater distances. Many companies have eliminated thousands of middle managers as a result of these changes.

Postindustrial Organizations

Postindustrial theories based more on history and sociology than economics also support the notion that IT should flatten hierarchies. In postindustrial societies, authority increasingly relies on knowledge and competence, and not merely on formal positions. Hence, the shape of organizations flattens because professional workers tend to be self-managing, and decision making should become more decentralized as knowledge and information become more widespread throughout the firm (Drucker, 1988).

Information technology may encourage task force–networked organizations in which groups of professionals come together—face to face or electronically— for short periods of time to accomplish a specific task (e.g., designing a new automobile); once the task is accomplished, the individuals join other task forces. The global consulting service Accenture is an example. It has no operational headquarters and no formal branches. Many of its 129,000 employees move from location to location to work on projects at client sites in 48 different countries.

FIGURE 9   **ORGANIZATIONAL RESISTANCE AND THE MUTUALLY ADJUSTING RELATIONSHIP BETWEEN TECHNOLOGY AND THE ORGANIZATION**

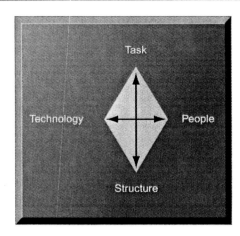

Implementing information systems has consequences for task arrangements, structures, and people. According to this model, to implement change, all four components must be changed simultaneously.
Source: Leavitt (1965).

Who makes sure that self-managed teams do not head off in the wrong direction? Who decides which person works on which team and for how long? How can managers evaluate the performance of someone who is constantly rotating from team to team? How do people know where their careers are headed? New approaches for evaluating, organizing, and informing workers are required, and not all companies can make virtual work effective.

Understanding Organizational Resistance to Change

Information systems inevitably become bound up in organizational politics because they influence access to a key resource—namely, information. Information systems can affect who does what to whom, when, where, and how in an organization. Many new information systems require changes in personal, individual routines that can be painful for those involved and require retraining and additional effort that may or may not be compensated. Because information systems potentially change an organization's structure, culture, business processes, and strategy, there is often considerable resistance to them when they are introduced.

There are several ways to visualize organizational resistance. Leavitt (1965) used a diamond shape to illustrate the interrelated and mutually adjusting character of technology and organization (see Figure 9). Here, changes in technology are absorbed, deflected, and defeated by organizational task arrangements, structures, and people. In this model, the only way to bring about change is to change the technology, tasks, structure, and people simultaneously. Other authors have spoken about the need to "unfreeze" organizations before introducing an innovation, quickly implementing it, and "refreezing" or institutionalizing the change (Alter and Ginzberg, 1978; Kolb, 1970).

Because organizational resistance to change is so powerful, many information technology investments flounder and do not increase productivity. Indeed, research on project implementation failures demonstrates that the most common reason for failure of large projects to reach their objectives is not the failure of the technology, but organizational and political resistance to change.

Therefore, as a manager involved in future IT investments, your ability to work with people and organizations is just as important as your technical awareness and knowledge.

THE INTERNET AND ORGANIZATIONS

The Internet, especially the World Wide Web, is beginning to have an important impact on the relationships between firms and external entities, and even on the organization of business processes inside a firm. The Internet increases the accessibility, storage, and distribution of information and knowledge for organizations. In essence, the Internet is capable of dramatically lowering the transaction and agency costs facing most organizations. For instance, brokerage firms and banks in New York can now deliver their internal operations procedures manuals to their employees at distant locations by posting them on the corporate Web site, saving millions of dollars in distribution costs. A global sales force can receive nearly instant price product information updates using the Web or instructions from management sent by e-mail. Vendors of some large retailers can access retailers' internal Web sites directly to find up-to-the-minute sales information and to initiate replenishment orders instantly.

Businesses are rapidly rebuilding some of their key business processes based on Internet technology and making this technology a key component of their IT infrastructures. If prior networking is any guide, one result will be simpler business processes, fewer employees, and much flatter organizations than in the past.

IMPLICATIONS FOR THE DESIGN AND UNDERSTANDING OF INFORMATION SYSTEMS

To deliver genuine benefits, information systems must be built with a clear understanding of the organization in which they will be used. In our experience, the central organizational factors to consider when planning a new system are the following:

- The environment in which the organization must function
- The structure of the organization: hierarchy, specialization, routines, and business processes
- The organization's culture and politics
- The type of organization and its style of leadership
- The principal interest groups affected by the system and the attitudes of workers who will be using the system
- The kinds of tasks, decisions, and business processes that the information system is designed to assist

 ## USING INFORMATION SYSTEMS TO ACHIEVE COMPETITIVE ADVANTAGE

In almost every industry you examine, you will find that some firms do better than most others. There's almost always a stand-out firm. In the automotive industry, Toyota is considered a superior performer. In pure online retail, Amazon.com is the leader. In off-line retail Wal-Mart, the largest retailer on earth, is the leader. In online music, Apple's iTunes is considered the leader with more than 75 percent of the downloaded music market, and in the related industry of digital music players, the iPod is the leader. In Web search, Google is considered the leader.

Firms that "do better" than others are said to have a competitive advantage over others: They either have access to special resources that others do not, or they are able to use commonly available resources more efficiently—usually because of superior knowledge and information assets. In any event, they do better in terms of revenue growth, profitability, or productivity growth (efficiency), all of which ultimately in the long run translate into higher stock market valuations than their competitors.

But why do some firms do better than others and how do they achieve competitive advantage? How can you analyze a business and identify its strategic advantages? How can you develop a strategic advantage for your own business? And how do information systems contribute to strategic advantages? One answer to that question is Michael Porter's competitive forces model.

PORTER'S COMPETITIVE FORCES MODEL

Arguably, the most widely used model for understanding competitive advantage is Michael Porter's **competitive forces model** (See Figure 10). This model provides a general view of the firm, its competitors, and the firm's environment. Earlier in this chapter, we described the importance of a firm's environment and the dependence of firms on environments. Porter's model is all about the firm's general business environment. In this model, five competitive forces shape the fate of the firm.

Traditional Competitors
All firms share market space with other competitors who are continuously devising new, more efficient ways to produce by introducing new products and services, and attempting to attract customers by developing their brands and imposing switching costs on their customers.

FIGURE 10   PORTER'S COMPETITIVE FORCES MODEL

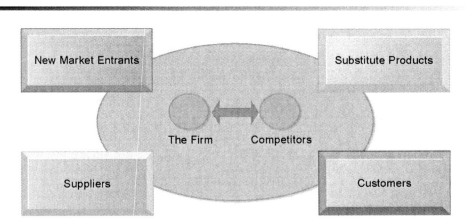

In Porter's competitive forces model, the strategic position of the firm and its strategies are determined not only by competition with its traditional direct competitors but also by four forces in the industry's environment: new market entrants, substitute products, customers, and suppliers.

New Market Entrants

In a free economy with mobile labor and financial resources, new companies are always entering the marketplace. In some industries, there are very low barriers to entry, whereas in other industries, entry is very difficult. For instance, it is fairly easy to start a pizza business or just about any small retail business, but it is much more expensive and difficult to enter the computer chip business, which has very high capital costs and requires significant expertise and knowledge that is hard to obtain. New companies have several possible advantages: They are not locked into old plants and equipment, they often hire younger workers who are less expensive and perhaps more innovative, they are not encumbered by old, worn-out brand names, and they are "more hungry" (more highly motivated) than traditional occupants of an industry. These advantages are also their weakness: They depend on outside financing for new plants and equipment, which can be expensive; they have a less experienced workforce; and they have little brand recognition.

Substitute Products and Services

In just about every industry, there are substitutes that your customers might use if your prices become too high. New technologies create new substitutes all the time. Even oil has substitutes: Ethanol can substitute for gasoline in cars; vegetable oil for diesel fuel in trucks; and wind, solar, coal, and hydro power for industrial electricity generation. Likewise, Internet telephone service can substitute for traditional telephone service, and fiber-optic telephone lines to the home can substitute for cable TV lines. And, of course, an Internet music service that allows you to download music tracks to an iPod is a substitute for CD-based music stores. The more substitute products and services in your industry, the less you can control pricing and the lower your profit margins.

Customers

A profitable company depends in large measure on its ability to attract and retain customers (while denying them to competitors), and charge high prices. The power of customers grows if they can easily switch to a competitor's products and services, or if they can force a business and its competitors to compete on price alone in a transparent marketplace where there is little **product differentiation**, and all prices are known instantly (such as on the Internet). For instance, in the used college textbook market on the Internet, students (customers) can find multiple suppliers of just about any current college textbook. In this case, online customers have extraordinary power over used-book firms.

Suppliers

The market power of suppliers can have a significant impact on firm profits, especially when the firm cannot raise prices as fast as can suppliers. The more different suppliers a firm has, the greater control it can exercise over suppliers in terms of price, quality, and delivery schedules. For instance, manufacturers of laptop PCs almost always have multiple competing suppliers of key components, such as keyboards, hard drives, and display screens.

INFORMATION SYSTEM STRATEGIES FOR DEALING WITH COMPETITIVE FORCES

What is a firm to do when it is faced with all these competitive forces? And how can the firm use information systems to counteract some of these forces?

Wal-Mart's continuous inventory replenishment system uses sales data captured at the checkout counter to transmit orders to restock merchandise directly to its suppliers. The system enables Wal-Mart to keep costs low while fine-tuning its merchandise to meet customer demands.

© Bob Daemmrich/PhotoEdit, Inc.

How do you prevent substitutes and inhibit new market entrants? There are four generic strategies, each of which often is enabled by using information technology and systems: low-cost leadership, product differentiation, focus on market niche, and strengthening customer and supplier intimacy.

Low-Cost Leadership

Use information systems to achieve the lowest operational costs and the lowest prices. The classic example is Wal-Mart. By keeping prices low and shelves well stocked using a legendary inventory replenishment system, Wal-Mart became the leading retail business in the United States. Wal-Mart's continuous replenishment system sends orders for new merchandise directly to suppliers as soon as consumers pay for their purchases at the cash register. Point-of-sale terminals record the bar code of each item passing the checkout counter and send a purchase transaction directly to a central computer at Wal-Mart headquarters. The computer collects the orders from all Wal-Mart stores and transmits them to suppliers. Suppliers can also access Wal-Mart's sales and inventory data using Web technology.

Because the system replenishes inventory with lightning speed, Wal-Mart does not need to spend much money on maintaining large inventories of goods in its own warehouses. The system also enables Wal-Mart to adjust purchases of store items to meet customer demands. Competitors, such as Sears, have been spending 24.9 percent of sales on overhead. But by using systems to keep operating costs low, Wal-Mart pays only 16.6 percent of sales revenue for overhead. (Operating costs average 20.7 percent of sales in the retail industry.)

Wal-Mart's continuous replenishment system is also an example of an efficient customer response system. An **efficient customer response system** directly links consumer behavior to distribution and production and supply chains. Wal-Mart's continuous replenishment system provides such an efficient customer response. Dell Computer Corporation's assemble-to-order system, described in the following discussion, is another example of an efficient customer response system.

Product Differentiation

Use information systems to enable new products and services, or greatly change the customer convenience in using your existing products and services. For instance, Google continuously introduces new and unique search services on its Web site, such as Google Maps. By purchasing PayPal, an electronic payment system, in 2003, eBay made it much easier for customers to pay sellers and expanded use of its auction marketplace. Apple created iPod, a unique portable digital music player, plus a unique online Web music service where songs can be purchased for 99 cents. Continuing to innovate, Apple recently introduced a portable iPod video player.

Manufacturers and retailers are using information systems to create products and services that are customized and personalized to fit the precise specifications of individual customers. Dell Computer Corporation sells directly to customers using assemble-to-order manufacturing. Individuals, businesses, and government agencies can buy computers directly from Dell, customized with the exact features and components they need. They can place their orders directly using a toll-free telephone number or by accessing Dell's Web site. Once Dell's production control receives an order, it directs an assembly plant to assemble the computer using components from an on-site warehouse based on the configuration specified by the customer.

Lands' End customers can use its Web site to order jeans, dress pants, chino pants, and shirts custom-tailored to their own specifications. Customers enter their measurements into a form on the Web site, which then transmits each customer's specifications over a network to a computer that develops an electronic made-to-measure pattern for that customer. The individual patterns are then transmitted electronically to a manufacturing plant, where they are used to drive fabric-cutting equipment. There are almost no extra production costs because the process does not require additional warehousing, production overruns, and inventories, and the cost to the customer is only slightly higher than that of a mass-produced garment. Fourteen percent of Lands' End shirt and pants sales are now customized. This ability to offer individually tailored products or services using the same production resources as mass production is called **mass customization**.

Table 2 lists a number of companies that have developed IS-based products and services that other firms have found difficult to copy, or at least took a long time to copy.

TABLE 2   IS-ENABLED NEW PRODUCTS AND SERVICES PROVIDING COMPETITIVE ADVANTAGE

Amazon.com: One-click shopping	Amazon holds a patent on one-click shopping that it licenses to other online retailers.
Online music: Apple iPod and iTunes	An integrated handheld player backed up with an online library of two million songs; one billion songs downloaded so far.
Search engine advertising: Google	Online search engine integrated with online advertising using text ads; two billion searches per month; Google holds several patents on its PageRank method of search response.
Golf club customization: Ping	Customers can select from more than one million different golf club options; a build-to-order system ships their customized clubs within 48 hours.
Online bill payment: CheckFree.com	Forty million households pay their bills online, as of 2006.
Online person-to-person payment: PayPal.com	Enables transfer of money between individual bank accounts and between bank accounts and credit card accounts.

Information systems make it possible for Ping Inc. to offer customers more than one million custom golf club options with different combinations of club heads, grips, shafts, and lie angles. Ping is able to fill many orders within 48 hours.

By permission, Ping, Inc.

Focus on Market Niche

Use information systems to enable a specific market focus, and serve this narrow target market better than competitors. Information systems support this strategy by producing and analyzing data for finely tuned sales and marketing techniques. Information systems enable companies to analyze customer buying patterns, tastes, and preferences closely so that they efficiently pitch advertising and marketing campaigns to smaller and smaller target markets.

The data come from a range of sources—credit card transactions, demographic data, purchase data from checkout counter scanners at supermarkets and retail stores, and data collected when people access and interact with Web sites. Sophisticated software tools find patterns in these large pools of data and infer rules from them to guide decision making. Analysis of such data drives one-to-one marketing that creates personal messages based on individualized preferences. Contemporary customer relationship management (CRM) systems feature analytical capabilities for this type of intensive data analysis.

Hilton Hotels uses a customer information system called OnQ, which contains detailed data about active guests in every property across the eight hotel brands owned by Hilton. Employees at the front desk tapping into the system instantly search through 180 million records to find out the preferences of customers checking in and their past experiences with Hilton so they can give these guests exactly what they want. OnQ establishes the value of each customer to Hilton, based on personal history and on predictions about the value of that person's future business with Hilton. OnQ can also identify customers who are clearly not profitable. Profitable customers receive extra privileges and attention, such as the ability to check out late without paying additional fees. After Hilton started using the system, the rate of staying at Hilton Hotels rather than at competing hotels soared from 41 percent to 61 percent (Kontzer, 2004).

The Interactive Session on Technology shows how 7-Eleven improved its competitive position by wringing more value out of its customer data. This company's early growth and strategy had been based on face-to-face relationships with its customers and intimate knowledge of exactly what they wanted to purchase. As the company grew over time, it was no longer

INTERACTIVE SESSION: TECHNOLOGY

7-ELEVEN STORES ASK THE CUSTOMER BY ASKING THE DATA

There is probably a 7-Eleven store in your neighborhood, and it's a convenient place for picking up a can of Coke or a quick ham-and-cheese sandwich. It's the largest convenience retailer in the world and the number one convenience store chain in the United States, with 5,300 stores.

This company started out about 75 years ago as an ice-dock operator. When refrigerators started replacing iceboxes, the manager of each store asked customers one-by-one what items they'd like to stock in their new appliances. By asking customers directly and stocking only the items customers most wanted, the company grew and prospered.

Over time, the company moved away from its roots, losing touch with customers along the way. It had no means of knowing what sold in each store and allowed vendors to decide what to stock on its shelves. Although large vendors, such as Coca-Cola and Frito-Lay, had powerful information systems for analyzing what they sold in individual stores, other vendors didn't have such systems. Moreover, the vendors' systems were designed to maximize opportunities for their businesses, not for 7-Eleven.

7-Eleven stores are not all alike. What their customers want depends a great deal on the neighborhood and region of the country where they are located. What sells well in Boston may not work in Texas.

Without detailed knowledge of its customer and sales patterns, 7-Eleven was unable to determine which items were selling well, or which items were most profitable to sell in the first place. This made a difference to the company's bottom line because of missed sales opportunities, lower profits, and excess store inventory, some of which consisted of perishable goods that had a very short shelf life. Profit margins are very thin in the convenience store business, so a quarter-point increase in sales volume can spell the difference between success and failure.

In 2004, 7-Eleven installed Hewlett-Packard servers and networking switches in all its U.S. stores to implement a Retail Information System. This system collects data from point-of-sale terminals in every store about each purchase made daily by its six million U.S customers and transmits the information in real time to a 7-terabyte Oracle database operated by Electronic Data Systems (EDS).

With this database, 7-Eleven keeps track of its purchase transactions and analyzes them to amass information about customer demand, pricing, and interest in new products, such as the Diet Pepsi Slurpee. Analysis of the data shows which items are selling well in which stores, which items customers are most interested in, seasonal demand for items, and which items are most profitable to sell in the first place.

Management uses this information to identify sales trends, improve product assortment, eliminate slow-moving products from inventory, and increase same-store sales by stocking products that are high in demand. Insights gleaned from the data also help 7-Eleven develop new products such as its fresh-food offerings that attract new customers and increase transaction size.

The system provides store managers with information on daily, weekly, and monthly sales of each item to help them determine which items to order and the exact quantities they will need for their stores. Managers use this information plus their on-the-spot knowledge of the neighborhood to make final ordering decisions.

Store managers enter orders into workstations or handheld computers by 10 A.M. each day. The system consolidates these orders and transmits them to 7-Eleven's suppliers. Orders are consolidated four times daily, one for each U.S. time zone in which 7-Eleven stores operate. 7-Eleven's orders for fresh food items are aggregated at 7-Eleven headquarters and transmitted to fresh food suppliers and bakeries for preparation and delivery the next day.

Thanks to information technology, 7-Eleven has come full circle in its ability to respond to the needs of the customer. By tracking and analyzing its data, it knows its customers as intimately as it did when store owners talked to each customer face-to-face. According to 7-Eleven President and CEO James Keyes, "Now we can use technology as a surrogate for being able to talk to every customer who walks in the door."

Sources: Oracle Corporation, "Streamlining Convenience," 2006 Shared Strategy Study and "7-Eleven Inc.," www.oracle.com, accessed July 15, 2006; Christopher Koch, "Who's Mining the Store?" *CIO*, May 15, 2005; James Keyes, "Data on the Fly," *Baseline*, August 2005; Laurie Sullivan, "Fine-Tuned Pricing," *Information Week*, August 15/22, 2005; and Steven Marlin, "The 24-Hour Supply Chain," InformationWeek, January 26, 2004.

CASE STUDY QUESTIONS

1. Why is knowing about the customer so important to a company such as 7-Eleven?
2. What are the benefits of 7-Eleven's Retail Information System?
3. In terms of Porter's model, what strategic forces does the Retail Information System seek to address?
4. Which of the strategies described in the chapter does the Retail Information System support?

MIS IN ACTION

Visit a nearby 7-Eleven store. Observe the items available for sale and the sales process at the store.

1. What technologies does the store use to process a purchase? Do you see any other technologies being used at the store?
2. Do you think the selection of items for sale is appropriate for the neighborhood and location of the particular 7-Eleven store you are visiting? What items might the Retail Information System have suggested for this store? Do you see any items that appear to be selling poorly at this store?
3. How well do you think 7-Eleven's Retail Information System works in stocking items for this store?

7-Eleven stores use a point-of-sale system to capture data about customer purchases and analyzes them to learn more about customer preferences and sales trends.

Photo courtesy of 7-Eleven, Inc.

able to discern customer preferences through personal face-to-face relationships. A new information system helped it obtain intimate knowledge of its customers once again by gathering and analyzing customer purchase transactions.

Strengthen Customer and Supplier Intimacy

Use information systems to tighten linkages with suppliers and develop intimacy with customers. Chrysler Corporation uses information systems to facilitate direct access from suppliers to production schedules, and even permits suppliers to decide how and when to ship suppliers to Chrysler factories. This

TABLE 3 FOUR BASIC COMPETITIVE STRATEGIES

STRATEGY	DESCRIPTION	EXAMPLE
Low-cost leadership	Use information systems to produce products and services at a lower price than competitors while enhancing quality and level of service.	Wal-Mart Dell Computer
Product differentiation	Use information systems to differentiate products, and enable new services and products.	Google, eBay, Apple, Lands' End
Focus on market niche	Use information systems to enable a focused strategy on a single market niche; specialize.	Hilton Hotels Harrah's
Customer and supplier intimacy	Use information systems to develop strong ties and loyalty with customers and suppliers.	Chrysler Corporation Amazon.com

allows suppliers more lead time in producing goods. On the customer side, Amazon.com keeps track of user preferences for book and CD purchases, and can recommend titles purchased by others to its customers. Strong linkages to customers and suppliers increase **switching costs** (the cost of switching from one product to a competing product), and loyalty to your firm. Table 3 summarizes the competitive strategies we have just described.

Some companies focus on one of these strategies, but you will often see companies pursuing several of them simultaneously. For example, Dell Computer tries to emphasize low cost as well as the ability to customize its personal computers. The new US Airways, described in the chapter-opening case, is trying to compete with quality of services as well as low cost.

THE INTERNET'S IMPACT ON COMPETITIVE ADVANTAGE

The Internet has nearly destroyed some industries and has severely threatened more. The Internet has also created entirely new markets and formed the basis for thousands of new businesses. The first wave of e-commerce transformed the business world of books, music, and air travel. In the second wave, eight new industries are facing a similar transformation scenario: telephone services, movies, television, jewelry, real estate, hotels, bill payments, and software. The breadth of e-commerce offerings grows, especially in travel, information clearinghouses, entertainment, retail apparel, appliances, and home furnishings.

For instance, the printed encyclopedia industry and the travel agency industry have been nearly decimated by the availability of substitutes over the Internet. Likewise, the Internet has had a significant impact on the retail, music, book, brokerage, and newspaper industries. At the same time, the Internet has enabled new products and services, new business models, and new industries to spring up every day, from eBay and Amazon.com to iTunes and Google. In this sense, the Internet is "transforming" entire industries, forcing firms to change how they do business.

Because of the Internet, the traditional competitive forces are still at work, but competitive rivalry has become much more intense (Porter, 2001). Internet technology is based on universal standards that any company can use, making it easy for rivals to compete on price alone and for new competitors to enter the market. Because information is available to everyone, the Internet raises the bargaining power of customers, who can quickly find the lowest-cost provider

TABLE 4 IMPACT OF THE INTERNET ON COMPETITIVE FORCES AND INDUSTRY STRUCTURE

COMPETITIVE FORCE	IMPACT OF THE INTERNET
Substitute products or services	Enables new substitutes to emerge with new approaches to meeting needs and performing functions.
Customers' bargaining power	Availability of global price and product information shifts; bargaining power to customers.
Suppliers' bargaining power	Procurement over the Internet tends to raise bargaining power over suppliers; suppliers can also benefit from reduced barriers to entry and from the elimination of distributors and other intermediaries standing between them and their users.
Threat of new entrants	The Internet reduces barriers to entry, such as the need for a sales force, access to channels, and physical assets; it provides a technology for driving business processes that makes other things easier to do.
Positioning and rivalry among existing competitors	Widens the geographic market, increasing the number of competitors, and reducing differences among competitors; makes it more difficult to sustain operational advantages; puts pressure to compete on price.

on the Web. Profits have been dampened. Some industries, such as the travel industry and the financial services industry, have been more impacted than others. Table 4 summarizes some of the potentially negative impacts of the Internet on business firms identified by Porter.

However, contrary to Porter's somewhat negative assessment, the Internet also creates new opportunities for building brands and building very large and loyal customer bases that are willing to pay a premium for the brand, for example, Yahoo!, eBay, BlueNile, RedEnvelope, Overstock.com, Amazon.com, Google, and many others. In addition, as with all IT-enabled business initiatives, some firms are far better at using the Internet than other firms are, which creates new strategic opportunities for the successful firms.

THE BUSINESS VALUE CHAIN MODEL

Although the Porter model is very helpful for identifying competitive forces and suggesting generic strategies, it is not very specific about what exactly to do, and it does not provide a methodology to follow for achieving competitive advantages. If your goal is to achieve operational excellence, where do you start? Here's where the business value chain model is helpful.

The **value chain model** highlights specific activities in the business where competitive strategies can best be applied (Porter, 1985) and where information systems are most likely to have a strategic impact. This model identifies specific, critical-leverage points where a firm can use information technology most effectively to enhance its competitive position. The value chain model views the firm as a series or chain of basic activities that add a margin of value to a firm's products or services. These activities can be categorized as either primary activities or support activities (see Figure 11).

Primary activities are most directly related to the production and distribution of the firm's products and services, which create value for the customer. Primary activities include inbound logistics, operations, outbound logistics, sales and marketing, and service. Inbound logistics includes receiving and storing materials for distribution to production. Operations transforms inputs into finished products. Outbound logistics entails storing and distributing finished products. Sales and marketing includes promoting and selling the firm's products. The service activity includes maintenance and repair of the firm's goods and services.

Support activities make the delivery of the primary activities possible and consist of organization infrastructure (administration and management), human

FIGURE 11   THE VALUE CHAIN MODEL

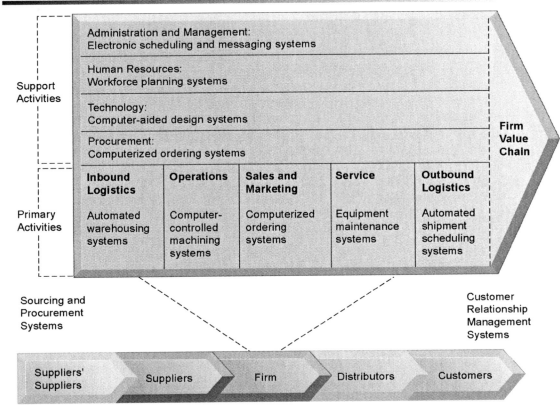

This figure provides examples of systems for both primary and support activities of a firm and of its value partners that can add a margin of value to a firm's products or services.

resources (employee recruiting, hiring, and training), technology (improving products and the production process), and procurement (purchasing input).

Now you can ask at each stage of the value chain, "How can we use information systems to improve operational efficiency, and improve customer and supplier intimacy?" This will force you to critically examine how you perform value-adding activities at each stage and how the business processes might be improved. You can also begin to ask how information systems can be used to improve the relationship with customers and with suppliers who lie outside the firm value chain but belong to the firm's extended value chain where they are absolutely critical to your success. Here, supply chain management systems that coordinate the flow of resources into your firm, and customer relationship management systems that coordinate your sales and support employees with customers are two of the most common system applications that result from a business value chain analysis.

Using the business value chain model will also cause you to consider benchmarking your business processes against your competitors or others in related industries, and identifying industry best practices. **Benchmarking** involves comparing the efficiency and effectiveness of your business processes against strict standards and then measuring performance against those standards. Industry **best practices** are usually identified by consulting companies, research organizations, government agencies, and industry associations as the most successful solutions or problem-solving methods for consistently and effectively achieving a business objective.

Once you have analyzed the various stages in the value chain at your business, you can come up with candidate applications of information systems. Then, once you have a list of candidate applications, you can decide which to develop first. By making improvements in your own business value chain that your competitors might miss, you can achieve competitive advantage by attaining operational excellence, lowering costs, improving profit margins, and forging a closer relationship with customers and suppliers. If your competitors are making similar improvements, then at least you will not be at a competitive disadvantage—the worst of all cases!

Extending the Value Chain: The Value Web

Figure 11 shows that a firm's value chain is linked to the value chains of its suppliers, distributors, and customers. After all, the performance of most firms depends not only on what goes on inside a firm but also on how well the firm coordinates with direct and indirect suppliers, delivery firms (logistics partners, such as FedEx or UPS), and, of course, customers.

How can information systems be used to achieve strategic advantage at the industry level? By working with other firms, industry participants can use information technology to develop industry-wide standards for exchanging information or business transactions electronically, which force all market participants to subscribe to similar standards. Such efforts increase efficiency, making product substitution less likely and perhaps raising entry costs—thus discouraging new entrants. Also, industry members can build industry-wide, IT-supported consortia, symposia, and communications networks to coordinate activities concerning government agencies, foreign competition, and competing industries.

Looking at the industry value chain encourages you to think about how to use information systems to link up more efficiently with your suppliers, strategic partners, and customers. Strategic advantage derives from your ability to relate your value chain to the value chains of other partners in the process. For instance, if you are Amazon.com, you want to build systems that

- Make it easy for suppliers to display goods and open stores on the Amazon site
- Make it easy for customers to pay for goods
- Develop systems that coordinate the shipment of goods to customers
- Develop shipment tracking systems for customers

In fact this is exactly what Amazon has done to become one of the Web's most satisfying online retail shopping sites. The Interactive Session on Technology discusses how Amazon.com developed and executes this business strategy. It also shows that Amazon.com had to revise its strategy several times in order to remain competitive.

Internet technology has made it possible to create highly synchronized industry value chains called value webs. A **value web** is a collection of independent firms that use information technology to coordinate their value chains to produce a product or service for a market collectively. It is more customer driven and operates in a less linear fashion than the traditional value chain.

INTERACTIVE SESSION: ORGANIZATIONS

AMAZON.COM: AN INTERNET GIANT FINE-TUNES ITS STRATEGY

Amazon.com made Internet history as one of the first large-scale retail companies to sell over the Web: in 2004 it hit $4 billion in online revenues, and by 2006 its sales guidance estimates $10 billion in revenue. It has grown to become one of the largest Internet retailers on earth. But the real significance of Amazon for this chapter is Amazon's continuous innovation in business strategy and information systems. In fact, the two are closely connected at Amazon: its business innovations are all driven by huge investments in information systems.

In 1995, former investment banker Jeff Bezos took advantage of new business opportunities created by the Internet by setting up a Web site to sell books directly to customers online. There were three million titles in print, and any one physical bookstore could only stock a fraction of them. A "virtual" bookstore offers a much larger selection of titles. Bezos believed consumers did not need to actually "touch and feel" a book before buying it, and Amazon.com provided online synopses, tables of contents, and reviews to help with selection. Amazon.com was able to charge lower prices than physical bookstores because it maintained very little of its own inventory (relying instead on distributors) and did not have to pay for maintaining physical storefronts or a large retail sales staff.

Amazon tried to provide superior customer service through e-mail and telephone customer support, automated order confirmation, online tracking and shipping information, and the ability to pay for purchases with a single click of the mouse using credit card and personal information a customer had provided during a previous purchase. This was called "1-Click" express shopping, and it made the shopping experience even more convenient.

In 1998, Amazon started selling music, CDs, videos, and DVDs, revising its business strategy "to become the best place to buy, find, and discover any product or service available online"—the online Wal-Mart. Its offerings grew to include electronics, toys, home improvement products, video games, apparel, gourmet food, travel services, personal care, and jewelry. It also introduced Amazon.com Auctions (similar to those offered by eBay), and zShops (online storefronts for small retailers). To service these new product lines, Amazon significantly expanded its warehouse and distribu-

tion capabilities and hired large numbers of employees. These moves strained its ability to adhere to its original vision of being a "virtual" retailer with lean inventories, low head count, and significant cost savings over traditional bookstores.

In 2001 and 2002, Amazon tried to increase revenue by cutting prices, offering free shipping, and leveraging its technology infrastructure to provide e-commerce services to other businesses. Amazon's Merchants@ and Amazon Marketplace allow other businesses to fully integrate their Web sites into Amazon's site to sell their branded goods using Amazon's fulfillment and payment systems. Nordstrom, The Gap, and Target stores use Amazon to sell their goods and then pay Amazon commissions and fees. In the Amazon Marketplace program, individuals are encouraged to sell their used or new goods on Amazon's Web site even when they compete directly with Amazon's sales of the same goods. Sales by third parties now represent 25 percent of Amazon's revenues.

Amazon refined its business model further to focus more on efficient operations while maintaining a steady commitment to keeping its 49 million customers satisfied. In early 2001, Amazon closed two of its eight warehouses, laid off 15 percent of its workforce, and consolidated orders from around the country prior to shipping to reduce shipping costs. Amazon used six sigma quality measures to reduce errors in fulfillment. These measures reduced fulfillment costs from 15 percent of revenue in 2000 to 10 percent by 2003.

Amazon finally became profitable in 2003 and remains an online retailing powerhouse growing at over 60 percent a year! It continues to innovate with IT-enabled services: free unlimited two-day shipping for $79 a year (Amazon Prime). Amazon entered the dry goods grocery business in 2006. These innovations increased its costs and reduced its profits, much to the disappointment of the stock market, which has depressed Amazon's stock from a high of $100 in 2000 down to the mid $20 range in 2006.

But Amazon faces powerful online retail competitors such as eBay and Yahoo! who also are very adept at using information systems to develop new products and services. Google is emerging as a competitor because so many consumers use its search engine—six billion searches are performed each month at Google—and in the process are exposed to search engine ads. Google is expanding into other shopping services: Google Base offers free classified listings of goods for sale and Google Checkout provides an online service that stores users' financial information to facilitate purchases from participating Internet vendors. Amazon is countering with new offerings, such as a digital mapping service with street-level photographs, a grocery store for non-perishable items sold in bulk, and selling short stories online for 49 cents apiece, along with additional expenditures to improve customer convenience and the shopping experience.

Recently, the company's profits have started to drop. The question is whether Amazon can turn its leadership in e-commerce into genuine long-term success. Can Amazon keep adapting its strategy to remain profitable and powerful?

Sources: Mary Crane, "Child's Play? Amazon Takes On Toys," Forbes.com, July 5, 2006; "Amazon Adds Groceries To Its Site," *The Wall Street Journal*, June 15, 2006; Randall Stross, "Trying to Get a Read on Amazon's Books," *The New York Times*, February 12, 2006; Bob Tedeschi, "Making Several Stops at Shops Online, but Paying All at Google," *The New York Times*, July 17, 2006; *The New York Times*, February 12, 2006; Gary Rivlin, "A Retail Revolution Turns 10," *The New York Times*, July 10, 2005; and Shaheen Pasha, "Amazon Has New Stories to Tell," *CNN Money*, August 22, 2005.

CASE STUDY QUESTIONS

1. Analyze Amazon.com using the competitive forces and value chain models. How has it responded to pressures from its competitive environment? How does it provide value to its customers?

2. Describe Amazon's evolving business strategy.

3. Why did the company change its strategy?

4. Do you think Amazon can continue to be successful? Explain your answer.

MIS IN ACTION

Search for an iPod nano on Amazon.com, eBay, and Yahoo! Shopping. Compare the shopping experience at these sites to answer the following questions.

1. Evaluate how each site offers information about a product, including information about the reliability of the vendor [seller].

2. Evaluate each of the sites in terms of how many sources for the product they offer.

3. Evaluate the sites in terms of pricing and availability of the product you have selected.

4. Which site would you choose for shopping for your nano? Why?

Amazon.com is an early e-commerce leader that has adjusted it strategy multiple times. It is trying to become a one-stop source for online shoppers.

© 2006 Amazon.com, Inc. or its affiliates. All Rights Reserved.

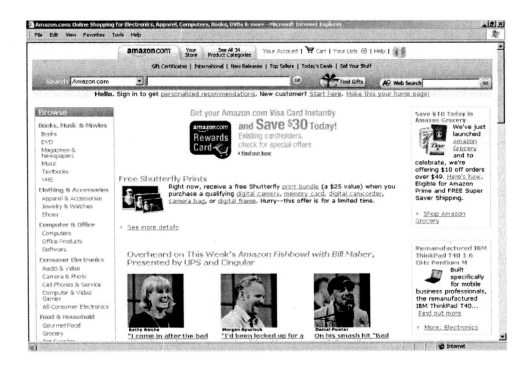

FIGURE 12   THE VALUE WEB

The value web is a networked system that can synchronize the value chains of business partners within an industry to respond rapidly to changes in supply and demand.

Figure 12 shows that this value web synchronizes the business processes of customers, suppliers, and trading partners among different companies in an industry or in related industries. These value webs are flexible and adaptive to changes in supply and demand. Relationships can be bundled or unbundled in response to changing market conditions. Firms will accelerate time to market and to customers by optimizing their value web relationships to make quick decisions on who can deliver the required products or services at the right price and location.

SYNERGIES, CORE COMPETENCIES, AND NETWORK-BASED STRATEGIES

A large corporation is typically a collection of businesses. Often, the firm is organized financially as a collection of strategic business units, and the returns to the firm are directly tied to the performance of all the strategic business units. Information systems can improve the overall performance of these business units by promoting synergies and core competencies.

Synergies

The idea of synergies is that when the output of some units can be used as inputs to other units, or two organizations pool markets and expertise, these relationships lower costs and generate profits. Recent bank and financial firm mergers, such as the mergers of JPMorgan Chase and BankOne

111

Corporation, Bank of America and FleetBoston Financial Corporation, and Deutsche Bank and Bankers Trust, occurred precisely for this purpose, as did the merger of US Airways and America West described in the chapter-opening case.

One use of information technology in these synergy situations is to tie together the operations of disparate business units so that they can act as a whole. For example, merging with Bank One provided JPMorgan Chase with a massive network of retail branches in the Midwest and Southwest. Information systems help the merged banks lower retailing costs and increase cross-marketing of financial products. The chapter-opening case describes the role of information systems in lowering costs and coordinating operations for US Airways after its merger.

Enhancing Core Competencies

Yet another way to use information systems for competitive advantage is to think about ways that systems can enhance core competencies. The argument is that the performance of all business units will increase insofar as these business units develop, or create, a central core of competencies. A **core competency** is an activity for which a firm is a world-class leader. Core competencies may involve being the world's best miniature parts designer, the best package delivery service, or the best thin-film manufacturer. In general, a core competency relies on knowledge that is gained over many years of experience and a first-class research organization or simply key people who follow the literature and stay abreast of new external knowledge.

Any information system that encourages the sharing of knowledge across business units enhances competency. Such systems might encourage or enhance existing competencies and help employees become aware of new external knowledge; such systems might also help a business leverage existing competencies to related markets.

For example, Procter & Gamble (P&G), a world leader in brand management and consumer product innovation, uses a series of systems to enhance its core competencies. P&G uses an intranet called InnovationNet to help people working on similar problems share ideas and expertise. The system connects those working in research and development (R&D), engineering, purchasing, marketing, legal affairs, and business information systems around the world, using a portal to provide browser-based access to documents, reports, charts, videos, and other data from various sources. In 2001, InnovationNet added a directory of subject-matter experts who can be tapped to give advice or collaborate on problem solving and product development, and created links to outside research scientists and 150 entrepreneurs who are searching for new, innovative products worldwide.

P&G sells more than 300 different branded products, with separate lines of business for Fabric and Home Care, Baby and Family Care, Beauty Care, Health Care, and Snacks and Beverages. It now uses custom-developed marketing management software to help all these groups share marketing ideas and data for marketing campaigns. This system supports strategic planning, research, advertising, direct mail, and events, and is able to analyze the impact of marketing projects on the business.

Network-Based Strategies

The availability of Internet and networking technologies has inspired strategies that take advantage of firms' abilities to create networks or network with each other. Network-based strategies include the use of network economics, a virtual company model, and business ecosystems.

Network Economics

Business models based on a network may help firms strategically by taking advantage of **network economics**. In traditional economics—the economics of factories and agriculture—production experiences diminishing returns. The more any given resource is applied to production, the lower the marginal gain in output, until a point is reached where the additional inputs produce no additional outputs. This is the law of diminishing returns, and it is the foundation for most of modern economics.

In some situations, the law of diminishing returns does not work. For instance, in a network, the marginal costs of adding another participant are about zero, whereas the marginal gain is much larger. The larger the number of subscribers in a telephone system or the Internet, the greater the value to all participants because each user can interact with more people. It is no more expensive to operate a television station with 1,000 subscribers than with 10 million subscribers. The value of a community of people grows with size, whereas the cost of adding new members is inconsequential.

From this network economics perspective, information technology can be strategically useful. Internet sites can be used by firms to build communities of users—like-minded customers who want to share their experiences. This builds customer loyalty and enjoyment, and builds unique ties to customers. eBay, the giant online auction site, and iVillage, an online community for women, are examples. Both businesses are based on networks of millions of users, and both companies have used the Web and Internet communication tools to build communities. The more people offering products on eBay, the more valuable the eBay site is to everyone because more products are listed, and more competition among suppliers lowers prices. Network economics also provides strategic benefits to commercial software vendors. The value of their software and complementary software products increases as more people use them, and there is a larger installed base to justify continued use of the product and vendor support.

Virtual Company Strategy

Another network-based strategy uses the model of a virtual company to create a competitive business. A **virtual company**, also known as a virtual organization, uses networks to link people, assets, and ideas, enabling it to ally with other companies to create and distribute products and services without being limited by traditional organizational boundaries or physical locations. One company can use the capabilities of another company without being physically tied to that company. The virtual company model is useful when a company finds it cheaper to acquire products, services, or capabilities from an external vendor or when it needs to move quickly to exploit new market opportunities and lacks the time and resources to respond on its own.

Fashion companies, such as GUESS, Ann Taylor, Levi Strauss, and Reebok, enlist Hong Kong-based Li & Fung to manage production and shipment of their garments. Li & Fung handles product development, raw material sourcing, production planning, quality assurance, and shipping. Li & Fung does not own any fabric, factories, or machines, outsourcing all of its work to a network of more than 7,500 suppliers in 37 countries all over the world. Customers place orders to Li & Fung over its private extranet. Li & Fung then sends instructions

113

to appropriate raw material suppliers and factories where the clothing is produced. The Li & Fung extranet tracks the entire production process for each order. Working as a virtual company keeps Li & Fung flexible and adaptable so that it can design and produce the products ordered by its clients in short order to keep pace with rapidly changing fashion trends.

Business Ecosystems: Keystone and Niche Firms

The Internet and the emergence of digital firms call for some modification of the industry competitive forces model. The traditional Porter model assumes a relatively static industry environment; relatively clear-cut industry boundaries; and a relatively stable set of suppliers, substitutes, and customers, with the focus on industry players in a market environment. Instead of participating in a single industry, some of today's firms are much more aware that they participate in industry sets—collections of industries that provide related services and products (see Figure 13). **Business ecosystem** is another term for these loosely coupled but interdependent networks of suppliers, distributors, outsourcing firms, transportation service firms, and technology manufacturers (Iansiti and Levien, 2004).

The concept of a business ecosystem builds on the idea of the value web described earlier, the main difference being that cooperation takes place across many industries rather than many firms. For instance, both Microsoft and Wal-Mart provide platforms composed of information systems, technologies, and services that thousands of other firms in different industries use to enhance their own capabilities. Microsoft has estimated that more than 40,000 firms use its Windows platform to deliver their own products, support Microsoft products, and extend the value of Microsoft's own firm. Wal-Mart's order entry and inventory management system is a platform used by thousands of suppliers to obtain real-time access to customer demand, track shipments, and control inventories.

FIGURE 13   AN ECOSYSTEM STRATEGIC MODEL

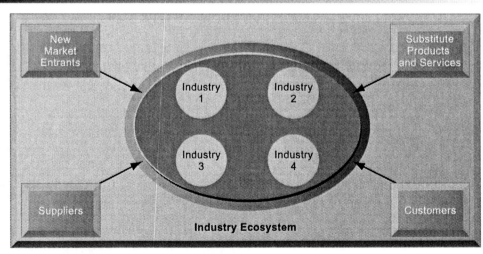

The digital firm era requires a more dynamic view of the boundaries among industries, firms, customers, and suppliers, with competition occurring among industry sets in a business ecosystem. In the ecosystem model, multiple industries work together to deliver value to the customer. IT plays an important role in enabling a dense network of interactions among the participating firms.

Business ecosystems can be characterized as having one or a few keystone firms that dominate the ecosystem and create the platforms used by other niche firms. Keystone firms in the Microsoft ecosystem include Microsoft and technology producers such as Intel and IBM. Niche firms include thousands of software application firms, software developers, service firms, networking firms, and consulting firms that both support and rely on the Microsoft products.

Information technology plays a powerful role in establishing business ecosystems. Obviously, many firms use information systems to develop into keystone firms by building IT-based platforms that other firms can use. For instance, eBay has created a platform for auctions and online stores used by over 400,000 small businesses every day. Amazon.com and portals such as Yahoo! have created online store business platforms used by Fortune 500 firms such as Dell (and thousands of smaller firms) to sell directly to the public. In the digital firm era, we can expect greater emphasis on the use of IT to build industry ecosystems because the costs of participating in such ecosystems will fall and the benefits to all firms will increase rapidly as the platform grows.

Individual firms should consider how their information systems will enable them to become profitable niche players in larger ecosystems created by keystone firms. For instance, in making decisions about which products to build or which services to offer, a firm should consider the existing business ecosystems related to these products and how it might use IT to enable participation in these larger ecosystems.

4 USING SYSTEMS FOR COMPETITIVE ADVANTAGE: MANAGEMENT ISSUES

Strategic information systems often change the organization as well as its products, services, and operating procedures, driving the organization into new behavioral patterns. Successfully using information systems to achieve a competitive advantage is challenging and requires precise coordination of technology, organizations, and management.

SUSTAINING COMPETITIVE ADVANTAGE

The competitive advantages strategic systems confer do not necessarily last long enough to ensure long-term profitability. Because competitors can retaliate and copy strategic systems, competitive advantage is not always sustainable. Markets, customer expectations, and technology change; globalization has made these changes even more rapid and unpredictable. The Internet can make competitive advantage disappear very quickly because virtually all companies can use this technology. Classic strategic systems, such as American Airlines's SABRE computerized reservation system, Citibank's ATM system, and FedEx's package tracking system, benefited by being the first in their industries. Then rival systems emerged. Amazon.com, discussed earlier in this chapter, was an e-commerce leader but now faces competition from eBay, Yahoo!, and Google. Information systems alone cannot provide an enduring business advantage. Systems originally intended to be strategic frequently become tools for survival, required by every firm to stay in business, or they may inhibit organizations from making the strategic changes essential for future success.

PERFORMING A STRATEGIC SYSTEMS ANALYSIS

Managers interested in using information systems for competitive advantage will need to perform a strategic systems analysis. To identify the types of systems that provide a strategic advantage to their firms, managers should ask the following questions:

1. What is the structure of the industry in which the firm is located?

- What are some of the competitive forces at work in the industry? Are there new entrants to the industry? What is the relative power of suppliers, customers, and substitute products and services over prices?
- Is the basis of competition quality, price, or brand?
- What are the direction and nature of change within the industry? From where are the momentum and change coming?
- How is the industry currently using information technology? Is the organization behind or ahead of the industry in its application of information systems?

2. What are the business, firm, and industry value chains for this particular firm?

- How is the company creating value for the customer—through lower prices and transaction costs or higher quality? Are there any places in the value chain where the business could create more value for the customer and additional profit for the company?
- Does the firm understand and manage its business processes using the best practices available? Is it taking maximum advantage of supply chain management, customer relationship management, and enterprise systems?
- Does the firm leverage its core competencies?
- Is the industry supply chain and customer base changing in ways that benefit or harm the firm?
- Can the firm benefit from strategic partnerships and value webs?
- Where in the value chain will information systems provide the greatest value to the firm?

MANAGING STRATEGIC TRANSITIONS

Adopting the kinds of strategic systems described in this chapter generally requires changes in business goals, relationships with customers and suppliers, and business processes. These sociotechnical changes, affecting both social and technical elements of the organization, can be considered **strategic transitions**—a movement between levels of sociotechnical systems.

Such changes often entail blurring of organizational boundaries, both external and internal. Suppliers and customers must become intimately linked and may share each other's responsibilities. Managers will need to devise new business processes for coordinating their firms' activities with those of customers, suppliers, and other organizations. The organizational change requirements surrounding new information systems are so important that they merit attention throughout this text.

5   HANDS-ON MIS

The projects in this section give you hands-on experience analyzing a company's competitive strategy, using a database to improve decision making about business strategy, and using Web tools to configure and price an automobile.

Analyzing Competitive Strategy

Software skills: Web browser software and presentation software
Business skills: Value chain and competitive forces analysis, business strategy formulation

This project provides an opportunity for you to develop the competitive strategy for a real-world business. You'll use the Web to identify Dirt Bikes's competitors and the competitive forces in its industry. You'll use value chain analysis to determine what kinds of information systems will provide the company with a competitive advantage.

Dirt Bikes's management wants to be sure it is pursuing the right competitive strategy. You have been asked to perform a competitive analysis of the company using the Web to find the information you need. Prepare a report that analyzes Dirt Bikes using the value chain and competitive forces models. You report should include the following:

- Which activities at Dirt Bikes create the most value? [Hint: review company description.]
- How does Dirt Bikes provide value to its customers? [Hint: review company description.]
- Who are Dirt Bikes's major competitors? How do their products compare in price to those of Dirt Bikes? What are some of the product features they emphasize?
- What are the competitive forces that can affect the industry? [Hint: research the dirt bikes and motor cycle industry online].
- What competitive strategy should Dirt Bikes pursue? [Hint: review discussion of Porter in this chapter.]
- What information systems best support that strategy?
- (Optional) Use electronic presentation software to summarize your findings for management.

Improving Decision Making: Using a Database to Clarify Business Strategy

Software skills: Database querying and reporting; database design
Business skills: Reservation systems; customer analysis

In this exercise, you will use database software to analyze the reservation transactions for a hotel and use that information to fine-tune the hotel's business strategy and marketing activities.

The Presidents' Inn is a small three-story hotel on the Atlantic Ocean in Cape May, New Jersey, a popular northeastern U.S. resort. Ten rooms overlook side streets, 10 rooms have bay windows that offer limited views of the ocean, and the remaining 10 rooms in the front of the hotel face the ocean. Room rates are based on room choice, length of stay, and number of guests per room. Room rates are the same for one to four guests. Fifth and sixth guests must pay an additional $20 charge each per day. Guests staying for seven days or more receive a 10 percent discount on their daily room rates.

Business has grown steadily during the past 10 years. Now totally renovated, the inn uses a romantic weekend package to attract couples, a vacation package to attract young families, and a weekday discount package to attract business travelers. The owners currently use a manual reservation and bookkeeping system, which has caused many problems. Sometimes two families have been booked in the same room at the same time. Management does not have immediate data about the hotel's daily operations and income.

At the Laudon Web site for this chapter, you will find a database for hotel reservation transactions developed in Microsoft Access. Illustrated below are some sample records from that database.

Develop several reports in Access that provide information to help management make the business more competitive and profitable. Your reports should answer the following questions:

- What is the average length of stay per room type?
- What is the average number of visitors per room type?
- What is the base income per room (i.e., length of visit multiplied by the daily rate) during a specified period of time?
- What is the strongest customer base?

After answering these questions, write a brief report describing what the database information reveals about the current business situation. Which specific business strategies might be pursued to increase room occupancy and revenue? How could the database be improved to provide better information for strategic decisions?

Improving Decision Making: Using Web Tools to Configure and Price an Automobile

Software skills: Internet-based software
Business skills: Researching product information and pricing

The Web is an online library of consumer information besides being a marketplace where goods and services are purchased. The Web has an extraordinary influence on off-line purchases: more than 80 percent of new car buyers research their dream cars online first (Laudon and Traver, 2006).

In this exercise, you will use software at Web sites for selling cars to find product information about a car of your choice and use that information to make an important purchase decision. You will also evaluate two of these sites as selling tools.

Let's assume your seven-year-old car has tried your patience one too many times, and you've decided to purchase a new automobile. You have been interested in a Ford family car and want to investigate the Ford Fusion (if you are personally interested in another car, domestic or foreign, investigate that one instead). Go to the Web site of CarsDirect (www.carsdirect.com) and begin your investigation. Locate the Ford Fusion. Research the various specific automobiles available in that model and determine which you prefer. Explore the full details about the specific car, including pricing, standard features, and options. Locate and read at least two reviews if possible. Investigate the safety of that model based on the U.S. government crash tests performed by the National Highway Traffic Safety Administration if those test results are available. Explore the features for locating a vehicle in inventory and purchasing directly. Finally, explore the other capabilities of the CarsDirect site for financing.

Having recorded or printed the information you need from CarsDirect for your purchase decision, surf the Web site of the manufacturer, in this case Ford (www.ford.com). Compare the information available on Ford's Web site with that of CarsDirect for the Ford Fusion. Be sure to check the price and any incentives being offered (which may not agree with what you found at CarsDirect). Next, find a dealer on the Ford site so that you can view the car before making your purchase decision. Try to locate the lowest price for the car you want in a local dealer's inventory. Which site would you use to purchase your car? Why? Suggest improvements for the sites of CarsDirect and Ford.

LEARNING TRACK MODULE

The Changing Business Environment for Information Technology. This Learning Track surveys the major changes in the global business environment facing firms today. You can find the Learning Track on the Laudon Web site for this chapter and on the Student CD-ROM.

Summary

1. *Identify and describe important features of organizations that managers need to know about in order to build and use information systems successfully.*

Managers need to understand certain essential features of organizations to build and use information systems successfully. All modern organizations are hierarchical, specialized, and impartial, using explicit routines to maximize efficiency. All organizations have their own cultures and politics arising from differences in interest groups, and they are affected by their surrounding environment. Organizations differ in goals, groups served, social roles, leadership styles, incentives, types of tasks performed, and type of structure. These features help explain differences in organizations' use of information systems.

2. *Evaluate the impact of information systems on organizations.*

Information systems and the organizations in which they are used interact with and influence each other. The introduction of a new information system will affect organizational structure, goals, work design, values, competition between interest groups, decision making, and day-to-day behavior. At the same time, information systems must be designed to serve the needs of important organizational groups and will be shaped by the organization's structure, tasks, goals, culture, politics, and management. Information technology can reduce transaction and agency costs, and such changes have been accentuated in organizations using the Internet.

Information systems are closely intertwined with an organization's structure, culture, and business processes. New systems disrupt established patterns of work and power relationships, so there is often considerable resistance to them when they are introduced. The complex relationship between information systems, organizational performance, and decision making must be carefully managed.

3. *Demonstrate how Porter's competitive forces model and the value chain model help businesses use information systems for competitive advantage.*

In Porter's competitive forces model, the strategic position of the firm, and its strategies, are determined by competition with its traditional direct competitors but also they are greatly affected by new market entrants, substitute products and services, suppliers, and customers. Information systems help companies compete by maintaining low costs, differentiating products or services, focusing on market niche, strengthening ties with customer and suppliers, and increasing barriers to market entry with high levels of operational excellence.

The value chain model highlights specific activities in the business where competitive strategies and information systems will have the greatest impact. The model views the firm as a series of primary and support activities that add value to a firm's products or services. Primary activities are directly related to production and distribution, whereas support activities make the delivery of primary activities possible. A firm's value chain can be linked to the value chains of its suppliers, distributors, and customers. A value web consists of information systems that enhance competitiveness at the industry level by promoting the use of standards and industry-wide consortia, and by enabling businesses to work more efficiently with their value partners.

4. *Demonstrate how information systems help businesses use synergies, core competences, and network-based strategies to achieve competitive advantage.*

Because firms consist of multiple business units, information systems achieve additional efficiencies or enhanced services by tying together the operations of disparate business units. Information systems help businesses leverage their core competencies by promoting the sharing of knowledge across business units. Information systems facilitate business models based on large networks of users or subscribers that take advantage of network economics. A virtual company strategy uses networks to link to other firms so that a company can use the capabilities of other companies to build, market, and distribute products and services. In business ecosystems, multiple industries work together to deliver value to the customer. Information systems support a dense network of interactions among the participating firms.

5. *Assess the challenges posed by strategic information systems and management solutions.*

Implementing strategic systems often requires extensive organizational change and a transition from one sociotechnical level to another. Such changes are called strategic transitions and are often difficult and painful to achieve. Moreover, not all strategic systems are profitable, and they can be expensive to build. Many strategic information systems are easily copied by other firms so that strategic advantage is not always sustainable. A strategic systems analysis is helpful.

Key Terms

Agency theory
Benchmarking
Best practices
Business ecosystem
Competitive forces model
Core competency
Efficient customer response systems
Mass customization
Network economics
Organization

Primary activities
Product differentiation
Routines
Strategic transitions
Support activities
Switching costs
Transaction cost theory
Value chain model
Value web
Virtual company

Review Questions

1. What is an organization? Compare the technical definition of organizations with the behavioral definition.

2. Identify and describe the features of organizations that help explain differences in organizations' use of information systems.

3. Describe the major economic theories that help explain how information systems affect organizations.

4. Describe the major behavioral theories that help explain how information systems affect organizations.

5. Why is there considerable organizational resistance to the introduction of information systems?

6. What is the impact of the Internet on organizations?

7. What is Porter's competitive forces model? How does it work? What does it explain about competitive advantage?

8. What are four competitive strategies enabled by information systems that firms can pursue? How

do information systems support each of these competitive strategies? Give examples.

9. What is the value chain model? How can it be used to identify opportunities for strategic information systems?

10. What is the value web? How is it related to the value chain? How does it help identify opportunities for strategic information systems?

11. How has the Internet changed competitive forces and competitive advantage?

12. How do information systems promote synergies and core competencies? How does this enhance competitive advantage?

13. How can businesses benefit by using network economics?

14. What is a virtual company? What are the benefits of pursuing a virtual company strategy?

15. Describe the management challenges posed by strategic information systems in organizations and suggest some ways of dealing with them.

Discussion Questions

1. It has been said that there is no such thing as a sustainable strategic advantage. Do you agree? Why or why not?

2. It has been said that the advantage that leading-edge retailers such as Dell and Wal-Mart have over their competition isn't technology; it's their management. Do you agree? Why or why not?

Video Case

You will find a video case illustrating some of the concepts in this chapter on the Laudon Web site and Student CD-ROM along with questions to help you analyze the case.

Teamwork: Identifying Opportunities for Strategic Information Systems

With a group of three or four students, select a company described in the *Wall Street Journal, Fortune, Forbes*, or another business publication. Visit the company's Web site to find additional information about that company and to see how the firm is using the Web. On the basis of this information, analyze the business. Include a description of the organization's features, such as important business processes, culture, structure, and environment, as well as its business strategy. Suggest strategic information systems appropriate for that particular business, including those based on Internet technology, if appropriate. Use electronic presentation software to present your findings to the class.

REFERENCES

Allison, Graham T. *Essence of Decision-Explaining the Cuban Missile Crisis*. Boston: Boston: Little Brown (1971).

Attewell, Paul, and James Rule. "Computing and Organizations: What We Know and What We Don't Know." *Communications of the ACM* 27, no. 12 (December 1984).

Beer, Michael, Russell A. Eisenstat, and Bert Spector. "Why Change Programs Don't Produce Change." *Harvard Business Review* (November-December 1990).

Bresnahan, Timohy F., Erik Brynjolfsson, and Lorin M. Hitt, "Information Technology, Workplace Organization, and the Demand for Skilled Labor," Quarterly Journal of Economics 117 (February 2002).

Camuffo, Arnaldo, Pietro Romano and AndreaVinellie. "Benetton Transforms Its Global Network." *Sloan Management Review* 43, no. 1 (Fall 2001)

Christensen, Clayton. "The Past and Future of Competitive Advantage." *Sloan Management Review* 42, no. 2 (Winter 2001).

Clemons, Eric K. "Evaluation of Strategic Investments in Information Technology." *Communications of the ACM* (January 1991).

———. "Sustaining IT Advantage: The Role of Structural Differences." *MIS Quarterly* 15, no. 3 (September 1991).

Coase, Ronald H. "The Nature of the Firm." (1937) in Putterman, Louis and Randall Kroszner. *The Economic Nature of the Firm: A Reader*, Cambridge University Press, 1995.

Davenport, Thomas H. "Competing on Analytics." *Harvard Business Review* (January 2006).

———. Jeanne G. Harris and Ajay K. Kohli, "How Do They Know Their Customers So Well?" *Sloan Management Review* 42, no. 2 (Winter 2001).

Erasala, Naveen and John "Skip" Benamati." Understanding the Electronic Commerce Cycles of Change" *Journal of Organizational Computing and Electronic Commerce* 13, no.1 (2003).

Farhoomand, Ali and Pauline S.P. Ng. "Creating Sustainable Competitive Advantage Through Internetworked Communities." *Communications of the ACM* 46, no. 9 (September 2003).

Feeny, David E., and Blake Ives. "In Search of Sustainability: Reaping Long-Term Advantage from Investments in Information Technology." *Journal of Management Information Systems* (Summer 1990).

Freeman, John, Glenn R. Carroll, and Michael T. Hannan. "The Liability of Newness: Age Dependence in Organizational Death Rates." *American Sociological Review* 48 (1983).

Fritz, Mary Beth Watson, Sridhar Narasimhan, and Hyeun-Suk Rhee. "Communication and Coordination in the Virtual Office." *Journal of Management Information Systems* 14, no. 4 (Spring 1998).

Gilbert, Clark and Joseph L. Bower, "Disruptive Change." *Harvard Business Review* (May 2002),

Gurbaxani, V., and S. Whang, "The Impact of Information Systems on Organizations and Markets." *Communications of the ACM* 34, no. 1 (Jan. 1991).

Hinds, Pamela, and Sara Kiesler. "Communication across Boundaries: Work, Structure, and Use of Communication Technologies in a Large Organization." *Organization Science* 6, no. 4 (July–August 1995).

Hitt, Lorin M. "Information Technology and Firm Boundaries: Evidence from Panel Data." *Information Systems Research* 10, no. 2 (June 1999).

Hitt, Lorin M., and Erik Brynjolfsson. "Information Technology and Internal Firm Organization: An Exploratory Analysis." *Journal of Management Information Systems* 14, no. 2 (Fall 1997).

Holweg, Matthias and Frits K. Pil. "Successful Build-to-Order Strategies Start with the Customer." *Sloan Management Review* 43, no. 1 (Fall 2001).

Iansiti, Marco. "Managing the Ecosystem." *Optimize Magazine* (February 2005).

Iansiti, Marco and Roy Levien, "Strategy as Ecology." *Harvard Business Review* (March 2004).

Jensen, M. C., and W. H. Meckling. "Specific and General Knowledge and Organizational Science." In *Contract Economics*, edited by L. Wetin and J. Wijkander. Oxford: Basil Blackwell (1992).

Jensen, Michael C., and William H. Meckling. "Theory of the Firm: Managerial Behavior, Agency Costs, and Ownership Structure." *Journal of Financial Economics* 3 (1976).

Kanter, Rosabeth Moss. "The New Managerial Work." *Harvard Business Review* (November-December 1989).

Kauffman, Robert J. and Yu-Ming Wang. "The Network Externalities Hypothesis and Competitive Network Growth." *Journal of Organizational Computing and Electronic Commerce* 12, no. 1 (2002).

Kettinger, William J., Varun Grover, Subashish Guhan, and Albert H. Segors. "Strategic Information Systems Revisited: A Study in Sustainability and Performance." *MIS Quarterly* 18, no. 1 (March 1994).

King, J. L., V. Gurbaxani, K. L. Kraemer, F. W. McFarlan, K. S. Raman, and C. S. Yap. "Institutional Factors in Information Technology Innovation." *Information Systems Research* 5, no. 2 (June 1994).

Kling, Rob. "Social Analyses of Computing: Theoretical Perspectives in Recent Empirical Research." *Computing Survey* 12, no. 1 (March 1980).

Kolb, D. A., and A. L. Frohman. "An Organization Development Approach to Consulting." *Sloan Management Review* 12, no. 1 (Fall 1970).

Kopczak, Laura Rock, and M. Eric Johnson. "The Supply-Chain Management Effect." *MIT Sloan Management Review* 44, no. 3 (Spring 2003).

Kraemer, Kenneth, John King, Debora Dunkle, and Joe Lane. *Managing Information Systems*. Los Angeles: Jossey-Bass (1989).

Lamb, Roberta and Rob Kling. "Reconceptualizing Users as Social Actors in Information Systems Research." *MIS Quarterly* 27, no. 2 (June 2003).

Laudon, Kenneth C. *Computers and Bureaucratic Reform*. New York: Wiley (1974).

———. "A General Model of the Relationship Between Information Technology and Organizations." Center for Research on Information Systems, New York University. Working paper, National Science Foundation (1989).

———. *Dossier Society: Value Choices in the Design of National Information Systems*. New York: Columbia University Press (1986).

———. "Environmental and Institutional Models of Systems Development." Communications of the ACM 28, no. 7 (July 1985).

———. "The Promise and Potential of Enterprise Systems and Industrial Networks." Working paper, The Concours Group. Copyright Kenneth C. Laudon (1999).

Laudon, Kenneth C. and Kenneth L. Marr, "Information Technology and Occupational Structure." (April 1995).

Laudon, Kenneth C. and Carol G. Traver, *E-Commerce. Business. Technology. Society.* Upper Saddle River, N.J.: Prentice Hall (2006).

Lawrence, Paul, and Jay Lorsch. *Organization and Environment*. Cambridge, MA: Harvard University Press (1969).

Levecq, Hugues and Bruce W. Weber, "Electronic Trading Systems: Strategic Implication of Market Design Choices." Journal of *Organizational Computing and Electronic Commerce* 12, no. 1 (2002).

Malone, Thomas W., JoAnne Yates, and Robert I. Benjamin. "Electronic Markets and Electronic Hierarchies." *Communications of the ACM* (June 1987).

March, James G., and Herbert A. Simon. *Organizations*. New York: Wiley (1958).

Markus, M. L. "Power, Politics, and MIS Implementation." *Communications of the ACM* 26, no. 6 (June 1983).

McAfee, Andrew and Francois-Xavier Oliveau. "Confronting the Limits of Networks." *Sloan Management Review* 43 no.4, (Summer 2002).

Mendelson, Haim, and Ravindra R. Pillai. "Clock Speed and Informational Response: Evidence from the Information Technology Industry." *Information Systems Research* 9, no. 4 (December 1998).

Mintzberg, Henry. *The Structuring of Organizations*. Englewood Cliffs, NJ: Prentice Hall (1979).

Mintzberg, Henry and Frances Westley. "Decision Making: It's Not What You Think." *Sloan Management Review* (Spring 2001).

Orlikowski, Wanda J., and Daniel Robey. "Information Technology and the Structuring of Organizations." *Information Systems Research* 2, no. 2 (June 1991).

Pindyck, Robert S., and Daniel L. Rubinfeld. *Microeconomics, Fifth Ed.* Upper Saddle River, NJ: Prentice Hall (2001).

Porter, Michael E. and Scott Stern. "Location Matters." *Sloan Management Review* 42, no. 4 (Summer 2001).

Porter, Michael E. *Competitive Advantage*. New York: Free Press (1985).

———. "How Information Can Help You Compete." *Harvard Business Review* (August–September 1985a).

———. "Strategy and the Internet." *Harvard Business Review* (March 2001).

Reich, Blaize Horner and Izak Benbasat. "Factors that Influence the Social Dimension of Alignment between Business and Information Technology Objectives." *MIS Quarterly* 24, no. 1 (March 2000).

Reinartz, Werner and V. Kumar. "The Mismanagement of Customer Loyalty." *Harvard Business Review* (July 2002).

Robey, Daniel and Marie-Claude Boudreau. "Accounting for the Contradictory Organizational Consequences of Information Technology: Theoretical Directions and Methodological Implications." *Information Systems Research* 10, no. 42 (June1999).

Shapiro, Carl, and Hal R. Varian. *Information Rules*. Boston, MA: Harvard Business School Press (1999).

Starbuck, William H. "Organizations as Action Generators." *American Sociological Review* 48 (1983).

Tversky, A., and D. Kahneman. "The Framing of Decisions and the Psychology of Choice." *Science* 211 (January 1981).

Weber, Max. *The Theory of Social and Economic Organization*. Translated by Talcott Parsons. New York: Free Press (1947).

Williamson, Oliver E. *The Economic Institutions of Capitalism*. New York: Free Press, (1985).

123

Blockbuster vs. Netflix: Which Will Win Out?
CASE STUDY

When Blockbuster entered the video rental business in 1985, the industry consisted mostly of independent, mom-and-pop-style stores whose entire reach may have been two towns or a few city blocks. In its first 20 years of business, the rental giant opened 9,100 stores in 25 countries, gaining a market share that has been enjoyed by few companies in any industry.

Blockbuster equipped each of its video rental stores with custom software it had designed to simplify rental and sale transactions. An automated point-of-sale system uses a laser bar code scanner to read data from items being rented or sold and from a Blockbuster customer's identification card. These data are transmitted to Blockbuster's corporate computer center. Management uses these data to monitor sales and to analyze the demographics, and rental and sales patterns for each store to improve its marketing decisions.

Blockbuster's success was based on video tape rentals and sales and rentals of DVDs. By 2004, Blockbuster possessed a 40-percent share of the U.S. video rental market, estimated to range from $7 billion of business per year to $9 billion; Blockbuster also had video sales of around $16 billion.

The greatest threat to Blockbuster's viability came from the emergence of a new business model in the video rental market. Launched in 1998, Netflix Inc. intended to cater to those video rental customers who valued convenience above all else. First, the upstart eliminated the need for a physical store. All interactions between Netflix and its customers took place on the Internet and through the postal service. Users could go online and create a wish list of movies they wanted to rent. For a monthly service fee, Netflix mailed up to three movies at a time, which the customer could keep for as long as he or she wanted without incurring late charges. When finished with a movie, the customer mailed it back to Netflix in pre-stamped packaging provided by the company. Returning a movie prompted Netflix to send the next title on the customer's wish list. For $19.95 a month, Netflix customers had access to thousands of movie titles without leaving their homes.

According to Kagan Research LLC, revenues from online movie rentals, which were basically nonexistent in 1998, rose to $522 million in 2004. Kagan projected that the total revenue would approach $1 billion in 2005 and $3 billion by 2009. As Netflix caught on and its subscription model became popular, Netflix's gains in market share, from 2 to 7 percent between 2003 and 2004, gave Blockbuster true cause for concern.

To compete in the changing marketplace, Blockbuster made some dramatic changes in its business beginning in 2003. It added an online rental service; Movie Pass, a monthly subscription service for in-store customers; Game Pass, a subscription service for video games; a trading service for movies and games; and the infamous "No More Late Fees" program. The entire question of how to address a new source of competition was a complicated matter. Blockbuster could have chosen to launch an online rental store similar to Netflix and leave it at that. Or, the company could have focused only on its traditional business in an attempt to lure customers back from the rising online tide. Instead, with the initiatives previously mentioned, Blockbuster tried to do both.

Blockbuster's $100 million increase in capital expenditures from 2003 to 2004 hints at the scale of the restructuring of the business. Many of those millions found their way to the information technology department, which took Netflix on directly by establishing the information systems supporting Blockbuster's own online subscription service. This venture required Blockbuster to construct a new business model within its existing operations.

Rather than meld the two channels, Blockbuster created a new online division with its own offices near corporate headquarters in Dallas. Part of Blockbuster's initial strategy for defeating the competition was to undercut Netflix in both pricing and distribution. Blockbuster set the price for its three-movies-at-a-time monthly subscription at $19.99, which was, at the time, two dollars less than Netflix's competing plan. Blockbuster had a strategic advantage in distribution as well. Netflix was serving its customers from 35 distribution centers around the country. Blockbuster had 30 such facilities but also had 4,500 stores in the United States to deliver DVDs to most of its customers in only a day or two at lower shipping costs. Blockbuster also enticed online customers to maintain a relationship with the physical stores by offering coupons for free in-store rentals. Blockbuster's original intent was to integrate the online and in-store services so that customers could float back and forth between the two channels with no restrictions. However, the disparate requirements for revenue recognition and inventory management have so far been too complex to make the plan a reality.

After a year in existence, the report card on Blockbuster's online store was mixed. The service had acquired one million subscribers and the company hoped to double that number within seven months or so. At the same time, Netflix had surpassed three million subscribers and was on its way to four million by the end of the year. Blockbuster continued to pursue gains through pricing, at one point lowering its three-movie plan to $14.99 per month versus $17.99 at Netflix. Both companies offer plan variations such as unlimited rentals of one DVD at a time for $5.99 per month and two at a time with a limit of 4 per month for $11.99.

In September 2005, research firm SG Cowen declared that Blockbuster's online DVD rental service "remains inferior" to Netflix. The researcher stated that Blockbuster had improved on movie availability but actually fell further behind in ratings of its user interface. The evaluation by SG Cowen came on the heels of rocky financial reports for Blockbuster. Blockbuster's most costly change was likely the "No More Late Fees" campaign it launched in January 2005. The goal of the program was to lure more customers and position Blockbuster better in the market alongside Netflix, which never charged late fees. However, the program may have created more problems than it solved. Blockbuster did measure an increase in in-store rentals after eliminating late fees, but early returns did not suggest that the increase offset the $250 million to $300 million in annual late fee revenue that was no longer being collected.

Well-known corporate raider Carl Icahn took advantage of Blockbuster's low share price and acquired 9 percent of the company, entitling him to a position on the board of directors. Icahn harshly criticized CEO John Antico's business strategy. Icahn believed that Blockbuster's new initiatives, such as online rentals, were too expensive and too risky. He believed that the company should take advantage of its prevailing position in the bricks-and-mortar rental industry, even if that industry were

slowly dying. Despite the presence of Icahn, Antico maintained that online rentals were the only segment of the industry open to growth.

Both Blockbuster and Netflix now face a new set of challenges. Fifteen million cable subscribers use video-on-demand (VOD) technology to watch movies and programs that are not yet available on DVD. TiVo and similar digital video recorders combined with VOD could make the rental of movies obsolete. Some analysts still insist that the economics do not make sense for movie studios to abandon DVD sales, which account for 50 percent of their profits, in favor of VOD. And technology does not currently permit the bandwidth for VOD suppliers to provide nearly the number of titles that Blockbuster can. Down the road, however, Blockbuster likely will have to address VOD, especially if the studios can eliminate companies like Blockbuster as an intermediary.

In April 2006, the Internet as a channel for movie distribution finally came into focus. Six movie studios, including Warner Brothers, Sony Pictures, Universal, MGM, and Paramount, reached an agreement with Web site Movielink to sell movies online via download. Until that time, Movielink had offered movie downloads as rentals, which, like the VOD model, the customer could watch for only 24 hours. Sony, MGM, and Lions Gate also reached agreements with a Movielink competitor, CinemaNow, which is partially owned by Lions Gate. Warner Brothers also expanded its presence by entering into relationships with Guba.com and BitTorrent. The studios moved to build on the momentum created by the success of the iTunes music store, which demonstrated that consumers were very willing to pay for legal digital downloads of copyrighted material. At the same time, they hoped that entering the download sales market would enable them to confront the piracy issue in their industry earlier in its development than the music industry was able to do.

While the studios' commitment to these ventures appeared clear, what remained a question was whether they could replicate the success of iTunes. The initial pricing schemes certainly did not offer the same appeal as Apple's $0.99 per song or $9.99 per CD. Movielink set the price for new movies at $20 to $30. Older movies were discounted to $10. Movielink was counting on the fact that customers would pay more for the immediacy of downloading a movie in their homes, as opposed to visiting a bricks-and-mortar store like Circuit City or an online store such as Amazon.com, both of which sell new DVDs for less than $15.00.

However, even if customers were willing to pay a little extra, they were getting less for their money. Most movie downloads did not come with the extra features that are common with DVD releases. Moreover, the downloaded movies were programmed for convenient viewing on computer screens, but transporting them from the computer to the TV screen involved a more complicated process than most consumers were willing to tackle. Neither Movielink nor CinemaNow offered a movie format that could be burned to a DVD and played on a regular DVD player. In fact, CinemaNow downloads were limited to use on a single computer. To watch these movies on a television screen, users would need to have Windows Media Center, which is designed to connect to a TV, or special jacks and cables.

An additional obstacle for both the technology and the consumer to overcome was bandwidth. Even using a broadband Internet connection, high-quality movie files, which generally surpassed 1 gigabyte in file size, required in the neighborhood of 90 minutes to download completely.

Considering these issues, the near-term outlook for the legal digital distribution of movies remains cloudy. Movielink, with only 75,000 downloads per month, was struggling to sustain itself. Neither Blockbuster nor Netflix seemed in a panic to adjust to this new source of competition. While locked in legal battles over patents and antitrust concerns, the two companies had few specific plans related to downloading, though Netflix was widely believed to be considering a set-top box. Netflix said only that downloading was part of its future plans, but expressed dissatisfaction with the terms the movie studios were offering in early discussions.

The one development that has the potential to force the hands of Blockbuster and Netflix is the entrance of Apple into the movie download market. Apple's iTunes store, like Netflix, already had a satisfied and loyal customer base, not to mention a pervasive "cool" factor. And, it was iTunes's successful transition from music-only to music and television downloads that paved the way for Movielink and CinemaNow to sell movie downloads in the first place. Apple is said to be on the verge of adding movies to its store and would stick to its flat-rate pricing model. Industry rumors indicated that Apple CEO Steve Jobs intended to sell downloads of all movies for $9.99. Industry experts characterized Apple's involvement as a possible "tipping point" for online movie distribution.

In the meantime, Antico wants Blockbuster to stay very close to the cutting edge of technology in his industry. Doing so, he believes will enable the company to replace directly any rental revenues lost to new technology. Meanwhile, add Amazon to the list of competitive threats on which Blockbuster must also keep a careful eye. Amazon.com already operates an online movie rental service in the United Kingdom. Could there be another player to compete with Blockbuster and Netflix? Or could a new partnership shake up the industry again?

Sources: Saul Hansell, "At Last, Movies to Keep Arrive on the Internet," The New York Times, April 3, 2006; Sarah McBride, "Movie Debut: Films for Sale by Download," The Wall Street Journal, April 3, 2006; Nate Mook, "Netflix Mulls Movie Download Service," BetaNews.com, June 21, 2006; "Guba Sells Sony Films," RedHerring.com, July 11, 2006; Michael Greeson, "iTunes' Movie Downloads the 'Tipping Point' for Online Movie Distribution," DigitalTrends.com, June 22, 2006; Mark Glaser, "Movie Download Services Still Need Work," PBS.org, June 30, 2006; Mike Snider, "Movie Downloads Can Be Fun, and the Technology Is Advancing," USA Today, accessed via Citizen-Times.com, July 4, 2006; "Guba to Distribute Warner Bros. Movies," Reuters, accessed via Yahoo! News, June 26, 2006; Janet Rae-Dupree, "Blockbuster: Movie Business Remains a Moving Target," CIO Insight, August 10, 2005; Dinesh C. Sharma,

CASE STUDY QUESTIONS

1. What is Blockbuster's business model? How successful has it been?

2. What industry and technology forces have challenged that business model? What problems have they created?

3. Is Blockbuster developing successful solutions to its problems? Are there other solutions it should have considered?

4. How successful is Netflix and its business model?

5. Do you think Blockbuster or Netflix will succeed in the future? Explain your answer.

Ethical and Social Issues in Information Systems

Ethical and Social Issues in Information Systems

LEARNING OBJECTIVES

After reading this chapter, you will be able to:

1. Analyze the relationships among ethical, social, and political issues that are raised by information systems.

2. Identify the main moral dimensions of an information society and specific principles for conduct that can be used to guide ethical decisions.

3. Evaluate the impact of contemporary information systems and the Internet on the protection of individual privacy and intellectual property.

4. Assess how information systems have affected everyday life.

Interactive Sessions:

Data for Sale

The Internet: Friend or Foe to Children?

CHAPTER OUTLINE

1 **UNDERSTANDING ETHICAL AND SOCIAL ISSUES RELATED TO SYSTEMS**
A Model for Thinking About Ethical, Social, and Political Issues
Five Moral Dimensions of the Information Age
Key Technology Trends that Raise Ethical Issues

2 **ETHICS IN AN INFORMATION SOCIETY**
Basic Concepts: Responsibility, Accountability, and Liability
Ethical Analysis
Candidate Ethical Principles
Professional Codes of Conduct
Some Real-World Ethical Dilemmas

3 **THE MORAL DIMENSIONS OF INFORMATION SYSTEMS**
Information Rights: Privacy and Freedom in the Internet Age
Property Rights: Intellectual Property
Accountability, Liability, and Control
System Quality: Data Quality and System Errors
Quality of Life: Equity, Access, and Boundaries

4 **HANDS-ON MIS**
Developing a Web Site Privacy Policy: Dirt Bikes USA
Achieving Operational Excellence: Creating a Simple Web Site Using Web Page Development Tools
Improving Decision Making: Using Internet Newsgroups for Online Market Research

LEARNING TRACK MODULE
Developing a Corporate Code of Ethics for Information Systems

For many years, parents of District of Columbia public school children complained about buses running late or not showing up. A federal court appointed an independent transportation administrator and enlisted Satellite Security Systems, or S3, to track the movements of the district's buses. S3 provides satellite tracking services to clients such as the District of Columbia, Fairfax County, state and federal government agencies, police departments, and private companies.

These services equip each vehicle or person they are monitoring with a tracking device using global positioning system (GPS) technology. GPS is a navigation system operated by the U.S. Department of Defense based on satellites that continually broadcast their position, time, and date. GPS receivers on the ground, which can be attached to vehicles, cell phones, or other equipment, use information from the satellite signals to calculate their own locations. Cell phones are now equipped with GPS.

The D.C. public school system is spending $6 million on its GPS tracking system. It is equipping buses with GPS locators and special-needs children riding those buses with ID cards that log when they get on and off their buses. Parents receive secret codes that enable them to use the Internet to track their children. S3's monitoring center picks up GPS information from the tracking devices and monitors the locations of the buses on video screens. Most of the monitoring is automated, and the S3 staff intervenes primarily in emergencies. S3 maintains each day's tracking data for long periods, and clients can access historical tracking data if they wish.

S3 provides detailed information to the D.C. public schools: each bus's route throughout the day, when the bus stops, when the doors open and close, the speed, and when the ignition is turned on and off. The S3 system includes a database with information on the bus passengers—each child's name, address, disabilities, allergies, contact information, and when their school days begin and end.

David Gilmore, the court-appointed transportation administrator for the D.C. public schools has seen improvement in bus driver performance. Reports of bus drivers making detours to banks or to take long lunches are diminishing.

Parents are also pleased. "I like that the system lets you watch them, because you never know what's going on in the bus," says Deneen Prior, whose three children ride D.C. public school buses. However, she also worries about the location tracking data being misused. "I don't want anybody watching them that's not supposed to be watching them," she notes.

Others feel the same way. Location tracking has benefits, but it also opens the door to potential invasion of privacy. Many people may not like having their physical move-

Photo courtesy of AP Wide World Photos

ments tracked so closely. Location information might help direct a tow truck to a broken-down car, but it could also be used to find out where the driver went during the lunch hour.

For similar reasons, privacy advocacy groups have opposed the use of radio-frequency identification (RFID) tags in consumer items. RFID tags are small silicon chips equipped with tiny antennas that enable them to communicate with RFID readers and track the location of items as they move. When placed on individual products, they allow companies to tell exactly when a product leaves a store or learn more about the actions of consumers buying the products.

Designer Lauren Scott had planned to add radio frequency tags to the childrens' clothing she designed to help parents keep track of their children. An RFID tag sewn into a child's clothing could store vital medical information or track the wearer's location to prevent children from being abducted or wandering away. As a result of the controversy surrounding RFID, however, several of Scott's major customers asked that the tags not be sewn directly into the clothing.

Sources: Mel Duvall, "At the Seams of RFID," *Baseline*, April 2006; Ariana Eunjung Cha, "To Protect and Intrude," *The Washington Post*, January 15, 2005; and Christopher Lindquist, "Watch Carefully," *CIO Magazine*, May 15, 2005.

The use of location tracking systems described in the chapter-opening case shows that technology can be a double-edged sword. It can be the source of many benefits, and it can also create new opportunities for breaking the law or taking benefits away from others.

The chapter-opening diagram calls attention to important points raised by this case and this chapter. The D.C. public school system faced a real problem in trying to make sure its drivers were transporting children safely and promptly to school. Location tracking technology provided a solution, but it also introduced the possibility that information about the people or vehicles S3 tracked could be used for the wrong purpose. Location tracking technology had a similar impact for designer Lauren Scott's children's clothing business.

This solution created what we call an "ethical dilemma," pitting the legitimate need to know what drivers of school buses were doing with the fear that such information could be used to threaten individual privacy. Another ethical dilemma might occur if you were implementing a new information system that reduced labor costs and eliminated employees' jobs. You need to be aware of the negative impacts of information systems and you need to balance the negative consequences with the positive ones.

HEADS UP

Information systems raise new and often-perplexing ethical problems. This is more true today than ever because of the challenges posed by the Internet and electronic commerce to the protection of privacy and intellectual property. Other ethical issues raised by widespread use of information systems include establishing accountability for the consequences of information systems, setting standards to safeguard system quality that protect the safety of individuals and society, and preserving values and institutions considered essential to the quality of life in an information society. Whether you run your own business or work in a large company, you'll be confronting these issues, and you'll need to know how to deal with them.

• If your career is in finance and accounting, you will need to ensure that the information systems you work with are protected from computer fraud and abuse.

• If your career is in human resources, you will be involved in developing and enforcing a corporate ethics policy and in providing special training to sensitize managers and employees to the new ethical issues surrounding information systems.

• If your career is in information systems, you will need to make management aware of the ethical implications of the technologies used by the firm and help management establish code of ethics for information systems.

• If your career is in manufacturing, production, or operations management, you will need to deal with data quality and software problems that could interrupt the smooth and accurate flow of information among disparate manufacturing and production systems and among supply chain partners.

• If your career is in sales and marketing, you will need to balance systems that gather and analyze customer data with the need for protecting consumer privacy.

---

1 UNDERSTANDING ETHICAL AND SOCIAL ISSUES RELATED TO SYSTEMS

In the past five years we have witnessed, arguably, one of the most ethically challenging periods for U.S. and global business. Table 1 provides a small sample of recent cases demonstrating failed ethical judgment by senior and middle managers. These lapses in management ethical and business judgment occurred across a broad spectrum of industries.

In today's new legal environment, managers who violate the law and are convicted will most likely spend time in prison. U.S. Federal Sentencing

TABLE 1   EXAMPLES OF FAILED ETHICAL JUDGMENT BY MANAGERS

Enron	Top three executives convicted for misstating earnings using illegal accounting schemes and making false representations to shareholders. Bankruptcy declared in 2001.
WorldCom	Second-largest U.S. telecommunications firm. Chief executive convicted for improperly inflating revenue by billions using illegal accounting methods. Bankruptcy declared in July 2002 with $41 billion in debts.
Merrill Lynch	Indicted for assisting Enron in the creation of financial vehicles that had no business purpose, enabling Enron to misstate its earnings.
Parmalat	Italy's eighth-largest industrial group indicted for misstating more than $5 billion in revenues, earnings, and assets over several years; senior executives indicted for embezzlement.
Bristol-Myers Squibb	Pharmaceutical firm agreed to pay a fine of $150 million for misstating its revenues by $1.5 billion and inflating its stock value.
Brocade Communications Systems, Inc.	Gregory Reyes, the CEO of Brocade Communications Systems Inc. until January 2005, indicted in criminal and civil cases in 2006 of backdating options and concealing millions of dollars of compensation expenses from shareholders. Nearly 100 other Silicon Valley tech firms are under investigation for similar practices.
KPMG LLP, Ernst & Young, and PricewaterhouseCoopers	Senior tax accountants of three of the leading "Big Four" public accounting firms are indicted by the Justice Department over the selling of abusive tax shelters to wealthy individuals in the period 2000-2005. This case is frequently referred to as the "largest tax fraud case in history."

Guidelines adopted in 1987 mandate that federal judges impose stiff sentences on business executives based on the monetary value of the crime, the presence of a conspiracy to prevent discovery of the crime, the use of structured financial transactions to hide the crime, and failure to cooperate with prosecutors (U.S. Sentencing Commission, 2004).

Although in the past, business firms would often pay for the legal defense of their employees enmeshed in civil charges and criminal investigations, now firms are encouraged to cooperate with prosecutors to reduce charges against the entire firm for obstructing investigations. These developments mean that, more than ever, as a manager or an employee, you will have to decide for yourself what constitutes proper legal and ethical conduct.

Although these major instances of failed ethical and legal judgment were not masterminded by information systems departments, information systems were instrumental in many of these frauds. In many cases, the perpetrators of these crimes artfully used financial reporting information systems to bury their decisions from public scrutiny in the vain hope they would never be caught. In this chapter we talk about the ethical dimensions of these and other actions based on the use of information systems.

Ethics refers to the principles of right and wrong that individuals, acting as free moral agents, use to make choices to guide their behaviors. Information systems raise new ethical questions for both individuals and societies because they create opportunities for intense social change, and thus threaten existing distributions of power, money, rights, and obligations. Like other technologies, such as steam engines, electricity, the telephone, and the radio, information technology can be used to achieve social progress, but it can also be used to commit crimes and threaten cherished social values. The development of information technology will produce benefits for many and costs for others.

Ethical issues in information systems have been given new urgency by the rise of the Internet and electronic commerce. Internet and digital firm technologies make it easier than ever to assemble, integrate, and distribute information, unleashing new concerns about the appropriate use of customer information, the protection of personal privacy, and the protection of intellectual property. Insiders with special knowledge can "fool" information systems by submitting phony records, and diverting cash, on a scale unimaginable in the pre-computer era.

Other pressing ethical issues raised by information systems include establishing accountability for the consequences of information systems, setting standards to safeguard system quality that protects the safety of the individual and society, and preserving values and institutions considered essential to the quality of life in an information society. When using information systems, it is essential to ask, "What is the ethical and socially responsible course of action?"

A MODEL FOR THINKING ABOUT ETHICAL, SOCIAL, AND POLITICAL ISSUES

Ethical, social, and political issues are closely linked. The ethical dilemma you may face as a manager of information systems typically is reflected in social and political debate. One way to think about these relationships is given in Figure 1. Imagine society as a more or less calm pond on a summer day, a delicate ecosystem in partial equilibrium with individuals and with social and political institutions. Individuals know how to act in this pond because social institutions (family, education, organizations) have developed well-honed rules of behavior, and these are supported by laws developed in the political sector that prescribe behavior and promise sanctions for violations. Now toss a rock into the center of the pond. But imagine instead of a rock that the disturbing force is a powerful shock of new information technology and systems hitting a society more or less at rest. What happens? Ripples, of course.

FIGURE 1   **THE RELATIONSHIP BETWEEN ETHICAL, SOCIAL, AND POLITICAL ISSUES IN AN INFORMATION SOCIETY**

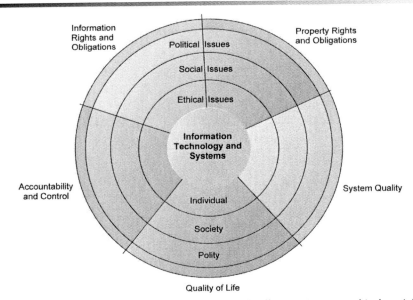

The introduction of new information technology has a ripple effect, raising new ethical, social, and political issues that must be dealt with on the individual, social, and political levels. These issues have five moral dimensions: information rights and obligations, property rights and obligations, system quality, quality of life, and accountability and control.

Suddenly individual actors are confronted with new situations often not covered by the old rules. Social institutions cannot respond overnight to these ripples—it may take years to develop etiquette, expectations, social responsibility, politically correct attitudes, or approved rules. Political institutions also require time before developing new laws and often require the demonstration of real harm before they act. In the meantime, you may have to act. You may be forced to act in a legal gray area.

We can use this model to illustrate the dynamics that connect ethical, social, and political issues. This model is also useful for identifying the main moral dimensions of the information society, which cut across various levels of action—individual, social, and political.

FIVE MORAL DIMENSIONS OF THE INFORMATION AGE

The major ethical, social, and political issues raised by information systems include the following moral dimensions:

Information rights and obligations. What **information rights** do individuals and organizations possess with respect to themselves? What can they protect? What obligations do individuals and organizations have concerning this information?

Property rights and obligations. How will traditional intellectual property rights be protected in a digital society in which tracing and accounting for ownership are difficult and ignoring such property rights is so easy?

Accountability and control. Who can and will be held accountable and liable for the harm done to individual and collective information and property rights?

System quality. What standards of data and system quality should we demand to protect individual rights and the safety of society?

Quality of life. What values should be preserved in an information- and knowledge-based society? Which institutions should we protect from violation? Which cultural values and practices are supported by the new information technology?

We explore these moral dimensions in detail in Section 3.

KEY TECHNOLOGY TRENDS THAT RAISE ETHICAL ISSUES

Ethical issues long preceded information technology. Nevertheless, information technology has heightened ethical concerns, taxed existing social arrangements, and made some laws obsolete or severely crippled. Information technologies and systems have also created new opportunities for criminal

TABLE 2 TECHNOLOGY TRENDS THAT RAISE ETHICAL ISSUES

TREND	IMPACT
Computing power doubles every 18 months	More organizations depend on computer systems for critical operations.
Data storage costs rapidly declining	Organizations can easily maintain detailed databases on individuals.
Data analysis advances	Companies can analyze vast quantities of data gathered on individuals to develop detailed profiles of individual behavior.
Networking advances and the Internet	Copying data from one location to another and accessing personal data from remote locations are much easier.

behavior and mischief. There are four key technological trends responsible for these ethical stresses and they are summarized in Table 2.

The doubling of computing power every 18 months has made it possible for most organizations to use information systems for their core production processes. As a result, our dependence on systems and our vulnerability to system errors and poor data quality have increased. The very same information systems that lead to high levels of productivity also create opportunities for abuse. Social rules and laws have not yet adjusted to this dependence. Standards for ensuring the accuracy and reliability of information systems are not universally accepted or enforced.

Advances in data storage techniques and rapidly declining storage costs have been responsible for the multiplying databases on individuals—employees, customers, and potential customers—maintained by private and public organizations. These advances in data storage have made the routine violation of individual privacy both cheap and effective. Already, massive data storage systems are cheap enough for regional and even local retailing firms to use in identifying customers. For instance, the major search firms like Google, America Online (AOL), MSN, and Yahoo! maintain detailed search histories on the more than 75 million Americans who use Internet search engines everyday and who generate more than 200 million searches each day. These huge collections of "consumer intentions" become the natural targets of private firms looking for market advantage, government agencies, and private investigators.

Advances in data analysis techniques for large pools of data are another technological trend that heightens ethical concerns because companies and government agencies are able to find out much detailed personal information about individuals. With contemporary data management tools, companies can assemble and combine the myriad pieces of information about you stored on computers much more easily than in the past.

Think of all the ways you generate computer information about yourself—credit card purchases; telephone calls; magazine subscriptions; video rentals; mail-order purchases; banking records; local, state, and federal government records (including court and police records); and visits to Web sites to read Web materials, use search engines, and write blogs. Put together and mined properly, this information could reveal not only your credit information but also your driving habits, your tastes, your associations, intended purchases, political views, and interests. What you thought was private, in fact, can quickly become public.

Companies with products to sell purchase relevant information from these sources to help them more finely target their marketing campaigns. Companies can analyze large pools of data from multiple sources to rapidly identify buying patterns of customers and suggest individual responses. The use of computers to combine data from multiple sources and create electronic dossiers of detailed information on individuals is called **profiling**.

For example, hundreds of Web sites allow DoubleClick (www.doubleclick.net), an Internet advertising broker, to track the activities of their visitors in exchange for revenue from advertisements based on visitor information DoubleClick gathers. DoubleClick uses this information to create a profile of each online visitor, adding more detail to the profile as the visitor accesses an associated DoubleClick site. Over time, DoubleClick can create a detailed dossier of a person's spending and computing habits on the Web that can be sold to companies to help them target their Web ads more precisely.

Credit card purchases can make personal information available to market researchers, telemarketers, and direct-mail companies. Advances in information technology facilitate the invasion of privacy.

Photo courtesy of Jon Feingersh/Masterfile Corporation

ChoicePoint, described in the Interactive Session on Management, gathers data from police, criminal, and motor vehicle records; credit and employment histories; current and previous addresses; professional licenses; and insurance claims to assemble and maintain electronic dossiers on almost every adult in the United Sates. The company sells this personal information to businesses and government agencies. Demand for personal data is so enormous that data broker businesses such as ChoicePoint are booming.

A new data analysis technology called **nonobvious relationship awareness (NORA)** has given both the government and the private sector even more powerful profiling capabilities. NORA can take information about people from many disparate sources, such as employment applications, telephone records, customer listings, and "wanted" lists, and correlate relationships to find obscure hidden connections that might help identify criminals or terrorists (see Figure 2). For instance, an applicant for a government security job might have received phone calls from a person wanted by the police. This diad (grouping of two) might also share the same religion, attend the same church, and be part of a small group with frequent telephone contacts.

NORA technology scans data and extracts information as the data are being generated so that it could, for example, instantly discover a man at an airline ticket counter who shares a phone number with a known terrorist before that person boards an airplane. The technology is considered a valuable tool for homeland security but does have privacy implications because it can provide such a detailed picture of the activities and associations of a single individual.

Finally, advances in networking, including the Internet, promise to reduce greatly the costs of moving and accessing large quantities of data and open the possibility of mining large pools of data remotely using small desktop machines, permitting an invasion of privacy on a scale and with a precision heretofore unimaginable. If computing and networking technologies continue to advance at the same pace as in the past, by 2023, large organizations will be

INTERACTIVE SESSION: MANAGEMENT

DATA FOR SALE

Want a list of 3,877 charity donors in Detroit? You can buy it from USAData for $465.24. Through USAData's Web site, which is linked to large databases maintained by Acxiom and Dun & Bradstreet, anyone with a credit card can buy marketing lists of consumers broken down by location, demographics, and interests. The College Board sells data on graduating high school seniors to 1,700 colleges and universities for 28 cents per student. These businesses are entirely legal. Also selling data are businesses that obtain credit card and cell phone records illegally and sell to private investigators and law enforcement. The buying and selling of personal data has become a multibillion dollar business that's growing by leaps and bounds.

Unlike banks or companies selling credit reports, these private data brokers are largely unregulated. There has been little or no federal or state oversight of how they collect, maintain, and sell their data. But they have been allowed to flourish because there is such a huge market for personal information and they provide useful services for insurance companies, banks, employers, and federal, state, and local government agencies.

For example, the Internal Revenue Service and departments of Homeland Security, Justice, and State paid data brokers $30 million in 2005 for data used in law enforcement and counterterrorism. The Internal Revenue Service signed a five-year $200 milllion deal to access ChoicePoint's databases to locate assets of delinquent taxpayers. After the September 11, 2001 terrorist attacks, ChoicePoint helped the U.S. government screen candidates for the new federally controlled airport security workforce.

ChoicePoint is one of the largest data brokers, with more than 5,000 employees serving businesses of all sizes as well as federal, state, and local governments. In 2004, ChoicePoint performed more than seven million background checks. It processes thousands of credit card transactions every second.

ChoicePoint builds its vast repository of personal data through an extensive network of contractors who gather bits of information from public filings, financial-services firms, phone directories, and loan application forms. The contractors use police departments, school districts, the department of motor vehicles, and local courts to fill their caches. All of the information is public and legal.

ChoicePoint possesses 19 billion records containing personal information on the vast majority of American adult consumers. According to Daniel J. Solove, associate professor of law at George Washington University, the company has collected information on nearly every adult American and "these are dossiers that J. Edgar Hoover would be envious of."

The downside to the massive databases maintained by ChoicePoint and other data brokers is the threat they pose to personal privacy and social well being. The quality of the data they maintain can be unreliable, causing people to lose their jobs and their savings. In one case, Boston Market fired an employee after receiving a background check from ChoicePoint that showed felony convictions. However, the report had been wrong. In another, a retired GE assembly-line worker was charged a higher insurance premium because another person's driving record, with multiple accidents, had been added to his ChoicePoint file.

ChoicePoint came under fire in early 2005 for selling information on 145,000 customers to criminals posing as legitimate businesses. The criminals then used the identities of some of individuals on whom ChoicePoint maintained data to open fraudulent credit card accounts.

Since then ChoicePoint curtailed the sale of products that contain sensitive data, such as social security and driver's license ID numbers, and limited access by small businesses, including private investigators, collection agencies, and non-bank financial institutions. ChoicePoint also implemented more stringent processes to verify customer authenticity.

Marc Rotenberg of the Electronic Privacy Information Center in Washington, D.C., believes that the ChoicePoint case is a clear demonstration that self-regulation does not work in the information business and that more comprehensive laws are needed. California, 22 other states, and New York City have passed laws requiring companies to inform customers when their personal data files have been compromised. More than a dozen data security bills were introduced in Congress in 2006 and some type of federal data security and privacy legislation will likely result. Privacy advocates are hoping for a broad federal law with a uniform set of standards for privacy protection practices.

Sources: Rick Whiting, "Who's Buying and Selling Your Data? Everybody," *Information Week*, July 10, 2006; Christopher Wolf,

"Dazed and Confused: Data Law Disarray," *Business Week*, June 8, 2006; Evan Perez and Rick Brooks, "For Big Vendor of Personal Data, A Theft Lays Bare the Downside," *The Wall Street Journal*, May 3, 2005; and "ChoicePoint Toughens Data Security," *CNN/Money*, July 5, 2005.

CASE STUDY QUESTIONS

1. Do data brokers pose an ethical dilemma? Explain your answer.

2. What are the problems caused by the proliferation of data brokers? What management, organization, and technology factors are responsible for these problems?

3. How effective are existing solutions to these problems?

4. Should the U.S. federal government regulate private data brokers? Why or why not? What are the advantages and disadvantages?

MIS IN ACTION

Explore the Web site of USAData (usadata.com). Click on Consumer Mailing Lists/Sales Leads to start the process of ordering a consumer mailing list online but do not use your credit card to pay for the list. Answer the following questions:

1. What kind of data does this company provide? How does it obtain the data?

2. Who uses the data sold by USAData? Are there any restrictions on who can use the data?

3. What kind of information can you obtain by ordering a mailing list online? How detailed is this information? How easy is it to purchase this information? Can someone use this online capability to find out how much money you make?

4. Does the capability of USAData raise privacy issues? What are they?

5. If your name and other personal information were in this database, what limitations on access would you want in order to preserve your privacy? Consider the following data users: (a) government agencies, (b) your employer, (c) private business firms, (d) other individuals.

able to devote the equivalent of a contemporary desktop personal computer to monitoring each of the 350 million individuals who will then be living in the United States (Farmer and Mann, 2003).

The development of global digital communication networks widely available to individuals and businesses poses many ethical and social concerns. Who will account for the flow of information over these networks? Will you be able to trace information collected about you? What will these networks do to the traditional relationships between family, work, and leisure? How will traditional job designs be altered when millions of "employees" become subcontractors using mobile offices for which they themselves must pay? In the next section we consider some ethical principles and analytical techniques for dealing with these kinds of ethical and social concerns.

FIGURE 2   NONOBVIOUS RELATIONSHIP AWARENESS (NORA)

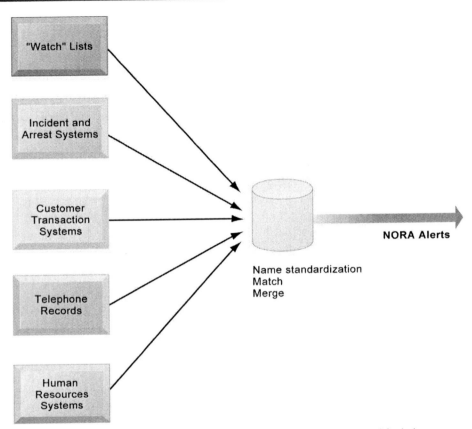

Name standardization
Match
Merge

NORA technology can take information about people from disparate sources and find obscure, nonobvious relationships. It might discover, for example, that an applicant for a job at a casino shares a telephone number with a known criminal and issue an alert to the hiring manager.

2   ETHICS IN AN INFORMATION SOCIETY

Ethics is a concern of humans who have freedom of choice. Ethics is about individual choice: When faced with alternative courses of action, what is the correct moral choice? What are the main features of ethical choice?

BASIC CONCEPTS: RESPONSIBILITY, ACCOUNTABILITY, AND LIABILITY

Ethical choices are decisions made by individuals who are responsible for the consequences of their actions. **Responsibility** is a key element of ethical action. Responsibility means that you accept the potential costs, duties, and obligations for the decisions you make.

Accountability is a feature of systems and social institutions: It means that mechanisms are in place to determine who took responsible action, who is responsible. Systems and institutions in which it is impossible to find out who took what action are inherently incapable of ethical analysis or ethical action. Liability extends the concept of responsibility further to the area of laws.

Liability is a feature of political systems in which a body of laws is in place that permits individuals to recover the damages done to them by other actors, systems, or organizations. **Due process** is a related feature of law-governed societies and is a process in which laws are known and understood and there is an ability to appeal to higher authorities to ensure that the laws are applied correctly.

These basic concepts form the underpinning of an ethical analysis of information systems and those who manage them. First, information technologies are filtered through social institutions, organizations, and individuals. Systems do not have impacts by themselves. Whatever information system impacts exist are products of institutional, organizational, and individual actions and behaviors. Second, responsibility for the consequences of technology falls clearly on the institutions, organizations, and individual managers who choose to use the technology. Using information technology in a socially responsible manner means that you can and will be held accountable for the consequences of your actions. Third, in an ethical, political society, individuals and others can recover damages done to them through a set of laws characterized by due process.

ETHICAL ANALYSIS

When confronted with a situation that seems to present ethical issues, how should you analyze it? The following five-step process should help.

1. *Identify and describe clearly the facts.* Find out who did what to whom, and where, when, and how. In many instances, you will be surprised at the errors in the initially reported facts, and often you will find that simply getting the facts straight helps define the solution. It also helps to get the opposing parties involved in an ethical dilemma to agree on the facts.

2. *Define the conflict or dilemma and identify the higher-order values involved.* Ethical, social, and political issues always reference higher values. The parties to a dispute all claim to be pursuing higher values (e.g., freedom, privacy, protection of property, and the free enterprise system). Typically, an ethical issue involves a dilemma: two diametrically opposed courses of action that support worthwhile values. For example, the chapter-ending case study illustrates two competing values: the need to protect citizens from terrorist acts and the need to protect individual privacy.

3. *Identify the stakeholders.* Every ethical, social, and political issue has stakeholders: players in the game who have an interest in the outcome, who have invested in the situation, and usually who have vocal opinions. Find out the identity of these groups and what they want. This will be useful later when designing a solution.

4. *Identify the options that you can reasonably take.* You may find that none of the options satisfy all the interests involved, but that some options do a better job than others. Sometimes arriving at a good or ethical solution may not always be a balancing of consequences to stakeholders.

5. *Identify the potential consequences of your options.* Some options may be ethically correct but disastrous from other points of view. Other options may work in one instance but not in other similar instances. Always ask yourself, "What if I choose this option consistently over time?"

CANDIDATE ETHICAL PRINCIPLES

Once your analysis is complete, what ethical principles or rules should you use to make a decision? What higher-order values should inform your judgment? Although you are the only one who can decide which among many ethical principles you will follow, and how you will prioritize them, it is helpful to consider some ethical principles with deep roots in many cultures that have survived throughout recorded history.

1. Do unto others as you would have them do unto you (the **Golden Rule**). Putting yourself into the place of others, and thinking of yourself as the object of the decision, can help you think about fairness in decision making.

2. If an action is not right for everyone to take, it is not right for anyone **(Immanuel Kant's Categorical Imperative)**. Ask yourself, "If everyone did this, could the organization, or society, survive?"

3. If an action cannot be taken repeatedly, it is not right to take at all **(Descartes' rule of change)**. This is the slippery-slope rule: An action may bring about a small change now that is acceptable, but if it is repeated, it would bring unacceptable changes in the long run. In the vernacular, it might be stated as "once started down a slippery path, you may not be able to stop."

4. Take the action that achieves the higher or greater value (the **Utilitarian Principle**). This rule assumes you can prioritize values in a rank order and understand the consequences of various courses of action.

5. Take the action that produces the least harm or the least potential cost **(Risk Aversion Principle)**. Some actions have extremely high failure costs of very low probability (e.g., building a nuclear generating facility in an urban area) or extremely high failure costs of moderate probability (speeding and automobile accidents). Avoid these high-failure-cost actions, paying greater attention obviously to high-failure-cost potential of moderate to high probability.

6. Assume that virtually all tangible and intangible objects are owned by someone else unless there is a specific declaration otherwise. (This is the **ethical "no free lunch" rule**.) If something someone else has created is useful to you, it has value, and you should assume the creator wants compensation for this work.

Although these ethical rules cannot be guides to action, actions that do not easily pass these rules deserve some very close attention and a great deal of caution. The appearance of unethical behavior may do as much harm to you and your company as actual unethical behavior.

PROFESSIONAL CODES OF CONDUCT

When groups of people claim to be professionals, they take on special rights and obligations because of their special claims to knowledge, wisdom, and respect. Professional codes of conduct are promulgated by associations of professionals, such as the American Medical Association (AMA), the American Bar Association (ABA), the Association of Information Technology Professionals (AITP), and the Association of Computing Machinery (ACM). These professional groups take responsibility for the partial regulation of their professions by determining entrance qualifications and competence. Codes of ethics are promises by professions to regulate themselves in the general interest of society. For example, avoiding harm to others, honoring property rights (including intellectual property), and respecting privacy are among the General Moral Imperatives of the ACM's Code of Ethics and Professional Conduct.

SOME REAL-WORLD ETHICAL DILEMMAS

Information systems have created new ethical dilemmas in which one set of interests is pitted against another. For example, many of the large telephone companies in the United States are using information technology to reduce the sizes of their workforces. Voice recognition software reduces the need for human operators by enabling computers to recognize a customer's responses to a series of computerized questions. Many companies monitor what their employees are doing on the Internet to prevent them from wasting company resources on nonbusiness activities.

In each instance, you can find competing values at work, with groups lined up on either side of a debate. A company may argue, for example, that it has a right to use information systems to increase productivity and reduce the size of its workforce to lower costs and stay in business. Employees displaced by information systems may argue that employers have some responsibility for their welfare. Business owners might feel obligated to monitor employee e-mail and Internet use to minimize drains on productivity. Employees might believe they should be able to use the Internet for short personal tasks in place of the

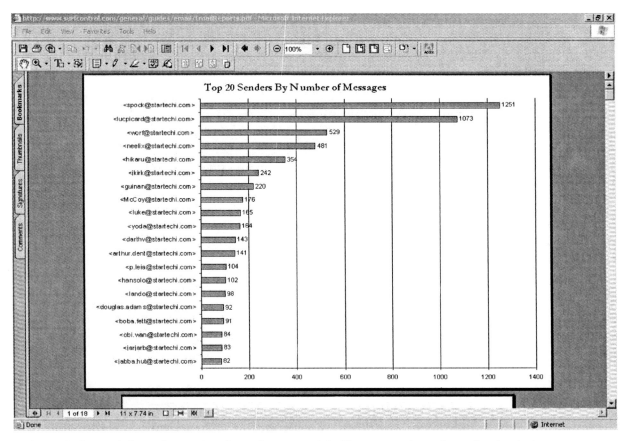

SurfControl offers tools for tracking Web and e-mail activity and for filtering unauthorized e-mail and Web site content. The benefits of monitoring employee e-mail and Internet use should be balanced with the need to respect employee privacy.

telephone. A close analysis of the facts can sometimes produce compromised solutions that give each side "half a loaf." Try to apply some of the principles of ethical analysis described to each of these cases. What is the right thing to do?

3 | THE MORAL DIMENSIONS OF INFORMATION SYSTEMS

In this section, we take a closer look at the five moral dimensions of information systems first described in Figure 1. In each dimension we identify the ethical, social, and political levels of analysis and use real-world examples to illustrate the values involved, the stakeholders, and the options chosen.

INFORMATION RIGHTS: PRIVACY AND FREEDOM IN THE INTERNET AGE

Privacy is the claim of individuals to be left alone, free from surveillance or interference from other individuals or organizations, including the state. Claims to privacy are also involved at the workplace: Millions of employees are subject to electronic and other forms of high-tech surveillance (Ball, 2001). Information technology and systems threaten individual claims to privacy by making the invasion of privacy cheap, profitable, and effective.

The claim to privacy is protected in the U.S., Canadian, and German constitutions in a variety of different ways and in other countries through various statutes. In the United States, the claim to privacy is protected primarily by the First Amendment guarantees of freedom of speech and association, the Fourth Amendment protections against unreasonable search and seizure of one's personal documents or home, and the guarantee of due process.

Table 3 describes the major U.S. federal statutes that set forth the conditions for handling information about individuals in such areas as credit reporting, education, financial records, newspaper records, and electronic communications. The Privacy Act of 1974 has been the most important of these laws, regulating the federal government's collection, use, and disclosure of information. At present, most U.S. federal privacy laws apply only to the federal government and regulate very few areas of the private sector.

TABLE 3 FEDERAL PRIVACY LAWS IN THE UNITED STATES

GENERAL FEDERAL PRIVACY LAWS	PRIVACY LAWS AFFECTING PRIVATE INSTITUTIONS
Freedom of Information Act of 1966 as Amended (5 USC 552)	Fair Credit Reporting Act of 1970
Privacy Act of 1974 as Amended (5 USC 552a)	Family Educational Rights and Privacy Act of 1974
Electronic Communications Privacy Act of 1986	Right to Financial Privacy Act of 1978
Computer Matching and Privacy Protection Act of 1988	Privacy Protection Act of 1980
Computer Security Act of 1987	Cable Communications Policy Act of 1984
Federal Managers Financial Integrity Act of 1982	Electronic Communications Privacy Act of 1986
Driver's Privacy Protection Act of 1994	Video Privacy Protection Act of 1988
E-Government Act of 2002	The Health Insurance Portability and Accountability Act of 1996 (HIPAA)
	Children's Online Privacy Protection Act of 1998 (COPPA)
	Financial Modernization Act (Gramm-Leach-Bliley Act) of 1999

Most American and European privacy law is based on a regime called Fair Information Practices (FIP) first set forth in a report written in 1973 by a federal government advisory committee (U.S. Department of Health, Education, and Welfare, 1973). **Fair Information Practices (FIP)** is a set of principles governing the collection and use of information about individuals. FIP principles are based on the notion of a mutuality of interest between the record holder and the individual. The individual has an interest in engaging in a transaction, and the record keeper—usually a business or government agency—requires information about the individual to support the transaction. Once information is gathered, the individual maintains an interest in the record, and the record may not be used to support other activities without the individual's consent. In 1998, the Federal Trade Commission (FTC) restated and extended the original FIP to provide guidelines for protecting online privacy. Table 4 describes the FTC's Fair Information Practice principles.

The FTC's FIP are being used as guidelines to drive changes in privacy legislation. In July 1998, the U.S. Congress passed the Children's Online Privacy Protection Act (COPPA), requiring Web sites to obtain parental permission before collecting information on children under the age of 13. The FTC has recommended additional legislation to protect online consumer privacy in advertising networks that collect records of consumer Web activity to develop detailed profiles, which are then used by other companies to target online ads. Other proposed Internet privacy legislation focuses on protecting the online use of personal identification numbers, such as social security numbers; protecting personal information collected on the Internet that deals with individuals not covered by the Children's Online Privacy Protection Act of 1998; and limiting the use of data mining for homeland security (see the chapter-ending case study).

Privacy protections have also been added to recent laws deregulating financial services and safeguarding the maintenance and transmission of health information about individuals. The Gramm-Leach-Bliley Act of 1999, which repeals earlier restrictions on affiliations among banks, securities firms, and insurance companies, includes some privacy protection for consumers of financial services. All financial institutions are required to disclose their policies and practices for protecting the privacy of nonpublic personal information and to allow customers to opt out of information-sharing arrangements with nonaffiliated third parties.

The Health Insurance Portability and Accountability Act of 1996 (HIPAA), which took effect on April 14, 2003, includes privacy protection for medical records. The law gives patients access to their personal medical records

TABLE 4 FEDERAL TRADE COMMISSION FAIR INFORMATION PRACTICE PRINCIPLES

1. *Notice/awareness (core principle).* Web sites must disclose their information practices before collecting data. Includes identification of collector; uses of data; other recipients of data; nature of collection (active/inactive); voluntary or required status; consequences of refusal; and steps taken to protect confidentiality, integrity, and quality of the data.

2. *Choice/consent (core principle).* There must be a choice regime in place allowing consumers to choose how their information will be used for secondary purposes other than supporting the transaction, including internal use and transfer to third parties.

3. *Access/participation.* Consumers should be able to review and contest the accuracy and completeness of data collected about them in a timely, inexpensive process.

4. *Security.* Data collectors must take responsible steps to assure that consumer information is accurate and secure from unauthorized use.

5. *Enforcement.* There must be in place a mechanism to enforce FIP principles. This can involve self-regulation, legislation giving consumers legal remedies for violations, or federal statutes and regulations.

maintained by healthcare providers, hospitals, and health insurers and the right to authorize how protected information about themselves can be used or disclosed. Doctors, hospitals, and other healthcare providers must limit the disclosure of personal information about patients to the minimum amount necessary to achieve a given purpose.

The European Directive on Data Protection

In Europe, privacy protection is much more stringent than in the United States. Unlike the United States, European countries do not allow businesses to use personally identifiable information without consumers' prior consent. On October 25, 1998, the European Commission's Directive on Data Protection went into effect, broadening privacy protection in the European Union (EU) nations. The directive requires companies to inform people when they collect information about them and disclose how it will be stored and used. Customers must provide their informed consent before any company can legally use data about them, and they have the right to access that information, correct it, and request that no further data be collected. **Informed consent** can be defined as consent given with knowledge of all the facts needed to make a rational decision. EU member nations must translate these principles into their own laws and cannot transfer personal data to countries, such as the United States, that do not have similar privacy protection regulations.

Working with the European Commission, the U.S. Department of Commerce developed a safe harbor framework for U.S. firms. A **safe harbor** is a private, self-regulating policy and enforcement mechanism that meets the objectives of government regulators and legislation but does not involve government regulation or enforcement.

U.S. businesses doing business with Europeans are allowed to use personal data from EU countries if they develop privacy protection policies that meet EU standards. Enforcement occurs in the United States using self-policing, regulation, and government enforcement of fair trade statutes. Firms must be certified by public accounting firms to be "safe harbor" for personal data on Europeans, and this certification is recognized (but not enforced) by the Department of Commerce. With this safe harbor policy, the Americans and Europeans have been able to overcome their differences on privacy matters, and permit trade to take place.

Internet Challenges to Privacy

Internet technology has posed new challenges for the protection of individual privacy. Information sent over this vast network of networks may pass through many different computer systems before it reaches its final destination. Each of these systems is capable of monitoring, capturing, and storing communications that pass through it.

It is possible to record all online activities of literally tens of millions of people, including which online newsgroups or files a person has accessed, which Web sites and Web pages he or she has visited, and what items that person has inspected or purchased over the Web. Much of this monitoring and tracking of Web site visitors occurs in the background without the visitor's knowledge. Tools to monitor visits to the World Wide Web have become popular because they help organizations determine who is visiting their Web sites and how to better target their offerings. Some firms also monitor the Internet usage of their employees to see how they are using company network resources. Web retailers now have access to software that lets them "watch" the online shopping behavior of individuals and groups while they are visiting a Web site

147

and making purchases. The commercial demand for this personal information is virtually insatiable.

Web sites can learn the identities of their visitors if the visitors voluntarily register at the site to purchase a product or service or to obtain a free service, such as information. Web sites can also capture information about visitors without their knowledge using cookie technology.

Cookies are tiny files deposited on a computer hard drive when a user visits certain Web sites. Cookies identify the visitor's Web browser software and track visits to the Web site. When the visitor returns to a site that has stored a cookie, the Web site software will search the visitor's computer, find the cookie, and know what that person has done in the past. It may also update the cookie, depending on the activity during the visit. In this way, the site can customize its contents for each visitor's interests. For example, if you purchase a book on the Amazon.com Web site and return later from the same browser, the site will welcome you by name and recommend other books of interest based on your past purchases. DoubleClick, described earlier in this chapter, uses cookies to build its dossiers with details of online purchases and to examine the behavior of Web site visitors. Figure 3 illustrates how cookies work.

Web sites using cookie technology cannot directly obtain visitors' names and addresses. However, if a person has registered at a site, that information can be combined with cookie data to identify the visitor. Web site owners can also combine the data they have gathered from cookies and other Web site monitoring tools with personal data from other sources, such as offline data collected from surveys or paper catalog purchases, to develop very detailed profiles of their visitors.

There are now even more subtle and surreptitious tools for surveillance of Internet users. Marketers use **Web bugs** as another tool to monitor online behavior. Web bugs are tiny graphic files embedded in e-mail messages and Web pages that are designed to monitor who is reading the e-mail message or Web page and transmit that information to another computer. Other **spyware** can secretly install itself on an Internet user's computer by piggybacking on larger

FIGURE 3   HOW COOKIES IDENTIFY WEB VISITORS

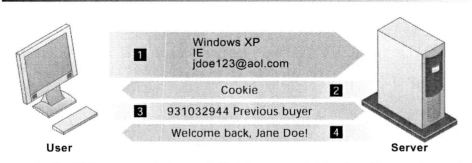

1. The Web server reads the user's Web browser and determines the operating system, browser name, version number, Internet address, and other information.
2. The server transmits a tiny text file with user identification information called a cookie, which the user's browser receives and stores on the user's computer hard drive.
3. When the user returns to the Web site, the server requests the contents of any cookie it deposited previously in the user's computer.
4. The Web server reads the cookie, identifies the visitor, and calls up data on the user.

Cookies are written by a Web site on a visitor's hard drive. When the visitor returns to that Web site, the Web server requests the ID number from the cookie and uses it to access the data stored by that server on that visitor. The Web site can then use these data to display personalized information.

applications. Once installed, the spyware calls out to Web sites to send banner ads and other unsolicited material to the user, and it can also report the user's movements on the Internet to other computers. Spyware also can log user keystrokes and send the information to other sites on the Web without the user's knowledge.

Google has been using tools to scan the contents of messages received by users of its free Web-based e-mail service called Gmail. Ads that users see when they read their e-mail are related to the subjects of these messages. Google's service offers users 1 gigabyte of storage space—far more than any of its competitors—but privacy advocates find the practice offensive.

The United States has allowed businesses to gather transaction information generated in the marketplace and then use that information for other marketing purposes without obtaining the informed consent of the individual whose information is being used. U.S. e-commerce sites are largely content to publish statements on their Web sites informing visitors about how their information will be used. Some have added opt-out selection boxes to these information policy statements. An **opt-out** model of informed consent permits the collection of personal information until the consumer specifically requests that the data not be collected. Privacy advocates would like to see wider use of an **opt-in** model of informed consent in which a business is prohibited from collecting any personal information unless the consumer specifically takes action to approve information collection and use.

The online industry has preferred self-regulation to privacy legislation for protecting consumers. In 1998, the online industry formed the Online Privacy Alliance to encourage self-regulation to develop a set of privacy guidelines for its members. The group promotes the use of online seals, such as that of TRUSTe, certifying Web sites adhering to certain privacy principles. Members of the advertising network industry, including DoubleClick, have created an additional industry association called the Network Advertising Initiative (NAI)

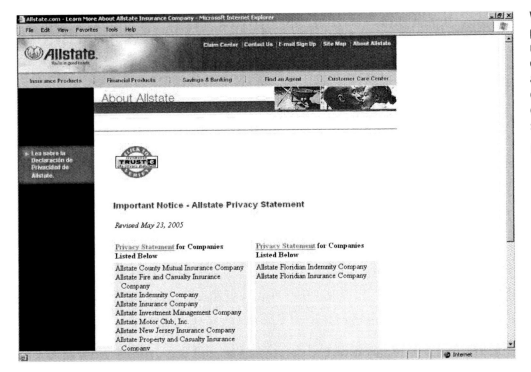

Web sites are posting their privacy policies for visitors to review. The TRUSTe seal designates Web sites that have agreed to adhere to TRUSTe's established privacy principles of disclosure, choice, access, and security.

Courtesy of The Allstate Corporation

to develop its own privacy policies to help consumers opt out of advertising network programs and provide consumers redress from abuses.

While nearly all the top 100 Web sites have privacy policies, you will quickly discover upon reading them that there are few limitations these firms place on their use of your personal information. In turn, consumers do not do as much as they could or should to protect themselves. Many companies with Web sites do not have privacy policies. Of the companies that do post privacy polices on their Web sites, about half do not monitor their sites to ensure they adhere to these policies. While the vast majority of online customers claim they are concerned about online privacy, less than half read the privacy statements on Web sites (Laudon and Traver, 2006).

Technical Solutions

In addition to legislation, new technologies are available to protect user privacy during interactions with Web sites. Many of these tools are used for encrypting e-mail, for making e-mail or surfing activities appear anonymous, for preventing client computers from accepting cookies, or for detecting and eliminating spyware.

There are now tools to help users determine the kind of personal data that can be extracted by Web sites. The Platform for Privacy Preferences, known as P3P, enables automatic communication of privacy policies between an e-commerce site and its visitors. **P3P** provides a standard for communicating a Web site's privacy policy to Internet users and for comparing that policy to the user's preferences or to other standards, such as the FTC's new FIP guidelines or the European Directive on Data Protection. Users can use P3P to select the level of privacy they wish to maintain when interacting with the Web site.

The P3P standard allows Web sites to publish privacy policies in a form that computers can understand. Once it is codified according to P3P rules, the privacy policy becomes part of the software for individual Web pages (see Figure 4). Users of Microsoft Internet Explorer Web browsing software can access and read the P3P site's privacy policy and a list of all cookies coming

FIGURE 4   THE P3P STANDARD

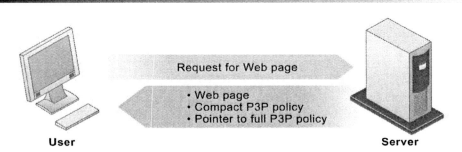

1. The user with P3P Web browsing software requests a Web page.
2. The Web server returns the Web page along with a compact version of the Web site's policy and a pointer to the full P3P policy. If the Web site is not P3P compliant, no P3P data are returned.
3. The user's Web browsing software compares the response from the Web site with the user's privacy preferences. If the Web site does not have a P3P policy or the policy does not match the privacy levels established by the user, it warns the user or rejects the cookies from the Web site. Otherwise, the Web page loads normally.

P3P enables Web sites to translate their privacy policies into a standard format that can be read by the user's Web browser software. The user's Web browser software evaluates the Web site's privacy policy to determine whether it is compatible with the user's privacy preferences.

from the site. Internet Explorer enables users to adjust their computers to screen out all cookies or let in selected cookies based on specific levels of privacy. For example, the "medium" level accepts cookies from first-party host sites that have opt-in or opt-out policies but rejects third-party cookies that use personally identifiable information without an opt-in policy.

However, P3P only works with Web sites of members of the World Wide Web Consortium who have translated their Web site privacy policies into P3P format. The technology will display cookies from Web sites that are not part of the consortium, but users will not be able to obtain sender information or privacy statements. Many users may also need to be educated about interpreting company privacy statements and P3P levels of privacy.

PROPERTY RIGHTS: INTELLECTUAL PROPERTY

Contemporary information systems have severely challenged existing law and social practices that protect private intellectual property. **Intellectual property** is considered to be intangible property created by individuals or corporations. Information technology has made it difficult to protect intellectual property because computerized information can be so easily copied or distributed on networks. Intellectual property is subject to a variety of protections under three different legal traditions: trade secrets, copyright, and patent law.

Trade Secrets

Any intellectual work product—a formula, device, pattern, or compilation of data-used for a business purpose can be classified as a **trade secret**, provided it is not based on information in the public domain. Protections for trade secrets vary from state to state. In general, trade secret laws grant a monopoly on the ideas behind a work product, but it can be a very tenuous monopoly.

Software that contains novel or unique elements, procedures, or compilations can be included as a trade secret. Trade secret law protects the actual ideas in a work product, not only their manifestation. To make this claim, the creator or owner must take care to bind employees and customers with nondisclosure agreements and to prevent the secret from falling into the public domain.

The limitation of trade secret protection is that, although virtually all software programs of any complexity contain unique elements of some sort, it is difficult to prevent the ideas in the work from falling into the public domain when the software is widely distributed.

Copyright

Copyright is a statutory grant that protects creators of intellectual property from having their work copied by others for any purpose during the life of the author plus an additional 70 years after the author's death. For corporate-owned works, copyright protection lasts for 95 years after their initial creation. Congress has extended copyright protection to books, periodicals, lectures, dramas, musical compositions, maps, drawings, artwork of any kind, and motion pictures. The intent behind copyright laws has been to encourage creativity and authorship by ensuring that creative people receive the financial and other benefits of their work. Most industrial nations have their own copyright laws, and there are several international conventions and bilateral agreements through which nations coordinate and enforce their laws.

In the mid-1960s, the Copyright Office began registering software programs, and in 1980 Congress passed the Computer Software Copyright Act, which clearly provides protection for software program code and for copies of the original sold in commerce, and sets forth the rights of the purchaser to use the software while the creator retains legal title.

Copyright protects against copying of entire programs or their parts. Damages and relief are readily obtained for infringement. The drawback to copyright protection is that the underlying ideas behind a work are not protected, only their manifestation in a work. A competitor can use your software, understand how it works, and build new software that follows the same concepts without infringing on a copyright.

"Look and feel" copyright infringement lawsuits are precisely about the distinction between an idea and its expression. For instance, in the early 1990s Apple Computer sued Microsoft Corporation and Hewlett-Packard for infringement of the expression of Apple's Macintosh interface, claiming that the defendants copied the expression of overlapping windows. The defendants countered that the idea of overlapping windows can be expressed only in a single way and, therefore, was not protectable under the merger doctrine of copyright law. When ideas and their expression merge, the expression cannot be copyrighted.

In general, courts appear to be following the reasoning of a 1989 case—Brown Bag Software vs. Symantec Corp.—in which the court dissected the elements of software alleged to be infringing. The court found that similar concept, function, general functional features (e.g., drop-down menus), and colors are not protectable by copyright law (*Brown Bag vs. Symantec Corp.*, 1992).

Patents

A **patent** grants the owner an exclusive monopoly on the ideas behind an invention for 20 years. The congressional intent behind patent law was to ensure that inventors of new machines, devices, or methods receive the full financial and other rewards of their labor and yet still make widespread use of the invention possible by providing detailed diagrams for those wishing to use the idea under license from the patent's owner. The granting of a patent is determined by the Patent Office and relies on court rulings.

The key concepts in patent law are originality, novelty, and invention. The Patent Office did not accept applications for software patents routinely until a 1981 Supreme Court decision that held that computer programs could be a part of a patentable process. Since that time, hundreds of patents have been granted and thousands await consideration.

The strength of patent protection is that it grants a monopoly on the underlying concepts and ideas of software. The difficulty is passing stringent criteria of nonobviousness (e.g., the work must reflect some special understanding and contribution), originality, and novelty, as well as years of waiting to receive protection.

Challenges to Intellectual Property Rights

Contemporary information technologies, especially software, pose severe challenges to existing intellectual property regimes and, therefore, create significant ethical, social, and political issues. Digital media differ from physical media like books, periodicals, CDs, and newspapers in terms of ease of replication; ease of transmission; ease of alteration; difficulty in classifying a software work as a program, book, or even music; compactness—making theft easy; and difficulties in establishing uniqueness.

The proliferation of electronic networks, including the Internet, has made it even more difficult to protect intellectual property. Before widespread use of networks, copies of software, books, magazine articles, or films had to be stored on physical media, such as paper, computer disks, or videotape, creating some hurdles to distribution. Using networks, information can be more widely reproduced and distributed. A study conducted by the International Data Corporation for the Business Software Alliance found that more than one-third of the software worldwide was counterfeit or pirated, and the Business Software Alliance reported $29 billion in yearly losses from software piracy (Geitner, 2004; Lohr, 2004).

The Internet was designed to transmit information freely around the world, including copyrighted information. With the World Wide Web in particular, you can easily copy and distribute virtually anything to thousands and even millions of people around the world, even if they are using different types of computer systems. Information can be illicitly copied from one place and distributed through other systems and networks even though these parties do not willingly participate in the infringement.

Individuals have been illegally copying and distributing digitized MP3 music files on the Internet for a number of years. File sharing services such as Napster, and later Grokster, Kazaa, and Morpheus sprung up to help users locate and swap digital music files, including those protected by copyright. Illegal file-sharing became so widespread that it threatened the viability of the music recording industry.

The recording industry won significant legal battles against Napster, and later against Grokster and all commercial P2P networks. The U.S. Supreme Court found in June 2005 that file-sharing networks that intentionally profited from illegal distribution of music could be held liable for their actions. This decision forced most of the large-scale commercial P2P networks to shut down, or to seek legal distribution agreements with the music publishers.

Despite these victories in court, illegal music file sharing abounds on the Internet: 27 percent of Internet users report downloading music from illegal sites (36 million Americans). This is down from a peak of 32 percent of Internet users downloading in 2002. The good news—if there is any in this area—is that legal music downloads from sites like iTunes has expanded to more than 43 percent of Internet users in the United States. (Madden and Rainie, 2005). As more and more homes adopt high-speed Internet access, illegal file sharing of videos will pose similar threats to the motion picture industry.

Mechanisms are being developed to sell and distribute books, articles, and other intellectual property legally on the Internet, and the **Digital Millennium Copyright Act (DMCA)** of 1998 is providing some copyright protection. The DMCA implemented a World Intellectual Property Organization Treaty that makes it illegal to circumvent technology-based protections of copyrighted materials. Internet service providers (ISPs) are required to take down sites of copyright infringers that they are hosting once they are notified of the problem.

Microsoft and 1,400 other software and information content firms are represented by the Software and Information Industry Association (SIIA), which lobbies for new laws and enforcement of existing laws to protect intellectual property around the world. (SIIA was formed on January 1, 1999, from the merger of the Software Publishers Association [SPA] and the Information Industry Association [IIA].) The SIIA runs an antipiracy hotline for individuals to report piracy activities and educational programs to help organizations combat software piracy and has published guidelines for employee use of software.

153

ACCOUNTABILITY, LIABILITY, AND CONTROL

Along with privacy and property laws, new information technologies are challenging existing liability law and social practices for holding individuals and institutions accountable. If a person is injured by a machine controlled, in part, by software, who should be held accountable and, therefore, held liable? Should a public bulletin board or an electronic service, such as AOL, permit the transmission of pornographic or offensive material (as broadcasters), or should they be held harmless against any liability for what users transmit (as is true of common carriers, such as the telephone system)? What about the Internet? If you outsource your information processing, can you hold the external vendor liable for injuries done to your customers? Some real-world examples may shed light on these questions.

Computer-Related Liability Problems

During the weekend of March 15, 2002, tens of thousands of Bank of America customers in California, Arizona, and Nevada were unable to use their paychecks and social security payments that had just been deposited electronically. Checks bounced. Withdrawals were blocked because of insufficient funds. Because of an operating error at the bank's computer center in Nevada, a batch of direct-deposit transactions was not processed. The bank lost track of money that should have been credited to customers' accounts, and it took days to rectify the problem (Carr and Gallagher, 2002). Who is liable for any economic harm caused to individuals or businesses that could not access their full account balances in this period?

This case reveals the difficulties faced by information systems executives who ultimately are responsible for any harm done by systems developed by their staffs. In general, insofar as computer software is part of a machine, and the machine injures someone physically or economically, the producer of the software and the operator can be held liable for damages. Insofar as the software acts like a book, storing and displaying information, courts have been reluctant to hold authors, publishers, and booksellers liable for contents (the exception being instances of fraud or defamation), and hence courts have been wary of holding software authors liable for booklike software.

In general, it is very difficult (if not impossible) to hold software producers liable for their software products when those products are considered like books are, regardless of the physical or economic harm that results. Historically, print publishers, books, and periodicals have not been held liable because of fears that liability claims would interfere with First Amendment rights guaranteeing freedom of expression.

What about software as service? ATM machines are a service provided to bank customers. Should this service fail, customers will be inconvenienced and perhaps harmed economically if they cannot access their funds in a timely manner. Should liability protections be extended to software publishers and operators of defective financial, accounting, simulation, or marketing systems?

Software is very different from books. Software users may develop expectations of infallibility about software; software is less easily inspected than a book, and it is more difficult to compare with other software products for quality; software claims actually to perform a task rather than describe a task, as a book does; and people come to depend on services essentially based on software. Given the centrality of software to everyday life, the chances are excellent that liability law will extend its reach to include software even when the software merely provides an information service.

Telephone systems have not been held liable for the messages transmitted because they are regulated common carriers. In return for their right to provide telephone service, they must provide access to all, at reasonable rates, and achieve acceptable reliability. But broadcasters and cable television systems are subject to a wide variety of federal and local constraints on content and facilities. Organizations can be held liable for offensive content on their Web sites; and online services, such as Prodigy or AOL, might be held liable for postings by their users. Although U.S. courts have increasingly exonerated Web sites and ISPs for posting material by third parties, the threat of legal action still has a chilling effect on small companies or individuals who cannot afford to take their cases to trial.

SYSTEM QUALITY: DATA QUALITY AND SYSTEM ERRORS

The debate over liability and accountability for unintentional consequences of system use raises a related but independent moral dimension: What is an acceptable, technologically feasible level of system quality? At what point should system managers say, "Stop testing, we've done all we can to perfect this software. Ship it!" Individuals and organizations may be held responsible for avoidable and foreseeable consequences, which they have a duty to perceive and correct. And the gray area is that some system errors are foreseeable and correctable only at very great expense, an expense so great that pursuing this level of perfection is not feasible economically—no one could afford the product.

For example, although software companies try to debug their products before releasing them to the marketplace, they knowingly ship buggy products because the time and cost of fixing all minor errors would prevent these products from ever being released. What if the product was not offered on the marketplace, would social welfare as a whole not advance and perhaps even decline? Carrying this further, just what is the responsibility of a producer of computer services—should it withdraw the product that can never be perfect, warn the user, or forget about the risk (let the buyer beware)?

Three principal sources of poor system performance are (1) software bugs and errors, (2) hardware or facility failures caused by natural or other causes, and (3) poor input data quality. Chapter 10 discusses why zero defects in software code of any complexity cannot be achieved and why the seriousness of remaining bugs cannot be estimated. Hence, there is a technological barrier to perfect software, and users must be aware of the potential for catastrophic failure. The software industry has not yet arrived at testing standards for producing software of acceptable but not perfect performance.

Although software bugs and facility catastrophes are likely to be widely reported in the press, by far the most common source of business system failure is data quality. Few companies routinely measure the quality of their data, but studies of individual organizations report data error rates ranging from 0.5 to 30 percent (Gilhooly, 2005).

QUALITY OF LIFE: EQUITY, ACCESS, AND BOUNDARIES

The negative social costs of introducing information technologies and systems are beginning to mount along with the power of the technology. Many of these negative social consequences are not violations of individual rights or property crimes. Nevertheless, these negative consequences can be extremely harmful to individuals, societies, and political institutions. Computers and information technologies potentially can destroy valuable elements of our culture and society even while they bring us benefits. If there is a balance of good and bad consequences of using information systems, who do we hold responsible for the bad consequences? Next, we briefly examine some of the negative social consequences of systems, considering individual, social, and political responses.

Balancing Power: Center Versus Periphery

An early fear of the computer age was that huge, centralized mainframe computers would centralize power at corporate headquarters and in the nation's capital, resulting in a Big Brother society, as was suggested in George Orwell's novel *1984*. The shift toward highly decentralized computing, coupled with an ideology of empowerment of thousands of workers, and the decentralization of decision making to lower organizational levels have reduced the fears of power centralization in institutions. Yet much of the empowerment described in popular business magazines is trivial. Lower-level employees may be empowered to make minor decisions, but the key policy decisions may be as centralized as in the past.

Rapidity of Change: Reduced Response Time to Competition

Information systems have helped to create much more efficient national and international markets. The now-more-efficient global marketplace has reduced the normal social buffers that permitted businesses many years to adjust to competition. Time-based competition has an ugly side: The business you work for may not have enough time to respond to global competitors and may be wiped out in a year, along with your job. We stand the risk of developing a "just-in-time society" with "just-in-time jobs" and "just-in-time" workplaces, families, and vacations.

Maintaining Boundaries: Family, Work, and Leisure

Parts of this text were produced on trains and planes, as well as on family vacations and during what otherwise might have been "family" time. The danger to ubiquitous computing, telecommuting, nomad computing, and the "do anything anywhere" computing environment is that it might actually come true. If so, the traditional boundaries that separate work from family and just plain leisure will be weakened.

Although authors have traditionally worked just about anywhere (typewriters have been portable for nearly a century), the advent of information systems, coupled with the growth of knowledge-work occupations, means that more and more people will be working when traditionally they would have been playing or communicating with family and friends. The work umbrella now extends far beyond the eight-hour day.

Even leisure time spent on the computer threatens these close social relationships. Extensive Internet use, even for entertainment or recreational purposes, takes people away from their family and friends. The Interactive Session on Organizations explores what happens to children and teenagers when time spent online is excessive or inappropriate.

Weakening these institutions poses clear-cut risks. Family and friends historically have provided powerful support mechanisms for individuals, and they act as balance points in a society by preserving private life, providing a

156

INTERACTIVE SESSION: ORGANIZATIONS

THE INTERNET: FRIEND OR FOE TO CHILDREN?

The Internet has so much to offer people of all ages, including children. School-age children typically use the Internet for school assignments, for downloading music, playing games, and for connecting with others. A child might use e-mail or instant messaging to stay in touch with friends who have moved away or family members in distant locations. Shy children may find an online community and set of "friends" with whom to share feelings that they are unable to express in person. Children living in rural areas can stay in touch with others who are isolated geographically.

But there's a dark side to all that Internet use. It can also socially isolate children and expose them to unhealthy activities and experiences.

According to child and adolescent psychiatrist Dr. David Bassler, certain children become too isolated as a result of heavy Internet use. A shy or overweight child can become a football star in an online game or a persona in MySpace. Bassler believes that "a degree of this is healthy, but if it starts to become the primary focus, it can become a problem." Staying online for long periods of time may make a shy or depressed child even more shy or depressed.

When children spend too much time online, they don't do their homework or can't focus on their work in school because their online activities have drained their energy. They miss out on sports and other activities and they don't spend enough time with their real-world peers and family members.

E-mail and instant messaging can help youngsters stay in touch with friends and family but they have also become instruments for "cyberbullying." Kids will use these tools to send insulting remarks to each other or to distribute personal details meant for a few close friends to a wide circle of strangers. One 16-year-old boy whose girlfriend had broken up with him over the telephone was shocked to find a detailed explanation for her actions on her instant messenger profile. She had used instant messaging to tell their entire network of social contacts, including friends of friends in different high schools, details about the reasons for the breakup. They boy was so upset he skipped school the next day.

Ten million young people use the Internet each day, and one in five have been solicited or approached by a child predator, according to the FBI. Federal arrests for online exploitation of children doubled from 863 to 1,649 between 2003 and 2005. Fifty percent of child victims of online sex abuse are in the seventh through ninth grades.

Online predators monitor screen names and scrutinize personal information on social networking sites such as MySpace, Friendster, and Facebook to find youngsters with self-esteem problems. They'll ask youngsters questions such as "Do you like this band? Can I help you with your homework?" Then they'll try to arrange a physical meeting with these juveniles.

Dr. Robert Kraut, a professor at Carnegie-Mellon University who has studied online behavior for more than a decade, found that the more people use the Internet, the less they socialize and the less they communicate with family members. High Internet usage among teenagers is associated with a decline in social support. Many hours spent online in casual conversation with other strangers don't translate into meaningful relationships.

Obesity, now an epidemic in the United States, is especially prevalent among youngsters who sit at their computers for hours at a time munching on snack food. And there are plenty of Web sites encouraging them to do just that.

Food companies aggressively use Internet games and other perks such as screen-saver downloads to entice children into buying their brands. Their Web sites offer childrens' games linked to snacks, such as Chips Ahoy Soccer Shootout, Pop-Tart Slalom, and Lucky Charms Wild Chocolate Mine. A Kaiser Family Foundation study found that between June and November 2005 more than 12.2 million children had visited 77 food company Web sites it examined.

According to the study's lead researcher Vicky Rideout, Internet advertising "still doesn't have the reach TV advertising has. But who it does reach, it reaches more deeply." This study is the first to investigate the scope of Internet advertising aimed at children.

Sources: Johanna Ambrosio, "Connected to Nowhere," *Information Week*, May 1, 2006; Jennifer B. McKim, "Keep Your Child Safe from Online Predators," *Orange County Register*, July 18, 2006; and Curtis L. Taylor, "Kids Swallowing Online Food Company Lures," *Newsday*, July 20, 2006.

CASE STUDY QUESTIONS

1. Does use of the Internet by children and teenagers pose an ethical dilemma? Why or why not?

2. Should parents restrict use of the Internet by children or teenagers? Why or why not?

MIS IN ACTION

Visit Nabiscoworld.com or another Web site from a food company that features games or other interactive features of interest to children and teenagers. Explore the site and answer the following questions.

1. What kinds of games and interactive features are available at this site? Are there any restrictions on who can play?

2. How do these sites help the company pitch food products to children?

3. Do these sites collect personal information? What kind of information?

4. Are these sites at all beneficial to consumers? What are the benefits?

5. Do these sites represent an ethical dilemma? Why or why not?

place for people to collect their thoughts, allowing people to think in ways contrary to their employer, and dream.

Dependence and Vulnerability

Today, our businesses, governments, schools, and private associations, such as churches, are incredibly dependent on information systems and are, therefore, highly vulnerable if these systems fail. With systems now as ubiquitous as the telephone system, it is startling to remember that there are no regulatory or standard-setting forces in place that are similar to telephone, electrical, radio, television, or other public-utility technologies. The absence of standards and the criticality of some system applications will probably call forth demands for national standards and perhaps regulatory oversight.

Computer Crime and Abuse

New technologies, including computers, create new opportunities for committing crime by creating new valuable items to steal, new ways to steal them, and new ways to harm others. **Computer crime** is the commission of illegal acts through the use of a computer or against a computer system. Computers or computer systems can be the object of the crime (destroying a company's computer center or a company's computer files), as well as the instrument of a crime (stealing computer lists by illegally gaining access to a computer system using a home computer). Simply accessing a computer system without authorization or with intent to do harm, even by accident, is now a federal crime.

Computer abuse is the commission of acts involving a computer that may not be illegal but that are considered unethical. The popularity of the Internet and e-mail has turned one form of computer abuse—spamming—into a serious problem for both individuals and businesses. **Spam** is junk e-mail sent by an organization or individual to a mass audience of Internet users who have expressed no interest in the product or service being marketed. Spammers tend

Although some people enjoy the convenience of working at home, the do-anything-any-where computing environment can blur the traditional boundaries between work and family time.

to market pornography, fraudulent deals and services, outright scams, and other products not widely approved in most civilized societies. Some countries have passed laws to outlaw spamming or to restrict its use. In the United States, it is still legal if it does not involve fraud and the sender and subject of the e-mail are properly identified.

Spamming has mushroomed because it only costs a few cents to send thousands of messages advertising wares to Internet users. Hundreds of CDs for sale on the Web offer spammers millions of e-mail addresses harvested by software robots that read message boards, chat rooms, and Web sites, or spammers use their own harvesting tools for this purpose. Spam now accounts for 70 percent of Internet e-mail traffic worldwide. Figure 5 provides data on

Spam consists of unsolicited e-mail messages, which can be bothersome, offensive, and even a drain on office worker productivity. Spam filtering software such as McAfee's SpamKiller blocks suspicious e-mail.

Courtesy of McAfee Corp.

FIGURE 5   THE SPAMMING PROBLEM

Spam for Everyone

Spam e-mail messages hawking many kinds of products and services, including scams, clog inboxes of employees in many industries.

What is being offered . . .

Products and services being sold with spam e-mail messages

. . . and to whom

Average number of spam e-mail messages received daily per user

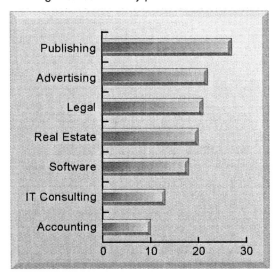

This figure shows the major types of products and services hawked through spam e-mail messages and the industries that receive the most spam.

Courtesy of New York Times Graphics

the scope of spamming and the types of industries most affected by the practice.

Spam costs for businesses are very high (an estimated $50 billion per year) because of the computing and network resources consumed by billions of unwanted e-mail messages and the time required to deal with them. Internet service providers and individuals can combat spam by using spam filtering software to block suspicious e-mail before it enters a recipient's e-mail inbox. However, spam filters may block legitimate messages, and many spammers skirt around filters by continually changing their e-mail accounts. Many spam messages are sent from one country while another country hosts the spam Web site.

Spamming is more tightly regulated in Europe than in the United States. On May 30, 2002, the European Parliament passed a ban on unsolicited commercial messaging. Electronic marketing can be targeted only to people who have given prior consent.

The U.S. CAN-SPAM Act of 2003, which went into effect on January 1, 2004, does not outlaw spamming but does ban deceptive e-mail practices by requiring commercial e-mail messages to display accurate subject lines, identify the true senders, and offer recipients an easy way to remove their names from e-mail lists. It also prohibits the use of fake return addresses. A few people have been prosecuted under the law, but spamming increased since it went into effect.

Employment: Trickle-Down Technology and Reengineering Job Loss

Reengineering work is typically hailed in the information systems community as a major benefit of new information technology. It is much less frequently noted that redesigning business processes could potentially cause millions of mid-level managers and clerical workers to lose their jobs. One economist has raised the possibility that we will create a society run by a small "high tech elite of corporate professionals . . . in a nation of the permanently unemployed" (Rifkin, 1993).

Other economists are much more sanguine about the potential job losses. They believe relieving bright, educated workers from reengineered jobs will result in these workers moving to better jobs in fast-growth industries. Missing from this equation are unskilled, blue-collar workers and older, less well-educated middle managers. It is not clear that these groups can be retrained easily for high-quality (high-paying) jobs. Careful planning and sensitivity to employee needs can help companies redesign work to minimize job losses.

Equity and Access: Increasing Racial and Social Class Cleavages

Does everyone have an equal opportunity to participate in the digital age? Will the social, economic, and cultural gaps that exist in the United States and other societies be reduced by information systems technology? Or will the cleavages be increased, permitting the better off to become even more better off relative to others?

These questions have not yet been fully answered because the impact of systems technology on various groups in society has not been thoroughly studied. What is known is that information, knowledge, computers, and access to these resources through educational institutions and public libraries are inequitably distributed along ethnic and social class lines, as are many other information resources. Several studies have found that certain ethnic and income groups in the United States are less likely to have computers or online Internet access even though computer ownership and Internet access have soared in the past five years. Although the gap is narrowing, higher-income families in each ethnic group are still more likely to have home computers and Internet access than lower-income families in the same group.

A similar **digital divide** exists in U.S. schools, with schools in high-poverty areas less likely to have computers, high-quality educational technology programs, or Internet access availability for their students. Left uncorrected, the digital divide could lead to a society of information haves, computer literate and skilled, versus a large group of information have-nots, computer illiterate and unskilled. Public interest groups want to narrow this digital divide by making digital information services—including the Internet—available to virtually everyone, just as basic telephone service is now.

Health Risks: RSI, CVS, and Technostress

The most important occupational disease today is **repetitive stress injury (RSI)**. RSI occurs when muscle groups are forced through repetitive actions often with high-impact loads (such as tennis) or tens of thousands of repetitions under low-impact loads (such as working at a computer keyboard).

The single largest source of RSI is computer keyboards. The most common kind of computer-related RSI is **carpal tunnel syndrome (CTS)**, in which pressure on the median nerve through the wrist's bony structure, called a

161

Repetitive stress injury (RSI) is the leading occupational disease today. The single largest cause of RSI is computer keyboard work.

carpal tunnel, produces pain. The pressure is caused by constant repetition of keystrokes: In a single shift, a word processor may perform 23,000 keystrokes. Symptoms of carpal tunnel syndrome include numbness, shooting pain, inability to grasp objects, and tingling. Millions of workers have been diagnosed with carpal tunnel syndrome.

RSI is avoidable. Designing workstations for a neutral wrist position (using a wrist rest to support the wrist), proper monitor stands, and footrests all contribute to proper posture and reduced RSI. New, ergonomically correct keyboards are also an option. These measures should be supported by frequent rest breaks and rotation of employees to different jobs.

RSI is not the only occupational illness computers cause. Back and neck pain, leg stress, and foot pain also result from poor ergonomic designs of workstations. **Computer vision syndrome (CVS)** refers to any eyestrain condition related to computer display screen use. Its symptoms, which are usually temporary, include headaches, blurred vision, and dry and irritated eyes.

The newest computer-related malady is **technostress**, which is stress induced by computer use. Its symptoms include aggravation, hostility toward humans, impatience, and fatigue. According to experts, humans working continuously with computers come to expect other humans and human institutions to behave like computers, providing instant responses, attentiveness, and an absence of emotion. Technostress is thought to be related to high levels of job turnover in the computer industry, high levels of early retirement from computer-intense occupations, and elevated levels of drug and alcohol abuse.

The incidence of technostress is not known but is thought to be in the millions and growing rapidly in the United States. Computer-related jobs now top the list of stressful occupations based on health statistics in several industrialized countries.

To date, the role of radiation from computer display screens in occupational disease has not been proved. Video display terminals (VDTs) emit nonionizing electric and magnetic fields at low frequencies. These rays enter the body and have unknown effects on enzymes, molecules, chromosomes, and cell membranes. Long-term studies are investigating low-level electromagnetic fields and birth defects, stress, low birth weight, and other diseases. All manufacturers have reduced display screen emissions since the early 1980s, and European countries, such as Sweden, have adopted stiff radiation emission standards.

The computer has become a part of our lives—personally as well as socially, culturally, and politically. It is unlikely that the issues and our choices will become easier as information technology continues to transform our world. The growth of the Internet and the information economy suggests that all the ethical and social issues we have described will be heightened further as we move into the first digital century.

4   HANDS-ON MIS

The projects in this section give you hands-on experience in developing a privacy policy for a real-world company, using Web page development tools to design and create a simple Web site, and using Internet newsgroups for market research.

Developing a Web Site Privacy Policy

Software skills: Web browser software and presentation software
Business skills: Corporate privacy policy formulation

Dirt Bikes's management wants to make sure it has policies and procedures in place to protect the privacy of visitors to its Web site. You have been asked to develop Dirt Bikes's Web site privacy policy. The TRUSTe Web site at www.truste.org has Model Privacy Disclosures in its Privacy Resources that you can download and review to help you draft Dirt Bikes's privacy policy. You can also examine specific companies' privacy policies by searching for Web site privacy policies on Yahoo!, Google, or another search engine. Prepare a report for management that addresses the following issues:

- How much data should Dirt Bikes collect on visitors to its Web site? What information could it discover by tracking visitors' activities at its Web site? What value would this information provide the company? What are the privacy problems raised by collecting such data?

- Should Dirt Bike use cookies? What are the advantages of using cookies for both Dirt Bikes and its Web site visitors? What privacy issues do they create for Dirt Bikes?

- Should Dirt Bikes join an organization such as TRUSTe to certify that it has adopted approved privacy practices? Why or why not?

- Should Dirt Bikes design its site so that it conforms to P3P standards? Why or why not?

- Should Dirt Bikes adopt an opt-in or opt-out model of informed consent?

- Include in your report a short (two to three pages) privacy statement for the Dirt Bikes Web site. You can use the categories of the TRUSTe Model Privacy Disclosures as a guideline if you wish.

- (Optional) Use electronic presentation software to summarize your recommendations for management.

Achieving Operational Excellence: Creating a Simple Web Site Using Web Page Development Tools

Software skills: Web page creation
Business skills: Web page design

In this project, you will learn how to build a simple Web site of your own design for a business using the Web page creation function of Microsoft Word, Microsoft FrontPage, or a Web page development tool of your choice.

Build a simple Web site for a business. The Web site should include a home page with a description of your business and at least one picture or graphic. From the home page, you must be able to link to a second Web page and, from there, link to a third Web page. Make the home page long enough so that when you arrive at the bottom of the page, you can no longer see the top. At the bottom of your Web page include a link back to the top. Also include a link to one of the secondary Web pages. On the secondary page, include a link to the top of that page and a link back to the top of the homepage. Also include a link to the third page, which should contain a link to its own top and a link back to the top of the home page. Finally, on one of the secondary pages, include another picture or graphic, and on the other page include an object that you create using Microsoft Excel or other spreadsheet software. The Laudon Web site for this chapter includes instructions for completing this project. If you have tested every function and all work to your satisfaction, save the pages you have created for submission to your instructor.

Improving Decision Making: Using Internet Newsgroups for Online Market Research

Software Skills: Web browser software and Internet newsgroups
Business Skills: Using Internet newsgroups to identify potential customers

This project will help develop your Internet skills in using newsgroups for marketing. It will also ask you to think about the ethical implications of using information in online discussion groups for business purposes.

You are producing hiking boots that you are selling through a few stores at this time. You think your boots are more comfortable than those of your competition. You believe you can undersell many of your competitors if you can significantly increase your production and sales. You would like to use Internet discussion groups interested in hiking, climbing, and camping both to sell your boots and to make them well known. Visit Google's Usenet archives (groups.google.com), which stores discussion postings from many thousands of newsgroups. Through this site you can locate all relevant newsgroups and search them by keyword, author's name, forum, date, and subject. Choose a message and examine it carefully, noting all the information you can obtain, including information about the author.

- How could you use these newsgroups to market your boots?
- What ethical principles might you be violating if you use these messages to sell your boots? Do you think there are ethical problems in using newsgroups this way? Explain your answer.
- Next use Google or Yahoo.com to search for the hiking boots industry and locate sites that will help you develop other new ideas for contacting potential customers.

- Given what you have learned in this and perhaps previous chapters, prepare a plan to use newsgroups and other alternative methods to begin attracting visitors to your site.

LEARNING TRACK MODULE

Developing a Corporate Code of Ethics for Information Systems. This Learning Track module describes the outline for a corporate code of ethics in information systems. What should be in a code of ethics? What ethical dimensions should be included? The Learning Track module is available at the Laudon Web site for this chapter and on the Student CD-ROM.

Summary

1. *Analyze the relationships among ethical, social, and political issues that are raised by information systems.*

    Information technology has raised new possibilities for behavior for which laws and rules of acceptable conduct have not yet been developed. Information technology is introducing changes that create new ethical issues for societies to debate and resolve. Increasing computing power, storage, and networking capabilities—including the Internet—can expand the reach of individual and organizational actions and magnify their impacts. The ease and anonymity with which information can be communicated, copied, and manipulated in online environments are challenging traditional rules of right and wrong behavior. Ethical, social, and political issues are closely related. Ethical issues confront individuals who must choose a course of action, often in a situation in which two or more ethical principles are in conflict (a dilemma). Social issues spring from ethical issues as societies develop expectations in individuals about the correct course of action. Political issues spring from social conflict and are mainly concerned with using laws that prescribe behavior to create situations in which individuals behave correctly.

2. *Identify the main moral dimensions of an information society and specific principles for conduct that can be used to guide ethical decisions.*

    The moral dimensions of information systems center around information rights and obligations, property rights and obligations, accountability and control, system quality, and quality of life. Six ethical principles are available to judge conduct. These principles are derived independently from several cultural, religious, and intellectual traditions and include the Golden Rule, Immanuel Kant's Categorical Imperative, Descartes' rule of change, the Utilitarian Principle, the Risk Aversion Principle, and the ethical "no free lunch" rule. These principles should be used in conjunction with an ethical analysis to guide decision making. The ethical analysis involves identifying the facts, values, stakeholders, options, and consequences of actions. Once completed, you can consider which ethical principle to apply to a situation to arrive at a judgment.

3. *Evaluate the impact of contemporary information systems and the Internet on the protection of individual privacy and intellectual property.*

    Contemporary information systems technology, including Internet technology, challenges traditional regimens for protecting individual privacy and intellectual property. Data storage and data analysis technology enables companies to easily gather personal data about individuals from many different sources and analyze these data to create detailed electronic profiles about individuals and their behaviors. Data flowing over the Internet can be monitored at many points. The activities of Web site visitors can be closely tracked using cookies and other Web monitoring tools. Not all Web sites have strong privacy protection policies, and they do not always allow for informed consent regarding the use of personal information. The online industry prefers self-regulation to the U.S. government tightening privacy protection legislation.

Traditional copyright laws are insufficient to protect against software piracy because digital material can be copied so easily. Internet technology also makes intellectual property even more difficult to protect because digital material can be copied easily and transmitted to many different locations simultaneously over the Net. Web pages can be constructed easily using pieces of content from other Web sites without permission.

4. *Assess how information systems have affected everyday life.*

Although computer systems have been sources of efficiency and wealth, they have some negative impacts. Errors in large computer systems are impossible to eradicate totally. Computer errors can cause serious harm to individuals and organizations, and existing laws and social practices are often unable to establish liability and accountability for these problems. Less serious errors are often attributable to poor data quality, which can cause disruptions and losses for businesses. Jobs can be lost when computers replace workers or tasks become unnecessary in reengineered business processes. The ability to own and use a computer may be exacerbating socioeconomic disparities among different racial groups and social classes. Widespread use of computers increases opportunities for computer crime and computer abuse. Computers can also create health problems, such as repetitive stress injury, computer vision syndrome, and technostress.

Key Terms

Accountability
Carpal tunnel syndrome (CTS)
Computer abuse
Computer crime
Computer vision syndrome (CVS)
Cookies
Copyright
Descartes' rule of change
Digital divide
Digital Millennium Copyright Act (DMCA)
Due process
Ethical "no free lunch" rule
Ethics
Fair Information Practices (FIP)
Golden Rule
Immanuel Kant's Categorical Imperative
Information rights
Informed consent
Intellectual property

Liability
Nonobvious relationship awareness (NORA)
Opt-in
Opt-out
P3P
Patent
Privacy
Profiling
Repetitive stress injury (RSI)
Responsibility, 135
Risk Aversion Principle
Safe harbor
Spam
Spyware
Technostress
Trade secret
Utilitarian Principle
Web bugs

Review Questions

1. In what ways are ethical, social, and political issues connected? Give some examples.

2. What are the key technological trends that heighten ethical concerns?

3. What are the differences between responsibility, accountability, and liability?

4. What are the five steps in an ethical analysis?

5. Identify and describe six ethical principles.

6. What is a professional code of conduct?

7. What are meant by privacy and fair information practices?

8. How is the Internet challenging the protection of individual privacy?

9. What role can informed consent, legislation, industry self-regulation, and technology tools play in protecting the individual privacy of Internet users?

10. What are the three different regimes that protect intellectual property rights? What challenges to intellectual property rights does the Internet pose?

11. Why is it so difficult to hold software services liable for failure or injury?

12. What is the most common cause of system quality problems?

13. Name and describe four quality-of-life impacts of computers and information systems.

14. What is technostress, and how would you identify it?

15. Name three management actions that could reduce RSI injuries.

Discussion Questions

1. Should producers of software-based services, such as ATMs, be held liable for economic injuries suffered when their systems fail?

2. Should companies be responsible for unemployment caused by their information systems? Why or why not?

Video Case

You will find a video case illustrating some of the concepts in this chapter on the Laudon Web site and Student CD-ROM along with questions to help you analyze the case.

Teamwork: Developing a Corporate Ethics Code

With three or four of your classmates, develop a corporate ethics code on privacy that addresses both employee privacy and the privacy of customers and users of the corporate Web site. Be sure to consider e-mail privacy and employer monitoring of worksites, as well as corporate use of information about employees concerning their off-the-job behavior (e.g., lifestyle, marital arrangements, and so forth). If possible, use electronic presentation software to present your ethics code to the class.

REFERENCES

Association of Computing Machinery. "ACM's Code of Ethics and Professional Conduct." *Communications of the ACM* 36, no. 12 (December 1993).

Ball, Kirstie S. "Situating Workplace Surveillance: *Ethics and Computer-based Performance Monitoring*." Ethics and Information Technology 3, no. 3 (2001)

Barrett, Larry and Sean Gallagher. "What Sin City Can Teach Tom Ridge." Baseline Magazine (April 2004).

Bellman, Steven, Eric J. Johnson and Gerald L. Lohse. "To Opt-in or Opt-out? It Depends on the Question". *Commumications of the ACM* 44, no. 2 (February 2001).

Bennett, Colin J. "Cookies, Web Bugs, Webcams, and Cue Cats: Patterns of Surveillance on the World Wide Web." *Ethics and Information Technology* 3, no. 3 (2001).

Bergstein, Brian. "Research Explores Data Mining, Privacy." Associated Press (June 17, 2006).

Bhattacharjee, Sudip, Ram D. Gopal, and G. Lawrence Sanders. "Digital Music and Online Sharing: Software Piracy 2.0?" *Communications of the ACM* 46, no.7 (July 2003).

Bowen, Jonathan. "The Ethics of Safety-Critical Systems." *Communications of the ACM* 43, no. 3 (April 2000).

Brown Bag Software vs. Symantec Corp. 960 F2D 1465 (Ninth Circuit, 1992).

Burk, Dan L. "Copyrightable Functions and Patentable Speech." *Communications of the ACM* 44, no. 2 (February 2001).

Carr, David F. and Sean Gallagher. "BofA's Direct-Deposit Debacle." *Baseline* (May 15, 2002).

Day, George S., Adam J. Fein, and Gregg Ruppersberger, "Shakeouts in Digital Markets," *California Management Review* 45, no. 3 (Winter 2003).

Earp, Julia B. and David Baumer. "Innovative Web Use to Learn About Consumer Behavior and Online Privacy." *Communications of the ACM* 46, no. 4 (April 2003).

Farmer, Dan and Charles C. Mann. "Surveillance Nation." Part I *Technology Review* (April 2003) and Part II *Technology Review* (May 2003).

Froomkin, A. Michael. "The Collision of Trademarks, Domain Names, and Due Process in Cyberspace." *Communications of the ACM* 44, no. 2 (February 2001).

Geitner, Paul. "Survey: 36 Percent of Software Pirated." Associated Press (July 7, 2004).

Gilhooly, Kym. "Dirty Data Blights the Bottom Line." *Computerworld* (November 7, 2005).

Hagerty, James R. and Dennis K. Berman. "New Battleground in Web Privacy War: Ads That Snoop." *The Wall Street Journal* (August 27, 2003).

Hansell, Saul. "The Internet Ad You Are About to See Has Already Read Your E-Mail." The New York Times (June 21, 2004).

Heingartner, Douglas. "Software Piracy is in Resurgence, with New Safeguards Eroded by File Sharing." *The New York Times* (January 19, 2004).

Jackson, Linda A., Alexander von Eye, Gretchen Barbatsis, Frank Biocca, Hiram E. Fitzgerald, and Yong Zhao. "The Impact of Internet Use on the Other Side of the Digital Divide." Communications of the ACM 47, no. 7 (July 2004).

Holmes, Allan. The Profits in Privacy." *CIO Magazine* (March 15, 2006).

Jackson, Thomas W., Ray Dawson, and Darren Wilson. "Understanding Email Interaction Increases Organizational Productivity." *Communications of the ACM* 46, no. 8 (August 2003).

Kapner, Suzanne. "Internet Site, Fearing Suit over Content, Curbs Activity." *The New York Times* (March 14, 2003).

Kling, Rob. "When Organizations Are Perpetrators: The Conditions of Computer Abuse and Computer Crime." In *Computerization & Controversy: Value Conflicts & Social Choices*, edited by Charles Dunlop and Rob Kling. New York: Academic Press (1991).

Kreie, Jennifer and Timothy Paul Cronan. "Making Ethical Decisions." *Communications of the ACM* 43, no. 12 (December 2000).

Laudon, Kenneth C. *Dossier Society: Value Choices in the Design of National Information Systems*. New York: Columbia University Press (1986).

———. "Ethical Concepts and Information Technology." *Communications of the ACM* 38, no. 12 (December 1995).

Laudon, Kenneth C. and Carol Guercio Traver. E-Commerce: *Business, Technology, Society*. Third Edition. Upper Saddle River, N.J.: Prentice Hall (2006).

Lee, Jintae. "An End-User Perspective on File-Sharing Systems," *Communications of the ACM* 46, no. 2 (February 2003).

Lenhart, Amanda, John Horrigan, Lee Rainie, Katherine Allen, Angie Boyce, Mary Madden, and Erin O'Grady. "The Ever-Shifting Internet Population." *The Pew Internet and American Life Project* (April 16, 2003).

Lohr, Steve. "Software Group Enters Fray over Proposed Piracy Law." *The New York Times* (July 19, 2004).

Madden, Mary and Lee Rainie. "Music and Video Downloading Moves Beyond P2P." Pew Internet and American Life Project (March 23, 2005).

Maltz, Elliott and Vincent Chiappetta. "Maximizing Value in the Digital World." *Sloan Management Review* 43, no. 3 (Spring 2002).

Mann, Catherine L. "What Global Sourcing Means for U.S. I.T. Workers and for the U.S. Economy." *Communications of the ACM* 47, no. 7 (July 2004).

Markoff, John. "Taking Snooping Further." *The New York Times* (February 25, 2006).

Martin, Jr. David M., Richard M. Smith, Michael Brittain, Ivan Fetch, and Hailin Wu. "The Privacy Practices of Web Browser Extensions." *Communications of the ACM* 44, no. 2 (February 2001).

Moores, Trevor and Gurpreet Dhillon. "Software Piracy: A View from Hong Kong." *Communications of the ACM* 43, no. 12, (December 2000).

National Telecommunications & Information Administration, U.S. Department of Commerce. " Falling Through the Net: Defining the Digital Divide." July 8, 1999.

Oz, Effy. "Ethical Standards for Information Systems Professionals," *MIS Quarterly* 16, no. 4 (December 1992).

Pear, Robert. "Survey Finds U.S. Agencies Engaged in 'Data Mining.'" The New York Times (May 27, 2004).

Rainie, Lee and Dan Packel. "More Online, Doing More." The Pew Internet and American Life Project (Febuary 18, 2001).

Reagle, Joseph, and Lorrie Faith Cranor. "The Platform for Privacy Preferences." *Communications of the ACM* 42, no. 2 (February 1999).

Redman, Thomas C. "The Impact of Poor Data Quality on the Typical Enterprise." *Communications of the ACM* 41, no. 2 (February 1998).

Rigdon, Joan E. "Frequent Glitches in New Software Bug Users." *The Wall Street Journal* (January 18, 1995).

Rotenberg, Marc. "Communications Privacy: Implications for Network Design." *Communications of the ACM* 36, no. 8 (August 1993).

Samuelson, Pamela. "Computer Programs and Copyright's Fair Use Doctrine." *Communications of the ACM* 36, no. 9 (September 1993).

Sewell, Graham and James R. Barker. "Neither Good, nor Bad, but Dangerous: Surveillance as an Ethical Paradox." *Ethics and Information Technology* 3, no. 3 (2001).

Sipior, Janice C., and Burke T. Ward. "The Dark Side of Employee Email." *Communications of the ACM* 42, no.7 (July 1999).

Smith, H. Jeff, Sandra J. Milberg, and Sandra J. Burke. "Information Privacy: Measuring Individuals' Concerns about Organizational Practices." *MIS Quarterly* 20, no. 2 (June 1996).

Payton, Fay Cobb. "Rethinking the Digital Divide." *Communications of the ACM* 46, no. 6 (June 2003)

Straub, Detmar W., Jr., and William D. Nance. "Discovering and Disciplining Computer Abuse in Organizations: A Field Study." *MIS Quarterly* 14, no. 1 (March 1990).

United States Department of Health, Education, and Welfare. *Records, Computers, and the Rights of Citizens*. Cambridge: MIT Press (1973).

United States Sentencing Commission, *U. S. Sentencing Commission's Sourcebook of Federal Sentencing Statistics*. http://www.ussc.gov/ANNRPT/2004 (2004)

Urbaczewski, Andrew and Leonard M. Jessup. "Does Electronic Monitoring of Employee Internet Usage Work?" *Communications of the ACM* 45, no. 1 (January 2002).

Volokh, Eugene. "Personalization and Privacy." *Communications of the ACM* 43, no. 8 (August 2000).

Wang, Huaiqing, Matthew K. O. Lee, and Chen Wang. "Consumer Privacy Concerns about Internet Marketing." *Communications of the ACM* 41, no. 3 (March 1998).

Wellman, Barry. "Designing the Internet for a Networked Society." *Communications of the ACM* 45, no. 5 (May 2002).

Whiting, Rick. "Who's Buying and Selling Your Data? Everybody." *Information Week* (July 10, 2006).

Wolf, Christopher. "Dazed and Confused: Data Law Disarray." *Business Week* (June 8, 2006).

Zeller, Tom Jr. "The Fight Against V1@gra (and other Spam)," *The New York Times*, May 21, 2006.

Is the Telephone Company Violating Your Privacy?
CASE STUDY

In May 2006, *USA Today* reported that three of the four major United States landline telecommunications companies had cooperated with the National Security Agency (NSA) fight against terrorism by turning over records of billions of phone calls made by Americans. AT&T, Verizon Communications, and BellSouth all contributed to the NSA's anti-terrorism program. Qwest Communications International was the only one of the big four to withhold its records.

The revelation by *USA Today* caused a firestorm of controversy. Media outlets, privacy advocates, and critics of the Bush administration expressed outrage over the program and questioned its legality. The *Washington Post* referred to the program as a "massive intrusion on personal privacy."

The issue received particularly strong scrutiny because it came to light only five months after President Bush said that he had authorized the NSA to listen in on international phone calls of Americans suspected of having ties to terrorism without obtaining a warrant. When combined, the two stories caused intense worry among privacy activists who feared that a widespread data mining effort was being carried out against American citizens by the administration.

President Bush would not acknowledge the existence of such an initiative. He said only that, "the intelligence activities I authorized are lawful and have been briefed to appropriate members of Congress." He added, "We are not mining or trolling through the personal lives of innocent Americans" and the privacy of citizens was being "fiercely protected."

What exactly did the phone companies do for the government? After September 11, 2001, they began turning over tens of millions of phone call records to the NSA, whose goal was to build a database of every call made inside the United States. The records that were turned over contained only phone numbers and calling information such as time, date, and the duration of the calls; they omitted names, addresses, and other personal data. Qwest was approached by the NSA at the same time as the others, but Joseph Nacchio, the company's CEO at the time (later involved in an insider trading scandal), refused to

cooperate. Nacchio based his decision on the fact that the NSA had not secured a warrant or submitted to other legal processes in requesting the data.

The ethical questions raised by this case prompted no shortage of opinions from executives, politicians, pundits, activists, and legal experts. The phone companies cited a strong belief in protecting the privacy of their customers but stated that the belief must co-exist with an obligation to cooperate with law enforcement and the government in matters of national security. A release from AT&T summed up the company's position as follows: "If and when AT&T is asked to help, we do so strictly within the law and under the most stringent conditions." Verizon made a similar statement but also declined to comment on having a connection to a "highly classified" national security plan. The company also indicated that press coverage of its data dealings contained factual errors.

After examining the issue, legal experts on both sides of it weighed in with their opinions on the actions taken by the phone companies. Lawmakers began to seek hearings on the matter almost immediately. Customers directed their anger and concern directly to customer support lines. Two lawyers in New Jersey filed a $5 billion suit against Verizon on behalf of the public accusing the company of violating privacy laws.

Some legal scholars and privacy advocates agree that the telecoms may have crossed the line. These experts cite the Electronic Privacy Act of 1986, which permits businesses to turn over calling data to the government only in extreme cases (for example, to protect individuals who are in immediate danger of being harmed). Creating a database from the records does not meet the criteria. James X. Dempsey of the Center for Democracy and Technology noted that the law allows for a minimum penalty of $1,000 per customer whose calling data were submitted to the government. Based on the number of records contributed to the NSA database, the phone companies faced civil penalties reaching hundreds of millions or possibly billions of dollars.

Dempsey shot down the idea that the phone companies did not break the law because the records they turned over included only phone numbers and not identifying information. According to Dempsey, the law does not specify that such personal information needs to be exchanged for the law to be broken. This was a popular position among critics of the NSA program. They asserted that phone numbers could easily be cross-referenced to personal information, such as names and addresses, using databases that are readily available to the public on the Internet.

A senior government official who spoke on condition of anonymity admitted that the NSA had access to most domestic telephone calls even though, according to Kate Martin of the Center for National Security Studies, the NSA would be prohibited by federal statutes from obtaining such data without judicial consent. The government official said that the scope of the program was small in the sense that the database was used only to track the communications of individuals who were known to have ties to terrorism.

The non-profit Electronic Frontier Foundation (EFF), a privacy watchdog, concurs with Martin's assessment. EFF supports its argument by referencing the Pen Register Statute, which prohibits the government from gathering calling data without a court order, and the Fourth Amendment, which covers privacy rights and unreasonable search and seizure. However, the impact of such a defense in court was unclear. In response to the wiretapping controversy of five months earlier, the Bush administration cited Article II of the Constitution as the derivation of its authority to employ wiretapping as a terror-fighting tool. Furthermore, Congress virtually wrote the President a blank check by empowering him to "use all necessary and appropriate force" in the war on terror.

It was not surprising that Congress had as much to say about the issue as anyone. Various senators weighed in both with opinions and calls for investigation. Opinions did not always fall along party lines.

Senator Dick Durbin, a Democrat from Illinois, believed that actions of the telephone companies put the privacy of American citizens at stake and that the companies should be compelled to appear before the Senate Judiciary Committee. Durbin was backed up by the chairman of that committee, Senator Arlen Specter, a Republican from Pennsylvania. Senator Specter intended to call upon executives from the participating companies to give their testimony about the NSA database program. House Majority Leader John Boehner of Ohio and Senator Lindsey Graham of South Carolina also crossed party lines in

questioning the necessity of such a program. Senator Graham asked, "The idea of collecting millions of thousands of phone numbers, how does that fit into following the enemy?"

Proponents of the program answer that question by saying that the purpose of the program is to discover patterns in the calling records that indicate the presence of terrorist activity. Intelligence analysts and commercial data miners refer to this as "link analysis," which is a technique for pulling meaningful patterns out of massive quantities of data. Defenders of the program were harshly critical of media outlets who exposed it. Representative Peter Hoekstra, a republican from Michigan and chairman of the House Intelligence Committee, insisted that reporting on the NSA's programs undermined national security. He stated, "Rather than allow our intelligence professionals to maintain a laser focus on the terrorists, we are once again mired in a debate about what our intelligence community may or may not be doing." President Bush echoed this sentiment by declaring that leaks of sensitive intelligence always hurt the government's ability to counter terrorism.

Republican Senator Jeff Sessions of Alabama also disputed the need to investigate the program. Senator Sessions answered the critics by emphasizing that the program did not involve actual surveillance of phone conversations and therefore did not merit the scrutiny it was receiving. In his statements, the president also went out of his way to distinguish between eavesdropping on telephone conversations and gathering call data.

In May 2006, senior intelligence officials revealed that the scope of the NSA's eavesdropping operations was strongly influenced by Vice President Dick Cheney and his office. The Vice President and his key legal adviser, David S. Addington, began pushing for surveillance of domestic phone calls and e-mails without warrants soon after September 11th. They believed that the Constitution gave the executive branch expansive powers that covered this type of domestic spying, as well as certain interrogation tactics for dealing with suspected terrorists. However, the NSA pushed back on advice from its own legal team. As a result, the NSA limited the eavesdropping to calls in which at least one participant was outside the United States.

Still, conducting such operations appeared to conflict with the 1978 Foreign Intelligence Surveillance Act (FISA), which required court authorization for any wiretapping done within the United

States. Nancy Libin of the Center for Democracy and Technology posits that listening in on any phone call without a warrant, regardless of whether it is domestic or international, is illegal according to FISA. However, while FISA covers wiretapping, it does not clearly prohibit the type of data mining was that done in the NSA database program.

In June 2006, a federal court in California released a document related to EFF's suit against AT&T that sheds light on how the phone company may have provided its data to the NSA. In the document, J. Scott Marcus, who had worked as a senior advisor for Internet technology to the Federal Communications Commission, evaluates evidence presented to EFF from a former AT&T technician named Mark Klein. Klein claimed that AT&T reconfigured its network in San Francisco and installed special computer systems in a secret room in order to divert and collect Internet traffic for use by the NSA. Marcus concluded that Klein's description of a private backbone network partitioned from AT&T's main Internet backbone was "not consistent with normal AT&T practice." Marcus further observed that at the time of the reconfiguration, AT&T was in poor shape financially and would have been very unlikely to have made such expensive infrastructure changes on its own.

In July 2006, Senator Specter announced that an agreement had been reached with the White House to give the Foreign Intelligence Surveillance Court the authority to review the constitutionality of the NSA's surveillance programs. The court would be empowered to determine whether wiretapping fell within the president's powers to fight the war on terrorism. The agreement allowed for the court's proceedings and rulings to be conducted in secret. Even though judicial oversight of the NSA's activities had been established, debate continued over the efficacy of the compromise. The American Civil Liberties Union and the ranking democrat on the House Intelligence Committee, Representative Jane Harman of California, accused Senator Specter of giving away too much, including a key Fourth Amendment protection.

The White House won several important points in the agreement, including the ability to appeal the court's decisions; changing the language so that submitting a program to the court was actually optional for the administration; and a guarantee that the agreement does not retract any of the president's existing constitutional authority. On the other hand, the lead judge on the court was known to have significant misgivings about the NSA's actions even before the program came to light. The bill to enact FISA's power over NSA wiretapping awaits Congressional approval.

Sources: Lauren Etter, "Is the Phone Company Violating Your Privacy?" *The Wall Street Journal*, May 13, 2006; Dionne Searcy, Amy Schatz, and Amol Sharma, "Phone Firms May Be On the Hook For Aiding U.S. Data-Mining Efforts," *The Wall Street Journal*, May 13, 2006; Eric Lichtblau and Scott Shane, "Bush Is Pressed Over New Report on Surveillance," *The New York Times*, May 11, 2006; "The Datamining Scare," *The Wall Street Journal*, May 13, 2006; Eric Lichtblau, "Bush Would Let Secret Court Sift Wiretap Process," *The New York Times*, July 14, 2006; Scott Shane and Eric Lichtblau, "Cheney Pushed U.S. to Widen Eavesdropping," *The New York Times*, May 14, 2006; "Deal Reached on Eavesdropping Program Oversight," CNN.com, July 13, 2006; John Markoff, "Questions Raised for Phone Giants in Spy Data Furor," *The New York Times*, May 13, 2006; Kim Zetter, "New Light on NSA Spying," Salon.com, June 23, 2006.

CASE STUDY QUESTIONS

1. Do the increased surveillance power and capability of the U.S. government present an ethical dilemma? Explain your answer.

2. Apply an ethical analysis to the issue of the U.S. government's use of telecommunications data to fight terrorism.

3. What are the ethical, social, and political issues raised by the U.S. government creating massive databases to collect the calling data of millions of Americans?

4. What is the responsibility of a business such as AT&T or Verizon in this matter? What are the ethical, social, and political issues raised by a business, such as a phone company, working with the government in this fashion?

5. State your opinion of the agreement reached by the White House and the Senate Judiciary Committee with regard to the NSA wiretapping program. Is this an effective solution?

IT Infrastructure and Emerging Technologies

From *Management Information Systems: Managing the Digital Firm, 10/e.* Kenneth C. Laudon, Jane P. Laudon.
Copyright © 2007 by Pearson Prentice Hall. All rights reserved.

IT Infrastructure and Emerging Technologies

Interactive Sessions:

Is It Time for Open-Source?

Application Service Providers: Two Tales

DREAMWORKS ANIMATION TURNS TO TECHNOLOGY FOR PRODUCTION SUPPORT

Can technology help DreamWorks Animation do better? Its management certainly sees it as a key factor in their success. It uses world-class creative talent and advanced computer technology to produce such successful computer-generated (CG) animated films as *Shrek, Shrek 2, Shark Tale,* and *Madagascar.* To date, *Shrek 2* is the third-highest-grossing movie ever, and the number one animated film of all time.

Nevertheless, DreamWorks has plenty of competition. Pixar Animation Studios, DreamWorks's archrival in computer animation, has prospered from a string of six blockbuster hits, including *The Incredibles, Finding Nemo,* and *Monsters, Inc.* Computer animation house Blue Sky Studios is another competitor, as is Disney. Sony Pictures Entertainment and Lucasfilm have also begun producing computer-animated films.

To gain an edge in this fiercely competitive market, DreamWorks Animation has set out to make entertaining films that appeal to all audiences, while leveraging the latest technology and finest talent available. With this strategy in mind, the company established a very ambitious production schedule that no other studio has ever tried before—the release of two animated movies per year. In order to meet this schedule, DreamWorks's staff often find themselves working on more than one movie at the same time, sharing technology among the various projects, and scaling up to work on multiple features.

How is DreamWorks able to make this happen? One of the solutions is to use the finest technology available. DreamWorks has implemented a high-speed network to link the powerful computers required for animation for three key animation pipelines, two in Los Angeles and one in Redwood City, California. A sophisticated video-teleconferencing system that projects nearly life-size images on the wall enables all three groups to collaborate as never before.

Additionally, DreamWorks animators use proprietary software developed in-house called EMO for nearly every stage of their work. In DreamWorks's *Madagascar,* this software enabled animators to adopt traditional "squash & stretch" techniques and place their characters in a digital environment. The software made each frame in *Madagascar* exquisitely detailed, right down to the animals' fur. According to the company's CEO Jeffrey Katzenberg, "Technically, we couldn't have made this movie a year ago."

DreamWorks Animation's management believes that its exclusive software and other technology infrastructure investments will not only pay off but also provide a strategic advantage. DreamWorks Animation's investments in technology are leveraged across all pipelines and all future films as well.

To render a CG film, DreamWorks technicians use a network of 2,700 Hewlett-Packard (HP) processors running the Linux operating system, which are organized to act as a single computer system

Photo courtesy of Kelvin Jones/DreamWorks

that is distributed among the company's studios and a HP research lab facility in Palo Alto, California.

At the end of the day, it takes approximately 400 artists, animators and technicians, over 200 characters modeled and surfaced, 15 terabytes of disk storage, 2,700 processors, over 10 million CPU rendering hours, and 18 months of core production to complete any one film. DreamWorks Animation has orchestrated its people, processes, and physical assets into an effective balance that produces world-class CG content effectively and efficiently.

Sources: Ed Leonard, "I.T. Gets Creative at Dreamworks," *Optimize Magazine,* April, 2006; Aaron Ricadela, "High-Tech Reveries," *Information Week,* May 23, 2005; www.dreamworksanimation.com, accessed September 29, 2005; and DreamWorks Animation, December 2, 2005.

DreamWorks Animation has an enviable track record in producing successful, high-quality CG animated films. But it also has a series of formidable competitors and a finicky mass audience to please. It was not as profitable as it could be. DreamWorks decided to outclass its competitors by investing heavily in computer hardware and software that increased animation quality and enabled it to produce animated films more rapidly. This case highlights the critical role that hardware and software investments can play in improving business performance and achieving strategic advantages by using information technology to create differentiated products more rapidly than competitors.

The chapter-opening diagram calls attention to important points raised by this case and this chapter. Computer-generated filmmaking requires an extraordinary amount of computing power and collaborative work. Management decided that investing in superior information technology would enable it to produce higher-quality animations and accelerate the pace at which films were produced.

1 IT INFRASTRUCTURE

We can define *information technology (IT) infrastructure* as the shared technology resources that provide the platform for the firm's specific information system applications. IT infrastructure includes investment in hardware, software, and services—such as consulting, education, and training—that are shared across the entire firm or across entire business units in the firm.

A firm's IT infrastructure provides the foundation for serving customers, working with vendors, and managing internal firm business processes (see Figure 1).

Supplying U.S. firms with IT infrastructure is a $1.8 trillion dollar industry when telecommunications, networking equipment, and telecommunications services (Internet, telephone, and data transmission) are included (Bureau of Economic Analysis, 2006). Investments in infrastructure account for between 25 and 35 percent of information technology expenditures in large firms (Weill et al., 2002).

DEFINING IT INFRASTRUCTURE

IT infrastructure consists of a set of physical devices and software applications that are required to operate the entire enterprise. But IT infrastructure is also a set of firmwide services budgeted by management and comprising both human and technical capabilities. These services include the following:

FIGURE 1   CONNECTION BETWEEN THE FIRM, IT INFRASTRUCTURE, AND BUSINESS CAPABILITIES

The services a firm is capable of providing to its customers, suppliers, and employees are a direct function of its IT infrastructure. Ideally, this infrastructure should support the firm's business and information systems strategy. New information technologies have a powerful impact on business and IT strategies, as well as the services that can be provided to customers.

- Computing platforms used to provide computing services that connect employees, customers, and suppliers into a coherent digital environment, including large mainframes, desktop and laptop computers, and personal digital assistants (PDAs) and Internet appliances.

- Telecommunications services that provide data, voice, and video connectivity to employees, customers, and suppliers.

- Data management services that store and manage corporate data and provide capabilities for analyzing the data.

- Application software services that provide enterprise-wide capabilities such as enterprise resource planning, customer relationship management, supply chain management, and knowledge management systems that are shared by all business units.

- Physical facilities management services that develop and manage the physical installations required for computing, telecommunications, and data management services.

- IT management services that plan and develop the infrastructure, coordinate with the business units for IT services, manage accounting for the IT expenditure, and provide project management services.

- IT standards services that provide the firm and its business units with policies that determine which information technology will be used, when, and how.

- IT education services that provide training in system use to employees and offer managers training in how to plan for and manage IT investments.

- IT research and development services that provide the firm with research on potential future IT projects and investments that could help the firm differentiate itself in the marketplace.

This "service platform" perspective makes it easier to understand the business value provided by infrastructure investments. For instance, the real business value of a fully loaded personal computer operating at 3 gigahertz that costs about $1,000 or a high-speed Internet connection is hard to understand without knowing who will use it and how it will be used. When we look at the services provided by these tools, however, their value becomes more apparent: The new PC makes it possible for a high-cost employee making $100,000 a year to connect to all the company's major systems and the public Internet. The high-speed Internet service saves this employee about one hour per day in reduced wait time for Internet information. Without this PC and Internet connection, the value of this one employee to the firm might be cut in half.

EVOLUTION OF IT INFRASTRUCTURE: 1950–2007

The IT infrastructure in organizations today is an outgrowth of over 50 years of evolution in computing platforms. We have identified five stages in this evolution, each representing a different configuration of computing power and infrastructure elements (see Figure 2). The five eras are electronic accounting machines, general-purpose mainframe and minicomputer computing, personal computers, client/server networks, and enterprise and Internet computing.

These eras do not necessarily end for all organizations at the same time, and the technologies that characterize one era may also be used in another time period for other purposes. For example, some companies still run traditional mainframe or minicomputer systems. Mainframe computers today are used as massive servers supporting large Web sites and corporate enterprise applications.

Electronic Accounting Machine Era: 1930–1950

The first era of business computing used specialized machines that could sort computer cards into bins, accumulate totals, and print reports (Columbia University, 2004). Although the electronic accounting machine was an efficient processor of accounting tasks, the machines were large and cumbersome. Software programs were hardwired into circuit boards, and they could be changed by altering the wired connections on a patch board. There were no programmers, and a human machine operator was the operating system, controlling all system resources.

General-Purpose Mainframe and Minicomputer Era: 1959 to Present

The first commercial all-electronic vacuum tube computers appeared in the early 1950s with the introduction of the UNIVAC computers and the IBM 700 Series. Not until 1959 with the introduction of the IBM 1401 and 7090 transistorized machines did widespread commercial use of **mainframe** computers begin in earnest. In 1965, the general-purpose commercial mainframe computer truly came into its own with the introduction of the IBM 360 series. The 360 was the first commercial computer with a powerful operating system that could provide time sharing, multitasking, and virtual memory in more advanced models.

Mainframe computers eventually became powerful enough to support thousands of online remote terminals connected to the centralized mainframe using proprietary communication protocols and proprietary data lines. The first airline reservation systems appeared in 1959 and became the prototypical

FIGURE 2   ERAS IN IT INFRASTRUCTURE EVOLUTION

Stages in IT Infrastructure Evolution

Illustrated here are the typical computing configurations characterizing each of the five eras of IT infrastructure evolution.

online, real-time interactive computing system that could scale to the size of an entire nation.

IBM dominated mainframe computing from 1965 onward and still dominates this $27 billion global market in 2007. Today, IBM mainframe systems can work with a wide variety of different manufacturers' computers and multiple operating systems on client/server networks and networks based on Internet technology standards.

The mainframe era was a period of highly centralized computing under the control of professional programmers and systems operators (usually in a corporate data center), with most elements of infrastructure provided by a single vendor, the manufacturer of the hardware and the software. This pattern began to change with the introduction of **minicomputers** produced by Digital Equipment Corporation (DEC) in 1965. DEC minicomputers (PDP-11 and later the VAX machines) offered powerful machines at far lower prices than IBM mainframes, making possible decentralized computing, customized to the specific needs of individual departments or business units rather than time sharing on a single huge mainframe.

Personal Computer Era: 1981 to Present

Although the first truly personal computers (PCs) appeared in the 1970s (the Xerox Alto, MIT's Altair, and the Apple I and II, to name a few), these machines had only limited distribution to computer enthusiasts. The appearance of the IBM PC in 1981 is usually considered the beginning of the PC era, because this machine was the first to be widely adopted by American businesses. At first using the DOS operating system, a text-based command language, and later the Microsoft Windows operating system, the **Wintel PC** computer (Windows operating system software on a computer with an Intel microprocessor) became the standard desktop personal computer. Today, 95 percent of the world's estimated 1 billion computers use the Wintel standard.

Proliferation of PCs in the 1980s and early 1990s launched a spate of personal desktop productivity software tools—word processors, spreadsheets, electronic presentation software, and small data management programs—that were very valuable to both home and corporate users. These PCs were standalone systems until PC operating system software in the 1990s made it possible to link them into networks.

Client/Server Era: 1983 to Present

In **client/server computing**, desktop or laptop computers called **clients** are networked to powerful **server** computers that provide the client computers with a variety of services and capabilities. Computer processing work is split between these two types of machines. The client is the user point of entry, whereas the server typically processes and stores shared data, serves up Web pages, or manages network activities. The term *server* refers to both the software application and the physical computer on which the network software runs. The server can be a mainframe, but today, server computers typically are more powerful versions of personal computers, based on inexpensive Intel chips and often using multiple processors in a single computer box.

The simplest client/server network consists of a client computer networked to a server computer, with processing split between the two types of machines. This is called a two-tiered client/server architecture. Whereas simple client/server networks can be found in small businesses, most corporations have more complex, **multitiered** (often called **N-tier**) **client/server architectures** in

181

FIGURE 3   A MULTITIERED CLIENT/SERVER NETWORK (N-TIER)

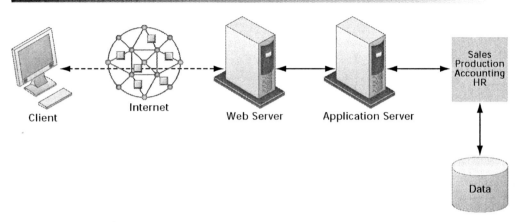

Client   Internet   Web Server   Application Server

Sales
Production
Accounting
HR

Data

In a multitiered client/server network, client requests for service are handled by different levels of servers.

which the work of the entire network is balanced over several different levels of servers, depending on the kind of service being requested (see Figure 3).

For instance, at the first level, a **Web server** serves a Web page to a client in response for a request for service. Web server software is responsible for locating and managing stored Web pages. If the client requests access to a corporate system (a product list or price information, for instance), the request is passed along to an **application server**. Application server software handles all application operations between a user and an organization's back-end business systems. The application server may reside on the same computer as the Web server or on its own dedicated computer.

Client/server computing enables businesses to distribute computing work across a series of smaller, inexpensive machines that cost much less than minicomputers or centralized mainframe systems. The result is an explosion in computing power and applications throughout the firm.

Novell NetWare was the leading technology for client/server networking at the beginning of the client/server era. Today, Microsoft is the market leader, with its **Windows** operating systems (Windows Server, Windows Vista, Windows XP, Windows 2000), dominating 78 percent of the local area network market. However, Linux is the fastest growing network operating system.

Enterprise Internet Computing Era: 1992 to Present

The success of the client/server model posed a new set of problems. Many large firms found it difficult to integrate all of their local area networks (LANs) into a single, coherent corporate computing environment. Applications developed by local departments and divisions in a firm, or in different geographic areas, could not communicate easily with one another and share data.

In the early 1990s, firms turned to networking standards and software tools that could integrate disparate networks and applications throughout the firm into an enterprise-wide infrastructure. As the Internet developed into a trusted communications environment after 1995, business firms began seriously using the *Transmission Control Protocol/Internet Protocol (TCP/IP)* networking standard to tie their disparate networks together.

The resulting IT infrastructure links different pieces of computer hardware and smaller networks into an enterprise-wide network so that information can flow freely across the organization and between the firm and other organizations. It can link different types of computer hardware, including mainframes, servers, PCs, mobile phones, and other handheld devices, and it includes public infrastructures such as the telephone system, the Internet, and public network services.

The enterprise infrastructure also requires software to link disparate applications and enable data to flow freely among different parts of the business. Other solutions for enterprise integration include enterprise application integration software, Web services, and outsourcing to external vendors that provide hardware and software for a comprehensive enterprise infrastructure. We discuss these solutions in detail in section 4.

The enterprise era promises to bring about a truly integrated computing and IT services platform for the management of global enterprises. The hope is to deliver critical business information painlessly and seamlessly to decision makers when and where they need it to create customer value. The reality is wrenchingly difficult because most firms have a huge tangled web of hardware systems and software applications inherited from the past. This makes achieving this level of enterprise integration a difficult, long-term process that can last perhaps as long as a decade and cost large companies hundreds of millions of dollars. Table 1 compares each era on the infrastructure dimensions introduced.

TECHNOLOGY DRIVERS OF INFRASTRUCTURE EVOLUTION

The changes in IT infrastructure we have just described have resulted from developments in computer processing, memory chips, storage devices, telecommunications and networking hardware and software, and software design that have exponentially increased computing power while exponentially reducing costs. Let's look at the most important developments.

Moore's Law and Microprocessing Power

In 1965, Gordon Moore, the director of Fairchild Semiconductor's Research and Development Laboratories, an early manufacturer of integrated circuits, wrote in *Electronics Magazine* that since the first microprocessor chip was introduced in 1959, the number of components on a chip with the smallest manufacturing costs per component (generally transistors) had doubled each year. This assertion became the foundation of **Moore's Law**. Moore later reduced the rate of growth to a doubling every two years (Tuomi, 2002).

This law would later be interpreted in multiple ways. There are at least three variations of Moore's Law, none of which Moore ever stated: (1) the power of microprocessors doubles every 18 months (Gates, 1997); (2) computing power doubles every 18 months; and (3) the price of computing falls by half every 18 months.

Figure 4 illustrates the relationship between number of transistors on a microprocessor and millions of instructions per second (MIPS), a common measure of processor power. Figure 5 shows the exponential decline in the cost of transistors and rise in computing power.

TABLE 1   STAGES IN THE IT INFRASTRUCTURE EVOLUTION

INFRASTRUCTURE DIMENSION	ELECTRONIC ACCOUNTING MACHINE ERA (1930–1950)	MAINFRAME ERA (1959 TO PRESENT)	PC ERA (1981 TO PRESENT)	CLIENT/SERVER ERA (1983 TO PRESENT)	ENTERPRISE ERA (1992 TO PRESENT)
Signature Firm(s)	IBM Burroughs NCR	IBM	Microsoft/Intel Dell HP IBM	Novell Microsoft	SAP Oracle PeopleSoft
Hardware Platform	Programmable card sorters	Centralized mainframe	Wintel computers	Wintel computers	Multiple: • Mainframe • Server • Client
Operating System	Human operators	IBM 360 IBM 370 Unix	DOS/Windows Linux IBM 390	Windows 3.1 Windows Server Linux	Multiple: • Unix/Linux • OS 390 • Windows Server
Application and Enterprise Software	None; application software created by technicians	Few enterprise-wide applications; departmental applications created by in-house programmers	No enterprise connectivity; boxed software	Few enterprise-wide applications; boxed software applications for workgroups and departments	Enterprise-wide applications linked to desktop and departmental applications: • mySAP • Oracle E-Business Suite
Networking/ Telecommunications	None	Vendor-provided: • Systems Network Architecture (IBM) • DECNET (Digital) • AT&T voice	None or limited	Novell NetWare Windows Server Linux AT&T voice	LAN Enterprise-wide area network (WAN) TCP/IP Internet standards-enabled
System Integration	Vendor-provided	Vendor-provided	None	Accounting and consulting firms Service firms	Software manufacturer Accounting and consulting firms System integration firms Service firms
Data Storage and Database Management	Physical card management	Magnetic storage Flat files Relational databases	DBase II and III Access	Multiple database servers with optical and magnetic storage	Enterprise database servers
Internet Platforms	None	Poor to none	None at first Later browser-enabled clients	None at first Later: • Apache server • Microsoft IIS	None in the early years Later: • Intranet- and Internet-delivered enterprise services • Large server farms

FIGURE 4   MOORE'S LAW AND MICROPROCESSOR PERFORMANCE

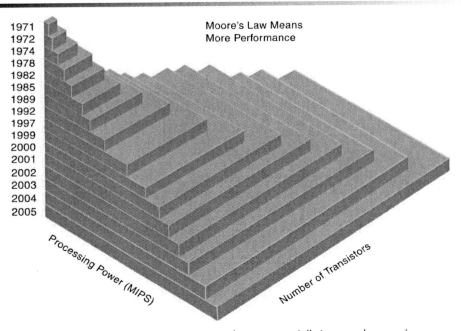

Packing more transistors into a tiny microprocessor has exponentially increased processing power.

Source: 2004 Intel Corporation; updated by the authors.

FIGURE 5   FALLING COST OF CHIPS

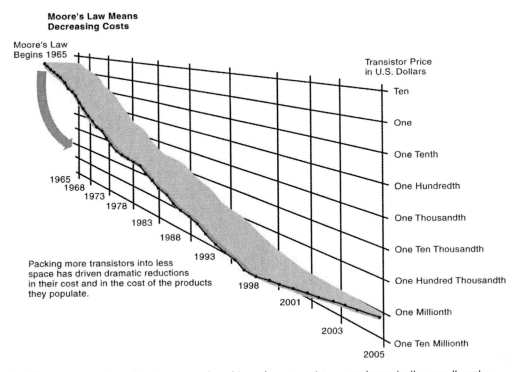

Packing more transistors into less space has driven down transistor cost dramatically as well as the cost of the products in which they are used. An Intel® processor today can contain as many as 1 billion transistors, run at 3.2 GHz and higher, deliver over 10,000 MIPS, and can be manufactured in high volumes with transistors that cost less than 1/10,000th of a cent. That's a little less than the cost of one printed character in this book.

Source: © 2004 Intel. All rights reserved.

There is reason to believe the exponential growth in the number of transistors and the power of processors coupled with an exponential decline in computing costs will continue into the future. Chip manufacturers continue to miniaturize components. Intel changed its manufacturing process from a 0.13-micron component size (a micron is a millionth of a meter), introduced in 2002, to a newer 90-nanometer process in 2004 (a nanometer is a billionth of a meter). Both IBM and Advanced Micro Devices (AMD), the other large manufacturers of processor chips, began producing 90-nanometer chips in 2006. With a size of about 50 nanometers, today's transistors should no longer be compared to the size of a human hair but rather to the size of a virus, the smallest form of organic life.

By using nanotechnology, Intel believes it can shrink the size of transistors down to the width of several atoms. **Nanotechnology** uses individual atoms and molecules to create computer chips and other devices that are thousands of times smaller than current technologies permit. IBM and other research labs have created transistors from nanotubes and other electrical devices and have developed a manufacturing process that could produce nanotube processors economically (Figure 6). Other new technologies include strained silicon, 300-millimeter production wafers (which decrease the costs of production), and denser interconnections among components.

Whereas the first Pentium microprocessors operated at 75 megahertz, today's Pentiums are available with close to 4-gigahertz speeds. However, increasing processor speeds at the same exponential rate as in the past may no longer be

FIGURE 6   EXAMPLES OF NANOTUBES

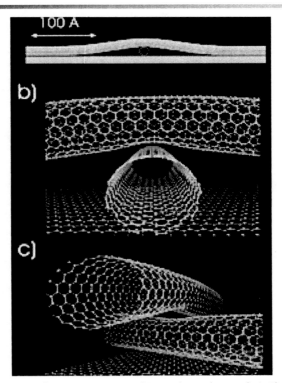

Nanotubes are tiny tubes about 10,000 times thinner than a human hair. They consist of rolled up sheets of carbon hexagons. Discovered in 1991 by researchers at NEC, they have the potential uses as minuscule wires or in ultrasmall electronic devices and are very powerful conductors of electrical current.

possible. As processor speeds increase, heat is generated that cannot be dissipated with air fans.

Another brake on future increases in microprocessor speed is consumer interest in low power consumption for longer battery life and low weight to increase laptop and handheld computer portability. For this reason, Intel and other firms are designing the next generation of chips to be less power hungry and lower in weight even if they are the same or even slower speeds. Other options include putting multiple processors on a single chip.

The Law of Mass Digital Storage

A second technology driver of IT infrastructure change is the Law of Mass Digital Storage. The world produces as much as 5 exabytes of unique information per year (an exabyte is a billion gigabytes, or 10^{18} bytes). The amount of digital information is roughly doubling every year (Lyman and Varian, 2003). Almost all of this information growth involves magnetic storage of digital data, and printed documents account for only 0.003 percent of the annual growth.

Fortunately, the cost of storing digital information is falling at an exponential rate. Figure 7 shows that PC hard drive capacity—beginning with a Seagate 506 in 1980 that had 5 megabytes of memory—has grown at a compound annual growth rate of 25 percent in the early years to over 60 percent a year since 1990. Today's PC hard drives have storage densities approaching 1 gigabyte per square inch and total capacities of over 500 gigabytes.

Figure 8 shows that the number of kilobytes that can be stored on magnetic disks for one dollar from 1950 to 2005 roughly doubled every 15 months.

Metcalfe's Law and Network Economics

Moore's Law and the Law of Mass Storage help us understand why computing resources are now so readily available. But why do people want more computing and storage power? The economics of networks and the growth of the Internet provide some answers.

FIGURE 7 **THE CAPACITY OF HARD DISK DRIVES GROWS EXPONENTIALLY 1980–2007**

From 1980 to 1990, hard disk drive capacities for PCs grew at the rate of 25 percent annual compound growth, but after 1990, growth accelerated to more than 65 percent each year.

FIGURE 8   THE COST OF STORING DATA DECLINES EXPONENTIALLY 1950–2005

Since the first magnetic storage device was used in 1955, the cost of storing a kilobyte of data has fallen exponentially, doubling the amount of digital storage for each dollar expended every 15 months on average.

© 2007 Kurzweill Technologies, Inc.

Source: Kurzweill, 2003; updated by the authors.

Robert Metcalfe—inventor of Ethernet LAN technology—claimed in 1970 that the value or power of a network grows exponentially as a function of the number of network members. Metcalfe and others point to the *increasing returns to scale* that network members receive as more and more people join the network. As the number of members in a network grows linearly, the value of the entire system grows exponentially and continues to grow forever as members increase. Demand for information technology has been driven by the social and business value of digital networks, which rapidly multiply the number of actual and potential links among network members.

Declining Communications Costs and the Internet

A fourth technology driver transforming IT infrastructure is the rapid decline in the costs of communication and the exponential growth in the size of the Internet. An estimated 1.1 billion people worldwide now have Internet access, with over 175 million of these in the United States. There are over 250 million Web host computers in the United States. Figure 9 illustrates the exponentially declining cost of communication both over the Internet and over telephone networks (which increasingly are based on the Internet). As communication costs fall toward a very small number and approach 0, utilization of communication and computing facilities explodes.

To take advantage of the business value associated with the Internet, firms must greatly expand their Internet connections, including wireless connectivity, and greatly expand the power of their client/server networks, desktop clients, and mobile computing devices. There is every reason to believe these trends will continue.

FIGURE 9   **EXPONENTIAL DECLINES IN INTERNET COMMUNICATIONS COSTS**

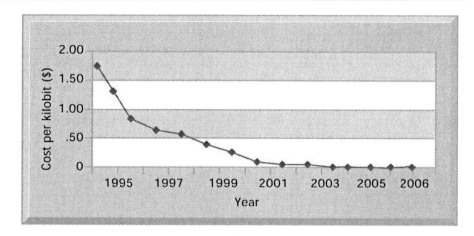

One reason for the growth in the Internet population is the rapid decline in Internet connection and overall communication costs. The cost per kilobit of Internet access has fallen exponentially since 1995. Digital Subscriber Line (DSL) and cable modems now deliver a kilobit of communication for a retail price of less than 2 cents.

Standards and Network Effects

Today's enterprise infrastructure and Internet computing would be impossible—both now and in the future—without agreements among manufacturers and widespread consumer acceptance of **technology standards**. Technology standards are specifications that establish the compatibility of products and the ability to communicate in a network (Stango, 2004).

Technology standards unleash powerful economies of scale and result in price declines as manufacturers focus on the products built to a single standard. Without these economies of scale, computing of any sort would be far more expensive than is currently the case. Table 2 describes just a few important standards that have shaped IT infrastructure. In fact, there are hundreds of standards besides those mentioned here, which are beyond the subject of this textbook.

Beginning in the 1990s, corporations started moving toward standard computing and communications platforms. The Wintel PC with the Windows operating system and Microsoft Office desktop productivity applications became the standard desktop and mobile client computing platform. Widespread adoption of Unix as the enterprise server operating system of choice made possible the replacement of proprietary and expensive mainframe infrastructure. In telecommunications, the Ethernet standard enabled PCs to connect together in small LANs, and the TCP/IP standard enabled these LANs to be connected into firmwide networks, and ultimately, to the Internet.

2   INFRASTRUCTURE COMPONENTS

IT infrastructure today is composed of seven major components. Figure 10 illustrates these infrastructure components and the major vendors within each component category. Table 3 describes the estimated overall spending on these infrastructure components in the United States for 2005. These components are

OME IMPORTANT STANDARDS IN COMPUTING

	SIGNIFICANCE
American Standard Code for Information Interchange (ASCII)(1958)	Made it possible for computer machines from different manufacturers to exchange data; later used as the universal language linking input and output devices such as keyboards and mice to computers. Adopted by the American National Standards Institute in 1963.
Common Business Oriented Language (COBOL) (1959)	An easy-to-use software language that greatly expanded the ability of programmers to write business-related programs and reduced the cost of software. Sponsored by the Defense Department in 1959.
Unix (1969–1975)	A powerful multitasking, multiuser, portable operating system initially developed at Bell Labs (1969) and later released for use by others (1975). It operates on a wide variety of computers from different manufacturers. Adopted by Sun, IBM, HP, and others in the 1980s and became the most widely used enterprise-level operating system.
Transmission Control Protocol/Internet Protocol (TCP/IP) (1974)	Suite of communications protocols and a common addressing scheme that enables millions of computers to connect together in one giant global network (the Internet). Later, it became the default networking protocol suite for local area networks and intranets. Developed in the early 1970s for the U.S. Department of Defense.
Ethernet (1973)	A network standard for connecting desktop computers into local area networks that enabled the widespread adoption of client/server computing and local area networks and further stimulated the adoption of personal computers.
IBM/Microsoft/Intel Personal Computer (1981)	The standard Wintel design for personal desktop computing based on standard Intel processors and other standard devices, Microsoft DOS, and later Windows software. The emergence of this standard, low-cost product laid the foundation for a 25-year period of explosive growth in computing throughout all organizations around the globe. Today, more than 1 billion PCs power business and government activities every day.
World Wide Web (1989–1993)	Standards for storing, retrieving, formatting, and displaying information as a worldwide web of electronic pages incorporating text, graphics, audio, and video enable the creation of a global repository of billions of Web pages.

investments that must be coordinated with one another to provide the firm with a coherent infrastructure.

In the past, technology vendors supplying these components were often in competition with one another, offering purchasing firms a mixture of incompatible, proprietary, partial solutions. But increasingly, the vendor firms have been forced by large customers to cooperate in strategic partnerships with one another. For instance, a hardware and services provider such as IBM cooperates with all the major enterprise software providers, has strategic relationships with system integrators (often accounting firms), and promises to work with whichever database products its client firms wish to use (even though it sells its own database management software called DB2). Let's examine the size and dynamics of each these infrastructure components and their markets.

COMPUTER HARDWARE PLATFORMS

U.S. firms spent about $145 billion in 2005 on computer hardware. This component includes client machines (desktop PCs, mobile computing devices such as PDAs and laptops) and server machines. The client machines use primarily Intel or AMD microprocessors. In 2005, 155 million PCs

FIGURE 10   THE IT INFRASTRUCTURE ECOSYSTEM

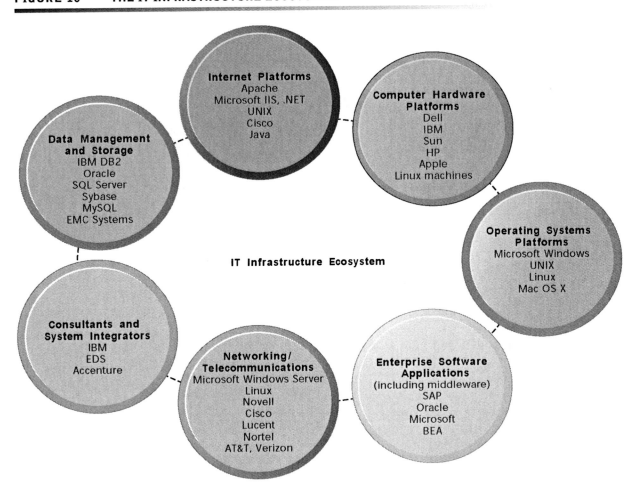

There are seven major components that must be coordinated to provide the firm with a coherent IT infrastructure. Listed here are major technologies and suppliers for each component.

TABLE 3   ESTIMATED SIZE OF U.S. INFRASTRUCTURE COMPONENTS, 2005

	EXPENDITURE ($ BILLIONS)	PERCENTAGE OF TOTAL
Computer hardware platforms	145	9%
Operating system platforms	110	7%
Enterprise and other IT software applications	297	19%
Database management and storage	42	3%
Networking and telecommunications equipment and services	769	50%
Internet platforms	35	2%
Consulting services and system integrators	130	9%
Total	1,528	

Sources: Author estimates; eMarketer, IT Spending and Trends, 2005; eMarketer, Telecom Spending, 2005.

A blade server is a thin, modular processing device that is intended for a single dedicated application (such as serving Web pages) that can be easily inserted into a space-saving rack with many similar servers.

were shipped to U.S. customers, and $30 billion was spent on clients (eMarketer, 2005).

The server market is more complex, using mostly Intel or AMD processors in the form of blade servers in racks, but also includes Sun SPARC microprocessors and IBM PowerPC chips specially designed for server use. **Blade servers** are ultrathin computers consisting of a circuit board with processors, memory, and network connections that are stored in racks. They take up less space than traditional box-based servers. Secondary storage may be provided by a hard drive in each blade server or by external, very large mass-storage drives.

The marketplace for computer hardware has increasingly become concentrated in top firms such as IBM, HP, Dell, and Sun Microsystems, which produce 90 percent of the machines, and three chip producers, Intel, AMD, and IBM, which account for over 90 percent of the processors sold in 2004. The industry has collectively settled on Intel as the standard processor, with major exceptions in the server market for Unix and Linux machines, which might use SUN or IBM Unix processors.

Mainframes have not disappeared. The mainframe market has actually grown steadily over the last decade, although the number of providers has dwindled to one: IBM. IBM has also repurposed its mainframe systems so they can be used as giant servers for massive enterprise networks and corporate Web sites. A single IBM mainframe can run up to 17,000 instances of Linux or Windows server software and is capable of replacing thousands of smaller blade servers

COMPUTER SOFTWARE PLATFORMS

In 2005, the U.S. market for **operating systems**, which manage the resources and activities of the computer, is expected to amount to $110 billion. At the client level, 95 percent of PCs and 45 percent of handheld devices use some form of Microsoft Windows operating system (such as Windows XP, Windows 2000, or Windows CE). In contrast, in the server marketplace, more than 85 percent of the corporate servers in the United States use some form of the **Unix** operating system or **Linux**, an inexpensive and robust open-source relative of Unix. Although Microsoft Windows Server 2003 is capable of providing enterprise-wide operating system and network services, it is generally not used when there are more than 3,000 client computers in a network.

Unix and Linux constitute the backbone of corporate infrastructure throughout much of the world because they are scalable, reliable, and much less expensive than mainframe operating systems. They can also run on many different types of processors. The major providers of Unix operating systems are IBM, HP, and Sun, each with slightly different and partially incompatible versions.

Although Windows continues to dominate the client marketplace, many corporations have begun to explore Linux as a low-cost desktop operating system provided by commercial vendors such as Red Hat. Linux is also available in free versions downloadable from the Internet as **open-source software**. Open-source software is described more fully later, but in essence it is software created and updated by a worldwide community of programmers and available for free.

Enterprise Software Applications

In addition to software for applications used by specific groups or business units, U.S. firms spent about $297 billion in 2005 on software. After telecommunications services, software is the largest single component of IT infrastructure. About $45 billion of the software budget will be spent on enterprise system software. The largest providers of enterprise application software are SAP and Oracle (which acquired PeopleSoft and many other smaller enterprise software firms in recent years). Also included in this category is middleware software supplied by vendors such as BEA for achieving firmwide integration by linking the firm's existing application systems. We describe both types of software in detail in section 4.

Microsoft is attempting to move into the lower ends of this market by focusing on small and medium-sized businesses. (There are over 35 million such businesses in the United States, and most have not yet implemented enterprise applications.) In general, most Fortune 500 large firms already have implemented enterprise applications and have developed long-term relationships with their providers. Once a firm decides to work with an enterprise vendor, switching can be difficult and costly, though not impossible.

DATA MANAGEMENT AND STORAGE

There are few choices for enterprise database management software, which is responsible for organizing and managing the firm's data so that it can be efficiently accessed and used. The leading database software providers are IBM (DB2), Oracle, Microsoft (SQL Server), and Sybase (Adaptive Server Enterprise), which supply more than 90 percent of the estimated $42 billion U.S. database management and storage marketplace. A growing new entrant is MySQL, a Linux open-source relational database product available for free on the Internet and increasingly supported by HP and others.

The physical data storage market is dominated by EMC Corporation for large-scale systems, and a small number of PC hard disk manufacturers led by Seagate, Maxtor, and Western Digital. In addition to traditional disk arrays and tape libraries, large firms are turning to network-based storage technologies. **Storage area networks (SANs)** connect multiple storage devices on a separate high-speed network dedicated to storage. The SAN creates a large central pool of storage that can be rapidly accessed and shared by multiple servers.

The amount of new digital information in the world is doubling every three years, driven in part by e-commerce and e-business and by statutes and regulations requiring firms to invest in extensive data storage and management facilities. Consequently, the market for digital data storage devices has been growing at more than 15 percent annually over the last five years.

NETWORKING/TELECOMMUNICATIONS PLATFORMS

U.S. firms spend a whopping $769 billon a year on networking and telecommunications hardware and services. The vast part of this budget, about $620 billion, is for telecommunications services (consisting mainly of telecommunications, cable, and telephone company charges for voice lines and Internet access; these are not included in this discussion but certainly could be counted as part of the firm's infrastructure). Windows Server is predominantly used as the local area network operating system, followed by Novell, Linux, and Unix. Large enterprise-wide area networks primarily use some variant of Unix. Nearly all local area networks, as well as wide area enterprise networks, use the TCP/IP protocol suite as a standard.

The leading networking hardware providers are Cisco, Lucent, Nortel, and Juniper Networks. Telecommunications platforms are typically provided by telecommunications/telephone services companies that offer voice and data connectivity, wide area networking, and Internet access. Leading telecommunications service vendors include MCI, AT&T, and regional telephone companies such as Verizon. This market is exploding with new providers of cellular wireless, Wi-Fi, and Internet telephone services.

INTERNET PLATFORMS

Internet platforms overlap with, and must relate to, the firm's general networking infrastructure and hardware and software platforms. U.S. firms spent an estimated $35 billion annually on Internet-related infrastructure. These expenditures were for hardware, software, and management services to support company Web sites, including Web hosting services, and for intranets and extranets. A **Web hosting service** maintains a large Web server, or series of servers, and provides fee-paying subscribers with space to maintain their Web sites. This category of technology expenditures is growing by approximately 10 percent per year.

The Internet revolution of the late 1990s led to a veritable explosion in server computers, with many firms collecting thousands of small servers to run their Internet operations. Since then there has been a steady push toward server consolidation, reducing the number of server computers by increasing the size and power of each. The Internet hardware server market has become increasingly concentrated in the hands of Dell, HP/Compaq, and IBM as prices have fallen dramatically.

The major Web software application development tools and suites are supplied by Microsoft (FrontPage and the Microsoft .NET family of development tools used to create Web sites using Active Server Pages for dynamic content), IBM's WebSphere line of Internet management tools, Sun (Sun's Java is the most widely used tool for developing interactive Web applications on both the server and client sides), and a host of independent software developers, including Macromedia/Adobe (Flash), media software (Real Media), and text tools (Adobe Acrobat).

CONSULTING AND SYSTEM INTEGRATION SERVICES

Although 20 years ago it might have been possible for a large firm to implement all its own IT infrastructure, today this is far less common. Even large firms do not have the staff, the skills, the budget, or the necessary experience to do so. Implementing new infrastructure requires significant changes in business processes and procedures, training and education, and software integration. For these reasons firms spend $130 billion a year on consulting services and system integrators.

Software integration means ensuring the new infrastructure works with the firm's older, so-called legacy systems and ensuring the new elements of the infrastructure work with one another. **Legacy systems** are generally older transaction processing systems created for mainframe computers that continue to be used to avoid the high cost of replacing or redesigning them. Replacing these systems is cost prohibitive and generally not necessary if these older systems can be integrated into a contemporary infrastructure.

Most companies in the past relied on their accounting firms to provide consulting and system integration services simply because the accounting firms were the only ones that truly understood a company's business processes and had the expertise to change its software. However, in the United States, accounting firms have been prohibited by law from providing these services and consequently have split off consulting services into separate entities, such as Accenture (formerly part of Arthur Andersen) and PwC Consulting (split off from the PricewaterhouseCoopers accounting firm and now part of IBM).

3 HARDWARE PLATFORM TRENDS AND EMERGING TECHNOLOGIES

Although the cost of computing has fallen exponentially, the cost of the IT infrastructure has actually expanded as a percentage of corporate budgets. Why? The costs of computing services (consulting, systems integration) and software are high, and the intensity of computing and communicating has increased as other costs have declined. For instance, employees now use much more sophisticated applications, requiring more powerful and expensive hardware of many different types (laptop, desktop, handheld, and tablet computers).

Firms face a number of other challenges. They need to integrate information stored in different applications, on different platforms (telephone, legacy systems, intranet, Internet sites, desktop, and mobile devices). Firms also need to build resilient infrastructures that can withstand huge increases in peak loads and routine assaults from hackers and viruses while conserving electrical power. Because customer and employee expectations for service are increasing, firms need to increase their service levels to meet customer demands. The trends in hardware and software platforms we now describe address some or all of these challenges.

THE INTEGRATION OF COMPUTING AND TELECOMMUNICATIONS PLATFORMS

Arguably the most dominant theme in hardware platforms today is the convergence of telecommunications and computing platforms to the point where, increasingly, computing takes place over the network. You can see this convergence at several levels.

At the client level, communication devices such as cell phones are taking on functions of handheld computers, whereas handheld PDAs are taking on cell phone functions. For instance, the Palm Treo 700w digital handheld integrates phone, camera, digital music player, and handheld computer in one device. High-end cell phones come equipped for downloading music and video clips and for playing 3-D games. Television, radio, and video are moving toward all-digital production and distribution. There is little doubt that personal computers of some sort will be the core of the home entertainment center and the mobile personal entertainment center of the next five years as a storage device and operating system.

At the server and network level, the growing success of Internet telephone systems (now the fastest-growing type of telephone service) demonstrates how historically separate telecommunications and computing platforms are converging toward a single network—the Internet.

Other major trends in hardware platforms described here are based in large part on computing over high-capacity networks. The network in many respects is becoming the source of computing power, enabling business firms to expand their computing power greatly at very little cost.

GRID COMPUTING

Grid computing involves connecting geographically remote computers into a single network to create a virtual supercomputer by combining the computational power of all computers on the grid. Grid computing takes advantage of the fact that most computers in the United States use their central processing units on average only 25 percent of the time for the work they have been assigned, leaving these idle resources available for other processing tasks. Grid computing was impossible until high-speed Internet connections enabled firms to connect remote machines economically and move enormous quantities of data.

The Palm Treo 700w combines a mobile phone, e-mail, messaging, personal organizer, Web access, digital camera, video recorder, and digital music player all in one device. Convergence of computing and communications technologies have turned cell phones into mobile computing platforms.

Photo courtesy of Jae C. Hong/AP Wide World Photos

Grid computing requires software programs to control and allocate resources on the grid, such as open-source software provided by Globus Alliance (www.globus.org) or private providers. Client software communicates with a server software application. The server software breaks data and application code into chunks that are then parceled out to the grid's machines. The client machines can perform their traditional tasks while running grid applications in the background.

The business case for using grid computing involves cost savings, speed of computation, and agility. For example, Royal Dutch/Shell Group is using a scalable grid computing platform that improves the accuracy and speed of its scientific modeling applications to find the best oil reservoirs. This platform, which links 1,024 IBM servers running Linux, in effect creates one of the largest commercial Linux supercomputers in the world. The grid adjusts to accommodate the fluctuating data volumes that are typical in this seasonal business. Royal Dutch/Shell Group claims the grid has enabled the company to cut processing time for seismic data, while improving output quality and helping its scientists pinpoint problems in finding new oil supplies.

ON-DEMAND COMPUTING (UTILITY COMPUTING)

On-demand computing refers to firms off-loading peak demand for computing power to remote, large-scale data processing centers. In this manner, firms can reduce their investment in IT infrastructure by investing just enough to handle average processing loads and paying for only as much additional computing power as the market demands. Another term for on-demand computing is **utility computing**, which suggests that firms purchase computing power from central computing utilities and pay only for the amount of computing power they use, much as they would pay for electricity. IBM, HP, Oracle, and Sun Microsystems all offer utility computing services on demand.

In addition to lowering the cost of owning hardware resources, on-demand computing gives firms greater agility to use technology, and greatly reduces the risk of over-investing in IT infrastructure. On-demand computing shifts firms from having a fixed infrastructure capacity toward a highly flexible infrastructure, some of it owned by the firm, and some of it rented from giant computer centers owned by computer hardware vendors. This arrangement frees firms to launch entirely new business processes that they would never attempt with a fixed infrastructure.

DreamWorks, described in the chapter-opening case, has used HP utility computing services for about four years. The company's demand for computing resources is cyclical and tied to events such as tight production deadlines for new films. Rather than purchase additional infrastructure to handle this peak load, DreamWorks rents this capacity when it needs from HP. (Krazit, 2005).

AUTONOMIC COMPUTING AND EDGE COMPUTING

Computer systems have become so complex today that some experts believe they may not be manageable in the future. With operating systems, enterprise, and database software weighing in at millions of lines of code, and large systems encompassing many thousands of networked devices, the problem of managing these systems looms very large (Kephardt and Chess, 2003).

It is estimated that one-third to one-half of a company's total IT budget is spent preventing or recovering from system crashes. About 40 percent of these crashes are caused by operator error. The reason is not because operators are not well trained or do not have the right capabilities. Rather, it is because the complexities of today's computer systems are too difficult to understand, and IT operators and managers are under pressure to make decisions about problems in seconds.

One approach to dealing with this problem from a computer hardware perspective is to employ autonomic computing. **Autonomic computing** is an industry-wide effort to develop systems that can configure themselves, optimize and tune themselves, heal themselves when broken, and protect themselves from outside intruders and self-destruction. Imagine, for instance, a desktop PC that could know it was invaded by a computer virus. Instead of blindly allowing the virus to invade, the PC would identify and eradicate the virus or, alternatively, turn its workload over to another processor and shut itself down before the virus destroyed any files. Table 4 describes the dimensions of autonomic computing.

A few of these capabilities are present in desktop operating systems. For instance, virus and firewall protection software can detect viruses on PCs, automatically defeat the viruses, and alert operators. These programs can be updated automatically as the need arises by connecting to an online virus protection service such as McAfee. IBM and other vendors are starting to build autonomic features into products for large systems (IBM, 2005).

Edge Computing

Edge computing is a multitier, load-balancing scheme for Web-based applications in which significant parts of Web site content, logic, and processing are performed by smaller, less-expensive servers located nearby the user in order to increase response time and resilience while lowering technology costs. In this sense, edge computing is another technique like grid computing and on-demand computing for using the Internet to share the workload experienced by a firm across many computers located remotely on the network.

Figure 11 illustrates the components of edge computing. There are three tiers in edge computing: the local client; the nearby edge computing platform, which consists of servers positioned at any of the 5,000-plus Internet service providers in the United States; and enterprise computers located at the firm's

TABLE 4   FOUR ASPECTS OF SELF-MANAGEMENT AS THEY ARE NOW AND WOULD BE WITH AUTONOMIC COMPUTING

CONCEPT	CURRENT COMPUTING	AUTONOMIC COMPUTING
Self-configuration	Corporate data centers have multiple vendors and and platforms. Installing, configuring, and integrating systems is time-consuming and error prone.	Automated configuration of components and systems follows high-level policies. Rest of system adjusts automatically and seamlessly.
Self-optimization	Systems have hundreds of manually set, nonlinear tuning parameters, and their number increases with each release.	Components and systems continually seek opportunities to improve their own performance and efficiency.
Self-healing	Problem determination in large, complex systems can take a team of programmers weeks.	System automatically detects, diagnoses, and repairs localized software and hardware problems.
Self-protection	Detection of and recovery from attacks and cascading failures is manual.	System automatically defends against malicious attacks or cascading failures. It uses early warning to anticipate and prevent systemwide failures.

FIGURE 11   EDGE COMPUTING PLATFORM

Edge computing involves the use of the Internet to balance the processing load of enterprise platforms across the client and edge computing platform.

main data center. The edge computing platform is owned by a service firm such as Akamai, which employs about 15,000 edge servers around the United States.

In an edge platform application, requests from the user client computer are initially processed by the edge servers. Presentation components such as static Web page content, reusable code fragments, and interactive elements gathered on forms are delivered by the edge server to the client. Database and business logic elements are delivered by the enterprise computing platform.

VIRTUALIZATION AND MULTICORE PROCESSORS

As companies deploy hundreds or thousands of servers, many have discovered that they are spending more on electricity to power and cool their systems than they did on acquiring the hardware. The average annual utility cost for a 100,000-square-foot data center has reached $5.9 million (Dunn, 2005). Google is building a new data center in Oregon in part because electricity costs are far cheaper there than other parts of the country. Cutting power consumption in data centers is now a priority for most CIOs.

One way of curbing hardware proliferation and power consumption is to use virtualization to reduce the number of computers required for processing. **Virtualization** is the process of presenting a set of computing resources (such as computing power or data storage) so that they can all be accessed in ways that are not restricted by physical configuration or geographic location. Server virtualization enables companies to run more than one operating system at the same time on a single machine. Most servers run at just 10 to 15 percent of capacity, and virtualization can boost server utilization rates to 70 percent or

199

higher. Higher utilization rates translate into fewer computers required to process the same amount of work.

For example, Denver Health and Hospital Authority servers mushroomed from 10 in 1996 to 220 in 2005, with server utilization rates averaging below 20 percent and 90 percent of the servers running a single application. The health care organization used virtualization to consolidate the work of 15 physical servers onto two machines running 15 virtual servers.

Server virtualization software runs between the operating system and the hardware, masking server resources, including the number and identity of physical servers, processors, and operating systems, from server users. VMware is the leading server virtualization software vendor for Windows and Linux systems. Microsoft offers its own Virtual Server product and has built virtualization capabilities into the newest version of Windows Server.

In addition to reducing hardware and power expenditures, virtualization allows businesses to run their legacy applications on older versions of an operating system on the same server as newer applications. Virtualization also facilitates centralization of hardware administration.

Multicore Processors

Another way to reduce power requirements and hardware sprawl is to use multicore processors. A **multicore processor** is an integrated circuit that contains two or more processors. In the past, chip makers increased the speed of processors by increasing their frequency, from a few megahertz to today's chips which operate at gigahertz frequencies. But this strategy increased both heat and power consumption to the point where very high gigahertz chips require water cooling. Dual core processors combine two or more slower processors in a single chip. This technology enables two processing engines with reduced power requirements and heat dissipation to perform tasks faster than a resource-hungry chip with a single processing core.

Intel and AMD now make dual-core microprocessors and are introducing quad-core processors. Sun Microsystems sells servers using its eight-core UltraSparc T1 processor.

The Tokyo Institute of Technology used dual-core processors to create the largest supercomputer in Japan. Using single-core processors would have required a data center that was twice as large as the Institute's current facility and would have generated nearly twice the heat. The dual-core implementation required half as many servers as the single-core approach and is less costly to maintain because there are fewer systems to monitor.

4 SOFTWARE PLATFORM TRENDS AND EMERGING TECHNOLOGIES

There are six major themes in contemporary software platform evolution:

- Linux and open-source software
- Java
- Enterprise software
- Web services and service-oriented architecture
- Mashups and Web-based software applications
- Software outsourcing

THE RISE OF LINUX AND OPEN-SOURCE SOFTWARE

Open-source software is software produced by a community of several hundred thousand programmers around the world. According to the leading open-source professional association, OpenSource.org, open-source software is free and can be modified by users. Works derived from the original code must also be free, and the software can be redistributed by the user without additional licensing. Open-source software is by definition not restricted to any specific operating system or hardware technology, although most open-source software is currently based on a Linux or Unix operating system (opensource.org, 2006).

Open-source software is based on the premise that it is superior to commercially produced proprietary software because thousands of programmers around the world working for no pay can read, perfect, distribute, and modify the source code much faster, and with more reliable results, than small teams of programmers working for a single software company.

Although it may seem that contributors to open-source software receive nothing in return, in fact they receive respect, prestige, and access to a network of knowledgeable programmers. Open-source contributors are dedicated professionals who have a well-defined organizational structure and set of procedures for getting the work done. The open-source movement has been evolving for more than 30 years and has demonstrated after many years of effort that it can produce commercially acceptable, high-quality software.

Now thousands of open-source programs are available from hundreds of Web sites. The range of open-source software extends from operating systems to desktop productivity suites, Web browsers, and games. Major hardware and software vendors, including IBM, Hewlett-Packard, Dell, Oracle, and SAP, now offer Linux-compatible versions of their products. You can find out more out more about the Open Source Definition from the Open Source Initiative and the history of open-source software at the Learning Tracks for this chapter.

Linux

Perhaps the most well-known open-source software is Linux, an operating system derived from Unix. Linux was created by the Finnish programmer Linus Torvalds and first posted on the Internet in August 1991. Linux is now the world's fastest-growing client and server operating system. In the United States Linux was installed in nearly 6 percent of new shipments of PCs in 2005, and this number is expected to grow to over 20 percent of new PC shipments by 2010 (Bulkeley, 2004). In Russia and China, over 40 percent of new PCs are shipped with Linux although in part this reflects a very high percentage of users who install pirated editions of Microsoft Windows on much less expensive Linux PCs.

Applications for the Linux operating system are rapidly growing also. Many of these applications are embedded in cell phones, PDAs, and other handheld devices. Although Linux is currently a small but rapidly growing presence on the desktop, it plays a major role in the back office running Web servers and local area networks. In the $50.9 billion U.S. server market, Linux is the most rapidly growing LAN server, with a current 23 percent market share, up from 1 percent in 1998.

IBM, HP, Intel, Dell, and Sun have made Linux a central part of their offerings to corporations. More than two dozen countries in Asia, Europe, and Latin America have adopted open-source software and Linux. Cost is a major driver, as discussed in the Interactive Session on Technology, as are reliability and flexibility. However the benefits are not always automatic, and managers

INTERACTIVE SESSION: TECHNOLOGY

IS IT TIME FOR OPEN-SOURCE?

During the late 1990s when E*Trade Financial's trading volume was mushrooming, the online trading company managed this growth by adding capacity in the form of large servers from Sun Microsystems running Sun Solaris, Sun's proprietary version of Unix. By the fall of 2001 the stock market was cooling, and trading volumes—and E*Trade's cash flow—dropped precipitously. The company decided to switch to Linux running on inexpensive Intel processor-based IBM x335 servers to rein in costs.

Preliminary tests running E*Trade's authentication, quote services, product services, and trading service applications on Linux showed that each Linux server could handle about 180 users at a time, compared to 300 to 400 users simultaneously on one of E*Trade's Sun 4500 servers. More than 180 users degraded performance, but with 180 users or fewer, the Linux server performed faster than the Sun server. The cost of a Sun 4500 server was about $250,000. Even though each Linux computer could only handle 180 users at a time, it only cost $4,000. E*Trade merely needed to purchase two Linux computers at a total cost of $8,000 to provide the same processing capabilities for 400 users as the expensive Sun machine.

Switching to Linux was a very easy decision to make. Using the open-source operating system on small inexpensive servers saves E*Trade $13 million annually while increasing computer performance. E*Trade's Sun servers were reallocated, retired, or sold to other companies.

Another obvious benefit of open-source is access to source code that companies can use to integrate Linux with their existing business applications and improve it for their purposes. Siegenia-Aubi KG, a German maker of windows, doors, and ventilating equipment, replaced the Windows operating system on its Compaq servers with Linux to run mySAP customer relationship management software, and the open-source Apache Web server and MySQL database software. Being able to manipulate Linux source code makes it easier to integrate with business applications the company uses. Linux is also more reliable than Windows, at least according to its supporters. The company had to reboot its Compaq servers every two weeks when they were running Windows because the operating system malfunctioned. Siegenia-Aubi is now trying to move more of its business systems to Linux.

Against these benefits, managers must weigh the issues and challenges that accompany the incorporation of open-source into an IT infrastructure. Arguably, a successful open-source deployment requires more expenditures on support and maintenance because the Linux tool set is not as well developed at that for Microsoft Windows Server, and the skills required of support staff are more esoteric and more expensive. If companies do not have access to resources that can provide support inexpensively, they may negate the advantages they gained by adopting open-source. Larry Kinder, CIO of Cendant, reflects, "You're always weighing the value of having a company like Microsoft behind you or relying on an open-source community you have no control over." If you're a large Microsoft Fortune 1000 user and you have a problem with Microsoft products, Microsoft can supply an army of support technicians to solve your problem often free of charge. The same cannot be said of Red Hat Linux, or free Linux downloaded from the Web.

Kamal Nasser, vice president of IT strategy for Nielsen Media Research, notes that adoption of Linux at his company has not progressed freely because the knowledge base of the IT staff is Sun Solaris. Florian Kainz, computer graphics principal engineer at Industrial Light & Magic, asserts that companies migrating from Unix to Linux are more likely to have better results than companies migrating from Windows because the technical support skills for Unix and Linux are similar. Vendors of open-source applications can provide support but may be stymied if customers have altered program code and created problems whose origins cannot be easily uncovered.

Communities that develop open-source applications are decentralized and unregulated. When an upgrade is released, mission-critical features may have disappeared without warning because the developers determined they lacked value.

The undefined structure of the development community also exposes companies to legal issues that they do not confront when using commercial applications. Large businesses fear that intellectual property lawsuits could result from using a product built by, in some cases, thousands of people across the globe who may claim ownership. License agreements for open-source do not always grant complete freedom for distributing and modifying code. Yahoo! and United Parcel Service (UPS), major adopters of Linux servers, both scrutinize and manage the usage rights and licenses of the open-source software they deploy.

Companies also need to ensure that the open-source offerings will fit into their operating environments. Most companies are not ripping out the commercial software in which they have invested quite heavily. For example, Yahoo! uses open-source to create and support the services that

its users are most drawn to, such as e-mail and Web page templates. However, Yahoo! has no plans to abandon the commercial applications that run its search technology, customer billing, and online ads. UPS, however, expects to run all of the traffic on UPS.com through Linux servers.

Sources: Jason Brooks, "Into the Great Wide Open," *eWeek Innovations*, Summer 2006; Larry Greenmeier, "Open Source Goes Corporate," *Information Week*, September 26, 2005; Laurie Sullivan, "Apps Migrate to Open Source," *Information Week*, September 5, 2005.

CASE STUDY QUESTIONS

1. What problems do Linux and other open-source software address? How does open-source software help solve these problems?
2. What issues and challenges do open-source software present? What can be done to address these issues?
3. What are the business as well as the technology issues that should be addressed when deciding whether to use open-source software?

MIS IN ACTION

Use the Web to research the cost of the Microsoft Office desktop productivity software and to identify comparable open-source software.

1. List and briefly describe the open-source spreadsheet programs, database, and word processing programs that compete with Microsoft Office software.
2. Create a table comparing the prices of traditional and open-source for each category of software.
3. Would you adopt the open-source software instead of Microsoft Office? Why or why not? On what criteria did you base your decision?

need to carefully assess whether open-source software will meet their business and computing requirements.

The rise of open-source software, particularly Linux and the applications it supports, has profound implications for corporate software platforms: cost reduction, reliability and resilience, and integration, because Linux works on all the major hardware platforms from mainframes to servers to clients. Linux has the potential to break Microsoft's monopoly of the desktop. Sun's StarOffice has an inexpensive Linux-based version that competes with Microsoft's Office productivity suite. And Web-based office applications now promoted by Google (discussed later in this chapter) that do not require a Windows operating system will offer Microsoft some competition in the coming years. However, the transition to open source, and Web-based office applications, will take many years because of the sunk costs of billions of spreadsheets, Word documents, and PowerPoint presentations, which cannot be easily converted to open-source office productivity suites.

JAVA IS EVERYWHERE

Java is an operating system–independent, processor-independent, object-oriented programming language that has become the leading interactive programming environment for the Web. If an object moves on the Web or takes input from the user, a Java applet is likely behind it.

Java was created by James Gosling and the Green Team at Sun Microsystems in 1992 as a programming environment to support interactive cable television content delivery. Widespread use of Java began in 1995 when large numbers of people started using the World Wide Web and Internet. Nearly all Web browsers come with a Java platform built in. More recently, the Java platform has migrated into cellular phones, automobiles, music players, game machines, and finally, into set-top cable television systems serving interactive content and pay-per-view services.

Java software is designed to run on any computer or computing device, regardless of the specific microprocessor or operating system the device uses. A Macintosh PC, an IBM PC running Windows, a Sun server running Unix, and even a smart cellular phone or PDA can share the same Java application. For each of the computing environments in which Java is used, Sun has created a Java Virtual Machine that interprets Java programming code for that machine. In this manner, the code is written once and can be used on any machine for which there exists a Java Virtual Machine.

Java is particularly useful in network environments such as the Internet. Here, Java is used to create miniature programs called applets that are designed to reside on centralized network servers. The network delivers to client computers only the applets required for a specific function. With Java applets residing on a network, a user can download only the software functions and data that he or she needs to perform a particular task, such as analyzing the revenue from one sales territory. The user does not need to maintain large software programs or data files on his or her desktop machine.

Java is also a very robust language that can handle text, data, graphics, sound, and video, all within one program if needed. Java enables PC users to manipulate data on networked systems using Web browsers, reducing the need to write specialized software. A **Web browser** is an easy-to-use software tool with a graphical user interface for displaying Web pages and for accessing the Web and other Internet resources. Microsoft's Internet Explorer, Mozilla Firefox, and Netscape Browser are examples. At the enterprise level, Java is being used for more complex e-commerce and e-business applications that require communication with an organization's back-end transaction processing systems.

The rapid deployment of Java was hindered in the past because of disagreements between Sun Microsystems and Microsoft over Java standards. In April 2004, under pressure from major customers such as General Motors, Microsoft agreed to stop distributing the Microsoft Java Virtual Machine (MSJVM) it had developed for its proprietary version of Java and to cooperate with Sun in the development of new technologies, including Java.

SOFTWARE FOR ENTERPRISE INTEGRATION

Without doubt, the single most urgent software priority for U.S. firms is integration of existing legacy software applications with newer Web-based applications into a coherent single system that can be rationally managed. In the past, business firms typically built their own custom software and made their own choices about their software platform. This strategy produced hundreds of thousands of computer programs that frequently could not communicate with other software programs, were difficult and expensive to maintain, and were nearly impossible to change quickly as business models changed.

One solution is to replace isolated systems that cannot communicate with enterprise applications for customer relationship management, supply chain management, knowledge management, and enterprise systems, which integrate multiple business processes.

Not all firms can jettison all of their legacy systems to convert to enterprise-wide platforms. These existing legacy mainframe applications are essential to daily operations and are very risky to change, but they can become more useful if their information and business logic can be integrated with other applications.

Some integration of legacy applications can be achieved by using special software called middleware to create an interface or bridge between two different systems. **Middleware** is software that connects two otherwise separate applications, enabling them to communicate with each other and to exchange data.

Firms may choose to write their own software to connect one application to another, but increasingly they are purchasing **enterprise application integration (EAI) software** packages for this purpose to connect disparate applications or application clusters. This software enables multiple systems to exchange data through a single software hub rather than building countless custom software interfaces to link each system (see Figure 12). WebMethods, Tibco, SeeBeyond, BEA, and Vitria are leading enterprise application software vendors.

Web Services and Service-Oriented Architecture (SOA)

Enterprise application integration software tools are product specific, meaning that they can work only with certain pieces of application software and operating systems. For example, one EAI tool to connect a specific piece of sales order entry software to manufacturing, shipping, and billing applications might not work with another vendor's order entry software. A middleware program developed by BEA systems, a large systems integrator, may not be able to communicate with another vendors middleware application that you purchased in previous years without a large expenditure of programming and design resources. Web services seek to provide a standardized alternative for

FIGURE 12   ENTERPRISE APPLICATION INTEGRATION (EAI) SOFTWARE VERSUS TRADITIONAL INTEGRATION

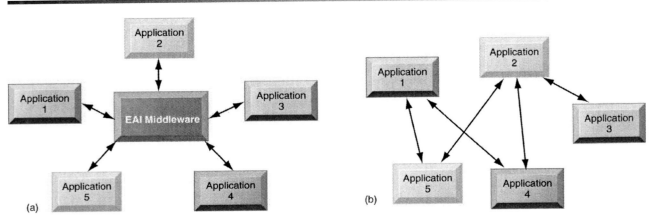

EAI software (a) uses special middleware that creates a common platform with which all applications can freely communicate with each other. EAI requires much less programming than traditional point-to-point integration (b).

dealing with integration problems like these by creating a communications environment that is vendor neutral.

Web services refer to a set of loosely coupled software components that exchange information with each other using standard Web communication standards and languages. They can exchange information between two different systems regardless of the operating systems or programming languages on which the systems are based. They can be fused to build open standard Web-based applications linking systems of two different organizations, and they can also be used to create applications that link disparate systems within a single company. Web services are not tied to any one operating system or programming language, and different applications can use them to communicate with each other in a standard way without time-consuming custom coding.

The foundation technology for Web services is **XML**, which stands for **Extensible Markup Language**. This language was developed in 1996 by the World Wide Web Consortium (W3C, the international body that oversees the development of the Web) as a more powerful and flexible markup language than Hypertext Markup Language for Web pages. **Hypertext Markup Language (HTML)** is a page description language for specifying how text, graphics, video, and sound are placed on a Web page document. Whereas HTML is limited to describing how data should be presented in the form of Web pages, XML can perform presentation, communication, and storage of data. In XML, a number is not simply a number; the XML tag specifies whether the number represents a price, a date, or a ZIP code. Table 5 illustrates some sample XML statements.

By tagging selected elements of the content of documents for their meanings, XML makes it possible for computers to manipulate and interpret their data automatically and perform operations on the data without human intervention. Web browsers and computer programs, such as order processing or enterprise resource planning (ERP) software, can follow programmed rules for applying and displaying the data. XML provides a standard format for data exchange, enabling Web services to pass data from one process to another.

Web services communicate through XML messages over standard Web protocols. **SOAP**, which stands for **Simple Object Access Protocol**, is a set of rules for structuring messages that enables applications to pass data and instructions to one another. **WSDL** stands for **Web Services Description Language**; it is a common framework for describing the tasks performed by a Web service and the commands and data it will accept so that it can be used by other applications. **UDDI**, which stands for **Universal Description, Discovery, and Integration**, enables a Web service to be listed in a directory of Web services so that it can be easily located. Companies discover and locate Web services through this directory much as they would locate services in the yellow pages of a telephone book. Using these protocols, a software application can connect freely to other

TABLE 5   EXAMPLES OF XML

PLAIN ENGLISH	XML
Subcompact	<AUTOMOBILETYPE="Subcompact">
4 passenger	<PASSENGERUNIT="PASS">4</PASSENGER>
$16,800	<PRICE CURRENCY="USD">16,800</PRICE>

applications without custom programming for each different application with which it wants to communicate. Everyone shares the same standards.

The collection of Web services that are used to build a firm's software systems constitutes what is known as a service-oriented architecture. A **service-oriented architecture (SOA)** is set of self-contained services that communicate with each other to create a working software application. Business tasks are accomplished by executing a series of these services. Software developers reuse these services in other combinations to assemble other applications as needed. In other words, SOA is an entirely new way of developing software for a firm. In the past, firms used to build software applications to serve a specific purpose, like calculate invoices and send out printed invoices. Often, there would be multiple programs that performed parts of or all of a task but used different code to accomplish their objectives. None of the programs could talk to each other.

In an SOA environment, it's different. For example, an "invoice service" can be written that is the only program in the firm responsible for calculating invoice information and reports. Whenever a different program in the firm needed invoice information, it would make use of this pre-defined, single invoice service.

If you want to see SOA at work in a single firm, go to Amazon.com for a demonstration. Amazon uses SOA to create a sales platform with 55 million active customers, and more than one million retail partners worldwide. Up to 2001, Amazon ran a monolithic application on a Web server that created the customer interface, the vendor interface, and a catalog that operated on a single database in the backend. By 2001, this approach could not scale up, was very inflexible, and vulnerable to failures at critical points. Today, Amazon's operation is a collection of hundreds of services delivered by a number of application servers that provide the customer interface, customer service interface, the seller interface, billing, and many third-party Web sites that run on Amazon's platform. So what you see on Amazon is the direct result of SOA services (Grey, 2006).

Here's a real-world example of an *inter-organizational* SOA at work. Dollar Rent A Car's systems use Web services to link its online booking system with Southwest Airlines's Web site. Although both companies' systems are based on different technology platforms, a person booking a flight on Southwest.com can reserve a car from Dollar without leaving the airline's Web site. Instead of struggling to get Dollar's reservation system to share data with Southwest's information systems, Dollar used Microsoft .NET Web services technology as an intermediary. Reservations from Southwest are translated into Web services protocols, which are then translated into formats that can be understood by Dollar's computers.

Other car rental companies have linked their information systems to airline companies' Web sites before. But without Web services, these connections had to be built one at a time. Web services provide a standard way for Dollar's computers to "talk" to other companies' information systems without having to build special links to each one. Dollar is now expanding its use of Web services to link directly to the systems of a small tour operator and a large travel reservation system as well as a wireless Web site for mobile phones and PDAs. It does not have to write new software code for each new partner's information systems or each new wireless device (see Figure 13).

Virtually all major software vendors such as IBM, Microsoft, Oracle, SAP, Sun, and HP provide tools and entire platforms for building and integrating software applications using Web services. IBM includes Web services tools in its

FIGURE 13   HOW DOLLAR RENT A CAR USES WEB SERVICES

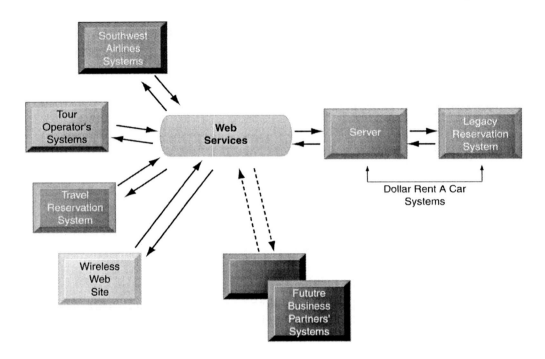

Dollar Rent A Car uses Web services to provide a standard intermediate layer of software to "talk" to other companies' information systems. Dollar Rent A Car can use this set of Web services to link to other companies' information systems without having to build a separate link to each firm's systems.

WebSphere e-business software platform, and Microsoft has incorporated Web services tools in its Microsoft .NET platform.

SOA is not a universal salve for all firms and it does raise issues all of its own. It's not clear what services to develop at first, and even Web services applications need to be rewritten as business firms develop and change. Once rewritten, all the programs that use these Web services need to be tested. In addition, SOA requires your staff to master an whole new set of tools and a new mentality about software development.

AJAX, MASHUPS, WEB 2.0, AND WEB-BASED SOFTWARE APPLICATIONS

Ever fill out a Web order form, make a mistake, and then have to start all over again after a long wait for a new order form page to appear on your screen? Ever visit a map site, click the North arrow once, and then wait some time for an entire new page to load? **Ajax** is a new software technique that prevents all this inconvenience and makes the user experience more seamless.

Ajax (Asynchronous JavaScript and XML) is a technique for allowing your client and the server you are working with to hold a conversation in the background, transferring your entries as they are made to the server without your awareness. Click North on a map site, like Google Maps, and the server downloads just that part of the application that changes with no wait for an entire new map. Make a mistake on forms at the iHotelier.com, TJMaxx.com, or HomeGoods.com Web sites and you'll be prompted just for clarifications on those entries without starting over again. Ajax, and a related set of techniques called RIA (rich Internet applications) use JavaScript or Adobe Flash (formerly Macromedia Flash) programs downloaded to your client to maintain a near continuous conversation with the server you are using. While making the life of consumers much easier, Ajax and RIA are even more important for another new software development: Web-based applications.

Imagine that instead of purchasing a suite of software tools in a box for word processing and spreadsheet development you could go out onto the Web and do all your writing and calculating online using free, Web-based software tools? You don't have to imagine anymore. In 2006, Google began delivering on its promise to provide online spreadsheet and word processing, along with calendar, e-mail, and instant messaging in a suite called Google Apps for Your Domain. While initially aimed at small businesses, there's no reason that once the bugs are worked out Google will try to extend this product to the same mass market where Microsoft's Office dominates more than 90 percent of the 1.5 billion PCs worldwide. Google will encourage people to share their Microsoft Word documents and spreadsheets with one another, but first they'll have to translate those documents into Google formats. Once that happens, users will no longer be so dependent on Word and Excel formats. They may end up dependent on Google formats, but Google promises to release all the tools necessary to users so they can integrate their Google applications and files into their existing infrastructure (e.g. Microsoft Office software and Microsoft Windows networks). Google will be using Ajax and related RIA tools to ensure that every time you move a cursor, or change a spreadsheet cell, you won't have to wait for the whole page to refresh itself!

Besides Google, there are many enterprise software firms such as salesforce.com, SAP, Oracle, and others who are delivering software services over the Web to client computers at their customer's sites. Increasingly over the next few years, software functionality will be delivered on the Web.

On a smaller scale, entrepreneurs are creating new software applications and services based on combining different online software applications. Called **mashups**, these new combined applications depend on high-speed data networks, universal communication standards, and open-source code. The idea is to take different sources and produce a new work that is "greater than" the sum of its parts.

Part of a movement called Web 2.0, and in the spirit of musical mashups, Web mashups combine the capabilities of two or more online applications to create a kind of hybrid that provides more customer value than the original sources alone. One area of great innovation is the mashup of mapping and satellite image software with local content. For instance, Paul Rademacher, a Silicon Valley programmer, opened a Web site called HousingMaps.com that makes it possible to display real estate listings in local areas from Craigslist.org overlaid on Google Maps, with pushpins showing the location of each listing. The site has attracted more than half a million visitors and receives about 10,000 visits a day.

Although building communication links among software applications using Web services is not new, online mapping applications are driving a whole new set of recombinant applications. Other map- and satellite-image-based mashups are in the works, encouraged by Google and Yahoo!, both of which in 2005 released for programmers the application programming interfaces (APIs) that allow other applications to pull in information from Google's and Yahoo!'s map and satellite images. Microsoft's competing map and satellite service is called Virtual Earth.

Google's service has simplified the process of using its mapping data down to the level of inserting four lines of JavaScript into a program. This simplification has made the process of integrating maps into other applications extremely easy for thousands of Web site designers. Publicly available APIs provide programmers with the tools for pulling data from many different Web sites and combining them with other information to make an entirely new Web service. The result is that instead of the Web being a collection of pages, it becomes a collection of capabilities, a platform where thousands of programmers can create new services quickly and inexpensively.

We've mentioned "Web 2.0" in the preceding text as part of a "movement." For us it's an expression of all the changes described previously, plus other changes in the way people and business use the Web and think about human interaction on the Web. Coined after the dot.com bubble burst in 2001 to refer to "the new Web applications," it's also the name of an annual conference. Web 2.0 can be summed up as (O'Reilly, 2005):

- Services, not packaged software, with cost-effective scalability
- Control over unique, hard-to-recreate data sources that get richer as more people use them
- Trusting users as co-developers
- Harnessing collective intelligence
- Leveraging the long tail through customer self-service
- Software above the level of a single device
- Lightweight user interfaces, development models, and business models

SOFTWARE OUTSOURCING

Today, most business firms continue to operate their legacy systems that continue to meet a business need and that would be extremely costly to replace. But they will purchase most of their new software applications from external sources. Figure 14 illustrates the rapid growth in external sources of software for U.S. firms.

Changing Sources of Software

U.S. firms will spend nearly $340 billion on software in 2006. In the past, most of this software was developed inside the firm by teams of programmers. While firms still retain sizable IT staffs, they are no longer exclusively in the software business. Instead firms in 2006 will turn over about one-third of their software development to outside developers, including enterprise software firms who will sell them pre-packaged solutions customized to their needs. Most of the outsourcing software is performed in the United States, but a growing portion of outsourced software projects are completed in off-shore, low-wage regions such as India, China, Eastern Europe, Africa, and Latin America. In addition, another 15 percent of the functionality of software will be obtained not by buying the software but purchasing the service—letting someone else develop the software. For instance, firms will purchase payroll processing services from application service providers, as well as sales force management services from Web providers like salesforce.com

Software Packages and Enterprise Software

We have already described software packages for enterprise applications as one of the major types of software components in contemporary IT infrastructures. A **software package** is a prewritten commercially available set of software

FIGURE 14   THE CHANGING SOURCES OF SOFTWARE

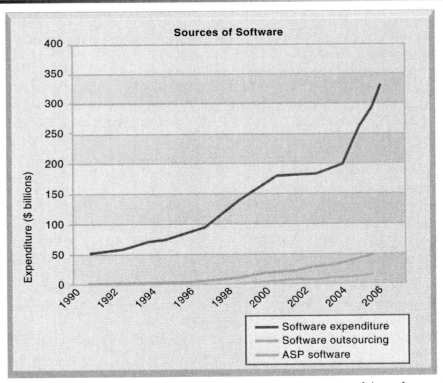

U.S. firms will spend nearly $340 billion on software in 2006. Over 30 percent of that software will come from outsourcing its development and operation to outside firms, and another 15 percent will come from purchasing the service from application service providers either on the Web or through traditional channels.

Sources: Authors estimates; Bureau of Economic Analysis, 2006; IT Spending and Trends, eMarketer, 2004; IT Spending and Trends, eMarketer, 2005; SEC 10K statements, various firms.

programs that eliminates the need for a firm to write its own software programs for certain functions, such as payroll processing or order handling.

Enterprise application software vendors such as SAP and Oracle-PeopleSoft have developed powerful software packages that can support the primary business processes of a firm worldwide from warehousing, customer relationship management, supply chain management, and finance to human resources. These large-scale enterprise software systems provide a single, integrated, worldwide software system for firms at a cost much less than they would pay if they developed it themselves. These systems are so complex, and require so much experience, that very few corporations have the expertise required to develop these packages.

Application Service Providers

A second external source of software is online application service providers. An **application service provider (ASP)** is a business that delivers and manages applications and computer services from remote computer centers to multiple users using the Internet or a private network. Instead of buying and installing software programs, subscribing companies can rent the same functions from these services. Users pay for the use of this software either on a subscription or per-transaction basis.

The ASP's solution combines package software applications and all of the related hardware, system software, network, and other infrastructure services that the customer otherwise would have to purchase, integrate, and manage independently. The ASP customer interacts with a single entity instead of an array of technologies and service vendors.

The time-sharing services of the 1970s, which ran applications such as payroll on their computers for other companies, were an earlier version of this application hosting. But today's ASPs run a wider array of applications than these earlier services and deliver many of these software services over the Web. At Web-based services, servers perform the bulk of the processing, and the only essential program needed by users is a desktop computer running either thin client software or a Web browser.

Large and medium-sized businesses are using ASPs for enterprise systems, sales force automation, or financial management, and small businesses are using them for functions such as invoicing, tax calculations, electronic calendars, and accounting. ASP vendors are starting to provide tools to integrate the applications they manage with clients' internal systems or with applications hosted by different vendors. In addition, enterprise software vendors such as SAP and Oracle have developed ASP versions of their enterprise software packages (such as www.mysap.com) for small and medium-sized firms that do not want to run this enterprise software on their own servers.

Some companies find it much easier to rent software from the ASP firm and avoid the expense and difficulty of installing, operating, and maintaining the hardware and software for complex systems, such as ERP systems. The ASP contracts guarantee a level of service and support to ensure that the software is available and working at all times. Today's Internet-driven business environment is changing so rapidly that getting a system up and running in three months instead of six could mean the difference between success and failure.

Application service providers also enable small and medium-sized companies to use applications that they otherwise could not afford. Small and midsize businesses have been drawn to these software-as-service solutions because the costs per user tend to be much cheaper than licensed on-premise software, which can cost anywhere from several hundred thousand dollars to several million dollars up front. But application service providers are not necessarily the best solution, even for these small companies. The Interactive Session on Technology explores this issue by examining two companies' experiences with hosted software, and why the results were so different.

Software Outsourcing

A third external source of software is **outsourcing**, in which a firm contracts custom software development or maintenance of existing legacy programs to outside firms, frequently firms that operate offshore in low-wage areas of the world. According to the Gartner Group, worldwide outsourcing totalled over $624 billion in 2005 (McDougall, 2006). The largest expenditure here is paid to domestic U.S. firms providing middleware, integration services, and other software support that are often required to operate larger enterprise systems.

For example, in early 2006, paper and packaging company MeadWestvaco hired Affiliated Computer Services (ACS) for $200 million to provide it with services and technology for five years. These services include software application maintenance and support and management of midrange and mainframe computers. Outsourcing gave the company access to highly trained technology specialists that were not available internally.

INTERACTIVE SESSION: TECHNOLOGY

APPLICATION SERVICE PROVIDERS: TWO TALES

Thermos is a midsize company, with less than 2,800 employees, but it is a widely known global brand, manufacturing Thermos bottles and other insulated food and beverage containers. Like other consumer package goods manufacturers, Thermos faces serious challenges from high fuel prices, rising costs for materials such as stainless steel and resin, and, of course, global competition. What's more, it has to meet the requirements of large retailers such as Wal-Mart and Target to deliver faster and more accurately while keeping costs low.

Consequently, Thermos needs to be both lean and innovative. The company's strategy focuses on finding ways to free up employees for high-value projects and strategic initiatives that focus on its core competencies, which are designing and manufacturing Thermos products. It doesn't want to waste these resources on operating its own IT infrastructure.

Thermos moved to a hosted on-demand service provided by Oracle Corporation. Using Oracle E-Business Suite on Demand, including Oracle Warehouse Management, Oracle Order Management, and Oracle Financials, all running on Oracle's computers, helped Thermos increase efficiencies in warehouse and inventory operations, marketing and brand management, and financial processes. In addition to the $665,000 Thermos saved in initial investment costs, the company estimates it saved another $300,000 from improved inventory control and warehouse labor productivity.

Thermos implemented the Oracle software without changing the software to make it work with its business processes. Instead, Thermos adopted the business processes of the Oracle systems. These processes turned out to be more efficient than Thermos's old ways of working.

ResortCom International's experience with an application service provider is quite different. This company is a small $15 million business providing financial and operational services for vacation property developers and managers. It needed a customer relationship management (CRM) system that could handle sales, marketing, customer support, self-service, and analytics. The software had to be flexible enough to meet changing needs of the company's sales and marketing staff yet integrate well with ResortCom's internal corporate applications containing customer contracts, invoices, and financial transactions.

ResortCom decided to use a hosted on-demand CRM system from RightNow Technologies that appeared to meet most of its requirements and had an especially user-friendly interface. The software service cost only $125 per user per month, which was much less than the $300,000 licensing fee plus additional implementation, infrastructure, and support costs to run software from a conventional vendor in-house.

Once ResortCom tried to implement the hosted RightNow system, it ran into problems. It took three months to get the system up and running instead of one because ResortCom wanted an automated capability for users to launch the RightNow applications as tabs within its back-office systems. Special programming was required. ResortCom's vice president of financial services Alex Marxer says that the integration of RightNow with the company's back-office system is satisfactory, although not ideal. To use the system to open up a customer incident report takes ten seconds because of the back and forth interaction between RightNow and the company's internal system.

What ResortCom found is that hosted CRM systems are not always as simple to implement as vendors promise. This solution is likely to work well for companies that want to implement standard CRM processes, that are able to use the software as is without modifications, and that don't require complex integration with back-office systems. Customizing the software to meet a company's unique requirements can be problematic, and the tools provided by the vendors to link their CRM software to subscribers' internal systems are usually not as powerful as onsite software.

Although it should take less time to get a hosted system working than in-house software or a traditional software package, larger and more complex implementations can still take a year or more. Even though an application service provider reduces the need for maintaining an in-house technical staff, applying upgrades to the software can sometimes be technically challenging, and there must be ongoing business support for the software.

As Rob Bois, senior research analyst for AMR Research observes, companies believe that using an application service provider "is like turning on a switch. But the integration and customization requirements are not that different from traditional software when you get into more complex implementations. There's still a lot of work involved."

Despite the implementation problems, the RightNow system still produced benefits for ResortCom. The customer self-service function provided by the system has reduced customer e-mails by 40 percent and the improved workflow between front- and back-office functions has increased

productivity by 40 percent as well. The Right Now system provided ResortCom with additional marketing functionality that should further enhance profitability. The company is sticking with the hosted CRM system, but it has held off on upgrading to any new versions of the software and hopes there won't be a problem when RightNow adapts a true Web-services integration platform.

Sources: Stephanie Overby, "The Truth about On-Demand CRM," *CIO Magazine*, January 15, 2006; Katheryn Potterf, "Keeping It Cool," *Profit Magazine*, February 2006; and "2005 CRM Elite," *Customer Relationship Management*, October 2005.

CASE STUDY QUESTIONS

1. Compare Thermos's experience with an application software provider with the experience of ResortCom.
2. Why do you think Thermos had an easier time with a hosted software service than ResortCom? What management, organization, and technology factors account for this difference?
3. If your company was considering using an application service provider, what management, organization, and technology factors should be addressed when making your decision?

MIS IN ACTION

Explore the Web sites of RightNow and Siebel CRM on Demand offered by Oracle.

1. Compare the services offered by both companies.
2. How could a business benefit from using these services?
3. What steps would a business need to take to use these hosted CRM systems?

Offshore firms provided about $8 billion in software services to the United States in 2004, which is about 2 percent of the combined U.S. software plus software services budget (around $400 billion). Until recently, this type of software development involved lower-level maintenance, data entry, and call center operations, but with the growing sophistication and experience of offshore firms, particularly in India, more and more new-program development is taking place offshore.

5 MANAGEMENT ISSUES

Creating and managing a coherent IT infrastructure raises multiple challenges: dealing with scalability and technology change, management and governance, and making wise infrastructure investments.

DEALING WITH INFRASTRUCTURE CHANGE

As firms grow, they can quickly outgrow their infrastructure. As firms shrink, they can get stuck with an excessive infrastructure purchased in better times. How can a firm remain flexible when most of the investments in IT infrastructure are fixed-cost purchases and licenses? How well does the infrastructure scale? **Scalability** refers to the ability of a computer, product, or system to expand to serve a large number of users without breaking down.

MANAGEMENT AND GOVERNANCE

A long-standing issue among information systems managers and CEOs has been the question of who will control and manage the firm's IT infrastructure. Should departments and divisions have the responsibility of making their own information technology decisions or should IT infrastructure be centrally controlled and managed? What is the relationship between central information systems management and business unit information systems management? How will infrastructure costs be allocated among business units? Each organization will need to arrive at answers based on its own needs.

MAKING WISE INFRASTRUCTURE INVESTMENTS

IT infrastructure is a major investment for the firm. If too much is spent on infrastructure, it lies idle and constitutes a drag on firm financial performance. If too little is spent, important business services cannot be delivered and the firm's competitors (who spent just the right amount) will outperform the underinvesting firm. How much should the firm spend on infrastructure? This question is not easy to answer.

A related question is whether a firm should purchase its own IT infrastructure components or rent them from external suppliers. As we discussed earlier, a major trend in computing platforms—both hardware and software—is to outsource to external providers. The decision either to purchase your own IT assets or rent them from external providers is typically called the *rent versus buy* decision.

Competitive Forces Model for IT Infrastructure Investment

Figure 15 illustrates a competitive forces model you can use to address the question of how much your firm should spend on IT infrastructure.

Market demand for your firm's services. Make an inventory of the services you currently provide to customers, suppliers, and employees. Survey each group, or hold focus groups, to find out if the services you currently offer are meeting the needs of each group. For example, are customers complaining of slow responses to their queries about price and availability? Are employees complaining about the difficulty of finding the right information for their jobs? Are suppliers complaining about the difficulties of discovering your production requirements?

Your firm's business strategy. Analyze your firm's five-year business strategy and try to assess what new services and capabilities will be required to achieve strategic goals.

Your firm's information technology (IT) strategy, infrastructure, and cost. Examine your firm's information technology plans for the next five years and assess its alignment with the firm's business plans. Determine total IT infrastructure costs. You will want to perform a total cost of ownership analysis (see the discussion later). If your firm has no IT strategy, you will need to devise one that takes into account the firm's five-year strategic plan.

Information technology assessment. Is your firm behind the technology curve or at the bleeding edge of information technology? Both situations are to be avoided. It is usually not desirable to spend resources on advanced

215

FIGURE 15   COMPETITIVE FORCES MODEL FOR IT INFRASTRUCTURE

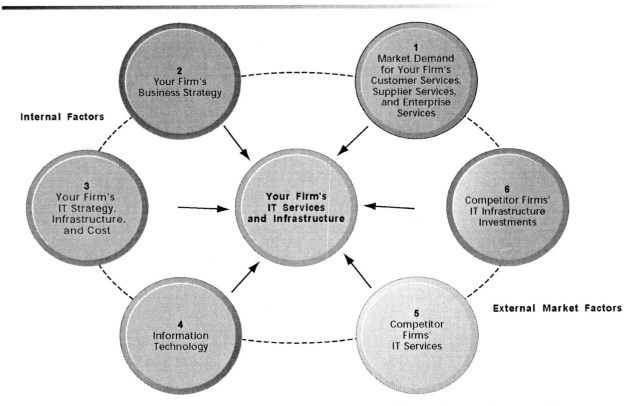

There are six factors you can use to answer the question, "How much should our firm spend on IT infrastructure?"

technologies that are still experimental, often expensive, and sometimes unreliable. You want to spend on technologies for which standards have been established and IT vendors are competing on cost, not design, and where there are multiple suppliers. However, you do not want to put off investment in new technologies or allow competitors to develop new business models and capabilities based on the new technologies.

Competitor firm services. Try to assess what technology services competitors offer to customers, suppliers, and employees. Establish quantitative and qualitative measures to compare them to those of your firm. If your firm's service levels fall short, your company is at a competitive disadvantage. Look for ways your firm can excel at service levels.

Competitor firm IT infrastructure investments. Benchmark your expenditures for IT infrastructure against your competitors. Many companies are quite public about their innovative expenditures on IT. If competing firms try to keep IT expenditures secret, you may be able to find IT investment information in public companies' SEC Form 10-K annual reports to the federal government when those expenditures impact a firm's financial results.

Your firm does not necessarily need to spend as much as, or more than, your competitors. Perhaps it has discovered much less expensive ways of providing services, and this can lead to a cost advantage. Alternatively, your firm may be spending far less than competitors and experiencing commensurate poor performance and losing market share.

TABLE 6   TOTAL COST OF OWNERSHIP (TCO) COST COMPONENTS

INFRASTRUCTURE COMPONENT	COST COMPONENTS
Hardware acquisition	Purchase price of computer hardware equipment, including computers, terminals, storage, and printers
Software acquisition	Purchase or license of software for each user
Installation	Cost to install computers and software
Training	Cost to provide training for information systems specialists and end users
Support	Cost to provide ongoing technical support, help desks, and so forth
Maintenance	Cost to upgrade the hardware and software
Infrastructure	Cost to acquire, maintain, and support related infrastructure, such as networks and specialized equipment (including storage backup units)
Downtime	Cost of lost productivity if hardware or software failures cause the system to be unavailable for processing and user tasks
Space and energy	Real estate and utility costs for housing and providing power for the technology

Total Cost of Ownership of Technology Assets

In benchmarking your firm's expenditures on IT infrastructure with that of your competitors, you will need to consider a wide range of costs. The actual cost of owning technology resources includes the original cost of acquiring and installing hardware and software, as well as ongoing administration costs for hardware and software upgrades, maintenance, technical support, training, and even utility and real estate costs for running and housing the technology. The **total cost of ownership (TCO)** model can be used to analyze these direct and indirect costs to help firms determine the actual cost of specific technology implementations.

Table 6 describes the most important TCO components to consider in a TCO analysis. When all these cost components are considered, the TCO for a PC might run up to three times the original purchase price of the equipment. Hidden costs for support staff, downtime, and additional network management can make distributed client/server architectures—especially those incorporating handheld computers and wireless devices—more expensive than centralized mainframe architectures.

Hardware and software acquisition costs account for only about 20 percent of TCO, so managers must pay close attention to administration costs to understand the full cost of the firm's hardware and software. It is possible to reduce some of these administration costs through better management. Many large firms are saddled with redundant, incompatible hardware and software because their departments and divisions have been allowed to make their own technology purchases.

These firms could reduce their TCO through greater centralization and standardization of their hardware and software resources. Companies could reduce the size of the information systems staff required to support their infrastructure if the firm minimizes the number of different computer models and pieces of software that employees are allowed to use. In a centralized infrastructure, systems can be administered from a central location and troubleshooting can be performed from that location (David, Schuff, and St. Louis, 2002).

6   HANDS-ON MIS

The projects in this section give you hands-on experience in using spreadsheet software to help a real-world company make a rent vs. buy decision about new manufacturing software, using spreadsheet software to evaluate alternative desktop systems, and using Web research to budget for a sales conference.

Improving Decision Making: Making the Rent vs. Buy Decision for Hardware and Software

> Software skills: Spreadsheet formulas, electronic presentation software (optional)
> Business skills: Technology rent vs. buy decision, TCO analysis

This project provides an opportunity for you to help a real-world company make a decision about whether to rent or buy new technology. You'll use spreadsheet software to compare the total three-year cost of licensing and maintaining new manufacturing software or renting the software from an application service provider.

Dirt Bikes would like to implement new production planning, quality control, and scheduling software for use by 25 members of its manufacturing staff. Management is trying to determine whether to purchase the software from a commercial vendor along with any hardware required to run the software or to use a hosted software solution from an application service provider. (The hosted software runs on the ASP's computer.) You have been asked to help management with this rent vs. buy decision by calculating the total cost of each option over a three-year period.

The costs of purchasing the software (actually for purchasing a license from the vendor to use its software package) include the initial purchase price of the software (licensing fee of $100,000 paid in the first year), the cost of implementing and customizing the software in the first year ($20,000), one new server to run the software (a first-year purchase of $4,000), one information systems specialist devoting half of his or her time to supporting the software ($55,000 in full-time annual salary and benefits with a 3 percent annual salary increase each year after the first year), user training in the first year ($10,000), and the cost of annual software upgrades ($5,000).

The costs of renting hosted software are the rental fees ($2,500 annually per user), implementation and customization costs ($12,000 in the first year), and training ($10,000 in the first year).

- Use your spreadsheet software to calculate the total cost of renting or purchasing this software over a three-year period. Identify the lowest-price alternative that meets Dirt Bikes's requirements.
- What other factors should Dirt Bikes consider besides cost in determining whether to rent or buy the hardware and software?
- (Optional) If possible, use electronic presentation software to summarize your findings for management.

Improving Decision Making: Using a Spreadsheet to Evaluate Hardware and Software Options

Software skills: Spreadsheet formulas
Business skills: Technology pricing

In this exercise, you will use spreadsheet software to calculate the cost of alternative desktop systems.

You have been asked to obtain pricing information on hardware and software for an office of 30 people. Using the Internet, get pricing for 30 PC desktop systems (monitors, computers, and keyboards) manufactured by Lenovo, Dell, and HP/Compaq as listed at their respective corporate Web sites. (For the purposes of this exercise, ignore the fact that desktop systems usually come with preloaded software packages). Also obtain pricing on 15 monochrome desktop printers manufactured by Hewlett-Packard and by Xerox. Each desktop system must satisfy the minimum specifications shown in the following table:

MINIMUM DESKTOP SPECIFICATIONS

Processor speed	3 GHz
Hard drive	250 GB
RAM	1 GB
CD-ROM speed	48 speed
Monitor (diagonal measurement)	17 inches

Each desktop printer must satisfy the minimum specifications shown in the following table:

MINIMUM MONOCHROME PRINTER SPECIFICATIONS

Print speed	12 pages per minute
Print resolution	600 ˘ 600
Network ready?	Yes
Maximum price/unit	$1,000

After pricing the desktop systems and printers, obtain pricing on 30 copies of the most recent versions of Microsoft Office, Lotus SmartSuite, and Sun StarOffice desktop productivity packages, and on 30 copies of Microsoft Windows XP Professional Edition or Windows Vista. The application software suite packages come in various versions, so be sure that each package contains programs for word processing, spreadsheet analysis, database analysis, graphics preparation, and e-mail.

Prepare a spreadsheet showing your research results for the desktop systems, printers, and software. Use your spreadsheet software to determine the desktop system, printer, and software combination that will offer both the best performance and pricing per worker. Because every two workers will share one printer (15 printers/30 systems), assume only half a printer cost per worker in the spreadsheet. Assume that your company will take the standard warranty and service contract offered by each product's manufacturer.

Improving Decision Making: Using Web Research to Budget for a Sales Conference

In this exercise, you will use software at various online travel sites to arrange transportation and lodging for a large sales force to attend a sales conference at two alternative locations. You will use that information to calculate total travel and lodging costs and decide where to hold the conference.

Software skills: Internet-based software
Business skills: Researching transportation and lodging costs

The Foremost Composite Materials Company is planning a two-day sales conference for October 15 and 16, starting with a reception on the evening of October 14. The conference consists of all-day meetings that the entire sales force, numbering 125 sales representatives and their 16 managers, must attend. Each sales representative requires his or her own room, and the company needs two common meeting rooms, one large enough to hold the entire sales force plus a few visitors (200) and the other able to hold half the force. Management has set a budget of $85,000 for the representatives' room rentals. The hotel must also have such services as overhead and computer projectors as well as business center and banquet facilities. It also should have facilities for the company reps to be able to work in their rooms and to enjoy themselves in a swimming pool or gym facility. The company would like to hold the conference in either Miami or Marco Island, Florida.

Foremost usually likes to hold such meetings in Hilton- or Marriott-owned hotels. Use the Hilton and Marriott Web sites to select a hotel in whichever of these cities that would enable the company to hold its sales conference within its budget.

Link to the Hilton and Marriott home pages, and search them to find a hotel that meets Foremost's sales conference requirements. Once you have selected the hotel, locate flights arriving the afternoon prior to the conference because the attendees will need to check in the day before and attend your reception the evening prior to the conference. Your attendees will be coming from Los Angeles (54), San Francisco (32), Seattle (22), Chicago (19), and Pittsburgh (14). Determine the costs of each airline ticket from these cities. When you are finished, create a budget for the conference. The budget will include the cost of each airline ticket, the room cost, and $60 per attendee per day for food.

- What was your final budget?
- Which did you select as the best hotel for the sales conference and why?

LEARNING TRACK MODULES

How Computer Hardware and Software Work. If you would like to review basic hardware and software concepts, you will find a Learning Track on this topic on the Student CD-ROM and on the Laudon Web site for this chapter.

The Open Source Software Initiative. If you want to learn more about the Open Source Definition from the Open Source Initiative and the history of open-source software, you will find a Learning Track on this topic on the Student CD-ROM and on the Laudon Web site for this chapter.

Summary ▬▬▬▬▬▬▬▬▬▬▬▬▬▬▬▬▬▬▬▬▬▬▬

1. *Define IT infrastructure and describe its components.*

   IT infrastructure is the shared technology resources that provide the platform for the firm's sp   s
   information system applications. IT infrastructure includes hardware, software, and services that are
   shared across the entire firm. Major IT infrastructure components include computer hardware
   platforms, operating system platforms, enterprise software platforms, networking and telecommunications platforms, database management software, Internet platforms, and consulting services and
   systems integrators. You can better understand the business value of IT infrastructure investments by
   viewing IT infrastructure as a platform of services as well as a set of technologies.

2. *Identify and describe the stages of IT infrastructure evolution.*

   There are five stages of IT infrastructure evolution. IT infrastructure in the earliest stage consisted
   of specialized electronic accounting machines that were primitive computers used for accounting
   tasks. IT infrastructure in the mainframe era (1959 to present) consists of a mainframe performing
   centralized processing that could be networked to thousands of terminals and eventually some
   decentralized and departmental computing using networked minicomputers. The personal computer
   era (1981 to present) in IT infrastructure has been dominated by the widespread use of standalone
   desktop computers with office productivity tools. The predominant infrastructure in the client/server
   era (1983 to present) consists of desktop or laptop clients networked to more powerful server
   computers that handle most of the data management and processing. The enterprise Internet
   computing era (1992 to present) is defined by large numbers of PCs linked into local area networks and
   growing use of standards and software to link disparate networks and devices linked into an enterprise-
   wide network so that information can flow freely across the organization.

3. *Identify and describe the technology drivers of IT infrastructure evolution.*

   A series of technology developments has driven the continuing transformation of IT infrastructure.
   Moore's Law deals with the exponential increase in processing power and decline in the cost of
   computer technology, stating that every 18 months the power of microprocessors doubles and the
   price of computing falls in half. The Law of Mass Digital Storage deals with the exponential decrease in
   the cost of storing data, stating that the number of kilobytes of data that can be stored on magnetic
   media for $1 roughly doubles every 15 months. Metcalfe's Law helps explain the mushrooming use of
   computers by showing that a network's value to participants grows exponentially as the network takes
   on more members. Also driving exploding computer use is the rapid decline in costs of communication and growing agreement in the technology industry to use computing and communications standards.

4. *Assess contemporary computer hardware platform trends.*

   Contemporary hardware and software platform trends address the overwhelming need to reduce IT
   infrastructure costs, to use computing resources more efficiently, to integrate information across
   platforms, and to provide a higher level of flexibility and service to the firm and its customers. The
   integration of computing and telecommunications platforms, grid computing, edge computing, and
   on-demand computing demonstrate that, increasingly, computing is taking place over a network. Grid
   computing involves connecting geographically remote computers into a single network to create a
   computational grid that combines the computing power of all the computers on the network with
   which to attack large computing problems. Edge computing balances the processing load for Web-
   based applications by distributing parts of the Web content, logic, and processing among multiple
   servers. On-demand computing also depends on networks for firms to purchase additional processing
   power from large computer service firms and to have that power delivered when they need it over a
   network. In autonomic computing, computer systems have capabilities for automatically configuring
   and repairing themselves.

   Virtualization organizes computing resources so that their use is not restricted by physical
   configuration or geographic location. Server virtualization enables companies to run more than one
   operating system at the same time. A multicore processor is an microprocessor to which two or more
   processors have been attached for enhanced performance, reduced power consumption, and more
   efficient simultaneous processing of multiple tasks.

Assess contemporary software platform trends.

Contemporary software platform trends include the growing use of Linux, open-source software, and Java, software for enterprise integration, and software outsourcing. Open-source software is produced and maintained by a global community of programmers and is downloadable for free. Linux is a powerful, resilient open-source operating system that can run on multiple hardware platforms and is used widely to run Web servers. Java is an operating-system- and hardware-independent programming language that is the leading interactive programming environment for the Web.

Software for enterprise integration includes enterprise applications and middleware such as enterprise application integration (EAI) software and Web services. Unlike EAI software, Web services are loosely coupled software components based on open Web standards that are not product-specific and can work with any application software and operating system. They can be used as components of Web-based applications linking the systems of two different organizations or to link disparate systems of a single company. Mashups are new software applications and services based on combining different online software applications using high-speed data networks, universal communication standards, and open-source code. Companies are purchasing their new software applications from outside sources, including software packages, by outsourcing custom application development to an external vendor (that may be offshore), or by renting software services from an application service provider.

6. *Evaluate the challenges of managing IT infrastructure and management solutions.*

Major infrastructure challenges include dealing with infrastructure change, agreeing on infrastructure management and governance, and making wise infrastructure investments. Solution guidelines include using a competitive forces model to determine how much to spend on IT infrastructure and where to make strategic infrastructure investments, and establishing the total cost of ownership (TCO) of information technology assets. The total cost of owning technology resources includes not only the original cost of computer hardware and software but also costs for hardware and software upgrades, maintenance, technical support, and training.

Key Terms

Ajax
Application server
Application service provider (ASP)
Autonomic computing
Blade servers
Client
Client/server computing
Edge computing
Enterprise application integration (EAI) software
Extensible Markup Language (XML)
Grid computing
Hypertext Markup Language (HTML)
Java
Legacy systems
Linux
Mainframe
Mashup
Middleware
Minicomputers
Moore's Law
Multicore processor
Multitiered (N-tier) client/server architecture
Nanotechnology, 180
On-demand computing

Open-source software
Operating systems
Outsourcing
Scalability
Server
Service-oriented architecture (SOA)
Simple Object Access Protocol (SOAP)
Software package
Storage area network (SAN)
Technology standards
Total cost of ownership (TCO)
Universal Description, Discovery, and Integration (UDDI)
Unix
Utility computing
Virtualization
Web browser
Web hosting service
Web server
Web services
Web Services Description Language (WSDL)
Windows
Wintel PC

Review Questions

1. Define IT infrastructure from both a technology and a services perspective. Which services does IT infrastructure comprise?

2. List each of the eras in IT infrastructure evolution and describe their distinguishing characteristics.

3. Define and describe the following: Web server, application server, and multitiered client/server architecture.

4. What are Moore's Law and the Law of Mass Digital Storage? What aspects of infrastructure change do they help explain?

5. How do network economics, declining communications costs, and technology standards affect IT infrastructure and the use of computers?

6. List and describe the components of IT infrastructure that firms need to manage.

7. Compare grid computing and edge computing.

8. How can businesses benefit from on-demand computing and autonomic computing?

9. How can businesses benefit from virtualization and multicore processors?

10. Define and describe open-source software and Linux. How can they benefit businesses?

11. What is Java? Why is it important today?

12. What is the difference between enterprise application integration software and Web services? What role is played by XML in Web services?

13. What are software mashups? How do they benefit businesses?

14. Name and describe the three external sources for software.

15. Name and describe the management challenges posed by IT infrastructure.

16. How would using a competitive forces model and calculating the TCO of technology assets help firms make infrastructure investments?

Discussion Questions

1. Why is selecting computer hardware and software for the organization an important management decision? What management, organization, and technology issues should be considered when selecting computer hardware and software?

2. Should organizations use ASPs for all their software needs? Why or why not? What management, organization, and technology factors should be considered when making this decision?

Video Case

You will find a video case illustrating some of the concepts in this chapter on the Laudon Web site and Student CD-ROM along with questions to help you analyze the case.

Teamwork: Evaluating Server Operating Systems

Form a group with three or four of your classmates. One group should research and compare the capabilities and costs of Linux versus the most recent version of the Windows operating system for servers. Another group should research and compare the capabilities and costs of Linux versus Unix. Each group should present its findings to the class, using electronic presentation software if possible.

REFERENCES

Aries, James A., Subhankar Banerjee, Marc S. Brittan, Eric Dillon, Janusz S. Kowalik, and John P. Lixvar. "Capacity and Performance Analysis of Distributed Enterprise Systems." *Communications of the ACM* 45, no. 6 (June 2002).

Babcock, Charles. "Virtualization's Next Stage." *Information Week* (March 20, 2006).

Barry, Douglas K. Web Services and Service-Oriented Architectures: The Savvy Manager's Guide. New York: Morgan Kaufman (2003).

Bell, Gordon and Jim Gray. What's Next in High-Performance Computing? *Communications of the ACM* 45, no. 1 (January 2002).

Bulkeley, William M. "New IBM Service Will Test Vision of Computing Power as Utility," *The Wall Street Journal* (July 1, 2002).

Bulkeley, William M. "Can LINUX Take Over the Desktop." The Wall Street Journal (May 24, 2004).

Bureau of Economic Analysis, National Income and Product Accounts, Table 5.3.5 Fixed Investment by Type. Washington, D.C. (2006).

Butler, Steve. "IT Spending and Trends." *eMarketer* (March 2005).

Butler, Steve. "Telecom Spending." *EMarketer* (April 2004).

Champy, James. "Re-examining the Infrastructure." *Optimize* 23 (September 2003).

Chari, Kaushal nand Saravanan Seshadri. "Demystifying Integration." *Communications of the ACM* 47, no. 7 (July 2004).

Columbia University. "A Chronology of Computing." http://www.columbia.edu/acis/history/ (November 2006).

Conry-Murray, Andrew . "Grid Computing's Promises and Perils." Network Magazine. com (February 5, 2004).

Cuomo, Jerry, et. al., "WebSphere Capacity — On Demand: Developing Edge Computing Applications." IBM Corporation and Akamai (2003). http://www-106.ibm.com/developerworks/websphere/library/techarticles/0310_haberkorn/haberkorn.html

David, Julie Smith, David Schuff, and Robert St. Louis. "Managing Your IT Total Cost of Ownership." Communications of the ACM 45, no. 1 (January 2002).

Dempsey, Bert J. Debra Weiss, Paul Jones, and Jane Greenberg. "What Is an Open Source Software Developer?" *Communications of the ACM* 45, no. 1 (January 2001).

Dunn, Darell. "Intel 'Core' Focuses On Power Consumption." InformationWeek (March 7, 2005)

eMarketer, "IT Spending and Trends," March 2005.

Ganek, A. G. and T.A. Corbi. "The Dawning of the Autonomic Computing Era." IBM Systems Journal. 42, No 1, (2003).

Gerlach, James, Bruce Neumann, Edwin Moldauer, Martha Argo, and Daniel Frisby. "Determining the Cost of IT Services." *Communications of the ACM* 45, no. 9 (September 2002).

Grey, Jim. "Learning from the Amazon Technology Platform." *ACM Queue* 4, No. 4 (May 2006).

Hagel III, John and John Seeley Brown. "Your Next IT Strategy." *Harvard Business Review* (October, 2001).

IBM. "IBM Launches New Autonomic Offerings for Self-Managing IT Systems." IBM Media Relations (June 30, 2005).

IBM. "20th Century Disk Storage Technology." http://www-1.ibm.com/ibm/history/exhibits/storage/storage_chrono20.html, accessed July 2004.

IBM. "Gridlines: The Intersection of Technology and Business." (July 2004) http://www-1.ibm.com/grid/gridlines/January2004/feature/teamwork.shtml.

IBM. "How Customers Are Making On Demand Real." (July 2004). http://www.ibm.com/news/us/2003/11/on_demand_real.html.

IBM, "The Mainframe Family Tree and Chronology." http://www-1.ibm.com/ibm/history/exhibits/mainframe/mainframe_FT1.html, accessed July 2004.

Intel Corporation. "Expanding Moore's Law: The Exponential Opportunity" (Fall 2002).

Intel Corporation. "Microprocessor Quick Reference Guide," www.intel.com/pressroom/kits/quickreffam.htm, July 2004.

International Technology Roadmap for Semiconductors Committee. "The International Technology Roadmap for Semiconductors 2003 Edition." http://public.itrs.net/., accessed July 2004.

Kern, Thomas, Leslie P. Willcocks, and Mary C. Lacity. "Application Service Provision: Risk Assessment and Mitigation." *MIS Quarterly Executive* 1, no. 2 (2002).

Kerstetter, Jim. "The Linux Uprising." Business Week Online (March 2003).

Kephart, Jeffrey O. and David M. Chess, "The Vision of Autonomic Computing." *IEEE Computer* (January 2003).

Krazit, Tom. "HP Bolsters Utility Services." *Network World*, (December 2005).

Lee, Jinyoul, Keng Siau, and Soongoo Hong. "Enterprise Integration with ERP and EAI," *Communications of the ACM* 46, no. 2 (February 2003)

Loo, Alfred W. "The Future of Peer-to-Peer Computing." *Communications of the ACM* 46, no. 9 (September 2003).

Lyman, Peter and Hal R. Varian. "How Much Information, 2003." http://www.sims.berkeley.edu/how-much-info-2003, accessed November 1, 2006.

Markoff, John and Jennifer L. Schenker. "Europe Exceeds U.S. in Refining Grid Computing." The New York Times (November 10, 2003).

McDougall, Paul. "Seven Fearless Predictions For Outsourcing In 2006," *InformationWeek* (December 20, 2005).

McDougall, Paul. "In Depth: Customers Analyze Outsourcing Vendors and Strategies." *Information Week* (June 19, 2006).

Moore, Gordon. "Cramming More Components Onto Integrated Circuits," Electronics 38, Number 8 (April 19, 1965).

National Science Foundation, "Revolutionizing Science and Engineering Through Cyberinfrastructure: Report of the National Science Foundation Blue-Ribbon Advisory Panel on Cyberinfrastructure." Washington D.C. (January, 2003).

Niemeyer,Alex, Misok H. Pak and Sanjay E. Ramaswamy. "Smart Tags for Your Supply Chain" *McKinsey Quarterly* 4 (2003).

O'Reilly, Tim. "What is Web 2.0: Design Patterns and Business Models for the Next Generation of Software." www.oreillynet.com/lpt/a/6228.

Patel, Samir and Suneel Saigal. "When Computers Learn to Talk: A Web Services Primer," *The McKinsey Quarterly* (2002, No. 1).

Phillips, Charles. "Stemming the Software Spending Spree." *Optimize Magazine* (April 2002).

Ricadela, Aaron. "Living on the Grid." *Information Week* (June 17, 2002).

Rogow, Rruce. "Tracking Core Assets." *Optimize Magazine* (April 2006).

Salkever, Alex with Olga Kharif. "Slowly Weaving Web Services Together." *Business Week* (June 24, 2003).

Schmerken, Ivy. "Girding for Grid." Wall Street & Technology (April 2003).

Schuff, David and Robert St. Louis. "Centralization vs. Decentralization of Application Software." *Communications of the ACM* 44, no. 6 (June 2001).

Shankland, Stephen. "IBM: On Demand Computing Has Arrived." CNET News (November 12, 2003).

Stango, Victor. "The Economics of Standards Wars." Review of Network Economics .3, Issue 1 (March 2004).

Susarla, Anjana, Anitesh Barus, and Andrew B. Whinston. "Understanding the Service Component of Application Service Provision: An Emprical Analysis of Satisfaction with ASP Services." *MIS Quarterly* 27, no. 1 (March 2003).

Tuomi, Ilkka. "The Lives and Death of Moore's Law." FirstMonday, Col 7, No. 11 (November 2002). www.firstmonday.org.

Weill, Peter, Mani Subramani and Marianne Broadbent. "Building IT Infrastructure for Strategic Agility." *Sloan Management Review* 44, no. 1 (Fall 2002).

Weill, Peter, and Marianne Broadbent. Leveraging the New Infrastructure. Cambridge, MA: Harvard Business School Press (1998).

———. "Management by Maxim: How Business and IT Managers Can Create IT Infrastructures," *Sloan Management Review* (Spring 1997).

Weitzel, Tim. Economics of Standards in Information Networks. Springer (2004).

Merrill Lynch Connects Past and Future Technology
CASE STUDY

Merrill Lynch is a worldwide leader in financial management and advisory services, employing 50,600 workers in 36 countries and territories. The company and its subsidiaries provide brokerage, investment banking, financing, wealth management, advisory, asset management, insurance, lending, and other related products and services to private, institutional, and government clients with assets of $1.6 trillion. In 2005, Merrill Lynch posted a record $5.1 billion in net earnings, a 15 percent increase over the previous year, on net revenues of $26 billion.

One of the most critical components of Merrill Lynch's operations is its information technology infrastructure. Over the last five years, that IT infra-structure has played a major role in the company's gains. Like many financial institutions, Merrill Lynch has had to modernize its technology infrastructure in order to remain competitive.

Merrill Lynch considered its IBM mainframe installation, which was one of the largest in the world, to be a strategic asset. The mainframe ran in the neighborhood of 23,000 programs to process the firm's 80 million daily online transactions for accessing customer accounts online or making stock trades.

In modernizing its technology, Merrill Lynch had to make choices regarding its legacy computers and applications. Internet-based applications that gave customers access to their portfolios and tools to work with them were a key to remaining competitive. But these applications did not use mainframe-based soft-ware. How could Merrill Lynch develop such applica-tions while leveraging the processing power and wealth of data in its mainframe?

The answer appeared to be Web services and a service-oriented architecture (SOA). Most corpora-tions developing a SOA typically use commercially available platforms such as those from BEA Systems and webMethods instead of creating their own development platforms. They rely on the vendor's expertise and access to consultants familiar with integrating mainframe and Web applications.

Project leader Jim Crew, then head of database infrastructure for Merrill Lynch, determined that on the surface, purchasing an SOA platform was much easier than building one, and would have enabled the firm to deploy its Web services relatively quickly. However, no SOA vendors that Crew researched offered products that met Crew's requirements for the project. They were offering SOA platforms that were geared toward distributed programming and recent development tools such as Java and .NET.

Merrill Lynch's 1200 mainframe programmers did not have experience with these tools. Retraining this huge staff did not make sense economically, nor did purchasing new workstations required for running the development software. According to research from Gartner Group consultants, retraining Merrill Lynch's mainframe programmers could have taken as much as a year and cost more than $80 million. To Crew, it was obvious that the firm should pursue a more unconventional approach; construct a proprietary Web development platform from the ground up to extend the capabilities of its legacy mainframe systems.

Merrill Lynch had initially tried to avoid these costs by copying the data stored in its mainframe installation into Oracle, Sybase, or Microsoft SQL Server databases. In those formats, the data were compatible with server-based applications. However, that technique was not entirely satisfactory. Copying large quantities of data often introduces errors based on disk failures and space issues. Furthermore, some data can become obsolete as soon as they are copied. For instance, a client who made several stock trades would have to wait until the next day to see an accurate balance in his or her account. Crew noted that the firm was spending money on copying data that could quickly be out-of-date while the accurate data were always residing on the mainframe.

Instead, Merrill Lynch created its own set of in-house proprietary tools that enable its mainframe legacy programs and the functions they perform to be exposed as Web services. XML tags are used to describe the data for other applications that are equipped to interpret XML. SOAP makes it possible for programs running under different operating systems to communicate with each other. Together, the two standards made it possible for online applica-tions to communicate effectively with the mainframe without an additional layer of middleware.

Merrill Lynch's Web services toolset was called X4ML, which stood for XML for Modernizing Legacy.

From *Management Information Systems: Managing the Digital Firm, 10/e.* Kenneth C. Laudon, Jane P. Laudon.

225

Crew challenged his team to increase the firm's savings from Web services ten-fold to $20 million. Crew's team established five criteria for the Web services project:

1. No new programming languages for the mainframe programmers to learn.

2. No new software tools for development that would require expensive workstations; tools would be accessible from a Web browser.

3. A central storage directory for the Web services that would be developed so that programmers could easily reuse and repackage them with each other.

4. Web services developed as a result of the project had to conform to the existing mainframe security standards as well as Web security standards for encryption, authentication, and authorization.

5. Inclusion of budding Web services standards in the Web services architecture to ensure future viability.

The project team prohibited the new platform from requiring changes to program code on the mainframe or hindering its operation in any respect. The team did not want to alter the mainframe in any way because of its track record, its complexity, and the fact that there was likely no one on staff who knew the inner workings of its deep-rooted code.

To maximize simplicity and speed, the team did not install a middleware server to translate requests made to it in other languages, such as Java, into instructions that could be understood by the mainframe applications. Instead, the translation software was written in Assembly Language (a programming language dating to the 1950s that is rarely used today for business applications) and installed directly on the mainframe This strategy reduced the number of things that could go wrong during translations and promised better performance.

The lack of middleware meant that the system's users, such as Merrill Lynch financial advisers, could request information directly from the mainframe from their desktops. For example, an adviser could use a Web browser to request a list of all clients who owned shares of a certain stock, such as General Electric (GE). The request arrives at the mainframe using SOAP, which instructs the mainframe to perform a particular operation, and the search is translated by XML.

A Merrill Lynch mainframe programmer can access the X4ML development tool from a desktop Web browser. Using X4ML, the programmer can create and name a new Web service, import the necessary application from the mainframe, and then pick and choose which parts of the operation in the legacy application to include in the Web service. Thus, a programmer is able to produce a Web service that pulls out all of the personal data for a client, or only the less sensitive data, such as name and address. Once a programmer creates a Web service, it is listed in a Universal Description, Discovery, and Integration (UDDI) directory, where it can be accessed by other programmers. The X4ML development tool also includes a testing capability, which enables programmers to correct errors before deploying a service, as well as utilize trial-and-error to perfect combinations of applications for new services.

Merrill Lynch earmarked $1 billion over a three-year period to use X4ML to provide its 14,000 financial advisers with a new suite of wealth management applications. For this initiative, the firm teamed with Thomson Financial and Siebel Systems (now owned by Oracle), which offered financial data and research services and client management expertise, respectively.

Merrill Lynch's investment in Web services saved the company $41 million in application development costs. The company wrung even more value out of X4ML by selling it in December 2005 to Web services vendor SOA Software Inc. of Los Angeles. As part of the deal, Crew and three other key members of the X4ML team shifted their employment to SOA Software to continue enhancing the tool, which was renamed Service Oriented Legacy Architecture (SOLA). Merrill Lynch had a long history of selling internally developed technology, and it viewed the sale of X4ML as a way of optimizing its investment.

Chief Technology Architect Andrew Brown did not think that turning the technology over to another company would hurt his firm's competitive advantage. He needed six months to convince management that selling to a software vendor was the right move. After the fact, management appreciated the value of the sale and the space that it created in the IT budget. At the time of the sale, X4ML was utilizing 600 Web services for 40 different core applications at Merrill Lynch and processing 1.5 million transactions daily. The price of the X4ML sale to SOA was not disclosed, but SOA Software began selling SOLA to customers in 2006 for $125,000. Purchasers of the tool were poised to gain unmatched scalability. Meanwhile, the success of X4ML gave a second life to Merrill Lynch's mainframe programmers and their work.

Sources: Mel Duvall, "Merrill Lynch & Co.: Web Services, Millions of Transactions, All Good," *Baseline Magazine*, February 2006; Charles Babcock, "Merrill Lynch Sells Its Web Services Vendor a Web Services Tool," *InformationWeek*, December 6, 2005; Elena Malykhina, "Merrill Lynch Embraces SOA," *InformationWeek*, November 8, 2005; China Martens, "SOA Software Snaps Up Blue Titan," IDG news service through www.techworld.com, May 8, 2006; Ann Bednarz, "SOA Software Buys Blue Titan," NetworkWorld, May 8, 2006.

CASE STUDY QUESTIONS

1. Why did Merrill Lynch need to update its IT infrastructure?

2. What is the relationship of information technology to Merrill Lynch's business strategy? How was its Web services initiative related to that strategy?

3. Evaluate Merrill Lynch's approach to Web services development. What are the advantages and disadvantages? Is it a good solution? Explain your answer.

4. Do you think that Merrill Lynch's decision to sell off its successful technology initiatives was a good idea? Why or why not?

Foundations of Business Intelligence: Databases and Information Management

From *Management Information Systems: Managing the Digital Firm, 10/e*. Kenneth C. Laudon, Jane P. Laudon.

Foundations of Business Intelligence: Databases and Information Management

The National Association for Stock Car Auto Racing, better known as NASCAR, is on its way to becoming America's most popular spectator sport. In 2005, 75 million people attended NASCAR races, the highest number of attendees of any sport in the United States. NASCAR racing is second only to the National Football League (NFL) in television ratings. From 1995 to 2004, NASCAR's fan base ballooned from 63 million to 75 million, and retail sales of NASCAR-licensed merchandise jumped more than 250 percent, from approximately $600 million to $2.1 billion. More Fortune 500 companies sponsor NASCAR than any other sport.

What's wrong with this picture? Not much, except NASCAR management thinks the company can still do better. It thinks it can grow NASCAR's fan base even more, especially in areas outside the South where NASCAR has traditionally been most popular. But NASCAR needs the right data to identify who its fans are, and it's having trouble putting all those data together.

Until about five years ago, NASCAR considered information systems a back-office function. Its entire race process—obtaining credentials for sponsors, running races, managing relationships with sponsors, and paying drivers and their teams—was heavily manual and paper-oriented. Race tracks did not have technology to transmit race data effectively.

The picture changed after NASCAR started recruiting top-notch executives from Fortune 500, sports, and media companies who appreciated what IT could do for a business. Roger Lovell, NASCAR's Managing Director of IT, was empowered to launch an IT-enabled business transformation.

Lovell and his team of information systems specialists developed a scalable, stable IT infrastructure, standardized NASCAR's desktop computing technology, and implemented a plan to beef up systems security. They began gathering more data electronically about driver performance during a race and analyzing the data so fans could follow drivers' performance similar to the way baseball uses batting averages. In 2006, NASCAR implemented a state-of-the-art Mobile Technology Center to collect and process timing and scoring data as races take place.

Now Lovell and Roger VanDerSnick, NASCAR's vice president of marketing, are working on building a single comprehensive database of racing car fans that could be shared with business partners and used for marketing to those fans. Such a database would provide a better understanding of NASCAR fans' demographic profiles, behaviors, and preferences for targeting offers such as NASCAR-branded jackets, opportunities to meet drivers at races, or products and services from sponsors. In addition to generating revenue, these initiatives would increase fan loyalty,

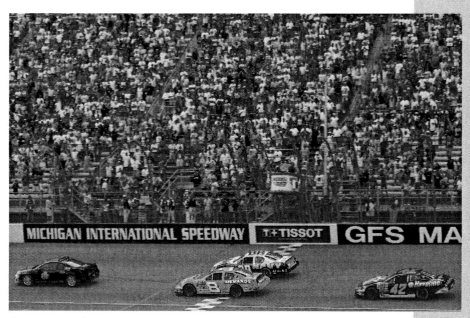

Photo courtesy of Getty Images, Inc.

helping NASCAR attract new sponsors and convince existing sponsors to increase their spending.

Creating a consolidated fan database is challenging because the data are housed in many disparate databases. NASCAR.com has its own database as does the NASCAR members club and each driver's fan club. It is likely that these databases do not store fan data in a consistent manner, so the data will need to be "cleansed" for discrepancies, inconsistencies, and errors, and restructured to fit a single standard format. NASCAR and its partners will have to establish rules for using a consolidated fan database so that NASCAR fans are not bombarded with excessive marketing appeals and the privacy agreements that racing teams, drivers, and sponsors have established with their own fans are respected. Stoneacre Partners, who built a relational database for the Official NASCAR Membership Club, is in charge of the project.

Sources: Meridith Levinson, "IT Supercharges NASCAR," *CIO Magazine*, February 1, 2006 and K.C. Jones, "NASCAR Revs Up Data Center on Wheels," *Information Week*, May 19, 2006.

NASCAR's experience illustrates the importance of data management and database systems for business. NASCAR has experienced phenomenal growth. But its future growth and business performance depend on what it can or can't do with its customer data. How businesses store, organize, and manage their data has a tremendous impact on organizational effectiveness.

The chapter-opening diagram calls attention to important points raised by this case and this chapter. Data about NASCAR fans and potential customers had been stored in a number of different databases where they could not be easily retrieved and analyzed. Management decided that NASCAR's business strategy needed to focus on creating customer intimacy, which necessitated integrating the data from all these disparate sources into a single comprehensive fan database. In addition to using appropriate technology, NASCAR had to correct and reorganize the data into a standard format and establish rules with its business partners for accessing information in the new database.

HEADS UP

This chapter focuses on data management and how businesses use database technology to achieve their objectives. Once businesses use database management systems to properly organize their data, the data can be analyzed. The resulting information can be used to develop new businesses, achieve operational excellence, inform management decision making, and help the firm fulfill its regulatory reporting requirements. Entire businesses, such as UPS, credit card companies, and Google, are based on databases. It would not be an overstatement to say that databases are the foundation of business today and that most businesses would fail should their databases cease to exist.

- If your career is in finance and accounting, you will be working with databases of financial transactions, such as payments, invoices, or credit history. If your job is in finance, you will work with massive databases housing data about securities prices, investment portfolios, and economic statistics.

- If your career is in human resources, you will work with databases maintaining data on employees, benefits plans, compensation plans, training programs, and compliance with governmental regulations on health, safety, and equal employment opportunity.

- If your career is in information systems, you will play a key role in providing data management tools and expertise to the firm. You'll design databases, implement and maintain database technology, and help promote data administration policies and procedures.

- If your career is in manufacturing, production, or operations management, you will be working with large databases with data on finished goods, raw materials in inventory, suppliers, product components, product quality, and goods in transit that can be used for supply chain management.

- If your career is in sales and marketing, you will be using databases for tracking customer purchases, analyzing customer data for targeted marketing campaigns, or identifying profitable customers and products.

1 ORGANIZING DATA IN A TRADITIONAL FILE ENVIRONMENT

An effective information system provides users with accurate, timely, and relevant information. Accurate information is free of errors. Information is timely when it is available to decision makers when it is needed. Information is relevant when it is useful and appropriate for the types of work and decisions that require it.

You might be surprised to learn that many businesses don't have timely, accurate, or relevant information because the data in their information systems have been poorly organized and maintained. That's why data management is so essential. To understand the problem, let's look how information systems arrange data in computer files and traditional methods of file management.

FILE ORGANIZATION CONCEPTS

A computer system organizes data in a hierarchy that starts with bits and bytes and progresses to fields, records, files, and databases (see Figure 1). A bit represents the smallest unit of data a computer can handle. A group of bits, called a byte, represents a single character, which can be a letter, a number, or another symbol. A grouping of characters into a word, a group of words, or a complete number (such as a person's name or age) is called a **field**. A group of related fields, such as the student's name, the course taken, the date, and the grade, comprises a **record**; a group of records of the same type is called a **file**.

For example, the records in Figure 1 could constitute a student course file. A group of related files makes up a **database**. The student course file illustrated in Figure 1 could be grouped with files on students' personal histories and financial backgrounds to create a student database.

A record describes an entity. An **entity** is a person, place, thing, or event on which we store and maintain information. Each characteristic or quality

FIGURE 1   THE DATA HIERARCHY

A computer system organizes data in a hierarchy that starts with the bit, which represents either a 0 or a 1. Bits can be grouped to form a byte to represent one character, number, or symbol. Bytes can be grouped to form a field, and related fields can be grouped to form a record. Related records can be collected to form a file, and related files can be organized into a database.

describing a particular entity is called an **attribute**. For example, Student_ID, Course, Date, and Grade are attributes of the entity COURSE. The specific values that these attributes can have are found in the fields of the record describing the entity COURSE.

PROBLEMS WITH THE TRADITIONAL FILE ENVIRONMENT

In most organizations, data files and systems tended to grow independently without a company-wide plan. Accounting, finance, manufacturing, human resources, and sales and marketing all developed their own systems and data files. Figure 2 illustrates the traditional approach to information processing.

Each application, of course, required its own files and its own computer program to operate. For example, the human resources department might have a personnel master file, a payroll file, a medical insurance file, a pension file, a mailing list file, and so forth until tens, perhaps hundreds, of files and programs existed. The finance department might also have a payroll file, a pension file, and an employee master list to run the payroll. In the company as a whole, this process led to multiple master files created, maintained, and operated by separate divisions or departments. As this process goes on for 5 or 10 years, the organization is saddled with hundreds of programs and applications that are very difficult to maintain and manage. The resulting problems are data redundancy and inconsistency, program-data dependence, inflexibility, poor data security, and an inability to share data among applications.

FIGURE 2   TRADITIONAL FILE PROCESSING

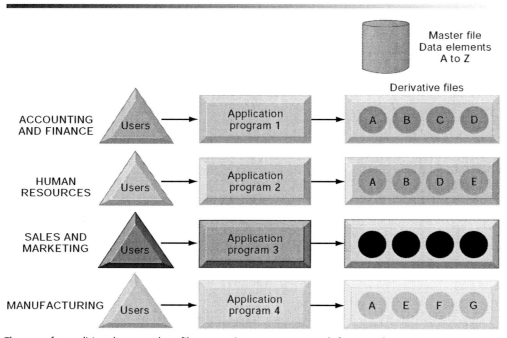

The use of a traditional approach to file processing encourages each functional area in a corporation to develop specialized applications and files. Each application requires a unique data file that is likely to be a subset of the master file. These subsets of the master file lead to data redundancy and inconsistency, processing inflexibility, and wasted storage resources.

235

Data Redundancy and Inconsistency

Data redundancy is the presence of duplicate data in multiple data files so that the same data are stored in more than one place or location. Data redundancy occurs when different groups in an organization independently collect the same piece of data and store it independently of each other. Data redundancy wastes storage resources and also leads to **data inconsistency**, where the same attribute may have different values. For example, in instances of the entity COURSE illustrated in Figure 1, the Date may be updated in some systems but not in others. The attribute Student_ID may have different names in different systems throughout the organization. Some systems might use Student_ID and others might use ID, for example.

Additional confusion might result from using different coding systems to represent values for an attribute. For instance, the sales, inventory, and manufacturing systems of a clothing retailer might use different codes to represent clothing size. One system might represent clothing size as "extra large," whereas another might use the code "XL" for the same purpose. The resulting confusion would make it difficult for companies to create customer relationship management, supply chain management, or enterprise systems that integrate data from different sources.

Program-Data Dependence

Program-data dependence refers to the coupling of data stored in files and the specific programs required to update and maintain those files such that changes in programs require changes to the data. Every traditional computer program has to describe the location and nature of the data with which it works. In a traditional file environment, any change in a software program could require a change in the data accessed by that program. One program might be modified from a five-digit to a nine-digit ZIP code. If the original data file were changed from five-digit to nine-digit ZIP codes, then other programs that required the five-digit ZIP code would no longer work properly. Such changes could cost millions of dollars to implement properly.

Lack of Flexibility

A traditional file system can deliver routine scheduled reports after extensive programming efforts, but it cannot deliver ad hoc reports or respond to unanticipated information requirements in a timely fashion. The information required by ad hoc requests is somewhere in the system but may be too expensive to retrieve. Several programmers might have to work for weeks to put together the required data items in a new file.

Poor Security

Because there is little control or management of data, access to and dissemination of information may be out of control. Management may have no way of knowing who is accessing or even making changes to the organization's data.

Lack of Data Sharing and Availability

Because pieces of information in different files and different parts of the organization cannot be related to one another, it is virtually impossible for information to be shared or accessed in a timely manner. Information cannot flow freely across different functional areas or different parts of the organization. If users find different values of the same piece of information in two different systems, they may not want to use these systems because they cannot trust the accuracy of their data.

236

2   THE DATABASE APPROACH TO DATA MANAGEMENT

Database technology cuts through many of the problems of traditional file organization. A more rigorous definition of a **database** is a collection of data organized to serve many applications efficiently by centralizing the data and controlling redundant data. Rather than storing data in separate files for each application, data are stored so as to appear to users as being stored in only one location. A single database services multiple applications. For example, instead of a corporation storing employee data in separate information systems and separate files for personnel, payroll, and benefits, the corporation could create a single common human resources database.

DATABASE MANAGEMENT SYSTEMS

A **database management system (DBMS)** is software that permits an organization to centralize data, manage them efficiently, and provide access to the stored data by application programs. The DBMS acts as an interface between application programs and the physical data files. When the application program calls for a data item, such as gross pay, the DBMS finds this item in the database and presents it to the application program. Using traditional data files, the programmer would have to specify the size and format of each data element used in the program and then tell the computer where they were located.

The DBMS relieves the programmer or end user from the task of understanding where and how the data are actually stored by separating the logical and physical views of the data. The *logical view* presents data as they would be perceived by end users or business specialists, whereas the *physical view* shows how data are actually organized and structured on physical storage media.

The database management software makes the physical database available for different logical views required by users. For example, for the human resources database illustrated in Figure 3, a benefits specialist might require a view consisting of the employee's name, social security number, and health insurance coverage. A payroll department member might need data such as the employee's name, social security number, gross pay, and net pay. The data for all these views are stored in a single database, where they can be more easily managed by the organization.

How a DBMS Solves the Problems of the Traditional File Environment

A DBMS reduces data redundancy and inconsistency by minimizing isolated files in which the same data are repeated. The DBMS may not enable the organization to eliminate data redundancy entirely, but it can help control redundancy. Even if the organization maintains some redundant data, using a DBMS eliminates data inconsistency because the DBMS can help the organization ensure that every occurrence of redundant data has the same values. The DBMS uncouples programs and data, enabling data to stand on their own. Access and availability of information will be increased and program development and maintenance costs reduced because users and programmers can perform ad hoc queries of data in the database. The DBMS enables the organization to centrally manage data, their use, and security.

FIGURE 3   HUMAN RESOURCES DATABASE WITH MULTIPLE VIEWS

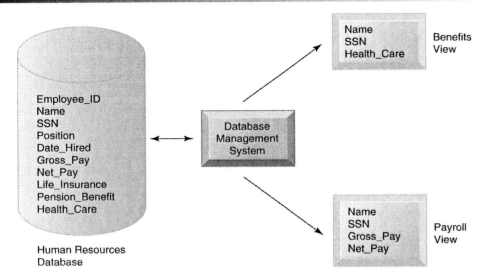

A single human resources database provides many different views of data, depending on the information requirements of the user. Illustrated here are two possible views, one of interest to a benefits specialist and one of interest to a member of the company's payroll department.

Relational DBMS

Contemporary DBMS use different database models to keep track of entities, attributes, and relationships. The most popular type of DBMS today for PCs as well as for larger computers and mainframes is the **relational DBMS**. Relational databases represent data as two-dimensional tables (called relations). Tables may be referred to as files. Each table contains data on an entity and its attributes. Microsoft Access is a relational DBMS for desktop systems, whereas DB2, Oracle Database, and Microsoft SQL Server are relational DBMS for large mainframes and midrange computers. MySQL is a popular open-source DBMS, and Oracle Database Lite is a DBMS for small handheld computing devices.

Let's look at how a relational database organizes data about suppliers and parts (see Figure 4). The database has a separate table for the entity SUPPLIER and a table for the entity PART. Each table consists of a grid of columns and rows of data. Each individual element of data for each entity is stored as a separate field, and each field represents an attribute for that entity. Fields in a relational database are also called columns. For the entity SUPPLIER, the supplier number, name, street, city, state, and ZIP code, are stored as a separate fields within the SUPPLIER table and each field represents an attribute for the entity SUPPLIER.

The actual information about a single supplier that resides in a table is called a row. Rows are commonly referred to as **records**, or in very technical terms, as **tuples**. Data for the entity PART have their own separate table.

The field for Supplier_Number in the SUPPLIER table uniquely identifies each record so that so that the record can be retrieved, updated or sorted and it is called a **key field**. Each table in a relational database has one field that is designated as its **primary key**. This key field is the unique identifier for all the information in any row of the table and this primary key cannot be duplicated. Supplier_Number is the primary key for the SUPPLIER table and Part_Number is the primary key for the PART table. Note that Supplier_Number appears in both the SUPPLIER and PART tables. In the SUPPLIER table, Supplier_Number

FIGURE 4   **RELATIONAL DATABASE TABLES**

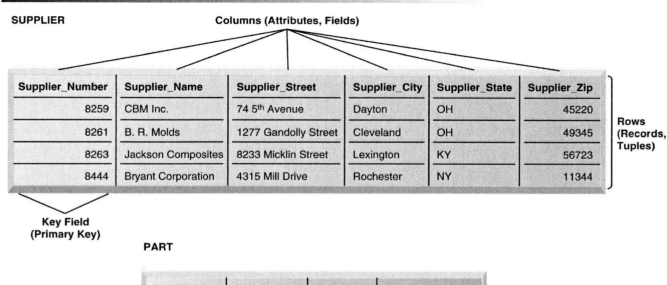

A relational database organizes data in the form of two-dimensional tables. Illustrated here are tables for the entities SUPPLIER and PART showing how they represent each entity and its attributes. Supplier_Number is a primary key for the SUPPLIER table and a foreign key for the PART table.

is the primary key. When the field Supplier_Number appears in the PART table it is called a **foreign key** and is essentially a look-up field to look up data about the supplier of a specific part.

Operations of a Relational DBMS

Relational database tables can be combined easily to deliver data required by users, provided that any two tables share a common data element. Suppose we wanted to find in this database the names and addresses of suppliers who could provide us with part number 137 or part number 150. We would need information from two tables: the SUPPLIER table and the PART table. Note that these two files have a shared data element: Supplier_Number.

In a relational database, three basic operations, as shown in Figure 5, are used to develop useful sets of data: select, project, and join. The *select* operation creates a subset consisting of all records (rows) in the table that meet stated criteria. In our example, we want to select records (rows) from the PART table where the Part_Number equals 137 or 150. The *join* operation combines relational tables to provide the user with more information than is available in indi-

FIGURE 5   THE THREE BASIC OPERATIONS OF A RELATIONAL DBMS

PART

Part_Number	Part_Name	Unit_Price	Supplier_Number
137	Door latch	22.00	8259
145	Side mirror	12.00	8444
150	Door molding	6.00	8263
152	Door lock	31.00	8259
155	Compressor	54.00	8261
178	Door handle	10.00	8259

Select Part_Number = 137 or 150

SUPPLIER

Supplier_Number	Supplier_Name	Supplier_Street	Supplier_City	Supplier_State	Supplier_Zip
8259	CBM Inc.	74 5th Avenue	Dayton	OH	45220
8261	B. R. Molds	1277 Gandolly Street	Cleveland	OH	49345
8263	Jackson Components	8233 Micklin Street	Lexington	KY	56723
8444	Bryant Corporation	4315 Mill Drive	Rochester	NY	11344

Join by Supplier_Number

Part_Number	Part_Name	Supplier_Number	Supplier_Name
137	Door latch	8259	CBM Inc.
150	Door molding	8263	Jackson Components

Project selected columns

The select, project, and join operations enable data from two different tables to be combined and only selected attributes to be displayed.

vidual tables. In our example, we want to join the now-shortened PART table (only parts 137 or 150 will be presented) and the SUPPLIER table into a single new table.

The *project* operation creates a subset consisting of columns in a table, permitting the user to create new tables that contain only the information required. In our example, we want to extract from the new table only the following columns: Part_Number, Part_Name, Supplier_Number, and Supplier_Name.

Hierarchical and Network DBMS

You may run across older systems that use a hierarchical or network DBMS. A hierarchical DBMS models one-to-many relationships, while a network DBMS models many-to-many relationships. Hierarchical and network DBMS are no longer used for building new database applications. They are much less flexible than relational DBMS and do not support ad hoc, natural language—like inquiries for information. You can find more detail on how these DBMS work in the Learning Track Modules for this chapter, which can be found on the Laudon Web site.

Relational DBMS have much more flexibility in providing data for ad hoc queries, combining information from different sources, and adding new data and records without disturbing existing programs and applications. However, these systems slow down if they require many accesses to the data stored on disk to carry out the select, join, and project commands. Of course, the database can be tuned to speed up prespecified queries.

Object-Oriented DBMS

Many applications today require databases that can store and retrieve not only records containing numbers and characters but also drawings, images, photographs, voice, and full-motion video. DBMS designed for organizing structured data into rows and columns are not well suited to handling graphics-based or multimedia applications. Object-oriented databases are better suited for this purpose. For instance, an architectural firm deals mostly with objects and drawings rather than structured text records.

An **object-oriented DBMS** stores the data and procedures that act on those data as objects that can be automatically retrieved and shared. Object-oriented database management systems (OODBMS) are becoming popular because they can be used to manage the various multimedia components or Java applets used in Web applications, which typically integrate pieces of information from a variety of sources.

Although object-oriented databases can store more complex types of information than relational DBMS, they are relatively slow compared with relational DBMS for processing large numbers of transactions or records. Hybrid **object-relational DBMS** systems are now available to provide capabilities of both object-oriented and relational DBMS.

CAPABILITIES OF DATABASE MANAGEMENT SYSTEMS

A DBMS includes capabilities and tools for organizing, managing, and accessing the data in the database. The most important are its data definition capability, data dictionary, and data manipulation language.

DBMS have a **data definition** capability to specify the structure of the content of the database. It would be used to create database tables and to define the characteristics of the fields in each table. This information about the database would be documented in a **data dictionary**. A data dictionary is an automated or manual file that stores definitions of data elements and their characteristics.

Microsoft Access has a built-in rudimentary data dictionary capability that displays information about the name, description, size, type, format, and other properties of each field in a table when it is in Design view or when the Documenter capability is employed. Data dictionaries for large corporate databases may capture additional information, such as ownership (who in the organization is responsible for maintaining the data); authorization; security; and the individuals, business functions, programs, and reports that use each data element (see Figure 6).

Querying and Reporting

DBMS includes tools for accessing and manipulating information in databases. Most DBMS have a specialized language called a **data manipulation language** that is used to add, change, delete, and retrieve the data in the database. This language contains commands that permit end users and programming specialists to extract data from the database to satisfy information requests and develop applications. The most prominent data manipulation language today is **Structured Query Language**, or **SQL**. Figure 7 illustrates the SQL query that would produce the new resultant table in Figure 5. You can find out more about how to perform SQL queries in our Learning Tracks for this chapter.

FIGURE 6   **SAMPLE DATA DICTIONARY REPORT**

NAME: Salary

DESCRIPTION: Employee's annual salary
SIZE: 9 bytes
TYPE: N (Numeric)
DATE CHANGED: 1/1/05
OWNERSHIP: Compensation

UPDATE SECURITY: Site Personnel
ACCESS SECURITY: Manager, Compensation Planning
                 Manager, Human Resources Planning
                 Manager, Equal Opportunity Affairs
                 Manager, Benefits Department

BUSINESS FUNCTIONS USED BY: Compensation
                            HR Planning
                            Employment
                            Insurance
                            Pension and 401K
PROGRAMS USING: PI01000
                PI02000
                PI03000

REPORTS USING: Salary Increase Tracking Report
                Salary Review Listing
                Pension Reference Listing

The sample data dictionary report for a human resources database provides helpful information, such as the size of the data element, which programs and reports use it, and which group in the organization is the owner responsible for maintaining it.

FIGURE 7   EXAMPLE OF AN SQL QUERY

SELECT PART.Part_Number, PART.Part_Name, SUPPLIER.Supplier_Number,
SUPPLIER.Supplier_Name
FROM PART, SUPPLIER
WHERE PART.Supplier_Number = SUPPLIER.Supplier_Number AND
Part_Number = 137 OR Part_Number = 150;

Illustrated here are the SQL statements for a query to select suppliers for parts 137 or 150.
They produce a list with the same results as Figure 5.

Users of DBMS for large and midrange computers, such as DB2, Oracle, or SQL Server, would employ SQL to retrieve information they needed from the database. Microsoft Access also uses SQL, but it provides its own set of user-friendly tools for querying databases and for organizing data from databases into more polished reports.

In Microsoft Access, you will find Query Wizard and Query Design View features that enable users to create queries by identifying the tables and fields they want and the results, and then selecting the rows from the database that meet particular criteria. These actions in turn are translated into SQL commands. Figure 8 illustrates how the same query as the SQL query to select parts and suppliers would be constructed using the Query Design View.

Microsoft Access and other DBMS include capabilities for report generation so that the data of interest can be displayed in a more structured and polished format than would be possible just by querying. Crystal Reports is a popular report generator for large corporate DBMS, although it can also be used with Access. Access also has capabilities for developing desktop system applications. These include tools for creating data entry screens, reports, and developing the logic for processing transactions.

FIGURE 8   AN ACCESS QUERY

Illustrated here is how the query in Figure 7 would be constructed using query-building tools in the Access Query Design View. It shows the tables, fields, and selection criteria used for the query.

DESIGNING DATABASES

To create a database, you must understand the relationships among the data, the type of data that will be maintained in the database, how the data will be used, and how the organization will need to change to manage data from a company-wide perspective. The database requires both a conceptual design and a physical design. The conceptual, or logical, design of a database is an abstract model of the database from a business perspective, whereas the physical design shows how the database is actually arranged on direct-access storage devices.

Normalization and Entity-Relationship Diagrams

The conceptual database design describes how the data elements in the database are to be grouped. The design process identifies relationships among data elements and the most efficient way of grouping data elements together to meet business information requirements. The process also identifies redundant data elements and the groupings of data elements required for specific application programs. Groups of data are organized, refined, and streamlined until an overall logical view of the relationships among all the data elements in the database emerges.

To use a relational database model effectively, complex groupings of data must be streamlined to minimize redundant data elements and awkward many-to-many relationships. The process of creating small, stable, yet flexible and adaptive data structures from complex groups of data is called **normalization**. Figures 9 and 10 illustrate this process.

In the particular business modeled here, an order can have more than one part but each part is provided by only one supplier. If we build a relation called ORDER with all the fields included here, we would have to repeat the name and address of the supplier for every part on the order, even though the order is for parts from a single supplier. This relationship contains what are called *repeating data groups* because there can be many parts on a single order to a given supplier. A more efficient way to arrange the data is to break down ORDER into smaller relations, each of which describes a single entity. If we go step by step and normalize the relation ORDER, we emerge with the relations illustrated in Figure 10. You can find out more about normalization, entity-relationship diagramming, and database design in the first Learning Track for this chapter.

Database designers document their data model with an **entity-relationship diagram**, illustrated in Figure 11. This diagram illustrates the relationship between the entities ORDER, LINE_ITEM, PART, and SUPPLIER. The boxes represent entities. The lines connecting the boxes represent relationships. A line connecting two entities that ends in two short marks designates a one-to-one relationship. A line connecting two entities that ends with a crow's foot topped by a short mark indicates a one-to-many relationship. Figure 11 shows

FIGURE 9   AN UNNORMALIZED RELATION FOR ORDER

ORDER (Before Normalization)

An unnormalized relation contains repeating groups. For example, there can be many parts and suppliers for each order. There is only a one-to-one correspondence between Order_Number and Order_Date.

FIGURE 10   NORMALIZED TABLES CREATED FROM ORDER

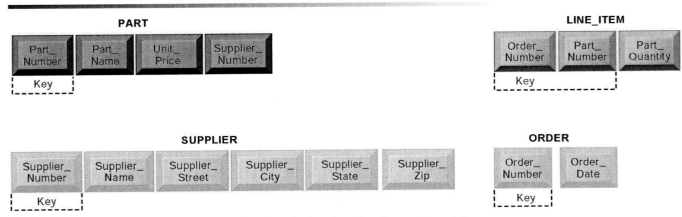

After normalization, the original relation ORDER has been broken down into four smaller relations. The relation ORDER is left with only two attributes and the relation LINE_ITEM has a combined, or concatenated, key consisting of Order_Number and Part_Number.

that one ORDER can contain many LINE_ITEMs. (A PART can be ordered many times and appear many times as a line item in a single order.) Each PART can have only one SUPPLIER, but many PARTs can be provided by the same SUPPLIER.

It can't be emphasized enough: If the business doesn't get its data model right, the system won't be able to serve the business well. The company's systems will not be as effective as they could be because they'll have to work with data that may be inaccurate, incomplete, or difficult to retrieve. Understanding the organization's data and how they should be represented in a database is perhaps the most important lesson you can learn from this course.

Distributing Databases

Database design also considers how the data are to be distributed. Information systems can be designed with a centralized database that is used by a single central processor or by multiple processors in a client/server network. Alternatively, the database can be distributed. A **distributed database** is one that is stored in more than one physical location.

There are two main methods of distributing a database (see Figure 12). In a *partitioned* database, parts of the database are stored and maintained physically in one location and other parts are stored and maintained in other locations (see Figure 12a) so that each remote processor has the necessary data to serve

FIGURE 11   AN ENTITY-RELATIONSHIP DIAGRAM

This diagram shows the relationships between the entities ORDER, LINE_ITEM, PART, and SUPPLIER that might be used to model the database in Figure 10.

FIGURE 12   DISTRIBUTED DATABASES

There are alternative ways of distributing a database. The central database can be partitioned (a) so that each remote processor has the necessary data to serve its own local needs. The central database also can be replicated (b) at all remote locations.

its local area. Changes in local files can be justified with the central database on a batch basis, often at night. Another strategy is to *replicate* (that is, duplicate in its entirety) the central database (Figure 12b) at all remote locations. For example, Lufthansa Airlines replaced its centralized mainframe database with a replicated database to make information more immediately available to flight dispatchers. Any change made to Lufthansa's Frankfort DBMS is automatically replicated in New York and Hong Kong. This strategy also requires updating the central database during off-hours.

Distributed systems reduce the vulnerability of a single, massive central site. They increase service and responsiveness to local users and often can run on smaller, less-expensive computers. However, local databases can sometimes depart from central data standards and definitions, and they pose security problems by widely distributing access to sensitive data. Database designers need to weigh these factors in their decisions.

3   USING DATABASES TO IMPROVE BUSINESS PERFORMANCE AND DECISION MAKING

Businesses use their databases to keep track of basic transactions, such as paying suppliers, processing orders, keeping track of customers, and paying employees. But they also need databases to provide information that will help the company run the business more efficiently, and help managers and employees make better decisions. If a company wants to know which product is the most popular or who is its most profitable customer, the answer lies in the data.

For example, by analyzing data from customer credit card purchases, Louise's Trattoria, a Los Angeles restaurant chain, learned that quality was more important than price for most of its customers, who were college-educated and liked fine wine. Acting on this information, the chain introduced vegetarian dishes, more seafood selections, and more expensive wines, raising sales by more than 10 percent.

In a large company, with large databases or large systems for separate functions, such as manufacturing, sales, and accounting, special capabilities and tools are required for analyzing vast quantities of data and for accessing data from multiple systems. These capabilities include data warehousing, data mining, and tools for accessing internal databases through the Web.

DATA WAREHOUSES

Suppose you wanted concise, reliable information about current operations, trends, and changes across the entire company. If you worked in a large company, obtaining this might be difficult because data are often maintained in separate systems, such as sales, manufacturing, or accounting. Some of the data you needed might be found in the sales system, and other pieces in the manufacturing system. Many of these systems are older legacy systems that use outdated data management technologies or file systems where information is difficult for users to access.

You might have to spend an inordinate amount of time locating and gathering the data you needed, or you would be forced to make your decision based on incomplete knowledge. If you wanted information about trends, you might also have trouble finding data about past events because most firms only make their current data immediately available. Data warehousing addresses these problems.

What Is a Data Warehouse?

A **data warehouse** is a database that stores current and historical data of potential interest to decision makers throughout the company. The data originate in many core operational transaction systems, such as systems for sales, customer accounts, and manufacturing, and may include data from Web site transactions. The data warehouse consolidates and standardizes information from different operational databases so that the information can be used across the enterprise for management analysis and decision making.

Figure 13 illustrates how a data warehouse works. The data warehouse makes the data available for anyone to access as needed, but it cannot be altered. A data warehouse system also provides a range of ad hoc and standardized query tools, analytical tools, and graphical reporting facilities. Many firms use intranet portals to make the data warehouse information widely available throughout the firm.

Data Marts

Companies often build enterprise-wide data warehouses, where a central data warehouse serves the entire organization, or they create smaller, decentralized warehouses called data marts. A **data mart** is a subset of a data warehouse in which a summarized or highly focused portion of the organization's data is placed in a separate database for a specific population of users. For example, a company might develop marketing and sales data marts to deal with customer information. A data mart typically focuses on a single subject area or line of business, so it usually can be constructed more rapidly and at lower cost than an enterprise-wide data warehouse.

FIGURE 13   COMPONENTS OF A DATA WAREHOUSE

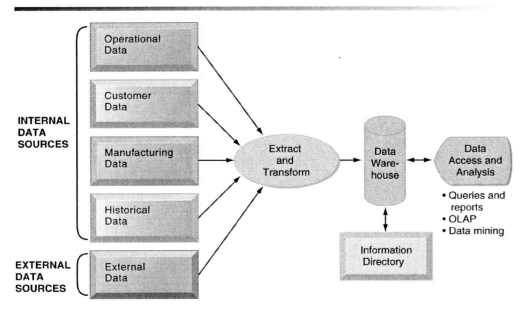

The data warehouse extracts current and historical data from multiple operational systems inside the organization. These data are combined with data from external sources and reorganized into a central database designed for management reporting and analysis. The information directory provides users with information about the data available in the warehouse.

BUSINESS INTELLIGENCE, MULTIDIMENSIONAL DATA ANALYSIS, AND DATA MINING

Once data have been captured and organized in data warehouses and data marts, they are available for further analysis. A series of tools enables users to analyze these data to see new patterns, relationships, and insights that are useful for guiding decision making. These tools for consolidating, analyzing, and providing access to vast amounts of data to help users make better business decisions are often referred to **business intelligence (BI)**. Principal tools for business intelligence include software for database query and reporting, tools for multidimensional data analysis (online analytical processing), and data mining.

When we think of *intelligence* as applied to humans, we typically think of people's ability to combine learned knowledge with new information and change behaviors in such a way that they succeed at their task or adapt to a new situation. Likewise, business intelligence provides firms with the capability to amass information; develop knowledge about customers, competitors, and internal operations; and change decision-making behavior to achieve higher profitability and other business goals.

For instance, Harrah's Entertainment, the second-largest gambling company in its industry, continually analyzes data about its customers gathered when people play its slot machines or use Harrah's casinos and hotels. Harrah's marketing department uses this information to build a detailed gambling profile, based on a particular customer's ongoing value to the company. This information guides management decisions about how to cultivate the most profitable customers, encourage those customers to spend more, and attract more customers with high revenue-generating potential. Business intelligence has improved Harrah's profits so much that it has become the centerpiece of the firm's business strategy.

Figure 14 illustrates how business intelligence works. The firm's operational databases keep track of the transactions generated by running the business. These databases feed data to the data warehouse. Managers use business intelligence tools to find patterns and meanings in the data. Managers then act on what they have learned from analyzing the data by making more informed and intelligent business decisions.

This section will introduce you to the most important business intelligence technologies and tools.

Online Analytical Processing (OLAP)

Suppose your company sells four different products—nuts, bolts, washers, and screws—in the East, West, and Central regions. If you wanted to ask a fairly straightforward question, such as how many washers sold during the past quarter, you could easily find the answer by querying your sales database. But what if you wanted to know how many washers sold in each of your sales regions and compare actual results with projected sales?

To obtain the answer, you would need **online analytical processing (OLAP)**. OLAP supports multidimensional data analysis, enabling users to view the same data in different ways using multiple dimensions. Each aspect of information—product, pricing, cost, region, or time period—represents a different dimension. So, a product manager could use a multidimensional data analysis tool to learn how many washers were sold in the East in June, how that compares with the previous month and the previous June, and how it compares with the sales forecast. OLAP enables users to obtain online answers to ad hoc questions such as these in a fairly rapid amount of time, even when the data are stored in very large databases, such as sales figures for multiple years.

FIGURE 14   BUSINESS INTELLIGENCE

A series of analytical tools works with data stored in databases to find patterns and insights for helping managers and employees make better decisions to improve organizational performance.

FIGURE 15   MULTIDIMENSIONAL DATA MODEL

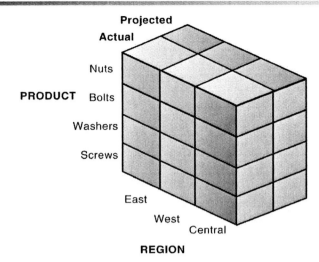

The view that is showing is product versus region. If you rotate the cube 90 degrees, the face that will show is product versus actual and projected sales. If you rotate the cube 90 degrees again, you will see region versus actual and projected sales. Other views are possible.

Figure 15 shows a multidimensional model that could be created to represent products, regions, actual sales, and projected sales. A matrix of actual sales can be stacked on top of a matrix of projected sales to form a cube with six faces. If you rotate the cube 90 degrees one way, the face showing will be product versus actual and projected sales. If you rotate the cube 90 degrees again, you will see region versus actual and projected sales. If you rotate 180 degrees from the original view, you will see projected sales and product versus region. Cubes can be nested within cubes to build complex views of data. A company would use either a specialized multidimensional database or a tool that creates multidimensional views of data in relational databases.

Data Mining

Traditional database queries answer such questions as, "How many units of product number 403 were shipped in February 2007?" OLAP, or multidimensional analysis, supports much more complex requests for information, such as, "Compare sales of product 403 relative to plan by quarter and sales region for the past two years." With OLAP and query-oriented data analysis, users need to have a good idea about the information for which they are looking.

Data mining is more discovery driven. Data mining provides insights into corporate data that cannot be obtained with OLAP by finding hidden patterns and relationships in large databases and inferring rules from them to predict future behavior. The patterns and rules are used to guide decision making and forecast the effect of those decisions. The types of information obtainable from data mining include associations, sequences, classifications, clusters, and forecasts.

- *Associations* are occurrences linked to a single event. For instance, a study of supermarket purchasing patterns might reveal that, when corn chips are purchased, a cola drink is purchased 65 percent of the time, but when there is a promotion, cola is purchased 85 percent of the time. This information helps managers make better decisions because they have learned the profitability of a promotion.

250

- In *sequences*, events are linked over time. We might find, for example, that if a house is purchased, a new refrigerator will be purchased within two weeks 65 percent of the time, and an oven will be bought within one month of the home purchase 45 percent of the time.

- *Classification* recognizes patterns that describe the group to which an item belongs by examining existing items that have been classified and by inferring a set of rules. For example, businesses such as credit card or telephone companies worry about the loss of steady customers. Classification helps discover the characteristics of customers who are likely to leave and can provide a model to help managers predict who those customers are so that the managers can devise special campaigns to retain such customers.

- *Clustering* works in a manner similar to classification when no groups have yet been defined. A data mining tool can discover different groupings within data, such as finding affinity groups for bank cards or partitioning a database into groups of customers based on demographics and types of personal investments.

- Although these applications involve predictions, *forecasting* uses predictions in a different way. It uses a series of existing values to forecast what other values will be. For example, forecasting might find patterns in data to help managers estimate the future value of continuous variables, such as sales figures.

These systems perform high-level analyses of patterns or trends, but they can also drill down to provide more detail when needed. There are data mining applications for all the functional areas of business, and for government and scientific work. One popular use for data mining is to provide detailed analyses of patterns in customer data for one-to-one marketing campaigns or for identifying profitable customers.

For example, Virgin Mobile Australia uses a data warehouse and data mining to increase customer loyalty and roll out new services. The data warehouse consolidates data from its enterprise system, customer relationship management system, and customer billing systems in a massive database. Data mining has enabled management to determine the demographic profile of new customers and relate it to the handsets they purchased. It has also helped management evaluate the performance of each store and point-of-sale campaigns, consumer reactions to new products and services, customer attrition rates, and the revenue generated by each customer.

Predictive analysis uses data mining techniques, historical data, and assumptions about future conditions to predict outcomes of events, such as the probability a customer will respond to an offer or purchase a specific product. For example, the U.S. division of The Body Shop International plc used predictive analysis with its database of catalog, Web, and retail store customers to identify customers who were more likely to make catalog purchases. That information helped the company build a more precise and targeted mailing list for its catalogs, improving the response rate for catalog mailings and catalog revenues.

Data mining is both a powerful and profitable tool, but it poses challenges to the protection of individual privacy. Data mining technology can combine information from many diverse sources to create a detailed "data image" about each of us—our income, our driving habits, our hobbies, our families, and our political interests. The Interactive Session on Organizations explores the debate about whether large databases housing DNA profiles used in crime fighting pose a threat to privacy and social well-being.

251

INTERACTIVE SESSION: ORGANIZATIONS

DNA DATABASES: CRIME-FIGHTING WEAPON OR THREAT TO PRIVACY?

On December 2, 1996, Cherie Morrisette, age 11, left her apartment on the south side of Jacksonville, Florida after arguing with her sister about washing the dishes. Six days later, her body was found 13 miles away in the St. Johns River. Detectives classified the case as a homicide, but could not locate a suspect for ten years. Then on March 16, 2006, detectives in Colchester, Connecticut announced that Robert Shelton Mitchell, age 43, of New Britain, Connecticut would be charged with the murder.

A DNA profile of bodily fluid left by the murderer at the crime scene had been developed by the Biology Laboratory of the Florida Department of Law Enforcement and sent to the nationwide DNA bank. There it matched a DNA sample provided by Mr. Mitchell to the Connecticut sex offenders' registry in 2003 while he was in prison on another charge.

DNA evidence has become a potent crime-fighting tool, allowing a criminal to be identified by his or her own genes. Computer analysis can discover the identity of a criminal by matching DNA from blood, hair, saliva, or other bodily fluids left at a crime scene with a DNA profile in a database. A laboratory creates a profile of specific agreed-upon genetic segments of the DNA molecule for a specific individual and stores that information in a database. To identify a particular individual, the laboratory compares the profile produced from a sample of unknown DNA with the profile produced from a sample belonging to an identified individual to see if there is a match.

Law enforcement agencies around the world are increasingly relying on DNA evidence. United States law enforcement agencies use databases of DNA profiles created by the states and linked through the FBI's Combined DNA Index System (CODIS). The CODIS system, authorized by Congress in 1994, allows law enforcement officials to exchange and compare DNA profiles at the local, state, and national levels. As of April 2004, CODIS had data on more than 1.8 million profiles. The samples on which the DNA profiles are based, primarily blood or saliva, are kept at forensic laboratories around the country. All 50 states, the FBI, and the U.S. Army work with this system.

The CODIS system has helped law enforcement officials identify suspects in more than 11,000 cases. It helped solve two "cold" murders in Kansas, identify two-decade-old remains of a missing California child, and capture a predator terrorizing young boys in Houston. Massachusetts authorities used DNA identification in the summer of 2005 to charge a convicted murderer in the 1998 death of a Foxboro woman who had been stabbed two times.

DNA identification is also helpful in proving innocence. Lawyer Barry Scheck's Innocence Project at the Cardozo School of Law in Yeshiva University has used DNA identification to free more than 100 people who had been wrongly convicted. Law schools at the University of Wisconsin, the University of Washington, and Santa Clara University have similar innocence projects.

According to Joseph M. Polisar, president of the International Association of Chiefs of Police, DNA testing "is the fingerprint technology of this century…The potential for us in the criminal justice field to solve crimes with this technology is boundless."

Despite all their benefits, DNA databases remain controversial. Privacy advocates and defense lawyers believe genetic databases pose risks to the innocent if they contain data on people who are not convicted criminals. In some instances, DNA has been collected from witnesses or others to eliminate them from police inquiries. DNA has also been collected from families of suspects to determine whether suspects should continue to be pursued. The Bush administration and some state legislators have advocated expanding the FBI national DNA database to include juveniles or people who have been accused of crimes but not convicted.

Most people aren't violent criminals, including those who commit misdemeanors, and their inclusion in a national DNA database exposes them to risks they would not otherwise face. People who collect and analyze DNA can make mistakes. (Sloppy DNA collection and laboratory procedures resulted in at least one wrongful conviction in Houston and may have affected the outcome of the O.J. Simpson trial.) There may be valid reasons for an innocent person's DNA to be at a crime scene that police might choose to disregard. Innocent people may be caught up in a criminal investigation when their DNA from a single hair or spot of saliva on a drinking glass appears in a public or private place where they had every right to be.

Sources: Stacey Stowe, "10 Years after Girl's Murder, DNA Link Results in Arrest," and Harlan Levy, "Caught Up in DNA's Growing Web," *The New York Times*, March 17, 2006; "Genetic Privacy," www.epic.org, accessed August 3, 2006; and John Solomon, "FBI's Massive DNA Database Helps ID Suspects," *USA Today*, March 8, 2004.

CASE STUDY QUESTIONS

1. What are the benefits of DNA databases?
2. What problems do DNA databases pose?
3. Who should be included in a national DNA database? Should it be limited to convicted felons? Explain your answer.
4. Who should be able to use DNA databases?

MIS IN ACTION

Explore the Web site for the Combined DNA Index System (CODIS) and answer the following questions.

1. How does CODIS work? How is it designed?
2. What information does CODIS maintain?
3. Who is allowed to use CODIS?
4. How does CODIS aid criminal investigations?

DATABASES AND THE WEB

Have you ever tried to use the Web to place an order or view a product catalog? If so, you were probably using a Web site linked to an internal corporate database. Many companies now use the Web to make some of the information in their internal databases available to customers and business partners.

Suppose, for example, a customer with a Web browser wants to search an online retailer's database for pricing information. Figure 16 illustrates how that customer might access the retailer's internal database over the Web. The user accesses the retailer's Web site over the Internet using Web browser software on his or her client PC. The user's Web browser software requests data from the organization's database, using HTML commands to communicate with the Web server.

Because many "back-end" databases cannot interpret commands written in HTML, the Web server passes these requests for data to software that translates HTML commands into SQL so that they can be processed by the DBMS working with the database. In a client/server environment, the DBMS resides on a dedicated computer called a **database server**. The DBMS receives the SQL requests and provides the required data. The middleware transfers information from the organization's internal database back to the Web server for delivery in the form of a Web page to the user.

Figure 16 shows that the middleware working between the Web server and the DBMS could be an application server running on its own dedicated computer. The application server software handles all application operations, including transaction processing and data access, between browser-based computers and a company's back-end business applications or databases. The application server takes requests from the Web server, runs the business logic to process transactions based on those requests, and provides connectivity to the organization's back-end systems or databases. Alternatively, the software for handling these operations could be a custom program or a CGI script. A CGI script is a compact program using the *Common Gateway Interface (CGI)* specification for processing data on a Web server.

FIGURE 16   LINKING INTERNAL DATABASES TO THE WEB

Users access an organization's internal database through the Web using their desktop PCs and Web browser software.

There are a number of advantages to using the Web to access an organization's internal databases. First, Web browser software is much easier to use than proprietary query tools. Second, the Web interface requires few or no changes to the internal database. It costs much less to add a Web interface in front of a legacy system than to redesign and rebuild the system to improve user access.

Accessing corporate databases through the Web is creating new efficiencies, opportunities, and business models. ThomasNet.com provides an up-to-date online directory of more than 650,000 suppliers of industrial products, such as chemicals, metals, plastics, rubber, and automotive equipment. Formerly called Thomas Register, the company used to send out huge paper catalogs with this information. iGo.com is an Internet-based business that sells batteries and accessories for mobile phones and computing devices. Its Web site links to a giant relational database with product information about batteries and peripherals for nearly every brand and model of mobile computer and portable electronic device.

The Internet Movie Database Web site is linked to a massive database that includes summaries, cast information, and actor biographies for almost every film ever released.

Courtesy of The Internet Movie Database (http://www.imdb.com). Used with permission.

4   MANAGING DATA RESOURCES

Setting up a database is only a start. In order to make sure that the data for your business remain accurate, reliable, and readily available to those who need it, your business will need special policies and procedures for data management.

ESTABLISHING AN INFORMATION POLICY

Every business, large and small, needs an information policy. Your firm's data are an important resource, and you don't want people doing whatever they want with them. You need to have rules on how the data are to be organized and maintained, and who is allowed to view the data or change them.

An **information policy** specifies the organization's rules for sharing, disseminating, acquiring, standardizing, classifying, and inventorying information. An information policy lays out specific procedures and accountabilities, identifying which users and organizational units can share information, where information can be distributed, and who is responsible for updating and maintaining the information. For example, a typical information policy would specify that only selected members of the payroll and human resources department would have the right to change and view sensitive employee data, such as an employee's salary or social security number, and that these departments are responsible for making sure that such employee data are accurate.

If you are in a small business, the information policy would be established and implemented by the owners or managers. In a large organization, managing and planning for information as a corporate resource often requires a formal data administration function. **Data administration** is responsible for the specific policies and procedures through which data can be managed as an organizational resource. These responsibilities include developing information policy, planning for data, overseeing logical database design and data dictionary development, and monitoring how information systems specialists and end-user groups use data.

You may hear the term **data governance** used to describe many of these activities. Promoted by IBM, data governance deals with the policies and processes for managing the availability, usability, integrity, and security of the data employed in an enterprise, with special emphasis on promoting privacy, security, data quality, and compliance with government regulations.

A large organization will also have a database design and management group within the corporate information systems division that is responsible for defining and organizing the structure and content of the database, and maintaining the database. In close cooperation with users, the design group establishes the physical database, the logical relations among elements, and the access rules and security procedures. The functions it performs are called **database administration**.

ENSURING DATA QUALITY

A well-designed database and information policy will go a long way toward ensuring that the business has the information it needs. However, additional steps must be taken to ensure that the data in organizational databases are accurate and remain reliable.

What would happen if a customer's telephone number or account balance were incorrect? What would be the impact if the database had the wrong price for the product you sold? Data that are inaccurate, untimely, or inconsistent with other sources of information lead to incorrect decisions, product recalls, and even financial losses.

According to Forrester Research, 20 percent of U.S. mail and commercial package deliveries were returned because of incorrect names or addresses. The Gartner Group consultants reported that more than 25 percent of the critical data in large Fortune 1000 companies' databases is inaccurate or incomplete, including bad product codes and product descriptions, faulty inventory descriptions, erroneous financial data, incorrect supplier information, and incorrect employee data. Gartner believes that customer data degrades at a rate of 2 percent per month, making poor data quality a major obstacle to successful customer relationship management (Gage and McCormick, 2005; Klau, 2003).

Think of all the times you've received several pieces of the same direct mail advertising on the same day. This is very likely the result of having your name maintained multiple times in a database. Your name may have been misspelled or you used your middle initial on one occasion and not on another or the information was initially entered onto a paper form and not scanned properly into the system. Because of these inconsistencies, the database would treat you as different people! We often receive redundant mail addressed to Laudon, Lavdon, Lauden, or Landon.

If a database is properly designed and enterprise-wide data standards established, duplicate or inconsistent data elements should be minimal. Most data quality problems, however, such as misspelled names, transposed numbers, or incorrect or missing codes, stem from errors during data input. The incidence of such errors is rising as companies move their businesses to the Web and allow customers and suppliers to enter data into their Web sites that directly update internal systems.

Before a new database is in place, organizations need to identify and correct their faulty data and establish better routines for editing data once their database is in operation. Analysis of data quality often begins with a **data quality audit**, which is a structured survey of the accuracy and level of completeness of the data in an information system. Data quality audits can be performed by surveying entire data files, surveying samples from data files, or surveying end users for their perceptions of data quality.

Data cleansing, also known as *data scrubbing*, consists of activities for detecting and correcting data in a database that are incorrect, incomplete, improperly formatted, or redundant. Data cleansing not only corrects errors but also enforces consistency among different sets of data that originated in separate information systems. NASCAR, described in the chapter-opening case, needed to use data cleansing to eliminate inconsistencies and errors in data from multiple sources when it created its comprehensive fan database. Specialized data-cleansing software is available to automatically survey data files, correct errors in the data, and integrate the data in a consistent companywide format.

The Interactive Session on Management describes some companies that experienced data quality problems and how they tried to solve them. These problems were multi-faceted. As you read this case, look for the managerial, organizational, and technology factors that produced these data quality problems and how they were addressed.

INTERACTIVE SESSION: MANAGEMENT

WHAT CAN BE DONE ABOUT DATA QUALITY?

BT Group, formerly British Telecom, struggled with data quality problems for a number of years. Poor product inventory data and customer billing errors were hindering its interactions with suppliers and customers. BT Group was spending too much time and effort correcting data.

BT Group started taking data quality seriously in 1997. Nigel Turner, project lead manager for BT data quality programs, identified a data quality "champion" in each of BT's major lines of business to lead an information management forum. Each information management group targeted specific projects with demonstrable returns on investment, such as improving private-inventory recordkeeping to increase the number of disconnected circuits returned to stock for reuse or correcting names and addresses in marketing data to reduce the number of letters sent to the wrong people. As the project expanded, Turner's group centralized data management and developed a data quality methodology that incorporated best practices from inside and outside the company.

By improving the quality of its data, BT Group saved as much as $800 million from improved inventory data and interactions with customers and suppliers and increased revenue through more accurate billing. To maintain a high level of data quality in its databases, BT uses data profiling and cleansing tools from Trillium Software to identify and remove erroneous data on an ongoing basis.

Emerson Process Management, a global supplier of measurement, analytical, and monitoring instruments and services based in Austin, Texas, had to retire a new data warehouse designed for analyzing customer activity to improve service and marketing because the warehouse was full of inaccurate and redundant data. The data in the warehouse came from numerous transaction processing systems in Europe, Asia, and other locations around the world. The group that had designed the warehouse had assumed that sales groups in all these areas would enter customer names and addresses the same way, regardless of their location. In fact, cultural differences combined with complications from absorbing companies that Emerson had acquired led to multiple ways of entering quote, billing, shipping, and other data.

Emerson implemented data quality software tools from Group 1 Software Inc. in Lanham, Maryland to help profile, cleanse, and merge records for the data warehouse. Customer information for quotations, billing, and shipping is linked to associated transactional records, duplicate records are eliminated, and the data are merged using Group 1 tools, custom software, and manual review processes.

Integrating data from multiple business operations also posed challenges at Cintas, which started out in the employee uniform business and then expanded into providing business cleaning supplies and document shredding and storage services. Cintas now has multiple divisions for these lines of business and wanted to integrate customer data from them in a data warehouse to improve cross-selling. But some customers were listed in multiple databases with enough variation in their names and addresses to be identified as different people, and those discrepancies sometimes led to existing customers being identified as new prospects. Such low-quality customer data could create embarrassing situations for sales reps and also make the reps distrust the sales leads provided by marketing. Alternatively, Cintas systems would identify two different customers with similar names as the same customer, depriving the company of a sales opportunity.

Cintas chose to overhaul its data warehouse by installing data quality management software from Dataflux to identify duplicate customer records and standardize customer data collected monthly from each division's database. It is considering how it can use the data matching capabilities provided by the Dataflux software to correct data as employees are entering them into its systems rather than when the data enter its data warehouse.

Bank of America had maintained a centralized data warehouse with account data from multiple sources used for marketing and cross-selling for a number of years. In 2002, it had to re-examine its data quality efforts to make sure it complied with the anti-money-laundering provisions of the Patriot Act. The bank established a common set of practices for capturing, integrating, and managing the data. Management designated data stewards in business units and the bank's information systems department to meet monthly and resolve data quality problems. The bank uses both commercial and home-grown data profiling and matching tools to examine and correct data sent to the warehouse.

Sources: Rick Whiting, "Aaww, Rubbish!" *Information Week*, May 8, 2006 and Kym Gilhooly, "Dirty Data Blights the Bottom Line," *Computerworld*, November 7, 2005.

CASE STUDY QUESTIONS

1. What was the impact of data quality problems on the companies described in this case study? What management, organization, and technology factors caused these problems?

2. How did the companies described in this case solve their data quality problems? What management, organization, and technology issues had to be addressed?

3. It has been said that the biggest obstacle to improving data quality is that business managers view data quality as a technical problem. Discuss how this statement applies to the companies described in this case study.

MIS IN ACTION

Visit the Web site of a data quality software vendor such as Dataflux, Trillium Software, or Group 1. Explore the site and answer the following questions:

1. What are the capabilities of the software for ensuring data completeness, accuracy, and consistency?

2. What steps would your business need to take to use this software?

5   HANDS-ON MIS

The projects in this section give you hands-on experience in redesigning a customer database for targeted marketing, creating a database for inventory management, and using the Web to search online databases for overseas business resources.

Improving Decision Making: Redesigning the Customer Database

Software skills: Database design, querying and reporting
Business skills: Customer profiling

Companies maintain data on their customers which could provide valuable insights about customer interests and buying preferences. Often, however, customer databases may not be capturing the right pieces of data for marketing decisions or their design may not allow the data to be analyzed. In this project, you will redesign a customer database so that it provides useful information for targeted marketing.

Dirt Bikes U.S.A. sells primarily through its distributors. It maintains a small customer database with the following data: customer name, address, telephone number, model purchased, date of purchase, and distributor. The database is illustrated below and you can find it on the Laudon Web site for this chapter and on the Student CD-ROM. These data are collected by its distributors when they make a sale and are then forwarded to Dirt Bikes. Dirt Bikes would like to be able to market more aggressively to its customers.

258

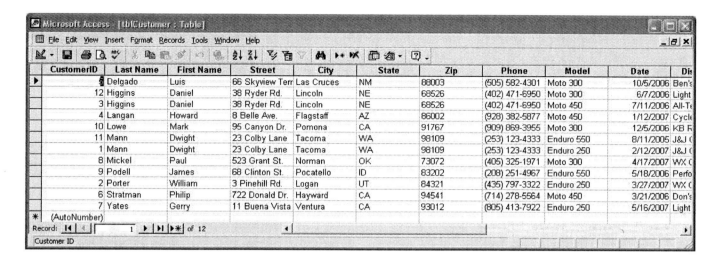

The Marketing Department would like to be able to send customers e-mail notices of special racing events and of sales on parts. It would also like to learn more about customers' interests and tastes: their ages, years of schooling, another sport in which they are interested, and whether they attend dirt bike racing events. Additionally, Dirt Bikes would like to know whether customers own more than one motorcycle. (Some Dirt Bikes customers own two or three motorcycles purchased from Dirt Bikes U.S.A. or other manufacturers.) If a motorcycle was purchased from Dirt Bikes, the company would like to know the date of purchase, model purchased, and distributor. If the customer owns a non-Dirt Bikes motorcycle, the company would like to know the manufacturer and model of the other motorcycle (or motorcycles) and the distributor from whom the customer purchased that motorcycle.

- Redesign Dirt Bikes's customer database so that it can store and provide the information needed for marketing. You will need to develop a design for the new customer database and then implement that design using database software. Consider using multiple tables in your new design. Populate each new table with 10 records.

- Develop several reports that would be of great interest to Dirt Bikes's marketing and sales department (for example, lists of repeat Dirt Bikes customers, Dirt Bikes customers who attend racing events, or the average ages and years of schooling of Dirt Bikes customers) and print them.

Achieving Operational Excellence: Building a Relational Database for Inventory Management

Software skills: Database design, querying and reporting
Business skills: Inventory management

Businesses today depend on databases to provide reliable information about items in inventory, items that need restocking, and inventory costs. In this exercise, you will use database software to design a database for managing inventory for a small business.

Sylvester's Bike Shop, located in San Francisco, California, sells road, mountain, hybrid, leisure, and children's bicycles. Currently, Sylvester's purchases bikes from three suppliers, but plans to add new suppliers in the near future. This rapidly growing business needs a database system to manage this information.

Initially, the database should house information about suppliers and products. The database will contain two tables: a supplier table and a product table. The reorder level refers to the number of items in inventory that triggers a decision to order more items to prevent a stockout. (In other words, if the number of units of a particular inventory item falls below the reorder level, the item should be reordered.) The user should be able to perform several queries and produce several managerial reports based on the data contained in the two tables.

Using the information found in the tables on the Student CD-ROM and the Laudon Web site for this chapter, build a simple relational database for Sylvester's. Once you have built the database, perform the following activities.

- Prepare a report that identifies the five most expensive bicycles. The report should list the bicycles in descending order from most expensive to least expensive, the quantity on hand for each, and the markup percentage for each.

- Prepare a report that lists each supplier, its products, the quantities on hand, and associated reorder levels. The report should be sorted alphabetically by supplier. Within each supplier category, the products should be sorted alphabetically.

- Prepare a report listing only the bicycles that are low in stock and need to be reordered. The report should provide supplier information for the items identified.

- Write a brief description of how the database could be enhanced to further improve management of the business. What tables or fields should be added? What additional reports would be useful?

Improving Decision Making: Searching Online Databases for Overseas Business Resources

Software skills: Online databases
Business skills: Researching services for overseas operations

Internet users have access to many thousands of Web-enabled databases with information on services and products in faraway locations. This project develops skills in searching these online databases.

Your company is located in Greensboro, North Carolina, and manufactures office furniture of various types. You have recently acquired several new customers in Australia, and a study you commissioned indicates that, with a presence there, you could greatly increase your sales. Moreover, your study indicates that you could do even better if you actually manufactured many of your products locally (in Australia). First, you need to set up an office in Melbourne to establish a presence, and then you need to begin importing from the United States. You then can plan to start producing locally.

You will soon be traveling to the area to make plans to actually set up an office, and you want to meet with organizations that can help you with your operation. You will need to engage people or organizations that offer many services necessary for you to open your office, including lawyers, accountants, import-export experts, telecommunications equipment and support, and even trainers who can help you to prepare your future employees to work for you. Start by searching for U.S. Department of Commerce advice on doing business in Australia. Then try the following online databases to locate companies that you would like to meet with during your coming trip: Australian Business Register (abr.gov.au), AustraliaTradeNow.com, and the Nationwide Business

Directory of Australia (www.nationwide.com.au). If necessary, you could also try search engines such as Yahoo! and Google.

- List the companies you would contact to interview on your trip to determine whether they can help you with functions you think are vital to establishing your office.
- Rate the databases you used for accuracy of name, completeness, ease of use, and general helpfulness.
- What does this exercise tell you about the design of databases?

LEARNING TRACK MODULES

Database Design, Normalization, and Entity-Relationship Diagramming. A well-designed relational database follows certain principles, which are described in this Learning Track module along with instructions on how to create an entity-relationship diagram. This module can be found on the Laudon Web site and Student CD-ROM for this chapter.

Introduction to SQL. SQL is the standard data manipulation language for relational database systems. This Learning Track module, which can be found on the Laudon Web site and Student CD-ROM for this chapter, describes basic SQL syntax and shows you how to construct a SQL query.

Hierarchical and Network Data Models. Many legacy systems still use these older data models. The Learning Track module, which can be found on the Laudon Web site and Student CD-ROM for this chapter, describes how these data models represent relationship, their strengths, and their limitations

Summary

1. *Describe basic file organization concepts and the problems of managing data resources in a traditional file environment.*

   A computer system organizes data in a hierarchy that starts with bits and bytes and progresses to fields, records, files, and databases. Traditional file management techniques make it difficult for organizations to keep track of all of the pieces of data they use in a systematic way and to organize these data so that they can be easily accessed. Different functional areas and groups were allowed to develop their own files independently. Over time, this traditional file management environment creates problems such as data redundancy and inconsistency, program-data dependence, inflexibility, poor security, and lack of data sharing and availability.

2. *Describe the principles of a database management system and the features of a relational database.*

   A database management system (DBMS) consists of software that permits centralization of data and data management so that businesses have a single consistent source for all their data needs. A single database services multiple applications. The most important feature of the DBMS is its ability to separate the logical and physical views of data. The user works with a logical view of data. The DBMS retrieves information so that the user does not have to be concerned with its physical location.

   The principal capabilities of a DBMS includes a data definition capability, a data dictionary capability, and a data manipulation language. The data definition capability specifies the structure and content of the database. The data dictionary is an automated or manual file that stores information about the data in the database, including names, definitions, formats, and descriptions of data elements. The data manipulation language, such as SQL, is a specialized language for accessing and manipulating the data in the database.

   The relational database is the primary method for organizing and maintaining data today in information systems. It organizes data in two-dimensional tables with rows and columns called relations. Each table contains data about an entity and its attributes. Each row represents a record and each column represents an attribute or field. Each table also contains a key field to uniquely identify each record for retrieval or manipulation.

3. *Apply important database design principles.*

   Designing a database requires both a logical design and a physical design. The logical design models the database from a business perspective. The organization's data model should reflect its key business processes and decision-making requirements. The process of creating small, stable, flexible, and adaptive data structures from complex groups of data when designing a relational database is termed normalization. A well-designed relational database will not have many-to-many relationships, and all attributes for a specific entity will only apply to that entity. An entity-relationship diagram graphically depicts the relationship between entities (tables) in a relational database. Database design also considers whether a complete database or portions of the database can be distributed to more than one location to increase responsiveness and reduce vulnerability and costs. There are two major types of distributed databases: replicated databases and partitioned databases.

4. *Evaluate tools and technologies for providing information from databases to improve business performance and decision making.*

   Powerful tools are available to analyze and access the information in databases. A data warehouse consolidates current and historical data from many different operational systems in a central database designed for reporting and analysis. Data warehouses support multidimensional data analysis, also known as online analytical processing (OLAP). OLAP represents relationships among data as a multidimensional structure, which can be visualized as cubes of data and cubes within cubes of data, enabling more sophisticated data analysis. Data mining analyzes large pools of data, including the contents of data warehouses, to find patterns and rules that can be used to predict future behavior and guide decision making. Conventional databases can be linked via middleware to the Web or a Web interface to facilitate user access to an organization's internal data.

5. *Assess the role of information policy, data administration, and data quality assurance in the management of organizational data resources.*

Developing a database environment requires policies and procedures for managing organizational data as well as a good data model and database technology. A formal information policy governs the maintenance, distribution, and use of information in the organization. In large corporations, a formal data administration function is responsible for information policy, as well as for data planning, data dictionary development, and monitoring data usage in the firm.

Data that are inaccurate, incomplete, or inconsistent create serious operational and financial problems for businesses because they may create inaccuracies in product pricing, customer accounts, and inventory data, and lead to inaccurate decisions about the actions that should be taken by the firm. Firms must take special steps to make sure they have a high level of data quality. These include using enterprise-wide data standards, databases designed to minimize inconsistent and redundant data, data quality audits, and data cleansing software.

Key Terms

Attribute	*Distributed database*
Business intelligence	*Entity*
Data administration	*Entity-relationship diagram*
Data cleansing	*Field*
Data definition	*File*
Data dictionary	*Foreign key*
Data governance	*Information policy*
Data inconsistency	*Key field*
Data manipulation language	*Normalization*
Data mart	*Object-oriented DBMS*
Data mining	*Object-relational DBMS*
Data quality audit	*Online analytical processing (OLAP)*
Data redundancy	*Predictive analysis*
Data warehouse	*Primary key*
Database	*Program-data dependence*
Database (rigorous definition)	*Record*
Database administration	*Relational DBMS*
Database management system (DBMS)	*Structured query language (SQL)*
Database server	*Tuple*

Review Questions

1. Why is file management important for overall system performance?

2. List and describe each of the components in the data hierarchy.

3. Define and explain the significance of entities, attributes, and key fields.

4. List and describe the problems of the traditional file environment.

5. Define a database and a database management system.

6. List some benefits of a DBMS and the solutions it provides for the problems of a traditional file environment.

7. What is a relational DBMS? How does it organize data? What are the three operations of a relational DBMS?

8. Name and briefly describe the capabilities of a DBMS.

9. What is normalization? How is it related to the features of a well-designed relational database?

10. What is a distributed database, and what are the two main ways of distributing data?

11. What is a data warehouse? How can it benefit organizations?

12. What is business intelligence? How is it related to database technology?

13. Describe the capabilities of online analytical processing (OLAP).

14. What is data mining? How does it differ from OLAP? What types of information can be obtained from data mining?

15. How can users access information from a company's internal databases through the Web?

16. What are the roles of information policy and data administration in information management?

17. Why are data quality audits and data cleansing essential?

Discussion Questions

1. It has been said that you do not need database management software to create a database environment. Discuss.
2. To what extent should end users be involved in the selection of a database management system and database design?

Video Case

You will find a video case illustrating some of the concepts in this chapter on the Laudon Web site and Student CD-ROM along with questions to help you analyze the case.

Teamwork: Identifying Entities and Attributes in an Online Database

With a group of two or three of your fellow students, select an online database to explore, such as AOL Music, iGo.com, or the Internet Movie Database. Explore these Web sites to see what information they provide. Then list the entities and attributes that they must keep track of in their databases. Diagram the relationship between the entities you have identified. If possible, use electronic presentation software to present your findings to the class.

REFERENCES

Cappiello, Cinzia, Chiara Francalanci, and Barbara Pernici. "Time-Related Factors of Data Quality in Multichannel Information Systems." Journal of Management Information Systems 20, No. 3 (Winter 2004).

Chen, Andrew N.K., Paulo B. Goes, and James R. Marsden. "A Query-Driven Approach to the Design and Management of Flexible Database Systems." Journal of Management Information Systems 19, No. 3 (Winter 2002–2003).

Eckerson, Wayne W. "Data Quality and the Bottom Line." The Data Warehousing Institute (2002).

Fayyad, Usama, Ramasamy Ramakrishnan, and Ramakrisnan Srikant. "Evolving Data Mining into Solutions for Insights." Communications of the ACM 45, no.8 (August 2002).

Jukic, Boris, Nenad Jukic, and Manoj Parameswaran. "Data Models for Information Sharing in E-Partnerships: Analysis, Improvements, and Relevance." Journal of Organizational Computing and Electronic Commerce 12, no. 2(2002).

Kroenke, David. Database Processing: Fundamentals, Design, and Implementation, 10th ed. Upper Saddle River, NJ: Prentice Hall (2006).

Lee, Yang W. and Diane M. Strong. "Knowing-Why about Data Processes and Data Quality." Journal of Management Information Systems 20, No. 3 (Winter 2004).

McFadden, Fred R., Jeffrey A. Hoffer and Mary B. Prescott. Modern Database Management, Sixth Edition. Upper Saddle River, NJ: Prentice-Hall (2002).

Morrison, Mike, Joline Morrison, and Anthony Keys. "Integrating Web Sites and Databases." Communications of the ACM 45, no.9 (September 2002).

Pierce, Elizabeth M. "Assessing Data Quality with Control Matrices," Communications of the ACM 47, no. 2 (February 2004).

Watson, Hugh J., and Barbara J. Haley. "Managerial Considerations." Communications of the ACM 41, no. 9 (September 1998).

Panasonic Creates a Single Version of the Truth from Its Data
CASE STUDY

Panasonic is one of the world's leading electronics manufacturers. It operates under the auspices of parent company Matsushita Electric Industrial Co. Ltd., a conglomeration of over 600 firms that is based in Kadoma, Japan. Collectively, the businesses of Matsushita manufacture 15,000 products for a global market and employ 330,000 people internationally. In Europe alone, Panasonic has 15 sales subsidiaries, 14 manufacturing facilities, five research and development centers, and seven administrative stations. Add in major presences around the world, including Asia and North America, and it is clear that Panasonic's operations cover the globe.

With so many different sources of data, the company found itself with product and customer data that were often inconsistent, duplicate, or incomplete. Different segments of the company used their own pools of data, which were completely isolated from the data that the rest of the company was using. These conditions combined to be a drag on operational efficiency and drained significant amounts of money from the corporation as a whole.

The types of data required to launch a new Panasonic product included photos, product specifications and descriptions, manuals, pricing data, and point-of-sale marketing information. Employees adapted product information to suit the needs of their country or region. It took considerable time and effort to sift through all the data and create a common set of data for launching products globally, which allowed competitors to infiltrate markets that Panasonic did not reach in its first phase of a launch.

To solve this problem, Panasonic decided to pursue a "single version of the truth." Daily activities required the data to pass though legacy systems, fax machines, e-mail, phone calls, and regular mail. With so many people handling the data in such a variety of formats, inefficiencies and inaccuracies were always a risk. Erasing these problems promised to increase Panasonic's speed of bringing products to market.

Panasonic was enjoying a number of successes: a market leadership in plasma TVs, a successful transition of company presidents, and a well-received marketing identity, "Panasonic: Ideas for Life." However, these positives were overshadowed by the administrative costs incurred by such an immense organization. Thus, when Fumio Otsubo took over as president in June 2006, he took over a company with an operating profit margin of only 5 percent. The board of directors saddled him with the goal of increasing the margin to 10 percent by 2010.

In Panasonic's industry, consumers expect the price of new technology to decrease over time, which it had for items that were strengths at Panasonic such as plasma TVs and DVD players. Therefore, Otsubo could not expect to increase the company's profit margin by increasing prices. Instead, he had to set his sights on reducing costs and increasing sales.

Starting in Europe, Panasonic sought to replace its "pull" model of data dissemination with a "push" model. Previously, employees in marketing and sales had to request data from numerous repositories. Under the push model, a centralized data bank sends the information to all employees who need it at the same time, ensuring uniformity. The recipients of the data include retail partners and e-commerce vendors, who receive complete product information at all stages of a product rollout. Panasonic employees receive data on a more targeted basis. The benefits to Panasonic Europe are more consistent product rollouts and product information. The latter ensures that customers do not become confused while researching their purchases, which could motivate them to abandon Panasonic for a competitor.

The technical force behind Panasonic Europe's data management overhaul was master-data-management (MDM) software from IBM's WebSphere line. The software enabled Panasonic Europe to consolidate data, as well as systematize the business processes related to the data. Overall, the company gained better control over its internal data.

Generally speaking, MDM software aims to merge disparate records into one authenticated master file. Many companies have adopted MDM to fix discrepancies among the databases used by their various departments (e.g., the accounting department having record of fewer customers than the number of customer IDs in the CRM database). MDM is particularly useful for companies that have data integration issues as a result of mergers or acquisitions. Small- and mid-size firms generally do not have the kinds of challenges that would require an MDM solution.

Implementing MDM is a multi-step process that includes business process analysis, data assessment, data cleansing, data consolidation and reconciliation, data migration, and development of a master data service layer. These steps produce a system of records that stores the master file for all of the company's data. It is critical for the organization to institute strict policies against computing activities that could compromise the authenticity of the data. Once the MDM is in place, employees and applications access a consolidated view of the company's data. The implementation should enforce standards for the formatting and storage of data, such as the number of fields in an address record or the number of digits in a ZIP code. The service layer of the MDM preserves the view of the master data for applications and synchronizes updates to the master file.

In the case of Panasonic, the deployment of the IBM MDM software paid quick dividends. Within a year and a half, Panasonic Europe was getting products to market faster and spending 50 percent less time creating and maintaining product information. Time-to-market for a product was reduced from five to six months to one to two months. According to internal calculations, Panasonic Europe improved its efficiency by a factor of 5 and anticipates saving a million euros a year while increasing sales by 3.5 percent.

However, analyst Paul Jackson of Forrester Inc., cautioned against high expectations of boosted sales based on data management improvements. He pointed to pricing, innovation, and strategic partnerships as better strategies for long-term market share increases.

When Panasonic North America had to reconcile its data, it did not have to confront the challenge of multiple countries with multiple languages and currencies complicating product launches, as had its European counterpart. However, the challenges of reorganizing workflow and consolidating product information were just as daunting.

Panasonic faced this issue when it needed to provide a consolidated view of product information for retail giant Wal-Mart. Panasonic started by identifying the information that Wal-Mart would need, which was data that adhered closely to industry standards. Then, the electronics maker searched its legacy systems for the sources of the required data. Finally, Panasonic worked with IBM to create an interface apparatus to collect the required data for a repository. Some information, such as that produced by newer business processes, was not available in the legacy systems. Panasonic had to add new interfaces in order to include this information, and then build an application-integration layer to send the whole package to Wal-Mart.

Each of the company's multiple facilities made its own contributions to new products. More importantly, the facilities had their own cultures and information infrastructures. They also valued their autonomy and the flexibility it furnished. Different Panasonic entities might be unwilling to give up control over information due to the perceived loss of power. The company required clear master data management rules to prevent too many hands from manipulating the data so that the master file would remain pristine. Panasonic North America Information Technology vice president Bob Schwartz hoped that the fierce competition threatening the standing of his company would help convince the traditionalists to support data-sharing. However, he expected that convincing the enterprise of this would be an uphill battle.

Besides all the units of Panasonic North America, there were manufacturing partners to bring aboard. Without them, the system could not fulfill its complete potential. This had been a serious challenge for Panasonic Europe, where most partners were based in Asia and were content with their manual processes for managing product data. Paul Bolton, senior manager for e-commerce and customer relationship management solutions, deployed the product information database at Panasonic first. Once it proved effective, he then presented its capabilities to the other manufacturers and won them over.

Schwartz therefore had a strategy and a roadmap to clear that hurdle. What remained was perhaps the biggest hurdle: convincing the corporate office in Japan that their data management strategy deserved global adoption. Only then would the application of MDM principles achieve its full benefit. In the meantime, Schwartz reached out to Panasonic's vendors in the U.S. and gained additional profits from the company's improved data. Panasonic was able to use the data to reduce the amount of time that vendors such as Best Buy and Circuit City kept high-cost inventory, such as large-model TVs, in stock from 35 to 7 days, thereby increasing their profit margins.

Sources: Duff McDonald, "Case Study: Panasonic Searches the Master Data for a Single Version of Truth," *CIO Insight*, May 22, 2006; Susana Schwartz, "Out of Many, One," *DB2 Magazine*, accessed via db2mag.com July 25, 2006; S. Jae Yang, "Primer: Master Data Management," *Baseline Magazine*, June 10, 2005.

CASE STUDY QUESTIONS

1. Evaluate Panasonic's business strategy using the competitive forces and value chain models.

2. How did Panasonic's information management problems affect its business performance and ability to execute its strategy? What management, organization, and technology factors were responsible for those problems?

3. How did master data management address these problems? How effective was this solution?

4. What challenges did Panasonic face in implementing this solution?

Telecommunications, the Internet, and Wireless Technology

From *Management Information Systems: Managing the Digital Firm, 10/e*. Kenneth C. Laudon, Jane P. Laudon.
Copyright © 2007 by Pearson Prentice Hall. All rights reserved.

Telecommunications, the Internet, and Wireless Technology

LEARNING OBJECTIVES

After reading this chapter, you will be able to:

1. Describe the features of telecommunications networks and identify key networking technologies.

2. Evaluate alternative transmission media, types of networks, and network services.

3. Demonstrate how the Internet and Internet technology work and how they support communication and e-business.

4. Identify and describe the principal technologies and standards for wireless networking, communication, and Internet access.

5. Assess the business value of wireless technology and important wireless applications in business.

Interactive Sessions:

Monitoring Employees on Networks: Unethical or Good Business?

Wal-Mart Grapples with RFID

CHAPTER OUTLINE

1   **TELECOMMUNICATIONS AND NETWORKING IN TODAY'S BUSINESS WORLD**
Networking and Communication Trends
What Is a Computer Network?
Key Digital Networking Technologies

2   **COMMUNICATIONS NETWORKS**
Signals: Digital vs. Analog
Types of Networks
Physical Transmission Media
Broadband Network Services and Technologies

3   **THE INTERNET**
What Is the Internet?
Internet Addressing and Architecture
Internet Services
The World Wide Web
Intranets and Extranets
Technologies and Tools for Communication and
    E-Business

4   **THE WIRELESS REVOLUTION**
Wireless Devices
Cellular Systems
Wireless Computer Networks and Internet Access
RFID and Wireless Sensor Networks

5   **HANDS-ON MIS**
Achieving Operational Excellence: Using Internet
    Tools to Increase Efficiency and Productivity:
    Dirt Bikes USA
Improving Decision Making: Using Spreadsheet
    Software to Evaluate Wireless Services
Achieving Operational Excellence: Using Web
    Search Engines for Business Research

LEARNING TRACK MODULES
Computing and Communications Services Provided
    by Commercial Telecommunications Vendors
Cellular System Generations
Wireless Applications for CRM, SCM, and
    Healthcare

HYATT REGENCY OSAKA USES WIRELESS NETWORKING FOR HIGH-TOUCH SERVICE

Hyatt Hotels are known for the "Hyatt Touch," and the Hyatt Regency Osaka (HRO) is no exception. This urban resort hotel in the Hyatt International hotel chain is located in the new Cosmo Square business district some distance from central Osaka. It features approximately 500 guest rooms and 19 rooms for conferences and other functions spread over 28 floors. With the hotel industry increasingly competitive, HRO searched for ways of providing a superior environment for guests and encouraging repeat visits despite its less convenient location. The hotel turned to technology for a solution.

Working with Nomura Research and Intel Corporation, HRO implemented a mobile wireless local area network (LAN) using Internet standards to provide integrated voice and data coverage across the entire hotel. The hotel initially deployed 25 wireless-enabled notebook computers using Intel Centrino mobile technology and 60 handheld mobile devices based on Intel XScale technology. Both types of devices can handle voice phone calls as well as data communication and their quality of service is comparable to HRO's wired voice system. The wireless infrastructure also provides guests with high-speed Internet access.

Before this system was installed, HRO staff members were only able to communicate using fixed-line telephones and pagers. The new wireless network enables these employees to communicate via handheld wireless PDAs or notebook PCs wherever they are working. HRO estimates its wireless network has saved 60 hours per year per staff member or a total of 4,800 hours annually. This time saved by higher employee productivity can be spent on more personal attention to guests.

The ability to access information online from anywhere in the hotel allows every employee to "act as a concierge," responding accurately and immediately to guest inquiries. If, for example, a guest asks a bell captain a question, the bell caption can access the information from HRO's intranet using his wireless PDA and reply to the guest on the spot. The ability to share and access information also makes it easier to provide customized services to guests. For example, if a guest reports she prefers a different kind of pillow than the one in her room, the staff can immediately check online the information maintained about that guest from past visits and provide exactly what she wants on the spot. That sort of memorable service makes guests want to visit again.

The wireless LAN has been a big hit with guests who use it to access the Internet from the hotel lobbies, conference center, meeting rooms, and guest rooms. Increasingly, the availability of high-speed Internet access in conference facilities has become an essential requirement for corporate conventions and seminars. Providing wireless Internet service

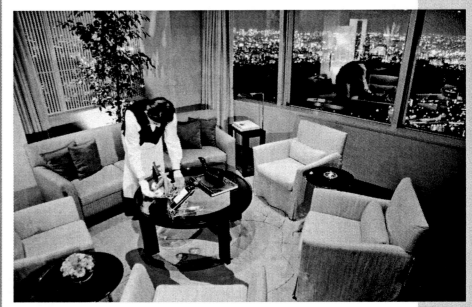

for conferences could potentially generate several million yen in additional revenue for the hotel.

Sources: Intel Corporation, "VoIP Enables VIP Service at Hyatt Regency Osaka," 2006; Intel Corporation, "Pilot Project Using Mobile IP-Centrex to Build an Integrated Voice and Data Environment," www. intel.com, accessed August 14, 2006; and Meru Networks, "Hyatt Regency Osaka Deploys Hotel-Wide Wireless VoIP System: New System Rivals Wired Dial-Tone Quality," 2005.

Hyatt Regency Osaka (HRO) illustrates some of the powerful new capabilities—and opportunities—provided by contemporary networking technology. HRO used Internet and wireless networking technology to provide staff and guests with voice and data communication capabilities, as well as wireless Internet access, anywhere in the hotel. The technology enabled HRO to provide superior customer service and made it a hotel of choice, even though its location is somewhat inconvenient.

The chapter-opening diagram calls attention to important points raised by this case and this chapter. The hotel industry is exceptionally competitve. HRO's management chose a strategy of focusing on a superior customer experience to distinguish it from competitors. Limitations of outdated networking and voice technology made it difficult to provide this experience. Using networks based on the Internet protocol and wireless technology saved staff time that was redirected to serving customers, and HRO had to redesign its processes for serving guests and redesign employee jobs to take advantage of the new technology.

HEADS UP

This chapter describes the key technologies for digital networking and communications and shows how they help business firms achieve operational excellence, strategic advantage, and close relationships with suppliers and customers. Businesses today could not survive without their computer and telecommunications networks.

- If your career is in finance or accounting, you will be working with networked systems and the Internet for accessing and updating account information, researching financial markets, trading securities, and transferring funds.

- If your career is in human resources, you will be using private corporate networks and intranets to access employee records and the Internet to research benefits and compensation plans.

- If your career is in information systems, you'll be supporting your company's network infrastructure and Web site and recommending new networking technologies and applications.

- If your career is in manufacturing and production, you will be working with networked systems for monitoring the factory floor, for scheduling work, for supply chain management, and for warehousing and delivery. Some of these systems will be based on intranets and extranets.

- If your career is in sales and marketing, you will be working with online sales systems that obtain order transactions from private networks or the Web and with marketing systems that use data generated by Web sites.

---

1 TELECOMMUNICATIONS AND NETWORKING IN TODAY'S BUSINESS WORLD

If you work in a business, chances are you've already learned that you can't stay in business without networks. You need to communicate rapidly with your customers, suppliers, and employees. Until about 1990, you would have used the postal system or telephone system with voice or fax for business communication. Today, however, you and your employees use computers and e-mail, instant messages, the Internet, cell phones, and mobile computers connected to wireless networks for this purpose. Networking and the Internet are now nearly synonymous with doing business.

NETWORKING AND COMMUNICATION TRENDS

Firms in the past used two fundamentally different types of networks: telephone networks and computer networks. Telephone networks historically handled voice communication, and computer networks handled data traffic. Telephone networks were built by telephone companies throughout the twentieth century using voice transmission technologies (hardware and software), and these companies almost always operated as regulated monopolies throughout the world. Computer networks were originally built by computer companies seeking to transmit data between computers in different locations.

Thanks to continuing telecommunications deregulation and information technology innovation, telephone and computer networks are slowly converging into a single digital network using shared Internet-based standards and equipment. Telecommunications providers, such as AT&T and Verizon, today offer data transmission, Internet access, wireless telephone service, and television programming as well as voice service. Cable companies, such as Cablevision and Comcast, now offer voice service and Internet access. Computer networks have expanded to include Internet telephone and limited video services. Increasingly, all of these voice, video, and data communications are based on Internet technology.

Both voice and data communication networks have also become more powerful (faster), more portable (smaller and mobile), and less expensive. For instance, the typical Internet connection speed in 2000 was 56 kilobits per second (Kbps), but today more than 60 percent of U.S. Internet users have high-speed **broadband** connections provided by telephone and cable TV companies running at one million bits per second. The cost for this service has fallen exponentially, from 25 cents in 2000, to less than 1 cent today.

Increasingly, voice and data communication as well as Internet access are taking place over broadband wireless platforms, such as cell phones, handheld digital devices, and PCs in wireless networks (eMarketer, 2005a). In fact, wireless broadband access is the fastest-growing form of Internet access, growing at 28 percent a year.

WHAT IS A COMPUTER NETWORK?

If you had to connect the computers for two or more employees together in the same office, you would need a computer network. Exactly what is a network? In its simplest form, a network consists of two or more connected computers. Figure 1 illustrates the major hardware, software, and transmission

FIGURE 1   COMPONENTS OF A SIMPLE COMPUTER NETWORK

Illustrated here is a very simple computer network, consisting of computers, a network operating system residing on a dedicated server computer, cable (wiring) connecting the devices, network interface cards (NIC), switches, and a router.

components used in a simple network: a client computer and a dedicated server computer, network interfaces, a connection medium, network operating system software, and either a hub or a switch. Each computer on the network contains a network interface device called a **network interface card (NIC)**. Most personal computers today have this card built into the motherboard. The connection medium for linking network components can be a telephone wire, coaxial cable, or radio signal in the case of cell phone and wireless local area networks (Wi-Fi networks).

The **network operating system (NOS)** routes and manages communications on the network and coordinates network resources. It can reside on every computer in the network, or it can reside primarily on a **dedicated server computer** for all the applications on the network. A network server computer is a computer on a network that performs important network functions for client computers, such as serving up Web pages, storing data, and storing the network operating system (and hence controlling the network). Network operating system software such as Linux, Microsoft Windows Server, and Novell NetWare, are the most widely used network operating systems.

Most networks also contain a switch or a hub acting as a connection point between the computers. **Hubs** are simple devices that connect network components, sending a packet of data to all other connected devices. A **switch** has more intelligence than a hub and can filter and forward data to a specified destination on a local area network. So hubs and switches link up the devices on a local area network.

But what if you want to communicate with another network (like the Internet)? **Routers** are network devices that connect two or more networks. So for instance, the cable modem in your house that brings you broadband Internet service is also a router that connects your local area network to the Internet. Routers are fairly intelligent devices that have to figure out where the packets of information you send are supposed to go. Routers maintain a routing table internally that keeps track of the addresses of destinations you frequently send packets towards. There's over one billion people connected to the Internet, and over 5 billion Internet addresses. Routers make sure your messages get to the right address.

Networks in Large Companies

The network we've just described might be suitable for a small business. But what about large companies with many different locations and thousands of employees? As a firm grows, and collects hundreds of small local area networks (LANs), these networks are linked together into a corporate-wide networking infrastructure. The network infrastructure for a large corporation consists of a large number of these small local area networks linked to other local area networks and to firmwide corporate networks. A number of powerful servers support a corporate Web site, a corporate intranet, and perhaps an extranet. Some of these servers link to other large computers supporting back-end systems for sales transactions, financial transactions, order entries, and purchasing transactions.

Figure 2 provides an illustration of these more complex, larger-scale corporate-wide networks. Here you can see that the corporate network infrastructure supports a mobile sales force using cell phones; mobile employees linking to the company Web site or internal company networks using mobile wireless local area networks (Wi-Fi networks); and a videoconferencing system to support managers across the world. In addition to these computer networks, the firm's infrastructure usually includes a separate telephone network that handles most

FIGURE 2   CORPORATE NETWORK INFRASTRUCTURE

Today's corporate network infrastructure is a collection of many different networks from the public switched telephone network; to the Internet; to corporate local area networks linking workgroups, departments, or office floors.

voice data. Many firms are dispensing with their traditional telephone networks and using Internet telephones that run on their existing data networks (described later).

As you can see from this figure, a large corporate network infrastructure uses a wide variety of technologies—everything from ordinary telephone service and corporate data networks to Internet service, wireless Internet, and wireless cell phones. One of the major problems facing corporations today is how to integrate all the different communication networks and channels into a coherent system that enables information to flow from one part of the corporation to another, from one system to another. As more and more communication networks become digital, and based on Internet technologies, it will become easier to integrate them.

KEY DIGITAL NETWORKING TECHNOLOGIES

Contemporary digital networks and the Internet are based on three key technologies: client/server computing, the use of packet switching, and the development of widely used communications standards (the most important of which is Transmission Control Protocol/Internet Protocol) for linking disparate networks and computers.

Client/Server Computing

Client/server computing is a distributed computing model in which some of the processing power is located within small, inexpensive client computers under user control, and resides literally on desktops, laptops, or in handheld devices. These powerful clients are linked to one another through a network that is controlled by a network server computer. The server sets the rule of communication for the network and provides every client with an address so others can find it on the network.

Client/server computing has largely replaced centralized mainframe computing in which nearly all of the processing takes place on a central large mainframe computer. Client/server computing has extended computing to departments, workgroups, factory floors, and other parts of the business that could not be served by a centralized architecture. The Internet is the largest implementation of client/server computing.

Packet Switching

Packet switching is a method of slicing digital messages into parcels called packets, sending the packets along different communication paths as they become available, and then reassembling the packets once they arrive at their destinations (see Figure 3). Prior to the development of packet switching, computer networks used leased, dedicated telephone circuits to communicate with other computers in remote locations. In circuit-switched networks, such as the telephone system, a complete point-to-point circuit is assembled, and then communication can proceed. These dedicated circuit-switching techniques were expensive and wasted available communications capacity—the circuit was maintained regardless of whether any data were being sent.

Packet switching makes much more efficient use of the communications capacity of a network. In packet-switched networks, messages are first broken down into small fixed bundles of data called packets. The packets include

FIGURE 3   PACKED-SWITCHED NETWORKS AND PACKET COMMUNICATIONS

Data are grouped into small packets, which are transmitted independently over various communications channels and reassembled at their final destination.

information for directing the packet to the right address and for checking transmission errors along with the data. The packets are transmitted over various communications channels using routers, each packet traveling independently. Packets of data originating at one source can be routed through many different paths and networks before being reassembled into the original message when they reach their destinations.

TCP/IP and Connectivity

In a typical telecommunications network, diverse hardware and software components need to work together to transmit information. Different components in a network communicate with each other only by adhering to a common set of rules called protocols. A **protocol** is a set of rules and procedures governing transmission of information between two points in a network.

In the past, many diverse proprietary and incompatible protocols often forced business firms to purchase computing and communications equipment from a single vendor. But today, corporate networks are increasingly using a single, common, worldwide standard called **Transmission Control Protocol/Internet Protocol (TCP/IP)**. TCP/IP was developed during the early 1970s to support U.S. Department of Defense Advanced Research Projects Agency (DARPA) efforts to help scientists transmit data among different types of computers over long distances.

TCP/IP uses a suite of protocols, the main ones being TCP and IP. TCP refers to the Transmission Control Protocol (TCP), which handles the movement of data between computers. TCP establishes a connection between the computers, sequences the transfer of packets, and acknowledges the packets sent. IP refers to the Internet Protocol (IP), which is responsible for the delivery of packets and includes the disassembling and reassembling of packets during transmission. Figure 4 illustrates the four-layered Department of Defense reference model for TCP/IP.

1. **Application layer**. The application layer enables client application programs to access the other layers and defines the protocols that applications use to exchange data. One of these application protocols is the Hypertext Transfer Protocol (HTTP), which is used to transfer Web page files.

FIGURE 4   THE TRANSMISSION CONTROL PROTOCOL/INTERNET PROTOCOL (TCP/IP) REFERENCE MODEL

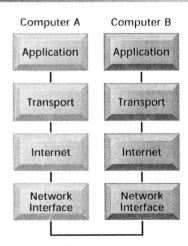

This figure illustrates the four layers of the TCP/IP reference model for communications.

2. **Transport layer.** The transport layer is responsible for providing the application layer with communication and packet services. This layer includes TCP and other protocols.

3. **Internet layer.** The Internet layer is responsible for addressing, routing, and packaging data packets called IP datagrams. The Internet Protocol is one of the protocols used in this layer.

4. **Network interface layer**. At the bottom of the reference model, the network interface layer is responsible for placing packets on and receiving them from the network medium, which could be any networking technology.

Two computers using TCP/IP can communicate even if they are based on different hardware and software platforms. Data sent from one computer to the other passes downward through all four layers, starting with the sending computer's application layer and passing through the network interface layer. After the data reach the recipient host computer, they travel up the layers and are reassembled into a format the receiving computer can use. If the receiving computer finds a damaged packet, it asks the sending computer to retransmit it. This process is reversed when the receiving computer responds.

2   COMMUNICATIONS NETWORKS

Let's look more closely at the alternative networking technologies available to businesses.

SIGNALS: DIGITAL VS. ANALOG

The most basic distinction in communication networks is that between analog and digital signals. There are two ways to communicate a message: either an analog signal or a digital signal. An *analog signal* is represented by a continuous waveform that passes through a communications medium and has been used for voice communication. The most common analog devices are the telephone hand set, the speaker on your computer, or your iPod earphone, all of which create analog wave forms that your ear can hear. Oh yes, your ear is an analog device also.

A *digital signal* is a discrete, binary waveform, rather than a continuous, waveform. Digital signals communicate information as strings of two discrete states: one bit and zero bits, which are represented as on-off electrical pulses. Computers use digital signals, so if you want to use the analog telephone system to send digital data, a device called a **modem** is required to translate digital signals into analog form. (see Figure 5). *Modem* stands for modulation/demodulation.

TYPES OF NETWORKS

There are many different kinds of networks and ways of classifying them. One way of looking at networks is in terms of their geographic scope (see Table 1).

Local Area Networks

If you work in a business that uses networking, you are probably connecting to other employees and groups via a local area network. A **local area network**

FIGURE 5   **FUNCTIONS OF THE MODEM**

A modem is a device that translates digital signals from a computer into analog form so that they can be transmitted over analog telephone lines. The modem also translates analog signals back into digital form for the receiving computer.

TABLE 1   TYPES OF NETWORKS

TYPE	AREA
Local area network (LAN)	Up to 500 meters (half a mile); an office or floor of a building
Campus area network (CAN)	Up to 1,000 meters (a mile); a college campus or corporate facility
Metropolitan area network (MAN)	A city or metropolitan area
Wide-area network (WAN)	A transcontinental or global area

(LAN) is designed to connect personal computers and other digital devices within a half-mile or 500-meter radius. LANs typically connect a few computers in a small office, all the computers in one building, or all the computers in several buildings in close proximity. LANs interconnected within multiple buildings or a geographic area, such as a school campus or military base, create a **campus area network (CAN)**. LANs can link to long-distance wide area networks (WANs, described later in this section) and other networks around the world using the Internet.

Review Figure 1, which could serve as a model for a small LAN that might be used in an office. One computer is a dedicated network file server, providing users with access to shared computing resources in the network, including software programs and data files. The server determines who gets access to what and in which sequence. The router connects the LAN to other networks, which could be the Internet or another corporate network, so that the LAN can exchange information with networks external to it. The most common LAN operating systems are Windows, Linux, and NetWare. Each of these network operating systems supports TCP/IP as its default networking protocol.

Ethernet is the dominant LAN standard at the physical network level, specifying the physical medium to carry signals between computers, access control rules, and a standardized frame or set of bits used to carry data over the system. Originally, Ethernet supported a data transfer rate of 10 megabits per second (Mbps). Newer versions, such as Fast Ethernet and Gigabit Ethernet, support data transfer rates of 100 Mbps and 1 gigabit per second (Gbps), respectively, and are used in network backbones.

The LAN illustrated in Figure 1 uses a client/server architecture where the network operating system resides primarily on a single file server, and the server provides much of the control and resources for the network. Alternatively, LANs may use a **peer-to-peer** architecture. A peer-to-peer network treats all processors equally and is used primarily in small networks with 10 or fewer users. The various computers on the network can exchange data by direct access and can share peripheral devices without going through a separate server.

In LANs using the Windows Server family of operating systems, the peer-to-peer architecture is called the *workgroup network model* in which a small group of computers can share resources, such as files, folders, and printers, over the network without a dedicated server. The Windows *domain network model*, in contrast, uses a dedicated server to manage the computers in the network.

Larger LANs have many clients and multiple servers, with separate servers for specific services, such as storing and managing files and databases (file servers or database servers), managing printers (print servers), storing and managing e-mail (mail servers), or storing and managing Web pages (Web servers).

Sometimes LANs are described in terms of the way their components are connected together, or their **topology**. There are three major LAN topologies: star, bus, and ring (see Figure 6).

In a star topology, all devices on the network connect to a single hub. Figure 6 illustrates a simple **star network** in which all network components connect to a single hub. All network traffic flows through the hub. In an *extended star network*, multiple layers or hubs are organized into a hierarchy.

In a bus topology, one station transmits signals, which travel in both directions along a single transmission segment. All of the signals are broadcast in both directions to the entire network. All machines on the network receive the same signals, and software installed on the clients enables each client to listen for messages addressed specifically to it. **Bus networks** are the most common Ethernet topology.

A ring topology connects network components in a closed loop. Messages pass from computer to computer in only one direction around the loop, and only one station at a time may transmit. **Ring networks** are used primarily in older LANs using Token Ring networking software.

FIGURE 6   NETWORK TOPOLOGIES

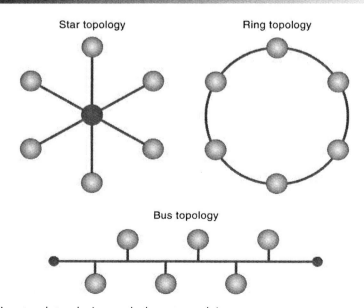

The three basic network topologies are the bus, star, and ring.

Metropolitan and Wide Area Networks

Wide area networks (WANs) span broad geographical distances—entire regions, states, continents, or the entire globe. The most universal and powerful WAN is the Internet. Computers connect to a WAN through public networks, such as the telephone system or private cable systems, or through leased lines or satellites. A **metropolitan area network (MAN)** is a large computer network that spans a metropolitan area or campus. Its geographic scope falls between a WAN and a LAN. MANs provide Internet connectivity for LANs in a metropolitan region, and connect them to wider area networks like the Internet.

PHYSICAL TRANSMISSION MEDIA

Networks use different kinds of physical transmission media, including twisted wire, coaxial cable, fiber optics, microwave, and other radio frequencies for wireless transmission. Each has advantages and limitations. A wide range of speeds is possible for any given medium depending on the software and hardware configuration.

Twisted Wire

Twisted wire consists of strands of copper wire twisted in pairs and is an older type of transmission medium. Many of the telephone systems in buildings had twisted wires installed for analog communication, but they can be used for digital communication as well. Although an older form of physical media, the twisted wires used in most of today's LANs can obtain speeds up to 1 Gbps. The most common local area network cabling today is CAT5 cable. CAT5 contains four pairs of copper wire and can transmit up to 1,000 Mbps. Twisted-pair cabling is limited to a maximum recommended run of 100 meters (328 feet).

Coaxial Cable

Coaxial cable, similar to that used for cable television, consists of a single, thickly insulated copper wire, which can transmit a larger volume of data than twisted wire. Coaxial cable was used in early local area networks and is still used today for longer (more than 100 meters) runs in large buildings. Coaxial is often referred to as "solid" CAT5 and has speeds similar to twisted wire, up to 1,000 Mbps.

Fiber Optics and Optical Networks

Fiber-optic cable consists of strands of clear glass fiber, each the thickness of a human hair, which are bound into cables. Data are transformed into pulses of light, which are sent through the fiber-optic cable by a laser device at rates varying from 500 kilobits to several trillion bits per second in experimental settings. Fiber-optic cable is considerably faster, lighter, and more durable than wire media, and is well suited to systems requiring transfers of large volumes of data. However, fiber-optic cable is more difficult to work with, more expensive, and harder to install.

Until recently, fiber-optic cable had been used primarily as the high-speed network backbone for the Internet, other wide area networks, and metropolitan area networks, whereas twisted wire and coaxial cable were used to connect the backbone to individual businesses and households. A **backbone** is the part of a network that handles the major traffic. It acts as the primary path for traffic flowing to or from other networks. Now, local cable companies and telephone companies are bringing fiber all the way into the basements of buildings and homes so they can provide a variety of new services to businesses and eventually residential customers.

These **optical networks** can transmit all types of traffic—voice, data, and video—over fiber cables and provide the massive bandwidth for new types of services and software. Using optical networks, on-demand video, software downloads, and high-quality digital audio can be accessed using set-top boxes and other information appliances without severe degradation in quality or delays.

Existing optical networks can boost capacity their capacity by using **dense wavelength division multiplexing (DWDM)**. **Multiplexing** enables a single communications channel to carry simultaneously data transmissions from multiple sources. This is accomplished by dividing a high-speed channel into multiple channels of slower speeds or by assigning each transmission source a very small slice of time for using a high-speed channel. DWDM boosts transmission capacity by using many different colors of light, or different wavelengths, to carry separate streams of data over the same fiber strand at the same time. DWDM combines up to 160 wavelengths per strand and can transmit up to 6.4 terabits per second (Tbps) over a single fiber. This technology adds transmission capacity to an existing fiber-optic network without having to lay more fiber-optic cable. Before wavelength division multiplexing, optical networks could use only a single wavelength per strand.

Wireless Transmission Media and Devices

Wireless transmission is based on radio signals of various frequencies. **Microwave** systems, both terrestrial and celestial, transmit high-frequency radio signals through the atmosphere and are widely used for high-volume, long-distance, point-to-point communication. Microwave signals follow a straight line and do not bend with the curvature of the earth; therefore, long-distance terrestrial transmission systems require that transmission stations be positioned about 37 miles apart, adding to the expense of microwave systems.

This problem can be solved by bouncing microwave signals off communication **satellites**, enabling them to serve as relay stations for microwave signals transmitted from terrestrial stations. Satellites are typically used for communications in large, geographically dispersed organizations that would be difficult to tie together through cabling media or terrestrial microwave transmission.

For instance, BP Amoco uses satellites for real-time data transfer of oil field exploration data gathered from searches of the ocean floor. Using geosynchronous satellites, exploration ships transfer these data to central computing centers in the United States for use by researchers in Houston, Tulsa, and suburban Chicago. Figure 7 illustrates how this system works.

Cellular telephones (cell phones) work by using radio waves to communicate with radio antennas (towers) placed within adjacent geographic areas called cells. Cell phones operate in a defined radio spectrum from 800–2,000 MHz (megahertz) depending on their generation. A telephone message is transmitted to the local cell by the cellular telephone and then is passed from antenna to antenna—cell to cell—until it reaches the its destination cell, where it is transmitted to the receiving telephone. As a cellular signal travels from one cell into another, a computer that monitors signals from the cells switches the conversation to a radio channel assigned to the next cell.

Older cellular systems are analog and used primarily for voice transmission. Contemporary cellular systems are digital, supporting data transmission as well as voice transmission.

Wireless transmission technology has matured to the point where wireless networks are supplanting traditional wired networks for many applications and

FIGURE 7   BP AMOCO'S SATELLITE TRANSMISSION SYSTEM

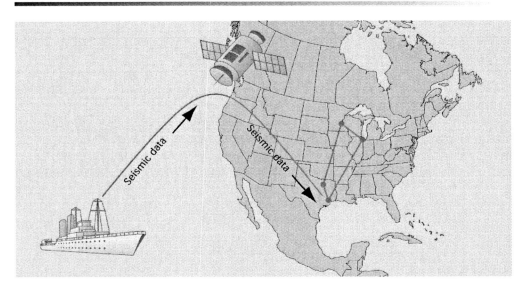

Satellites help BP Amoco transfer seismic data between oil exploration ships and research centers in the United States.

creating new applications, services, and business models. In Section 4, we provide a detailed description of the applications and technology standards driving the "wireless revolution."

Transmission Speed

The total amount of digital information that can be transmitted through any telecommunications medium is measured in bits per second (bps). One signal change, or cycle, is required to transmit one or several bits; therefore, the transmission capacity of each type of telecommunications medium is a function of its frequency. The number of cycles per second that can be sent through that medium is measured in **hertz**—one hertz is equal to one cycle of the medium.

The range of frequencies that can be accommodated on a particular telecommunications channel is called its **bandwidth**. The bandwidth is the difference between the highest and lowest frequencies that can be accommodated on a single channel. The greater the range of frequencies, the greater the bandwidth and the greater the channel's transmission capacity. Table 2 compares the transmission speeds of the major types of media.

BROADBAND NETWORK SERVICES AND TECHNOLOGIES

A number of network services and technologies are available to companies that need high-speed transmission or access to the Internet.

Frame relay is a shared network service that is faster and less expensive than packet switching and can achieve transmission speeds ranging from 56 Kbps to more than 40 Mbps. Frame relay packages data into frames similar to packets but takes advantage of higher-speed, more reliable digital circuits that require less error checking than packet switching. The major

TABLE 2 TYPICAL SPEEDS AND COSTS OF TELECOMMUNICATIONS TRANSMISSION MEDIA

MEDIUM	SPEED
Twisted wire (unshielded)	Up to 1,000 Mbps (1 Gbps)
Microwave	Up to 600+ Mbps
Satellite	Up to 600+ Mbps
Coaxial cable	Up to 1 Gbps
Fiber-optic cable	Up to 6+ Tbps

Mbps = megabits per second

Gbps = gigabits per second

Tbps = terabits per second

telecommunications carriers provide frame relay services. Many organizations use frame relay services in their international data communication networks.

A technology called **Asynchronous Transfer Mode (ATM)** can handle many types of network traffic and provides transmission speeds ranging from 1.5 Mbps to more than 9 Gbps. Like frame relay, ATM takes advantage of high-bandwidth digital circuits, parceling information into fixed 53-byte cells, of which 48 bytes are for data and 5 are for header information. ATM can pass data among computers from different vendors and is popular for transmitting data, video, and audio over the same network. Many telecommunications carriers and large enterprise backbone networks use ATM.

Integrated Services Digital Network (ISDN) is an older, international telephone standard for network access that integrates voice, data, image, and video services. It is still very effective for supporting interactive teleconferencing over long distances (say New York to São Paulo, Brazil). There are two levels of ISDN service: basic rate ISDN (which can transmit at 128 Kbps) and primary rate ISDN (which can transmit at 1.5 Mbps).

Other high-capacity services include digital subscriber line technologies, cable, and T1 lines. Like ISDN, **digital subscriber line (DSL)** technologies also operate over existing telephone lines to carry voice, data, and video, but they have higher transmission capacities than ISDN. (By 2005, most small businesses had converted from ISDN to either cable or DSL Internet services, which are cheaper and more powerful.) There are several categories of DSL. Asymmetric digital subscriber lines (ADSLs) support a transmission rate of 1.5 to 9 Mbps when receiving data and over 700 Kbps when sending data. Symmetric digital subscriber lines (SDSLs) support the same transmission rate for sending and receiving data of up to 3 Mbps.

Cable Internet connections provided by cable television vendors use digital cable coaxial lines to deliver high-speed Internet access to homes and businesses. They can provide high-speed access to the Internet of up to 10 Mbps. More than 60 percent of U.S. broadband households use cable (eMarketer, 2005b) as opposed to DSL telephone Internet service.

But what if you have large amounts of very sensitive information to send out from one continent to another? Would you use the Internet, or a public telephone service? Chances are you would not use either because the risk of failure or security losses is too great. The Internet does not guarantee any level of service, just "best effort." Most Fortune 1000 Firms that have large amounts of data to move across the continent, or around the world, or that have high-security or guaranteed service level requirements, lease high-speed data lines from communication providers, typically long-distance telephone companies. These lines are designated as **T lines**.

T1 lines offer up to twenty-four 64-Kbps channels that can support a total data transmission rate of 1.544 Mbps. Each of these 64-Kbps channels can be configured to carry voice or data traffic. A T3 line is a very high-speed connection capable of transmitting data at a whopping rate of 45 million bps. You will rarely encounter a T3 line unless you work in the networking department of a major corporation or university. For instance, the Internet backbone operates using multiple T3 lines. Leasing a T1 line costs about $1,000 per month, whereas T3 line costs start around $10,000 per month. Table 3 summarizes these network services.

3   THE INTERNET

We all use the Internet, and many of us can't do without it. It's become an indispensable personal and business tool. But what exactly is the Internet? How does it work, and what does Internet technology have to offer for business? Let's look at the most important Internet features.

TABLE 3   BROADBAND NETWORK SERVICES

SERVICE	DESCRIPTION	BANDWIDTH
Frame relay	Packages data into frames for high-speed transmission over reliable circuits that require less error checking than packet switching	56 Kbps to 40+ Mbps
Asynchronous Transfer Mode (ATM)	Parcels data into uniform 53-byte cells for high-speed transmission; can transmit data, video, and audio over the same network	1.5 Mbps to 9+ Gbps
Integrated Services Digital Network (ISDN)	Dial-up network access standard that can integrate voice, data, and video services	Basic rate ISDN: 128 Kbps Primary rate ISDN: 1.5 Mbps
Digital subscriber line (DSL)	Dedicated telephone network broadband Internet access	ADSL: Up to 9 Mbps for receiving and over 700 Kbps for sending data SDSL: Up to 3 Mbps for both sending and receiving
Cable Internet connection	Dedicated cable network broadband access	Up to 10 Mbps
T lines	Dedicated lines for high-speed data transmission and Internet connection	T1: 1.544 Mbps T3: 45 Mbps

WHAT IS THE INTERNET?

The Internet has become the world's most extensive, public communication system that now rivals the global telephone system in reach and range. It's also the world's largest implementation of client/server computing and internetworking, linking hundreds of thousands of individual networks all over the world and more than 1 billion people worldwide. The word *Internet* derives from the word **internetworking**, or the linking of separate networks, each of which retains its own identity, into an interconnected network. This gigantic network of networks began in the early 1970s as a U.S. Department of Defense network to link scientists and university professors around the world.

Individuals connect to the Internet in two ways. Most homes connect to the Internet by subscribing to an Internet service provider. An **Internet service provider (ISP)** is a commercial organization with a permanent connection to the Internet that sells temporary connections to retail subscribers. Telephone lines, cable lines, or wireless connections can provide these connections. Major ISPs include Earthlink, Comcast, Verizon, and NetZero. Individuals also connect to the Internet through their business firms, universities, or research centers that have designated Internet domains, such as www.ibm.com.

INTERNET ADDRESSING AND ARCHITECTURE

The Internet is based on the TCP/IP networking protocol suite described earlier in this chapter. Every computer on the Internet is assigned a unique **Internet Protocol (IP) address**, which currently is a 32-bit number represented by four strings of numbers ranging from 0 to 255 separated by periods. For instance, the IP address of www.microsoft.com is 207.46.250.119.

When a user sends a message to another user on the Internet, the message is first decomposed into packets using the TCP protocol. Each packet contains its destination address. The packets are then sent from the client to the network server, then to a local router, and from there on to as many other routers and servers as necessary to arrive at a specific computer with the correct IP address. At the destination address, the packets are reassembled into the original message.

The Domain Name System

Because it would be incredibly difficult for Internet users to remember strings of 12 numbers, a **Domain Name System (DNS)** converts IP addresses to domain names. The **domain name** is the English-like name that corresponds to the unique 32-bit numeric IP address for each computer connected to the Internet. DNS servers maintain a database containing IP addresses mapped to their corresponding domain names. To access a computer on the Internet, users need only specify its domain name.

DNS has a hierarchical structure (see Figure 8). At the top of the DNS hierarchy is the root domain. The child domain of the root is called a top-level domain, and the child domain of a top-level domain is called is a second-level domain. Top-level domains are two- and three-character names you are familiar with from surfing the Web, for example, .com, .edu, .gov, and the various country codes such as .ca for Canada or .it for Italy. Second-level domains have two parts—designating a top-level name and a second-level name—such as buy.com, nyu.edu, or amazon.ca. A host name at the bottom of the hierarchy designates a specific computer on either the Internet or a private network.

The most common domain extensions currently available and officially approved are shown in the following list. Countries also have domain names

FIGURE 8   THE DOMAIN NAME SYSTEM

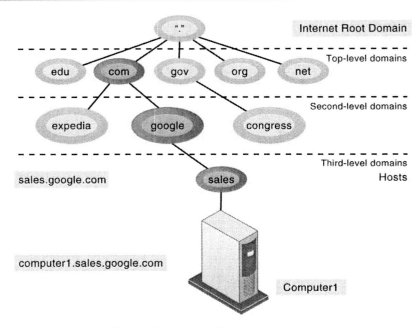

The Domain Name System is a hierarchical system with a root domain, top-level domains, second-level domains, and host computers at the third level.

such as .uk, .au, and .fr (United Kingdom, Australia, and France, respectively). In the future, this list will expand to include many more types of organizations and industries.

.com	Commercial organizations/businesses
.edu	Educational institutions
.gov	U.S. government agencies
.mil	U.S. military
.net	Network computers
.org	Nonprofit organizations and foundations
.biz	Business firms
.info	Information providers

Internet Architecture and Governance

Internet data traffic is carried by transcontinental high-speed backbone networks that generally operate today in the range of 45 Mbps to 2.5 Gbps (see Figure 9). These trunk lines are typically owned by long-distance telephone companies (called *network service providers*) or by national governments. Local connection lines are owned by regional telephone and cable television companies in the United States that connect retail users in homes and businesses to the Internet. The regional networks lease access to ISPs, private companies, and government institutions.

No one "owns" the Internet, and it has no formal management. However, worldwide Internet policies are established by a number of professional organizations and government bodies, including the Internet Architecture Board (IAB), which helps define the overall structure of the Internet; The

FIGURE 9   INTERNET NETWORK ARCHITECTURE

The Internet backbone connects to regional networks, which in turn provide access to Internet service providers, large firms, and government institutions. Network access points (NAPs) and metropolitan area exchanges (MAEs) are hubs where the backbone intersects regional and local networks and where backbone owners connect with one another. MAEs are also referred to as Internet Exchange Points.

Internet Corporation for Assigned Names and Numbers (ICANN), which assigns IP addresses; and The World Wide Web Consortium (W3C), which sets Hypertext Markup Language (HTML) and other programming standards for the Web.

These organizations influence government agencies, network owners, ISPs, and software developers with the goal of keeping the Internet operating as efficiently as possible. The Internet must also conform to the laws of the sovereign nation-states in which it operates, as well as the technical infrastructures that exist within the nation-states. Although in the early years of the Internet and the Web there was very little legislative or executive interference, this situation is changing as the Internet plays a growing role in the distribution of information and knowledge, including content that some find objectionable. In some countries, the Internet is censored just like traditional broadcast media.

The Internet is not "free," even though many people, such as students and employees, do not pay for their access. In fact, everyone who uses the Internet pays some fee—hidden or otherwise—to maintain the network. Each organization and business firm pays for its own networks and its own local Internet connection services, a part of which is paid to the long-distance trunk line owners. The costs of e-mail and other Internet connections tend to be far lower than equivalent voice, postal, or overnight delivery costs, making the Internet a very inexpensive communications medium. It is also a very fast method of communication, with messages arriving anywhere in the world in a matter of seconds, or a minute or two at most.

The Future Internet: IPv6 and Internet2

The Internet was not originally designed to handle the transmission of massive quantities of data and billions of users. Because many corporations and governments have been given large blocks of millions of IP addresses to accommodate current and future workforces, and because of sheer Internet population growth, the world is running out of available IP addresses using the existing addressing convention called IPv4. IPv4 uses a 32-bit addressing scheme and contains only 4.5 billion addresses, not enough for each of the 6.5 billion people on Earth.

Internet engineers believe the world will start running out of addresses beginning in 2009. To avoid this unpleasant outcome, the Internet Engineering Task Force adopted a new Internet Protocol Version 6 (IPv6), which uses a 128-bit addressing scheme and produces 3.4×10^{38} addresses. This is a large enough number to give each person on Earth several million addresses.

The existing Internet has many shortcomings chief among which are poor security, no service level guarantees, no differential service, no differential pricing, and bandwidth limitations that would prevent the emergence of wide-scale Internet television or Internet video distribution. **Internet2** and Next-Generation Internet (NGI) are consortia representing 200 universities, private businesses, and government agencies in the United States that are working on a new, robust, high-bandwidth version of the Internet. They have established several new high-performance backbone networks with bandwidths ranging from 2.5 Gbps to 9.6 Gbps.

Internet2 research groups are developing and implementing new technologies for more effective routing practices; different levels of service, depending on the type and importance of the data being transmitted; and advanced applications for distributed computation, virtual laboratories, digital libraries, distributed learning, and tele-immersion. These networks would not replace the public Internet, but they do provide test beds for leading-edge technology that may eventually migrate to the public Internet.

INTERNET SERVICES

The Internet is based on client/server technology. Individuals using the Internet control what they do through client applications on their computers, such as Web browser software. The data, including e-mail messages and Web pages, are stored on servers. A client uses the Internet to request information from a particular Web server on a distant computer, and the server sends the requested information back to the client over the Internet.

Client platforms today include not only PCs and other computers but also cell phones, small handheld digital devices, and other information appliances. An **information appliance** is a device, such as an Internet-enabled cell phone or a TV Internet receiver for Web access and e-mail, that has been designed to perform a few specialized computing tasks well with minimal user effort. People are increasingly relying on these easy-to-use specialized information appliances to connect to the Internet.

A client computer connecting to the Internet has access to a variety of services. These services include e-mail, electronic discussion groups (Usenet newsgroups), chatting and instant messaging, **Telnet, File Transfer Protocol**

TABLE 4 MAJOR INTERNET SERVICES

CAPABILITY	FUNCTIONS SUPPORTED
E-mail	Person-to-person messaging; document sharing
Usenet newsgroups	Discussion groups on electronic bulletin boards
Chatting and instant messaging	Interactive conversations
Telnet	Logging on to one computer system and doing work on another
File Transfer Protocol (FTP)	Transferring files from computer to computer
World Wide Web	Retrieving, formatting, and displaying information (including text, audio, graphics, and video) using hypertext links

(FTP), and the World Wide Web. Table 4 provides a brief description of these services.

Each Internet service is implemented by one or more software programs. All of the services may run on a single server computer, or different services may be allocated to different machines. Figure 10 illustrates one way that these services might be arranged in a multitiered client/server architecture.

THE WORLD WIDE WEB

You've probably used the World Wide Web to download music, to find information for a term paper, or to obtain news and weather reports. The Web is the most popular Internet service. It's a system with universally accepted standards for storing, retrieving, formatting, and displaying information using a

FIGURE 10   CLIENT/SERVER COMPUTING ON THE INTERNET

Client computers running Web browser and other software can access an array of services on servers over the Internet. These services may all run on a single server or on multiple specialized servers.

client/server architecture. Web pages are formatted using hypertext with embedded links that connect documents to one another and that also link pages to other objects, such as sound, video, or animation files. When you click a graphic and a video clip plays, you have clicked a hyperlink.

Hypertext

Web pages are based on a standard Hypertext Markup Language (HTML), which formats documents and incorporates dynamic links to other documents and pictures stored in the same or remote computers. Web pages are accessible through the Internet because Web browser software operating your computer can request Web pages stored on an Internet host server using the **Hypertext Transfer Protocol (HTTP)**. HTTP is the communications standard used to transfer pages on the Web. For example, when you type a Web address in your browser, such as www.sec.gov, your browser sends an HTTP request to the sec.gov server requesting the home page of sec.gov.

HTTP is the first set of letters at the start of every Web address, followed by the domain name, which specifies the organization's server computer that is storing the document. Most companies have a domain name that is the same as or closely related to their official corporate name. The directory path and document name are two more pieces of information within the Web address that help the browser track down the requested page. Together, the address is called a **uniform resource locator (URL)**. When typed into a browser, a URL tells the browser software exactly where to look for the information. For example, in the following URL

http://www.megacorp.com/content/features/082602.html

http names the protocol used to display Web pages, *www.megacorp.com* is the domain name, *content/features* is the directory path that identifies where on the domain Web server the page is stored, and *082602.html* is the document name and the name of the format it is in (it is an HTML page).

Web Servers

A Web server is software for locating and managing stored Web pages. It locates the Web pages requested by a user on the computer where they are stored and delivers the Web pages to the user's computer. Server applications usually run on dedicated computers, although they can all reside on a single computer in small organizations.

The most common Web server in use today is Apache HTTP Server, which controls 70 percent of the market. Apache is an open-source product that is free of charge and can be downloaded from the Web. Microsoft's product Internet Information Services (IIS) is the second most commonly used Web server, with a 21 percent market share.

A typical **Web site** is a collection of Web pages linked to a **home page**—a text and graphical screen display that usually welcomes the user and provides a brief description of the organization that has established the Web site. Most home pages offer a way to contact the organization or individual. The person in charge of an organization's Web site is called a **Webmaster**.

Searching for Information on the Web

No one knows for sure how many Web pages there really are. The surface Web is the part of the Web that search engines visit and about which information is recorded. For instance, Google visited about eight billion pages in 2005. But there is a "deep Web" that contains an estimated 800 billion additional pages, many of them proprietary (such as the pages of *The Wall Street Journal Online*, which cannot be visited without an access code) or that are stored in protected corporate databases.

Search Engines

Obviously, with so many Web pages, finding specific Web pages that can help you or your business, nearly instantly, is an important problem. The question is, how can you find the one or two pages you really want and need out of billions of indexed Web pages? **Search engines** solve the problem of finding useful information on the Web nearly instantly, and, arguably, they are the "killer app" of the Internet era. There are hundreds of different search engines in the world, but the vast majority of search results are supplied by three top providers (see Figure 11).

Web search engines started out in the early 1990s as relatively simple software programs that roamed the nascent Web, visiting pages, and gathering information about the content of each page. These early programs were called variously crawlers, spiders, and wanderers. AltaVista, launched in 1995, was the first to allow "natural language" queries, such as "history of web search engines" rather than "history + web search + search engine".

The first search engines were simple keyword indexes of all the pages they visited. They would count the number of times a word appeared on the pages and store this information in an index, leaving the user with lists of pages that may not have been truly relevant to their search.

In 1994, Stanford University computer science students David Filo and Jerry Yang created a hand-selected list of their favorite Web pages and called it "Yet Another Hierarchical Officious Oracle," or Yahoo!. Yahoo! was never a real search engine but rather an edited selection of Web sites organized by categories the editors found useful. Yahoo! has since developed its own search engine capabilities.

In 1998, Larry Page and Sergey Brin, two other Stanford computer science students, released their first version of Google. This search engine was different: Not only did it index each Web page's words but it also ranked search results based on the relevance of each page. Page patented the idea of a page ranking system (PageRank System), which essentially measures the popularity of a Web page by calculating what other sites link to that page. Brin contributed a unique Web crawler program that indexed not only keywords on a page but

FIGURE 11   MAJOR WEB SEARCH ENGINES

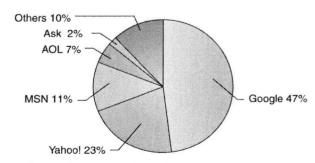

Google is the most popular search engine on the Web, handling nearly 50 percent of all Web searches.

Sources: http://searchenginewatch.com, accessed August 19, 2006 and Kevin J. Delaney, "Search Engines Find a Role for Humans," *The Wall Street Journal*, May 11, 2006.

also combinations of words (such as authors and the titles of their articles). These two ideas became the foundation for the Google search engine. Figure 12 illustrates how Google works.

Web sites for locating information such as Yahoo!, Google, and MSN have become so popular and easy to use that they also serve as major portals for the Internet. The search marketplace has become very competitive. Microsoft has unleashed its MSN search tool; Amazon.com has entered the fray with A9; and Overture.com (now owned by Yahoo!) transformed the search world by charging advertisers for placement and ranking.

The spectacular increase in Internet advertising revenues has made search engines major shopping tools by offering what is now called **search engine marketing**. When users enter a search term at Google, MSN, Yahoo!, or any of the other sites serviced by these search engines, they receive two types of listings: sponsored links, for which advertisers have paid to be listed (usually at the top of the search results page) and unsponsored "organic" search results. In addition, advertisers can purchase tiny text boxes on the right side of the Google and MSN search results page. The paid, sponsored advertisements are the fastest-growing form of Internet advertising and are powerful new marketing tools that precisely match consumer interests with advertising messages at the right moment (see the chapter-ending case study).

FIGURE 12   HOW GOOGLE WORKS

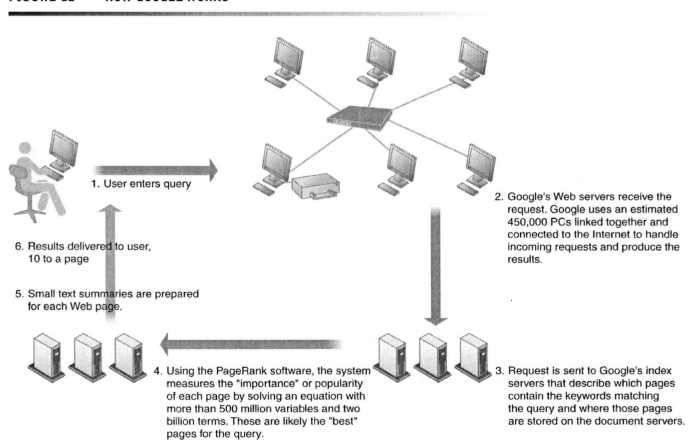

1. User enters query

6. Results delivered to user, 10 to a page

5. Small text summaries are prepared for each Web page.

2. Google's Web servers receive the request. Google uses an estimated 450,000 PCs linked together and connected to the Internet to handle incoming requests and produce the results.

4. Using the PageRank software, the system measures the "importance" or popularity of each page by solving an equation with more than 500 million variables and two billion terms. These are likely the "best" pages for the query.

3. Request is sent to Google's index servers that describe which pages contain the keywords matching the query and where those pages are stored on the document servers.

The Google search engine is continuously crawling the Web, indexing the content of each page, calculating its popularity, and storing the pages so that it can respond quickly to user requests to see a page. The entire process takes about one-half second.

Search engines have become crucial tools within individual e-commerce sites. Customers can search easily for the product information they want with the help of an internal search program. However, within Web sites, the search engine is limited to finding matches from that one site.

Intelligent Agent Shopping Bots

Software agents with built-in intelligence can gather or filter information and perform other tasks to assist users. **Shopping bots** use intelligent agent software for searching the Internet for shopping information. Shopping bots such as MySimon or Froogle can help people interested in making a purchase filter and retrieve information about products of interest, evaluate competing products according to criteria the users have established, and negotiate with vendors for price and delivery terms. Many of these shopping agents search the Web for pricing and availability of products specified by the user and return a list of sites that sell the item along with pricing information and a purchase link.

Web 2.0

If you have shared photos over the Internet at Flickr or another photo site, blogged, looked up a word on Wikipedia, or contributed information yourself, you've used services that are part of **Web 2.0**. Today's Web sites don't just contain static content—they enable people to collaborate, share information, and create new services online. Web 2.0 refers to these second-generation interactive Internet-based services.

The innovations that distinguish Web 2.0 are mashups, blogs, RSS, and wikis. Mashups are software services that enable users and system developers to mix and match content or software components to create something entirely new. For example, Yahoo!'s photo storage and sharing site Flickr combines photos with other information about the images provided by users and tools to make it usable within other programming environments.

With mashups, the Web is not just a collection of destination sites but a source of data and services that can be combined to create applications users need. Web 2.0 software applications run on the Web itself instead of the desktop and bring the vision of Web-based computing closer to realization.

A **blog**, the popular term for a Weblog, is an informal yet structured Web site where subscribing individuals can publish stories, opinions, and links to other Web sites of interest. Blogs have become popular personal publishing tools, but they also have business uses. For example, GM Vice President Bob Lutz uses a blog to communicate directly with customers.

If you are an avid blog reader, you might use RSS to keep up with your favorite blogs without constantly checking them for updates. **RSS**, which stands for Rich Site Summary or Really Simple Syndication, syndicates Web site content so that it can be used in another setting. RSS technology pulls specified content from Web sites and feeds it automatically to users' computers, where it can be stored for later viewing.

To receive an RSS information feed, you need to install aggregator or news reader software that can be downloaded from the Web. (Microsoft Internet Explorer 7 includes RSS reading capabilities.) Alternatively, you can establish an account with an aggregator Web site. You tell the aggregator to collect all updates from a given Web page, or list of pages, or gather information on a given subject by conducting Web searches at regular intervals. Once subscribed, you automatically receive new content as it is posted to the specified Web site. A number of businesses use RSS internally to distribute updated corporate information.

Blogs allow visitors to add comments to the original content, but they do not allow visitors to change the original posted material. **Wikis**, in contrast, are collaborative Web sites where visitors can add, delete, or modify content on the site, including the work of previous authors. Wiki comes from the Hawaiian word for "quick." Probably the best-known wiki site is Wikipedia, the massive online open-source encyclopedia to which anyone can contribute. But wikis also are used for business. For example, investment bank Dresdner Kleinwort Wasserstein uses wikis instead of e-mail to create meeting agendas and post training videos for new hires.

INTRANETS AND EXTRANETS

Organizations use Internet networking standards and Web technology to create private networks called *intranets*. An intranet is an internal organizational network that provides access to data across the enterprise. It uses the existing company network infrastructure along with Internet connectivity standards and software developed for the World Wide Web. Intranets create networked applications that can run on many different kinds of computers throughout the organization, including mobile handheld computers and wireless remote access devices.

Whereas the Web is available to anyone, an intranet is private and is protected from public visits by **firewalls**—security systems with specialized software to prevent outsiders from entering private networks. Intranet software technology is the same as that of the World Wide Web. A simple intranet can be created by linking a client computer with a Web browser to a computer with Web server software using a TCP/IP network with software to keep unwanted visitors out.

Extranets

A firm creates an extranet to allow authorized vendors and customers to have limited access to its internal intranet. For example, authorized buyers could link to a portion of a company's intranet from the public Internet to obtain information about the costs and features of the company's products. The company uses firewalls to ensure that access to its internal data is limited and remains secure; firewalls also authenticate users, making sure that only authorized users access the site.

Both intranets and extranets reduce operational costs by providing the connectivity to coordinate disparate business processes within the firm and to link electronically to customers and suppliers. Extranets often are employed for collaborating with other companies for supply chain management, product design and development, and training efforts.

TECHNOLOGIES AND TOOLS FOR COMMUNICATION AND E-BUSINESS

You've probably used e-mail and instant messaging at home and at work. They are some of the Internet-based tools that today's businesses use for communication and coordination. Others include electronic discussion groups, groupware, electronic conferencing, Internet telephony, and virtual private networks.

E-Mail, Chat, Instant Messaging, and Electronic Discussions

E-mail enables messages to be exchanged from computer to computer, eliminating costly long-distance telephone charges while expediting communication among different parts of the organization. E-mail software has capabilities for routing messages to multiple recipients, forwarding messages, and attaching text documents or multimedia files to messages. Although some organizations operate their own internal electronic mail systems, a great deal of e-mail today is sent through the Internet.

Nearly 90 percent of U.S. workplaces have employees communicating interactively using **chat** or instant messaging tools. Chatting enables two or more people who are simultaneously connected to the Internet to hold live, interactive conversations. Chat groups are divided into channels, and each is assigned its own topic of conversation. Chat systems now support voice and video chat as well as written conversations. Many online retail businesses offer chat services on their Web sites to attract visitors, to encourage repeat purchases, and to improve customer service.

Instant messaging is a type of chat service that enables participants to create their own private chat channels. The instant messaging system alerts the user whenever someone on his or her private list is online so that the user can initiate a chat session with other individuals. Instant messaging systems for consumers include Yahoo! Messenger, Windows Live Messenger, and AOL Instant Messenger. Companies concerned with security are building proprietary instant messaging systems with tools such as Lotus Sametime. Instant messaging has migrated to cell phones and wireless handhelds.

Usenet newsgroups are worldwide discussion groups posted on Internet electronic bulletin boards on which people share information and ideas on a defined topic, such as radiology or rock bands. Anyone can post messages on these bulletin boards for others to read. Many thousands of groups exist that discuss almost all conceivable topics.

Employee use of e-mail, instant messaging, and the Internet is supposed to increase worker productivity, but the accompanying Interactive Session on Management shows that this may not always be the case. Many company managers now believe they need to monitor their employees' online activity. But is this ethical? Although there are some strong business reasons why companies may need to monitor their employees' e-mail and Web activities, what does this mean for employee privacy?

Groupware and Electronic Conferencing

Groupware provides capabilities for supporting enterprise-wide communication and collaborative work. Individuals, teams, and workgroups at different locations in the organization use groupware for writing and commenting on group projects, sharing ideas and documents, conducting electronic meetings, tracking the status of tasks and projects, scheduling, and sending e-mail. Any group member can review the ideas of other group members at any time and add to them, or an individual can post a document for others to comment on or edit. Commercial groupware products, such as Lotus Notes and OpenText's LiveLink, are Internet based. Microsoft Office Groove 2007 is an interesting groupware tool based on peer-to-peer technology that enables people to work directly with other people over the Internet without going through a central server sharing files, conversations, and project documents.

A growing number of companies are using Internet conferencing tools to stage meetings, conferences, and presentations online. Web conferencing

INTERACTIVE SESSION: MANAGEMENT

MONITORING EMPLOYEES ON NETWORKS: UNETHICAL OR GOOD BUSINESS?

As Internet use has exploded worldwide, so have the use of e-mail and the Web for personal business at the workplace. A number of studies have concluded that at least 25 percent of employee online time is spent on non-work-related Web surfing, and perhaps as many as 90 percent of employees receive or send personal e-mail at work.

Many companies have begun monitoring their employee use of e-mail and the Internet, often without employee knowledge. A study by Forrester Consulting found that 37.8 percent of U.S. companies with 1,000 or more workers employ people to read through employees' out-bound e-mail. A similar study by the American Management Association concluded that 55 percent of U.S. companies retain and review employee e-mail messages and that 76 percent monitor their Web connections. Although U.S. companies have the legal right to monitor employee Internet and e-mail activity, is such monitoring unethical, or is it simply good business?

Managers worry about the loss of time and employee productivity when employees are focusing on personal rather than company business. A recent survey by America Online and Salary.com found that the average U.S. worker wastes more than two hours per day on non-work-related business, and 45 percent of respondents cited personal Internet use as their primary time-wasting activity at work.

If personal traffic on company networks is too high, it can also clog the company's network so that business work cannot be performed. Potomac Hospital in Woodridge, Virginia found its computing resources were limited by a lack of bandwidth caused by employees using the hospital's Internet connections to access radio stations and download music and video files.

Too much time on personal business, on the Internet or not, can mean lost revenue or over-billed clients. Some employees may be charging time they spend trading their personal stocks online or pursuing other personal business to clients, thus overcharging the clients.

When employees use e-mail or the Web at employer facilities or with employer equipment, anything they do, including anything illegal, carries the company's name. Therefore, the employer can be traced and held liable. Management in many firms fear that racist, sexually explicit, or other potentially offensive material accessed or traded by their employees could result in adverse publicity and even lawsuits for the firm. Even if the company is found not to be liable, responding to lawsuits could cost the company tens of thousands of dollars. Companies also fear e-mail leakage of trade secrets.

Companies that allow employees to use personal e-mail accounts at work could face legal and regulatory trouble if they do not retain those messages. E-mail today is an important source of evidence for lawsuits, and companies are now required to retain all of their e-mail messages for longer periods than in the past. Courts do not discriminate about whether e-mails involved in lawsuits were sent via personal or business e-mail accounts. Not producing those e-mails could result in a five- to six-figure fine.

Companies have the legal right to monitor what employees are doing with company equipment during business hours. The question is whether electronic surveillance is an appropriate tool for maintaining an efficient and positive workplace. Some companies try to ban all personal activities on corporate networks—zero tolerance. Others block employee access to specific Web sites or limit personal time on the Web using software that enables IT departments to track the Web sites employees visit, the amount of time employees spend at these sites, and the files they download. Some firms have fired employees who have stepped out of bounds. Nearly one-third of the companies surveyed in the Forrester Consulting study had fired at least one employee within the last year for breaking company e-mail rules.

No solution is problem free, but many consultants believe companies should write corporate policies on employee e-mail and Internet use. The policies should include explicit ground rules that state, by position or level, under what circumstances employees can use company facilities for e-mail or Internet use. The policies should also inform employees whether these activities are monitored and explain why.

The rules should be tailored to specific business needs and organizational cultures. For example, although some companies may exclude all employees from visiting sites that have explicit sexual material, law firm or hospital employees may require access to these sites. Investment firms will need to allow many of their employees access to other investment sites. A company dependent on widespread information sharing, innovation, and independence could very well find that monitoring creates more problems than it solves.

Sources: Alex Mindlin, "You've Got Someone Reading Your E-Mail," *The New York Times*, June 12, 2006; Darrell Dunn, "Who's Watching Now?" *Information Week*, February 27, 2006; and Jack M. Germain, "Monitoring Employee Communications in the Enterprise," NewsFactor Network, April 10, 2006.

CASE STUDY QUESTIONS

1. Should managers monitor employee e-mail and Internet usage? Why or why not?

2. Describe an effective e-mail and Web use policy for a company.

MIS IN ACTION

Explore the Web site of a company selling online employee-monitoring software such as NetVizor, SpyAgent, or Activity Monitor and answer the following questions.

1. What employee activities does this software track? What can an employer learn about an employee by using this software?

2. How can businesses benefit from using this software?

3. How would you feel if your employer used this software where you work to monitor what you are doing on the job? Explain your response.

and collaboration software provide virtual conference tables for participants to view and modify documents and slides, write or draw on an electronic whiteboard, or share their thoughts and comments using chat or voice conferencing. The current generation of such tools from Lotus, Microsoft, and WebEx work through a standard Web browser. Web videoconferencing tools enable meeting participants equipped with Web cameras to see and talk to each other using their PCs and Web browsers. These forms of electronic conferencing are growing in popularity because they reduce the need for face-to-face meetings, saving travel time and cost.

Internet Telephony

Internet telephony enables companies to use Internet technology for telephone voice transmission over the Internet or private networks. (Internet telephony products sometimes are called *IP telephony* products.) **Voice over IP (VoIP)** technology uses the Internet Protocol (IP) to deliver voice information in digital form using packet switching, avoiding the tolls charged by local and long-distance telephone networks (see Figure 13). Calls that would ordinarily be transmitted over public telephone networks would travel over the corporate network based on the Internet Protocol, or the public Internet. IP telephony calls can be made and received with a desktop computer equipped with a microphone and speakers or with a VoIP-enabled telephone.

VoIP is the fastest-growing form of telephone service in the United States. The number of lines is roughly doubling each year and is expected to reach 30 million

FIGURE 13   HOW IP TELEPHONY WORKS

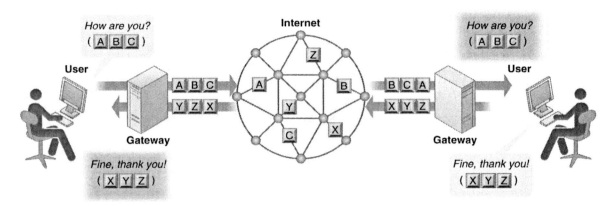

An IP phone call digitizes and breaks up a voice message into data packets that may travel along different routes before being reassembled at the final destination. A processor nearest the call's destination, called a *gateway*, arranges the packets in the proper order and directs them to the telephone number of the receiver or the IP address of the receiving computer.

lines by 2008 (eMarketer, 2005c). Vonage, the early VoIP mover, competes with baby Bells (such as Verizon) and cable firms (such as Time Warner and Cablevision). Skype, which offers free VoIP worldwide using a peer-to-peer network, was acquired by eBay and Google has its own free VoIP service.

Although there are up-front investments required for an IP phone system, VoIP can reduce communication and network management costs by 20 to 30 percent. For example, VoIP saves Virgin Entertainment Group $700,000 per year in long-distance bills (Hoover, 2006). In addition to lowering long-distance costs and eliminating monthly fees for private lines, an IP network provides a single voice-data infrastructure for both telecommunications and computing services. Companies no longer have to maintain separate networks or provide support services and personnel for each different type of network.

Another advantage of VoIP is its flexibility. Unlike the traditional telephone network, phones can be added or moved to different offices without rewiring or reconfiguring the network. With VoIP, a conference call is arranged by a simple click-and-drag operation on the computer screen to select the names of the conferees. Voice mail and e-mail can be combined into a single directory.

Virtual Private Networks

What if you had a marketing group charged with developing new products and services for your firm with members spread across the United States? You would want to be able to e-mail each other and communicate with the home office without any chance that outsiders could intercept the communications. In the past, one answer to this problem was to work with large private networking firms who offered secure, private, dedicated networks to customers. But this was an expensive solution. A much less expensive solution is to create a virtual private network within the public Internet.

A **virtual private network (VPN)** is a secure, encrypted, private network that has been configured within a public network to take advantage of the economies of scale and management facilities of large networks, such as the Internet (see Figure 14). A VPN provides your firm with secure, encrypted communications at a much lower cost than the same capabilities offered by

FIGURE 14   A VIRTUAL PRIVATE NETWORK USING THE INTERNET

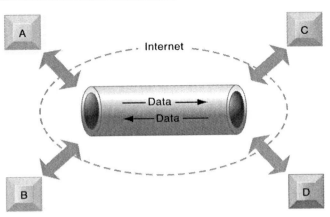

This VPN is a private network of computers linked using a secure "tunnel" connection over the Internet. It protects data transmitted over the public Internet by encoding the data and "wrapping" them within the Internet Protocol (IP). By adding a wrapper around a network message to hide its content, organizations can create a private connection that travels through the public Internet.

traditional non-Internet providers who use their private networks to secure communications. VPNs also provide a network infrastructure for combining voice and data networks.

Several competing protocols are used to protect data transmitted over the public Internet, including Point-to-Point Tunneling Protocol (PPTP). In a process called *tunneling*, packets of data are encrypted and wrapped inside IP packets. By adding this wrapper around a network message to hide its content, business firms create a private connection that travels through the public Internet.

4   THE WIRELESS REVOLUTION

If you have a cell phone, do you use it for taking and sending photos, sending text messages, or downloading music clips? Do you take your laptop to class or to the library to link up to the Internet? If so, you're part of the wireless revolution! Cell phones, laptops, and small handheld devices have morphed into portable computing platforms that let you perform some of the computing tasks you used to do at your desk.

Wireless communication helps businesses more easily stay in touch with customers, suppliers, and employees and provides more flexible arrangements for organizing work. Wireless technology has also created new products, services, and sales channels.

WIRELESS DEVICES

If you require mobile communication and computing power or remote access to corporate systems, you can work with an array of wireless devices: PCs, cell phones, personal digital assistants (PDAs), e-mail handhelds, and smart phones.

We introduced cell phones in Section 2. **Personal digital assistants (PDAs)** are small, handheld computers featuring applications such as electronic schedulers, address books, memo pads, and expense trackers. Many models feature e-mail messaging, wireless access to the Internet, voice communication, and digital cameras. **E-mail handhelds**, such as the BlackBerry Handheld, are a special type of handheld that is optimized for wireless text messaging. Hybrid devices combining the functionality of a PDA with that of a digital cell phone are called **smart phones**.

CELLULAR SYSTEMS

Mobile phones are not only for voice communication—they have become mobile platforms for delivering digital data. Mobile phones enable many millions of people to communicate and access the Internet in Africa and other countries where conventional telephone or Internet service is expensive or unavailable.

Cellular Network Standards and Generations

Digital cellular service uses several competing standards that are incompatible. This means that digital cellular handsets cannot work on networks that use another wireless standard.

In Europe and much of the rest of the world outside the United States, the standard is **Global System for Mobile Communication (GSM)**. GSM's strength is its international roaming capability. Users have seamless same-number roaming in more than 170 countries. Most GSM systems outside North America operate in the 900 MHz and 1.8 gigahertz (GHz) frequency bands. (In North America, they operate in the 1.9 GHz band.)

There are GSM cell phone systems in the United States, including T-Mobile and Cingular. However, the most widely used standard in the United States is **Code Division Multiple Access (CDMA)**, which is the system used by Verizon and Sprint. CDMA was developed by the military during World War II. It transmits over several frequencies, occupies the entire spectrum, and randomly assigns users to a range of frequencies over time. In general, CDMA is cheaper to implement, is more efficient in its use of spectrum, and provides higher quality voice and data than GSM.

Cellular Generations

Most digital cellular systems today are used primarily for voice, but they are able to transmit data at rates ranging from 9.6 to 2 Mbps. Most cellular users in the U.S. with Web service adopt plans which offer 384 Kbps, which is acceptable for e-mail but not for downloading large files or entire Web pages. The most economical use of cellular technology for data transmission is SMS messaging. **Short message service (SMS)** is a text message service used by a number of digital cell phone systems to send and receive short alphanumeric messages less than 160 characters in length. Like e-mail, SMS messages can be forwarded and stored for later retrieval.

More powerful cellular networks called **third-generation (3G) networks** have transmission speeds ranging from 384 Kbps for mobile users in, say, a car, to more than 2 Mbps for stationary users. This is sufficient transmission capacity for video, graphics, and other rich media, in addition to voice, making 3G networks suitable for wireless broadband Internet access and always-on data transmission.

Wireless carriers are starting to roll out 3G services. In the meantime, those interested in high-speed Internet access and data transmission where 3G is unavailable are relying on an interim solution called **2.5G networks**. 2.5G networks use upgrades to the existing cellular infrastructure and feature data transmission rates ranging from 30 to 144 Kbps.

Mobile Wireless Standards for Web Access

There are also multiple standards and technologies governing how cellular phones access the Internet and the World Wide Web. **Wireless Application Protocol (WAP)** is a system of protocols and technologies that enables cell phones and other wireless devices with tiny display screens, low-bandwidth connections, and minimal memory to access Web-based information and services. WAP uses Wireless Markup Language (WML), which is based on XML and is optimized for tiny displays.

A person with a WAP-compliant phone uses the built-in microbrowser to make a request in WML. A **microbrowser** is an Internet browser with a small file size that works with the low-memory constraints of handheld wireless devices and the low bandwidth of wireless networks. The request is passed to a WAP gateway, which retrieves the information from an Internet server in either standard HTML format or WML. The gateway translates HTML content back into WML for the WAP client to receive it. WAP supports most wireless network standards and operating systems for handheld computing devices.

I-mode is a wireless service offered by Japan's NTT DoCoMo mobile phone network that uses a different set of standards. Instead of using WAP, i-mode uses compact HTML to deliver content, making it easier for businesses to convert their HTML Web sites to mobile service. I-mode enables users to be connected constantly to the network and content providers to broadcast relevant information to users. (WAP users have to dial in to see if a site has changed—see Figure 15).

FIGURE 15   WIRELESS APPLICATION PROTOCOL (WAP) VERSUS I-MODE

WAP and i-mode use alternative standards for accessing information from the wireless Web.

WIRELESS COMPUTER NETWORKS AND INTERNET ACCESS

If you have a laptop computer, you might be able to use it to access the Internet as you move from room to room in your dorm, or table to table in your university library. An array of technologies provide high-speed wireless access to the Internet for PCs and other wireless handheld devices as well as for cell phones. These new high-speed services have extended Internet access to numerous locations that could not be covered by traditional wired Internet services.

The Institute of Electrical and Electronics Engineers (IEEE) has established a hierarchy of complementary standards for wireless computer networks. These standards include IEEE 802.15 for the personal area network (Bluetooth), IEEE 802.11 for the local area network (LAN; Wi-Fi), and 802.16 for the metropolitan-area network (MAN; WiMax).

Bluetooth

Bluetooth is the popular name for the 802.15 wireless networking standard, which is useful for creating small **personal area networks (PANs).** It links up to eight devices within a 10-meter area using low-power, radio-based communication and can transmit up to 722 Kbps in the 2.4-GHz band.

Wireless phones, pagers, computers, printers, and computing devices using Bluetooth communicate with each other and even operate each other without direct user intervention (see Figure 16). For example, a person could direct a notebook computer to send a document file wirelessly to a printer. Bluetooth connects wireless keyboards and mice to PCs or cell phones to earpieces without wires. Bluetooth has low-power requirements, making it appropriate for battery-powered handheld computers, cell phones, or PDAs.

FIGURE 16   A BLUETOOTH NETWORK (PAN)

Bluetooth enables a variety of devices, including cell phones, PDAs, wireless keyboards and mice, PCs, and printers, to interact wirelessly with each other within a small 30-foot (10-meter) area. In addition to the links shown, Bluetooth can be used to network similar devices to send data from one PC to another, for example.

Although Bluetooth lends itself to personal networking, it has uses in large corporations. For example, Federal Express drivers use Bluetooth to transmit the delivery data captured by their handheld PowerPad computers to cellular transmitters, which forward the data to corporate computers. Drivers no longer need to spend time docking their handheld units physically in the transmitters, and Bluetooth has saved FedEx $20 million per year.

Wi-Fi

The IEEE set of standards for wireless LANs is the 802.11 family, also known as **Wi-Fi** (for wireless fidelity). There are three standards in this family: 802.11a, 802.11b, and 802.11g. 802.11n is an emerging standard for increasing the speed and capacity of wireless networking.

The 802.11a standard can transmit up to 54 Mbps in the unlicensed 5 GHz frequency range and has an effective distance of 10 to 30 meters. The 802.11b standard can transmit up to 11 Mbps in the unlicensed 2.4 GHz band and has an effective distance of 30 to 50 meters, although this range can be extended outdoors by using tower-mounted antennas. The 802.11g standard can transmit up to 54 Mbps in the 2.4 GHz range. 802.11n will transmit at more than 200 Mbps.

Because 802.11b and 802.11g operate in the 2.4 GHz frequency, products built for either of these two standards are compatible. Products designed for the 802.11a specification won't work with either 802.11b or 802.11g, because 802.11a uses a different frequency band.

802.11b was the first wireless standard to be widely adopted for wireless LANs and wireless Internet access. 802.11g is increasingly used for this purpose, and dual-band systems capable of handling 802.11b and 802.11g are available.

A Wi-Fi system can operate in two different modes. In infrastructure mode, wireless devices communicate with a wired LAN using access points. An **access point** is a box consisting of a radio receiver/transmitter and antennas that links to a wired network, router, or hub.

In ad hoc mode, also known as peer-to-peer mode, wireless devices communicate with each other directly and do not use an access point. Most Wi-Fi communication uses infrastructure mode. (Ad hoc mode is used for very small LANs in the home or small business offices.)

Figure 17 illustrates an 802.11 wireless LAN operating in infrastructure mode that connects a small number of mobile devices to a larger wired LAN. Most wireless devices are client machines. The servers that the mobile client stations need to use are on the wired LAN. The access point controls the wireless stations and acts as a bridge between the main wired LAN and the wireless LAN. (A bridge connects two LANs based on different technologies.) The access point also controls the wireless stations.

Mobile wireless stations often need an add-in card called a *wireless network interface card (NIC)* that has a built-in radio and antenna. **Wireless NICs** can be credit card–size cards that snap into the Personal Computer Memory Card International Association (PCMCIA) card slot (also called the PC card slot) on a PC or external adapters that plug into the PC's universal serial bus (USB) port. Newer laptop PCs come equipped with chips that can receive Wi-Fi signals.

Wi-Fi and Wireless Internet Access

The 802.11 standard also provides wireless access to the Internet using a broadband connection. In this instance, an access point plugs into an Internet connection, which could come from a cable TV line or DSL telephone service.

FIGURE 17   AN 802.11 WIRELESS LAN

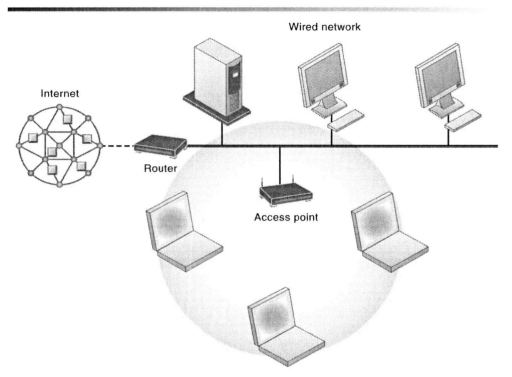

Mobile laptop computers equipped with wireless NICs link to the wired LAN by communicating with the access point. The access point uses radio waves to transmit network signals from the wired network to the client adapters, which convert them into data that the mobile device can understand.
The client adapter then transmits the data from the mobile device back to the access point, which forwards the data to the wired network.

Computers within a range of the access point use it to link wirelessly to the Internet.

Large corporations and small businesses are using Wi-Fi networks to provide low-cost wireless LANs and Internet access. Wi-Fi hotspots are springing up in hotels, airport lounges, libraries, cafes, and college campuses to provide mobile access to the Internet. Dartmouth College is one of many campuses where students now use Wi-Fi for research, course work, and entertainment.

Hotspots typically consist of one or more access points positioned on a ceiling, wall, or other strategic spot in a public place to provide maximum wireless coverage for a specific area. Users in range of a hotspot are able to access the Internet from their laptops. Some hotspots are free or do not require any additional software to use; others may require activation and the establishment of a user account by providing a credit card number over the Web.

Wi-Fi technology poses several challenges, however. Right now, users cannot freely roam from hotspot to hotspot if these hotspots use different Wi-Fi network services. Unless the service is free, users would need to log on to separate accounts for each service, each with its own fees.

One major drawback of Wi-Fi is its weak security features, which make these wireless networks vulnerable to intruders.

Another drawback of Wi-Fi networks is susceptibility to interference from nearby systems operating in the same spectrum, such as wireless phones, microwave ovens, or other wireless LANs. Wireless networks based on the 802.11n specification will solve this problem by using multiple wireless antennas in tandem to transmit and receive data and technology called *MIMO* (multiple input multiple output) to coordinate multiple simultaneous radio signals.

WiMax

A surprisingly large number of areas in the United States and throughout the world do not have access to Wi-Fi or fixed broadband connectivity. The range of Wi-Fi systems is no more than 300 feet from the base station, making it difficult for rural groups that don't have cable or DSL service to find wireless access to the Internet.

The IEEE developed a new family of standards known as WiMax to deal with these problems. **WiMax**, which stands for Worldwide Interoperability for Microwave Access, is the popular term for IEEE Standard 802.16, known as the "Air Interface for Fixed Broadband Wireless Access Systems." WiMax has a wireless access range of up to 31 miles, compared to 300 feet for Wi-Fi and 30 feet for Bluetooth, and a data transfer rate of up to 75 Mbps. The 802.16 specification has robust security and quality-of-service features to support voice and video.

WiMax antennas are powerful enough to beam high-speed Internet connections to rooftop antennas of homes and businesses that are miles away. Spring Nextel is building a national WiMax network to support video, video calling, and other data-intensive wireless services and Intel has a special chips that facilitate WiMax access from mobile computers.

Broadband Cellular Wireless and Emerging Wireless Services

Suppose your sales force needs to access the Web or use e-mail but can't always find a convenient Wi-Fi hotspot? You can now plug a small card into your laptop and use your PC on a cellular network. Major cellular telephone carriers have configured their 3G networks to provide anytime, anywhere broadband access for PCs and other handheld devices. Cingular offers a service called EDGE. Verizon's service is called BroadBand Access and is based on a technology called **EV-DO**, which stands for Evolution Data Optimized. EV-DO provides wireless access to the Internet over a cellular network at an average speed of 300 to 500 Kbps. Sprint offers a similar EV-DO wireless service.

Increasingly, cell phones, wireless PDAs, and laptops offer the ability to switch from one type of network to another. For example, most new cell phone handsets now have Bluetooth capabilities or the ability to support wireless calls over the Internet.

RFID AND WIRELESS SENSOR NETWORKS

Mobile technologies are creating new efficiencies and ways of working throughout the enterprise. In addition to the wireless systems we have just described, radio frequency identification (RFID) systems and wireless sensor networks are having a major impact.

Radio Frequency Identification (RFID)

Radio frequency identification (RFID) systems provide a powerful technology for tracking the movement of goods throughout the supply chain. RFID systems use tiny tags with embedded microchips containing data about an item and its location to transmit radio signals over a short distance to special RFID readers. The RFID readers then pass the data over a network to a computer for processing. Unlike bar codes, RFID tags do not need line-of-sight contact to be read.

The transponder, or RFID tag, is electronically programmed with information that can uniquely identify an item plus other information about the item, such as its location, where and when it was made, or its status during production. Embedded in the tag is a microchip for storing the data. The rest of the tag is an antenna that transmits data to the reader.

The reader unit consists of an antenna and radio transmitter with a decoding capability attached to a stationary or handheld device. The reader emits radio waves in ranges anywhere from 1 inch to 100 feet, depending on its power output, the radio frequency employed, and surrounding environmental conditions. When an RFID tag comes within the range of the reader, the tag is activated and starts sending data. The reader captures these data, decodes them, and sends them back over a wired or wireless network to a host computer for further processing (see Figure 18). Both RFID tags and antennas come in a variety of shapes and sizes.

RFID systems operate in a number of unlicensed frequency bands worldwide. Low-frequency systems (30 to 500 kilohertz) have short reading ranges (inches to a few feet); lower system costs; and are often used in security, asset tracking, or animal identification applications. High-frequency RFID systems (850 to 950 MHz and 2.4 to 2.5 GHz) offer reading ranges that can extend beyond 90 feet and are useful for applications such as railroad car tracking or automated toll collection for highways or bridges.

In inventory control and supply chain management, RFID systems capture and manage more detailed information about items in warehouses or in

FIGURE 18   HOW RFID WORKS

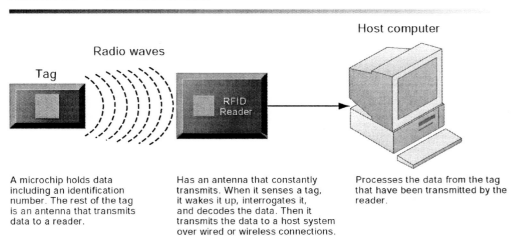

| A microchip holds data including an identification number. The rest of the tag is an antenna that transmits data to a reader. | Has an antenna that constantly transmits. When it senses a tag, it wakes it up, interrogates it, and decodes the data. Then it transmits the data to a host system over wired or wireless connections. | Processes the data from the tag that have been transmitted by the reader. |

RFID uses low-powered radio transmitters to read data stored in a tag at distances ranging from 1 inch to 100 feet. The reader captures the data from the tag and sends them over a network to a host computer for processing.

production than bar coding systems. If a large number of items are shipped together, RFID systems track each pallet, lot, or even unit item in the shipment. Manufacturers using RFID will be able to track the production history of each product for a better understanding of product defects and successes.

RFID has been available for decades, but widespread use was held back by the expense of the tags, which ranged from just under $1.00 to $20.00 each. Now the cost of a tag has dropped to about 19 cents and will drop to 5 cents within a few years. At these prices for tags, RFID becomes cost effective for many companies.

In addition to installing RFID readers and tagging systems, companies may need to upgrade their hardware and software to process the massive amounts of data produced by RFID systems—transactions that could add up to tens or hundreds of terabytes.

Special middleware is required to filter, aggregate, and prevent RFID data from overloading business networks and system applications. Applications will need to be redesigned to accept massive volumes of RFID-generated data frequently and to share those data with other applications. Major enterprise software vendors, including SAP and Oracle-PeopleSoft, now offer RFID-ready versions of their supply chain management applications.

The Interactive Session on Organizations deals with these issues. Wal-Mart has required its top suppliers to use passive RFID tags on cases and pallets shipped to its stores to help it track and record inventory flow. Suppliers have been proceeding slowly because of difficulties in RFID implementation.

Wireless Sensor Networks

If your company wanted state-of-the art technology to monitor building security or detect hazardous substances in the air, it might deploy a wireless sensor network. **Wireless sensor networks (WSNs)** are networks of interconnected wireless devices that are embedded into the physical environment to provide measurements of many points over large spaces. These devices have built-in processing, storage, and radio frequency sensors and antennas. They are linked into an interconnected network that routes the data they capture to a computer for analysis.

These networks range from hundreds to thousands of nodes. Because wireless sensor devices are placed in the field for years at a time without any maintenance or human intervention, they must have very low power requirements and batteries capable of lasting for years.

Sensor networks typically have a tiered architecture, such as that used by the wireless security system illustrated in Figure 19. This particular wireless sensor network starts with low-level sensors and progresses toward nodes for high-level data aggregation, analysis, and storage. Both simple and complex data are routed over a network to an automated facility that provides continuous building monitoring and control.

Wireless sensor networks are valuable in areas such as monitoring environmental changes; monitoring traffic or military activity; protecting property; efficiently operating and managing machinery and vehicles; establishing security perimeters; monitoring supply chain management; or detecting chemical, biological, or radiological material.

INTERACTIVE SESSION: ORGANIZATIONS

WAL-MART GRAPPLES WITH RFID

On February 1, 2005, Wal-Mart began rolling out its first radio-frequency identification (RFID) applications in seven of its Texas stores. Wal-Mart had ordered its top suppliers to place RFID tags on all products shipped to specific distribution centers. The objective was to reduce out-of-stock items by tracking item location more precisely as goods moved from the receiving dock to store shelves.

Wal-Mart wanted RFID readers installed at store receiving docks to record the arrival of cases of goods that had been shipped with RFID tags. The RFID reader would read the tags a second time just as the cases were brought to the sales floor from back-room storage areas. Software would use sales data from Wal-Mart's point-of-sale systems and the RFID data about the number of cases brought out the sales floor to figure out which items would soon be depleted and automatically generate a list of items to pick in the warehouse to replenish store shelves. This information would help Wal-Mart reduce out-of-stock items, increase sales, and further reduce its costs.

Wal-Mart is sharing all its RFID data with suppliers through its Retail Link extranet. The RFID data improve inventory management because suppliers know exactly where their goods are located within 30 minutes of the goods' movement from one part of a Wal-Mart store to another. Sales improve because the system allows Wal-Mart to always have products in stock.

Despite these benefits, the RFID implementations did not go exactly as planned. In late 2004, Wal-Mart scaled back its original demands, requiring suppliers to attach RFID tags to only 65 percent of their products. Even then, not all suppliers could comply. Only 30 percent made the major technology and business process changes to integrate RFID into their IT infrastructures and information systems. The rest were practicing what's called "slap and ship," sticking an RFID tag to a small percentage of cases and pallets slated for Wal-Mart. They did not make further changes to their systems so that they could actually use the data generated by RFID to track product movement and inventory.

Why was there such supplier resistance to RFID? Some industry analysts believe Wal-Mart tried to impose a top-down mandate for suppliers to use RFID before the technology matured and was cost-effective.

"We don't have a business case for RFID," commented a supply chain executive for one of the world's largest consumer goods manufacturers who did not want to be identified. "Because the standards are not complete, the equipment isn't developed...I can't fulfill Wal-Mart's demand, " he said.

RFID tags in early 2005 were costing suppliers between 25 and 75 cents each, still too expensive to be cost-effective. RFID-tagging a case of goods might easily cost a supplier an additional 40 to 50 cents per case—about 20 to 30 cents for the tag, and the remainder for labor costs to affix the tags. A large supplier that shipped 15 million cases and pallets to Wal-Mart each year would be spending an extra $6 million in tag costs.

Wal-Mart wanted all the cases on a pallet RFID-tagged and did not distinguish between a case containing video games or one containing toothpaste. RFID tagging would obviously contribute much more to costs for suppliers of low-cost items than for suppliers of high-value merchandise.

Moreover, RFID tags, particularly the least expensive types, may not perform properly when they are near certain liquids, metals, or porous objects. Kimberly-Clark's baby wipes absorbed radio-frequency signals, and Unilever had similar problems with liquid-containing products. To ensure accuracy and proper performance, suppliers may have to use more expensive tags. Integrating the new RFID data with legacy systems amplifies the costs.

Acknowledging these difficulties, Wal-Mart is working with suppliers individually to help them get up to speed. Today, Wal-Mart has over 300 suppliers that use RFID tags on cases and pallets. Over 500 Wal-Mart stores handle more than 3 million RFID-tagged cases and pallets per week. RFID helped Wal-Mart reduce out-of-stock merchandise in its stores by 30 percent in the fall of 2005 compared with a year earlier. In 2006, the company expects to install RFID readers at receiving docks and on sales floors of 500 additional stores.

Sources: Laurie Sullivan, "Hey, Wal-Mart, New Case of Pampers Is on the Way," *Information Week*, January 23, 2006; Elena Malykhina, "RFID: Beyond the Pallet," *Information Week*, June 19, 2006; Mark Roberti, "Wal-Mart Begins RFID Process Changes, *RFID Journal*, February 1, 2005; and Thomas Wailgum, "Tag, You're Late," *CIO Magazine*, November 15, 2004.

CASE STUDY QUESTIONS

MIS IN ACTION

1. How is RFID technology related to Wal-Mart's business model? How does it benefit suppliers?
2. What management, organization, and technology factors explain why Wal-Mart suppliers had trouble implementing RFID systems?
3. What conditions would make adopting RFID more favorable for suppliers?
4. Should Wal-Mart require all its suppliers to use RFID? Why or why not? Explain your answer.

Explore the RFID Privacy Page at the Electronic Privacy Information Center (EPIC) (www.epic.org/privacy/rfid) and answer the following questions.

1. Describe some RFID applications that might pose a threat to privacy. What information does RFID enable them to track?
2. How do these applications threaten personal privacy? How serious is this threat?
3. Should these RFID applications be deployed? Why or why not? Justify your answer.

FIGURE 19   A WIRELESS SENSOR NETWORK FOR A SECURITY SYSTEM

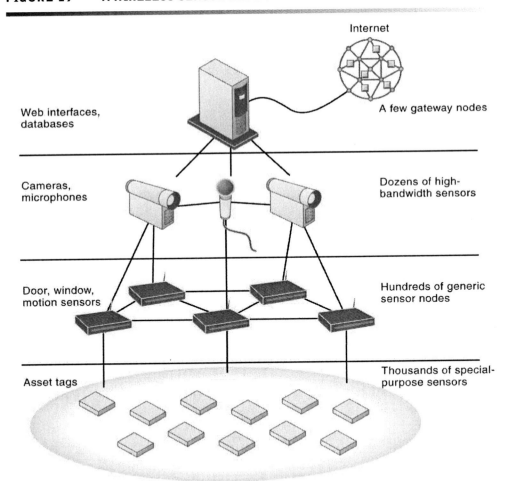

Each level of this wireless sensor network handles different types of sensing. Lower-level sensors for monitoring events, such as doors opening and closing, motion, and breakage of windows and doors, are complemented by a small group of more advanced sensors placed in key locations, such as cameras and acoustic and chemical detectors.

Source: From Jason Hill, Mike Horton, Ralph Kling, and Lakshman Krishamurthy, "The Platforms Enabling Wireless Sensor Networks," *Communications of the ACM 47*, no. 6 (June 2004).

5 HANDS-ON MIS

The projects in this section give you hands-on experience designing Internet applications to increase employee efficiency, using spreadsheet software to improve selection of telecommunications services, and using Web search engines for business research.

Achieving Operational Excellence: Using Internet Tools to Increase Efficiency and Productivity

Software skills: Web browser software and presentation software
Business skills: Employee productivity analysis

In this project, you will suggest applications of Internet technology to help employees at a real-world company work more efficiently.

Dirt Bikes's management is concerned about how much money is being spent communicating with people inside and outside the company and on obtaining information about developments in the motorcycle industry and the global economy. You have been asked to investigate how Internet tools and technology could be used to help Dirt Bikes employees communicate and obtain information more efficiently. Dirt Bikes provides Internet access to all its employees who use desktop computers.

- How could the various Internet tools help employees at Dirt Bikes? Create a matrix showing what types of employees and business functions would benefit from using each type of tool and why.

- How could Dirt Bikes benefit from intranets for its sales and marketing, human resources, and manufacturing and production departments? Select one of these departments and describe the kind of information that could be provided by an intranet for that department. How could this intranet increase efficiency and productivity for that department?

- (Optional) Use electronic presentation software to summarize your findings for management.

Improving Decision Making: Using Spreadsheet Software to Evaluate Wireless Services

Software skills: Spreadsheet formulas, formatting
Business skills: Analyzing telecommunications services and costs

In this project, you will use the Web to research alternative wireless services and use spreadsheet software to calculate wireless service costs for a sales force.

You would like to equip your sales force of 35 based in Cincinnati, Ohio, with mobile phones that have capabilities for voice transmission, text messaging, and taking and sending photos. Use the Web to select a wireless service provider that provides nationwide service as well as good service in your home area. Examine the features of the mobile handsets offered by each of these vendors. Assume that each of the 35 salespeople will need to spend three hours per day during business hours (8 A.M. to 6 P.M.) on mobile voice communication, and send 30 text messages per day and five photos per week. Use your spreadsheet software to determine the wireless service and handset that will offer both the best pricing per user over a two-year period. For the purposes of this exercise, you do not need to consider corporate discounts.

Achieving Operational Excellence: Using Web Search Engines for Business Research

Software skills: Web search tools
Business skills: Researching new technologies

This project will help develop your Internet skills in using Web search engines for business research.

With the price of home heating oil and natural gas skyrocketing, you believe that fuel cells might be a reasonable, cost-effective alternative for home heating systems as well as co-generation of electricity. Yet you don't know much about fuel cells, their current cost per kilowatt of output, or their BTU heat output. You would like to explore a possible new business model for supplying heating and electricity to homes. Your first step will be to figure out how fuel cells work. Second, you want some information on the economics of small fuel cells. For instance, how much do they cost? Finally, you want to know how much heat and electricity could they potentially generate for a home. Use the following four search engines to obtain that information: Yahoo!, Google, MSN, and Ask.com. If you wish, try some other search engines as well. Compare the volume and quality of information you find with each search tool. Which tool is the easiest to use? Which produced the best results for your research? Why do the results differ if all search engines search the same Web?

LEARNING TRACK MODULES

Computing and Communications Services Provided by Commercial Telecommunications Vendors. This Learning Track module on the Student CD-ROM and Web site for this chapter describes the communication and computing services from major U.S. telecommunications vendors that are now available to individuals and businesses.

Cellular System Generations. This Learning Track module on the Student CD-ROM and Web site for this chapter compares the transmission technologies and capacities of first, second, and third-generation wireless cellular systems.

Wireless Applications for CRM, SCM, and Health Care. This Learning Track module on the Student CD-ROM and Web site for this chapter describes how wireless systems are used in customer relationship management, supply chain management, and health care.

Summary

1. *Describe the features of telecommunications networks and identify key networking technologies.*

   A simple network consists of two or more connected computers. Basic network components include computers, network interfaces, a connection medium, network operating system software, and either a hub or a switch. The networking infrastructure for a large company relies on both public and private infrastructures to support the movement of information across diverse technological platforms. It includes the traditional telephone system, mobile cellular communication, wireless local area networks, videoconferencing systems, a corporate Web site, intranets, extranets, and an array of local and wide area networks, including the Internet. This collection of networks evolved from two fundamentally different types of networks: telephone networks and computer networks.

   Contemporary networks have been shaped by the rise of client/server computing, the use of packet switching, and the adoption of Transmission Control Protocol/Internet Protocol (TCP/IP) as a universal communications standard for linking disparate networks and computers. Client/server networks have distributed much of the organization's computing power to the desktop and factory floor. Packet switching makes more efficient use of network communications capacity by breaking messages into small packets that are sent independently along different paths in a network and then reassembled at their destinations. Protocols provide a common set of rules that enable communication among diverse components in a telecommunications network. TCP/IP is a suite of protocols that has become the dominant model of achieving connectivity among different networks and computers. It is the connectivity model used in the Internet.

2. *Evaluate alternative transmission media, types of networks, and network services.*

   The principal physical transmission media are twisted copper telephone wire, coaxial copper cable, fiber-optic cable, and wireless transmission. The choice of transmission medium depends on the distance and volume of communication required by the organization and its financial resources. Twisted wire enables companies to use existing wiring for telephone systems for digital communication. Fiber-optic and coaxial cable are used for high-volume transmission but are expensive to install. Microwave and satellite are used for wireless communication over long distances. The transmission capacity of a medium, known as the bandwidth, is determined by the range of frequencies it can accommodate.

   There are different types of networks and network services available to organizations. Network selection and design should be based on the organization's information requirements and the distance required for transmission. Local area networks (LANs) connect PCs and other digital devices together within a 500-meter radius and are used today for many corporate computing tasks. Network components may be connected together using a star, bus, or ring topology. Wide area networks (WANs) span broad geographical distances, ranging from several miles to continents, and are private networks that are independently managed. Metropolitan area networks (MANs) span a single urban area, whereas campus area networks (CANs) span a campus of buildings or a military base.

   A number of network services are available to organizations requiring high-bandwidth transmission. Frame relay is a shared network service with transmission speeds ranging from 56 Kbps to more than 40 Mbps; it relies on digital circuits that require less error checking than packet switching. Asynchronous Transfer Mode (ATM) provides transmission speeds of 1.5 Mbps to more than 9 Gbps, parceling data into fixed 53-byte cells. ATM can pass data between computers from different vendors and is popular for transmitting data, video, and audio over the same network. Integrated Services Digital Network (ISDN) is an international standard for dial-up network access that uses existing local telephone lines to integrate voice, data, image, and video services. Basic rate ISDN can transmit data at a rate of 128 Kbps.

   Digital subscriber line (DSL) technologies, cable Internet connections, and T1 lines are often used for high-capacity Internet connections. Like ISDN, DSL technologies also operate over existing copper telephone lines to carry voice, data, and video, but they have higher transmission capacities than ISDN. Asymmetric Digital Subscriber Line (ADSL) supports a transmission rate of 1.5 to 9 Mbps when receiving data and up over 700 Kbps when sending data. Symmetric Digital Subscriber Line (SDSL) supports the same transmission rate for sending and receiving data of up to 3 Mbps.

   Cable Internet connections provide high-speed access to the Web or corporate intranets at speeds of up to 10 Mbps. T lines are high-speed data lines leased from communications providers. A T1 line supports a data transmission rate of 1.544 Mbps.

3. *Demonstrate how the Internet and Internet technology work and how they support communication and e-business.*

The Internet is a worldwide network of networks that uses the client/server model of computing and the TCP/IP network reference model. Every computer on the Internet is assigned a unique numeric IP address. The Domain Name System (DNS) converts IP addresses to domain names so that users only need to specify a domain name to access a computer on the Internet instead of typing in the numeric IP address. No one owns the Internet and it has no formal management organization. However, worldwide Internet policies are established by organizations and government bodies, such as the Internet Architecture Board and the World Wide Web Consortium. The Internet must also conform to the laws of the sovereign nation-states in which it operates, as well as the technical infrastructures that exist within the nation-state.

Major Internet services include e-mail, Usenet, chatting, instant messaging, Telnet, FTP, and the World Wide Web. Web pages are based on Hypertext Markup Language (HTML) and can display text, graphics, video, and audio. Web site directories, search engines, and RSS technology help users locate the information they need on the Web. RSS, blogs, and wikis are features of Web 2.0. Web technology and Internet networking standards provide the connectivity and interfaces for internal private intranets and private extranets that be accessed by many different kinds of computers inside and outside the organization.

Internet-based groupware and electronic conferencing software provide tools to support communication and collaboration when people work together in groups or work teams, often in different locations. Firms are also starting to realize economies by using Internet telephony, which enables Internet technology to be used for telephone voice transmission. Internet technology can also reduce communication costs by enabling companies to create virtual private networks (VPNs) as low-cost alternatives to private WANs.

4. *Identify and describe the principal technologies and standards for wireless networking, communication, and Internet access.*

Cellular networks have evolved from slow-speed (1G) analog networks to high-speed, high-bandwidth, digital, third-generation (3G) networks with speeds ranging from 144 Kbps to more than 2 Mbps for data transmission. Second-generation (2G) cellular networks are digital circuit-switched networks used primarily for voice transmission, but they can also transmit data at rates ranging from 9.6 to 14.4 Kbps. 2.5G networks are packet switched, use many existing infrastructure elements, and have data transmission rates ranging from 50 to 144 Kbps.

Major cellular standards include Code Division Multiple Access (CDMA), which is used primarily in the United States, and Global System for Mobile Communication (GSM), which is the standard in Europe and much of the rest of the world.

Alternative standards governing the way wireless mobile devices access the Internet and the World Wide Web include Wireless Application Protocol (WAP) and i-mode.

Standards for wireless computer networks include Bluetooth (802.15) for small personal area networks (PANs), Wi-Fi (802.11) for local area networks (LANs), and WiMax (802.16) for metropolitan area networks (MANs). Bluetooth can link up to eight devices within a 10-meter area using low-power, radio-based communication and can transmit up to 722 Kbps in the 2.4 GHz band. Wireless phones, keyboards, computers, printers, and PDAs using Bluetooth can communicate with each other and even operate each other without direct user intervention.

The most popular of the 802.11 standards are 802.11b and 802.11g. 802.11b can transmit up to 11 Mbps in the unlicensed 2.4 GHz band. 802.11g can transmit up to 54 Mbps in the same frequency range. The 802.11b standard has been the most widely used standard for creating wireless LANs and providing broadband wireless Internet access. However, 802.11b is vulnerable to penetration by outsiders and interference from other wireless devices in the same frequency spectrum.

WiMax has a wireless access range of up to 31 miles and a data transfer rate of up to 75 Mbps, making it suitable for providing broadband Internet access in areas lacking DSL and cable lines. The 802.16 specification also has robust security and quality-of-service features to support voice and video.

Major cellular carriers are also upgrading their networks to provide wireless broadband access to the Internet at an average speed of 300 to 500 Kbps. Verizon's service, called BroadBand Access, uses a technology called EV-DO to provide Internet access over a cellular network.

5. *Assess the business value of wireless technology and important wireless applications in business.*

Wireless technology increases productivity and worker output by providing anytime, anywhere communication and access to information, including the information resources of the Internet. Wireless communication helps businesses stay more easily in touch with customers, suppliers, and employees and provides more flexible arrangements for organizing work.

Mobile wireless technology facilitates supply chain management by capturing data on the movement of goods as these events take place and by providing detailed, immediate information as goods move among supply chain partners. Radio frequency identification (RFID) systems provide a powerful technology for this purpose. These systems use tiny tags that have embedded microchips that contain data about an item and its location. The tags transmit radio signals over a short distance to special RFID readers. The RFID readers then pass the data over a network to a computer for processing.

Wireless sensor networks (WSNs) are networks of interconnected wireless devices with some processing and radio-transmitting capability that are embedded into the physical environment to provide measurements of many points over large spaces. Wireless sensor networks are valuable for monitoring environmental changes, traffic patterns, security incidents, or supply chain events.

Key Terms

2.5G networks
3G networks
Access point
Asynchronous Transfer Mode (ATM)
Backbone
Bandwidth
Blog
Bluetooth
Broadband
Bus networks
Cable Internet connections
Campus area network (CAN)
Cellular telephones (cell phones)
Chat
Coaxial cable
Code Division Multiple Access (CDMA)
Dedicated server computer
Dense wavelength division multiplexing (DWDM)
Digital subscriber line (DSL)
Domain Name System (DNS)
Domain name
E-mail handhelds
E-mail
EV-DO
Fiber-optic cable
File Transfer Protocol (FTP)
Firewalls
Frame relay
Global System for Mobile Communication (GSM)
Groupware
Hertz
Home page
Hotspots
Hubs
Hypertext Transfer Protocol (HTTP)
I-mode
Information appliance
Instant messaging
Integrated Services Digital Network (ISDN)
Internet Protocol (IP) address
Internet service provider (ISP)

Internet telephony
Internet2
Internetworking
Local area network (LAN)
Metropolitan area network (MAN)
Microbrowser
Microwave
Modem
Multiplexing
Network interface card (NIC)
Network operating system (NOS)
Optical networks
Packet switching
Peer-to-peer
Personal area networks (PANs)
Personal digital assistants (PDAs)
Protocol
Radio frequency identification (RFID)
Ring networks
Router
RSS
Satellites
Search engines
Search engine marketing
Shopping bots
Short message service (SMS)
Smart phones
Star network
Switch
T lines
Telnet
Topology
Transmission Control Protocol/Internet Protocol (TCP/IP)
Twisted wire
Uniform resource locator (URL)
Usenet
Virtual private network (VPN)
Voice over IP (VoIP)
Web 2.0
Web site

Webmaster
Wide area networks (WANs)
Wi-Fi
Wiki

WiMax
Wireless Application Protocol (WAP)
Wireless NICs
Wireless sensor networks (WSNs)

Review Questions

1. Describe the features of a simple network and the network infrastructure for a large company.

2. Name and describe the principal technologies and trends that have shaped contemporary telecommunications systems.

3. What is a local area network (LAN)? What are the components of a typical LAN? What are the functions of each component?

4. Name and describe the principal network topologies.

5. Name the different types of physical transmission media and compare them in terms of speed and cost.

6. Define the following: WAN, MAN, 3G, modem, protocol, optical network, bandwidth, and Internet2.

7. List and describe the various broadband network services.

8. What is the Internet? How does it work? How does it provide business value?

9. Explain how the domain name and IP addressing system work.

10. List and describe the principal Internet services.

11. List and describe alternative ways of locating information on the Web.

12. What are intranets and extranets? How do they provide value to businesses?

13. Name and describe the principal technologies and tools that support communication and electronic business.

14. What are Internet telephony and virtual private networks? How do they provide value to businesses?

15. Compare Bluetooth, Wi-Fi, WiMax, and EV-DO. What are their capabilities? For what types of applications is each best suited?

16. Compare the WAP and i-mode standards for wireless access to the Web.

17. What is RFID? How does it work? How does it provide value to businesses?

18. What are wireless sensor networks? How do they work? What applications use them?

Discussion Questions

1. Network design is a key business decision as well as a technology decision. Why?

2. Should all major retailing and manufacturing companies switch to RFID? Why or why not?

Video Case

You will find a video case illustrating some of the concepts in this chapter on the Laudon Web site and Student CD-ROM along with questions to help you analyze the case.

Teamwork: Comparing Mobile Internet Access Devices

Form a group with three or four of your classmates. Evaluate mobile devices with Internet access from two different vendors, such as Palm, BlackBerry, Nokia, Samsung, or Motorola. Your analysis should consider the purchase cost of each device, the wireless networks where each device can operate, the cost of wireless Internet services, and what other services are available for each device. You should also consider other capabilities of each device, including the ability to integrate with existing corporate or PC applications. Which device would you select? What criteria would you use to guide your selection? If possible, use electronic presentation software to present your findings to the class.

REFERENCES

Bose, Indranil and Raktim Pal. "Auto-ID: Management Anything Anywhere, Anytime in the Supply Chain." *Communications of the ACM* 48, No.8 (August 2005).

Brandt, Richard. "Net Assets." Stanford Magazine (November–December 2004).

Carr, David F. "How Google Works." *Baseline Magazine* (July 2006).

Claburn, Thomas. "Google Revealed." *Information Week* (August 28,2006).

Dignan, Larry. "RFID: Hit or Myth?" Baseline Magazine (February 2004).

eMarketer, Inc. (Ben Macklin). "Broadband: Demographics and Usage." (July 2005a).

eMarketer, Inc. (Steve Butler). "VoIP: Spending and Trends." (June 2005c).

eMarketer, Inc. (Noah Elkin). "Wireless Broadband: The Future Around the Corner." (May 2005b).

Greenstein, Howard. "Web 2.0 Meets the Enterprise." *Optimize Magazine* (May 2006)

Grover, Varun and Khawaja Saeed. "The Telecommunication Industry Revisited." *Communications of the ACM* 46, no.7 (July 2003).

Hof, Robert. "Web 2.0 Has Corporate America Spinning." *Business Week* (June 5, 2006).

Hoover, J. Nicholas. "5 Things You Must Know About VoIP." *Information Week* (July 3, 2006)

Hoover, J. Nicholas. "In Your Face." *Information Week* (May 8, 2006).

Housel, Tom and Eric Skopec. *Global Telecommunication Revolution: The Business Perspective.* New York: McGraw-Hill (2001).

Johnson, Keith. "Europe Picks Up 3G, as Phone Hopes Lift." Wall Street Journal (August 25, 2005)

LaFraniere, Sharon. *"Cellphones Catapult Rural Africa to 21st Century." New York Times (August 25, 2005).*

Li Yuan. "Text Messages Sent by Cellphone Finally Catch on in U.S." *Wall Street Journal* (August 11, 2005).

Malykhina, Elena. "Bold Bet on WiMax." *Information Week* (August 14, 2006).

Malykhina, Elena and J. Nicholas Hoover. "Clear Signal for Wimax." *Information Week* (July 3, 2006).

Madden, Mary and Lee Rainie. "America's Online Pursuits." Pew Internet and American Life Project (April 25, 2004).

Nasaw, Daniel. "Instant Messages Are Popping Up All Over." *Wall Street Journal* (June 12, 2003).

National Research Council. "The Internet's Coming of Age. Washington, D.C.: National Academy Press (2000).

Netcraft. "Netcraft August 2005 Web Server Survey." (August 2005).

Niemeyer,Alex, Misok H. Pak and Sanjay E. Ramaswamy. "Smart Tags for Your Supply Chain" *McKinsey Quarterly* 4 (2003).

Nicopolitidis,Petros, Georgios Papademitriou, Mohammad S. Obaidat, and Adreas S. Pomportsis. "The Economics of Wireless Networks." *Communications of the ACM* 47, no. 4(April 2004).

Niemeyer, Alex, Minsok H. Pak, and Sanjay E. Ramaswamy. "Smart Tags for Your Supply Chain." The McKinsey Quarterly 4 (2003).

Overby, Christine Spivey. "RFID at What Cost?" Forrester Research (March 1, 2004).

Papazoglou, Mike P.. "Agent-Oriented Technology in Support of E-Business." *Communications of the ACM* 44, no. 4 (April 2001).

Richtel, Matt. "The Wi-Fi in Your Handset." *The New York Times* (July 29, 2006).

Rothfeder, Jeffrey. "What's Wrong with RFID?" *CIO Insight* (August 1, 2004).

Roush, Wade. "The Internet Reborn." *Technology Review* (October 2003).

Talbot, David. "The Internet Is Broken." *Technology Review* (December 2005/January 2006).

Werbach, Kevin. "Using VoIP to Compete." *Harvard Business Review* (September 2005).

Young, Shawn. "Market for Internet Calling, Once Tiny, Gets Crowded Fast." Wall Street Journal (August 26, 2005)

Google Takes on the World
CASE STUDY

The rise of Google, now a $6.1 billion company, has been fast and fierce. Founders Sergey Brin and Larry Page met in 1995 as Stanford University graduate students. They created a search engine that combined the technologies of Page's PageRank system, which evaluates a page's importance based on the external links to it, and Brin's Web crawler, which visits Web sites and records a summary of their content. Because Google was so effective, it quickly became the search engine of choice for Web users. Today, Google handles nearly 50 percent of Web searches.

Google stopped displaying the number of Web pages it indexed after the number surpassed 8 billion in 2005, but some estimates now place the number at 25 billion. Google's index also includes one billion images and one billion Usenet newsgroup messages. In addition to searching for Web pages, Google users can search for PDF, PostScript, text, Microsoft Office, Lotus, PowerPoint, and Shockwave files. Google claims to be one of the five most popular sites on the Internet with more than 380 million unique users per month and more than 50 percent of its traffic coming from outside the United States.

Google's IT infrastructure is a closely guarded secret because it is part of its competitive advantage. The best guess is that Google has up to 450,000 servers spread over at least 25 locations around the world. These servers use inexpensive off-the-shelf hardware to run a customized version of the Linux operating system and other critical pieces of custom software. These include MapReduce, a programming model to simplify processing and create large data sets; Google WorkQueue, a system that groups queries and schedules them for distributed processing; and the Google File System, which keeps copies of data in several places so that the data will always be available even if a server fails.

According to a widely cited estimate, Google only needs to spend $1 for every $3 its competitors spend to deliver a comparable amount of computing power. This inexpensive, flexible infrastructure explains the speed of Google Web searches and its ability to provide its users with such a vast array of Web-based services and software tools.

Most of Google's revenue comes from online advertising and online search services. Google Search Services enable organizations to include the Google search engine on their own Web pages. This is a straightforward technology licensing arrangement—not groundbreaking, but profitable.

The side of Google that has driven its phenomenal growth and profits is its advertising program. In a fraction of a second, Google's technology can evaluate millions of variables about its users and advertisers, correlate them with millions of potential ads, and deliver the message to which each user is most likely to respond. Because this technology makes ads more relevant, users click on ads 50 to 100 percent more often on Google than on Yahoo!, creating a better return for advertisers. According to eMarketer, Google grabbed about 70 percent of all paid search advertising.

In 2000, Google launched AdWords, a self-service advertising program in which vendors bid to have their ads placed alongside the search results for specific keyword queries. In 2002, AdWords Select introduced cost-per-click (CPC) pricing so that advertisers only pay for their ads when users actually click on them. Google determines the placement of ads through a combination of the CPC and click-through (total number of clicks) rates so that the most relevant ads for a keyword string appear in the most prominent positions. The keyword-targeted ads appear throughout the Google Network, which includes America Online, Shopping.com, Ask.com, The New York Times on the Web, and many other high-profile Web sites.

AdWords has come under some fire for being vulnerable to a practice known as click-fraud. A business whose ad receives thousands of clicks from sources that have no intention of making a purchase may run through its marketing budget quickly and have to drop out of the ad game altogether. Unscrupulous businesses have tried to use click fraud to drive up the cost of competitors' ads and put them at a competitive disadvantage.

Google and its competitor Yahoo!, have been criticized for their vague response to the problem.

From *Management Information Systems: Managing the Digital Firm, 10/e*. Kenneth C. Laudon, Jane P. Laudon. Copyright © 2007 by Pearson Prentice Hall. All rights reserved.

Google credits customers for invalid clicks. It also has a system in place to detect click-fraud before customers are charged. Google does not disclose details about its antifraud methods to advertisers because of concerns about security

Although advertising customers are worried about fraud attacks, Google must be concerned with legitimate offensives from its rivals. Yahoo! has been sponsoring prominent academic economists and other researchers to find new ways of using its data about online consumer behavior to increase market share for its services and the revenue generated by its searches.

Microsoft has a history of diminishing or destroying its competitors by exploiting the fact that its Microsoft Windows operating system can be found on 95 percent of the world's personal computers. Netscape Navigator, Lotus 1-2-3, and WordPerfect have all been defeated in this manner.

Microsoft launched MSN Search in November 2004, but this search service made only a marginal dent in the market, accounting for 13 percent of worldwide search requests. Still, that 13 percent could double once Microsoft's Windows Vista operating system enters the marketplace. Microsoft plans to integrate search technology into Windows Vista and into upcoming versions of Office.

Two other areas where Microsoft can vault ahead of Google are context-aware searches and "deep Web" searches. By personalizing search technology, a search engine can return results that accurately match the context of the user's query, producing more relevant search outcomes. Because Microsoft has the capital to purchase the rights to copyrighted material and owns powerful digital rights management software, the company is considered a good candidate to become the gateway to the Deep Web's massive quantity of documents and data that are not indexed by search engines.

Microsoft's battle for Google's market share goes beyond search engines. To Microsoft, Google has ceased being a search technology company and is now a software company, capable of infringing on the markets that Microsoft dominates. In the past, Microsoft has thwarted competition through strategic pricing and feature enhancements, as well as by tying its products together so that they are the most convenient to use. Microsoft may not find it so easy to thwart Google. Other software manufacturers had to rely on Windows as a platform on which to run their products. Since Google's applications are Web-based and not tied to the Windows operating system, Microsoft can't use its operating system

monopoly to limit access to Google. Google is giving away its Linux-based programs over the Internet for free.

In the spring of 2006, Google introduced Google Spreadsheets, a Web-based spreadsheet application, and also acquired the company Writely, which offers a Web-based word processor. In late August of that year, Google offered a package targeting businesses called Google Apps for Your Domain that bundles e-mail, calendar, instant messaging, and Web page creation services that run on Google's computers. Competition with Microsoft will intensify when Google adds its online spreadsheet, word-processing, and collaboration applications to the Apps suite and markets the whole package to large companies.

How far Google can eat into Microsoft's software franchise is uncertain. But Microsoft fears Google's Web-based computing model could make it possible for computer users to bypass its products entirely.

Google is constantly looking for new ways to grow. Its AdSense program scans Web pages for target words and displays appropriate advertisements, enabling Web site operators to generate revenue from their sites. Google introduced the Google Toolbar, which enables Web surfers to search the Google index without visiting the Google home page. The toolbar also provided one of the Web's earliest defenses against pop-up ads. Google's image search index launched in 2001 and now archives more than one billion images. In 2002, Google News appeared, becoming the first Internet news service compiled completely by computer algorithms, and offering customized news alerts by e-mail.

In April 2004, Google announced its Gmail, Web-based e-mail service, offering free online storage to users. Google made headlines later that year when it released Google Desktop Search, a downloadable program for searching personal files on a computer, including e-mail, productivity files, browsing history, and instant message conversations. The latest version of Google Desktop introduced Gadgets, small applications that bring specific content such as news, weather, or cartoons, along with highly targeted ads, directly to the user's desktop.

Other popular services that Google has introduced include Froogle, a consumer product locator, and Google Maps, which includes dynamic online mapping and satellite pictures of searchable addresses. Google also acquired and improved Picasa digital photo management software, which is downloadable free of charge and introduced a free instant messaging and voice communication service for personal computers called Google Talk. Instant messaging is now fully integrated with Gmail so users can chat in the same window in which they compose and read e-mail. Taking advantage of the social networking craze started by Web sites such as Friendster and MySpace, Google partnered with Nike to create an online, invitation-only community for soccer fans worldwide called Joga.com.

Not all of Google's products have been met with unanimous enthusiasm. Gmail, for instance, raised the ire of privacy advocates because it uses the same technology as AdSense to place advertisements alongside messages. The selection of ads is based on the actual text of the messages, meaning that every Gmail message is read by an automated scanner.

Google Checkout, which stores users' credit card numbers and shipping information to facilitate online purchases, is forging new relationships with online merchants, who receive a more favorable transaction charge from Google than they would get from credit card companies. Google's roster of paying advertisers continues to grow.

Google Video allows users to search for and then purchase TV shows, sports broadcasts, film clips, and music videos. In this area, Google has less experience than Yahoo! in negotiating with content providers, who are particularly concerned with piracy in the digital age. Eric Schmidt, Google's CEO, says that video search and its corresponding rights issues "will be a major story for Google for years." In the meantime, profits continue to soar, and Google will continue to innovate. Schmidt estimates that Google will need 300 years to organize all of the information in the world.

Sources: Thomas Claburn, "Google Revealed," *Information Week*, August 28, 2006; Ben Worthen, "The Enterprise Gets Googled," *CIO Magazine*, May 1, 2006; Thomas Claburn, "Google Goes to Work," *Information Week*, February 27, 2006; Ben Elgin and Jay Greene, "The Counterattack on Google," *Business Week*, May 8, 2006; Steve Lohr and Saul Hansell, "Microsoft and Google Set to Wage Arms Race," *The New York Times*, May 2, 2006; David F. Carr, "How Google Works," *Baseline*, July, 2006; Kevin J. Delaney, "Hoping to Ovetake Its Rivals, Yahoo Stocks Up on Academics," *The Wall Street Journal*, August 25, 2006 and "Google Bundles Package of Tools for Business, Education Markets," *The Wall Street Journal*, August 28, 2006; Saul Hansell, "Your Ads Here (All of Them)," *The New York Times*, October 30, 2005; John Markoff, "Google to Offer Instant Messaging and Voice Communications on Web," *The New York Times*, August 24, 2005; Fred Vogelstein, "Search and Destroy," *Fortune*, May 2, 2005; Kevin J. Delaney, "Web Start-Ups Vie to Detect 'Click Fraud,'" *The Wall Street Journal*, June 9, 2005; and Kevin J. Delaney and Mylene Mangalindan, "Google Plans Online-Payment Service," *The Wall Street Journal*, June 20, 2005.

CASE STUDY QUESTIONS

1. Evaluate Google using the competitive forces and value chain models.

2. What are Google's sources of competitive advantage? How does it provide value to its users?

3. What problems and challenges does Google face in this case? What management, organization, and technology factors are responsible for these problems and challenges?

4. Does Google's business strategy effectively address these challenges? Explain your answer.

5. How successful do you think Google will be in the future?

Securing Information Systems

From *Management Information Systems: Managing the Digital Firm, 10/e*. Kenneth C. Laudon, Jane P. Laudon.
Copyright © 2007 by Pearson Prentice Hall. All rights reserved.

Securing Information Systems

PHISHING: A COSTLY NEW SPORT FOR INTERNET USERS

Elizabeth Owen almost lost her identity. A frequent eBay user, she received an e-mail that appeared to come from eBay's payment service PayPal asking her to update her credit information or be barred from future purchases. She immediately started assembling the data. Right before she was to transmit it, she stopped. Her office, the National Association of Consumer Agency Administrators, had received constant complaints of e-mail scams. Even with this knowledge, she had almost become a victim of a special type of identify theft called phishing.

A phishing attack sends e-mail that claims to be from a bank, credit card company, retailer, or other company directing the recipient to a Web site where that person is asked to enter vital information, such as bank account numbers, social security numbers, credit card details, or online passwords. The Web site appears to be legitimate, but it's actually bogus. Scam artists use information obtained through phishing to drain bank or credit card accounts or sell the information to others to do the same.

According to FraudWatch International, a vendor of anti-phishing products, JPMorgan Chase, Citibank, Visa, and Bank of America top the list of financial brand names hijacked by phishers. Most phishing losses have been absorbed by the banks and credit card companies, but fear of identity theft has discouraged a significant number of people from using online financial services.

What can be done to combat phishing and prevent confidence from disappearing? A number of approaches are helpful. First, companies can educate their consumers about phishing scams. Citigroup's Citibank unit warns its Web site visitors about the dangers of phishing along with providing warning signs of potentially fraudulent e-mails. Citibank asserts that it won't ever send customers e-mail requesting sensitive information.

Individual Web sites and Internet service providers (ISPs) have started using antiphishing products and services. Some services sift through junk e-mail. Others scour the Web for bogus sites, issuing blacklists of known phishing sites to warn consumers about them. Some monitor online banking sites for signs the sites are being cased as possible targets and even contact Internet service providers to remove offending sites.

Banks are starting to blunt phishing attacks by requiring two-factor authentication of online customers—their user names and passwords plus something extra, such as a tiny, unique photo. Bank of America implemented a system called SiteKey that requires Internet customers to choose a digital image (such as a picture of a cat) from an archive, name that image, and answer various secret questions, such as "What is your first pet's name?" to help the bank verify their identity. The software will not allow users to

Example of a bogus phishing site.

enter their password into the bank's Web site until they see and acknowledge their image, which proves they are on the real Bank of America site rather than a bogus site.

However, other banks are hesitant to adopt such measures, for fear that they will make Internet banking too difficult. Bank of America itself has experienced some problems. Although SiteKey cut down on phishing attacks, the bank experienced a spike in customer service calls because online users forgot their answers to the secret questions.

Sources: Sarah D. Scalet, "Two-Factor Too Scarce at Consumer Banks," *CIO Magazine*, July, 2006; Deborah Gage, "Helping Customers Help Themselves," *Baseline*, May 15, 2006; Robin Arnfield, "Online Banking: How Safe Is Your Money?" NewsFactor Network, January 20, 2006; and Kimberly Morrison, "Internet Sees Increase in 'Phishing' for Online Victims," *Knight Ridder Newspapers*, February 28, 2005.

The problems created by phishing for companies such as Bank of America and eBay and for individual consumers illustrate some of the reasons why businesses need to pay special attention to information system security. Phishing and identity theft have cost banks and financial services billions of dollars and individual victims much agony and worry. They also discourage individuals from making Internet purchases or from using online financial services, thereby lowering revenues and profits.

The chapter-opening diagram calls attention to important points raised by this case and this chapter. Phishing has proliferated because so many people use online financial services and the technology for phishing is readily available. Combating phishing is a complex problem that involves multiple approaches, including education, new tools and technologies, and better authentication procedures. No single approach is sufficient. Moreover, some approaches, such as multi-step authentication procedures for accessing online systems, are helpful, but they are not always effective if they discourage people from visiting a Web site or using a system because it is too complicated.

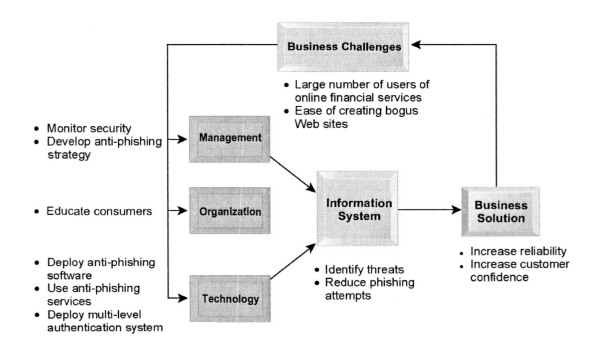

This is not only true of anti-phishing efforts but for information system security as a whole. Securing information systems from unauthorized access, abuse, destruction, or tampering of assets requires a combination of training, procedures, and technologies. The cost and difficulty of using all of these must be balanced with the net benefits to the business in the form of greater customer trust, uninterrupted operations, compliance with government regulations, and protection of financial assets.

HEADS UP

This chapter focuses on how to secure your information systems and the information inside them. As e-commerce and e-business have grown to encompass so much of our lives, we have all become much more aware of the need to secure digital information. Your customers expect you to keep their digital private information secure and confidential. As your business increasingly relies on the Internet, you will become vulnerable to a variety of attacks against your systems that could, if successful, put you out of business in a very short time. To protect your business, you will need to pay more attention to security and control than ever before.

• If your career is in finance or accounting, you will need to work with information system controls to prevent errors, fraud, and disruption of services that lead to large monetary losses and the erosion of customer confidence.

• If your career is in human resources, you will be dealing with "people factors," which are as important as technology in establishing the security and reliability of the firm's information systems. Many security breaches and system errors are caused by legitimate company insiders, and the human resources function is responsible for training programs and establishing security awareness among employees.

• If your career is in information systems, you will be working with technologies and procedures to ensure your company's systems are reliable and secure.

• If your career is in manufacturing and production or operations management, you will be concerned with preventing security breaches and downtime as your firm links with the systems of other firms for supply chain management.

• If your career is in sales and marketing, you will be concerned with secure payment systems for online purchases, as well as measures for ensuring that customer data are secure and properly used.

---

1   SYSTEM VULNERABILITY AND ABUSE

Can you imagine what would happen if you tried to link to the Internet without a firewall or antivirus software? Your computer would be disabled in a few seconds, and it might take you many days to recover. If you used the computer to run your business, you might not be able to sell to your customers or place orders with your suppliers while it was down. And you might find that your computer system had been penetrated by outsiders, who perhaps stole or destroyed valuable data, including confidential payment data from your customers. If too much data were destroyed or divulged, your business might never be able to operate!

In short, if you operate a business today, you need to make security and control a top priority. **Security** refers to the policies, procedures, and technical measures used to prevent unauthorized access, alteration, theft, or physical damage to information systems. **Controls** consist of all the methods, policies, and organizational procedures that ensure the safety of the organization's assets; the accuracy and reliability of its accounting records; and operational adherence to management standards.

WHY SYSTEMS ARE VULNERABLE

When large amounts of data are stored in electronic form, they are vulnerable to many more kinds of threats than when they existed in manual form. Through communications networks, information systems in different locations are interconnected. The potential for unauthorized access, abuse, or fraud is not limited to a single location but can occur at any access point in the network.

Figure 1 illustrates the most common threats against contemporary information systems. They can stem from technical, organizational, and environmental factors compounded by poor management decisions. In the multitier client/server computing environment illustrated here, vulnerabilities exist at each layer and in the communications between the layers. Users at the client layer can cause harm by introducing errors, accessing the system without authorization, or unknowingly downloading spyware and viruses. Hackers can, through a variety of ruses, access data flowing over networks, steal valuable data during transmission, or alter messages without authorization. Needless to say, the Internet and other networks are highly vulnerable to disruptions from radiation. Intruders can launch denial-of-service attacks or malicious software to disrupt the operation of Web sites. Those capable of penetrating corporate systems can destroy or alter corporate data stored in databases or files.

FIGURE 1   CONTEMPORARY SECURITY CHALLENGES AND VULNERABILITIES

Client (User)	Communications Lines	Corporate Servers	Corporate Systems
• Unauthorized access • Errors • Viruses and spyware	• Tapping • Sniffing • Message alteration • Theft and fraud • Radiation	• Hacking • Viruses and worms • Theft and fraud • Vandalism • Denial-of-service attacks	Hardware Operating Systems Software • Theft of data • Copying data • Alteration of data • Hardware failure • Software failure

The architecture of a Web-based application typically includes a Web client, a server, and corporate information systems linked to databases. Each of these components presents security challenges and vulnerabilities. Floods, fires, power failures, and other electrical problems can cause disruptions at any point in the network.

Systems malfunction if computer hardware breaks down, is not configured properly, or is damaged by improper use or criminal acts. Errors in programming, improper installation, or unauthorized changes cause computer software to fail. Power failures, floods, fires, or other natural disasters can also disrupt computer systems.

Domestic or offshore partnering with another company adds to system vulnerability if valuable information resides on networks and computers outside the organization's control. Without strong safeguards, valuable data could be lost or destroyed, or could fall into the wrong hands, revealing important trade secrets or information that violates personal privacy.

Internet Vulnerabilities

Large public networks, such as the Internet, are more vulnerable than internal networks because they are open to anyone. The Internet is so huge and so fast that when abuses do occur, they can have an enormously widespread impact in a matter of minutes. When corporate networks link to the Internet, the firm's information systems are vulnerable to attacks from outsiders.

Modern high-speed broadband networks do not help matters. Computers that are constantly connected to the Internet by cable or digital subscriber line (DSL) modems are more open to penetration by outsiders than older dial-up lines. Computers with high-speed access are typically connected for a greater number of hours per day; attacks can take place much faster; and for DSL lines which offer clients fixed IP addresses, the identity of the local computer is easier to establish. A fixed Internet address creates a fixed target for hackers.

Telephone service based on Internet technology can be more vulnerable than the switched voice network if it does not run over a secure, private network. Most voice over IP (VoIP) traffic over the public Internet is not encrypted, so hackers can potentially listen in on conversations at a number of points from the local area network (LAN) modem to neighborhood servers. Hackers can intercept conversations to obtain credit card and other confidential personal information or shut down voice service by flooding servers supporting VoIP with bogus traffic.

Vulnerability has also increased from widespread use of e-mail and instant messaging (IM). E-mail may contain attachments that serve as springboards for malicious software or unauthorized access to internal corporate systems. Employees may use e-mail messages to transmit valuable trade secrets, financial data, or confidential customer information to unauthorized recipients. Popular instant messaging applications for consumers do not use a secure layer for text messages, so they can be intercepted and read by outsiders during transmission over the public Internet. IM activity over the Internet can in some cases be used as a back door to an otherwise secure network.

Wireless Security Challenges

Is it safe to log onto a wireless fidelity (Wi-Fi) hotspot network at an airport, library, or other public location? Generally not, because these networks are "open" and "unsecured," meaning that anyone can gain access, and the communication between your laptop and the wireless server is not encrypted. Wireless networks in homes are frequently not secured by encryption (although this is an option for all home wireless networks), and hackers driving by in cars or on bicycles can easily use your network, and listen to your communications with your wireless router. Even Bluetooth communication devices have notorious holes in the security of their communications.

Although the range of Wi-Fi networks is only several hundred feet, it can be extended up to one-fourth of a mile using external antennae. LANs using the 802.11 standard can be easily penetrated by outsiders armed with laptops, wireless cards, external antennae, and hacking software. Hackers use these tools to detect unprotected networks, monitor network traffic, and, in some cases, gain access to the Internet or to corporate networks.

Wi-Fi transmission technology was designed to make it easy for stations to find and hear one another. The *service set identifiers (SSIDs)* identifying the access points in a Wi-Fi network are broadcast multiple times and can be picked up fairly easily by intruders' sniffer programs (see Figure 2). Wireless networks in many locations do not have basic protections against **war driving**, in which eavesdroppers drive by buildings or park outside and try to intercept wireless network traffic.

A hacker can employ an 802.11 analysis tool to identify the SSID. (Windows XP has capabilities for detecting the SSID used in a network and automatically configuring the radio NIC within the user's device.) An intruder that has associated with an access point by using the correct SSID can then access other resources on the network, using the Windows operating system to determine which other users are connected to the network, access their computer hard drives, and open or copy their files.

FIGURE 2   WI-FI SECURITY CHALLENGES

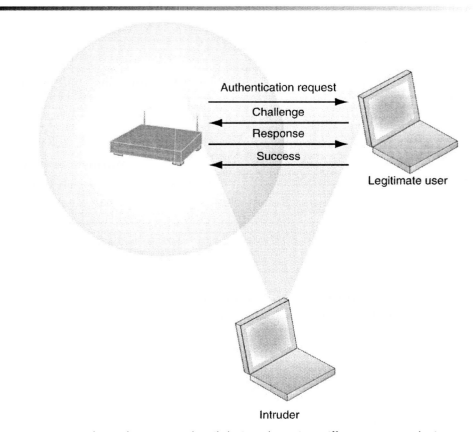

Authentication request

Challenge

Response

Success

Legitimate user

Intruder

Many Wi-Fi networks can be penetrated easily by intruders using sniffer programs to obtain an address to access the resources of a network without authorization.

Intruders also use the information they have gleaned to set up rogue access points on a different radio channel in physical locations close to users to force a user's radio NIC to associate with the rogue access point. Once this association occurs, hackers using the rogue access point can capture the names and passwords of unsuspecting users.

The initial security standard developed for Wi-Fi, called Wired Equivalent Privacy (WEP), is not very effective. WEP is built into all standard 802.11 products, but its use is optional. Many users neglect to use WEP security features, leaving them unprotected. The basic WEP specification calls for an access point and all of its users to share the same 40-bit encrypted password, which can be easily decrypted by hackers from a small amount of traffic. Manufacturers of wireless networking products are now beefing up their security by offering stronger encryption and authentication systems.

MALICIOUS SOFTWARE: VIRUSES, WORMS, TROJAN HORSES, AND SPYWARE

Malicious software programs are referred to as **malware** and include a variety of threats, such as computer viruses, worms, and Trojan horses. A **computer virus** is a rogue software program that attaches itself to other software programs or data files in order to be executed, usually without user knowledge or permission. Most computer viruses deliver a "payload." The payload may be relatively benign, such as the instructions to display a message or image, or it may be highly destructive—destroying programs or data, clogging computer memory, reformatting a computer's hard drive, or causing programs to run improperly. Viruses typically spread from computer to computer when users take an action, such as sending an e-mail attachment or copying an infected file.

Most recent attacks have come from **worms**, which are independent computer programs that copy themselves from one computer to other computers over a network. Unlike viruses, worms operate on their own without attaching to other computer program files and rely less on human behavior in order to spread from computer to computer. This explains why computer worms spread much more rapidly than computer viruses. Worms destroy data and programs as well as disrupt or even halt the operation of computer networks.

Worms and viruses are often spread over the Internet from files of downloaded software, from files attached to e-mail transmissions, or from compromised e-mail messages or instant messaging. Viruses have also invaded computerized information systems from "infected" disks or infected machines. E-mail worms are currently the most problematic.

Now viruses and worms are spreading to wireless computing devices. For example, the Cabir worm, which first appeared in early 2005, targets mobile devices running the popular Symbian mobile operating system and spreads through Bluetooth wireless networks. Cabir continually seeks other Bluetooth devices and eventually runs down a device's battery. Mobile device viruses pose serious threats to enterprise computing because so many wireless devices are now linked to corporate information systems. Table 1 describes the characteristics of some of the most harmful worms and viruses that have appeared to date.

331

TABLE 1 EXAMPLES OF MALICIOUS CODE

NAME	TYPE	DESCRIPTION
Sasser.ftp	Worm	First appeared in May 2004. Spread over the Internet by attacking random IP addresses. Causes computers to continually crash and reboot, and infected computers to search for more victims. Affected millions of computers worldwide, disrupting British Airways flight check-ins, operations of British coast guard stations, Hong Kong hospitals, Taiwan post office branches, and Australia's Westpac Bank. Sasser and its variants caused an estimated $14.8 billion to $18.6 billion in damages worldwide.
MyDoom.A	Worm	First appeared January 26, 2004. Spreads as an e-mail attachment. Sends e-mail to addresses harvested from infected machines, forging the sender's address. At its peak this worm lowered global Internet performance by 10 percent and Web page loading times by as much as 50 percent. Was programmed to stop spreading after February 12, 2004.
Bagle	Worm	First appeared January 18, 2004. Infected PCs via an e-mail attachment, then used the PC e-mail addresses for replicating itself. Infected PCs and their data could be accessed by remote users and applications. Bagle.B stopped spreading after January 28, 2004, but other variants are still active. Has caused tens of millions of dollars in damage already.
Sobig.F	Worm	First detected on August 19, 2003. Spreads via e-mail attachments and sends massive amounts of mail with forged sender information. Deactivated itself on September 10, 2003, after infecting more than 1 million PCs and doing $5 to $10 billion in damage.
ILoveYou	Virus	First detected on May 3, 2000. Script virus written in Visual Basic script and transmitted as an attachment to e-mail with the subject line ILOVEYOU. Overwrites music, image, and other files with a copy of itself and did an estimated $10 billion to $15 billion in damage.
Melissa	Macro virus/ worm	First appeared in March 1999. Word macro script mailing infected Word file to first 50 entries in user's Microsoft Outlook address book. Infected 15 to 29 percent of all business PCs, causing $300 million to $600 million in damage.
CIH (Chernobyl)	Virus	Unleashed in June 1998. Infected Windows executable files and overwrote the data on a PC hard drive. Destroyed huge amounts of PC data, creating $20 to $80 million in damage worldwide.

Over the past decade, worms and viruses have caused billions of dollars of damage to corporate networks, e-mail systems, and data. Among the companies surveyed in the ICSA Labs Tenth Annual Virus Prevalence Survey, recovering from virus and malware attacks took respondents an average of seven person days and cost an average of $130,000 (ICSA Labs, 2005).

A **Trojan horse** is a software program that appears to be benign but then does something other than expected. The Trojan horse is not itself a virus because it does not replicate but is often a way for viruses or other malicious code to be introduced into a computer system. The term *Trojan horse* is based on the huge wooden horse used by the Greeks to trick the Trojans into opening the gates to their fortified city during the Trojan War. Once inside the city walls, Greek soldiers hidden in the horse revealed themselves and captured the city.

An example of a modern-day Trojan horse is DSNX-05, detected in early 2005. It was unleashed by a bogus e-mail message appearing to come from

Microsoft, which directed recipients to visit a Web site designed to look like the Microsoft Windows Update page. The Web site downloaded and installed malicious code on the compromised computer. Once this Trojan horse was installed, hackers could access the computer remotely without detection and use it for their own purposes.

Some types of **spyware** also act as malicious software. These small programs install themselves surreptitiously on computers to monitor user Web surfing activity and serve up advertising. Thousands of forms of spyware have been documented. Harris Interactive found that 92 percent of the companies surveyed in its Web@Work study reported detecting spyware on their networks (Mitchell, 2006).

Spyware is not just annoying. It offers outsiders the possibility of invading your privacy and stealing your personal identity, including PIN codes, logins, and account information. **Key loggers** record every keystroke made on a computer to steal serial numbers for software, to launch Internet attacks, to gain access to e-mail accounts, to obtain passwords to protected computer systems, or to pick up personal information such as credit card numbers. Other spyware programs reset Web browser home pages, redirect search requests, or slow computer performance by taking up too much memory.

HACKERS AND CYBERVANDALISM

A **hacker** is an individual who intends to gain unauthorized access to a computer system. Within the hacking community, the term **cracker** is typically used to denote a hacker with criminal intent, although in the public press, the terms *hacker* and *cracker* are used interchangeably. Hackers and crackers gain unauthorized access by finding weaknesses in the security protections employed by Web sites and computer systems, often taking advantage of various features of the Internet that make it an open system that is easy to use.

Hacker activities have broadened beyond mere system intrusion to include theft of goods and information, as well as system damage and **cybervandalism**, the intentional disruption, defacement, or even destruction of a Web site or corporate information system. For example, on August 20, 2006, Pakistani hackers broke into the computer hosting the Web site of Kevin Mitnick, an ex-hacker turned security consultant, and replaced the home page with one displaying a vulgar message (Evers, 2006).

Spoofing and Sniffing

Hackers attempting to hide their true identities often spoof, or misrepresent, themselves by using fake e-mail addresses or masquerading as someone else. **Spoofing** also may involve redirecting a Web link to an address different from the intended one, with the site masquerading as the intended destination. For example, if hackers redirect customers to a fake Web site that looks almost exactly like the true site, they can then collect and process orders, effectively stealing business as well as sensitive customer information from the true site. We provide more detail on other forms of spoofing in our discussion of computer crime.

A **sniffer** is a type of eavesdropping program that monitors information traveling over a network. When used legitimately, sniffers help identify potential network trouble spots or criminal activity on networks, but when used for criminal purposes, they can be damaging and very difficult to detect. Sniffers enable hackers to steal proprietary information from anywhere on a network, including e-mail messages, company files, and confidential reports.

Denial-of-Service Attacks

In a **denial-of-service (DoS) attack**, hackers flood a network server or Web server with many thousands of false communications or requests for services to crash the network. The network receives so many queries that it cannot keep up with them and is thus unavailable to service legitimate requests. A **distributed denial-of-service (DDoS)** attack uses hundreds or even thousands of computers to inundate and overwhelm the network from numerous launch points.

Although DoS attacks do not destroy information or access restricted areas of a company's information systems, they often cause a Web site to shut down, making it impossible for legitimate users to access the site. For busy e-commerce sites, these attacks are costly; while the site is shut down, customers cannot make purchases. Especially vulnerable are small and midsize businesses whose networks tend to be less protected than those of large corporations.

Perpetrators of DoS attacks often use thousands of "zombie" PCs infected with malicious software without their owners' knowledge and organized into a **botnet**. Hackers create these botnets infecting other people's computers with bot malware that opens a back door through which an attacker can give instructions. The infected computer then becomes a slave, or zombie, serving a master computer belonging to someone else. Once a hacker infects enough computers, her or she can use the amassed resources of the botnet to launch distributed denial-of-service attacks, phishing campaigns, or unsolicited "spam" e-mail.

Experts estimate that there are over 3 million bots active around the world in any given day, and each day those bots infect hundreds of thousands of Internet-connected devices. (Gage and Nash, 2006). The Interactive Session on Technology describes some of these bot attacks, illustrating their scope and severity.

Figure 3 illustrates the estimated worldwide damage from all forms of digital attack, including hacking, malware, and spam between 1999 and 2005.

FIGURE 3   WORLDWIDE DAMAGE FROM DIGITAL ATTACKS

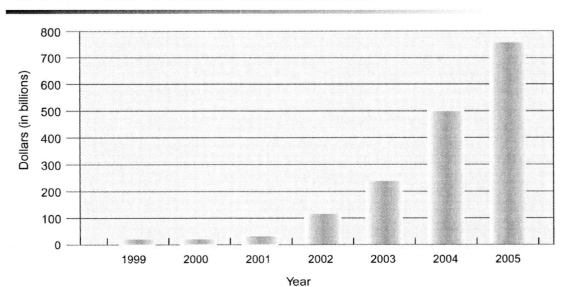

This chart shows estimates of the average annual worldwide damage from hacking, malware, and spam since 1999. These data are based on figures from mi2G and the authors.

INTERACTIVE SESSION: TECHNOLOGY

BOT ARMIES AND NETWORK ZOMBIES

On July 7, 2004, Gary Chiacco reported to federal authorities that customers had difficulty accessing his Jersey-Joe.com online sports apparel site for several days. Unable to conduct business, Jersey-Joe lost hundreds of thousands of dollars in sales. Jersey-Joe had become the victim of a denial-of-service attack, in which the Web site was bombarded by so many requests that the site overloaded and went offline. As investigators worked on the case into the fall of 2004, the attacks worsened to such a degree that the company hosting the Jersey-Joe Web site asked Chiacco to take his site elsewhere because the attacks were affecting service to other Web sites hosted by the company.

Investigators discovered that the attacks came from computers belonging to college students in Massachusetts and Pennsylvania that were infected with software that made them "zombies." These computers were receiving instructions from a user whose IP address was traced to a high school student in Edison, New Jersey, named Jasmine Singh. The teenager had been hired to launch these attacks by 18-year-old Jason Arabo, another online seller of sports apparel who wanted to harm his competition. The government gave Singh a five-year prison sentence, which it believes was justified by the widespread harm to Chiacco and other businesses affected by Singh and Arabo's actions. Arabo could be imprisoned up to ten years.

Building and selling bots for malicious purposes has become a serious money-making enterprise. James Ancheta, a self-taught computer expert, pleaded guilty on January 23, 2006, in the U.S. District Court in Los Angeles to building and selling bots and using his network of thousands of bots to commit crimes. His botnet infected at least 400,000 computers, including machines at two U.S. Department of Defense facilities, and had installed unauthorized adware that earned him more than $60,000.

Adware companies pay other companies for each digital advertisement they install on a PC. The adware tries to display pop-up ads related to the user's activity, such as what terms that person searched for at Google. Ancheta abused this system by instructing his bots to install ads on computers they had taken over so he could collect fees for placing the ads—as much as 40 cents per successful placement.

Ancheta also rented or sold bots to people interested in using them to send spam or launch DoS attacks to disable specific Web sites. Ancheta's botz4sale Web site offered access to up to 10,000 compromised PCs at one time for as little as 4 cents each. He even provided his "customers" with tips for using his product.

To outwit law enforcement, Ancheta continually changed e-mail addresses, ISPs, domain names, and instant messaging handles. Eventually his luck ran out. The FBI arrested him on November 3, 2005, and shut down his operations. Ancheta was sentenced to 57 months in federal prison.

Could bot attacks like these be prevented? It's getting increasingly difficult. According to Michael Lines, chief security officer at credit reporting firm TransUnion, "There is no single technology or strategy to [solve] the problem." Even if people use antivirus and antispyware software and patch software vulnerabilities, new bots appear that target different vulnerabilities. In 2005, 175 new bots were detected.

Hackers don't even have to write their own bot programs. They can download bot toolkits for free on the Internet. Ancheta modified Rxbot, a bot strain available for download at several Web sites and had his bots report to an Internet Relay Chat (IRC) channel that he controlled. And as the Ancheta case revealed, people can even buy access to bots.

Having a strategy in place before a bot attack hits is crucial to mitigating the damage of the attack. When DNS servers that keep track of Internet addresses and domain names at Akamai Technologies were flooded in June 2004 with bogus requests for connections from a zombie army, the damage to Akamai's business could have been severe. However, the staff at Akamai was prepared to respond.

When Akamai's Network Operations Command Center (NOCC) detected spikes in traffic volume on company DNS servers, Akamai's first response team, known as the White Hat team, initiated its emergency response procedure. The team made its initial diagnosis of who and what was under attack, and then the team split into subgroups. One group was put in charge of capturing the incoming requests, decoding their patterns, creating a profile of the attack, and recommending countermeasures.

A second group began notifying federal law enforcement officials and Internet service providers, who offered guidance and helped shut down secondary attacks. Another group measured the impact of the attack on customers. Still another group deployed a custom-built application to identify and filter the bogus incoming data packets.

Sources: Deborah Gage and Kim S. Nash, "When Bots Attack," *Baseline*, April 2006; Robert Lemos, "Major Prison Time for Bot Master," *Security Focus*, May 9, 2006; "Computer Attacks-Jason Salah Arabo," *Federal Crimes Blog*, April 13, 2006; and Cassell Bryan-Low, "Tech-Savvy Blackmailers Hone a New Form of Extortion," *The Wall Street Journal*, May 5, 2005.

CASE STUDY QUESTIONS

1. What is the business impact of botnets?
2. What management, organization, and technology factors should be addressed in a plan to prevent botnet attacks?
3. How easy would it be for a small business to combat botnet attacks? A large business?

MIS IN ACTION

Read the article on "Robot Wars-How Botnets Work" by Massimiliano Romano, Simone Rosignoli, and Ennio Giannini at WindowsSecurity.com. Prepare an electronic presentation that summarizes your answers to the following questions:

1. What are botnets and how do they work?
2. What features do the most popular botnets offer?
3. How does a bot infect and control a host computer?
4. How can a bot attack be prevented?

COMPUTER CRIME AND CYBERTERRORISM

Most hacker activities are criminal offenses, and the vulnerabilities of systems we have just described make them targets for other types of computer crime as well. Computer crime is defined by the U.S. Department of Justice as "any violations of criminal law that involve a knowledge of computer technology for their perpetration, investigation, or prosecution." Table 2 provides examples of the computer as a target of crime and as an instrument of crime.

TABLE 2 EXAMPLES OF COMPUTER CRIME

COMPUTERS AS TARGETS OF CRIME	COMPUTERS AS INSTRUMENTS OF CRIME
Breaching the confidentiality of protected computerized data	Theft of trade secrets and unauthorized copying of software or copyrighted intellectual property, such as articles, books, music, and video
Accessing a computer system without authority	Schemes to defraud
Knowingly accessing a protected computer to commit fraud	Using e-mail for threats or harassment
Intentionally accessing a protected computer and causing damage, negligently or deliberately	Intentionally attempting to intercept electronic communication
Knowingly transmitting a program, program code, or command that intentionally causes damage to a protected computer	Illegally accessing stored electronic communications, including e-mail and voice mail
Threatening to cause damage to a protected computer	Transmitting or possessing child pornography using a computer

No one knows the magnitude of the computer crime problem—how many systems are invaded, how many people engage in the practice, or the total economic damage. According to one study by the Computer Crime Research Center, U.S. companies lose approximately $14 billion annually to cybercrimes. Many companies are reluctant to report computer crimes because the crimes may involve employees or the company fears that publicizing its vulnerability will hurt its reputation. The most economically damaging kinds of computer crime are DoS attacks, introducing viruses, theft of services, and disruption of computer systems.

Identity Theft

With the growth of the Internet and electronic commerce, identity theft has become especially troubling. **Identity theft** is a crime in which an imposter obtains key pieces of personal information, such as social security identification numbers, driver's license numbers, or credit card numbers, to impersonate someone else. The information may be used to obtain credit, merchandise, or services in the name of the victim or to provide the thief with false credentials. According to Javelin Strategy and Research, 9 million Americans were victims of identity theft in 2005 and they suffered losses totaling $56.6 billion (Leland and Zeller, 2006).

Identify theft has flourished on the Internet. Credit card files are a major target of Web site hackers. Moreover, e-commerce sites are wonderful sources of customer personal information—name, address, and phone number. Armed with this information, criminals can assume new identities and establish new credit for their own purposes.

One increasingly popular tactic is a form of spoofing called **phishing**, which we described in the chapter opening case. Phishing involves setting up fake Web sites or sending e-mail messages that look like those of legitimate businesses to ask users for confidential personal data. The e-mail message instructs recipients to update or confirm records by providing social security numbers, bank and credit card information, and other confidential data either by responding to the e-mail message, by entering the information at a bogus Web site, or by calling a telephone number.

Phishing scams have posed as PayPal, the online payment service; online service provider America Online (AOL); Citibank; American Express; the Federal Deposit Insurance Corporation; the Bank of England; and other banks around the world. Phishing is increasing at an alarming rate. In May 2006 alone, the Anti-Phishing Working Group received reports of 20,109 phishing e-mail messages, 11,976 phishing Web sites, and 137 "hijacked" brands (Anti-Phishing Working Group, 2006).

New phishing techniques called evil twins and pharming are harder to detect. **Evil twins** are wireless networks that pretend to offer trustworthy Wi-Fi connections to the Internet, such as those in airport lounges, hotels, or coffee shops. The bogus network looks identical to a legitimate public network. Fraudsters try to capture passwords or credit card numbers of unwitting users who log on to the network.

Pharming redirects users to a bogus Web page, even when the individual types the correct Web page address into his or her browser. This is possible if pharming perpetrators gain access to the Internet address information stored by Internet service providers to speed up Web browsing and the ISP companies have flawed software on their servers that allows the fraudsters to hack in and change those addresses.

The U.S. Congress addressed the threat of computer crime in 1986 with the Computer Fraud and Abuse Act. This act makes it illegal to access a computer system without authorization. Most states have similar laws, and nations in Europe have comparable legislation. Congress also passed the National Information Infrastructure Protection Act in 1996 to make virus distribution and hacker attacks intended to disable Web sites federal crimes. U.S. legislation, such as the Wiretap Act, Wire Fraud Act, Economic Espionage Act, Electronic Communications Privacy Act, E-Mail Threats and Harassment Act, and Child Pornography Act, covers computer crimes involving intercepting electronic communication, using electronic communication to defraud, stealing trade secrets, illegally accessing stored electronic communications, using e-mail for threats or harassment, and transmitting or possessing child pornography.

Click Fraud

When you click on an ad displayed by a search engine, the advertiser typically pays a fee for each click, which is supposed to direct potential buyers to its products. **Click fraud** occurs when an individual or computer program fraudulently clicks on an online ad without any intention of learning more about the advertiser or making a purchase. Click fraud has become a serious problem at Google and other Web sites that feature pay-per-click online advertising.

Some companies hire third parties (typically from low-wage countries) to fraudulently click on a competitor's ads to weaken them by driving up their marketing costs. Click fraud can also be perpetrated with software programs doing the clicking, and bot networks are often used for this purpose (review the Interactive Session on Technology). Search engines such as Google attempt to monitor click fraud but have been reluctant to publicize their efforts to deal with the problem. How big is the click fraud problem? Some, including Google executives, believe it is the single largest threat to search engine marketing. Estimates of the percentage of clicks that are fraudulent vary from less than 5 percent to over 20 percent, with some keywords exceeding 25 percent on occasion.

Cyberterrorism and Cyberwarfare

Concern is mounting that the vulnerabilities of the Internet or other networks could be exploited by terrorists, foreign intelligence services, or other groups to create widespread disruption and harm. Such cyberattacks might target the software that runs electrical power grids, air traffic control systems, or networks of major banks and financial institutions. At least twenty countries are believed to be developing offensive and defensive cyberwarfare capabilities. U.S. military networks and U.S. government agencies suffer hundreds of hacker attacks each year.

To deal with this threat, the U.S. Department of Homeland Security has an Information Analysis and Infrastructure Protection Directorate to coordinate cybersecurity. The directorate's National Cyber Security Division is responsible for protecting critical infrastructure. It conducts cyberspace analysis, promotes information sharing, issues alerts, and aids in national recovery efforts. The U.S. Department of Defense has joint task forces for computer network defense and for managing computer network attacks.

INTERNAL THREATS: EMPLOYEES

We tend to think the security threats to a business originate outside the organization. In fact, company insiders pose serious security problems. Employees have access to privileged information, and in the presence of sloppy internal security procedures, they are often able to roam throughout an organization's systems without leaving a trace.

Studies have found that user lack of knowledge is the single greatest cause of network security breaches. Many employees forget their passwords to access computer systems or allow co-workers to use them, which compromises the system. Malicious intruders seeking system access sometimes trick employees into revealing their passwords by pretending to be legitimate members of the company in need of information. This practice is called **social engineering**.

Both end users and information systems specialists are also a major source of errors introduced into information systems. End users introduce errors by entering faulty data or by not following the proper instructions for processing data and using computer equipment. Information systems specialists may create software errors as they design and develop new software or maintain existing programs.

SOFTWARE VULNERABILITY

Software errors pose a constant threat to information systems, causing untold losses in productivity. Symantec, a leading vendor of security software, found 3,758 vulnerabilities in software in 2005, up 42 percent from the previous year (Vara, 2006). The U.S. Department of Commerce National Institute of Standards and Technology (NIST) reported that software flaws (including vulnerabilities to hackers and malware) cost the U.S. economy $59.6 billion each year (NIST, 2005).

Commercial software often contains flaws that create not only performance but also security vulnerabilities that open networks to intruders. These vulnerabilities enable malware to slip past antivirus defenses. A great deal of malware has been trying to exploit vulnerabilities in the Microsoft Windows operating system and other Microsoft products, but malware targeting the Linux operating system is on the rise as well.

To correct software flaws once they are identified, the software vendor creates small pieces of software called **patches** to repair the flaws without disturbing the proper operation of the software. An example is Microsoft's XP Service Pack 2 (SP2) introduced in 2004, which features added firewall protection against viruses and intruders, capabilities for automatic security updates, and an easy-to-use interface for managing the security applications on the user's computer. It is up to users of the software to track these vulnerabilities, test, and apply all patches. This process is called *patch management*.

Because a company's IT infrastructure is typically laden with multiple business applications, operating system installations, and other system services, maintaining patches on all devices and services used by a company is often time-consuming and costly. Malware is being created so rapidly that companies have very little time to respond between the time a vulnerability and a patch are announced and the time malicious software appears to exploit the vulnerability.

2   BUSINESS VALUE OF SECURITY AND CONTROL

Many firms are reluctant to spend heavily on security because it is not directly related to sales revenue. However, protecting information systems is so critical to the operation of the business that it deserves a second look.

Companies have very valuable information assets to protect. Systems often house confidential information about individuals' taxes, financial assets, medical records, and job performance reviews. They also can contain information on corporate operations, including trade secrets, new product development plans, and marketing strategies. Government systems may store information on weapons systems, intelligence operations, and military targets. These information assets have tremendous value, and the repercussions can be devastating if they are lost, destroyed, or placed in the wrong hands. A recent study estimated that when the security of a large firm is compromised, the company loses approximately 2.1 percent of its market value within two days of the security breach, which translates into an average loss of $1.65 billion in stock market value per incident (Cavusoglu, Mishra, and Raghunathan, 2004).

Inadequate security and control can also create serious legal liability. Businesses must protect not only their own information assets but also those of customers, employees, and business partners. Failure to do so may open the firm to costly litigation for data exposure or theft. An organization can be held liable for needless risk and harm created if the organization fails to take appropriate protective action to prevent loss of confidential information, data corruption, or breach of privacy (see the chapter-ending case study). A sound security and control framework that protects business information assets can thus produce a high return on investment.

LEGAL AND REGULATORY REQUIREMENTS FOR ELECTRONIC RECORDS MANAGEMENT

Recent U.S. government regulations are forcing companies to take security and control more seriously by mandating the protection of data from abuse, exposure, and unauthorized access. Firms face new legal obligations for electronic records management and document retention as well as for privacy protection. **Electronic records management (ERM)** consists of policies, procedures, and tools for managing the retention, destruction, and storage of electronic records.

If you work in the healthcare industry, your firm needs to comply with the Health Insurance Portability and Accountability Act **(HIPAA)** of 1996. HIPAA outlines medical security and privacy rules and procedures for simplifying the administration of healthcare billing and automating the transfer of healthcare data between healthcare providers, payers, and plans. It requires members of the healthcare industry to retain patient information for six years and ensure the confidentiality of those records. It specifies privacy, security, and electronic transaction standards for healthcare providers handling patient information, providing penalties for breaches of medical privacy, disclosure of patient records by e-mail, or unauthorized network access.

If you work in a firm providing financial services, your firm will need to comply with the **Gramm-Leach-Bliley Act**. The Financial Services Modernization Act of 1999, better known as the Gramm-Leach-Bliley Act after its congressional sponsors, requires financial institutions to ensure the security and confidentiality of customer data. Data must be stored on a secure medium. Special security measures must be enforced to protect such data on storage media and during transmittal.

If you work in a publicly traded company, your company will need to comply with the **Sarbanes-Oxley Act**. The Public Company Accounting Reform and Investor Protection Act of 2002, better known as Sarbanes-Oxley after its sponsors Senator Paul Sarbanes of Maryland and Representative Michael Oxley of Ohio, was designed to protect investors after the financial scandals at Enron, WorldCom, and other public companies. It imposes responsibility on companies and their management to safeguard the accuracy and integrity of financial information that is used internally and released externally.

Sarbanes-Oxley is fundamentally about ensuring that internal controls are in place to govern the creation and documentation of information in financial statements. Because information systems are used to generate, store, and transport such data, the legislation requires firms to consider information systems security and other controls required to ensure the integrity, confidentiality, and accuracy of their data. Each system application that deals with critical financial reporting data requires controls to make sure the data are accurate. Controls to secure the corporate network, prevent unauthorized access to systems and data, and ensure data integrity and availability in the event of disaster or other disruption of service are essential as well.

ELECTRONIC EVIDENCE AND COMPUTER FORENSICS

Security, control, and electronic records management have become essential for responding to legal actions. Much of the evidence today for stock fraud, embezzlement, theft of company trade secrets, computer crime, and many civil cases is in digital form. In addition to information from printed or typewritten pages, legal cases today increasingly rely on evidence represented as digital data stored on portable floppy disks, CDs, and computer hard disk drives, as well as in e-mail, instant messages, and e-commerce transactions over the Internet. E-mail is currently the most common type of electronic evidence.

In a legal action, a firm is obligated to respond to a discovery request for access to information that may be used as evidence, and the company is required by law to produce those data. The cost of responding to a discovery request can be enormous if the company has trouble assembling the required data or the data have been corrupted or destroyed. Likewise, the cost of not responding is very high. Courts now impose severe financial and even criminal penalties for improper destruction of electronic documents, failure to produce records, and failure to store records properly.

An effective electronic document retention policy ensures that electronic documents, e-mail, and other records are well organized, accessible, and neither retained too long nor discarded too soon. It also reflects an awareness of how to preserve potential evidence for computer forensics. **Computer forensics** is the scientific collection, examination, authentication, preservation, and analysis of data held on or retrieved from computer storage media in such a way that the information can be used as evidence in a court of law. It deals with the following problems:

- Recovering data from computers while preserving evidential integrity
- Securely storing and handling recovered electronic data
- Finding significant information in a large volume of electronic data
- Presenting the information to a court of law

Electronic evidence may reside on computer storage media in the form of computer files and as *ambient data*, which are not visible to the average user.

341

An example might be a file that has been deleted on a PC hard drive. Data that a computer user may have deleted on computer storage media can be recovered through various techniques. Computer forensics experts try to recover such hidden data for presentation as evidence.

An awareness of computer forensics should be incorporated into a firm's contingency planning process. The CIO, security specialists, information systems staff, and corporate legal counsel should all work together to have a plan in place that can be executed if a legal need arises.

3   ESTABLISHING A FRAMEWORK FOR SECURITY AND CONTROL

Technology is not the key issue in information systems security and control. The technology provides a foundation, but in the absence of intelligent management policies, even the best technology easily can be defeated. For instance, experts believe that more than 90 percent of successful cyberattacks could have been prevented by technology available at the time. Inadequate human attention made these attacks so prevalent.

Protection of information resources requires a sound security policy and set of controls. **ISO 17799**, an international set of standards for security and control, provides helpful guidelines. It specifies best practices in information systems security and control, including security policy, business continuity planning, physical security, access control, compliance, and creating a security function within the organization.

RISK ASSESSMENT

Before your company commits resources to security, it must know which assets require protection and the extent to which these assets are vulnerable. A risk assessment helps answer these questions and determine the most cost-effective set of controls for protecting assets.

A **risk assessment** determines the level of risk to the firm if a specific activity or process is not properly controlled. Business managers working with information systems specialists can determine the value of information assets, points of vulnerability, the likely frequency of a problem, and the potential for damage. For example, if an event is likely to occur no more than once a year, with a maximum of a $1,000 loss to the organization, it is not feasible to spend $20,000 on the design and maintenance of a control to protect against that event. However, if that same event could occur at least once a day, with a potential loss of more than $300,000 a year, $100,000 spent on a control might be entirely appropriate.

Table 3 illustrates sample results of a risk assessment for an online order processing system that processes 30,000 orders per day. The likelihood of each exposure occurring over a one-year period is expressed as a percentage. The next column shows the highest and lowest possible loss that could be expected each time the exposure occurred and an average loss calculated by adding the highest and lowest figures together and dividing by two. The expected annual loss for each exposure can be determined by multiplying the average loss by its probability of occurrence.

This risk assessment shows that the probability of a power failure occurring in a one-year period is 30 percent. Loss of order transactions while power is

TABLE 3 ONLINE ORDER PROCESSING RISK ASSESSMENT

EXPOSURE	PROBABILITY OF OCCURRENCE (%)	LOSS RANGE/AVERAGE ($)	EXPECTED ANNUAL LOSS ($)
Power failure	30%	$5,000–$200,000 ($102,500)	$30,750
Embezzlement	5%	$1,000–$50,000 ($25,500)	$1,275
User error	98%	$200–$40,000 ($20,100)	$19,698

down could range from $5,000 to $200,000 (averaging $102,500) for each occurrence, depending on how long processing is halted. The probability of embezzlement occurring over a yearly period is about 5 percent, with potential losses ranging from $1,000 to $50,000 (and averaging $25,500) for each occurrence. User errors have a 98 percent chance of occurring over a yearly period, with losses ranging from $200 to $40,000 (and averaging $20,100) for each occurrence.

Once the risks have been assessed, system builders will concentrate on the control points with the greatest vulnerability and potential for loss. In this case, controls should focus on ways to minimize the risk of power failures and user errors because anticipated annual losses are highest for these areas.

SECURITY POLICY

Once you've identified the main risks to your systems, your company will need to develop a security policy for protecting the company's assets. A **security policy** consists of statements ranking information risks, identifying acceptable security goals, and identifying the mechanisms for achieving these goals. What are the firm's most important information assets? Who generates and controls this information in the firm? What existing security policies are in place to protect the information? What level of risk is management willing to accept for each of these assets? Is it willing, for instance, to lose customer credit data once every 10 years? Or will it build a security system for credit card data that can withstand the once-in-a-hundred-year disaster? Management must estimate how much it will cost to achieve this level of acceptable risk.

In larger firms, you may see a formal corporate security function headed by a **chief security officer (CSO)**. The security group educates and trains users, keeps management aware of security threats and breakdowns, and maintains the tools chosen to implement security. The chief security officer is responsible for enforcing the firm's security policy.

The security policy drives policies determining acceptable use of the firm's information resources and which members of the company have access to its information assets. An **acceptable use policy (AUP)** defines acceptable uses of the firm's information resources and computing equipment, including desktop and laptop computers, wireless devices, telephones, and the Internet. The policy should clarify company policy regarding privacy, user responsibility, and personal use of company equipment and networks. A good AUP defines unacceptable and acceptable actions for every user and specifies consequences for noncompliance.

Authorization policies determine differing levels of access to information assets for different levels of users. **Authorization management systems** establish where and when a user is permitted to access certain parts of a Web site or a corporate database. Such systems allow each user access only to those portions of a system that person is permitted to enter, based on information established by a set of access rules.

The authorization management system knows exactly what information each user is permitted to access as shown in Figure 4. This figure illustrates the security allowed for two sets of users of an online personnel database containing sensitive information, such as employees' salaries, benefits, and medical histories. One set of users consists of all employees who perform clerical functions, such as inputting employee data into the system. All individuals with this type of profile can update the system but can neither read nor update sensitive fields, such as salary, medical history, or earnings data. Another profile applies to a divisional manager, who cannot update the system but who can read all employee data fields for his or her division, including medical history and salary. These profiles are based on access rules supplied by business groups. The system illustrated in Figure 4 provides very fine-grained security restrictions, such as allowing authorized personnel users to inquire about all employee information except that in confidential fields, such as salary or medical history.

ENSURING BUSINESS CONTINUITY

As companies increasingly rely on digital networks for revenue and operations, they need to take additional steps to ensure that their systems and applications are always available. Firms such as those in the airline and financial services

FIGURE 4   SECURITY PROFILES FOR A PERSONNEL SYSTEM

SECURITY PROFILE 1

User: Personnel Dept. Clerk

Location: Division 1

Employee Identification
Codes with This Profile: 00753, 27834, 37665, 44116

Data Field Restrictions	Type of Access
All employee data for Division 1 only	Read and Update
• Medical history data	None
• Salary	None
• Pensionable earnings	None

SECURITY PROFILE 2

User: Divisional Personnel Manager

Location: Division 1

Employee Identification
Codes with This Profile: 27321

Data Field Restrictions	Type of Access
All employee data for Division 1 only	Read Only

These two examples represent two security profiles or data security patterns that might be found in a personnel system. Depending on the security profile, a user would have certain restrictions on access to various systems, locations, or data in an organization.

industries with critical applications requiring online transaction processing have traditionally used fault-tolerant computer systems for many years to ensure 100 percent availability. In **online transaction processing**, transactions entered online are immediately processed by the computer. Multitudinous changes to databases, reporting, and requests for information occur each instant.

Fault-tolerant computer systems contain redundant hardware, software, and power supply components that create an environment that provides continuous, uninterrupted service. Fault-tolerant computers use special software routines or self-checking logic built into their circuitry to detect hardware failures and automatically switch to a backup device. Parts from these computers can be removed and repaired without disruption to the computer system.

Fault tolerance should be distinguished from **high-availability computing**. Both fault tolerance and high-availability computing try to minimize downtime. **Downtime** refers to periods of time in which a system is not operational. However, high-availability computing helps firms recover quickly from a system crash, whereas fault tolerance promises continuous availability and the elimination of recovery time altogether. High-availability computing environments are a minimum requirement for firms with heavy electronic commerce processing or for firms that depend on digital networks for their internal operations.

High-availability computing requires backup servers, distribution of processing across multiple servers, high-capacity storage, and good disaster recovery and business continuity plans. The firm's computing platform must be extremely robust with scalable processing power, storage, and bandwidth.

Researchers are exploring ways to make computing systems recover even more rapidly when mishaps occur, an approach called **recovery-oriented computing**. This work includes designing systems that recover quickly, and implementing capabilities and tools to help operators pinpoint the sources of faults in multicomponent systems and easily correct their mistakes (Fox and Patterson, 2003).

Disaster Recovery Planning and Business Continuity Planning

Disaster recovery planning devises plans for the restoration of computing and communications services after they have been disrupted by an event such as an earthquake, flood, or terrorist attack. Disaster recovery plans focus primarily on the technical issues involved in keeping systems up and running, such as which files to back up and the maintenance of backup computer systems or disaster recovery services.

For example, MasterCard maintains a duplicate computer center in Kansas City, Missouri, to serve as an emergency backup to its primary computer center in St. Louis. Rather than build their own backup facilities, many firms contract with disaster recovery firms, such as Comdisco Disaster Recovery Services in Rosemont, Illinois, and SunGard Recovery Services, headquartered in Wayne, Pennsylvania. These disaster recovery firms provide hot sites housing spare computers at locations around the country where subscribing firms can run their critical applications in an emergency.

Business continuity planning focuses on how the company can restore business operations after a disaster strikes. The business continuity plan identifies critical business processes and determines action plans for handling mission-critical functions if systems go down.

Business managers and information technology specialists need to work together on both types of plans to determine which systems and business processes are most critical to the company. They must conduct a business impact analysis to identify the firm's most critical systems and the impact a systems outage would have on the business. Management must determine the maximum amount of time the business can survive with its systems down and which parts of the business must be restored first.

Security Outsourcing

Many companies, especially small businesses, lack the resources or expertise to provide a secure high-availability computing environment on their own. They can outsource many security functions to **managed security service providers (MSSPs)** that monitor network activity and perform vulnerability testing and intrusion detection. Guardent, Counterpane, VeriSign, and Symantec are leading providers of MSSP services.

THE ROLE OF AUDITING

How does management know that information systems security and controls are effective? To answer this question, organizations must conduct comprehensive and systematic audits. An **MIS audit** examines the firm's overall security environment as well as controls governing individual information systems. The auditor should trace the flow of sample transactions through the system and perform tests, using, if appropriate, automated audit software.

Security audits review technologies, procedures, documentation, training, and personnel. A thorough audit will even simulate an attack or disaster to test the response of the technology, information systems staff, and business employees.

An auditor often traces the flow of sample transactions through an information system and may perform tests using automated audit software. MIS audits help management identify security vulnerabilities and determine whether information system controls are effective.

© Chuck Savage.

FIGURE 5   SAMPLE AUDITOR'S LIST OF CONTROL WEAKNESSES

Function: Loans Location: Peoria, IL	Prepared by: J. Ericson Date: June 16, 2007		Received by: T. Benson Review date: June 28, 2007	
Nature of Weakness and Impact	Chance for Error/Abuse		Notification to Management	
	Yes/No	Justification	Report date	Management response
User accounts with missing passwords	Yes	Leaves system open to unauthorized outsiders or attackers	5/10/07	Eliminate accounts without passwords
Network configured to allow some sharing of system files	Yes	Exposes critical system files to hostile parties connected to the network	5/10/07	Ensure only required directories are shared and that they are protected with strong passwords
Software patches can update production programs without final approval from Standards and Controls group	No	All production programs require management approval; Standards and Controls group assigns such cases to a temporary production status		

This chart is a sample page from a list of control weaknesses that an auditor might find in a loan system in a local commercial bank. This form helps auditors record and evaluate control weaknesses and shows the results of discussing those weaknesses with management, as well as any corrective actions taken by management.

The audit lists and ranks all control weaknesses and estimates the probability of their occurrence. It then assesses the financial and organizational impact of each threat. Figure 5 is a sample auditor's listing of control weaknesses for a loan system. It includes a section for notifying management of such weaknesses and for management's response. Management is expected to devise a plan for countering significant weaknesses in controls.

4   TECHNOLOGIES AND TOOLS FOR SECURITY

An array of tools and technologies are available to secure systems and data. They include tools for authentication, firewalls, intrusion detection systems, antivirus and antispyware software, and encryption.

ACCESS CONTROL

Access control consists of all the policies and procedures a company uses to prevent improper access to systems by unauthorized insiders and outsiders. To gain access a user must be authorized and authenticated. **Authentication** refers to the ability to know that a person is who he or she claims to be. Access control software is designed to allow only authorized users to use systems or to access data using some method for authentication.

Authentication is often established by using passwords known only to authorized users. An end user uses a password to log on to a computer system and may also use passwords for accessing specific systems and files. However, users often forget passwords, share them, or choose poor passwords that are easy to guess, which compromises security. Password systems that are too rigorous hinder employee productivity. When employees must change complex passwords frequently, they often take shortcuts, such as choosing passwords that are easy to guess or writing down their passwords at their workstations in plain view. Passwords can also be "sniffed" if transmitted over a network or stolen through social engineering.

New authentication technologies, such as tokens, smart cards, and biometric authentication, overcome some of these problems. A **token** is a physical device, similar to an identification card, that is designed to prove the identity of a single user. Tokens are small gadgets that typically fit on key rings and display passcodes that change frequently. A **smart card** is a device about the size of a credit card that contains a chip formatted with access permission and other data. (Smart cards are also used in electronic payment systems.) A reader device interprets the data on the smart card and allows or denies access.

Biometric authentication uses systems that read and interpret individual human traits, such as fingerprints, irises, and voices, in order to grant or deny access. Biometric authentication is based on the measurement of a physical or behavioral trait that makes each individual unique. It compares a person's unique characteristics, such as the fingerprints, face, or retinal image, against a stored set profile of these characteristics to determine whether there are any differences between these characteristics and the stored profile. If the two profiles match, access is granted. The technology is expensive, and fingerprint and facial recognition technologies are just beginning to be used for information system security applications.

Biometric identification uses technologies that read and interpret individual human traits, such as fingerprints, voices, or facial images, in order to grant or deny access to systems.

© ITAR-TASS/Sergey Smolsky/NewsCom.

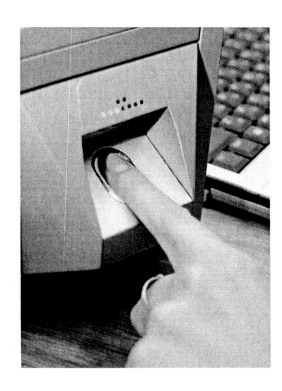

FIREWALLS, INTRUSION DETECTION SYSTEMS, AND ANTIVIRUS SOFTWARE

Without protection against malware and intruders, connecting to the Internet would be very dangerous. Firewalls, intrusion detection systems, and antivirus software have become essential business tools.

Firewalls

Firewalls are used to prevent unauthorized users from accessing private networks. A firewall is a combination of hardware and software that controls the flow of incoming and outgoing network traffic. It is generally placed between the organization's private internal networks and distrusted external networks, such as the Internet, although firewalls can also be used to protect one part of a company's network from the rest of the network (see Figure 6).

The firewall acts like a gatekeeper who examines each user's credentials before access is granted to a network. The firewall identifies names, IP addresses, applications, and other characteristics of incoming traffic. It checks this information against the access rules that have been programmed into the system by the network administrator. The firewall prevents unauthorized communication into and out of the network.

In large organizations, the firewall often resides on a specially designated computer separate from the rest of the network, so no incoming request

FIGURE 6   A CORPORATE FIREWALL

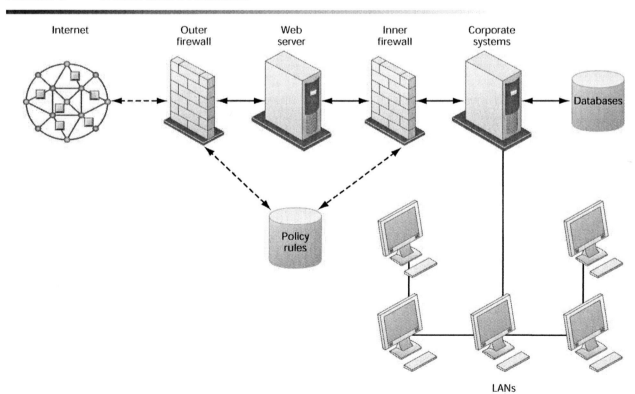

The firewall is placed between the firm's private network and the public Internet or another distrusted network to protect against unauthorized traffic.

directly accesses private network resources. There are a number of firewall screening technologies, including static packet filtering, stateful inspection, Network Address Translation, and application proxy filtering. They are frequently used in combination to provide firewall protection.

Packet filtering examines selected fields in the headers of data packets flowing back and forth between the trusted network and the Internet, examining individual packets in isolation. This filtering technology can miss many types of attacks. **Stateful inspection** provides additional security by determining whether packets are part of an ongoing dialogue between a sender and a receiver. It sets up state tables to track information over multiple packets. Packets are accepted or rejected based on whether they are part of an approved conversation or whether they are attempting to establish a legitimate connection.

Network Address Translation (NAT) can provide another layer of protection when static packet filtering and stateful inspection are employed. NAT conceals the IP addresses of the organization's internal host computer(s) to prevent sniffer programs outside the firewall from ascertaining them and using that information to penetrate internal systems.

Application proxy filtering examines the application content of packets. A proxy server stops data packets originating outside the organization, inspects them, and passes a proxy to the other side of the firewall. If a user outside the company wants to communicate with a user inside the organization, the outside user first "talks" to the proxy application and the proxy application communicates with the firm's internal computer. Likewise, a computer user inside the organization goes through the proxy to talk with computers on the outside.

To create a good firewall, an administrator must maintain detailed internal rules identifying the people, applications, or addresses that are allowed or rejected. Firewalls can deter, but not completely prevent, network penetration by outsiders and should be viewed as one element in an overall security plan.

Intrusion Detection Systems

In addition to firewalls, commercial security vendors now provide intrusion detection tools and services to protect against suspicious network traffic and attempts to access files and databases. **Intrusion detection systems** feature full-time monitoring tools placed at the most vulnerable points or "hot spots" of corporate networks to detect and deter intruders continually. The system generates an alarm if it finds a suspicious or anomalous event. Scanning software looks for patterns indicative of known methods of computer attacks, such as bad passwords, checks to see if important files have been removed or modified, and sends warnings of vandalism or system administration errors. Monitoring software examines events as they are happening to discover security attacks in progress. The intrusion detection tool can also be customized to shut down a particularly sensitive part of a network if it receives unauthorized traffic.

Antivirus and Antispyware Software

Defensive technology plans for both individuals and businesses must include antivirus protection for every computer. **Antivirus software** is designed to check computer systems and drives for the presence of computer viruses. Often the software eliminates the virus from the infected area. However, most antivirus software is effective only against viruses already known when the software was written. To remain effective, the antivirus software must be continually updated.

Leading antivirus software vendors, such as McAfee, Symantec and Trend Micro, have enhanced their products to include protection against spyware. Anti-spyware software tools such as Ad-Aware, Spybot, and Spyware Doctor are also very helpful.

SECURING WIRELESS NETWORKS

Despite its flaws, WEP provides some margin of security if Wi-Fi users remember to activate it. Corporations can further improve Wi-Fi security by using it in conjunction with virtual private network (VPN) technology when accessing internal corporate data.

In June 2004, the Wi-Fi Alliance industry trade group finalized the 802.11i specification that tightens security for wireless LAN products. It replaces the static encryption keys used in WEP with much longer keys that continually change, making them harder to crack. A central authentication server authenticates each user on the network. 802.11i also employs mutual authentication so that a wireless user does not get pulled into a rogue network that might steal the user's network credentials. Data packets are checked to make sure they are part of a current network session and not repeated by hackers to fool network users.

To be effective, wireless security technology should be accompanied by appropriate policies and procedures for using wireless devices securely. The Interactive Session on Management shows how Unilever PLC handled this issue.

ENCRYPTION AND PUBLIC KEY INFRASTRUCTURE

Many businesses use encryption to protect digital information that they store, physically transfer, or send over the Internet. **Encryption** is the process of transforming plain text or data into cipher text that cannot be read by anyone other than the sender and the intended receiver. Data are encrypted by using a secret numerical code, called an encryption key, that transforms plain data into cipher text. The message must be decrypted by the receiver.

Two methods for encrypting network traffic on the Web are SSL and S-HTTP. **Secure Sockets Layer (SSL)** and its successor **Transport Layer Security (TLS)** enable client and server computers to manage encryption and decryption activities as they communicate with each other during a secure Web session. **Secure Hypertext Transfer Protocol (S-HTTP)** is another protocol used for encrypting data flowing over the Internet, but it is limited to individual messages, whereas SSL and TLS are designed to establish a secure connection between two computers.

The capability to generate secure sessions is built into Internet client browser software and servers. The client and the server negotiate what key and what level of security to use. Once a secure session is established between the client and the server, all messages in that session are encrypted.

There are two alternative methods of encryption: symmetric key encryption and public key encryption. In symmetric key encryption, the sender and receiver establish a secure Internet session by creating a single encryption key and sending it to the receiver so both the sender and receiver share the same key. The strength of the encryption key is measured by its bit length. Today, a typical key will be 128 bits long (a string of 128 binary digits).

The problem with all symmetric encryption schemes is that the key itself must be shared somehow among the senders and receivers, which exposes the

INTERACTIVE SESSION: MANAGEMENT

UNILEVER SECURES ITS MOBILE DEVICES

Unilever is a $54 billion global manufacturer and supplier of fast-moving consumer goods, including brands such as Q-Tips, Lipton tea, and Dove personal care products. It operates in 57 countries, with regional teams for Europe, the Americas, and Asia/Africa (including Australia.) Unilever also has teams for its Foods and Home and Personal Care products.

This global giant is known for its ability to leverage products and brands throughout the world by tailoring them to local conditions and for its commitment to top-quality management. Unilever recruits its managers from all over the world and carefully trains them to serve as a unifying force for its operations.

In March 2004, Unilever's senior management ordered the company's thousand top executives to be equipped with mobile handheld devices to increase their productivity. The devices had to provide both voice and data transmission, operate on different wireless networks, be able to view e-mail attachments, such as Word files, and run on battery power for more than four hours.

The company selected BlackBerry 7100, 7290, and 8700 handhelds from Research in Motion because they were the leader in their category and they worked with heterogeneous e-mail servers and multiple wireless network standards, including CDMA and Wi-Fi.

Selecting the handheld was the easy part. The hard part was making sure Unilever's handhelds were secure. Wireless handhelds are easy to lose or steal because they're so portable, and they are penetrable by hackers and other outsiders. PDAs and smart phones, especially those used by senior executives, often store sensitive corporate data such as sales figures, social security numbers, customer names, phone numbers, and e-mail addresses. Unauthorized users may be able to access internal corporate networks through these devices. Downloading unauthorized data or messages may introduce disabling malware.

Tony Farah, Unilever's director of global solutions, and his team were charged with developing the security for these mobile devices to make sure Unilever did not suffer any data theft or financial losses. The team decided that a mobile handheld

required the same level of security as Unilever's laptops.

Under Unilever's corporate security policy, every employee equipped with a laptop or handheld must use a company-specified device. Users who log onto the corporate network must be able to identify themselves using a password or some other method of authentication.

BlackBerry devices use a proprietary operating system that allows an information technology manager to establish automated restrictions, such as not allowing users to open e-mail attachments sent from their desktops. This reduces the chances of a virus infecting the company network. The security settings also prevent the use of alternative e-mail or Web browser services. All e-mail and browser traffic are routed through BlackBerry Enterprise Servers, which use strong data encryption technology. Applications running on the BlackBerry operating system can't open both internal and external connections to the Internet, which would allow a malicious application to gather data from inside the company firewall and transmit the data outside the firewall without any auditing.

Unilever's firewall monitors all traffic and tracks user attempts to forward their e-mail to non-corporate accounts. If the firewall detects an employee who is doing this, the company orders the employee to stop. E-mail that passes from a person's home network to Unilever's corporate network is not secure.

Unilever configured the BlackBerrys so that users can't install any third-party applications. The handheld devices must be cradled every 30 days to create a new security key. The handhelds were set to time out after being idle for 15 minutes. After that amount of time has elapsed, a user must re-enter his or her password to regain access to e-mail or the telephone. Another security feature triggers a lockout and complete wipe of the device after ten unsuccessful attempts to log in or submit a password.

Although an overwhelming majority of Unilever executives believed that the BlackBerry security procedures were reasonable, not everyone was pleased. Some executives balked at having to enter a password when using the BlackBerry as a phone. Although management originally stipulated that the

BlackBerrys were to be used both as phones and for data transmission, Unilever allows recalcitrant executives to use their BlackBerry for data and a cell phone or smart phone for voice transmission.

Unilever's wireless handheld security program costs $70,000 annually to support over 450 executives. An additional 550 executives were added in 2006. Although there have been a few lost or stolen handhelds, Unilever has not experienced any security breaches.

Sources: Beth McFadden, "Security from Scratch," *Baseline*, May 15, 2006; Mary Lisbeth D'Amico, "Call Security," *The Wall Street Journal*, February 13, 2006; and www.unilever.com, accessed August 25, 2006.

CASE STUDY QUESTIONS

1. How are Unilever executives' wireless handhelds related to the company's business performance?
2. Discuss the potential impact of a security breach at Unilever.
3. What management, organization, and technology factors had to be addressed in developing security policies and procedures for Unilever's wireless handhelds?
4. Is it a good idea to allow Unilever executives to use both BlackBerrys and cell phones? Why or why not?

MIS IN ACTION

Explore the BlackBerry Web site, paying particular attention to the security features of the BlackBerry Enterprise Solution. Then answer these questions:

1. What security does BlackBerry provide for wireless data and stored data?
2. How do BlackBerry Enterprise Solution tools help protect BlackBerry devices against malware?

key to outsiders who might just be able to intercept and decrypt the key. A more secure form of encryption called **public key encryption** uses two keys: one shared (or public) and one totally private as shown in Figure 7. The keys are mathematically related so that data encrypted with one key can be decrypted using only the other key. To send and receive messages, communicators first create separate pairs of private and public keys. The public key is kept in a directory and the private key must be kept secret. The sender encrypts a message with the recipient's public key. On receiving the message, the recipient uses his or her private key to decrypt it.

FIGURE 7   PUBLIC KEY ENCRYPTION

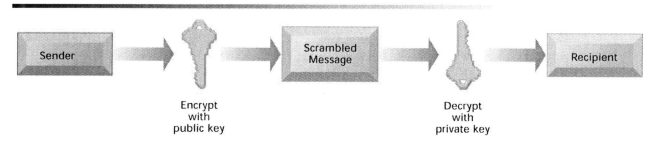

A public key encryption system can be viewed as a series of public and private keys that lock data when they are transmitted and unlock the data when they are received. The sender locates the recipient's public key in a directory and uses it to encrypt a message. The message is sent in encrypted form over the Internet or a private network. When the encrypted message arrives, the recipient uses his or her private key to decrypt the data and read the message.

Digital signatures and digital certificates further help with authentication. A **digital signature** is an encrypted message (such as the sender's name) that only the sender using his or her private key can create. A digital signature is used to verify the origin and contents of a message. It provides a way to associate a message with a sender, performing a function similar to a written signature.

Digital certificates are data files used to establish the identity of users and electronic assets for protection of online transactions (see Figure 8). A digital certificate system uses a trusted third party, known as a certificate authority (CA), to validate a user's identity. There are many CAs in the United States and around the world, including VeriSign, IdenTrust, and Australia's KeyPost.

The CA verifies a digital certificate user's identity offline. This information is put into a CA server, which generates an encrypted digital certificate containing owner identification information and a copy of the owner's public key. The certificate authenticates that the public key belongs to the designated owner. The CA makes its own public key available publicly either in print or perhaps on the Internet. The recipient of an encrypted message uses the CA's public key to decode the digital certificate attached to the message, verifies it was issued by the CA, and then obtains the sender's public key and identification information contained in the certificate. Using this information, the recipient can send an encrypted reply. The digital certificate system would enable, for example, a credit card user and a merchant to validate that their digital certificates were issued by an authorized and trusted third party before they exchange data. **Public key infrastructure (PKI)**, the use of public key cryptography working with a certificate authority, is now widely used in e-commerce.

FIGURE 8   DIGITAL CERTIFICATES

Digital certificates help establish the identity of people or electronic assets. They protect online transactions by providing secure, encrypted, online communication.

5   HANDS-ON MIS

The projects in this section give you hands-on experience developing a disaster recovery plan, using spreadsheet software for risk analysis, and using Web tools to research security outsourcing services.

Achieving Operational Excellence: Developing a Disaster Recovery Plan

Software skills: Web browser and presentation software
Business skills: Disaster recovery planning

This project requires you to develop a disaster recovery plan for a real-world company.

Management is concerned that Dirt Bikes's computer systems could be vulnerable to power outages, vandalism, computer viruses, natural disasters, or telecommunications disruptions. You have been asked to perform an analysis of system vulnerabilities and disaster recovery planning for the company. Your report should answer the following questions:

- What are the most likely threats to the continued operation of Dirt Bikes's systems?

- What would you identify as Dirt Bikes's most critical systems? What is the impact on the company if these systems cannot operate? How long could the company survive if these systems were down? Which systems are the most important to back up and restore in the event of a disaster?

- Use the Web to locate two disaster recovery services that could be used by a small business such as Dirt Bikes. Compare them in terms of the services they offer. Which should Dirt Bikes use? Exactly how could these services help Dirt Bikes recover from a disaster?

- (Optional) If possible, use electronic presentation software to summarize your findings for management.

Improving Decision Making: Using Spreadsheet Software to Perform a Security Risk Assessment

Software skills: Spreadsheet formulas and charts
Business skills: Risk assessment

This project uses spreadsheet software to calculate anticipated annual losses from various security threats identified for a small company.

Mercer Paints is a small but highly regarded paint manufacturing company located in Alabama. The company has a network in place linking many of its business operations. Although the firm believes that its security is adequate, the recent addition of a Web site has become an open invitation to hackers. Management requested a risk assessment. The risk assessment identified a number of potential exposures. These exposures, their associated probabilities, and average losses are summarized in the following table.

- In addition to the potential exposures listed, you should identify at least three other potential threats to Mercer Paints, assign probabilities, and estimate a loss range.

- Use spreadsheet software and the risk assessment data to calculate the expected annual loss for each exposure.

MERCER PAINTS RISK ASSESSMENT

EXPOSURE	PROBABILITY OF OCCURRENCE (%)	AVERAGE LOSS ($)
Malware attack	60%	$75,000
Data loss	12%	$70,000
Embezzlement	3%	$30,000
User errors	95%	$25,000
Threats from hackers	95%	$90,000
Improper use by employees	5%	$5,000
Power failure	15%	$300,000

- Present your findings in the form of a chart. Which control points have the greatest vulnerability? What recommendations would you make to Mercer Paints? Prepare a written report that summarizes your findings and recommendations.

Improving Decision Making: Evaluating Security Outsourcing Services

Software skills: Web browser and presentation software
Business skills: Evaluating business outsourcing services

Businesses today have a choice of whether to outsource the information systems security function or maintain their own internal staff for this purpose. This project will help develop your Internet skills in using the Web to research and evaluate information system security outsourcing services.

As an information systems expert in your firm, you have been asked to help management decide whether to outsource security or keep the security function within the firm. Search the Web to find information to help you decide whether to outsource security and to locate security outsourcing services.

- Present a brief summary of the arguments for and against outsourcing system security for your company.
- Select two firms that offer system security outsourcing services, and compare them and their services.
- Prepare an electronic presentation for management summarizing your findings. Your presentation should make the case on whether or not your company should outsource system security. If you believe your company should outsource, the presentation should identify which security outsourcing service should be selected and justify your selection.

LEARNING TRACK MODULES

General and Application Controls for Information Systems. If you want to learn more about the various types of controls used in information systems, you will find a Learning Track on general and application controls on the Laudon Web site and Student CD-ROM for this chapter.

Management Challenges of Security and Control. If you want to learn more about management challenges and decisions concerning security and control, you will find a Learning Track on that topic on the Laudon Web site and Student CD-ROM for this chapter.

Software Vulnerability and Reliability. If you want to learn more about software vulnerability and measures to ensure software reliability, you will find a Learning Track on these topics on the Laudon Web site and Student CD-ROM for this chapter.

Summary

1. *Analyze why information systems need special protection from destruction, error, and abuse.*

    With data concentrated into electronic form and many procedures invisible through automation, computerized information systems are vulnerable to destruction, misuse, error, fraud, and hardware or software failures. Corporate systems using the Internet are especially vulnerable because the Internet is designed to be an open system and makes internal corporate systems more vulnerable to actions from outsiders. Hackers can unleash denial-of-service (DoS) attacks or penetrate corporate networks, causing serious system disruptions. Wi-Fi networks easily can be penetrated by intruders using sniffer programs to obtain an address to access the resources of the network. Computer viruses and worms can spread rampantly from system to system, clogging computer memory or destroying programs and data. Software presents problems because software bugs may be impossible to eliminate and because software vulnerabilities can be exploited by hackers and malicious software. End users can introduce errors.

2. *Assess the business value of security and control.*

    Security and control are important but often-neglected areas for information systems investment. Firms relying on computer systems for their core business functions can lose sales and productivity. Information assets, such as confidential employee records, trade secrets, or business plans, lose much of their value if they are revealed to outsiders or if they expose the firm to legal liability. New laws, such as HIPAA, the Sarbanes-Oxley Act, and the Gramm-Leach-Bliley Act, require companies to practice stringent electronic records management and adhere to strict standards for security, privacy, and control. Legal actions requiring electronic evidence and computer forensics also require firms to pay more attention to security and electronic records management.

3. *Design an organizational framework for security and control.*

    Firms need to establish an appropriate organizational and managerial framework for security and control to use technologies effectively to protect their information resources. A risk assessment evaluates information assets, identifies control points and control weaknesses, and determines the most cost-effective set of controls.

    Firms must also develop a coherent corporate security policy and plans for continuing business operations in the event of disaster or disruption. The security policy includes policies for acceptable use and authorization. A disaster recovery plan provides procedures and facilities for restoring computing and communication services after they have been disrupted, whereas a business continuity plan focuses on how the company can restore business operations.

    Comprehensive and systematic MIS auditing helps organizations determine the effectiveness of security and controls for their information systems.

4. *Evaluate the most important tools and technologies for safeguarding information resources.*

    Companies require special measures to support electronic commerce and digital business processes. They can use fault-tolerant computer systems or create high-availability computing environments to make sure that their information systems are always available and performing without interruptions. Firewalls are placed between an organization's private network and external networks, such as the Internet, to prevent unauthorized users from accessing the private network. Intrusion detection systems monitor private networks from suspicious network traffic and attempts to access corporate systems. Passwords, tokens, smart cards, and biometric authentication are used to authenticate system users. Antivirus software checks computer systems for infections by viruses and worms and often eliminates the malicious software, while antispyware software combats intrusive and harmful spyware programs. Encryption, the coding and scrambling of messages, is a widely used technology for securing electronic transmissions over the Internet and over Wi-Fi networks. Digital certificates combined with public key encryption provide further protection of electronic transactions by authenticating a user's identity.

Key Terms

Acceptable use policy (AUP)
Access control
Antivirus software
Application proxy filtering
Authentication
Authorization management systems
Authorization policies
Biometric authentication
Botnet
Business continuity planning
Chief security officer (CSO)
Click fraud
Computer forensics
Computer virus
Controls
Cracker
Cybervandalism
Denial-of-service (DoS) attack
Digital certificates
Digital signature
Disaster recovery planning
Distributed denial-of-service (DDoS) attack
Downtime
Electronic records management (ERM)
Encryption
Evil twin
Fault-tolerant computer systems
Gramm-Leach-Bliley Act
Hacker
High-availability computing
HIPAA
Identity theft

Intrusion detection systems
ISO 17799
Key loggers
Malware
Managed security service providers (MSSPs)
MIS audit
Network Address Translation (NAT)
Online transaction processing
Packet filtering
Patches
Pharming
Phishing
Public key encryption
Public key infrastructure (PKI)
Recovery-oriented computing
Risk assessment
Sarbanes-Oxley Act
Secure Hypertext Transfer Protocol (S-HTTP)
Secure Sockets Layer (SSL)
Security
Security policy
Smart card
Sniffer
Social engineering
Spoofing
Spyware
Stateful inspection
Token
Transport Layer Security (TLS)
Trojan horse
War driving
Worms

Review Questions

1. Why are computer systems so vulnerable? Describe the most common threats against contemporary information systems.

2. Why are the Internet and Wi-Fi networks so difficult to secure?

3. What is malware? Distinguish among a virus, a worm, and a Trojan horse.

4. What is a hacker? How do hackers create security problems and damage systems?

5. How can software affect system reliability and security?

6. What is computer crime? Provide two examples of crime in which computers are targets and two examples in which computers are used as instruments of crime.

7. What is identity theft? Why is it such a big problem today? How does phishing promote identity theft?

8. How can computer systems and networks be used for cyberterrorism and cyberwarfare?

9. What security problems are created by employees?

10. Define security and control. How do they provide business value? How are security and control related to recent U.S. government regulatory requirements and to computer forensics?

11. What is the function of risk assessment? How is it conducted for information systems?

12. Define and describe the following: security policy, acceptable use policy, authorization policy.

13. Distinguish between fault-tolerant and high-availability computing, and between disaster recovery planning and business continuity planning.

14. How does MIS auditing promote security and control?

15. Name and describe three authentication methods.

16. Describe the roles of firewalls, intrusion detection systems, and antivirus software in promoting security.

17. How can encryption be used to protect information? Describe the role of encryption and digital certificates in a public key infrastructure.

Discussion Questions

1. Security isn't simply a technology issue, it's a business issue. Discuss.

2. If you were developing a business continuity plan for your company, where would you start? What aspects of the business would the plan address?

Video Case

You will find a video case illustrating some of the concepts in this chapter on the Laudon Web site and Student CD-ROM along with questions to help you analyze the case.

Teamwork: Evaluating Security Software Tools

With a group of three or four students, use the Web to research and evaluate security products from two competing vendors, such antivirus software, firewalls, or antispyware software. For each product, describe its capabilities, for what types of businesses it is best suited, and its cost to purchase and install. Which is the best product? Why? If possible, use electronic presentation software to present your findings to the class.

REFERENCES

Anti-Phishing Working Group. "Phishing Activity Trends." (May 2006).

Associated Press. "Worm Damage Could Have Been Reduced." (May 5, 2004).

Austin, Robert D. and Christopher A. R. Darby. "The Myth of Secure Computing." *Harvard Business Review* (June 2003).

Backhouse, James, Carol Hsu, and Aidan McDonnell, *"Toward Public-Key Infrastructure Interoperability." Communications of the ACM 46, no. 6 (June 2003).*

Bank, David. "Mydoom Worm Renews Debate On Cybetr-Ethics." Wall Street Journal (November 11, 2004).

———. "Outbreak!" *The Wall Street Journal* (November 15, 2004).

Bank, David and Riva Richmond. "Where the Dangers Are." *Wall Street Journal Technology Report* (July 18, 2005).

———. "What's That Sneaking into Your Computer?" *Wall Street Journal* (April 26, 2004).

Berghel, Hal. "The Discipline of Internet Forensics." *Communications of the ACM* 46, no. 8 (August 2003).

Biever, Celeste. "Instant Messaging Falls Prey to Worms." (May 14, 2005).

Borzo, Jeannette. "Something's Phishy." *Wall Street Journal* (November 15, 2004).

Brenner, Susan W. "U.S. Cybercrime Law: Defining Offenses." Information Systems Frontiers 6, no. 2 (June 2004).

Byers, Simon and Dave Kormann. "802.11b Access Point Mapping." *Communications of the ACM* 46, no. 5 (May 2003).

Cam Winget, Nancy, Russ Housley, David Wagner, and Jesse Walker. "Security Flaws in 802.11b Data Link Protocols." *Communications of the ACM* 46, no. 5 (May 2003).

Cavusoglu, Huseyin, Birendra Mishra, and Srinivasan Raghunathan, "A Model for Evaluating IT Security Investments." *Communications of the ACM* 47, no. 7 (July 2004).

Chawki, Mohamed. "Phishing in Cyberspace: Issues and Solutions." Computer Crime Research Center (August 19, 2006).

Cox, Mark. "Internet Security Threats Increasing in Maliciousness and Criminal Intent: CompTIA," eChannel Line Daily New (June 19, 2005).

D'Amico, Mary Lisbeth. "Call Security." *The Wall Street Journal* (February 13, 2006).

Darby, Christopher. "The Dollars and Cents of Security." *Optimize Magazine* 12 (October 2002).

Datz,, Todd. "The Interactive Nightmare" CSO Magazine (April 2004).

Delaney, Kevin J. "'Evil Twins' and 'Pharming'." *Wall Street Journal* (May 17, 2005).

Di Pietro, Roberto and Luigi V. Mancini. "Security and Privacy Issues of Handheld and Wearable Wireless Devices." *Communications of the ACM* 46, no. 9 (September 2003).

Evers, Joris. "Kevin Mitnick Web Site Hacked." *ZDNet* (August 21, 2006).

Foley, John. "You Call This Trustworthy Computing?" *Information Week* (February 14, 2005).

Gage, Deborah and Kim S. Nash. "When Bots Attack." Baseline Magazine (April 2006).

Golden, G. Richard III and Vassil Roussev. "Next-Generation Digital Forensics." *Communications of the ACM* 49, No., 2 (February 2006).

Gordon, Lawrence A., Martin P. Loeb, William Lucyshyn, and Robert Richardson. "2006 CSI/FBI Computer Crime and Security Survey." Computer Security Institute (2006).

Gordon, Lawrence A., Martin P. Loeb, William Lucyshyn, and Robert Richardson, "2005 CSI/FBI Computer Crime and Security Survey." Computer Security Institute (2005).

Gordon, Lawrence A., Martin P. Loeb and Tashfeen Sohail. "A Framework for Using Insurance for Cyber-Risk Management. "*Communications of the ACM* 46, no. 3 (March 2003).

Hartman, Amir with Craig LeGrande and Tom Goff. "Lock Out Business Risks." *Optimize Magazine* (December 2005).

Horowitz, Alan S. "Biting Back." *Computerworld* (January 13, 2003).

Housley, Russ and William Arbaugh. "Security Problems in 802.11b Networks." *Communications of the ACM* 46, no. 5 (May 2003).

Hulme, George V. "Dial V for Virus," *Information Week*, December 6, 2004;

ICSA Labs. "Tenth Annual Computer Virus Prevalence Survey." www.icsalabs.com, www.cybertrust.com, accessed June 17, 2005.

Jones, George. "The Absolute Worst (So Far)." *Information Week* (July 10, 2006).

Joshi, James B.D., Walid G. Aref, Arif Ghafoor, and Eugene H. Spafford. "Security Models for Web-Based Applications." *Communications of the ACM* 44, no. 2 (February 2001).

Laudon, Kenneth C. "Data Quality and Due Process in Large Interorganizational Record Systems." *Communications of the ACM* 29 (January 1986a).

Leland, John and Tom Zeller Jr.. "Technology and Easy Credit Give Identity Thieves an Edge." *The New York Times* (May 30, 2005).

Mercuri, Rebeca T. "Analyzing Security Costs." *Communications of the ACM* 46, no. 6 (June 2003)

Mercuri, Rebecca T. "The HIPAA-potamus in Health Care Data Security." *Communications of the ACM* 47, no. 7 (July 2004).

Mitchell, Dan. "It's Here: It's There; It's Spyware." *The New York Times* (May 20, 2006).

Newman, Robert. *Enterprise Security*. Upper Saddle River, NY: Prentice-Hall (2003).

NIST, "Software Vulnerabilities." Workshop on Software Security Assurance Tools, Techniques, and Metrics (November 2005).

Panko, Raymond R. *Corporate Computer and Network Security*. Upper Saddle River, N.J.: Pearson Prentice-Hall (2004).

Reuters. "Sasser Computer Worm Author Confesses in Trial."(July 5, 2005).

Roberts, Paul. "Fake Microsoft Security Trojan on the Loose, Antivirus Firm Says," ID News Service, April 8, 2005.

Roche, Edward M. and George Van Nostrand. *Information Systems, Computer Crime and Criminal Justice*. New York: Barraclough Ltd. (2004).

Schwerha, Joseph J. IV. "Cybercrime: Legal Standards Governing the Collection of Digital Evidence." *Information Systems Frontiers* 6, no. 2 (June 2004).

Searcey, Dionne and Shawn Young, "Arrests Indicate Vulnerability of Web Phone Service to Fraud," *The Wall Street Journal* (June 8, 2006).

Shukla, Sudhindra and Fiona Fui-Hoon Nah. "Web Browsing and Spyware Intrusion." *Communications of the ACM* 48, no. 8 (August 2005).

Straub, Detmar W., and Richard J. Welke. "Coping with Systems Risk: Security Planning Models for Management Decision Making." *MIS Quarterly* 22, no. 4 (December 1998).

Thompson, Roger. "Why Spyware Poses Multiple Threats to Security." *Communications of the ACM* 48, no. 8 (August 2005).

Thomson, Iain. "Akamai Investigates Denial of Service Attack." vunet.com (June 17, 2004).

Vara, Vauhini. "Tech Companies Check Software Earlier for Flaws." *The Wall Street Journal* (May 4, 2006).

Vara, Vauhini. "Lurking in the Shadows." *Wall Street Journal Technology Report* (July 18, 2005).

Volonino, Linda and Stephen R. Robinson. *Principles and Practices of Information Security*. Upper Saddle River, NJ: Prentice-Hall (2004)

Wang, Huaiqing and Chen Wang. "Taxonomy of Security Considerations and Software Quality." *Communications of the ACM* 46, no. 6 (June 2003).

Warkentin, Merrill, Xin Luo, and Gary F. Templeton. "A Framework for Spyware Assessement." *Communications of the ACM* 48, no. 8 (August 2005).

Zeller, Tom Jr. "The Scramble to Protect Personal Data." *New York Times* (June 9, 2005).

Zhou, Jianying. "Achieving Fair Nonrepudiation in Electronic Transactions." *Journal of Organizational Computing and Electronic Commerce* 11, no. 4 (2001).

A Stolen Laptop at the Department of Veterans Affairs: The Worst Data Theft Ever?
CASE STUDY

The Department of Veterans Affairs (VA) is responsible for dispensing federal benefits such as healthcare, burial, disability compensation, and pensions to U.S. military veterans and their families. It serves roughly 63 million people who are eligible for benefits.

On May 22, 2006, the VA revealed that a laptop and disks containing the personal electronic files of 26.5 million military veterans had been stolen from the home of a longtime Veterans Affairs employee on May 3. The employee, a data analyst, brought the materials home in order to work on a project from his residence in Aspen Hill, Maryland. At that time it was believed that the analyst had done this without authorization. The data stolen included names, social security numbers, and birth dates of veterans who were discharged from the military starting in 1975. Also involved were files of veterans who were discharged earlier and later filed claims with the VA. The stolen data were not related to health records or financial information, but they were not encrypted.

The VA announced that it could find no evidence suggesting that the stolen data had been used illegally. The department went on to assert that the perpetrators of the burglary might not even know what they possessed or how to use it. Jim Nicholson, Secretary of Veterans Affairs, wrote a letter to the veterans whose data were potentially exposed, advising these veterans to be "extra vigilant" in monitoring their bank and credit card statements. The VA set up a call center and a Web site to field queries from veterans. In the first few days after the theft was announced, the VA received over 100,000 calls to its toll-free information line.

The theft of the VA data occurred at a time when the nation's confidence in the security of personal data was at an all-time low. Security breaches at ChoicePoint in February 2005 and at CardSystems Solutions the following June had shaken the belief that companies entrusted with sensitive personal data could adequately protect them. ChoicePoint, the world's largest commercial data broker, failed to properly screen its customers, enabling thieves to gain access to the personal data of over 150,000 consumers. At CardSystems, a payment processor that handles transactions for major credit card companies, a hacking incident compromised the credit card accounts of 40 million consumers. In the wake of these and other scandals, a number of states enacted laws to compel organizations that process private data to inform consumers when their data have been compromised. Though Congress has debated a number of similar bills, it has been unable to come to a consensus on the issue, so no federal statute exists.

With 26.5 million records exposed, the VA breach was the second largest such case after CardSystems and the largest unauthorized disclosure of social security identification data. Such data are particularly useful to anyone intent on identity theft because they are used for accessing credit reports, bank accounts, and credit card accounts.

The acting VA inspector general reported to Congress that his office had been concerned with the department's security controls since 2001. The inspector general had concluded that the operating system, password system, and detection alerts were all vulnerable to security breaches. The leadership of the VA was more seriously called into question for the way it initially responded to the data theft. The department did not report the incident to law enforcement until two weeks after it found out about it. Officials from the Justice Department and the Federal Bureau of Investigation (FBI) felt that the delay may have inhibited their ability to perform a thorough investigation and solve the case.

The VA did not initially offer a statement explaining why it waited before informing law enforcement or the public. Nicholson himself did not learn about the theft until 13 days after it occurred. It was unclear how many people knew about the theft before Nicholson did, and who eventually made the decision to tell him.

When the burglary occurred, the data analyst informed his supervisors, but they did not tell the inspector general's office right away. VA Inspector General George Opfer became aware of the issue as a result of office gossip. The inspector general's office was only able to begin an investigation on May 10 because one of its employees heard discussion about a burglary during a regular meeting. In testimony before Senate and House panels investigating the breach, Opfer revealed that the employee whose house was burglarized had been routinely transporting the data to his home for three years, unbeknownst to his supervisors. The data analyst was placed on administrative leave for the investigation. He was not thought to have broken any laws.

According to Opfer, a 2004 audit of the VA included recommendations to centralize IT security programs, to ensure that employee job descriptions contained proper rules about what data they could access, and to complete work on intrusion detection systems, infrastructure protection actions, and better access controls. None of these recommendations were fully implemented.

Two former CIOs from the VA, John Gauss and Robert McFarland, appeared before the House Committee on Veterans' Affairs and offered opinions on how to improve information security at the department. They agreed that centralized management of all IT programs and activities was paramount. McFarland noted that decentralized management is deep-rooted at the agency, making it resistant to change. Gauss cited such "cultural impediments" as reasons why he was unable to institute central management of IT at the departmental level or a strong information security program during his tenure. Gauss wanted to introduce a horizontal structure that would be less susceptible to delays, budget overruns, and performance failures.

Both former CIOs stressed that the VA CIO and the chief information security officer needed to have greater direct authority to enforce security policies and mandates. They agreed with the recommendation of Committee Chairman Steve Buyer that the CIO be raised in rank to undersecretary and the chief information security officer be raised to the assistant secretary level. McFarland left the agency in April 2006 when he became frustrated with the implementation of a new "federated" IT management system whose purpose was to reduce costs and make the department more efficient.

Nicholson approved the reorganization in October 2005, enabling the VA to divide its IT operations into two domains. Congress also passed a bill that gave a single executive control over all of the department's IT spending. The VA planned to merge the two IT domains to finally centralize IT programs and activities completely. McFarland testified that such a

consolidation was the only hope for ensuring a secure IT environment.

These actions were of little consolation to veterans. Five veterans' groups came together to file a class-action suit against the federal government in response to the burglary and the delayed actions of the VA in its aftermath. The suit required the VA to provide full disclosure of which veterans were affected by the theft and asked for damages awards of $1,000 for each—a potential payout of $26.5 billion. Language in the complaint accused the VA of disregarding the privacy rights of veterans and "recklessly failing to make even the most rudimentary effort to safeguard" their personal information.

The VA consulted credit-monitoring services to plan assistance for those that might be affected—a list which had grown to include as many as 50,000 Navy and National Guard personnel. The Bush administration later asked Congress to approve a $160.5 million package to cover the cost of free credit monitoring for all of the veterans and military personnel whose records were in the stolen database. In the weeks following the disclosure of the breach, the VA also announced that the stolen data included disability codes and, perhaps, phone numbers and addresses.

The VA finally had some good news in late June 2006 when the stolen laptop and storage media were recovered. Initial forensic analysis indicated that the database had not been accessed since the date of the theft, but further tests would determine if the data had been duplicated or accessed in any way. Nicholson said that law enforcement officials had told him that there was reason to be optimistic that the data had not been utilized. Lawmakers, while pleased with the progress of the investigation, were not prepared to let the VA off the hook. Representative Lane Evans, the ranking Democrat on the Veterans Affairs Committee, summed up their feelings by stating, "Today's announcement does not relieve the Department of Veterans Affairs from fixing its broken data security system and failed leadership."

The leadership of the agency was again called into question when the Veterans Affairs Committee revealed that documents obtained from the VA showed that the data analyst did have authorization to take home a laptop and use a software package to work with the data. The Associated Press detailed three such documents dating back to 2002. The documents respectively authorized the analyst to use at home special software designed to manipulate large amounts of data, to access the social security numbers of millions of veterans, and to remove a laptop and other accessories from the VA building for outside work. The documents weakened the agency's defense that it had security policies in place, but the employee violated the policies. Nonetheless, Nicholson had by this time decided to fire the employee, a decision which the analyst formally challenged.

On August 5, 2006, authorities arrested two teenagers from Rockville, Maryland, for the theft of the laptop and hard drive. They were charged with first-degree burglary and theft over $500. A third suspect, a juvenile, was also facing charges. The burglary was committed randomly and the teenagers did not realize what data were on the stolen equipment until the case gained notoriety.

With that chapter of the case closed, Congress and the VA itself could turn their full attention to what went wrong and how to prevent it from happening again. Those goals were made all the more urgent just a few days after the arrests when the VA announced that a desktop computer containing the personal information of 38,000 veterans was missing from an office of Unisys Corp in Reston, Virginia. The VA had subcontracted Unisys to perform insurance collection tasks for VA medical centers in Pittsburgh and Philadelphia. The computer may have contained records of patients' names, addresses, social security numbers, dates of birth, insurance company names, billing information, dates of military service, claims data, and medical information. The data were not classified, nor were they encrypted—the contract did not require encryption. The VA teamed with Unisys to notify the veterans who might be affected and offered them credit-monitoring services. Unisys could not immediately determine whether the computer had been stolen or simply misplaced. The company was reviewing security tapes, records, and logs as well as conducting interviews in its quest to resolve the issue.

Sources: Hope Yen, "Veterans' ID Theft May Be Largest Ever," The Associated Press, accessed via Forbes.com, May 23, 2006; David Stout and Tom Zeller Jr., "Vast Data Cache About Veterans Is Stolen," *The New York Times*, May 23, 2006; David Stout and Tom Zeller Jr., "Agency Delayed Reporting Theft of Veterans' Data," *The New York Times*, May 24, 2006; David Stout, "Veterans Chief Voices Anger on Data Theft," *The New York Times*, May 25, 2006; Hope Yen, "VA Breach Discovered Through Office Gossip," The Associated Press, accessed via Washingtonpost.com, May 25, 2006; David Stout, "Veteran Data Was Removed Routinely, Official Says," *The New York Times*, May 26, 2006; Hope Yen, "Veterans' Groups Sue Over Data Theft," The Associated Press, accessed via Msnbc.com, June 6, 2006; Jaikumar Vijayan, "IT Centralization at VA Key to Security, Former Agency CIOs Say," *Computerworld*, June 29, 2006; Christopher Lee and Zachary A. Goldfarb, "Stolen VA Laptop and Hard Drive Recovered," *The Washington Post*, June 30, 2006; Brian Westley, "2 Teens Arrested in Theft of VA Laptop," The Associated Press, accessed via Yahoo News, August 5, 2006; Linda Rosencrance, "Update: Another VA Computer Missing," *Computerworld*, August 8, 2006; and Larry Greenemeier, "No More Excuses," *Information Week*, May 29, 2006.

CASE STUDY QUESTIONS

1. List and describe the security weaknesses at the Department of Veterans Affairs.
2. What management, organization, and technology factors contributed to these weaknesesses?
3. How effectively did the VA deal with these problems?
4. What solutions would you suggest to prevent these security problems?

Achieving Operational Excellence and Customer Intimacy: Enterprise Applications

From *Management Information Systems: Managing the Digital Firm, 10/e*. Kenneth C. Laudon, Jane P. Laudon. Copyright © 2007 by Pearson Prentice Hall. All rights reserved.

Achieving Operational Excellence and Customer Intimacy: Enterprise Applications

LEARNING OBJECTIVES

After reading this chapter, you will be able to:

1. Demonstrate how enterprise systems achieve operational excellence by integrating and coordinating diverse functions and business processes in the firm.

2. Demonstrate how supply chain management systems coordinate planning, production, and logistics with suppliers.

3. Demonstrate how customer relationship management systems achieve customer intimacy by integrating all customer information and making it available throughout the firm.

4. Assess the challenges posed by enterprise applications.

5. Describe how enterprise applications can be used in platforms for new cross-functional services.

Interactive Sessions:

IHOP Cooks Customer Data to Order

Invacare Struggles with Its Enterprise System Implementation

CHAPTER OUTLINE

1 **ENTERPRISE SYSTEMS**
What Are Enterprise Systems?
Enterprise Software
Business Value of Enterprise Systems

2 **SUPPLY CHAIN MANAGEMENT SYSTEMS**
The Supply Chain
Information and Supply Chain Management
Supply Chain Management Applications
Supply Chain Management and the Internet
Business Value of Supply Chain Management Systems

3 **CUSTOMER RELATIONSHIP MANAGEMENT SYSTEMS**
What Is Customer Relationship Management?
Customer Relationship Management Software
Operational and Analytical CRM
Business Value of Customer Relationship Management Systems

4 **ENTERPRISE APPLICATIONS: NEW OPPORTUNITIES AND CHALLENGES**
Enterprise Application Challenges
Extending Enterprise Software

5 **HANDS-ON MIS**
Achieving Operational Excellence: Identifying Supply Chain Management Solutions: Dirt Bikes USA
Improving Decision Making: Using Database Software to Manage Customer Service Requests
Achieving Operational Excellence: Evaluating Supply Chain Management Services

LEARNING TRACK MODULES
SAP Business Process Map
Best Practices Business Processes in CRM Software

WHIRLPOOL FIXES ITS SUPPLY CHAIN

Whirlpool, based in Benton Harbor, Michigan, is the number one U.S. home appliance maker, producing washers, dryers, refrigerators, ovens, and more under brand names such as Whirlpool, Kitchen Aid, Roper, and Speed Queen. Whirlpool manages nearly 50 manufacturing and research centers and 80 distribution centers all over the world. The company had grown so much by acquisition and geographic expansion that it strained its old systems for supply chain management.

By 2000, Whirlpool's supply chain "system" had become what salespeople called a "sales disabler." Whirlpool's inventory of finished goods was very high, yet the percentage of time that Whirlpool's products were available when customers needed them was an unacceptably low 87 percent. Staff grimly joked that among the four major U.S. appliance makers, Whirlpool ranked fifth in delivery performance.

The systems Whirlpool used at that time to manage its North American supply chain consisted of aging custom-developed systems for production scheduling and distribution planning; demand forecasting software from i2 Technologies that had been installed in 1997; and SAP's R/3 enterprise resource planning (ERP) software for accounting and order processing. The homegrown systems were very outdated and not well integrated with the ERP system or each other. They also weren't integrated with the systems of major suppliers of parts and materials and of wholesale customers. As a result, Whirlpool's supply chain management systems lacked precision and could only balance priorities and constraints through slow and cumbersome manual procedures.

One solution tried by Whirlpool was to overstock its warehouses to ensure items were in plentiful supply, even if there were more than enough for customer orders. However, this raised inventory carrying costs, further eroding profits. Moreover, the company continued to lose sales because its systems still made the wrong decisions about which specific items to stock in warehouses. Retail sellers still did not have the appliances customers wanted at the time of purchase.

In 2001, Whirlpool began a global overhaul of its supply chain systems. Manufacturing companies typically think about their supply chains as something that originates with suppliers. Whirlpool's management decided its supply chain solution should focus on serving the customer. A world-class solution that would surpass the performance of Whirlpool's best competitors on every front would cost $85 million, which was much too expensive. So managers settled on alternative solutions where the company could meet—and sometimes beat—the competition at a minimum cost.

Whirlpool implemented an advanced planning and scheduling (APS) system that

Photo courtesy of AP Wide World Photos

included a suite of supply chain integration and optimization software from i2 Technologies. These tools consisted of Supply Chain Planner for Master Scheduling, Deployment Planner, Inventory Planner, and Demand Planner. These modules were implemented in phases during 2001 and 2002.

In 2002, Whirlpool installed i2 TradeMatrix Collaborative Planning, Forecasting, and Replenishment (CPFR), a Web-based tool for sharing and combining the sales forecasts of Whirlpool and its major sales partners—Sears, Roebuck and Co., Lowe's, and Best Buy.

Even before Whirlpool's supply chain project was completed, it had already produced huge improvements in customer service and reduced supply chain costs. APS boosted availability in North America to 97 percent while reducing finished-goods inventories by more than 20 percent, and freight and warehouse costs by 5 percent. CPFR cut the number of forecasting errors in half.

Sources: I2 Technologies, "Whirlpool Achieves Maximum Supply Chain Value with i2 BOS," www.i2.com, accessed September 1, 2006; Gary H. Anthes, "Supply Chain Whirl," *Computerworld*, June 6, 2005; and www.whirlpool.com, accessed September 3, 2006.

Whirlpool's problems with its supply chain illustrate the critical role of supply chain management in business. Whirlpool lost sales because it couldn't balance supply with demand across multiple distribution sites and locations to make sure the right products required by customers were in the right stores and warehouses at the right time. The company needed better control over its supply chain.

The chapter-opening diagram calls attention to important points raised by this case and this chapter. Like all large firms, Whirlpool has several hundred main suppliers of parts, and these suppliers in turn have hundreds of suppliers of basic parts and raw materials. Altogether, Whirlpool deals with several thousand firms that sell everything from steel and plastic assemblies, to computer chips and controls that end up in Whirlpool appliances. Coordinating all these firms so that the right parts show up at the Whirlpool factories just at the right time and that the right amount of finished appliances actually ordered by customers are in the warehouses was a major problem. Replacing outdated systems with supply chain management software from i2 Technologies improved coordination of Whirlpool inventory with demand, raising sales, lowering costs, and ultimately increasing profitability.

HEADS UP

This chapter focuses on how firms use enterprise-wide systems to achieve operational excellence, customer intimacy, and improved decision making. Enterprise systems and systems for supply chain management and customer relationship management help companies integrate information from many different parts of the business, forge closer ties with customers, and coordinate firm activities with those of suppliers and other business partners.

- If your career is in finance and accounting, you will be working with enterprise resource planning systems with comprehensive financial modules that integrate financial information from manufacturing, marketing, and sales.
- If your career is in human resources, you will be helping your firm deal with the "people" issues that are critical to the successful implementation of enterprise applications, such as changing job responsibilities, new training, and overcoming resistance to the change.
- If your career is in information systems, you will be evaluating and installing software for enterprise applications and helping your company redesign its business processes to work with the new software.
- If your career is in manufacturing, production, or operations management, you will be using enterprise systems and supply chain management systems to plan, make, and deliver products and services to customers more rapidly and accurately at lower cost.
- If your career is in sales and marketing, you will be using customer relationship management systems to plan marketing campaigns, identify profitable customers, advance new products and services, generate sales leads, and fine-tune customer service.

1 ENTERPRISE SYSTEMS

Around the globe, companies are increasingly becoming more connected, both internally and with other companies. If you run a business, you want to be able to react instantaneously when a customer places a large order or when a shipment from a supplier is delayed. You may also want to know the impact of these events on every part of the business and how the business is performing at any point in time, especially if you're running a large company. Enterprise systems provide the integration to make this possible. Let's look at how they work and what they can do for the firm.

WHAT ARE ENTERPRISE SYSTEMS?

Imagine that you had to run a business based on information from tens or even hundreds of different databases and systems, none of which could speak to one another? Imagine your company had 10 different major product lines, each produced in separate factories, and each with separate and incompatible sets of systems controlling production, warehousing, and distribution. Your decision making would often be based on manual hard copy reports, often out of date, and it would be difficult to really understand what was happening in the business as whole. You would have a very poor grasp of how profitable the firm was as a whole, or what your costs were. You now have a good idea of why firms need a special enterprise system to integrate information.

Enterprise systems, also known as enterprise resource planning (ERP) systems, are based on a suite of integrated software modules and a common central database. The database collects data from many different divisions and departments in a firm, and from a large number of key business processes in manufacturing and production, finance and accounting, sales and marketing, and human resources, making the data available for applications that support nearly all of an organization's internal business activities. When new information is entered by one process, the information is made immediately available to other business processes (see Figure 1).

If a sales representative places an order for tire rims, for example, the system verifies the customer's credit limit, schedules the shipment, identifies the best shipping route, and reserves the necessary items from inventory. If inventory stock were insufficient to fill the order, the system schedules the manufacture of more rims, ordering the needed materials and components from suppliers. Sales and production forecasts are immediately updated. General ledger and corporate cash levels are automatically updated with the revenue and cost information from the order. Users could tap into the system and find out where that particular order was at any minute. Management could obtain information at any point in time about how the business was operating. The system could also generate enterprise-wide data for management analyses of product cost and profitability.

FIGURE 1   HOW ENTERPRISE SYSTEMS WORK

Enterprise systems feature a set of integrated software modules and a central database that enables data to be shared by many different business processes and functional areas throughout the enterprise.

ENTERPRISE SOFTWARE

Enterprise software is built around thousands of predefined business processes that reflect best practices. **Best practices** are the most successful solutions or problem-solving methods in an industry for consistently and effectively achieving a business objective. Best practices emerge from two sources: consulting firms who work for many firms in an industry and enterprise software firms that develop industry expertise working with many clients. When your firm hires a consulting company or enterprise software firm to help you build your own enterprise system, you are in reality hiring the knowledge base of best practices accumulated by these companies over many years. Table 1 describes some of the major business processes supported by enterprise software.

Companies implementing this software would have to first select the functions of the system they wished to use and then map their business processes to the predefined business processes in the software. (The first Learning Track for this chapter shows how SAP enterprise software handles the procurement process for a new piece of equipment.) A firm would use configuration tables provided by the software to tailor a particular aspect of the system to the way it does business. For example, the firm could use these tables to select whether it wants to track revenue by product line, geographical unit, or distribution channel.

If the enterprise software does not support the way the organization does business, companies can rewrite some of the software to support the way their business processes work. However, enterprise software is unusually complex, and extensive customization may degrade system performance, compromising the information and process integration that are the main benefits of the system. If companies want to reap the maximum benefits from enterprise software, they must change the way they work to conform to the business processes in the software.

Major enterprise software vendors include SAP, Oracle (with its acquisition of PeopleSoft), SSA Global, Lawson Software, and Microsoft (which sells the Dynamics software suite). There are versions of enterprise software packages designed for small businesses and versions obtained through application service providers over the Web. Although initially designed to automate the firm's internal back-office business processes, enterprise systems have become

TABLE 1   BUSINESS PROCESSES SUPPORTED BY ENTERPRISE SYSTEMS

Financial and accounting processes, including general ledger, accounts payable, accounts receivable, fixed assets, cash management and forecasting, product-cost accounting, cost-center accounting, asset accounting, tax accounting, credit management, and financial reporting

Human resources processes, including personnel administration, time accounting, payroll, personnel planning and development, benefits accounting, applicant tracking, time management, compensation, workforce planning, performance management, and travel expense reporting

Manufacturing and production processes, including procurement, inventory management, purchasing, shipping, production planning, production scheduling, material requirements planning, quality control, distribution, transportation execution, and plant and equipment maintenance

Sales and marketing processes, including order processing, quotations, contracts, product configuration, pricing, billing, credit checking, incentive and commission management, and sales planning more externally oriented and capable of communicating with customers, suppliers, and other organizations.

BUSINESS VALUE OF ENTERPRISE SYSTEMS

Enterprise systems provide value both by increasing operational efficiency and by providing firm-wide information to help managers make better decisions. Large companies with many operating units in different locations have used enterprise systems to enforce standard practices and data so that everyone does business the same way worldwide.

Coca-Cola, for instance, implemented a SAP enterprise system to standardize and coordinate important business processes in 200 countries. Lack of standard, company-wide business processes prevented the company from leveraging its worldwide buying power to obtain lower prices for raw materials and from reacting rapidly to market changes.

Enterprise systems help firms respond rapidly to customer requests for information or products. Because the system integrates order, manufacturing, and delivery data, manufacturing is better informed about producing only what customers have ordered, procuring exactly the right amount of components or raw materials to fill actual orders, staging production, and minimizing the time that components or finished products are in inventory.

Enterprise software includes analytical tools for using data captured by the system to evaluate overall organizational performance. Enterprise system data have common standardized definitions and formats that are accepted by the entire organization. Performance figures mean the same thing across the company. Enterprise systems allow senior management to easily find out at any moment how a particular organizational unit is performing or to determine which products are most or least profitable.

2   SUPPLY CHAIN MANAGEMENT SYSTEMS

If you manage a small firm that makes a few products or sells a few services, chances are you will have a small number of suppliers. You could coordinate your supplier orders and deliveries using a telephone and fax machine. But if you manage a firm that produces more complex products and services, then you will have hundreds or even thousands of suppliers, and your suppliers will each have their own set of suppliers. Suddenly, you are in a situation where you will need to coordinate the activities of many supplier firms in order to produce your products and services. Supply chain management systems are an answer to these problems of supply chain complexity and scale.

THE SUPPLY CHAIN

A firm's **supply chain** is a network of organizations and business processes for procuring raw materials, transforming these materials into intermediate and finished products, and distributing the finished products to customers. It links suppliers, manufacturing plants, distribution centers, retail outlets, and customers to supply goods and services from source through consumption. Materials, information, and payments flow through the supply chain in both directions.

Goods start out as raw materials and, as they move through the supply chain, are transformed into intermediate products (also referred to as components or parts), and finally, into finished products. The finished products are shipped to distribution centers and from there to retailers and customers. Returned items flow in the reverse direction from the buyer back to the seller.

Let's look at the supply chain for Nike sneakers as an example. Nike designs, markets, and sells sneakers, socks, athletic clothing, and accessories throughout the world. Its primary suppliers are contract manufacturers with factories in China, Thailand, Indonesia, Brazil, and other countries. These companies fashion Nike's finished products.

Nike's contract suppliers do not manufacture sneakers from scratch. They obtain components for the sneakers—the laces, eyelets, uppers, and soles—from other suppliers and then assemble them into finished sneakers. These suppliers in turn have their own suppliers. For example, the suppliers of soles have suppliers for synthetic rubber, suppliers for chemicals used to melt the rubber for molding, and suppliers for the molds into which to pour the rubber. Suppliers of laces have suppliers for their thread, dyes, and for the plastic lace tips.

Figure 2 provides a simplified illustration of Nike's supply chain for sneakers. It shows the flow of information and materials among suppliers, Nike, and Nike's distributors, retailers, and customers. Nike's contract manufacturers are its primary suppliers. The suppliers of soles, eyelets, uppers, and laces are the secondary (Tier 2) suppliers. Suppliers to these suppliers are the tertiary (Tier 3) suppliers.

The *upstream* portion of the supply chain includes the company's suppliers, the suppliers' suppliers, and the processes for managing relationships with them. The *downstream* portion consists of the organizations and processes for distributing and delivering products to the final customers. Companies doing manufacturing, such as the Nike's contract suppliers of sneakers, also manage their own *internal supply chain* processes for transforming materials, components, and services furnished by their suppliers into finished products or intermediate products (components or parts) for their customers and for managing materials and inventory.

The supply chain illustrated in Figure 2 has been simplified. It only shows two contract manufacturers for sneakers and only the upstream supply chain for sneaker soles. Nike has hundreds of contract manufacturers turning out finished sneakers, socks, and athletic clothing, each with its own set of suppliers. The upstream portion of Nike's supply chain would actually comprise thousands of entities. Nike also has numerous distributors and many thousands of retail stores where its shoes are sold, so the downstream portion of its supply chain is also large and complex.

INFORMATION AND SUPPLY CHAIN MANAGEMENT

Inefficiencies in the supply chain, such as parts shortages, underutilized plant capacity, excessive finished goods inventory, or high transportation costs, are caused by inaccurate or untimely information. For example, manufacturers may keep too many parts in inventory because they do not know exactly when they will receive their next shipments from their suppliers. Suppliers may order too few raw materials because they do not have precise information on demand. These supply chain inefficiencies waste as much as 25 percent of a company's operating costs.

FIGURE 2   NIKE'S SUPPLY CHAIN

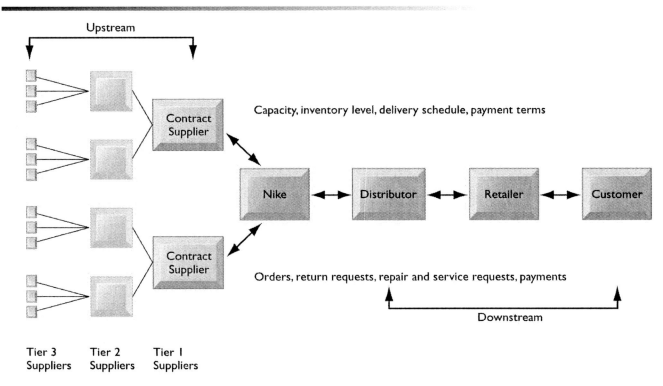

This figure illustrates the major entities in Nike's supply chain and the flow of information upstream and downstream to coordinate the activities involved in buying, making, and moving a product. Shown here is a simplified supply chain, with the upstream portion focusing only on the suppliers for sneakers and sneaker soles.

If a manufacturer had perfect information about exactly how many units of product customers wanted, when they wanted them, and when they could be produced, it would be possible to implement a highly efficient **just-in-time** strategy. Components would arrive exactly at the moment they were needed and finished goods would be shipped as they left the assembly line.

In a supply chain, however, uncertainties arise because many events cannot be foreseen—uncertain product demand, late shipments from suppliers, defective parts or raw materials, or production process breakdowns. To satisfy customers, manufacturers often deal with such uncertainties and unforeseen events by keeping more material or products in inventory than what they think they may actually need. The safety stock acts as a buffer for the lack of flexibility in the supply chain. Although excess inventory is expensive, low fill rates are also costly because business may be lost from canceled orders.

One recurring problem in supply chain management is the **bullwhip effect**, in which information about the demand for a product gets distorted as it passes from one entity to the next across the supply chain. A slight rise in demand for an item might cause different members in the supply chain—distributors, manufacturers, suppliers, secondary suppliers (suppliers' suppliers), and tertiary suppliers (suppliers' suppliers' suppliers)—to stockpile inventory so each has enough "just in case." These changes ripple throughout the supply chain, magnifying what started out as a small change from planned orders, creating excess inventory, production, warehousing, and shipping costs (see Figure 3).

374

FIGURE 3   THE BULLWHIP EFFECT

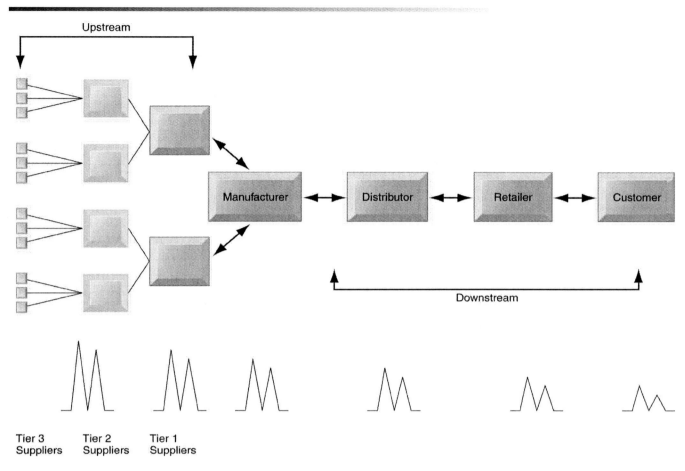

Inaccurate information can cause minor fluctuations in demand for a product to be amplified as one moves further back in the supply chain. Minor fluctuations in retail sales for a product can create excess inventory for distributors, manufacturers, and suppliers.

For example, Procter & Gamble (P&G) found it had excessively high inventories of its Pampers disposable diapers at various points along its supply chain because of such distorted information. Although customer purchases in stores were fairly stable, orders from distributors would spike when P&G offered aggressive price promotions. Pampers and Pampers components accumulated in warehouses along the supply chain to meet demand that did not actually exist. To eliminate this problem, P&G revised its marketing, sales, and supply chain processes and used more accurate demand forecasting (Lee, Padmanabhan, and Wang, 1997).

The bullwhip is tamed by reducing uncertainties about demand and supply when all members of the supply chain have accurate and up-to-date information. If all supply chain members share dynamic information about inventory levels, schedules, forecasts, and shipments, they have more precise knowledge about how to adjust their sourcing, manufacturing, and distribution plans. Supply chain management systems provide the kind of information that helps members of the supply chain make better purchasing and scheduling decisions.

SUPPLY CHAIN MANAGEMENT APPLICATIONS

Supply chain software is classified as either software to help businesses plan their supply chains (supply chain planning) or software to help them execute the supply chain steps (supply chain execution). **Supply chain planning systems** enable the firm to generate demand forecasts for a product and to develop sourcing and manufacturing plans for that product. Such systems help companies make better operating decisions, such as determining how much of a specific product to manufacture in a given time period; establishing inventory levels for raw materials, intermediate products, and finished goods; determining where to store finished goods; and identifying the transportation mode to use for product delivery.

For example, if a large customer places a larger order than usual or changes that order on short notice, it can have a widespread impact throughout the supply chain. Additional raw materials or a different mix of raw materials may need to be ordered from suppliers. Manufacturing may have to change job scheduling. A transportation carrier may have to reschedule deliveries. Supply chain planning software makes the necessary adjustments to production and distribution plans. Information about changes is shared among the relevant supply chain members so that their work can be coordinated. One of the most important—and complex—supply chain planning functions is **demand planning**, which determines how much product a business needs to make to satisfy all of its customers' demands.

Supply chain execution systems manage the flow of products through distribution centers and warehouses to ensure that products are delivered to the right locations in the most efficient manner. They track the physical status of goods, the management of materials, warehouse and transportation operations, and financial information involving all parties. Manugistics (acquired by JDA Software Group) and i2 Technologies are major supply chain management software vendors, and enterprise software vendors SAP and Oracle-PeopleSoft offer supply chain management modules. Table 2 provides more details on supply chain planning and execution systems.

An important use of SmartForecasts demand planning software from Smart Software is to forecast future demand for products where demand is intermittent or irregular. Shown here is a forecast graph for the distribution of total cumulative demand for a spare part over a four-month lead time.

Reprinted with permission of Smart Software, Inc.

TABLE 2   SUPPLY CHAIN PLANNING AND EXECUTION SYSTEMS

CAPABILITIES OF SUPPLY CHAIN PLANNING SYSTEMS

Order planning. Select an order fulfillment plan that best meets the desired level of service to the customer given existing transportation and manufacturing constraints.

Advanced scheduling and manufacturing planning. Provide detailed coordination of scheduling based on an analysis of changing factors, such as customer orders, equipment outages, or supply interruptions. Scheduling modules create job schedules for the manufacturing process and supplier logistics.

Demand planning. Generate demand forecasts from all business units using statistical tools and business forecasting techniques.

Distribution planning. Create operating plans for logistics managers for order fulfillment based on input from demand and manufacturing planning modules.

Transportation planning. Track and analyze inbound, outbound, and intracompany movement of materials and products to ensure that materials and finished goods are delivered at the right time and place at the minimum cost.

CAPABILITIES OF SUPPLY CHAIN EXECUTION SYSTEMS

Order commitments. Enable vendors to quote accurate delivery dates to customers by providing more real-time detailed information on the status of orders from availability of raw materials and inventory to production and shipment status.

Final production. Organize and schedule final subassemblies required to make each final product.

Replenishment. Coordinate component replenishment work so that warehouses remain stocked with the minimum amount of inventory in the pipeline.

Distribution management. Coordinate the process of transporting goods from the manufacturer to distribution centers to the final customer. Provide online customer access to shipment and delivery data.

Reverse distribution. Track the shipment and accounting for returned goods or remanufactured products.

SUPPLY CHAIN MANAGEMENT AND THE INTERNET

Before the Internet, supply chain coordination was hampered by the difficulties of making information flow smoothly among disparate internal supply chain systems for purchasing, materials management, manufacturing, and distribution. It was also difficult to share information with external supply chain partners because the systems of suppliers, distributors, or logistics providers were based on incompatible technology platforms and standards. Enterprise systems could supply some integration of internal supply chain processes but they were not designed to deal with external supply chain processes.

Some supply chain integration is supplied inexpensively using Internet technology. Firms use *intranets* to improve coordination among their internal supply chain processes, and they use *extranets* to coordinate supply chain processes shared with their business partners (see Figure 4).

Using intranets and extranets, all members of the supply chain are instantly able to communicate with each other, using up-to-date information to adjust purchasing, logistics, manufacturing, packaging, and schedules. A manager will use a Web interface to tap into suppliers' systems to determine whether inventory and production capabilities match demand for the firm's products. Business partners will use Web-based supply chain management tools to collaborate online on forecasts. Sales representatives will access suppliers' production schedules and logistics information to monitor a customer's order status. Many companies now use suppliers from many different countries, and the Internet helps them coordinate overseas sourcing, transportation, communications, financing, and compliance with customs regulations.

FIGURE 4   INTRANETS AND EXTRANETS FOR SUPPLY CHAIN MANAGEMENT

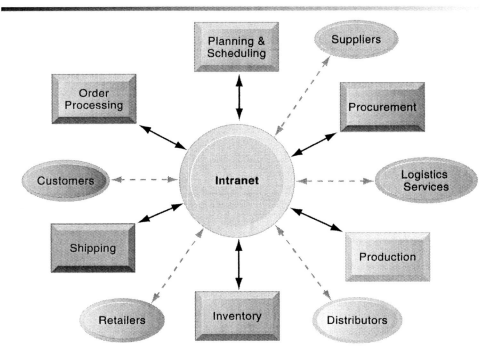

Intranets integrate information from isolated business processes within the firm to help manage its internal supply chain. Access to these private intranets can also be extended to authorized suppliers, distributors, logistics services, and, sometimes, to retail customers to improve coordination of external supply chain processes.

Demand-Driven Supply Chains: From Push to Pull Manufacturing and Efficient Customer Response

In addition to reducing costs, supply chain management systems facilitate efficient customer response, enabling the workings of the business to be driven more by customer demand.

Earlier supply chain management systems were driven by a push-based model (also known as *build-to-stock*). In a **push-based** model, production master schedules are based on forecasts or best guesses of demand for products, and products are "pushed" to customers. With new flows of information made possible by Web-based tools, supply chain management more easily follows a pull-based model. In a **pull-based model**, also known as a *demand-driven model* or *build-to-order*, actual customer orders or purchases trigger events in the supply chain. Transactions to produce and deliver only what customers have ordered move up the supply chain from retailers to distributors to manufacturers and eventually to suppliers. Only products to fulfill these orders move back down the supply chain to the retailer. Manufacturers use only actual order demand information to drive their production schedules and the procurement of components or raw materials, as illustrated in Figure 5. Wal-Mart's continuous replenishment system and Dell Computer's build-to-order system are examples of the pull-based model.

The Internet and Internet technology make it possible to move from sequential supply chains, where information and materials flow sequentially from company to company, to concurrent supply chains, where information

FIGURE 5   PUSH- VERSUS PULL-BASED SUPPLY CHAIN MODELS

Push-Based Model

Supplier ← Manufacturer → Distributor → Retailer → Customer

| Supply to forecast | Production based on forecasts | Inventory based on forecasts | Stock based on forecasts | Purchase what is on shelves |

Pull-Based Model

Supplier ← Manufacturer ← Distributor ← Retailer ← Customer

| Supply to order | Produce to order | Automatically replenish warehouse | Automatically replenish stock | Customer orders |

The difference between push- and pull-based models is summarized by the slogan "Make what we sell, not sell what we make."

flows in many directions simultaneously among members of a supply chain network. Members of the network immediately adjust to changes in schedules or orders. Ultimately, the Internet could create a "digital logistics nervous system" throughout the supply chain. This system permits simultaneous, multidirectional communication of information about participants' inventories, orders, and capacities, optimizing the activities of individual firms and groups of firms interacting in e-commerce marketplaces (see Figure 6).

FIGURE 6   THE FUTURE INTERNET-DRIVEN SUPPLY CHAIN

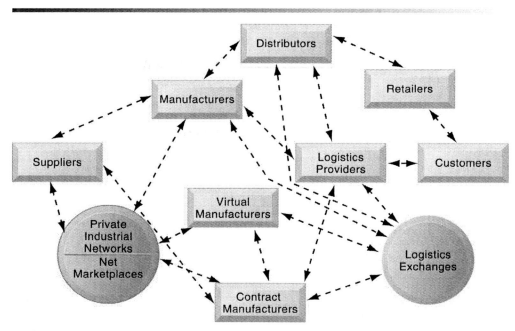

The future Internet-driven supply chain operates like a digital logistics nervous system. It provides multidirectional communication among firms, networks of firms, and e-marketplaces so that entire networks of supply chain partners can immediately adjust inventories, orders, and capacities.

BUSINESS VALUE OF SUPPLY CHAIN MANAGEMENT SYSTEMS

You've just seen how supply chain management systems enable firms to streamline both their internal and external supply chain processes and provide management with more accurate information about what to produce, store, and move. By implementing a networked and integrated supply chain management system, companies match supply to demand, reduce inventory levels, improve delivery service, speed product time to market, and use assets more effectively.

Total supply chain costs represent the majority of operating expenses for many businesses and in some industries approach 75 percent of the total operating budget (Handfield and Nichols, 2002). Reducing supply chain costs may have a major impact on firm profitability.

In addition to reducing costs, supply chain management systems help increase sales. If a product is not available when a customer wants it, customers often try to purchase it from someone else. More precise control of the supply chain enhances the firm's ability to have the right product available for customer purchases at the right time, as illustrated by the chapter-opening case on Whirlpool.

3 CUSTOMER RELATIONSHIP MANAGEMENT SYSTEMS

You've probably heard phrases such as "the customer is always right" or "the customer comes first." Today these words ring more true than ever. Because competitive advantage based on an innovative new product or service is often very short lived, companies are realizing that their only enduring competitive strength may be their relationships with their customers. Some say that the basis of competition has switched from who sells the most products and services to who "owns" the customer, and that customer relationships represent a firm's most valuable asset. Even manufactured goods, like automobiles, come with significant customer service and support content from warranties and road side repairs and towing services built into the purchase price. The distinction between a manufactured product and a service is increasingly difficult to maintain.

WHAT IS CUSTOMER RELATIONSHIP MANAGEMENT?

What kinds of information would you need to build and nurture strong, long-lasting relationships with customers? You'd want to know exactly who your customers are, how to contact them, whether they are costly to service and sell to, what kinds of products and services they are interested in, and how much money they spend on your company. If you could, you'd want to make sure you knew your each of your customers well, as if you were running a small-town store. And you'd want to make your good customers feel special.

In a small business operating in a neighborhood, it is possible for business owners and managers to really know their customers on a personal, face-to-face basis. But in a large business operating on a metropolitan, regional, national, or even global basis, it is impossible to "know your customer" in this intimate way. In these kinds of businesses there are too many customers and too many different ways that customers interact with the firm (over the Web, the phone, fax, and face-to-face). It becomes especially difficult to integrate information from all theses sources and to deal with the large numbers of customers.

This is where customer relationship management systems help. Customer relationship management (CRM) systems capture and integrate customer data from all over the organization, consolidate the data, analyze the data, and then distribute the results to various systems and customer touch points across the enterprise. A **touch point** (also known as a *contact point*) is a method of interaction with the customer, such as telephone, e-mail, customer service desk, conventional mail, Web site, wireless device, or retail store.

Well-designed CRM systems provide a single enterprise view of customers that is useful for improving both sales and customer service. Such systems likewise provide customers with a single view of the company regardless of what touch point the customer uses (see Figure 7).

Good CRM systems provide data and analytical tools for answering questions such as these: "What is the value of a particular customer to the firm over his or her lifetime?" "Who are our most loyal customers?" (It can cost six times more to sell to a new customer than to an existing customer.) "Who are our most profitable customers?" and "What do these profitable customers want to buy?" Firms use the answers to these questions to acquire new customers, provide better service and support to existing customers, customize their offerings more precisely to customer preferences, and provide ongoing value to retain profitable customers.

The Interactive Session on Technology describes how the International House of Pancakes (IHOP) used customer relationship management systems to learn more about its customers and improve customer communication. IHOP installed Oracle Corporation's Customer Data Hub to integrate customer data from multiple sources and Oracle Teleservice software to manage telephone communication about customer service.

FIGURE 7   CUSTOMER RELATIONSHIP MANAGEMENT (CRM)

CRM systems examine customers from a multifaceted perspective. These systems use a set of integrated applications to address all aspects of the customer relationship, including customer service, sales, and marketing.

INTERACTIVE SESSION: TECHNOLOGY

IHOP COOKS CUSTOMER DATA TO ORDER

The International House of Pancakes (IHOP) is known best for serving an estimated three-quarter billion pancakes annually to diners across the United States and Canada. The chain, which is based in Glendale, California, has expanded its menu over the years to include a growing number of traditional lunch and dinner items as well. The promise of a simple, economical, and taste-bud-satisfying dining experience has enabled IHOP to maintain its position as one of the top family restaurant chains in the United States. More than 90 percent of Americans are familiar with the IHOP brand name. The chain includes approximately 1,200 restaurants, more than 90 percent of which are owned by independent franchisees.

IHOP's slogan is "Come Hungry, Leave Happy." But IHOP didn't know as much as it wanted about its customers and how to make them happier. IHOP had been conducting extensive research into demographic trends, spending patterns, and customer preferences. However, according to Patrick Piccininno, IHOP's vice president of information technology, the information in its systems "wasn't available in a useful, easy-to-access way." Each IHOP division worked with a different slice of customer data. In fact, the company employed five different systems for processing sales data, and there was no method for synchronizing or cleansing the data. Piccininno had no idea if separate franchises were finding the same problems or trends.

What IHOP needed was a single central company-wide repository of all of its customer information that could provide a quantifiable picture of customer behavior. "Instead of using gut feel and conjecture, we want to find out what is actually driving customers to us," Piccininno stated.

IHOP could have built an entirely new system based on a centralized company-wide database that was a single source of customer information. This approach would have been prohibitively costly and complicated. Instead, it chose to use Oracle Customer Data Hub middleware to integrate its customer data from its various legacy systems.

Data hubs pull together data from many different applications and make them available for operational systems. Oracle's Customer Data Hub creates a single company-wide view of the customer so that every single customer touch point displays current and consistent information without disrupting existing systems. This integration makes it possible for a call center representative, for instance, to find out whether

the customer on the line does a lot of business with the company.

IHOP's Oracle's Customer Data Hub collects and integrates customer data from six point-of-sales systems, human resources, and financial systems based on Lawson software and an Oracle data warehouse. It also cleans and enriches the customer data as they are collected from source applications. In the past, the company required separate data cleansing, support, and processing work for each of its systems, which was quite costly. Duplicate and inconsistent data have been eliminated.

IHOP adopted Oracle TeleService to improve communication with its customers through a call center. Previously, diners communicated with IHOP via e-mail. However, the company lacked a central process for tracking the e-mail. Consequently, some e-mail was not addressed in a timely manner. There was no mechanism for knowing how long it would take to solve a problem or if specific problems that had been reported were ever solved at all.

With Oracle TeleService, IHOP receives comments and feedback from restaurant guests on a toll-free number. Its information systems department is able to log the calls, route the collected data to the appropriate resource, and track the progress of resolutions to customers' questions and problems. Now restaurant guests who report problems receive a resolution in three days on average. The centralized and encompassing nature of TeleService also enables IHOP to notice trends among its clientele, based on its messages, and take the appropriate action to address the trends.

Individual franchisees have access to the CRM system through portals created with Oracle AS Portal 10g software. Users connect to the portal through a Web browser. IHOP restaurant franchisees are able to see daily sales data, the average check for each day, how promotions are performing, and figures on how well they manage their operations. The portal is customizable to help restaurant owners access the specific types of information they need, while giving IHOP an improved ability to measure customer service.

Sources: "Fresh Guest Data Helps IHOP Franchises Thrive," www.oracle.com, accessed September 5, 2006; Colin Beasty, "CRM Where You Least Expect It," *Customer Relationship Management*, March 2005; Robert Westervelt, "Customer Data Hub Keeps IHOP Stats Hot," searchoracle.techtarget.com, accessed June 7, 2005; and Charles Babcock, "Customer-Data Hubs Inch Ahead," *InformationWeek*, April 25, 2005.

CASE STUDY QUESTIONS   MIS IN ACTION

1. How does knowledge of customers impact IHOP's business performance?

2. Why did IHOP have trouble getting to know its customers?

3. How has the company chosen to improve its knowledge of customers? Analyze the management, organization, and technology dimensions of the solution.

4. Did IHOP choose the best solution? Explain your answer.

Explore IHOP's Web site and answer the following questions:

1. Does this Web site provide opportunities for IHOP to gather data about its customers? Describe the customer data collected at the Web site and explain how IHOP can use the data to improve its business performance.

2. Is this Web site well-designed for interacting with customers and gathering customer data? What other customer data could this Web site collect?

3. How would you redesign the Web site to increase interactions with customers?

CUSTOMER RELATIONSHIP MANAGEMENT SOFTWARE

Commercial CRM software packages range from niche tools that perform limited functions, such as personalizing Web sites for specific customers, to large-scale enterprise applications that capture myriad interactions with customers, analyze them with sophisticated reporting tools, and link to other major enterprise applications, such as supply chain management and enterprise systems. The more comprehensive CRM packages contain modules for **partner relationship management (PRM)** and **employee relationship management (ERM)**.

PRM uses many of the same data, tools, and systems as customer relationship management to enhance collaboration between a company and its selling partners. If a company does not sell directly to customers but rather works through distributors or retailers, PRM helps these channels sell to customers directly. It provides a company and its selling partners with the ability to trade information and distribute leads and data about customers, integrating lead generation, pricing, promotions, order configurations, and availability. It also provides a firm with tools to assess its partners' performance so it can make sure its best partners receive the support they need to close more business.

ERM software deals with employee issues that are closely related to CRM, such as setting objectives, employee performance management, performance-based compensation, and employee training. Major CRM application software vendors include Siebel Systems (acquired by Oracle Corp.), Clarify, and Salesforce.com. Enterprise software vendors, such as SAP and Oracle-PeopleSoft, are also active in customer relationship management and feature tools for integrating their enterprise system modules with their customer relationship management modules.

Customer relationship management systems typically provide software and online tools for sales, customer service, and marketing. We briefly describe some of these capabilities.

Sales Force Automation (SFA)

Sales force automation modules in CRM systems help sales staff increase their productivity by focusing sales efforts on the most profitable customers, those who are good candidates for sales and services. CRM systems provide sales prospect and contact information, product information, product configuration capabilities, and sales quote generation capabilities. Such software can assemble information about a particular customer's past purchases to help the salesperson make personalized recommendations. CRM software enables sales, marketing, and delivery departments to easily share customer and prospect information. It increases each salesperson's efficiency in reducing the cost per sale as well as the cost of acquiring new customers and retaining old ones. CRM software also has capabilities for sales forecasting, territory management, and team selling.

Customer Service

Customer service modules in CRM systems provide information and tools to increase the efficiency of call centers, help desks, and customer support staff. They have capabilities for assigning and managing customer service requests.

One such capability is an appointment or advice telephone line: When a customer calls a standard phone number, the system routes the call to the correct service person, who inputs information about that customer into the system only once. Once the customer's data are in the system, any service representative can handle the customer relationship. Improved access to consistent and accurate customer information helps call centers handle more calls per day and decrease the duration of each call. Thus, call centers and customer service groups achieve greater productivity, reduced transaction time, and higher quality of service at lower cost. The customer is happier because he or she spends less time on the phone restating his or her problem to customer service representatives.

CRM systems may also include Web-based self-service capabilities: The company Web site can be set up to provide inquiring customers personalized support information as well as the option to contact customer service staff by phone for additional assistance.

Marketing

CRM systems support direct-marketing campaigns by providing capabilities for capturing prospect and customer data, for providing product and service information, for qualifying leads for targeted marketing, and for scheduling and tracking direct-marketing mailings or e-mail (see Figure 8). Marketing modules also include tools for analyzing marketing and customer data—identifying profitable and unprofitable customers, designing products and services to satisfy specific customer needs and interests, and identifying opportunities for cross-selling.

Cross-selling is the marketing of complementary products to customers. (For example, in financial services, a customer with a checking account might be sold a money market account or a home improvement loan.) CRM tools also help firms manage and execute marketing campaigns at all stages, from planning to determining the rate of success for each campaign.

Figure 9 illustrates the most important capabilities for sales, service, and marketing processes that would be found in major CRM software products. Like enterprise software, this software is business-process driven, incorporating hundreds of business processes thought to represent best practices in each of these areas. To achieve maximum benefit, companies need to revise and model

FIGURE 8   HOW CRM SYSTEMS SUPPORT MARKETING

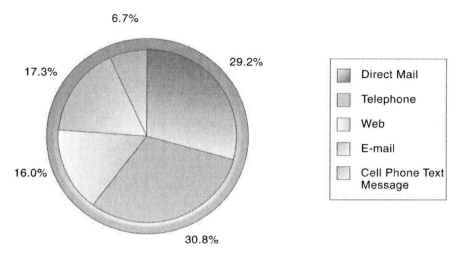

Customer relationship management software provides a single point for users to manage and evaluate marketing campaigns across multiple channels, including e-mail, direct mail, telephone, the Web, and wireless messages.

FIGURE 9   CRM SOFTWARE CAPABILITIES

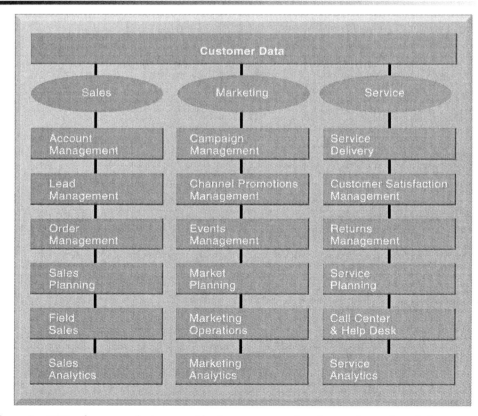

The major CRM software products support business processes in sales, service, and marketing, integrating customer information from many different sources. Included are support for both the operational and analytical aspects of CRM.

their business processes to conform to the best-practice business processes in the CRM software.

Figure 10 illustrates how a best practice for increasing customer loyalty through customer service might be modeled by CRM software. Directly servicing customers provides firms with opportunities to increase customer retention by singling out profitable long-term customers for preferential treatment. CRM software can assign each customer a score based on that person's value and loyalty to the company and provide that information to help call centers route each customer's service request to agents who can best handle that customer's needs. The system would automatically provide the service agent with a detailed profile of that customer that included his or her score for value and loyalty. The service agent would use this information to present special offers or additional service to the customer to encourage the customer to keep transacting business with the company. You will find more information on other best-practice business processes in CRM systems in the second Learning Track for this chapter.

OPERATIONAL AND ANALYTICAL CRM

All of the applications we have just described support either the operational or analytical aspects of customer relationship management. **Operational CRM** includes customer-facing applications, such as tools for sales force automation, call center and customer service support, and marketing automation. **Analytical CRM** includes applications that analyze customer data generated by operational CRM applications to provide information for improving business performance.

Analytical CRM applications are based on data warehouses that consolidate the data from operational CRM systems and customer touch points for use with online analytical processing (OLAP), data mining, and other data analysis

FIGURE 10   CUSTOMER LOYALTY MANAGEMENT PROCESS MAP

This process map shows how a best practice for promoting customer loyalty through customer service would be modeled by customer relationship management software. The CRM software helps firms identify high-value customers for preferential treatment.

FIGURE 11   ANALYTICAL CRM DATA WAREHOUSE

Analytical CRM uses a customer data warehouse and tools to analyze customer data collected from the firm's customer touch points and from other sources.

techniques. Customer data collected by the organization might be combined with data from other sources, such as customer lists for direct-marketing campaigns purchased from other companies or demographic data. Such data are analyzed to identify buying patterns, to create segments for targeted marketing, and to pinpoint profitable and unprofitable customers (see Figure 11).

Another important output of analytical CRM is the customer's lifetime value to the firm. **Customer lifetime value (CLTV)** is based on the relationship between the revenue produced by a specific customer, the expenses incurred in acquiring and servicing that customer, and the expected life of the relationship between the customer and the company.

BUSINESS VALUE OF CUSTOMER RELATIONSHIP MANAGEMENT SYSTEMS

Companies with effective customer relationship management systems realize many benefits, including increased customer satisfaction, reduced direct-marketing costs, more effective marketing, and lower costs for customer acquisition and retention. Information from CRM systems increases sales revenue by identifying the most profitable customers and segments for focused marketing and cross-selling.

Customer churn is reduced as sales, service, and marketing better respond to customer needs. The **churn rate** measures the number of customers who stop using or purchasing products or services from a company. It is an important indicator of the growth or decline of a firm's customer base.

4 ENTERPRISE APPLICATIONS: NEW OPPORTUNITIES AND CHALLENGES

Many firms have implemented enterprise systems and systems for supply chain management and customer relationship management because they are such powerful instruments for achieving operational excellence and enhancing decision making. But precisely because they are so powerful in changing the way the organization works, they are challenging to implement. Let's briefly examine some of these challenges, as well as new ways of obtaining value from these systems.

ENTERPRISE APPLICATION CHALLENGES

Promises of dramatic reductions in inventory costs, order-to-delivery time, as well as more efficient customer response and higher product and customer profitability make enterprise systems and systems for supply chain management and customer relationship management very alluring. But to obtain this value, you must clearly understand how your business has to change to use these systems effectively.

Enterprise applications involve complex pieces of software that are very expensive to purchase and implement. It might take a large company several years to complete a large-scale implementation of an enterprise system or a system for supply chain management or customer relationship management. The total implementation cost of a large system, including software, database tools, consulting fees, personnel costs, training, and perhaps hardware costs, might amount to four to five times the initial purchase price for the software.

Enterprise applications require not only deep-seated technological changes but also fundamental changes in the way the business operates. Companies must make sweeping changes to their business processes to work with the software. Employees must accept new job functions and responsibilities. They must learn how to perform a new set of work activities and understand how the information they enter into the system can affect other parts of the company. This requires new organizational learning.

Supply chain management systems require multiple organizations to share information and business processes. Each participant in the system may have to change some of its processes and the way it uses information to create a system that best serves the supply chain as a whole.

Some firms experienced enormous operating problems and losses when they first implemented enterprise applications because they did not understand how much organizational change was required. Kmart had trouble getting products to store shelves when it implemented supply chain management software from i2 Technologies in July 2000. The i2 software did not work well with Kmart's promotion-driven business model, which creates sharp spikes and drops in demand for products, and it was not designed to handle the massive number of products stocked in Kmart stores.

Hershey Foods' profitability dropped when it tried to implement SAP enterprise software, Manugistics SCM software, and Siebel Systems CRM software on a crash schedule in 1999 without thorough testing and employee training. Shipments ran two weeks late and many customers did not receive enough candy to stock shelves during the busy Halloween selling period. Hershey lost sales and customers during that period, although the new systems eventually improved operational efficiency.

The Interactive Session on Organizations describes another company's struggle to implement enterprise software. Invacare, a leading health care products manufacturer, had trouble making some of the modules of Oracle's E-Business Suite perform properly. Its experience illustrates some of the problems that occur when a company tries to make enterprise software work with its unique business processes.

Enterprise applications also introduce "switching costs." Once you adopt an enterprise application from a single vendor, such as SAP, Oracle, or others, it is very costly to switch vendors, and your firm becomes dependent on the vendor to upgrade its product and maintain your installation.

Enterprise applications are based on organization-wide definitions of data. You'll need to understand exactly how your business uses its data and how the data would be organized in a customer relationship management, supply chain management, or enterprise system. CRM systems typically require some data cleansing work.

In a nutshell, it takes a lot of work to get enterprise applications to work properly. Everyone in the organization must be involved. Of course, for those companies that have successfully implemented CRM, SCM, and enterprise systems, the results have justified the effort.

EXTENDING ENTERPRISE SOFTWARE

Today many experienced business firms are looking for ways to wring more value from their enterprise applications. One way is to make them more flexible, Web-enabled, and capable of integration with other systems. The major enterprise software vendors have created what they call *enterprise solutions*, *enterprise suites*, or *e-business suites* to make their customer relationship management, supply chain management, and enterprise systems work closely with each other, and to link to systems of customers and suppliers. SAP's mySAP and Oracle's E-Business Suite are examples.

Service Platforms

Another way of leveraging investments in enterprise applications is to use them to create service platforms for new or improved business processes that integrate information from multiple functional areas. These enterprise-wide service platforms provide a greater degree of cross-functional integration than the traditional enterprise applications. A **service platform** integrates multiple applications from multiple business functions, business units, or business partners to deliver a seamless experience for the customer, employee, manager, or business partner.

For instance, the order-to-cash process involves receiving an order and seeing it all the way through obtaining payment for the order. This process begins with lead generation, marketing campaigns, and order entry, which are typically supported by CRM systems. Once the order is received, manufacturing is scheduled and parts availability is verified—processes that are usually supported by enterprise software. The order then is handled by processes for distribution planning, warehousing, order fulfillment, and shipping, which are usually supported by supply chain management systems. Finally, the order is billed to the customer, which is handled by either enterprise financial applications or accounts receivable. If the purchase at some point required customer service, customer relationship management systems would again be invoked.

INTERACTIVE SESSION: ORGANIZATIONS:

INVACARE STRUGGLES WITH ITS ENTERPRISE SYSTEM IMPLEMENTATION

Invacare, headquartered in Elyria, Ohio, is the world's leading manufacturer and distributor of non-acute health care products, including wheel chairs, motorized scooters, home care beds, portable compressed oxygen systems, bath safety products, and skin and wound care products. It conducts business in over eighty countries, maintaining manufacturing plants in the United States and eleven other nations. Invacare sells its products primarily to over 25,000 home health care and medical equipment provider locations in the United States, Europe, Australia, New Zealand, and Canada, with the remainder of its sales primarily to government agencies and distributors. The company also distributes medical equipment and related supplies manufactured by other companies.

Invacare does not maintain much inventory. It manufactures most of its products to meet near-term demands, and it builds some of its products to order. It is constantly revising and expanding its numerous product lines.

In 2004, Invacare began working on replacing a collection of homemade legacy systems for purchase to payable processes with modules from Oracle's 11i E-Business Suite. Invacare had been using Oracle database software and had implemented the financial modules from Oracle E-Business Suite four years earlier. The company experienced no problems implementing and using the Oracle E-Business financial modules.

However, Invacare ran into problems when it went live with new order-to-cash modules, which let a company receive an order, allocate supplies to build it, and provide customer access to order status. Invacare's information systems specialists had tested the software under real-world business conditions and everyone felt the software was ready to be used in actual business operations.

When the new system went live in October 2005, the software would not perform properly. "Our systems were locking up," observed Greg Thompson, Invacare's chief financial officer. Invacare call center representatives were unable to answer customer telephone calls in a timely manner. When they did talk with customers, they could not find complete information in the system about stock availability and shipment dates for products. The company was unable to ship products to customers within required

lead times. Invacare's management never expected the implementation to be trouble-free, but it clearly did not foresee the magnitude of the problems it experienced with the new system.

As a result of the malfunctioning software, Invacare lost sales and had higher than usual levels of returned goods. It also incurred extra expenses for expediting product orders and for paying for employee overtime in its manufacturing, distribution, and customer service departments. Two months of sales disruptions caused Invacare to cut its fourth-quarter 2005 revenue estimate to between $370 million and $380 million, lower than the previous year and well below the 2 percent sales increase the company had previously projected. Losses totaled $30 million for the quarter and extended into the first quarter of 2006.

The new system also changed some of the company's internal controls over financial reporting, and some of these controls did not function as intended. During the final quarter of 2005, Invacare had to perform a physical year-end inventory count for its North American operations, and take special steps to validate the figures used in financial statements.

According to Thompson, Invacare's problems were not caused by the Oracle software but by the way that Invacare configured the software and integrated its business processes with the new system. He and other Invacare management also believe that the company should have done more testing work.

Oracle worked closely with Invacare to resolve the problems and Thompson was pleased by Oracle's response. "Oracle has been very helpful in working with our teams to resolve the issues we've identified," he said. Thompson anticipated all ordering and invoicing problems to be cleared up by early 2006.

Thompson also expressed hope that the new ERP system will provide enough value to offset the company's losses from the system. Invacare spent $20 million on its ERP implementation. It's still too early to tell whether Invacare's ERP system will justify its costs.

Sources: Marc Songini, "Faulty ERP App Results in Shortfall for Medical Firm," *Computerworld*, January 2, 2006 and "Medical Products Maker Invacare Faces Rough ERP Ride," *Computerworld*, December 20, 2006; "Invacare Corporation 10-K Annual Report" filed March 14, 2006; "Invacare Corporation Reports First-Quarter Earnings," April 27, 2006; and Stacy Cowley, "Invacare Blames Botched Oracle ERP Project for Q4 Miss," *IDG News Service*, December 14, 2005.

CASE STUDY QUESTIONS   MIS IN ACTION

1. How did problems implementing the Oracle enterprise software affect Invacare's business performance?

2. What management, organization, and technology factors affected Invacare's ERP implementation?

3. If you were Invacare's management, what steps would you have taken to prevent these problems?

Visit the Oracle Web site and explore its section on Oracle E-Business Suite. Listen to one of Oracle's podcasts about this software. Then answer the following questions:

1. List and describe the capabilities of the Order Management modules.

2. How would the Order Management modules benefit a company such as Invacare? Describe how Invacare would use these capabilities.

A service such as order-to-cash requires data from enterprise applications and financial systems to be further integrated into an enterprise-wide composite process. To accomplish this, firms need software tools that use existing applications as building blocks for new cross-enterprise processes (see Figure 12). Enterprise application vendors provide middleware and tools that use XML and Web services for integrating enterprise applications with older legacy applications and systems from other vendors.

Increasingly, these new services will be delivered through portals. Today's portal products provide frameworks for building new composite services. Portal software can integrate information from enterprise applications and disparate in-house legacy systems, presenting it to users through a Web interface so that the information appears to be coming from a single source.

FIGURE 12   ORDER-TO-CASH SERVICE

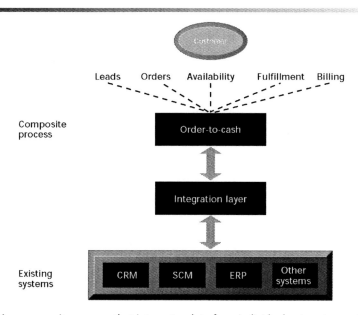

Order-to-cash is a composite process that integrates data from individual enterprise applications and legacy financial applications. The process must be modeled and translated into a software system using application integration tools.

5 HANDS-ON MIS
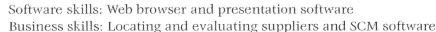

The projects in this section give you hands-on experience evaluating supply chain management software for a real-world company, using database software to manage customer service requests, and evaluating supply chain management business services.

Achieving Operational Excellence: Identifying Supply Chain Management Solutions

> Software skills: Web browser and presentation software
> Business skills: Locating and evaluating suppliers and SCM software

Businesses are always seeking suppliers who can fulfill orders promptly at the lowest possible cost. In this project, you will use the Web to identify the best suppliers for one component of a dirt bike and appropriate supply chain management software for a small manufacturing company.

A growing number of Dirt Bikes orders cannot be fulfilled on time because of delays in obtaining some important components and parts for its motorcycles, especially their fuel tanks. Complaints are mounting from distributors who fear losing sales if the dirt bikes they have ordered are delayed too long. Dirt Bikes's management has asked you to help it address some of its supply chain issues.

- Use the Internet to locate alternative suppliers for motorcycle fuel tanks. Identify two or three suppliers. Find out the amount of time and cost to ship a fuel tank (weighing about five pounds) by ground (surface delivery) from each supplier to Dirt Bikes in Carbondale, Colorado. Which supplier is most likely to take the shortest amount of time and cost the least to ship the fuel tanks?

- Dirt Bikes's management would like to know if there is any supply chain management software for a small business that would be appropriate for Dirt Bikes. Use the Internet to locate two supply chain management software providers for companies such as Dirt Bikes. Briefly describe the capabilities of the two software applications and indicate how they could help Dirt Bikes. Which supply chain management software product would be more appropriate for Dirt Bikes? Why?

- (Optional) Use electronic presentation software to summarize your findings for management.

Improving Decision Making: Using Database Software to Manage Customer Service Requests

> Software skills: Database design; querying and reporting
> Business skills: Customer service analysis

Companies specializing in service need a way to monitor and manage the numerous requests for their services that they receive each day. It is usually advantageous while providing service to give priority to the customers who have generated the most revenue for the business. In this exercise, you will use database software to develop an application that tracks customer service requests and analyzes customer data to identify customers meriting priority treatment.

Prime Service is a large service company that provides maintenance and repair services for close to 1,200 commercial businesses in New York, New Jersey, and Connecticut. Its customers include businesses of all sizes. Customers with service needs call into its customer service department with requests for repairing heating ducts, broken windows, leaky roofs, broken water pipes, and other problems. The company assigns each request a number and writes down the service request number, identification number of the customer account, the date of the request, the type of equipment requiring repair, and a brief description of the problem. The service requests are handled on a first-come-first-served basis. After the service work has been completed, Prime calculates the cost of the work, enters the price on the service request form, and bills the client.

Management is not happy with this arrangement because the most important and profitable clients—those with accounts of more than $70,000—are treated no differently from its clients with small accounts. It would like to find a way to provide its best customers with better service. Management would also like to know which types of service problems occur the most frequently so that it can make sure it has adequate resources to address them.

Prime Service has a small database with client account information, which can be found on the Laudon Web site for this chapter. It includes fields for the account ID, company (account) name, street address, city, state, ZIP code, account size (in dollars), contact last name, contact first name, and contact telephone number. The contact is the name of the person in each company who is responsible for contacting Prime about maintenance and repair work. Use your database software to design a solution that would enable Prime's customer service representatives to identify the most important customers so that they could receive priority service. Your solution will require more than one table. Populate your database with at least 15 service requests. Create several reports that would be of interest to management, such as a list of the highest- and lowest-priority accounts or a report showing the most frequently occurring service problems. Create a report showing customer service representatives which service calls they should respond to first on a specific date.

ACCT_ID	NAME	ADDR	CITY	STATE	ZIP	DOLLAR_SIZE	CONTACT_FIRS	CONTACT_LAS	PHONE
1	Able Association	123 Axion Stree	Albertown	NY	11444-4444	$50,000	Alison	Ableson	(209) 111-1111
2	Briggs Bakery	123 Boggs Stre	Brimstone	CT	11200-1234	$94,000	Barry	Berryman	(210) 111-1212
3	Constant Carriers	31 Carmine Le	Carver	NJ	20111-1212	$200,000	Carl	Compress	(202) 123-1222
4	Darning Drapers	1234 Dante Ave	Dribble	NY	12345-6849	$60,000	Delilah	Dilman	(209) 123-4321
5	Eagle Engineers	Eagle Park	Edmonton	CT	11222-2313	$45,000	Eddie	Exeter	(210) 212-2233
(AutoNumber)						$0			

Achieving Operational Excellence: Evaluating Supply Chain Management Services

Software skills: Web browser and presentation software
Business skills: Evaluating supply chain management services

Trucking companies no longer merely carry goods from one place to another. Some also provide supply chain management services to their customers and help them manage their information. In this project, you will use the Web to research and evaluate two of these business services.

Investigate the Web sites of two companies, J.B. Hunt and Schneider Logistics, to see how these companies' services can be used for supply chain management. Then respond to the following questions:

- What supply chain processes can each of these companies support for their clients?
- How can customers use the Web sites of each company to help them with supply chain management?
- Compare the supply chain management services provided by these companies. Which company would you select to help your firm manage its supply chain? Why?

LEARNING TRACK MODULES

SAP Business Process Map. If you want to learn more about how SAP enterprise software works, you will find a Learning Track on SAP's Business Process Map at the Laudon Web site for this chapter and on the Student CD-ROM.

Best Practices Business Processes in CRM Software. If you want to learn more about customer-related business processes supported by CRM software, you will find a Learning Track on Siebel Systems's best practice business processes at the Laudon Web site for this chapter and on the Student CD-ROM.

Summary

1. *Demonstrate how enterprise systems achieve operational excellence by integrating and coordinating diverse functions and business processes in the firm.*

   Enterprise systems integrate the key business processes of a firm into a single software system so that information can flow seamlessly throughout the organization, improving coordination, efficiency, and decision making. Enterprise software is based on a suite of integrated software modules and a common central database. The database collects data from and feeds the data into numerous applications that can support nearly all of an organization's internal business activities. When new information is entered by one process, the information is made available immediately to other business processes. Organizations implementing enterprise software would have to adopt the business processes embedded in the software and, if necessary, change their business processes to conform to those in the software.

   Enterprise systems support organizational centralization by enforcing uniform data standards and business processes throughout the company and a single unified technology platform. The firmwide data generated by enterprise systems helps managers evaluate organizational performance. By integrating business processes in sales, production, finance, and logistics, the entire organization will more efficiently respond to customer requests for products or information, forecast new products, and build and deliver them as demand requires.

2. *Demonstrate how supply chain management systems coordinate planning, production, and logistics with suppliers.*

   Supply chain management systems automate the flow of information among members of the supply chain so they can use it to make better decisions about when and how much to purchase, produce, or ship. More accurate information from supply chain management systems reduces uncertainty and the impact of the bullwhip effect. The correct movement of information makes it possible to time orders, shipments, and production properly to minimize inventory levels and expedite deliveries to customers.

   Supply chain management software includes software for supply chain planning and for supply chain execution. Supply chain planning systems enable the firm to generate demand forecasts for a product and to develop sourcing, manufacturing, and distribution plans. Supply chain execution systems manage the flow of products through the final stages of production, distribution, and delivery. Firms can use intranets to improve coordination among their internal supply chain processes, and they can use extranets to coordinate supply chain processes shared with their business partners. Internet technology facilitates the management of global supply chains by providing the connectivity for organizations in different countries to share supply chain information. Improved communication among supply chain members also facilitates efficient customer response and movement toward a demand-driven model.

3. *Demonstrate how customer relationship management systems achieve customer intimacy by integrating all customer contact information and making it available throughout the firm.*

Customer relationship management (CRM) systems integrate and automate many customer-facing processes in sales, marketing, and customer service, providing an enterprise-wide view of customers. These systems track all of the ways in which a company interacts with its customers and analyze these interactions to maximize customer lifetime value for the firm. CRM systems capture and integrate customer data from all over the organization, analyzing the data and distributing the results to customer-related systems and customer touch points across the enterprise. Companies can use this customer knowledge when they interact with customers to provide them with better service or to sell new products and services. These systems also identify profitable or nonprofitable customers or opportunities to reduce the churn rate.

The major customer relationship management software packages integrate customer-related processes in sales, marketing, and customer service and provide capabilities for both operational CRM and analytical CRM. They often include modules for managing relationships with selling partners (partner relationship management) and for employee relationship management.

If they are properly implemented, CRM systems help firms increase customer satisfaction, reduce direct-marketing costs, and lower costs for customer acquisition and retention. Information from CRM systems increases sales revenue by identifying the most profitable customers and segments for focused marketing and cross-selling. Customer churn will be reduced as sales, service, and marketing better respond to customer needs.

4. *Assess the challenges posed by enterprise applications.*

Enterprise applications are difficult to implement. They require extensive organizational change, large new software investments, and careful assessment of how these systems will enhance organizational performance. Enterprise applications create new interconnections among myriad business processes and data flows inside the firm (and in the case of supply chain management systems, between the firm and its external supply chain partners). Enterprise applications cannot provide value if they are implemented atop flawed processes or if firms do not know how to use these systems to measure performance improvements. Employees require training to prepare for new procedures and roles. Attention to data management is essential.

5. *Describe how enterprise applications can be used in platforms for new cross-functional services.*

Enterprise applications can serve as building blocks for new cross-functional services for customers, suppliers, or business partners. Service platforms integrate data and processes from the various enterprise applications (customer relationship management, supply chain management, and enterprise systems), as well as from disparate legacy applications to create new composite business processes. Application integration middleware or Web services tie various systems together. The new services are delivered through enterprise portals, which can integrate disparate applications so that information appears to be coming from a single source.

Key Terms

Analytical CRM	*Operational CRM*
Best practices	*Partner relationship management (PRM)*
Bullwhip effect	*Pull-based model*
Churn rate	*Push-based model*
Cross-selling	*Service platform*
Customer lifetime value (CLTV)	*Supply chain*
Demand planning	*Supply chain execution systems*
Employee relationship management (ERM)	*Supply chain planning systems*
Enterprise software	*Touch point*
Just-in-time	

Review Questions

1. What is an enterprise system? How does enterprise software work?

2. How do enterprise systems provide value for a business?

3. What is a supply chain? What entities does it comprise?

4. What is the bullwhip effect? How can supply chain management systems deal with it?

5. What are supply chain planning systems and supply chain execution systems? What functions do they perform?

6. How can the Internet and Internet technology facilitate supply chain management?

7. Distinguish between a push-based and pull-based model of supply chain management. How can contemporary supply chain management systems facilitate a pull-based model?

8. How do supply chain management systems provide value for a business?

9. What is customer relationship management? Why are customer relationships so important today?

10. How are partner relationship management (PRM) and employee relationship management (ERM) related to customer relationship management (CRM)?

11. Describe the tools and capabilities of customer relationship management software for sales, marketing, and customer service.

12. Distinguish between operational and analytical CRM.

13. Define the following terms and explain why they are important for customer relationship management: churn rate, customer lifetime value (CLTV), best practices.

14. What are the challenges posed by enterprise applications? How can these challenges be addressed?

15. How can enterprise applications be extended to provide more value to businesses? Describe the role of service platforms and portals.

Discussion Questions

1. Supply chain management is less about managing the physical movement of goods and more about managing information. Discuss the implications of this statement.

2. If a company wants to implement an enterprise application, it had better do its homework. Discuss the implications of this statement.

Video Case

You will find a video case illustrating some of the concepts in this chapter on the Laudon Web site and Student CD-ROM along with questions to help you analyze the case.

Teamwork: Analyzing Enterprise Application Vendors

With a group of three or four students, use the Web to research and evaluate the products of two vendors of enterprise application software. You could compare, for example, the SAP and Oracle enterprise systems, the supply chain management systems from i2 and JDA Software's Manugistics, or the customer relationship management systems of Oracle's Siebel Systems and salesforce.com. Use what you have learned from these companies' Web sites to compare the software packages you have selected in terms of business functions supported, technology platforms, cost, and ease of use. Which vendor would you select? Why? Would you select the same vendor for a small business as well as a large one? If possible, use electronic presentation software to present your findings to the class.

REFERENCES

Anderiz, Diego. "The Rebirth of CRM." *IT Adviser* 44 (July/August 2006).

Anderson, James C. and James A. Narus. "Selectively Pursuing More of Your Customer's Business." *MIT Sloan Management Review* 44, no. 3 (Spring 2003).

D'Avanzo, Robert, Hans von Lewinski, and Luk N. Van Wassenhove. "The Link Between Supply Chain and Financial Performance." Supply Chain Management Review". (November 1, 2003).,

Davenport, Thomas H. *Mission Critical: Realizing the Promise of Enterprise Systems.* Boston, MA: Harvard Business School Press (2000).

———. "Putting the Enterprise into Enterprise Systems." *Harvard Business Review* (July–August 1998).

Day, George S. "Creating a Superior Customer-Relating Capability." *MIT Sloan Management Review* 44, no. 3 (Spring 2003).

Dowling, Grahame. "Customer Relationship Management: In B2C Markets, Often Less is More." *California Management Review* 44, no. 3 (Spring 2002).

Fleisch, Elgar, Hubert Oesterle, and Stephen Powell. "Rapid Implementation of Enterprise Resource Planning Systems." *Journal of Organizational Computing and Electronic Commerce* 14, no. 2 (2004).

Gosain, Sanjay, Arvind Malhotra, and Omar A. ElSawy. "Coordinating for Flexibility in e-Business Supply Chains." *Journal of Management Information System*s 21, No. 3 (Winter 2004–2005).

Goodhue, Dale L., Barbara H. Wixom, and Hugh J. Watson. "Realizing Business Benefits through CRM: Hitting the Right Target in the Right Way." *MIS Quarterly Executive* 1, no. 2 (June 2002).

Handfield, Robert B. and Ernest L. Nichols. *Supply Chain Redesign: Transforming Supply Chains into Integrated Value Systems.* Financial Times Press (2002).

Hitt, Lorin, D.J. Wu, and Xiaoge Zhou. "Investment in Enterprise Resource Planning: Business Impact and Productivity Measures." *Journal of Management Information Systems* 19, no. 1 (Summer 2002).

Kalakota, Ravi and Marcia Robinson. *E-Business* 2.0 Boston: Addison-Wesley (2001).

———. *Services Blueprint: Roadmap for Execution.* Boston: Addison-Wesley (2003).

Kanakamedala, Kishore, Glenn Ramsdell, and Vats Srivatsan. "Getting Supply Chain Software Right." *McKinsey Quarterly* (2003 No. 1).

Kopczak, Laura Rock, and M. Eric Johnson. "The Supply-Chain Management Effect." *MIT Sloan Management Review* 44, no. 3 (Spring 2003).

Lee, Hau. "The Triple-A Supply Chain." *Harvard Business Review* (October 2004).

Lee, Hau, L., V. Padmanabhan, and Seugin Whang. "The Bullwhip Effect in Supply Chains." *Sloan Management Review* (Spring 1997).

Malhotra, Arvind, Sanjay Gosain, and Omar A. El Sawy. "Absorptive Capacity Configurations in Supply Chains: Gearing for Partner-Enabled Market Knowledge Creation." *MIS Quarterly* 29, No. 1 (March 2005).

Rai, Arun, Ravi Patnayakuni, and Nainika Seth. "Firm Performance Impacts of Digitally Enabled Supply Chain Integration Capabilities." *MIS Quarterly* 30 No. 2 (June 2006).

Ranganathan, C. and Carol V. Brown. "ERP Iinvestments and the Market Value of Firms: Toward an Understanding of Influential ERP Project Variables." *Information Systems Research* 17, No. 2 (June 2006).

Ranganathan, C., Jasbir S. Dhaliwal, and Thompson S.H. Teo. "Assimilation and Diffusion of Web Technologies in Supply-Chain Management: An Examination of Key Drivers and Performance Impacts." *International Journal of Electronic Commerce* 9, no. 1 (Fall 2004).

Robey, Daniel, Jeanne W. Ross, and Marie-Claude Boudreau. "Learning to Implement Enterprise Systems: An Exploratory Study of the Dialectics of Change." *Journal of Management Information Systems* 19, no. 1 (Summer 2002).

Scott, Judy E. and Iris Vessey. "Managing Risks in Enterprise Systems Implementations." *Communications of the ACM* 45, no. 4 (April 2002).

Slone, Reuben E. "Leading a Supply Chain Turnaround." *Harvard Business Review* (October 2004).

Whiting, Rick. "You Look Marvelous!" *Information Week* (July 24, 2006).

Winer, Russell S. "A Framework for Customer Relationship Management." *California Management Review* 43, no. 4 (Summer 2001).

Yu, Larry. "Successful Customer Relationship Management." *Sloan Management Review* 42, no. 4 (Summer 2001).

Limited Brands Consolidates Its Supply Chain Management
CASE STUDY

Limited Brands, Inc. is a specialty retail business based in Columbus, Ohio. As of 2006, the Limited Brands family included 3,500 stores divided among seven retail brands. Most of the brands should be familiar to the average consumer: Victoria's Secret, Express, Bath & Body Works, C.O. Bigelow, The Limited, the White Barn Candle Co., and Henri Bendel.

Since the first Limited store opened in 1963, the business grew dramatically, launching new stores and acquiring other companies for its retail empire. In 2002, The Limited Inc. and Intimate Brands Inc., which had been established as a fully independent company in 1995, merged as The Limited Inc., with Intimate Brands becoming a wholly owned subsidiary. The Limited then renamed itself Limited Brands.

Fortune Magazine named Limited Brands number one in the specialty retail category of its "World's Most Admired Companies" survey for 2002. However, behind the scenes, operations were not always running so smoothly. Specifically, problems with the enterprise's supply chain that year led to what senior vice president of supply chain transformation Paul Matthews called "a pretty significant catastrophe." A combination of circumstances conspired to create a traffic jam of 400 merchandise trailers at the parking lot of a distribution center that was designed to hold only 150 trailers. The logistics disaster clogged up a main highway. Aside from the public relations nightmare, the incident occurred at the beginning of a sales period.

Matthews described the environment surrounding the catastrophe as one in which planning systems crashed, corporate executives made assumptions, and different segments of the enterprise were not maintaining proper communication with each other. No one had any knowledge of the origin of inventory or where it was going. Matthews admitted that the company never really figured out how this happened. It was clear that the logjam was a symptom of a larger problem.

Leading up to 2002, the growth rate of Limited Brands since its inception was very rapid. However, acquisitions, rather than organic growth, were responsible for a large percentage of this growth. Thus, Limited Brands's information technology infrastructure included a mishmash of systems and software from the various retailers that Limited Brands had brought into the fold.

Sixty major systems were in place with hundreds of applications running on a variety of platforms, including computers and servers from IBM, Hewlett-Packard, Sun Microsystems, and Tandem. Redundancies were not uncommon. Given the makeup of the infrastructure, it would be extremely difficult to make supply chain information flow between applications to coordinate Limited's supply chain. Establishing better control over the supply chain so that such incidents would not happen again would be a major challenge.

Limited Brands had already begun to contemplate its supply chain needs a year earlier when discount retailers were pushing Limited stores out of their market space. The company reacted to the threat by focusing on higher-end products, which carried the potential for higher profit margins. In order to get the most out of this strategy, the company needed to increase its speed to market for these products. Improved supply chain technologies that integrate and leverage the supply chain and logistics for the overall benefit of the brand were required. Leonard A. Schlesinger, the company's vice chairman and chief operating officer, referred to the solution as "integrated brand delivery."

And, so, Limited Brands initiated the process of upgrading its supply chain and eliminating the jumble of legacy systems complicating the infrastructure. The company hoped to reap numerous rewards from the effort, including: increased sales; better flexibility for responding to market trends and customer needs; and freeing up employees to concentrate on sales rather than on tasks related to supply chain and logistics. Matthews explained that with over 1,000 suppliers around the world and multiple distribution channels it was imperative for Limited Brands to develop an enterprise-wide view of the supply chain. Such a view required visibility in the supply chain—often described as seeing it as a glass pipeline—views of the inventory and customer buying patterns, raw material transportation, and, most importantly, the ability to look at all of these components simultaneously.

Developing this type of supply chain presented a number of challenges. Limited Logistics Services (LLS), which supplies global logistics management and leadership for the supply chains used by Limited's brands, ran into resistance from brand executives when it first tried to integrate the supply chain logistics operations of all the Limited companies. Rick Jackson, executive vice president of LLS, won the brand executives over by showing them one by one how supply chain transformation would produce significant savings and strategic benefits. Jackson and his team also developed for each brand a customer service agreement and metrics for evaluating results.

Jackson and his team launched several cross-functional projects to bolster their credibility. They built regional docking centers on the East and West Coasts to funnel products directly to stores, reducing costs and time to get products to market by as much as 10 days. This helped brand managers make much quicker decisions about which products to reorder. Brand executives embraced the transformation after they saw these results.

Limited Brands also faced technical and business process obstacles, as illustrated by its work with Tibco Software, one of many supply chain software vendors with which the company worked. Tibco is a leading vendor of enterprise application integration software (see Chaper 5) and was contracted to develop a global application integration platform for Limited Brands. The purpose of the platform was to improve the company's ability to track and manage the flow of information through its worldwide supply chain. Tibco and Limited Brands began the project by performing an assessment of the relevant business processes. Dean Hidalgo, Tibco's senior manager of product marketing, said that such an assessment was a typical first step for a large project because his company needed to understand fully the functioning of the existing business processes.

The assessment revealed that Limited Brands was struggling with scheduling issues and processing delays. These problems were attributable to overly simple point-to-point interfaces that linked one system to another, for example, a shipping facility to a distribution center. The interfaces existed for very specific purposes, such as transmitting data between the two systems on a batch schedule. Hidalgo pointed out the weaknesses of such an arrangement, which he called "the classic spaghetti dilemma." The infrastructure lacked flexibility because its robust software applications were hard-wired point-by-point to different application programming interfaces (APIs). Changing one API resulted in a chain reaction necessitating changes to all of the APIs in communication with the connected applications.

Tibco worked with Limited Brands to install real-time reporting and communications with delivery agents. They also integrated the outbound supply chain accountability and reporting (OSCAR) application with the logistics applications. Tibco extolled the value of its business integration framework because of the ease with which it could be replicated when new delivery agents entered the network. Tibco's installation introduced real-time communications between Limited Brands and its suppliers, and provided a secure environment for transmitting documents. The technology also enhanced the shipment tracking and order visibility capabilities of Limited Brands' partners using a booking information module (BIM).

According to Darrell S. Riekena, Limited Brands's director of logistics systems, Tibco met his company's expectations for the project and positioned the business "to support future business initiatives and reduce development time and the cost of solutions." Limited Brands was able unite all of its brands' technology operations under a central entity, a subsidiary called Limited Technology Services, overseen by CIO Jon Ricker with a budget of $150 million and 750 employees.

Matthews said there was still plenty of work to do before the transformation of Limited Brands would be complete. Among the company's additional technology goals were a reusable framework to enable the replication of software solutions and an enterprise resource planning (ERP) deployment. In 2005, Limited Brands adopted Web-based demand and supply chain management tools from Manugistics (acquired by JDA Software Group) to improve collaborative logistics management for both the inbound and outbound chains.

In the meantime, Matthews parlayed his experience with the project into support for the supply chain strategy that he had been promoting for 25 years: bringing supply chain management (SCM) closer to the boardroom. Matthews had always believed that the corporate level of many businesses was mistakenly ambivalent toward supply chain management concerns. SCM had been found to be a major drain on revenues and was closely linked to other success-related factors such as pricing, quality, lead times, and customer satisfaction. Matthews was therefore very pleased to make SCM a large part of the corporate culture at Limited Brands, where he said it contributed significantly to overall corporate strategy.

Matthews's ultimate goal was to create a "supply chain that begins and ends with the customer." He also emphasized the impact of the supply chain on shareholder value. With the supply chain better aligned with the goals of the boardroom, the company was able to focus on improving revenue rather than simply keeping costs down.

Sources: Laton McCartney, "The Limited Designs Supply Chain to Begin and End with the Customer," *Baseline Magazine*, April 3, 2006; "Supply Chain Management Value: Time to Align the Supply Chain to the Boardroom, Says the Limited Brands' Paul Matthews," scdigest.com, March 31, 2006; Anne Field, "Making the Sale," *Harvard Business Review*, March 2005; "Manugistics Strategic Demand and Supply Chain Management Solutions Selected by Limited Brands," TMCnet.com, January 17, 2005; "Limited Brands Sees Tough Quarter Ahead," CNNMoney.com, August 17, 2006; "Limited Sees Challenging Qtr; Keeps Aug Forecast," Reuters.com, August 17, 2006; LimitedBrands.com, accessed August 25, 2006; and Limited Brands, Inc., Annual Report on Form 10-K for the Fiscal Year Ended January 28, 2006.

CASE STUDY QUESTIONS

1. Analyze Limited Brands using the competitive forces and value chain models. How is supply chain management related to the company's business strategy?

2. Describe the supply chain management problems encountered by Limited Brands in this case. What was their business impact?

3. What management, organization, and technology factors were responsible for these problems?

4. How did Limited Brands solve these problems? What management, organization, and technology issues were addressed by the solution?

E-Commerce: Digital Markets, Digital Goods

E-Commerce: Digital Markets, Digital Goods

LEARNING OBJECTIVES

After reading this chapter, you will be able to:

1. Describe the unique features of e-commerce, digital markets, and digital goods.

2. Analyze how Internet technology has changed value propositions and business models.

3. Describe the various types of e-commerce and how e-commerce has changed consumer retailing and business-to-business transactions.

4. Evaluate the role of m-commerce in business and describe the most important m-commerce applications.

5. Compare the principal payment systems for electronic commerce.

Interactive Sessions:

The Allure of MySpace

Stonyfield Farm Blogs for Organic Communication

CHAPTER OUTLINE

MAJOR LEAGUE BASEBALL HITS A HOME RUN WITH INFORMATION SYSTEMS

Technology is helping Major League Baseball (MLB) raise its batting average. MLB is responsible for operating the two top baseball leagues in North America—the National League and the American League. Although baseball is a sport, Major League Baseball is also a big business, requiring revenue from tickets to games, television broadcasts, and other sources to pay for its stadiums and teams. One of the functions of MLB is to promote and grow that business.

Major League Baseball has its own set of business challenges. As salaries for top players ballooned, so have ticket prices. Many fans now watch games on television rather than attending them in person. Although some teams fill the stadiums, others, such as the Chicago White Sox, have seen their fan base dwindle. Shea Stadium, the home field of the New York Mets, was half empty most of the 2004 baseball season.

MLB still uses traditional print and broadcast media—newspapers, television, and radio—to publicize games, and retail outlets and stadiums to sell baseball tickets and souvenirs. But its new emphasis is on using the Internet and information technology. It now runs a high-tech production/Internet spin-off based in New York called MLB Advanced Media (MLBAM), which oversees MLB video productions, the Web sites for each of MLB's 30 teams, and its own Web site, MLB.com.

Bib Bowman, CEO and president of MLBAM, wants to find more customers and turn them into devoted fans who will go to more games and buy more baseball-related merchandise. "A lot of people just go to one game per year, and we need to encourage that fan to be more active with his or her favorite team," he says. Teams such as the Mets, which had ranked seventeenth in attendance among MLB's 30 teams, have benefited. The MLB Web sites have helped publicize information about the Mets and increased season ticket sales.

It's easy to see why. At MLB.com, for example, fans can check game scores; purchase game tickets; shop for caps, jerseys, baseball cards, and memorabilia; post opinions on electronic message boards; use e-mail; and find out more about their favorite teams and players. The site features fantasy baseball games, where fans compete with each other by managing "fantasy teams" based on real players' statistics. About 800,000 subscribers pay $79.95 per year for live streaming video of baseball games that play on their computers. During the baseball season, MLB.com streams 10-15 live baseball games a day.

MLBAM is trying to boost ticket sales further by broadcasting offers to fans' cell phones. For instance, Mets fans who have shown interest in ticket offers may receive a text message that there are still seats available for a Mets game at Shea Stadium and they can purchase tickets using their cell phones. If the fan purchases, a bar code is

Photo courtesy of AP Wide World Photos

transmitted to his or her cell phone to use as a ticket that will be accepted at the gate. MLBAM also sold more than one million cell phone wallpapers, ring tones, and other content during that baseball season. It has started to offer live audio broadcast feeds of games and fantasy games to owners of color-screen phones at all the major cellular services.

To learn more about who its customers were and what they wanted, MLBAM worked with SAS Inc. on software to collect and analyze its customer data. These data come from subscriptions; e-commerce transactions on MLB Web sites; and e-mail addresses collected from sweepstakes, online newsletters, and other offers. Special Web site tracking tools provide information on the most popular parts of MLB Web sites, which ball games participants watch or download, which online games they play, and which team merchandise or tickets they buy.

MLB has leveraged its expertise in streaming live video baseball games to offer streaming video services to other businesses. CBS, Major League Soccer, the World Championship Sports Network, and entertainer Jimmy Buffet have hired MLB.com to stream their video events. About 15 percent of MLB.com's total revenue of $195 million in 2005 came from managing Web sites and streaming video partnerships.

Sources: Bobby White, "Major League Baseball Steps Out as Coach in the Game of Web Video," *The Wall Street Journal*, March 27, 2006; Jon Surmacz, "In a League of Its Own," *CIO Magazine*, April 15, 2005; W. David Gardner, "Fans Say 'Take Me Out to the Web Site,'" *InformationWeek*, August 22, 2005; and Peter J. Howe, "Major League Baseball Pitches Cellphone Content," *Boston Globe*, March 14, 2005.

Major League Baseball's Web-based ventures show why e-commerce is becoming so important. The Internet has breathed new life into MLB, as well as many other companies, by providing new online channels for reaching customers, new digital products and services, and new marketing tools. Internet technology has transformed its business model.

The chapter-opening diagram calls attention to important points raised by this case and this chapter. Baseball ticket prices have risen, costs are up, and baseball must compete with other forms of entertainment, including electronic games. MLB set up a series of Web sites that offer extensive information about teams, games, and players; video and audio broadcasts, the ability to purchase tickets via computer or cell phone; and the ability to purchase souvenirs and memorabilia over the Web. The Web sites include community-building features, such as e-mail and electronic messaging, and new products for sale, such as cell phone content and fantasy games, that are not available through traditional channels. Use of the Internet and the Web makes it possible for MLB to use new tools for analyzing customers. Knowledge of this technology has opened up a new line of business supplying technology services. Thanks to all of these new e-commerce initiatives, MLB revenue has increased.

HEADS UP

This chapter focuses on e-commerce and how businesses use e-commerce to achieve operational excellence and customer intimacy. E-commerce is also transforming business and industries. E-commerce advertising revenues are growing faster than other forms of advertising. Every large company, and most medium and small companies, have Web sites that speak directly to customers. If you work in business today, you need to know about e-commerce.

- If your career is in finance and accounting, you will be working with systems for receiving payments electronically over the Internet and for delivering new online financial services based on the Web.

- If your career is in human resources, you will be using online job-hunting sites to attract new employees.

- If your career is in information systems, you will be helping to design and maintain e-commerce Web sites.

- If your career is in manufacturing, production, or operations management, you will be using the Internet for sourcing, and using a variety of network exchanges and private industrial networks for procurement and management of your supply chain.

- If your career is in sales and marketing, you will be using the Web to provide digital products and services, and to sell and promote products by using personalization, customization, and community marketing techniques.

---

1   ELECTRONIC COMMERCE AND THE INTERNET

Have you ever downloaded music over the Web? Ever purchased books and CDs online? Have you ever used the Web to search for information about personal clothing items before you bought anything in a retail store? If so, you've participated in e-commerce. So have hundreds of millions of people around the globe. And although most purchases still take place through traditional channels, e-commerce continues to be the fastest growing form of retail trade, and continues to transform the way companies do business.

E-COMMERCE TODAY

E-commerce refers to the use of the Internet and the Web to transact business. More formally, e-commerce is about digitally enabled commercial transactions between and among organizations and individuals. For the most part, this means transactions that occur over the Internet and the Web. Commercial transactions involve the exchange of value (e.g., money) across organizational or individual boundaries in return for products and services.

E-commerce began in 1995 when one of the first Internet portals, Netscape.com, accepted the first ads from major corporations and popularized the idea that the Web could be used as a new medium for advertising and sales. No one envisioned at the time what would turn out to be an exponential growth curve for e-commerce retail sales, which tripled and doubled in the early years. Only since 2006 has consumer e-commerce "slowed" to a 25 percent annual growth rate (Figure 1).

Mirroring the history of commercial innovations, such as the telephone, radio, and television, the very rapid growth in e-commerce in the early years created a stock market bubble in e-commerce stocks. Like all bubbles, the "dot-com" bubble burst in March 2001. A large number of e-commerce companies failed during this process. Yet for many others, such as Amazon, eBay, Expedia, and Google, the results have been more positive: soaring revenues, fine-tuned business models that produce profits, and rising stock prices. In 2007, the overall e-commerce revenues picture is very positive:

- Online consumer sales will increase by more than 23 percent in 2007 to an estimated $180 billion (including travel) , with 106 million people purchasing online (eMarketer, 2006).

- The number of individuals online in the United States will expand to 160 million in 2007, up from 147 million in 2004 (eMarketer, 2005). In the world, over 1 billion people are now connected to the Internet. Growth in the overall Internet population has spurred growth in e-commerce.

- On the average day, 70 million people go online, 140 million send e-mail, 5 million write on their blogs, 4 million share music on peer-to-peer networks, and 3 million use the Internet to rate a person, product, or service.

- The number of people who have purchased something online expanded to about 106 million, with additional millions shopping (gathering information) but not purchasing.

FIGURE 1   THE GROWTH OF E-COMMERCE

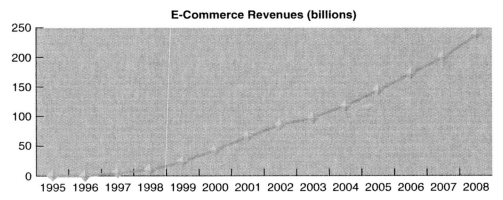

Retail e-commerce revenues have grown exponentially since 1995 and have only recently "slowed" to a very rapid 25 percent annual increase, which is projected to remain the same until 2008.

Source: Based on data from eMarketer, 2006; Shop.org and Forrester Research, 2005; and authors.

TABLE 1 NEW DEVELOPMENTS IN E-COMMERCE

BUSINESS TRANSFORMATION

The first wave of e-commerce transformed the business world of books, music, and air travel. In the second wave, eight new industries are facing a similar transformation scenario: telephones, movies, television, jewelry, real estate, hotels, bill payments, and software.

The breadth of e-commerce offerings grows, especially in travel, information clearinghouses, entertainment, retail apparel, appliances, and home furnishings.

The online demographics of shoppers continue to broaden to match that of ordinary shoppers.

Pure e-commerce business models will be refined further to achieve higher levels of profitability, whereas traditional retail brands, such as Sears, J.C.Penney, and Wal-Mart, will use e-commerce to retain their dominant retail positions.

Small businesses and entrepreneurs continue to flood the e-commerce marketplace, often riding on the infrastructures created by industry giants, such as Amazon, eBay, and Overture.

TECHNOLOGY FOUNDATIONS

Wireless Internet connections (Wi-Fi, WiMax, and 3G mobile phone) grow rapidly.

Podcasting takes off as a new medium for distribution of radio and user-generated content.

The Internet broadband foundation becomes stronger in households and businesses as transmission prices fall. More than 42 million households had broadband cable or DSL access to the Internet in 2005—about 38 percent of all households (eMarketer, 2006).

RSS (Rich Site Summary or Really Simple Syndication) grows to become a major new form of user-controlled information distribution that rivals e-mail in some applications.

Computing and networking component prices continue to fall dramatically.

New Internet-based models of computing, such as .NET and Web services, expand B2B opportunities.

NEW BUSINESS MODELS EMERGE

User-generated content and syndication in the form of blogs and social networks grow to form an entirely new self-publishing forum. Advertisers begin taking advantage of blogs and social sites as a new commercial medium.

Newspapers and other traditional media adopt online, interactive models.

More than half the Internet user population join a social group on the Internet.

- B2B e-commerce—use of the Internet for business-to-business commerce—will continue to expand by about 25 percent in 2007 to more than $2 trillion and continues to strengthen (Laudon and Traver, 2006).

The e-commerce revolution is still just beginning. Individuals and businesses will increasingly use the Internet to conduct commerce as more products and services come online and more households switch to broadband telecommunications. More industries will be transformed by e-commerce, including travel reservations, music and entertainment, news, software, education, and finance. Table 1 highlights these new e-commerce developments.

WHY E-COMMERCE IS DIFFERENT

Why has e-commerce grown so rapidly? The answer lies in the unique nature of the Internet and the Web. Simply put, the Internet and e-commerce technologies are much more rich and powerful than previous technology revolutions. Table 2 describes the unique features of the Internet and Web as a commercial medium.

Let's explore each of these unique features in more detail.

TABLE 2   SEVEN UNIQUE FEATURES OF E-COMMERCE TECHNOLOGY

E-COMMERCE TECHNOLOGY DIMENSION	BUSINESS SIGNIFICANCE
Ubiquity. Internet/Web technology is available everywhere: at work, at home, and elsewhere via mobile devices, anytime.	The marketplace is extended beyond traditional boundaries and is removed from a temporal and geographic location. "Marketspace" is created; shopping can take place anywhere. Customer convenience is enhanced, and shopping costs are reduced.
Global Reach. The technology reaches across national boundaries, around the Earth.	Commerce is enabled across cultural and national boundaries seamlessly and without modification. The marketspace includes, potentially, billions of consumers and millions of businesses worldwide.
Universal Standards. There is one set of technology standards, namely Internet standards.	With one set of technical standards across the globe, disparate computer systems can easily communicate with each other.
Richness. Video, audio, and text messages are possible.	Video, audio, and text marketing messages are integrated into a single marketing message and consumer experience.
Interactivity. The technology works through interaction with the user.	Consumers are engaged in a dialog that dynamically adjusts the experience to the individual, and makes the consumer a co-participant in the process of delivering goods to the market.
Information Density. The technology reduces information costs and raises quality.	Information processing, storage, and communication costs drop dramatically, whereas currency, accuracy, and timeliness improve greatly. Information becomes plentiful, cheap, and more accurate.
Personalization/Customization. The technology allows personalized messages to be delivered to individuals as well as groups.	Personalization of marketing messages and customization of products and services are based on individual characteristics.

Ubiquity

In traditional commerce, a marketplace is a physical place, such as a retail store, that you visit to transact business. E-commerce is ubiquitous, meaning that is it available just about everywhere, at all times. It makes it possible to shop from your desktop, at home, at work, or even from your car, using mobile commerce. The result is called a **marketspace**—a marketplace extended beyond traditional boundaries and removed from a temporal and geographic location.

From a consumer point of view, ubiquity reduces transaction costs—the costs of participating in a market. To transact business, it is no longer necessary that you spend time or money traveling to a market, and much less mental effort is required to make a purchase.

Global Reach

E-commerce technology permits commercial transactions to cross cultural and national boundaries far more conveniently and cost effectively than is true in traditional commerce. As a result, the potential market size for e-commerce merchants is roughly equal to the size of the world's online population (more than 1.1 billion in 2006, and growing rapidly).

In contrast, much traditional commerce is local or regional—it involves local merchants or national merchants with local outlets. Television and radio stations and newspapers, for instance, are primarily local and regional institutions with limited, but powerful, national networks that can attract a national audience but not easily cross national boundaries to a global audience.

Universal Standards

One strikingly unusual feature of e-commerce technologies is that the technical standards of the Internet and, therefore, the technical standards for conducting e-commerce are universal standards. They are shared by all nations around the world and enable any computer to link with any other computer regardless of the technology platform each is using. In contrast, most traditional commerce technologies differ from one nation to the next. For instance, television and radio standards differ around the world, as does cell telephone technology.

The universal technical standards of the Internet and e-commerce greatly lower **market entry costs**—the cost merchants must pay simply to bring their goods to market. At the same time, for consumers, universal standards reduce **search costs**—the effort required to find suitable products.

Richness

Information **richness** refers to the complexity and content of a message. Traditional markets, national sales forces, and small retail stores have great richness: They are able to provide personal, face-to-face service using aural and visual cues when making a sale. The richness of traditional markets makes them powerful selling or commercial environments. Prior to the development of the Web, there was a trade-off between richness and reach: The larger the audience reached, the less rich the message. The Web makes it possible to deliver rich messages with text, audio, and video simultaneously to large numbers of people.

Interactivity

Unlike any of the commercial technologies of the twentieth century, with the possible exception of the telephone, e-commerce technologies are interactive, meaning they allow for two-way communication between merchant and consumer. Television, for instance, cannot ask viewers any questions or enter into conversations with them, and it cannot request that customer information be entered into a form. In contrast, all of these activities are possible on an e-commerce Web site. Interactivity allows an online merchant to engage a consumer in ways similar to a face-to-face experience but on a massive, global scale.

Information Density

The Internet and the Web vastly increase **information density**—the total amount and quality of information available to all market participants, consumers, and merchants alike. E-commerce technologies reduce information collection, storage, processing, and communication costs while greatly increasing the currency, accuracy, and timeliness of information.

Information density in e-commerce markets makes prices and costs more transparent. **Price transparency** refers to the ease with which consumers can find out the variety of prices in a market; **cost transparency** refers to the ability of consumers to discover the actual costs merchants pay for products.

There are advantages for merchants as well. Online merchants can discover much more about consumers than in the past. This allows merchants to segment the market into groups who are willing to pay different prices and permits the merchants to engage in **price discrimination**—selling the same goods, or nearly the same goods, to different targeted groups at different prices. For instance, an online merchant can discover a consumer's avid interest in expensive, exotic vacations and then pitch high-end vacation plans to that consumer at a premium price, knowing this person is willing to pay extra for such a vacation. At the same time, the online merchant can pitch the same vacation plan at a lower price to a more price-sensitive consumer. Information density also helps merchants differentiate their products in terms of cost, brand, and quality.

Personalization/Customization

E-commerce technologies permit **personalization**: Merchants can target their marketing messages to specific individuals by adjusting the message to a person's name, interests, and past purchases. The technology also permits **customization**—changing the delivered product or service based on a user's preferences or prior behavior. Given the interactive nature of e-commerce technology, much information about the consumer can be gathered in the marketplace at the moment of purchase. With the increase in information density, a great deal of information about the consumer's past purchases and behavior can be stored and used by online merchants.

The result is a level of personalization and customization unthinkable with traditional commerce technologies. For instance, you may be able to shape what you see on television by selecting a channel, but you cannot change the content of the channel you have chosen. In contrast, the *Wall Street Journal Online* allows you to select the type of news stories you want to see first and gives you the opportunity to be alerted when certain events happen.

KEY CONCEPTS IN E-COMMERCE: DIGITAL MARKETS AND DIGITAL GOODS

The location, timing, and revenue models of business are based in some part on the cost and distribution of information. When communication is limited to people moving along paths that connect villages, the cost of gathering information is extremely high, and village markets provide the location of business and the business model. The Internet has greatly reduced the cost of obtaining and distributing information, and created a digital marketplace where millions of people are able to exchange massive amounts of information directly, instantly, and for free. As a result, the Internet has changed the way companies conduct business.

The Internet shrinks information asymmetry. An **information asymmetry** exists when one party in a transaction has more information that is important for the transaction than the other party. That information helps determine their relative bargaining power. In digital markets, consumers and suppliers can "see" the prices being charged for goods, and in that sense digital markets are said to be more "transparent" than traditional markets.

For example, until auto retailing sites appeared on the Web, there was a pronounced information asymmetry between auto dealers and customers. Only the auto dealers knew the manufacturers' prices, and it was difficult for consumers to shop around for the best price. Auto dealers' profit margins depended on this asymmetry of information. Today's consumers have access to a legion of Web sites providing competitive pricing information, and three-fourths of U.S. auto buyers use the Internet to shop around for the best deal. Thus, the Web has reduced the information asymmetry surrounding an auto purchase. The Internet has also helped businesses seeking to purchase from other businesses reduce information asymmetries and locate better prices and terms.

Digital markets are very flexible and efficient because they operate with reduced search and transaction costs, lower **menu costs** (merchants' costs of changing prices), price discrimination, and the ability to change prices dynamically based on market conditions. In **dynamic pricing**, the price of a product varies depending on the demand characteristics of the customer or the supply situation of the seller.

These markets may either reduce or increase switching costs, depending on the nature of the product or service being sold, and they may cause some extra delay in gratification. Unlike a physical market, you can't immediately consume a product such as clothing purchased over the Web (although immediate consumption is possible with digital music downloads and other digital products.)

Digital markets provide many opportunities to sell directly to the consumer, bypassing intermediaries, such as distributors or retail outlets. Eliminating intermediaries in the distribution channel can significantly lower purchase transaction costs. To pay for all the steps in a traditional distribution channel, a product may have to be priced as high as 135 percent of its original cost to manufacture.

Figure 2 illustrates how much savings result from eliminating each of these layers in the distribution process. By selling directly to consumers or reducing the number of intermediaries, companies are able to raise profits while charging lower prices. The removal of organizations or business process layers responsible for intermediary steps in a value chain is called **disintermediation.**

Disintermediation is also taking place in the market for services. Airlines and hotels operating their own reservation sites online earn more per ticket because they have eliminated travel agents as intermediaries. Table 3 summarizes the differences between digital markets and traditional markets.

FIGURE 2   THE BENEFITS OF DISINTERMEDIATION TO THE CONSUMER

				Cost per Sweater
Manufacturer	Distributor	Retailer	Customer	$48.50
Manufacturer		Retailer	Customer	$40.34
Manufacturer			Customer	$20.45

The typical distribution channel has several intermediary layers, each of which adds to the final cost of a product, such as a sweater. Removing layers lowers the final cost to the consumer.

413

TABLE 3   DIGITAL MARKETS COMPARED TO TRADITIONAL MARKETS

	DIGITAL MARKETS	TRADITIONAL MARKETS
Information asymmetry	Asymmetry reduced	Asymmetry high
Search costs	Low	High
Transaction costs	Low (sometimes virtually nothing)	High (time, travel)
Delayed gratification	High (or lower in the case of a digital good)	Lower: purchase now
Menu costs	Low	High
Dynamic Pricing	Low cost, instant	High cost, delayed
Price discrimination	Low cost, instant	High cost, delayed
Market segmentation	Low cost, moderate precision	High cost, less precision
Switching costs	Higher/lower (depending on product characteristics)	High
Network effects	Strong	Weaker
Disintermediation	More possible/likely	Less possible/unlikely

Digital Goods

The Internet digital marketplace has greatly expanded sales of digital goods. **Digital goods** are goods that can be delivered over a digital network. Music tracks, video, software, newspapers, magazines, and books can all be expressed, stored, delivered, and sold as purely digital products. Currently, most of these products are sold as physical goods, for example, CDs, DVDs, and hard copy books. But the Internet offers the possibility of delivering all these products on demand as digital products.

In general, for digital goods, the marginal cost of producing another unit is about zero (it costs nothing to make a copy of a music file). However, the cost of producing the original first unit is relatively high—in fact it is nearly the total cost of the product because there are few other costs of inventory and distribution. Costs of delivery over the Internet are very low; marketing costs remain the same; and pricing can be highly variable. (On the Internet, the merchant can changes prices as often as desired because of low menu costs.)

The impact of the Internet on the market for these kinds of digital goods is nothing short of revolutionary, and we see the results around us every day. Businesses dependent on the physical products for sales—such as bookstores, book publishers, music labels, and film studios—face the possibility of declining sales and even destruction of their businesses. Newspapers and magazines are losing readers to the Internet, and losing advertisers. Record label companies are losing sales to Internet piracy and record stores are going out of business. Video rental firms, such as Blockbuster, based on a physical DVD market and physical stores, are losing sales to NetFlix using an Internet model. Hollywood studios as well face the prospect that Internet pirates will distribute their product as digital streaming video, bypassing Hollywood's monopoly on DVD rentals and sales, which now accounts for more than half of industry film revenues. Table 4 describes digital goods and how they differ from traditional physical goods.

TABLE 4 HOW THE INTERNET CHANGES THE MARKETS FOR DIGITAL GOODS

TABLE 4 HOW THE INTERNET CHANGES THE MARKETS FOR DIGITAL GOODS

	DIGITAL GOODS	TRADITIONAL GOODS
Marginal cost/unit	Zero	Greater than zero , high
Cost of production	High (most of the cost)	Variable
Copying cost	Approximately 0	Greater than zero, high
Distributed delivery cost	Low	High
Inventory cost	Low	High
Marketing cost	Variable	Variable

INTERNET BUSINESS MODELS

The bottom line result of these changes in the economics of information is nearly a revolution in commerce, with many new business models appearing and many old business models no longer tenable. Table 5 describes some of the most important Internet business models that have emerged. All, in one way or another, use the Internet to add extra value to existing products and services or to provide the foundation for new products and services.

TABLE 5 INTERNET BUSINESS MODELS

CATEGORY	DESCRIPTION	EXAMPLES
Virtual storefront	Sells physical products directly to consumers or to individual businesses.	Amazon.com RedEnvelope.com
Information broker	Provides product, pricing, and availability information to individuals and businesses. Generates revenue from advertising or from directing buyers to sellers.	Edmunds.com Insweb.com, Realtor.com
Transaction broker	Saves users money and time by processing online sales transactions and generating a fee each time a transaction occurs. Also provides information on rates and terms.	E*Trade.com Expedia.com
Online marketplace	Provides a digital environment where buyers and sellers can meet, search for products, display products, and establish prices for those products. Can provide online auctions or reverse auctions in which buyers submit bids to multiple sellers to purchase at a buyer-specified price as well as negotiated or fixed pricing. Can serve consumers or B2B e-commerce, generating revenue from transaction fees.	eBay.com Priceline.com ChemConnect.com
Content provider	Creates revenue by providing digital content, such as digital news, music, photos, or video, over the Web. The customer may pay to access the content, or revenue may be generated by selling advertising space.	WSJ.com GettyImages.com iTunes.com Games.com
Online service provider	Provides online service for individuals and businesses. Generates revenue from subscription or transaction fees, from advertising, or from collecting marketing information from users.	Streamload.com Xdrive.com, Ofoto.com salesforce.com
Virtual community	Provides an online meeting place where people with similar interests can communicate and find useful information.	YouTube.com MySpace.com, iVillage.com
Portal	Provides initial point of entry to the Web along with specialized content and other services.	Yahoo.com MSN.com, StarMedia.com

Communication and Community

Some of these new business models take advantage of the Internet's rich communication capabilities. eBay is an online auction forum that uses e-mail and other interactive features of the Web. The system accepts bids entered on the Internet, evaluates the bids, and notifies the highest bidder. eBay collects a small commission on each listing and sale. eBay has become so popular that its site serves as a huge trading platform for other companies, hosting hundreds of thousands of "virtual storefronts." The case study concluding this chapter discusses eBay and its business model in greater detail.

Business-to-business auctions have also emerged. GoIndustry, for instance, features Web-based auction services for business-to-business sales of industrial equipment and machinery.

The Internet has created online communities where people with similar interests exchange ideas from many different locations. Some of these virtual communities are providing the foundation for new businesses. iVillage.com provides an online community for women sharing similar interests, such as diet and fitness, pregnancy, parenting, home and garden, and food. Members participate in online discussions and join online "communities" with other like-minded people.

A major source of revenue for these communities involves providing ways for corporate clients to target customers, including the placement of banner ads and pop-up ads on their Web sites. A **banner ad** is a graphic display on a Web page used for advertising. The banner is linked to the advertiser's Web site so that a person clicking the banner is transported to a Web page with more information about the advertiser. **Pop-up ads** work in the opposite manner. They automatically open up when a user accesses a specific Web site, and the user must click the ad to make it disappear.

Social networking sites are a type of online community that has become extremely popular. Social networking is the practice of expanding the number

YouTube is a free online streaming video service enabling users to upload, tag, and share videos worldwide. Members can join and create video groups to connect to people with similar interests.

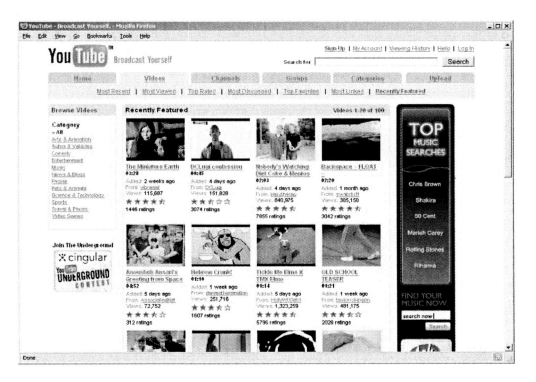

of one's business or social contacts by making connections through individuals. Social networking sites link people through their mutual business or personal connections, enabling them to mine their friends (and their friends' friends) for sales leads, job-hunting tips, or new friends. MySpace.com, Facebook.com. and Friendster.com appeal to people who are primarily interested in extending their friendships, while LinkedIn.com focuses on job networking.

Members of social networking sites spend hours surfing pages, checking out other members, and exchanging messages, and they reveal a great deal of information about themselves. Businesses harvest this information to create carefully targeted promotions that far surpass the typical text and display ads found on the Web. They also use the sites to interact with potential customers. The most popular of these sites attract so many visitors and are so "sticky" that they have become very powerful marketing tools. The Interactive Session on Management discusses MySpace as a business model.

Social networking is so appealing that it has inspired a new type of e-commerce experience called **social shopping**. Social shopping sites such as Kaboodle, ThisNext, Wists.com, and StyleHive.com provide online meeting places for people to swap shopping ideas. These sites provide tools for users to create their own Web pages with information and images about items they like to help other shoppers.

Digital Content, Entertainment, and Services

The ability to deliver digital goods and digital content over the Web has created new alternatives to traditional print and broadcast media. There are Web sites for digital versions of print publications, such as the *New York Times* or *The Wall Street Journal*, and for new online journals such as Salon.com.

Some of the most popular Web sites deliver entertainment in digital form. Online games attract huge numbers of players. For example, Blizzard Entertainment's online role-playing game World of Warcraft earned $1 billion in 2006 alone, from 7 million players worldwide (Wireless Week, 2006).

You can listen to some of your favorite radio channels, such as Classic Rock or the BBC, on the Web as well as many independent channels. Because the radio signal is relayed over the Internet, it is possible to access stations from anywhere in the world. Services such as Yahoo!'s LAUNCHcast and RealNetworks' Rhapsody even put together individualized radio channels for listeners.

Broadband connections now make it possible for Web sites to display full-length films and television shows. Apple, Amazon.com, Movielink, and CinemaNow have downloading services for full-length movies. The chapter-opening case describes online broadcasts of MLB baseball games. For viewers outside North America, the National Football League (NFL) started streaming a full season of live games over the Internet.

Many of you use the Web to preview and download music. Although some of this Internet music is free of charge, Apple's iTunes and other sites are generating revenue by charging for each song or album downloaded from their Web sites. The phenomenal popularity of Apple's iTunes music service and Apple's iPod portable music player has inspired a new form of digital content delivery called *podcasting*. **Podcasting** is a method of publishing audio broadcasts via the Internet, allowing subscribing users to download audio files onto their personal computers or portable music players. Video clips designed to be downloaded and viewed on a portable device are called vcasts.

Podcasting enables independent producers to self-publish their own audio content and gives broadcast media a new distribution method. Podcasts also have internal uses for businesses who want to distribute information in audio

417

INTERACTIVE SESSION: MANAGEMENT

THE ALLURE OF MYSPACE

MySpace.com has become nothing short of a phenomenon. Next to Yahoo! it's the most highly visited Web site in the United States, and the destination of nearly 4.5 percent of all online visits. And it has only been in business since January 2004!

MySpace offers a rich array of features, including message boards, e-mail, instant messaging, video clips, classified ads, online games, blogs, job searches, music, and, of course, the ability to network with other people online and perhaps meet them in person. Although MySpace touts itself as a private community favoring bands and musicians seeking audiences for their music, it's also big business. News Corp paid $580 million to acquire MySpace in late 2005.

Advertisers are enthralled with the opportunity to create personal relationships with millions of young people. "What we really struck upon is the power of friendship," said Michael Barrett, chief revenue officer for News Corp.'s Fox Interactive Media. And MySpace's circle of friends is huge. According to Nielsen/NetRatings, MySpace logged close to 457 million unique visitors in June 2006 alone, with users spending an average of nearly two hours on each visit to the site. By early August 2006, MySpace was hosting 100 million profiles.

Companies can pay MySpace to set up profiles of their products as if they were members of the community. MySpace users can become "friends" of Toyota Motor's Yaris car or entire movies, such as Full Metal Alchemist. Profile sponsors see exactly who is interested in their product and gather rich data on age, marital status, location language, gender, occupation, and personal interests.

Procter & Gamble used MySpace to launch its Secret Sparkle deodorant for 16- to 24-year-old women by linking the product to the Web pages of musicians that used MySpace and appealed to the same demographic group. When users listened to new songs by The Donnas and Bonnie McKey, they were exposed to ads for Secret Sparkle and offered a chance to participate in a Secret Sparkle sweepstakes.

On August 8, 2006, Google agreed to pay Fox Interactive Media $900 million to have MySpace use its search engine so that it could place text ads alongside search results generated by MySpace users.

Besides the Google deal, MySpace will be able to generate revenue display advertising, video advertising, and ads on key MySpace destinations such as the music page, the main comedy page, or the home page. Pali Research analyst Richard Greenfield expects MySpace to generate $300 million in revenue for fiscal year 2007 and at least $450 million the following year.

Sounds like good business—except that MySpace is also very controversial. Many teenage subscribers post suggestive photos of themselves and lie about their age. About one-fourth of all MySpace users are registered as minors under 18 years of age, but that number could be much larger. Parents, politicians, and police worry that sexual predators use MySpace to stalk potential victims. In June 2006, the mother of a 14-year-old girl who was sexually assaulted by a 19-year-old user sued MySpace and News Corp for $30 million. The lawsuit, filed in Texas, claimed the 19-year-old lied about being a high school senior to gain the young girl's trust and phone number. Other similar incidents have been reported.

In response, MySpace is trying to restrict how adults contact its younger users. It already prohibits children under 13 from setting up accounts and displays only partial profiles of registered 14- or 15-year-olds unless the person viewing the profile is already on the teen's list of friends. (Partial profiles display gender, age, and city, while full profiles describe hobbies, schools, and other personal details.) Friends' lists are no longer available to MySpace users over 18 unless they already know the youth's full name or e-mail address. However, users under 18 can still make contact, and MySpace has no mechanism for verifying that users submit their true age when registering. So adults can sign up as minors and join a 14-year-old's list of friends. MySpace is also fine-tuning its ad targeting to avoid displaying gambling and other adult-themed sites on minors' profile pages.

Sources: Elizabeth Holmes, "On MySpace, Millions of Users Make 'Friends' with Ads," *The Wall Street Journal*, August 7, 2006; Jessica Sebor, "MySpace Cadets," *Customer Relationship Management*, September 2006; Steve Rosenbush, "Fox to Make MySpace More Spacious," *Business Week*, August 8, 2006; Steve Rosenbush, "Socializing for Dollars," *Business Week*, April 10, 2006; "MySpace Plans New Age Restritions," Associated Press, June 21, 2006; Anick Jesdanun, "Online Age Verification May Prove Complex," Associated Press, July 17, 2006.

CASE STUDY QUESTIONS

1. How do businesses benefit from MySpace?
How do MySpace members benefit?

2. Does MySpace create an ethical dilemma?
Why or why not?

3. Do parent and schools' objections to MySpace
have any merit? Should a site like MySpace be
allowed to operate? Why or why not?

4. Is there anything that MySpace management can
do to make the site less controversial?

MIS IN ACTION

Explore MySpace.com, examining the features and
tools that are not restricted to registered members.
View the profile created for a product such as the
Toyota Yaris or a movie of your choice and related
profiles about individuals who are "friends" of that
product. Then answer the following questions:

1. What information can you find out about the
product from its MySpace profile?

2. What features of the profile would attract teenage
and college buyers? How does this profile differ
from display advertising on the Web?

3. Explore some of the profiles of "friends" of this
product. What kind of information is available
about them?

4. Is using MySpace a good way to promote this
product? Why or why not?

form to their employees. Internet security firm SonicWall uses podcasts to
demonstrate its expertise to customers and to provide new product information
to its resellers.

The Web's information resources are so vast and rich that portals have
emerged as an Internet business model. Portals help individuals and organizations locate information more efficiently and also seek to become destination
sites by aggregating content on their sites. A portal is a Web interface for presenting integrated, personalized information from a variety of sources. As an e-
commerce business model, a *portal* is a "supersite" that provides a comprehensive entry point for a huge array of resources and services on the Internet.

Yahoo! is an example. It provides capabilities for locating information on the
Internet along with news, sports, weather, telephone directories, maps, games,
shopping, e-mail, chat, discussion boards, and links to other sites. Specialized portals help users with specific interests. For example, StarMedia is a portal
customized for Latin American Internet users, and the portal Sina.com is
customized for Chinese users.

Yahoo! and other portals and Web content sites often combine content and
applications from many different sources and service providers. Other Internet
business models use syndication as well, providing additional value. For
example, E*Trade, the discount Web trading site, purchases most of its content
from outside sources such as Reuters (news) and BigCharts.com (charts).
Online **syndicators**, who aggregate content or applications from multiple
sources, package them for distribution, and resell them to third-party Web sites,
have emerged as another variant of the online content provider business
model. The Web makes it much easier for companies to aggregate, repackage,
and distribute information and information-based services.

Application service providers, such as salesforce.com, feature software that
runs over the Web. They provide online services to subscribing businesses.
Other online service providers offer services to individual consumers, such as
remote storage of data at Xdrive.com or online photo storage and digital photo

printouts at Ofoto.com. Service providers generate revenue through subscription fees or from advertising.

Most of the business models described in Table 5 are called **pure-play** business models because they are based purely on the Internet. These firms did not have an existing bricks-and-mortar business when they designed their Internet business. However, many existing retail firms, such as L.L.Bean, Office Depot, REI, and *The Wall Street Journal*, have developed Web sites as extensions of their traditional bricks-and-mortar businesses. Such businesses represent a hybrid **clicks-and-mortar** business model.

ELECTRONIC COMMERCE

Although most commercial transactions still take place through traditional retail channels, rising numbers of consumers and businesses are using the Internet for electronic commerce. Today, e-commerce revenue represents about 2 percent of all retail sales in the United States, and there is tremendous upside potential for growth.

TYPES OF ELECTRONIC COMMERCE

There are many ways to classify electronic commerce transactions. One is by looking at the nature of the participants in the electronic commerce transaction. The three major electronic commerce categories are business-to-consumer (B2C) e-commerce, business-to-business (B2B) e-commerce, and consumer-to-consumer (C2C) e-commerce.

- **Business-to-consumer (B2C) electronic commerce** involves retailing products and services to individual shoppers. Barnesandnoble.com, which sells books, software, and music to individual consumers, is an example of B2C e-commerce.

- **Business-to-business (B2B) electronic commerce** involves sales of goods and services among businesses. ChemConnect's Web site for buying and selling natural gas liquids, refined and intermediate fuels, chemicals, and plastics is an example of B2B e-commerce.

- **Consumer-to-consumer (C2C) electronic commerce** involves consumers selling directly to consumers. For example, eBay, the giant Web auction site, enables people to sell their goods to other consumers by auctioning the merchandise off to the highest bidder.

Another way of classifying electronic commerce transactions is in terms of the participants' physical connection to the Web. Until recently, almost all e-commerce transactions took place over wired networks. Now mobile phones and other wireless handheld digital appliances are Internet-enabled to send text messages and e-mail, access Web sites, and make purchases. Companies are offering new types of Web-based products and services that can be accessed by these wireless devices. The use of handheld wireless devices for purchasing goods and services from any location has been termed **mobile commerce** or **m-commerce**. Both business-to-business and business-to-consumer e-commerce transactions can take place using m-commerce technology, which we discuss in detail in Section 3.

ACHIEVING CUSTOMER INTIMACY: INTERACTIVE MARKETING, PERSONALIZATION, AND SELF-SERVICE

The unique dimensions of e-commerce technologies that we have just described offer many new possibilities for marketing and selling. The Internet provides companies with additional channels of communication and interaction for closer yet more cost-effective relationships with customers in sales, marketing, and customer support.

Interactive Marketing and Personalization

The Internet and e-commerce have helped some merchants achieve the holy grail of marketing: making products for millions of consumers that are personal, an impossible task in traditional markets. Web sites, such as those for Lands' End (shirts and pants) and VistaPrint (business cards, note cards, and labels), feature online tools that allow consumers to purchase products tailored to their individual specifications.

Web sites have become a bountiful source of detailed information about customer behavior, preferences, needs, and buying patterns that companies can use to tailor promotions, products, services, and pricing. Some customer information may be obtained by asking visitors to "register" online and provide information about themselves, but many companies also collect customer information using software tools that track the activities of Web site visitors.

Clickstream tracking tools collect data on customer activities at Web sites and store them in a log. The tools record the site that users visited prior to coming to a particular Web site and where these users go when they leave that site. They also record the specific pages visited on the particular site, the time spent on each page of the site, the types of pages visited, and what the visitors purchased (see Figure 3). Firms analyze this information about customer interests and behavior to develop precise profiles of existing and potential customers.

FIGURE 3   WEB SITE VISITOR TRACKING

Click 1	The shopper clicks on the home page. The store can tell that the shopper arrived from the Yahoo! portal at 2:30 PM (which might help determine staffing for customer service centers) and how long she lingered on the home page (which might indicate trouble navigating the site).
Click 2	
Click 3	The shopper clicks on blouses, clicks to select a woman's white blouse, then clicks to view the same item in pink. The shopper clicks to select this item in a size 10 in pink and clicks to place it in her shopping cart. This information can help the store determine which sizes and colors are most popular.
Click 4	
Click 5	
Click 6	From the shopping cart page, the shopper clicks to close the browser to leave the Web site without purchasing the blouse. This action could indicate the shopper changed her mind or that she had a problem with the Web site's checkout and payment process. Such behavior might signal that the Web site was not well designed.

E-commerce Web sites have tools to track a shopper's every step through an online store. Close examination of customer behavior at a Web site selling women's clothing shows what the store might learn at each step and what actions it could take to increase sales.

Such information enables firms to create unique personalized Web pages that display content or ads for products or services of special interest to each user, improving the customer's experience and creating additional value (see Figure 4). By using personalization technology to modify the Web pages presented to each customer, marketers achieve the benefits of using individual salespeople at dramatically lower costs.

One technique for Web personalization is **collaborative filtering**, which compares information gathered about a specific user's behavior at a Web site to data about other customers with similar interests to predict what the user would like to see next. The software then makes recommendations to users based on their assumed interests. For example, Amazon.com and Barnesandnoble.com use collaborative filtering software to prepare personalized book recommendations: "Customers who bought this book also bought . . .." These recommendations are made just at the point of purchase, an ideal time to prompt a consumer into purchasing a related product.

Blogs

Blogs have emerged as another promising Web-based tool for marketing. A blog, the popular term for a Weblog, is a personal Web page that typically contains a series of chronological entries (newest to oldest) by its author, and links to related Web pages.

The blog may include a blogroll (a collection of links to other blogs) and TrackBacks (a list of entries in other blogs that refer to a post on the first blog). Most blogs allow readers to post comments on the blog entries as well.

FIGURE 4   WEB SITE PERSONALIZATION

Firms can create unique personalized Web pages that display content or ads for products or services of special interest to individual users, improving the customer experience and creating additional value.

The act of creating a blog is often referred to as "blogging." Blogs are either hosted by a third-party site such as Blogger.com (owned by Google and formerly called Blogspot.com), LiveJournal.com, Typepad.com, and Xanga.com, or prospective bloggers can download software such as Moveable Type and bBlog to create a blog that is hosted by the user's ISP. Blog pages are usually variations on templates provided by the blogging service or software and hence require no knowledge of HTML. Therefore, millions of people without HTML skills of any kind can post their own Web pages, and share content with friends and relatives. The totality of blog-related Web sites is often referred to as the **blogosphere**.

The content of blogs range from individual musings to corporate communications. Blogs have had a significant impact on political affairs, and have gained increasing notice for their role in breaking and shaping the news. Blogs have become hugely popular. Some research firms put the number of blogs at more than 25 million as of January 2006. According to comScore Networks, nearly 50 million Americans visited a blog during the first quarter of 2005 and around 7 percent of the U.S. online population (8 million people) have created blogs (comScore Networks, 2005; Pew Internet & American Life Project, 2005d).

Companies that maintain public blogs use them as a new channel for reaching customers. These corporate blogs provide a personal and conversational way for businesses to present information to the public and prospective customers about new products and services. Readers are often invited to post comments. The Interactive Session on Organizations describes how organic yogurt company Stonyfield Farm Inc. is taking advantage of these capabilities to create tighter relationships with its customers.

Marketers are starting to analyze blogs as well as chat groups and message boards to see what is being said online about new products, old brands, and ad campaigns. Blog-watching services that monitor popular blogs claim that "blog watching" can be cheaper and faster for analyzing consumer interests and sentiment than traditional focus groups and surveys. For example, Polaroid learned from blogs that consumers online frequently discuss photo longevity and archiving, prompting it to pay more attention to long-lasting photos in its product development. Companies are also posting ads on some of the most popular blogs published by individuals or by other organizations.

As of September 2006, about 6 percent of Fortune 500 companies had active public blogs. Many more, such as McDonalds and Cannondale Bicycle, use them for internal corporate communication (Business Week, 2006; Fortune 500 Business Blogging Wiki, 2006). Also useful for internal communication are wikis.

Customer Self-Service

Many companies use their Web sites and e-mail to answer customer questions or to provide customers with product information, reducing the need for human customer-support experts. For instance, American, Northwest, and other major airlines have created Web sites where customers can review flight departure and arrival times, seating charts, and airport logistics; check frequent-flyer miles; and purchase tickets online. Customers of UPS use its Web site to track shipments, calculate shipping costs, determine time in transit, and arrange for a package pickup. FedEx and other package delivery firms provide similar Web-based services. Automated self-service or other Web-based responses to customer questions cost only a fraction of what a live customer service representative on the telephone would cost.

INTERACTIVE SESSION: ORGANIZATIONS

STONYFIELD FARM BLOGS FOR ORGANIC COMMUNICATION

The story of Stonyfield Farm is something of a legend. In 1983, friends and social activists Gary Hirschberg and Samuel Kaymen started out with a great yogurt recipe, seven cows, and a dream. They set up an organic yogurt company in Wilton, New Hampshire, to capitalize on baby boomers' growing concerns with pure foods and health, and to revitalize the New England dairy industry. Stonyfield Farms has grown to become the third largest organic company in the world, with more than $50 million in annual sales in 50 states. It produces more than 18 million cups of yogurt each month.

Stonyfield Farm's phenomenal growth is in part attributable to its ability to provide a product for a special niche market—people who treasure healthy foods and want to protect the environment. These values have become embedded in the company's "personality." Stonyfield pledges to use in its products only natural ingredients and milk that have not been produced with antibiotics, synthetic growth hormones, and toxic pesticides and fertilizers. The company donates 10 percent of its profits each year to efforts that help protect or restore the Earth.

As the company expanded, management feared it would lose touch with its loyal and committed customer base. Traditional media-based advertising was expensive and wouldn't really help the company "connect" with the kinds of people it was trying to reach. This company prefers word-of-mouth approaches that get its message to customers in ways that are more compatible with its grassroots, organic, activist people-friendly image. Stonyfield has several active e-mail newsletters with more than 500,000 subscribers, and it regularly places messages promoting causes it supports on the lids of its yogurt cups. Now it is turning to blogs to further personalize its relationship with customers and reach even more people.

Inspired by Howard Dean's presidential campaign and tutorials from Dean's bloggers, CEO Hirschberg became convinced that Stonyfield could use blogs to create a more personal relationship with consumers that is different from the traditional selling relationship. "The blogs give us what we call a handshake with consumers" and "a little more access to us as a people with a mission," he says.

Stonyfield now publishes two different blogs on its Web site—Baby Babble and the Bovine Bugle. At one time Stonyfield was managing five blogs, but decided to retire three of them because they were not attracting enough readers.

Baby Babble provides a forum for Stonyfield employees and other parents of young children to meet and talk about child development and balancing work with family. Stonyfield started that blog because baby yogurts are one of its most popular product lines and blogs about parenting seem to draw large numbers of readers.

The Bovine Bugle provides reports from Jonathan Gates's organic dairy farm in Franklin, Vermont, a member of the organic cooperative that supplies the milk for Stonyfield products. This blog elicits a large number of nostalgic comments from readers remembering their childhood on a farm. As organic foods go mainstream, these blogs help the company show how its brand differs from others and invite customers to help them in that effort.

Stonyfield continually posts new content to each of the blogs. Readers can subscribe to any of these blogs and automatically receive updates when they become available. And of course, they can respond to the postings.

At this point, the benefits of Stonyfield's blogs have not yet been quantified, but management has faith that there are real benefits. The blogs have created a positive response to the Stonyfield brand by providing readers with something that inspires them or piques their interest. If the blogs give readers new information, inspire them to take environmental actions, or ask for opinions, management believes they will remember the brand when they stand in front of the yogurt case at the supermarket or grocery store and that they will reach for Stonyfield rather than a competing product when given the choice.

Stonyfield has a very large Web site. The blogs provide a way to highlight some of the Web content that might otherwise get lost. This, too, helps steer some blog readers to buy Stonyfield products.

Sources: "Stonyfield Farm's Chief Blogger Leaves," Backbone Corporate Blogging Survey, March 24, 2006; "Online Extra: Stonyfield Farm's Blog Culture," *Business Week*, May 2, 2005; Sarah Needleman, "Blogging Becomes a Corporate Job: Digital 'Handshake'?" *The Wall Street Journal*, May 31, 2005; and www.stonyfieldfarms.com, accessed September 12, 2006.

CASE STUDY QUESTIONS

1. What are Stonyfield Farm's business model and business strategy? What challenges and problems does the company face?
2. How do blogs help the company solve these problems and compete in the industry?
3. What are the advantages and disadvantages of using blogs for a company such as Stonyfield Farm?

MIS IN ACTION

Visit Stonyfield Farm's Web site and explore each of its blogs. Read some of the postings and related material. Then answer these questions:

1. Describe the kind of topics discussed on Stonyfield Farm's blogs. Are they closely related to Stonyfield's products? What kinds of people would they attract?
2. Is there any other content on the blog pages to promote Stonyfield products? Describe what you see and how it might help the company.
3. Should all companies use blogs to reach their customers? Why or why not?

New software products are even integrating the Web with customer call centers, where customer service problems have been traditionally handled over the telephone. A **call center** is an organizational department responsible for handling customer service issues by telephone and other channels. For example, a visitor to the Lands' End Web site can request a phone call from customer service by entering his or her telephone number. A call-center system directs a customer service representative to place a voice telephone call to the user's phone.

Visitors to the United States Postal Service Web site can calculate postage, print shipping labels, schedule package pickups, and track shipments. Web sites for customer self-service are convenient for customers and help firms lower their customer service and support costs.

BUSINESS-TO-BUSINESS (B2B) ELECTRONIC COMMERCE: NEW EFFICIENCIES AND RELATIONSHIPS

About 80 percent of B2B e-commerce is still based on proprietary systems for **electronic data interchange (EDI)**, which enables the computer-to-computer exchange between two organizations of standard transactions such as invoices, bills of lading, shipment schedules, or purchase orders. Transactions are automatically transmitted from one information system to another through a network, eliminating the printing and handling of paper at one end and the inputting of data at the other. Each major industry in the United States and much of the rest of the world has EDI standards that define the structure and information fields of electronic documents for that industry.

EDI originally automated the exchange of documents such as purchase orders, invoices, and shipping notices. Although some companies still use EDI for document automation, firms engaged in just-in-time inventory replenishment and continuous production use EDI as a system for continuous replenishment. Suppliers have online access to selected parts of the purchasing firm's production and delivery schedules and automatically ship materials and goods to meet prespecified targets without intervention by firm purchasing agents (see Figure 5).

Although many organizations still use private networks for EDI, companies are increasingly turning to the Internet for this purpose because it provides a much more flexible and low-cost platform for linking to other firms. Using the Internet, businesses are able to extend digital technology to a wider range of activities and broaden their circle of trading partners.

Take procurement, for example. **Procurement** involves not only purchasing goods and materials but also sourcing, negotiating with suppliers, paying for goods, and making delivery arrangements. Businesses can now use the Internet to locate the most low-cost supplier, search online catalogs of supplier products, negotiate with suppliers, place orders, make payments, and arrange transportation. They are not limited to partners linked by traditional EDI networks.

The Internet and Web technology enable businesses to create new electronic storefronts for selling to other businesses with multimedia graphic displays and interactive features similar to those for B2C commerce. Alternatively, businesses can use Internet technology to create extranets or electronic marketplaces for linking to other businesses for purchase and sale transactions.

FIGURE 5   ELECTRONIC DATA INTERCHANGE (EDI)

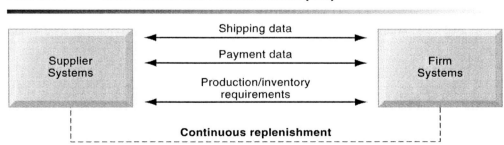

Companies use EDI to automate transactions for B2B e-commerce and continuous inventory replenishment. Suppliers can automatically send data about shipments to purchasing firms. The purchasing firms can use EDI to provide production and inventory requirements and payment data to suppliers.

FIGURE 6   A PRIVATE INDUSTRIAL NETWORK

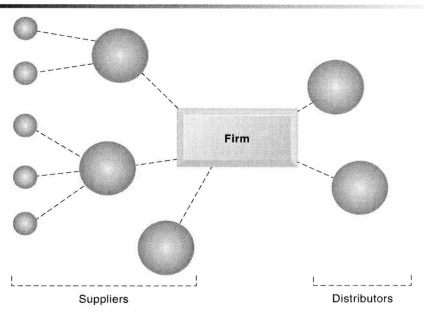

Suppliers   Distributors

A private industrial network, also known as a private exchange, links a firm to its suppliers, distributors, and other key business partners for efficient supply chain management and other collaborative commerce activities.

Private industrial networks typically consist of a large firm using an extranet to link to its suppliers and other key business partners (see Figure 6). The network is owned by the buyer, and it permits the firm and designated suppliers, distributors, and other business partners to share product design and development, marketing, production scheduling, inventory management, and unstructured communication, including graphics and e-mail. Another term for a private industrial network is a **private exchange**.

An example is VWGroupSupply.com, which links the Volkswagen Group and its suppliers. VWGroupSupply.com handles 90 percent of all global purchasing for Volkswagen, including all automotive and parts components.

Net marketplaces, which are sometimes called *e-hubs*, provide a single, digital marketplace based on Internet technology for many different buyers and sellers (see Figure 7). They are industry owned or operate as independent intermediaries between buyers and sellers. Net marketplaces generate revenue from purchase and sale transactions and other services provided to clients. Participants in Net marketplaces can establish prices through online negotiations, auctions, or requests for quotations, or they can use fixed prices.

There are many different types of Net marketplaces and ways of classifying them. Some Net marketplaces sell *direct goods* and some sell *indirect goods*. Direct goods are goods used in a production process, such as sheet steel for auto body production. Indirect goods are all other goods not directly involved in the production process, such as office supplies or products for maintenance and repair. Some Net marketplaces support contractual purchasing based on long-term relationships with designated suppliers, and others support short-term spot purchasing, where goods are purchased based on immediate needs, often from many different suppliers.

FIGURE 7   A NET MARKETPLACE

- Catalogs
- Sourcing
- Automated purchasing
- Processing and fulfillment

Suppliers   Buyers

Net marketplaces are online marketplaces where multiple buyers can purchase from multiple sellers.

Some Net marketplaces serve vertical markets for specific industries, such as automobiles, telecommunications, or machine tools, whereas others serve horizontal markets for goods and services that can be found in many different industries, such as office equipment or transportation.

Exostar is an example of an industry-owned net marketplace, focusing on long-term contract purchasing relationships and on providing common networks and computing platforms for reducing supply-chain inefficiencies. This aerospace and defense industry-sponsored Net marketplace was founded jointly by BAE Systems, Boeing, Lockheed Martin, Raytheon, and Rolls-Royce PLC to connect these companies to their suppliers and facilitate collaboration on major projects. More than 16,000 trading partners in the commercial, military, and government sectors use Exostar's sourcing, e-procurement, and collaboration tools for both direct and indirect goods. Exostar includes capabilities for auctioning, purchase forecasting, issuing electronic payments and receipts, and linking to participants' internal corporate systems. Also featured are capabilities for collaboration on joint development projects and sharing engineering product data.

Exchanges are independently owned third-party Net marketplaces that connect thousands of suppliers and buyers for spot purchasing. Many exchanges provide vertical markets for a single industry, such as food, electronics, or industrial equipment, and they primarily deal with direct goods. For example, FoodTrader.com automates spot purchases among buyers and sellers from more than 180 countries in the food and agriculture industry.

Exchanges proliferated during the early years of e-commerce, but many have failed. Suppliers were reluctant to participate because the exchanges encouraged competitive bidding that drove prices down and did not offer any long-term relationships with buyers or services to make lowering prices worthwhile. Many essential direct purchases are not conducted on a spot basis because they require contracts and consideration of issues such as delivery timing, customization, and quality of products.

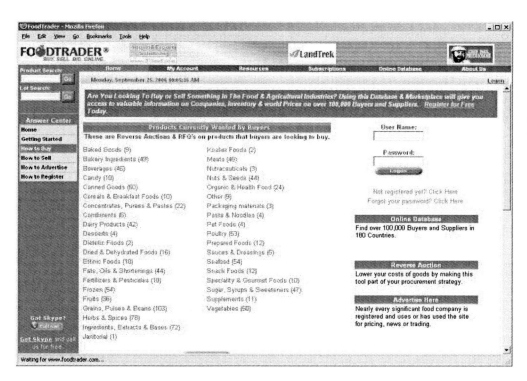

FoodTrader.com is a Net marketplace serving the food and agricultural industries. Over 100,000 growers, packers, processors, and retail chains in 170 countries use the site as a one-stop source to buy and sell food products directly.

Courtesy of FoodTrader.com

3 M-COMMERCE

Wireless mobile devices are starting to be used for purchasing goods and services as well as for transmitting messages. Although m-commerce represents a small fraction of total e-commerce transactions, revenue has been steadily growing (see Figure 8). In 2006, there were an estimated 175 million cell phone users in the United States and over 2 billion wireless and mobile subscribers worldwide.

M-COMMERCE SERVICES AND APPLICATIONS

M-commerce applications have taken off for services that are time-critical, that appeal to people on the move, or that accomplish a task more efficiently than other methods. They are especially popular in Europe, Japan, South Korea, and other countries where fees for conventional Internet usage are very expensive. Here are some examples.

Content and Location-Based Services

Subscribers to NTT DoCoMo wireless services in Japan can access wireless Web sites to check train schedules, obtain movie listings, browse restaurant guides, purchase tickets on Japan Airlines, trade stocks, view new cartoons, and read Japan's largest daily newspaper. Go2 Mobile Directory users can search for local businesses, movie shows, and restaurants; obtain driving directions; check local weather forecasts; and find detailed information about hotels, airlines, and car rental agencies.

FIGURE 8   GLOBAL M-COMMERCE REVENUE, 2000-2009

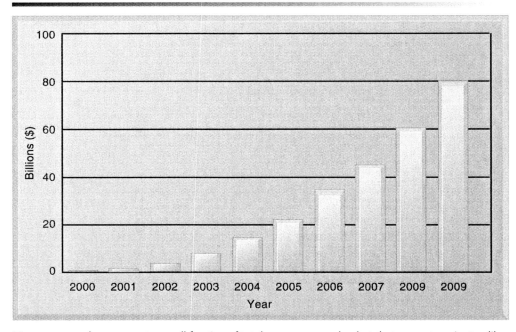

M-commerce sales represent a small fraction of total e-commerce sales, but that percentage is steadily growing. (Totals for 2006–2009 are estimated.)

Sources: Jupiter Research; eMarketer, 2006; eMarketer, 2005; authors.

Banking and Financial Services

Citibank offers wireless alerts about changes in account information on digital cell phones that support text messaging or Web access. Customers of Bank Asia in Bangladesh can use their mobile phones to check account balances, transfer funds between accounts, and pay bills from their accounts.

Wireless Advertising

Wireless service providers in the United States are starting to include advertising on their sites. Yahoo! and go2 Directory Systems arranged to put Yahoo-sponsored listings on the go2 Mobile Directory search site carried by Verizon Wireless, Sprint, and Cingular Wireless. When consumers use go2 Mobile Directory to search for local restaurants or movie theaters, Yahoo-sponsored advertisers appear in the list of search results.

Games and Entertainment

Cell phones are quickly turning into portable entertainment platforms. Mobile phone services offer downloadable digital games and **ringtones** (digitized snippets of music that play on mobile phones when a user receives or places a call). Some handset models combine the features of a cell phone and a portable music player. Users of broadband services from the major wireless vendors can download on-demand movie clips, news clips, and weather reports. MobiTV, offered by Sprint and Cingular Wireless, features live TV programs, including MSNBC and Fox Sports. Film companies are starting to produce short films explicitly designed to play on mobile phones.

Nokia's N91 mobile handset combines the features of a cell phone and a portable music player. It can store up to 3,000 songs.

Photo courtesy of Hugh Threlfall/ Alamy.com

ACCESSING INFORMATION FROM THE WIRELESS WEB

Although cell phones, PDAs, and other handheld mobile devices are able to access the Web at anytime and from anyplace, the amount of information that they can actually handle at one time is very limited. Until 3G broadband service comes into widespread use, these devices will not be able to transmit or receive large amounts data. The information must fit onto small display screens.

Some Web sites have been specifically designed for m-commerce. They feature Web pages with very few graphics and just enough information to fit on a small mobile handheld screen. Special **wireless portals** (also known as *mobile portals*) feature content and services optimized for mobile devices to steer users to the information they are most likely to need. For example, the MSN mobile portal provides access to news from MSNBC, sports from ESPN, movie times, local traffic reports, restaurant listings, Yellow Pages, and stock market reports, as well as capabilities for managing e-mail messages and instant messaging.

M-COMMERCE CHALLENGES

The number of Wi-Fi hotspots for wireless Internet access has been mushrooming in many countries because the technology combines high-speed Internet access with a measure of flexibility and mobility. Rollout of mobile m-commerce services, however, has proved more problematic. Keyboards and screens on cell phones are still tiny and awkward to use. The data transfer speeds on second-generation cellular networks are very slow compared to dial-up and high-speed Internet connections for PCs. Each second waiting for data to download costs the customer money. Most Internet-enabled phones have limited memory and power supplies. M-commerce will benefit from 3G networks and other cellular broadband services and from standardized mobile payment systems.

4   ELECTRONIC COMMERCE PAYMENT SYSTEMS

Special electronic payment systems have been developed to pay for goods electronically on the Internet. Electronic payment systems for the Internet include systems for digital credit card payments, digital wallets, accumulated balance digital payment systems, stored value payment systems, digital cash, peer-to-peer payment systems, digital checking, and electronic billing presentment and payment systems.

TYPES OF ELECTRONIC PAYMENT SYSTEMS

Credit cards account for 80 percent of online payments in the United States and about 50 percent of online purchases outside the United States. The more sophisticated electronic commerce software has capabilities for processing credit card purchases on the Web. Businesses can also contract with services that extend the functionality of existing credit card payment systems. **Digital credit card payment systems** extend the functionality of credit cards so they can be used for online shopping payments. They make credit cards safer and more convenient for online merchants and consumers by providing mechanisms for authenticating the purchaser's credit card to make sure it is valid and arranging for the bank that issued the credit card to deposit money for the amount of the purchase in the seller's bank account.

Digital wallets make paying for purchases over the Web more efficient by eliminating the need for shoppers to enter their address and credit card information repeatedly each time they buy something. A **digital wallet** securely stores credit card and owner identification information, and provides that information at an electronic commerce site's "checkout counter." The digital wallet enters the shopper's name, credit card number, and shipping information automatically when invoked to complete the purchase. Q*Wallet and Google Toolbar AutoFill are examples of digital wallets.

Micropayment systems have been developed for purchases of less than $10, such as downloads of individual articles or music clips, which would be too small for conventional credit card payments. Accumulated balance digital payment systems or stored value payment systems are useful for such purposes.

Accumulated balance digital payment systems enable users to make micropayments and purchases on the Web, accumulating a debit balance that they must pay periodically on their credit card or telephone bills. QPass enables wireless customers to charge ringtones, games, and other digital products and services to their monthly phone bills.

Stored value payment systems such as eCount enable consumers to make instant online payments to merchants and other individuals based on value stored in a digital account. Online value systems rely on the value stored in a consumer's bank, checking, or credit card account, and some of these systems require the use of a digital wallet.

Smart cards are another type of stored value system used for micropayments. A smart card is a plastic card the size of a credit card that stores digital information. The smart card can store health records, identification data, or telephone numbers, or it can serve as an "electronic purse" in place of cash. The Mondex smart card contains electronic cash and can be used to transfer funds to merchants in physical storefronts and to merchants on the Internet. It requires use of a special card-reading device whenever the card needs to transfer cash to either an online or offline merchant.

Digital cash (also known as *electronic cash* or *e-cash*) can also be used for micropayments or larger purchases. **Digital cash** is currency represented in electronic form that moves outside the normal network of money (paper currency, coins, checks, and credit cards). Users are supplied with client software and can exchange money with another e-cash user over the Internet or with a retailer accepting e-cash. ClearBIT is an example of a digital cash service. In addition to facilitating micropayments, digital cash can be useful for people who do not have credit cards and wish to make Web purchases.

New Web-based **peer-to-peer payment systems**, such as PayPal, serve people who want to send money to vendors or individuals who are not set up to accept credit card payments. The party sending money uses his or her credit card to create an account with the designated payment at a Web site dedicated to peer-to-peer payments. The recipient "picks up" the payment by visiting the Web site and supplying information about where to send the payment (a bank account or a physical address).

Digital checking payment systems, such as eCheck, extend the functionality of existing checking accounts so they can be used for online shopping payments. Digital checks are less expensive than credit cards and much faster than traditional paper-based checking. These checks are encrypted with a digital signature that can be verified and used for payments in electronic commerce. Electronic check systems are useful in business-to-business electronic commerce.

Electronic billing presentment and payment systems are used for paying routine monthly bills. They enable users to view their bills electronically and pay them through electronic fund transfers from bank or credit card accounts. These services support payment for online and physical store purchases of goods or services after the purchase has taken place. They notify purchasers about bills that are due, present the bills, and process the payments. Some of these services, such as CheckFree, consolidate subscribers' bills from various sources so that they can all be paid at one time. Table 6 summarizes the features of some of these e-commerce payment systems.

DIGITAL PAYMENT SYSTEMS FOR M-COMMERCE

With a Wi-Fi connection, you can take advantage of all existing forms of Internet payment—the fact that you are connected wirelessly should have no impact. Many m-commerce transactions, however, are small, frequent purchases for items such as soft drinks, sports scores, newspapers, or mobile games that require special micropayment systems.

Micropayment systems are working well in Europe and Asia, where mobile operators and Internet service providers handle small payments by adding them up and presenting them on a single bill, such as the mobile telephone bill. In London, you can buy Virgin Cola using a Virgin Mobile phone by simply dialing a number posted on the vending machine (the cost of the drink is simply charged to your cell phone account). eBay's PayPal Mobile Text2Buy service allows consumers to send payments to PayPal Mobile accounts, purchase items from select retailers, or donate money to some charities by punching a short text code into a cell phone. Japan's NTT DoCoMo offers a cell phone with a stored payment system for purchases in designated stores, restaurants, and vending machines and another handset model with an embedded credit card. Motorola, MasterCard, and Visa are developing mobile wallet services.

TABLE 6 EXAMPLES OF ELECTRONIC PAYMENT SYSTEMS FOR E-COMMERCE

PAYMENT SYSTEM	DESCRIPTION	COMMERCIAL EXAMPLE
Digital credit card payment systems	Secure services for credit card payments on the Internet protect information transmitted among users, merchant sites, and processing banks	eCharge
Digital wallet	Software that stores credit card and other information to facilitate form completion and payment for goods on the Web	Q*Wallet, Google Toolbar AutoFill
Accumulated balance digital payment systems	Accumulates micropayment purchases as a debit balance that must be paid periodically on credit card or telephone bills	QPass, Valista, Peppercoin
Stored value payment systems	Enables consumers to make instant payments to merchants based on value stored in a digital account	eCount, Mondex card
Digital cash	Digital currency that can be used for micropayments or larger purchases	ClearBit
Peer-to-peer payment systems	Sends money using the Web to individuals or vendors who are not set up to accept credit card payments	PayPal
Digital checking	Electronic check with a secure digital signature	eCheck
Electronic billing presentment and payment systems	Supports electronic payment for online and physical store purchases of goods or services after the purchase has taken place	CheckFree, Yahoo! Bill Pay

In both the United States and Europe, individual micropayment service providers run their own separate payment systems. A common secure platform for wireless m-commerce payments would help m-commerce take off.

5 HANDS-ON MIS

The projects in this section give you hands-on experience developing an e-commerce strategy for a real-world company, using spreadsheet software to analyze the profitability of an e-commerce company, and using Web tools to research and evaluate e-commerce hosting services.

Achieving Operational Excellence: Developing an E-Commerce Strategy

Software skills: Web browser software, Web page development software
Business skills: Strategic analysis

This project provides an opportunity for you to develop an e-commerce strategy for a real-world business and to use a Web page development tool to create part of the company's Web site.

Dirt Bikes's management believes that the company could benefit from e-commerce. The company has sold motorcycles and parts primarily through authorized dealers. Dirt Bikes advertises in various magazines catering to dirt bike enthusiasts and maintains booths at important off-road motorcycle racing events. You have been asked to explore how Dirt Bikes could benefit from e-commerce and a Dirt Bikes Web site. Prepare a report for management that answers the following questions:

- How could Dirt Bikes benefit from e-commerce? Should it sell motorcycles or parts over the Web? Should it use its Web site primarily to advertise its products and services? Should it use the Web for customer service?

- How would a Web site provide value to Dirt Bikes? Use the Web to research the cost of an e-commerce site for a small to medium-sized company. How much revenue or cost savings would the Web site have to produce to make it a worthwhile investment for Dirt Bikes?

- Prepare specifications describing the functions that should be performed by Dirt Bikes's Web site. Include links to other Web sites or other systems in your specifications.

- (Optional) Design the home page for Dirt Bikes's Web site and an important secondary page linked to the home page using the Web page creation capabilities of word processing software or a Web page development tool of your choice.

Improving Decision Making: Using Spreadsheet Software to Analyze a Dot-Com Business

Software skills: Spreadsheet downloading, formatting, and formulas
Business skills: Financial statement analysis

Publicly traded companies, including those specializing in e-commerce, are required to file financial data with the Securities and Exchange Commission. By analyzing this information, you can determine the profitability of an e-commerce company and the viability of its business model.

Pick one e-commerce company on the Internet, for example, Ashford.com, Buy.com, Yahoo.com, or Priceline.com. Study the Web pages that describe the company and explain its purpose and structure. Use the Web to find articles that comment on the company. Then visit the Securities and Exchange Commission's Web site at www.sec.gov and select Filings and Forms to access the company's 10-K (annual report) form showing income statements and balance sheets. Select only the sections of the 10-K form containing the desired portions of financial statements that you need to examine, and download them into your spreadsheet. Create simplified spreadsheets of the company's balance sheets and income statements for the past three years.

- Is the company a dot-com success, borderline business, or failure? What information forms the basis of your decision? Why? When answering these questions, pay special attention to the company's three-year trends in revenues, cost of sales, gross margins, operating expenses, and net margins. See the Laudon Web site for this chapter for definitions of these terms and how they are calculated.

- Prepare an overhead presentation (with a minimum of five slides), including appropriate spreadsheets or charts, and present your work to your professor and classmates.

Achieving Operational Excellence: Evaluating E-Commerce Hosting Services

Software skills: Web browser software
Business skills: Evaluating e-commerce hosting services

This project will help develop your Internet skills in evaluating services for hosting an e-commerce site for a small startup company.

You would like to set up a Web site to sell towels, linens, pottery, and tableware from Portugal and are examining services for hosting small business Internet storefronts. Your Web site should be able to take secure credit card payments and to calculate shipping costs and taxes. Initially, you would like to display photos and descriptions of 40 different products. Visit Yahoo! Small Business and Freemerchant.com and compare the range of e-commerce hosting services they offer to small business, their capabilities, and costs. Also examine the tools they provide for creating an e-commerce site. Compare both of these services and decide which of the two you would use if you were actually establishing a Web store. Write a brief report indicating your choice and explaining the strengths and weaknesses of both.

LEARNING TRACK MODULES

E-Commerce Challenges: The Story of Online Groceries. This Learning Track explores the history of the online grocery business and examines the business model of FreshDirect, a new generation online grocery business. You can find this material on the Student CD-ROM and Laudon Web site for this chapter.

Build an E-commerce Business Plan. This Learning Track outlines the process of building an e-commerce business plan, including the development of a marketing plan and a financial plan. You can find this material on the Student CD-ROM and Laudon Web site for this chapter.

Summary

1. *Describe the unique features of e-commerce, digital markets, and digital goods.*

E-commerce involves digitally enabled commercial transactions between and among organizations and individuals. There are seven unique features of e-commerce technology: E-commerce technology is ubiquitous, meaning that is it available just about everywhere a computer can connect to the Internet. It has global reach, permitting commercial transactions to cross cultural and national boundaries far more conveniently and cost effectively than is true in traditional commerce. It operates according to universal standards shared by all nations around the world, whereas most traditional commerce technologies differ from one nation to the next. It provides information richness, enabling an online merchant to deliver to an audience of millions complex and rich marketing messages with text, video, and audio in a way not possible with traditional commerce technologies, such as radio, television, or magazines. It is interactive, meaning it allows for two-way communication between merchant and consumer and enables the merchant to engage a consumer in ways similar to a face-to-face experience but on a much more massive, global scale. It increases information density (the total amount and quality of information available to all market participants). It permits personalization and customization: Merchants can target their marketing messages to specific individuals by adjusting the message to a person's name, interests, and past purchases.

The Internet has created a digital marketplace where millions of people are able to exchange massive amounts of information directly, instantly, and for free. Digital markets are said to be more "transparent" than traditional markets. Information asymmetry is reduced. Digital markets are very flexible and efficient, with reduced search and transaction costs, lower menu costs, and the ability to change prices dynamically based on market conditions. Digital markets provide many opportunities to sell directly to the consumer, bypassing intermediaries, such as distributors or retail outlets.

Digital goods are goods, such as music, video, software, newspapers, magazines, and books, that can be delivered over a digital network. Once a digital product has been produced, the cost of delivering that product digitally is extremely low. New business models based on delivering digital goods are challenging bookstores, publishers, music labels, and film studios that depend on delivery of traditional goods.

2. *Analyze how Internet technology has changed value propositions and business models.*

The Internet radically reduces the cost of creating, sending, and storing information while making that information more widely available. Information is not limited to traditional physical methods of delivery. This unbundling of information from traditional value chain channels is having a disruptive effect on old business models, and it is creating new business models. Some of the traditional channels for exchanging product information have become unnecessary or uneconomical, and business models based on the coupling of information with products and services may no longer be necessary.

The Internet can help companies create and capture profits in new ways by adding extra value to existing products and services or by providing the foundation for new products and services. Many different business models for electronic commerce on the Internet have emerged, including virtual storefronts, information brokers, transaction brokers, Net marketplaces, content providers, online service providers, virtual communities, and portals. Business models that take advantage of the Internet's capabilities for communication, community-building capabilities, and digital goods distribution have become especially prominent.

3. *Describe the various types of e-commerce and how e-commerce has changed consumer retailing and business-to-business transactions.*

The three major types of electronic commerce are business-to-consumer (B2C), business-to-business (B2B), and consumer-to-consumer (C2C). Another way of classifying electronic commerce transactions is in terms of the participants' physical connections to the Web. Conventional e-commerce transactions, which take place over wired networks, can be distinguished from mobile commerce, or m-commerce, which is the purchase of goods and services using handheld wireless devices.

The Internet provides a universally available set of technologies for electronic commerce that can be used to create new channels for marketing, sales, and customer support and to eliminate intermediaries in buy-and-sell transactions. Interactive capabilities on the Web can be used to build closer relationships with customers in marketing and customer support. Firms can use various Web personalization technologies to deliver Web pages with content geared to the specific interests of each user, including technologies that deliver personalized information and ads through m-commerce channels. Companies can also reduce costs and improve customer service by using Web sites, as well as e-mail and even telephone access to customer service representatives, to provide helpful information.

B2B e-commerce generates efficiencies by enabling companies to locate suppliers, solicit bids, place orders, and track shipments in transit electronically. Businesses can use their own Web sites to sell to other businesses or use Net marketplaces or private industrial networks. Net marketplaces provide a single, digital marketplace based on Internet technology for many buyers and sellers. Net marketplaces can be differentiated by whether they sell direct or indirect goods, support spot or long-term purchasing, or serve vertical or horizontal markets. Private industrial networks link a firm with its suppliers and other strategic business partners to develop highly efficient supply chains and to respond quickly to customer demands.

4. *Evaluate the role of m-commerce in business and describe the most important m-commerce applications.*

M-commerce uses the Internet for purchasing goods and services as well as for transmitting messages using wireless mobile devices. It is especially well-suited for location-based applications, such as finding local hotels and restaurants, monitoring local traffic and weather, and providing personalized location-based marketing. Mobile phones and handhelds are being used for mobile bill payment; banking; securities trading; transportation schedule updates; and downloads of digital content, such as music, games, and video clips.

Wireless portals (mobile portals) feature content and services optimized for mobile devices to steer users to the information they are most likely to need. M-commerce requires special digital payment systems that can handle micropayments because most m-commerce purchases today are for very small amounts.

M-commerce represents a tiny fraction of all online purchases because wireless mobile devices can't display merchandise very well. Mobile phones have tiny keyboards, small screens, and slow data transfer speeds (9.6 to 14.4 Kbps). M-commerce will benefit from interoperable payment systems for wireless devices and faster wireless networks to support more data-rich communication.

5. *Compare the principal payment systems for electronic commerce.*

The principal electronic payment systems for electronic commerce are digital credit card payment systems, digital wallets, accumulated balance digital payment systems, stored value payment systems, digital cash, peer-to-peer payment systems, digital checking, and electronic billing presentment and payment systems. Accumulated balance systems, stored value systems (including smart cards), and digital cash are useful for small micropayments.

Key Terms

Accumulated balance digital payment systems	Electronic data interchange (EDI)
Banner ad	Exchanges
Blogosphere	Information asymmetry
Business-to-business (B2B) electronic commerce	Information density
Business-to-consumer (B2C) electronic commerce	Market entry costs
Call center	Marketspace
Clicks-and-mortar	Menu costs
Clickstream tracking	Micropayment
Collaborative filtering	Mobile commerce (m-commerce)
Consumer-to-consumer (C2C) electronic commerce	Net marketplaces
Cost transparency	Peer-to-peer payment systems
Customization	Personalization
Digital cash	Podcasting
Digital checking	Pop-up ads
Digital credit card payment systems	Price discrimination
Digital goods	Price transparency
Digital wallet	Private exchange
Disintermediation	Private industrial networks
Dynamic pricing	Procurement
Electronic billing presentment and payment systems	Pure-play

Richness
Ringtones
Search costs
Social networking sites

Social shopping
Stored value payment systems
Syndicators
Wireless portals

Review Questions

1. Name and describe four business trends and three technology trends shaping e-commerce today.

2. List and describe the seven unique features of e-commerce technology.

3. Define a digital market and describe its distinguishing features.

4. Define digital goods and describe their distinguishing features.

5. How is the Internet changing the economics of information and business models?

6. Name and describe six Internet business models for electronic commerce. Distinguish between a pure-play Internet business model and a clicks-and-mortar business model.

7. Name and describe the various categories of electronic commerce.

8. How can the Internet facilitate sales and marketing for individual customers? Describe the role played by Web personalization.

9. How can the Internet enhance customer service?

10. How can Internet technology support business-to-business electronic commerce?

11. What are Net marketplaces? Why do they represent an important business model for B2B e-commerce? How do they differ from private industrial networks?

12. List and describe important types of m-commerce services and applications.

13. How do wireless portals help users access information on the wireless Web?

14. What are some of the barriers to m-commerce?

15. Name and describe the principal electronic payment systems used on the Internet. What types of payment systems are used in m-commerce?

Discussion Questions

1. How does the Internet change consumer and supplier relationships?

2. The Internet may not make corporations obsolete, but the corporations will have to change their business models. Do you agree? Why or why not?

Video Case

You will find a video case illustrating some of the concepts in this chapter on the Laudon Web site and Student CD-ROM along with questions to help you analyze the case.

Teamwork: Performing a Competitive Analysis of E-Commerce Sites

Form a group with three or four of your classmates. Select two businesses that are competitors in the same industry and that use their Web sites for electronic commerce. Visit these Web sites. You might compare, for example, the Web sites for iTunes and Napster, Amazon.com and BarnesandNoble.com, or E*Trade and Scottrade. Prepare an evaluation of each business's Web site in terms of its functions, user friendliness, and ability to support the company's business strategy. Which Web site does a better job? Why? Can you make some recommendations to improve these Web sites?

REFERENCES

Adomavicius, Gediminas and Alexander Tuzhilin. "Personalization Technologies: A Process-Oriented Perspective." *Communications of the ACM* 48, no. 10 (October 2005).

Ba, Sulin and Paul A. Pavlou. "Evidence of the Effect of Trust Building Technology i Electronic Markets: Price Premiums and Buyer Behavior." *MIS Quarterly* 26, no. 3 (September 2002).

Bakos, Yannis. "The Emerging Role of Electronic Marketplaces and the Internet." *Communications of the ACM* 41, no. 8 (August 1998).

Bright, Beckey. "Clip Quest." *Wall Street Journal* (September 12, 2005).

Bhargava, Hemant K. and Vidyanand Chourhary. "Economics of an Information Intermediary with Aggregation Benefits." *Information Systems Research* 15, no. 1 (March 2004).

Brynjolfsson, Erik, Yu Hu, and Michael D. Smith. "Consumer Surpus in the Digital Economy: Estimating the Value of Increased Product Variety at Online Booksellers." *Management Science* 49, no. 11 (November 2003).

Chaudhury, Abhijit,, Debasish Mallick and H. Raghav Rao. "Web Channels in E-Commerce." *Communications of the ACM* 44, No. 1 (January 2001).

Chopra, Anand. "Let Me Help You with That." *KMWorld* (September 2006).

Christiaanse, Ellen. "Performance Benefits Through Integration Hubs." *Communications of the ACM* 48, No.5 (April 2005).

Crockett, Roger O. et. al., "IPod Killers?" *Business Week Online* (April 21, 2005).

Markoff, John. "Apple Unveils a New IPod and a Phone Music Player." *New York Times* (September 8, 2005.)

Cuneo, Eileen Colkin. "Web Ads Upend Industry Practices." *Information Week* (June 13, 2005).

ComScore Networks, "Digital Calculator Report: Top 100 List." www.Comscore.com (September 2005).

DeFelice, Alexandra. "A New Marketing Medium." *Customer Relationship Management* (January 2006).

Devaraj, Sarv, Ming Fan and Rajiv Kohli. "Antecedents of B2C Channel Satisfaction and Preference: Validating e-Commerce Metrics." *Information Systems Research* 13, no.3 (September 2002).

Dewan, Rajiv M., Marshall L. Freimer, and Jie Zhang. "Management and Valuation of Advertisement-Supported Web Sites." *Journal of Management Information Systems* 19, no. 3 (Winter 2002–2003).

Elliott, Stuart. "Shopping by Phone, on the Move." *The New York Times* (June 24, 2006).

eMarketer, Inc., "E-Commerce Retail Trends." (January, 2006)

eMarketer, Inc., "Worldwide Online Access." (May 2006).

eMarketer, Inc., "Comparative Estimates: B2C E-commerce" Revenues in the United States, 1997–2010 (in billions). (August 26, 2005a)

eMarketer, Inc. (Noah Elkin). "Mobile Marketing and M-Commerce: Global Spending and Trends." (February 2005c).

"E-Tailing's Next Lift." Optimize, July, 2005.

Evans, Philip and Thomas S. Wurster. *Blown to Bits: How the New Economics of Information Transforms Strategy.* Boston, MA: Harvard Business School Press (2000).

Huang, Gregory T. "The Web's New Currency." Technology Review (November 2003).

Hui, Kai Lung and Patrick Y.K. Chau. "Classifying Digital Products." *Communications of the ACM* 45, no.6 (June 2002).

Iansiti, Marco, F. Warren McFarlan and George Wessterman. "Leveraging the Incumbent's Advantage." *MIS Sloan Management Review* 44, no. 4 (Summer 2003).

Kaplan, Steven and Mohanbir Sawhney. "E-Hubs: the New B2B Marketplaces." *Harvard Business Review* (May-June 2000).

Kauffman, Robert J. and Bin Wang. "New Buyers' Arrival Under Dynamic Pricing Market Microstructure: The Case of Group-Buying Discounts on the Internet, *Journal of Management Information Systems* 18, no. 2 (Fall 2001).

Kenny, David and John F. Marshall. "Contextual Marketing." *Harvard Business Review* (November–December 2000.

Kesmodel, David. "More Marketers Place Web Ads by Time of Day." *The Wall Street Journal* (June 23, 2006).

Kingson, Jennifer A. "Wireless Moves the Cash Register Where You Are." *New York Times* (November 26, 2005).

Koufaris, Marios. "Applying the Technology Acceptance Model and Flow Theory to Online Consumer Behavior." *Information Systems Research* 13, no. 2 (2002).

Laudon, Kenneth C. and Carol Guercio Traver. *E-Commerce: Business, Technology, Society. 3rd Edition.* Upper Saddle River, N.J.: Prentice Hall (2006).

Lee, Hau L. and Seungin Whang. "Winning the Last Mile of E-Commerce." *Sloan Management Review* 42, no. 4 (Summer 2001).

Li Yuan and Cassell Bryan-Low. "Coming Soon to Cellphone Screens-More Ads Than Ever." *The Wall Street Journal* (August 16, 2006).

Li Yuan. "Can't Talk Now, I'm Winning," *Wall Street Journal* (October 11, 2005).

———. "Now, the Very Small Screen." *Wall Street Journal*, September 22, 2005.

———"TV-Anytime, Anywhere." *Wall Street Journal* (September 12, 2005).

Lim, Gyoo Gun and Jae Kyu Lee. "Buyer-Carts for B2B EC: The b-Cart Approach." *Journal of Organizational Computing and Electronic Commerce* 13, no. 3 & 4 (2003).

Madden, Andrew P. "The Business of Blogging." *Technology Review* (August 2005).

Magretta, Joan. "Why Business Models Matter." *Harvard Business Review* (May 2002).

Mangalindan, Mylene and Jessica E. Vascellaro. "You've Got Money: Paying via Text Message." *The Wall Street Journal* (April 26, 2006).

Markillie, Paul. "A Perfect Market." *The Economist* (May 15–21, 2004).

Mc Knight, D. Harrison, Vivek Choudhury, and Charlea Kacmar. "Developing and Validating Trust Measures for e-Commerce: An Integrative Typology." *Information Systems Research* 13, no.3 (September 2002).

McWilliam, Gil. "Building Stronger Brands through Online Communities." *Sloan Management Review* 41, no. 3 (Spring 2000).

Mossberg, Walter H. "Sprint Brings Music Direct to Cellphones, But Price Is Too High," *Wall Street Journal*, (November 17, 2005.)

Pavlou, Paul A. and David Gefen. "Building Effective Online Marketplaces with Institution-Based Trust." *Information Systems Research* 15, no. 1 (March 2004).

Pew Internet and American Life Project. "The State of Blogging." *Pew Internet & American Life Project* (January 2005).

Pinker, Edieal, Abraham Seidmann, and Riginald C. Foster. "Strategies for Transitioning 'Old Economy' Firms to E-Business." *Communications of the ACM* 45, no. 5 (May 2002).

Prahalad, C.K. and Venkatram Ramaswamy. "Coopting Consumer Competence." *Harvard Business Review* (January–February 2000).

Riggins, Frederic J., "Market Segmentation and Information Development Costs in a Two-Tiered Fee-Based and Sponsorship-Based Web Site." *Journal of Management Information Systems* 19, no. 3 (Winter 2002–2003).

Roush, Wade. "Social Machines." *Technology Review* (August 2005).

Roy, Cayce. "E-tailing's Next Lift." *Optimize* (July 2005).

Sawhney, Mohanbir, Emanuela Prandelli, and Gianmario Verona. "The Power of Innomediation." *MIT Sloan Management Review* (Winter 2003).

Schultze, Ulrike and Wanda J. Orlikowski. "A Practice Perspective on Technology-Mediated Network Relations: The Use of Internet-Based Self-Serve Technologies." *Information Systems Research* 15, no. 1 (March 2004).

Smith, Michael D., Joseph Bailey and Erik Brynjolfsson. *"Understanding Digital Markets*: Review and Assessment" in Erik Brynjolfsson and Brian Kahin, ed. Understanding the Digital Economy. Cambridge, MA: MIT Press (1999).

Sultan, Fareena and Andrew Rohm. "The Coming Era of 'Brand in Hand' Marketing." *MIT Sloan Management Review* 47, No. 1 (Fall 2005).

Tedeschi, Bob. "Like Shopping? Social Networking? Try Social Shopping." *The New York Times* (September 11, 2006).

"The MySpace Generation." *Business Week* (December 12, 2005).

Thomke, Stefan and Eric von Hippel. "Customers as Innovators." *Harvard Business Review* (April 2002).

Urbaczewski, Andrew, Leonard M. Jessup, and Bradley Wheeler. "Electronic Commerce Research: A Taxonomy and Synthesis." *Journal of Organizational Computing and Electronic Commerce* 12, no. 2 (2002).

Werbach,Kevin. "Syndication: The Emerging Model for Business in the Internet Era." *Harvard Business Review* (May–June 2000).

Westland, J. Christopher. "Preference Ordering Cash, Near-Cash and Electronic Cash." *Journal of Organizational Computing and Electronic Commerce* 12, no. 3 (2002).

Wireless Week. "World of Warcraft Hits 7 Million Players." *Digital Trends* (September 7, 2006).

Yen, Benjamin P.-C. and Elsie O.S. Ng. "The Impact of Electronic Commerce on Procurement." *Journal of Organizational Computing and Electronic Commerce* 13, no. 3 & 4 (2003).

Yoo, Byungjoon, Vidyanand Choudhary, and Tridas Mukhopadhyay. "A Model of Neutral B2B Intermediaries." *Journal of Management Information Systems* 19, no. 3 (Winter 2002–2003).

Can eBay Continue Growing?
CASE STUDY

eBay.com is an online auction service whose business model is ideally suited to the Web. eBay stores no inventory and ships no products. Instead, it derives its revenue from the movement of information, an ideal task for the Internet. Since eBay was founded in 1995 by Pierre Omidyar and Jeff Skoll, the company has been profitable, attracting more than 200 million users by 2006. eBay now employs more than 8,000 full-time workers and has operations in 32 countries, including an equity investment in MercadoLibre, which services Mexico and eight South American countries. In 2005, eBay users listed 1.8 billion items for auction, resulting in $40 billion worth of goods changing hands. The number of items listed in 2006 was expected to surpass 2 billion.

eBay has mass appeal because its fully automated auction service helps buyers and sellers trade high-end articles, such as fine art, automobiles, and jewelry, as well as more mundane and practical items, such as clothing, consumer electronics, and housewares. Users can list their goods under more than 30 main categories and tens of thousands of subcategories.

The success of eBay relies on a unique formula. eBay derives the bulk of its revenue from fees and commissions associated with its trading services. This revenue, however, is only made possible by the hundreds of thousands of people who put time and effort into selling goods on eBay but do not work for the company. Nearly half a million people rely on eBay auctions as their main source of income. The seller pays an insertion fee for listing goods that operates on a sliding scale. For example, if the opening bid price starts between 1 cent and 99 cents, eBay charges the seller a 25-cent insertion fee. The fee increases as the opening price increases all the way up to $4.80 for goods starting at $500 or more. eBay also collects a fee from the seller when an auction is successful. These final fees begin at 5.25 percent of the closing price.

A portion of eBay's revenue also comes from direct advertising on the site, as well as end-to-end service providers whose services increase the ease and speed of eBay transactions. The acquisition of PayPal, whose service enables the exchange of money between individuals over the Internet, brings additional transaction-based fee revenue. PayPal charges the recipients of payments a flat fee plus a percentage of the total transaction size and has more than 70 million user accounts.

eBay's growth strategy focuses on expansion in geography and scope and on continuing innovation to enhance the variety and appeal of products on its sites. eBay has taken its model to numerous foreign markets and been successful, particularly in England, France, and Germany. It is also working hard to gain a foothold in the Chinese online auction market. Growth rates have been hindered somewhat in the United States and Germany by an increase in seller fees, but these losses have been covered by rapid growth in places such as France and Italy. Although eBay's domestic growth has slowed to about 20 to 30 percent annually, the company's international business is growing at 50 percent per year. By 2005, transactions completed on international Web sites accounted for approximately half of eBay's business.

In 2000, eBay introduced eBay Motors to encourage the sale of bulky items that are too expensive to ship. Critics believed that consumers would find purchasing a used car over the Web too risky. However, eBay added extra measures of protection in the form of used-vehicle warranties and purchase protection up to $20,000. These measures, combined with the standard eBay seller feedback ratings, gave users enough security to buy one million cars within four years. eBay Motors now includes subcategories for boats, motorcycles, parts and accessories, and more.

Also in 2000, eBay implemented the "Buy It Now" feature, which enables sellers to name a price at which they would be willing to sell an item to any buyer. Buyers have the option to purchase the item instantly without waiting for an auction to end. Additionally, eBay acquired Half.com, which offers person-to-person selling of goods such as books, CDs, videos, and games without the auction process. On Half.com, listings are free but eBay collects a commission for completed sales

In 2001, the company launched eBay Stores. eBay Stores enable sellers with a proven track record, a verified ID, or a PayPal account to set up an online

From *Management Information Systems: Managing the Digital Firm, 10/e.* Kenneth C. Laudon, Jane P. Laudon.

storefront and offer fixed-price merchandise. eBay Store owners pay subscription fees (from $15.95 to $499.95 per month), insertion fees, and final value fees on a sliding scale.

In another attempt to reinvigorate its growth, eBay agreed to buy Shopping.com, an online shopping comparison site, for $620 million in mid-2005. In September of that year, eBay acquired VoIP service provider Skype Technologies for $2.6 billion. Skype provides a service for free or low-cost voice calls over the Internet. eBay is betting heavily that Internet telephony will become an integral part of the e-commerce experience and accelerate trade on its Web site. The service could potentially generate $3.5 billion in revenue from markets that eBay traditionally had trouble penetrating, such as real estate, travel, new-car sales, and expensive collectibles. Those markets require more communication among buyers and sellers than eBay currently offers, and Skype will provide voice communication services to help. Internet companies such as Google and Microsoft are now offering VoIP services, and VoIP may become a required capability for all major companies that do business online.

However, some analysts report that many of eBay's top sellers aren't interested in adding voice calls to their sales models. They can barely keep up with the e-mail they receive on eBay and may like the simplicity and anonymity that eBay provided pre-Skype. VoIP could also stimulate eBay's "gray market," consisting of items sold outside the eBay structure to avoid seller fees.

eBay faces other challenges. Yahoo is trying to edge it out of the Asian market by setting up competing auction sites. eBay's growing international presence may make it difficult to monitor compliance with the variety of laws and regulations that apply in different jurisdictions. The law related to the liability of providers of online services for the activities of their users is unsettled. Even though eBay has taken steps to prohibit the listing of certain items, it may be liable if its members nonetheless manage to use it to sell unlawful goods, such as weapons, drugs, alcohol, adult material, and cigarettes, or if its members defame or libel one another in eBay's Feedback Forum.

In response to growing domestic and international competition, eBay has entered into a number of relationships with other major players in the e-commerce field, including competitors Yahoo! and Google. Google gained the exclusive right to display text advertisements on eBay's international auction sites despite having recently added shopping services that compete with eBay auctions. eBay was willing to look beyond its rivalry with Google to secure the potential windfall of revenue from Google's first-rate advertising technology. The deal with Google followed by just a few months a similar deal with Yahoo!, giving that company exclusive rights to provide advertisements for eBay's sites in the U.S. As part of that agreement, Yahoo! will promote PayPal on its sites. The pair reached the accord despite their battle for shares of the auction market in Asia.

eBay is optimistic that its partnership with Google will also enable the auction house to generate more revenue from its acquisition of Skype. The partnership includes the introduction of a "click-to-call" feature, which enables consumers to talk to merchants and advertisers directly using Skype by clicking a connection embedded in their ads. The strategy embraces the idea that some goods, such as mortgages and homes, are not well-suited to the traditional eBay transaction model. Advertisers of these goods seem willing to pay a fee, perhaps as much as $15, for each call received from a potential customer in order to establish better dialogues that are more likely to result in sales.

Meanwhile, eBay is competing directly with Google by introducing its AdContext service. The service is similar to Google AdSense in that it runs online contextual ads based on keywords in Web pages. eBay sellers can use AdContext to display contextual ads and auction promotions on linked Web sites.

Clearly, the largest threat to eBay is the honesty and integrity of its auctions, over which it has some—but not total—control. As eBay ventured into the realm of higher-priced antiques and collectibles, it opened itself up to lawsuits from buyers claiming to have been defrauded by online sellers. Some buyers have alleged that eBay does not do enough to prevent unscrupulous sellers from collecting inflated fees for goods that are not legitimate, or worse, do not exist. eBay users have also been the victims of identity theft scams that resulted in the unauthorized use of their accounts—and hundreds of thousands of dollars worth of fraudulent sales.

With online crime becoming more and more sophisticated, the onus is on eBay to provide its users with a secure trade environment. Some users, and former users, believe that the company has not adequately addressed the issue of fraud. The growing scale of eBay makes fraud protection prohibitive. eBay insists that the percentage of listings on its site that are fraudulent is tiny and that the success of the marketplace bears that out.

Another area in which the sheer size of eBay may be a hindrance is customer service. The company understandably struggles with the task of satisfying two types of "customers": online buyers and online sellers. What's good for one isn't always good for the other. Fraud complaints often result in an automated response from eBay that encourages buyers and sellers to resolve disputes on their own. As eBay has seen, one unilateral policy decision can set off a negative chain reaction. When eBay Store fees were raised, some 7,000 storeowners shut down their stores and looked for other means to conduct their businesses. But eBay is in a bind because addressing customer service issues costs money. The more money eBay spends, the more it cuts into its profits, which also makes Wall Street nervous.

eBay does make an effort to remain in touch with its community of users. A program called Voices brings buyers and sellers together 10 times a year at corporate headquarters. The users engage in two full days of give-and-take with company officials about the best and worst aspects of eBay's services. eBay also monitors every transaction and usage statistics in real time, enabling timely troubleshooting. A Rules, Trust, and Safety committee judges whether questionable listings should be permitted on the site (human organs have been banned, for example).

Indeed, the sustained growth of eBay may rely on the continued enhancement of the technology available to the eBay community rather than on major acquisitions. Recent partnerships with JotSpot and Kaboodle seek to improve the overall value of the eBay experience for members of the community. JotSpot is a provider of wiki applications and, with eBay, is developing the eBay Community Wiki. The wiki serves as an information source that buyers and sellers can update and edit with entries on best practices and tips and tricks for effective auctioning. Kaboodle is teaming with eBay to create an online "social collecting" destination named MyCollectibles where users can promote and share information about the items they collect and trade.

Keeping the community happy is of utmost importance to the future of eBay. A loyal user base may be the company's most valuable asset, and one which competitors will be challenged to replicate. While investors and analysts mostly maintain their confidence in the company's management, cries for change have gone up from the merchant population. Sellers are concerned about the declining number of transactions and a coinciding drop in sales prices. eBay must find a way to secure the confidence of its merchant population or it will risk losing business to other online marketplaces.

Sources: Mylene Mangalindan, "eBay Merchants Seek Management Change," *The Wall Street Journal*, August 21, 2006; Stacy Cowley, "eBay Turns to Partners, ISPs to Jack Up Sales," *InformationWeek*, July 24, 2006; Thomas Claburn, "eBay Is Sold on Wikis," *InformationWeek*, June 14, 2006; Thomas Claburn, "Analysis: eBay's Growth to Come from Community, Not Acquisitions," *InformationWeek*, June 19, 2006; Stacy Cowley, "eBay Opens More PayPal Tools to Developer Partners," *InformationWeek*," June 12, 2006; Saul Hansell, "eBay Gambles on Google Partnership for Success of Skype, the Internet Phone Service," *The New York Times*, August 29, 2006; Mylene Mangalindan, "eBay, Google Reach Overseas Text-Ad Alliance," *The Wall Street Journal*, August 28, 2006; Laurie Sullivan, "eBay to Go Head to Head Against Google for Online Ad Market," *InformationWeek*, June 12, 2006; Nicholas Hoover, "eBay Bets on VoIP, but Do Sellers Want to Chat?" *InformationWeek*, September 19, 2005; and CNBC, "Ten Things You Didn't Know About eBay," msnbc.com, accessed June 29, 2005.

CASE STUDY QUESTIONS

1. What is eBay's business model and business strategy? How successful has it been?
2. What are the problems that eBay is currently facing?
3. How is eBay trying to solve these problems? Are these good solutions? Are there any other solutions that eBay should consider?
4. What management, organization, and technology factors play a role in eBay's response to its problems?
5. Will eBay be successful in the long run? Why or why not?

Managing Knowledge

Managing Knowledge

CONTENT MANAGEMENT MAKES SOUTHERN COMPANY A TOP UTILITY PERFORMER

Southern Company is one of the largest electricity generators in the United States and provides power to more than 4 million people in Alabama, Georgia, and parts of Florida and Mississippi. It has 272 coal, oil, gas, and hydro generating units at 68 power plants. Running these operating companies generates millions of documents, including engineering drawings of boilers and other plant assets and personnel data.

Until late 2002, Southern Company had to store and access all this information with a hodgepodge of legacy systems, custom applications, and manual processes. The content resided in mainframe applications, homegrown databases, local area networks, and old-fashioned filing cabinets. Southern Company had no central location for storing all this content and no control over who was making changes to documents and what versions of documents they were using. Standard procedures change frequently in the energy business. But Southern's engineers had no way of knowing for sure if the procedures they were using were current or outdated.

When a technician needed to repair or replace a component at a power plant, such as a boiler, that person needed to locate documentation on the boiler and all related systems. Often that information existed solely on paper, where it was very difficult and time-consuming to locate. Engineers looking for drawings had to first search one system to find a drawing number and then key that number into another system to access the drawing. The resulting loss of productivity increased operating costs and also hampered the company's efforts to restore power after outages.

All that changed in November 2002 when Southern installed an enterprise content management system from Documentum (now part of EMC Corporation) to serve its fossil-fuel and hydroelectric plants and its power generation and energy marketing units. More than 2 million documents, including engineering drawings, maintenance data, procedure instructions, and vendor manuals, were converted to digital format, consolidated, and stored in the Documentum system. Drawings stored in one legacy system had to be matched with text data relating to the drawings in another system. The content management system runs on a server farm housing Windows-based Web, file, and content servers and an Oracle database.

Having all this information stored and organized at a central repository cut down the average search time for engineering drawings from two hours to less than 10 minutes. The rate of success for locating the correct content on the first try increased from 50 percent to 90 percent.

When Hurricane Katrina struck the Gulf Coast in the late summer of 2005, Southern was much better prepared than other utility companies to serve customers. Workers copied drawings and other information from the content management system onto CD-ROMs and distributed them to laptop-equipped field engineers.

Photo courtesy of Stephen Morton/AP Wide World Photos

449

These engineers were immediately able to access design plans for repairing damaged substations and restoring power.

A *Baseline* magazine study of major power outages in the United States found that Southern Company restored power faster than other utilities. Utility companies that reported major outages to the U.S. Department of Energy in 2004 took an average of 3 days and 5 hours to restore power to customers. During the same period, Southern Company was able to restore power on average within 1 day and 20 hours.

Sources: Bob Violino, "Power Play," *Baseline*, January 2006 and www.documentum.com, accessed September 16, 2006.

Southern Company's experience shows how organizational performance can benefit by making organizational knowledge more easily available. By organizing its knowledge about how to run its power-generating companies and making it more accessible, Southern increased its efficiency and ability to serve customers.

The chapter-opening diagram calls attention to important points raised by this case and this chapter. Southern Company is highly document-intensive. Much of the essential information and knowledge for running the company was not easily accessible because it was stored in many different documents and legacy systems. Delays in accessing design documents and other vital information created inefficiencies that impaired Southern Company's business performance, including its response to emergency power outages. In order to benefit from enterprise content management technology, Southern Company had to develop a classification scheme for its documents and tie documents to data housed in other systems. This took a great deal of time and effort. By making maintenance and repair information immediately available, the new system has made Southern Company much more efficient and profitable.

- Monitor service level and costs
- Develop document access rules

- Coordinate documents and maintenance data
- Develop document access procedures
- Revise repair and maintenance procedures

- Implement Oracle database
- Deploy Windows-based servers
- Implement Documentum content management software
- Deploy laptops

Business Problems

- Document-intensive business
- Fragmented information in legacy systems and manual processes

Management

Organization

Technology

Information System

- Immediately access and design plans and equipment maintenance information

Business Solution

- Reduce time
- Reduce cost

HEADS UP

Collaborating and communicating with practitioners and experts, creating new knowledge, facilitating access to knowledge, and using that knowledge to improve business processes and decision making have become vital to organizational innovation and survival. This chapter shows how you and your firm can benefit from information systems for knowledge management.

- If your career is in finance and accounting, you may use rule-based expert systems for evaluating the credit risk of loan applicants and for investment portfolio selection, and you may use neural networks for securities trading and for detecting credit card fraud.

- If your career is in human resources, you will run employee training programs to help employees use knowledge management systems and may be responsible for operating the firm's learning management systems.

- If your career is in information systems, you will be evaluating software for knowledge management applications and intelligent techniques as well as helping business professionals classify and organize knowledge for knowledge management systems.

- If your career is in manufacturing, production, or operations management, you will use knowledge work and group collaboration tools for creating and sharing product design and manufacturing specifications, and you may also use expert and case-based reasoning systems for diagnostic and repair work.

- If your career is in sales and marketing, you will use corporate portals and repositories for structured and unstructured knowledge to access and share information about customers, sales leads, competitors, and changes in product pricing and specifications.

1   THE KNOWLEDGE MANAGEMENT LANDSCAPE

Knowledge management systems have become one of the fastest-growing areas of corporate and government software investment. Figure 1 shows that sales of enterprise content management software for knowledge management are expected to grow 35 percent annually through 2006, even though overall software sales are projected to grow only 6 percent annually during the same period (eMarketer, 2003). The past decade has likewise shown an explosive growth in research on knowledge and knowledge management in the economics, management, and information systems fields (Alavi and Leidner, 2001; Cole, 1998).

We live in an information economy in which the major source of wealth and prosperity is the production and distribution of information and knowledge. About 55 percent of the U.S. labor force consists of knowledge and information workers, and 60 percent of the gross domestic product of the United States comes from the knowledge and information sectors, such as finance and publishing.

Knowledge management has become an important theme at many large business firms as managers realize that much of their firm's value depends on the firm's ability to create and manage knowledge. Studies have found that a substantial part of a firm's stock market value is related to its intangible assets, of which knowledge is one important component, along with brands, reputations, and unique business processes (Gu and Lev, 2001). Well-executed knowledge-based projects have been known to produce extraordinary returns on investment, although knowledge-based investments are difficult to measure (Blair and Wallman, 2001).

FIGURE 1 **U.S. ENTERPRISE KNOWLEDGE MANAGEMENT SOFTWARE REVENUES, 2001–2008**

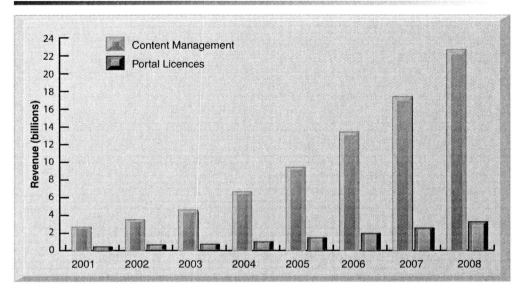

Enterprise knowledge management software includes sales of content management and portal licenses, which have been growing at a rate of 35 percent annually, making it among the fastest-growing software applications.

Sources: Based on data in "Portals and Content Management Solutions," eMarketer, June 2003, and author estimates.

IMPORTANT DIMENSIONS OF KNOWLEDGE

There is an important distinction between data, information, knowledge, and wisdom. **Data** can be defined as a flow of events or transactions captured by an organization's systems that, by itself, is useful for transacting but little else. To turn data into useful *information*, a firm must expend resources to organize data into categories of understanding, such as monthly, daily, regional, or store-based reports of total sales. To transform information into **knowledge**, a firm must expend additional resources to discover patterns, rules, and contexts where the knowledge works. Finally, **wisdom** is thought to be the collective and individual experience of applying knowledge to the solution of problems. Wisdom involves where, when, and how to apply knowledge.

Knowledge is both an individual attribute and a collective attribute of the firm. Knowledge is a cognitive, even a physiological, event, that takes place inside peoples' heads. It is also stored in libraries and records, shared in lectures, and stored by firms in the form of business processes and employee know-how. Knowledge residing in the minds of employees that has not been documented is called **tacit knowledge**, whereas knowledge that has been documented is called **explicit knowledge**. Knowledge can reside in e-mail, voice mail, graphics, and unstructured documents as well as structured documents. Knowledge is generally believed to have a location, either in the minds of humans or in specific business processes. Knowledge is "sticky" and not universally applicable or easily moved. Finally, knowledge is thought to be situational and contextual. For example, you must know when to perform a procedure as well as how to perform it. Table 1 reviews these dimensions of knowledge.

TABLE 1 IMPORTANT DIMENSIONS OF KNOWLEDGE

KNOWLEDGE IS A FIRM ASSET

Knowledge is an intangible asset.

The transformation of data into useful information and knowledge requires organizational resources.

Knowledge is not subject to the law of diminishing returns as are physical assets, but instead experiences network effects as its value increases as more people share it.

KNOWLEDGE HAS DIFFERENT FORMS

Knowledge can be either tacit or explicit (codified).

Knowledge involves know-how, craft, and skill.

Knowledge involves knowing how to follow procedures.

Knowledge involves knowing why, not simply when, things happen (causality).

KNOWLEDGE HAS A LOCATION

Knowledge is a cognitive event involving mental models and maps of individuals.

There is both a social and an individual basis of knowledge.

Knowledge is "sticky" (hard to move), situated (enmeshed in a firm's culture), and contextual (works only in certain situations).

KNOWLEDGE IS SITUATIONAL

Knowledge is conditional: Knowing when to apply a procedure is just as important as knowing the procedure (conditional).

Knowledge is related to context: You must know how to use a certain tool and under what circumstances.

We can see that knowledge is a different kind of firm asset from, say, buildings and financial assets; that knowledge is a complex phenomenon; and that there are many aspects to the process of managing knowledge. We can also recognize that knowledge-based core competencies of firms—the two or three things that an organization does best—are key organizational assets. Knowing how to do things effectively and efficiently in ways that other organizations cannot duplicate is a primary source of profit and competitive advantage that cannot be purchased easily by competitors in the marketplace.

For instance, having a unique build-to-order production system constitutes a form of knowledge and perhaps a unique asset that other firms cannot copy easily. With knowledge, firms become more efficient and effective in their use of scarce resources. Without knowledge, firms become less efficient and less effective in their use of resources and ultimately fail.

Organizational Learning and Knowledge Management

Like humans, organizations create and gather knowledge using a variety of organizational learning mechanisms. Through collection of data, careful measurement of planned activities, trial and error (experimentation), and feedback from customers and the environment in general, organizations gain experience. Organizations that learn then adjust their behavior to reflect that learning by creating new business processes and by changing patterns of management decision making. This process of change is called **organizational learning**. Arguably, organizations that can sense and respond to their environments rapidly will survive longer than organizations that have poor learning mechanisms.

THE KNOWLEDGE MANAGEMENT VALUE CHAIN

Knowledge management refers to the set of business processes developed in an organization to create, store, transfer, and apply knowledge. Knowledge management increases the ability of the organization to learn from its environment and to incorporate knowledge into its business processes. Figure 2 illustrates the five value-adding steps in the knowledge management value chain. Each stage in the value chain adds value to raw data and information as they are transformed into usable knowledge.

In Figure 2, a line divides information systems activities and related management and organizational activities, with information systems activities on the top of the graphic and organizational and management activities below. One apt slogan of the knowledge management field is "Effective knowledge management is 80 percent managerial and organizational, and 20 percent technology."

We can define *organizational and management capital* as the set of business processes, culture, and behavior required to obtain value from investments in information systems. In the case of knowledge management, as with other information systems investments, supportive values, structures, and behavior patterns must be built to maximize the return on investment in knowledge management projects. In Figure 2, the management and organizational activities in the lower half of the diagram represent the investment in organizational capital required to obtain substantial returns on the information technology (IT) investments and systems shown in the top half of the diagram.

FIGURE 2   THE KNOWLEDGE MANAGEMENT VALUE CHAIN

Knowledge management today involves both information systems activities and a host of enabling management and organizational activities.

Knowledge Acquisition

Organizations acquire knowledge in a number of ways, depending on the type of knowledge they seek. The first knowledge management systems sought to build corporate repositories of documents, reports, presentations, and best practices. These efforts have been extended to include unstructured documents (such as e-mail). In other cases, organizations acquire knowledge by developing online expert networks so that employees can "find the expert" in the company who has the knowledge in his or her head.

In still other cases, firms must create new knowledge by discovering patterns in corporate data or by using knowledge workstations where engineers can discover new knowledge. These various efforts are described throughout this chapter. A coherent and organized knowledge system also requires systematic data from the firm's transaction processing systems that track sales, payments, inventory, customers, and other vital data, as well as data from external sources such as news feeds, industry reports, legal opinions, scientific research, and government statistics.

Knowledge Storage

Once they are discovered, documents, patterns, and expert rules must be stored so they can be retrieved and used by employees. Knowledge storage generally involves the creation of a database. Document management systems that digitize, index, and tag documents according to a coherent framework are large databases adept at storing collections of documents. Expert systems also help corporations preserve the knowledge that is acquired by incorporating that knowledge into organizational processes and culture.

Management must support the development of planned knowledge storage systems, encourage the development of corporate-wide schemas for indexing documents, and reward employees for taking the time to update and store documents properly. For instance, it would reward the sales force for submitting names of prospects to a shared corporate database of prospects where all sales personnel can identify each prospect and review the stored knowledge.

Knowledge Dissemination

Portal, e-mail, instant messaging, and search engine technology have added to an existing array of collaboration technologies and office systems for sharing calendars, documents, data, and graphics. Contemporary technology seems to have created a deluge of information and knowledge. How can managers and employees discover, in a sea of information and knowledge, that which is really important for their decisions and their work? Here, training programs, informal networks, and shared management experience communicated through a supportive culture help managers focus their attention on the important knowledge and information.

Knowledge Application

Regardless of what type of knowledge management system is involved, knowledge that is not shared and applied to the practical problems facing firms and managers does not add business value. To provide a return on investment, organizational knowledge must become a systematic part of management decision making and become situated in decision-support systems. Ultimately, new knowledge must be built into a firm's bus-iness processes and key application systems, including enterprise applications for managing key internal business processes and relationships with customers and suppliers. Management supports this process by creating—based on new knowledge—new business practices, new products and services, and new markets for the firm.

Building Organizational and Management Capital: Collaboration, Communities of Practice, and Office Environments

In addition to the activities we have just described, managers can help by developing new organizational roles and responsibilities for the acquisition of knowledge, including the creation of chief knowledge officer executive positions, dedicated staff positions (knowledge managers), and communities of practice. The **chief knowledge officer (CKO)** is a senior executive who is responsible for the firm's knowledge management program. The CKO helps design programs and systems to find new sources of knowledge or to make better use of existing knowledge in organizational and management processes.

Communities of practice (COPs) are informal social networks of professionals and employees within and outside the firm who have similar work-related activities and interests. The activities of these communities include self- and group education, conferences, online newsletters, and day-to-day sharing of experiences and techniques to solve specific work problems. Many organizations, such as IBM, the U.S. Federal Highway Administration, and the World Bank have encouraged the development of thousands of online communities of practice.

COPs can make it easier for people to reuse knowledge by pointing community members to useful documents, creating document repositories, and filtering information for newcomers. COP members act as facilitators, encouraging contributions and discussion. COPs can also reduce the learning curve for new employees by providing contacts with subject matter experts and access to a community's established methods and tools. Finally, COPs can act as a spawning ground for new ideas, techniques, and decision-making behavior.

TYPES OF KNOWLEDGE MANAGEMENT SYSTEMS

There are essentially three major types of knowledge management systems: enterprise-wide knowledge management systems, knowledge work systems, and intelligent techniques. Figure 3 shows the knowledge management system applications for each of these major categories.

Enterprise-wide knowledge management systems are general-purpose firmwide efforts to collect, store, distribute, and apply digital content and knowledge. Such systems provide databases and tools for organizing and storing structured and unstructured documents and other knowledge objects, directories and tools for locating employees with expertise in a particular area, and, increasingly, Web-based tools for collaboration and communication. Section 2 discusses enterprise-wide knowledge management systems in more detail.

The development of powerful networked workstations and software for assisting engineers and scientists in the discovery of new knowledge has led to the creation of knowledge work systems such as computer-aided design, visualization, simulation, and virtual reality systems. **Knowledge work systems (KWS)** are specialized systems built for engineers, scientists, and other knowledge workers charged with discovering and creating new knowledge for a company. We discuss knowledge work applications in detail in Section 3.

FIGURE 3   MAJOR TYPES OF KNOWLEDGE MANAGEMENT SYSTEMS

There are three major categories of knowledge management systems, and each can be broken down further into more specialized types of knowledge management systems.

Knowledge management also includes a diverse group of **intelligent techniques**, such as data mining, expert systems, neural networks, fuzzy logic, genetic algorithms, and intelligent agents. These techniques have different objectives, from a focus on discovering knowledge (data mining and neural networks), to distilling knowledge in the form of rules for a computer program (expert systems and fuzzy logic), to discovering optimal solutions for problems (genetic algorithms). Section 4 provides more detail about these intelligent techniques.

2   ENTERPRISE-WIDE KNOWLEDGE MANAGEMENT SYSTEMS

Figure 4 provides an overview of the technologies and capabilities found in enterprise-wide knowledge management systems. They include capabilities for storing both structured and unstructured data; tools for locating employee expertise within the firm; and capabilities for obtaining data and information from key transaction systems, such as enterprise applications and from Web sites. They also include supporting technologies such as portals, search engines, and collaboration tools (including e-mail, instant messaging, groupware, blogs, wikis, and social bookmarking) to help employees search the corporate knowledge base, communicate and collaborate with others inside and outside the firm, and apply the stored knowledge to new situations. Systems for managing employee learning are emerging as another supporting technology for enterprise-wide knowledge management.

Managers and firms must deal with many different kinds of knowledge and knowledge issues. There are three major categories of enterprise-wide knowledge management systems for dealing with these different kinds of knowledge. Some knowledge exists already somewhere in the firm in the form of structured text documents and reports or presentations, and the central problem is organizing this existing structured knowledge into a library and

FIGURE 4   ENTERPRISE-WIDE KNOWLEDGE MANAGEMENT SYSTEMS

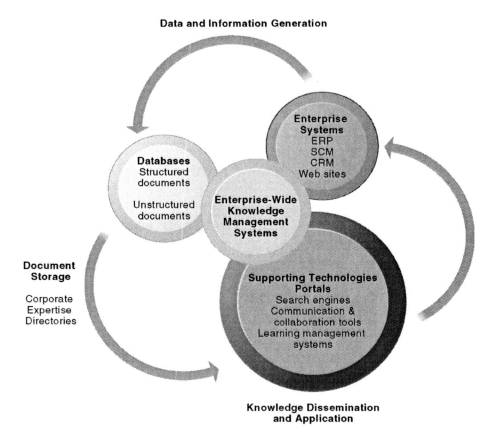

Enterprise-wide knowledge management systems use an array of technologies for storing structured and unstructured documents, locating employee expertise, searching for information, disseminating knowledge, and using data from enterprise applications and other key corporate systems.

making it accessible throughout the firm. We will call this type of knowledge **structured knowledge**, and we can refer to these types of systems as **structured knowledge systems**.

Managers may also need information that may exist somewhere inside the firm in the form of less-structured documents, such as e-mail, voice mail, chat room exchanges, videos, digital pictures, brochures, or bulletin boards. We can call this knowledge **semistructured knowledge**, and we can refer to the systems that focus on this type of knowledge as **semistructured knowledge systems** (the industry name is *digital asset management systems*).

Systems for structured and semistructured knowledge function as knowledge repositories. A **knowledge repository** is a collection of internal and external knowledge in a single location for more efficient management and utilization by the organization. Knowledge repositories provide access through enterprise portals and search engine technology and may include tools for accessing information from corporate databases.

In still other cases there are no formal or digital documents of any kind, and the knowledge resides in the heads of experienced employees somewhere in the company. Much of this knowledge is *tacit knowledge* and is rarely written down. Here, the problem faced by managers is building a network that con-

TABLE 2   CATEGORIES OF ENTERPRISE-WIDE KNOWLEDGE MANAGEMENT SYSTEMS

TYPE OF KNOWLEDGE	KNOWLEDGE CONTENT	CATEGORY OF ENTERPRISE KNOWLEDGE MANAGEMENT SYSTEM
Structured knowledge	Formal documents	Structured knowledge systems
Semistructured knowledge	E-mail, voice mail, memos, brochures, digital pictures, bulletin boards, and other unstructured documents	Semistructured knowledge systems
Network (tacit) knowledge	Expertise of individuals	Knowledge networks

nects knowledge demand with knowledge supply. **Knowledge network systems**, also known as *expertise location and management systems,* attempt to perform this function. Knowledge network systems provide an online directory of corporate experts in well-defined knowledge domains and use communication technologies to make it easy for employees to find the appropriate expert in a company. Some knowledge network systems go further by systematizing the solutions being developed by experts and then storing the solutions in a knowledge database as a best practices or frequently asked questions (FAQ) repository.

Table 2 compares the major categories of enterprise-wide knowledge management systems.

STRUCTURED KNOWLEDGE SYSTEMS

The essential problem in managing structured knowledge is creating an appropriate classification scheme to organize information into meaningful categories in a knowledge database that can be easily accessed by employees. Once the categories for classifying knowledge have been created, each document needs to be "tagged," or coded, so that search engines can retrieve it and the quality of search results can be improved. Structured knowledge systems perform the function of implementing the tagging, interfacing with corporate databases where the documents are stored, and creating an enterprise portal environment for employees to use when searching for corporate knowledge.

All the major accounting and consulting firms have developed structured document and engagement-based (case-based) repositories of reports from consultants who are working with particular clients. The reports typically are created after the consulting engagement is completed and include detailed descriptions of the consulting objective, participants, and the practices used to achieve the client's objectives. These reports are placed in a massive database to be used later for training new consultants in the company's best practices and for preparing new consultants joining an existing on-site consulting team.

One of the world's largest structured knowledge systems is KPMG's KWorld. KPMG International is an international tax and accounting firm with 97,000 professionals serving clients through 1,100 offices in 144 countries. With such a large global base of employees and clients, KPMG faced a number of problems in sharing knowledge, preventing the loss of knowledge as consultants retired or left the firm, disseminating best practices, and coping with information overload of individual consultants.

KWorld addresses these problems by providing an integrated set of knowledge content and collaboration tools for use worldwide. Although it is primarily a document repository, KWorld also provides online collaboration capabilities for the firm's consultants and an internal reporting system. KWorld stores white papers, presentations, best-practice proposals, articles, presentations, internal discussions, marketing materials, engagement histories, news feeds, external industry research, and other intellectual capital.

The content is organized into nine levels by KPMG products and market segments (see Figure 5). Within each of these levels are many subcategories of knowledge. For instance, the client knowledge domain includes entries on financials, industry dynamics, change dynamics, client organizations, client products and customers, and KPMG's history of engagements. Consultants use KWorld to coordinate their work as a team with a client, and the client is allowed access to the collaboration environment as well.

KPMG has invested heavily in organizational and management capital required to make use of the millions of documents stored in KWorld. KPMG has created a division of knowledge management, headed by a chief knowledge officer. An extensive staff of analysts and librarians assesses the quality of incoming information, ensures its proper categorization, and provides some analysis of its importance.

SEMISTRUCTURED KNOWLEDGE SYSTEMS

Semistructured information is all the digital information in a firm that does not exist in a formal document or a formal report. It has been estimated that at least 80 percent of an organization's business content is unstructured—information in folders, messages, memos, proposals, e-mails, graphics, electronic slide

FIGURE 5   KWORLD'S KNOWLEDGE DOMAINS

KPMG's KWorld is organized into nine levels of content that are further classified by product, market segment, and geographic area.

presentations, and even videos created in different formats and stored in many locations.

Increasingly, firms are required to track and manage this semistructured content in order to comply with the Sarbanes-Oxley Act of 2002 and other government legislation, and to manage their information assets more efficiently. Firms subject to Sarbanes-Oxley, for instance, must retain digital records of employee e-mail and phone conversations for a minimum of five years. Large firms such as Coca-Cola need to keep track of all the images of the Coca-Cola brand that have been created in the past at all their worldwide offices, both to avoid duplicating efforts and to avoid variation from a standard brand image.

A number of vendors have responded to this need with semistructured knowledge systems that track, store, and organize semistructured documents, as well as more structured traditional documents. For example, OpenText Livelink ECM™ specializes in "integrated knowledge management systems" (see Figure 6). In addition to providing centralized repositories for document management, OpenText LiveLink ECM™ provides a rules-based e-mail management program that automatically profiles incoming and outgoing mail messages using rules developed by line managers.

FIGURE 6   OPENTEXT LIVELINK ECM INTEGRATED KNOWLEDGE MANAGEMENT SYSTEM

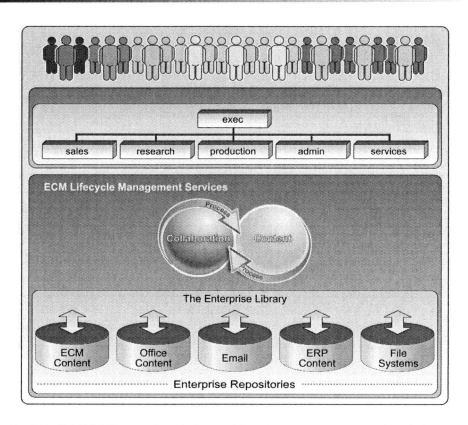

OpenText's Livelink ECM™ enterprise solution combines document management, knowledge management, business intelligence, and portal technologies and can be used for managing semistructured as well as structured knowledge.

Courtesy of OpenText Corporation

INTERACTIVE SESSION: ORGANIZATIONS

STIKEMAN ELLIOTT COMPUTERIZES ITS BRAINPOWER

Stikeman Elliott is an international business law firm based in Toronto, Ontario, Canada, noted for its work in mergers and acquisitions, antitrust, banking and finance, insolvency, intellectual property, and technology. The firm started with two lawyers in 1952 and today operates with more than 440 lawyers in eight offices in Canada, New York, London, and Sydney. It is one of the top business law firms in Canada.

Stikeman Elliott tries to promote a culture of initiative and high-performance standards. The key to creating and maintaining such a culture is in finding the best way to share the vast repositories of knowledge that reside in the brains of the lawyers and in the documents and files that the lawyers have been collecting throughout their careers. Foremost among the forms of knowledge critical to lawyers are precedents, which can include documents, forms, guidelines, and best practices.

Stikeman Elliott realized that an effective knowledge management (KM) system would enable the firm's lawyers to be more productive and contribute to sustaining the growth of the firm over the long term. In 2001, Stikeman Elliott selected Hummingbird Enterprise Webtop from Hummingbird Ltd. to build a portal for the firm's corporate intranet. The portal officially launched in 2002 under the name STELLA, which is a play on the name of the firm.

With STELLA in place, all of the firm's lawyers have easy access to the firm's knowledge assets, including important precedents, through a single access point using a Web browser. STELLA includes an expertise database, identifying lawyers with proficiency in specific areas. The portal also codifies the generation and organization of new precedents. Margaret Grottenthaler, the co-chair of Stikeman Elliott's national knowledge management committee, points out the importance of STELLA to the firm's junior employees: "It's the way to access all our research, all the legal how-tos. It's absolutely critical they use it. The more junior they are, the more likely they are to use it for those purposes."

An additional benefit of STELLA has been its ability to encourage the sense of community that Stikeman Elliott wishes to foster in its firm by growing organically rather than through mergers or acquisitions. Everyone in the firm, regardless of which office they work in, has access to the same resources. With everyone on equal footing, the multiple-office structure maintains the feel of a single organization. Stikeman Elliott believes that this working atmosphere positions the firm well among its competitors. The increased level of communication among the offices also prevents lawyers from duplicating work that has already been done. Lawyers can customize the portal's home page so that they have quick access to the information they need most, whether it is their case files, news about their clients, or news about their clients' industries.

Stikeman Elliott integrated its portal closely with its document management (DM) system, which was also based on Hummingbird DOCS Open software. (Hummingbird has since been acquired by OpenText™). Stikeman employees use the Hummingbird SearchServer search engine to search through the firm's document repository and internal legal and business content, including e-mail, and some external resources, such as LexisNexis.

Of course, a KM system is only useful if it is populated with the knowledge of its users. Some firms have difficulty with partners who hoard their knowledge, it being a valuable commodity. At Stikeman Elliott, the greater obstacle has been time. Partners are often too busy to contribute their work to the system. To combat this problem, the firm is building tools to automate the population of the knowledge database. With these tools, lawyers can easily create Web sites for their cases, clients, and industry research. STELLA has extranet capabilities that enable Stikeman Elliott to create sites on which clients can review and work with documents pertaining to their cases in a collaborative manner. Grottenthaler points out that the firm's KM system is actually geared toward the client, not the lawyer, because the ultimate goal is to serve the client better.

The KM team at Stikeman Elliott includes library staff and law clerks in addition to lawyers. All three groups can add precedents, memos, and even meeting notes to the system. The team emphasizes the importance of the human presence in KM and keeps in close contact with the firm's lawyers to make sure they have access to the knowledge they need. A human subject matter expert also reviews content that has been added and categorized by automated procedures, which ensures the quality of the information.

Sources: "Stikeman Elliott Collaborates with Hummingbird and ii3," www.hummingbird.com, accessed September 19, 2006; Judith Lamont, "Smart by Any Name—Enterprise Suites Offer Broad Benefits," *KMWorld Magazine*, April 2005; and Hugh McKellar, "Business and Practice: KM and the Law," *KM World*, October 2006.

CASE STUDY QUESTIONS

1. What are the problems and challenges that a law firm such as Stikeman Elliott faces?

2. What solutions are available to solve these problems?

3. How did implementing Hummingbird address these problems? How successful was the solution? Did Stikeman Elliott choose the best alternative?

MIS IN ACTION

Visit the OpenText Livelink ECM™ Web site and explore the sections on Hummingbird Enterprise Management and the ROI Case Studies. Then answer the following questions:

1. List and describe the components of OpenText Livelink ECM™ that are most useful for knowledge work. What additional OpenText Livelink ECM™ capabilities might benefit a company such as Stikeman Elliott? Explain how each of these capabilities would help.

2. How did Hummingbird provide value for the companies discussed in the ROI case studies? How could OpenText Livelink ECM™ increase ROI for Stikeman Elliott?

One user of Hummingbird's enterprise knowledge management system is Canadian law firm Stikeman Elliott, which is described in the Interactive Session on Organizations. Like other law firms, Stikeman Elliott is a knowledge-intensive company, but its employees, offices, and knowledge resources are distributed in many different locations. It implemented Hummingbird tools to help it leverage this knowledge and use it more efficiently.

Organizing Knowledge: Taxonomies and Tagging

One of the first challenges that firms face when building knowledge repositories of any kind is the problem of identifying the correct categories to use when classifying documents. Firms are increasingly using a combination of internally developed taxonomies and search engine techniques. A **taxonomy** is a scheme for classifying information and knowledge in such a way that it can be easily accessed. A taxonomy is like a table of contents in a book or like the Library of Congress system for classifying books and periodicals according to subject matter and author. A business firm can access information much more easily if it devises its own taxonomy for classifying information into logical categories. The more precise the taxonomy, the more relevant are the search results produced by search engines. Once a knowledge taxonomy is produced, documents are all *tagged* with the proper classification.

Products such as Autonomy Taxonomy attempt to reduce the burden on users by categorizing documents using an existing corporate taxonomy. Such products consider the user's prior searches, the context of the search term in the document (the relationships between words in a document), related concepts the user may not have entered, as well as keyword frequency and the popularity of the document.

Several tools perform auto tagging and reduce the need for managers to develop their own unique taxonomies. Entrieva's SemioTagger software is a categorization and indexing engine that identifies key phrases in documents, assigns relevance factors to these phrases, and organizes the documents into categories, creating XML-based document tags using rules that users can see and modify. Users can add, delete, or merge categories after examining how the system responds.

One user of Semio's auto-tagging tools is Stanford University's HighWire Press, which publishes 324 online journals containing more than 12 million articles. HighWire needed a way to automate and expand its indexing process. It also needed to provide researchers with better browsing and searching capabilities to support the discovery of unexpected relationships, to link articles from a variety of disciplines, to identify concepts in articles, and to link these concepts in logical categories. Currently, the system has developed 22,000 categories and more than 300,000 concepts. The system supports 84 million hits each week with a database of 6 terabytes (Semio, 2006). The system requires some active management. HighWire Press reviews its classification scheme every quarter and makes changes based on user feedback and management insight.

KNOWLEDGE NETWORK SYSTEMS

Knowledge network systems address the problem that arises when the appropriate knowledge is tacit knowledge residing in the memory of expert individuals in the firm. Because such knowledge cannot be conveniently found, employees expend significant resources rediscovering knowledge. An International Data Corporation (IDC) study estimated that the average cost of redundant effort in Fortune 500 companies exceeds $60 million per year per firm (AskMe, 2003a).

Knowledge network systems provide an online directory of corporate experts in well-defined knowledge domains and use communication technologies to make it easy for employees to find the appropriate expert in a company. Some knowledge network systems go further by systematizing the solutions developed by experts and then storing the solutions in a knowledge database as a best-practices or frequently asked questions (FAQ) repository.

AskMe, Inc., offers a widely adopted enterprise knowledge network system. Its users include Procter & Gamble and Intec Engineering Partnership, a project management company with more than 500 employees worldwide serving the global oil and gas industry. The software, AskMe Enterprise, enables firms to develop a database of employee expertise and know-how, documents, best practices, and FAQs, and then to share that information across the firm using whichever portal technology the firm has adopted. Content can be further categorized through community spaces that organize expertise and knowledge around a common discipline. Federated search capabilities ensure the reuse of existing knowledge from internal repositories, third-party repositories, and external sources on the Web. Users can subscribe to RSS feeds to receive notifications about new content.

Figure 7 illustrates how AskMe Enterprise works. An Intec engineer with a question, for instance, could access relevant documents, Web links, and answers to previous related questions by initiating a keyword search. If no answer was found, that person could post a general question on a Web page for categories, such as Pipeline or Subsea, for other engineers accessing that page to answer. Alternatively, the person could review the profiles of all company engineers

FIGURE 7   ASKME ENTERPRISE KNOWLEDGE NETWORK SYSTEM

A knowledge network maintains a database of firm experts, as well as accepted solutions to known problems. The AskMe Enterprise system facilitates the communication between employees looking for knowledge and internal solution providers through the Web-based system, standard e-mail such as Outlook, PDAs, BlackBerry handhelds, or instant messaging. Solutions created in this communication are then added to a database of solutions in the form of FAQs, best practices, or other documents.

with relevant expertise and send a detailed e-mail query to experts who might have the answer. All questions and answers are automatically incorporated into the knowledge database.

SUPPORTING TECHNOLOGIES: PORTALS, COLLABORATION TOOLS, AND LEARNING MANAGEMENT SYSTEMS

The major commercial knowledge management system vendors have integrated their content and document management capabilities with powerful portal and collaboration technologies. Enterprise knowledge portals can provide access to external sources of information, such as news feeds and research, as well as to internal knowledge resources along with capabilities for e-mail, chat/instant messaging, discussion groups, and videoconferencing.

Groupware can be used for organizational information—sharing and collaboration. Companies are now starting to use consumer Web technologies such as blogs, wikis, and social bookmarking for internal use to facilitate the exchange of information between individuals and teams.

Intel CEO Paul Otellini uses a blog for conveying his thoughts to employees and for soliciting their opinions. Internal teams at Ernst & Young use blogs to collaborate and share knowledge about clients and projects, while French pharmaceutical company Ipsen uses blogs for reputation management and for gathering competitive intelligence.

INTERACTIVE SESSION: TECHNOLOGY

SHARING KNOWLEDGE WITH SOCIAL BOOKMARKING

Most Web users know the value of bookmarks, which allow Web surfers to store and annotate links to useful Web sites. Bookmarks make it much easer to relocate information. But they're tied to a single machine and Web browser, so you can't bring them with you or share them easily with people in other locations.

Enter social bookmarking. Instead of storing bookmarks on desktops, users store them on shared sites, where they can be accessed from any location with Web access and also shared with other people. The shared sites can be sites for bookmarking pages on the public Web or internal corporate sites for bookmarking pages on the corporate intranet. The bookmarks are "tagged" with keywords to help organize and classify them. Other people can use these tags to find bookmarks relevant to their interests that may help them find information more easily, including new sources of information that might be missed by search engines.

For example, suppose you're on a corporate team doing research on wind power. If you did a Web search and found relevant Web pages on wind power, you'd click on a bookmarking button on the social networking site and create a tag identifying each Web document in such a way that it would be linked to wind power. You can click on the "tags" button at the social networking site to see a list of all the tags you created and select the documents you need.

Some even use these tags to identify other users with similar interests. Because social bookmarking sites indicate the author of each bookmark and provide access to that person's other bookmarked resources, users can make social connections with other individuals interested in a particular topic. This process allows like-minded individuals to find one another and create new communities of users. It could be said that social bookmarking creates a network of resources and connections that represents the interests and judgments of a community of users.

Web-based social bookmarking sites are on the rise, including del.icio.us (pronounced delicious), which was acquired by Yahoo! in 2005. Del.icio.us is targeted at individual consumers, but there are other social bookmarking sites offering services to academic and business users. Academics use

CiteULike.org to share and store academic papers, while medical researchers and practitioners use Connotea.org to track references. Visitors to social bookmarking sites can search for resources by keyword, person, or popularity and see the public bookmarks, tags, and classification schemes that registered bookmark users have created.

IBM developed Dogear, a social bookmarking service for businesses. It includes a user authentication feature, which is important for ensuring only selected employees collaborate. Dogear allows users in a business to search and bookmark information on either the public Web or an internal corporate intranet. Users can decide whether to make all their tagged bookmarks public or only selected bookmarks. (The rest are kept private.) In addition to facilitating document-sharing, Dogear connects people in large organizations who would otherwise never meet and promotes information sharing between individuals in a team. According to David Millen, manager of IBM's Collaborative User Experience group, social bookmarking "allows you to see who is interested in the topics you're interested in." If you think a particular person's bookmarks are especially useful, you can subscribe to those bookmarks. Dogear users can subscribe to particular tags and have newly tagged items delivered automatically.

There are downsides. Public social bookmarking sites provide no oversight about how resources are organized or tagged. In some instances, this will lead to inconsistent or disorganized uses of tags. For example, if a user saves a bookmark for a site with information about wind power, but only tags the site with the term wind power and not with the terms alternative energy or renewable energy, that information might never be found by someone looking for information about wind power as a source of alternative energy. Social bookmarking reflects the values of a community of users, so there's always a chance they will present a skewed view of a particular topic.

Sources: Michael Totty, "Information Found - and Shared." *The Wall Street Journal*, September 11, 2006; Shamus McGillicudy, "Social Bookmarking: Pushing Collaboration to the Edge," SearchCIO.com, June 21, 2006; and Vauhini Vara, "Offices Co-Opt Consumer Web Tools Like 'Wikis' and Social Networking." *The Wall Street Journal*, September 12, 2006.

CASE STUDY QUESTIONS

1. What are the advantages and disadvantages of using social bookmarking for knowledge management?

2. What management, organization, and technology issues should be addressed when considering whether to use social bookmarking for knowledge management at a business?

3. Should there be different standards for posting bookmarks to public Web pages at a public Web site and posting bookmarks to internal corporate Web pages on a corporate social bookmarking site?

MIS IN ACTION

Visit the social bookmarking site Del.icio.us and search for bookmarks on a topic of your choice, such as global warming, bird flu, ethanol, or open-source. Then answer the following questions:

1. How easy was it to find bookmarks about your topic? How many bookmarks did you find?

2. Compare these bookmarks to the results of a search on your topic of choice using Google, Yahoo!, or another search engine. Which tools were the most useful in pointing you to good information?

3. Would you use Del.icio.us to find information for a research paper or business presentation? Why or why not?

Wikis are inexpensive, easy to implement and use, and do not require a massive software rollout. They are meant to stimulate collaboration. Users determine the content, eliminating the need for a central distribution center with extensive management. Wikis can centralize all types of corporate data that can be displayed in a Web browser, including Microsoft Word documents, spreadsheets, Microsoft PowerPoint slides, and electronic pages of documents, and can embed e-mail and instant messages. Heavy-duty wikis are able to directly interface with corporate databases to import audio and picture files. Although users can modify wiki content contributed by others, wikis have some built-in version control. No changes can be made without recording the author of those changes and it is possible to revert to an earlier version.

These features of wikis make them especially appealing to small businesses with limited technology staffs and budgets, but they are also being deployed by large enterprises. Nokia has been using Socialtext wiki software to facilitate information exchange within its Insight and Foresight Group. Intel Corp. created a wiki called Intelpedia that lets employees collect information and collaborate on projects instead of having to send countless e-mails. (Vara, 2006). Socialtext, JotSpot, and Atlassian are leading wiki software vendors, while Twiki and Perspective are non-commercial open-source tools.

Social bookmarking makes it easier to search for, and also to share information by allowing users to save their bookmarks to Web pages on a public Web site and tag these bookmarks with keywords. These tags can be used to organize and search for the documents, and lists of tags can be shared with other people to help them find information of interest. The Interactive Session on Technology describes how this technology works and its benefits for knowledge management.

Learning Management Systems

Companies need ways to keep track of and manage employee learning and to integrate it more fully into their knowledge management and other corporate systems. **Learning management systems (LMS)** provide tools for the management, delivery, tracking, and assessment of various types of employee learning and training.

Contemporary LMS support multiple modes of learning, including CD-ROM, downloadable videos, Web-based classes, live instruction in classes or online, and group learning in online forums and chat sessions. LMS consolidate mixed-media training, automate the selection and administration of courses, assemble and deliver learning content, and measure learning effectiveness.

For example, the Naval Education Training Command (NETC) uses the THINQ Training Server Learning Management System to manage electronic and instructor-led training for 47,000 officers and enlisted people enrolled in 3,600 different courses. The system provides tools to assess individual skills and competencies, manage personalized learning plans, and track required certifications. The system saves the Navy about $40 million in travel costs per year and has also reduced the amount of time required for training (Hollis, 2004).

3   KNOWLEDGE WORK SYSTEMS

The enterprise-wide knowledge systems we have just described provide a wide range of capabilities that can be used by many if not all the workers and groups in an organization. Firms also have specialized systems for knowledge workers to help them create new knowledge and to ensure that this knowledge is properly integrated into the business.

KNOWLEDGE WORKERS AND KNOWLEDGE WORK

Knowledge workers include researchers, designers, architects, scientists, and engineers who primarily create knowledge and information for the organization. Knowledge workers usually have high levels of education and memberships in professional organizations and are often asked to exercise independent judgment as a routine aspect of their work. For example, knowledge workers create new products or find ways of improving existing ones. Knowledge workers perform three key roles that are critical to the organization and to the managers who work within the organization:

- Keeping the organization current in knowledge as it develops in the external world—in technology, science, social thought, and the arts
- Serving as internal consultants regarding the areas of their knowledge, the changes taking place, and opportunities
- Acting as change agents, evaluating, initiating, and promoting change projects

REQUIREMENTS OF KNOWLEDGE WORK SYSTEMS

Most knowledge workers rely on office systems, such as word processors, voice mail, e-mail, videoconferencing, and scheduling systems, which are designed to increase worker productivity in the office. However, knowledge workers also require highly specialized knowledge work systems with powerful graphics, analytical tools, and communications and document management capabilities.

These systems require substantial computing power to handle the sophisticated graphics or complex calculations necessary for such knowledge workers as scientific researchers, product designers, and financial analysts. Because knowledge workers are so focused on knowledge in the external world, these

FIGURE 8   REQUIREMENTS OF KNOWLEDGE WORK SYSTEMS

Knowledge work systems require strong links to external knowledge bases in addition to specialized hardware and software.

systems also must give the worker quick and easy access to external databases. They typically feature user-friendly interfaces that enable users to perform needed tasks without having to spend a great deal of time learning how to use the system. Knowledge workers are highly paid—wasting a knowledge worker's time is simply too expensive. Figure 8 summarizes the requirements of knowledge work systems.

Knowledge workstations often are designed and optimized for the specific tasks to be performed. For example, a design engineer requires a different workstation setup than a financial analyst. Design engineers need graphics with enough power to handle three-dimensional computer-aided design systems. However, financial analysts are more interested in access to a myriad of external databases and technology for efficiently storing and accessing massive amounts of financial data.

EXAMPLES OF KNOWLEDGE WORK SYSTEMS

Major knowledge work applications include computer-aided design systems, virtual reality systems for simulation and modeling, and financial workstations. **Computer-aided design (CAD)** automates the creation and revision of designs, using computers and sophisticated graphics software. Using a more traditional physical design methodology, each design modification requires a mold to be made and a prototype to be tested physically. These steps must be repeated many times, which is a very expensive and time-consuming process. Using a CAD workstation, the designer need only make a physical prototype toward the end of the design process because the design can be easily tested and changed on the computer. The ability of CAD software to provide design specifications for the tooling and the manufacturing processes also saves a great deal of time and money while producing a manufacturing process with far fewer problems.

Computer-aided design CAD systems improve the quality and precision of product design by performing much of the design and testing work on the computer.

Photo courtesy of ndx photos/ NewsCom

For example, architects from Skidmore, Owings, & Merrill LLP used a 3-D design program called Revit to work out the creative and technical details of the design for the Freedom Tower at the site of the former World Trade Center. The software enabled the architects to strip away the outer layer to manipulate the shape of the floors. Changes appeared immediately in the entire model, and the software automatically recalculated the technical details in the blueprints (Frangos, 2004).

Virtual reality systems have visualization, rendering, and simulation capabilities that go far beyond those of conventional CAD systems. They use interactive graphics software to create computer-generated simulations that are so close to reality that users almost believe they are participating in a real-world situation. In many virtual reality systems, the user dons special clothing, headgear, and equipment, depending on the application. The clothing contains sensors that record the user's movements and immediately transmit that information back to the computer. For instance, to walk through a virtual reality simulation of a house, you would need garb that monitors the movement of your feet, hands, and head. You also would need goggles containing video screens and sometimes audio attachments and feeling gloves so that you can be immersed in the computer feedback.

Virtual reality is just starting to provide benefits in educational, scientific, and business work. For example, neuroradiologists at New York's Beth Israel Medical Center can use the Siemens Medical Systems 3D Virtuoso System to peek at the interplay of tiny blood vessels or take a fly-through of the aorta. Surgeons at New York University School of Medicine can use three-dimensional modeling to target brain tumors more precisely, thereby reducing bleeding and trauma during surgery.

Virtual reality applications developed for the Web use a standard called **Virtual Reality Modeling Language (VRML)**. VRML is a set of specifications for interactive, three-dimensional modeling on the World Wide Web that can organize multiple media types, including animation, images, and audio, to put users in a simulated real-world environment. VRML is platform-independent, operates over a desktop computer, and requires little bandwidth.

TABLE 3 EXAMPLES OF KNOWLEDGE WORK SYSTEMS

KNOWLEDGE WORK SYSTEM	FUNCTION IN ORGANIZATION
CAD/CAM (computer-aided design/computer-aided manufacturing)	Provides engineers, designers, and factory managers with precise control over industrial design and manufacturing
Virtual reality systems	Provide architects, engineers, and medical workers with precise, photorealistic simulations of objects
Investment workstations	High-end PCs used in financial sector to analyze trading situations instantaneously and facilitate portfolio management

DuPont, the Wilmington, Delaware, chemical company, created a VRML application called HyperPlant, which enables users to access three-dimensional data over the Internet using Web browser software. Engineers can go through three-dimensional models as if they were physically walking through a plant, viewing objects at eye level. This level of detail reduces the number of mistakes they make during construction of oil rigs, oil plants, and other structures.

The financial industry is using specialized **investment workstations** to leverage the knowledge and time of its brokers, traders, and portfolio managers. Firms such as Merrill Lynch and UBS Financial Services have installed investment workstations that integrate a wide range of data from both internal and external sources, including contact management data, real-time and historical market data, and research reports. Previously, financial professionals had to spend considerable time accessing data from separate systems and piecing together the information they needed. By providing one-stop information faster and with fewer errors, the workstations streamline the entire investment process from stock selection to updating client records. Table 3 summarizes the major types of knowledge work systems.

4 INTELLIGENT TECHNIQUES

Artificial intelligence and database technology provide a number of intelligent techniques that organizations can use to capture individual and collective knowledge and to extend their knowledge base. Expert systems, case-based reasoning, and fuzzy logic are used for capturing tacit knowledge. Neural networks and data mining are used for **knowledge discovery**. They can discover underlying patterns, categories, and behaviors in large data sets that could not be discovered by managers alone or simply through experience. Genetic algorithms are used for generating solutions to problems that are too large and complex for human beings to analyze on their own. Intelligent agents can automate routine tasks to help firms search for and filter information for use in electronic commerce, supply chain management, and other activities.

Data mining helps organizations capture undiscovered knowledge residing in large databases, providing managers with new insight for improving business performance. It has become an important tool for management decision making.

The other intelligent techniques discussed in this section are based on **artificial intelligence (AI)** technology, which consists of computer-based systems (both hardware and software) that attempt to emulate human behavior. Such systems are able to learn languages, accomplish physical tasks, use a perceptual apparatus, and emulate human expertise and decision making. Although AI applications do not exhibit the breadth, complexity, originality, and generality of human intelligence, they play an important role in contemporary knowledge management.

CAPTURING KNOWLEDGE: EXPERT SYSTEMS

Expert systems are an intelligent technique for capturing tacit knowledge in a very specific and limited domain of human expertise. These systems capture the knowledge of skilled employees in the form of a set of rules in a software system that can be used by others in the organization. The set of rules in the expert system adds to the memory, or stored learning, of the firm.

Expert systems lack the breadth of knowledge and the understanding of fundamental principles of a human expert. They typically perform very limited tasks that can be accomplished by professionals in a few minutes or hours, such as diagnosing a malfunctioning machine or determining whether to grant credit for a loan. Problems that cannot be solved by human experts in the same short period of time are far too difficult for an expert system. However, by capturing human expertise in limited areas, expert systems can provide benefits, helping organizations make high-quality decisions with fewer people. Today expert systems are widely used in business in discrete, highly structured decision-making situations.

How Expert Systems Work

Human knowledge must be modeled or represented in a way that a computer can process. Expert systems model human knowledge as a set of rules that collectively are called the **knowledge base**. Expert systems have from 200 to many thousands of these rules, depending on the complexity of the problem. These rules are much more interconnected and nested than in a traditional software program (see Figure 9).

The strategy used to search through the knowledge base is called the **inference engine**. Two strategies are commonly used: forward chaining and backward chaining (see Figure 10).

In **forward chaining**, the inference engine begins with the information entered by the user and searches the knowledge base to arrive at a conclusion. The strategy is to fire, or carry out, the action of the rule when a condition is true. In Figure 10, beginning on the left, if the user enters a client's name with income greater than $100,000, the engine will fire all rules in sequence from left to right. If the user then enters information indicating that the same client owns real estate, another pass of the knowledge base will occur and more rules will fire. Processing continues until no more rules can be fired.

In **backward chaining**, the strategy for searching the knowledge base starts with a hypothesis and proceeds by asking the user questions about selected facts until the hypothesis is either confirmed or disproved. In our example, in Figure 10, ask the question, "Should we add this person to the prospect database?" Begin on the right of the diagram and work toward the left. You can see that the person should be added to the database if a sales representative is sent, term insurance is granted, or a financial adviser visits the client.

FIGURE 9 **RULES IN AN EXPERT SYSTEM**

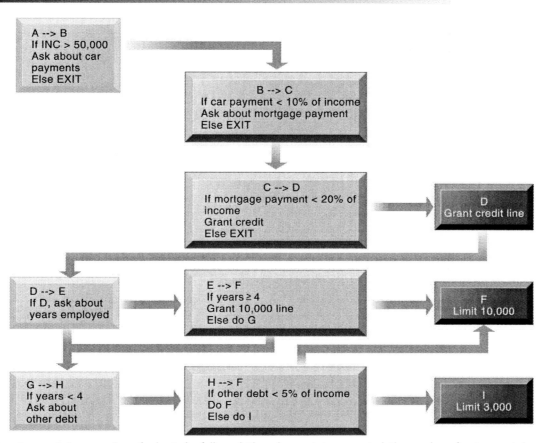

An expert system contains a number of rules to be followed. The rules are interconnected; the number of outcomes is known in advance and is limited; there are multiple paths to the same outcome; and the system can consider multiple rules at a single time. The rules illustrated are for simple credit-granting expert systems.

FIGURE 10 **INFERENCE ENGINES IN EXPERT SYSTEMS**

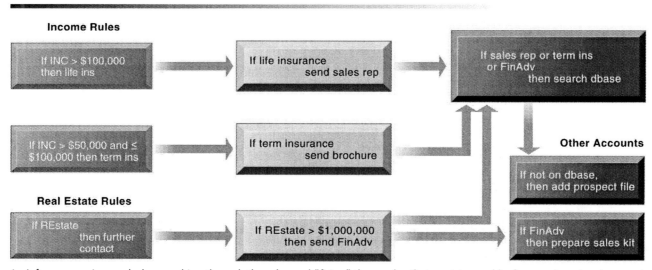

An inference engine works by searching through the rules and "firing" those rules that are triggered by facts gathered and entered by the user.

Developing an expert system requires input from one or more experts who have a thorough command of the knowledge base, and one or more knowledge engineers who can translate the knowledge (as described by the expert) into a set of rules. A **knowledge engineer** is similar to a traditional systems analyst but has special expertise in eliciting information and expertise from other professionals.

Examples of Successful Expert Systems

Expert systems provide businesses with an array of benefits including improved decisions, reduced errors, reduced costs, reduced training time, and higher levels of quality and service. Here are several examples:

Countrywide Funding Corporation in Pasadena, California, uses an expert system to improve decisions about granting loans. This loan-underwriting firm employs about 400 underwriters in 150 offices around the country. The company developed a PC-based expert system in 1992 to make preliminary creditworthiness decisions on loan requests. The company had experienced rapid, continuing growth and wanted the system to help ensure consistent, high-quality loan decisions. Countrywide's Loan Underwriting Expert System (CLUES) has about 400 rules. Countrywide tested the system by sending every loan application handled by a human underwriter to CLUES as well. The system was refined until it agreed with the underwriters in 95 percent of the cases.

Countrywide does not rely on CLUES to reject loans because the expert system cannot be programmed to handle exceptional situations, such as those involving a self-employed person or complex financial arrangements. An underwriter must review all rejected loans and makes the final decision. CLUES has other benefits. Traditionally, an underwriter could handle six or seven applications a day. Using CLUES, the same underwriter can evaluate at least 16 per day. Countrywide now uses the rules in its expert system to answer inquiries from visitors to its Web site who want to know if they qualify for a loan.

Con-Way Transportation built an expert system called Line-haul to automate and optimize planning of overnight shipment routes for its nationwide freight-trucking business. The expert system captures the business rules that dispatchers follow when assigning drivers, trucks, and trailers to transport 50,000 shipments of heavy freight each night across 25 states and Canada and when plotting their routes. Line-haul runs on a Sun platform and uses data on daily customer shipment requests, available drivers, trucks, trailer space, and weight stored in an Oracle database. The expert system uses thousands of rules and 100,000 lines of program code written in C++ to crunch the numbers and create optimum routing plans for 95 percent of daily freight shipments. Con-Way dispatchers tweak the routing plan provided by the expert system and relay final routing specifications to field personnel responsible for packing the trailers for their nighttime runs. Con-Way recouped its $3 million investment in the system within two years by reducing the number of drivers, packing more freight per trailer, and reducing damage from rehandling. The system also reduces dispatchers' arduous nightly tasks (Pastore, 2003).

Although expert systems lack the robust and general intelligence of human beings, they can provide benefits to organizations if their limitations are well understood. Only certain classes of problems can be solved using expert systems. Virtually all successful expert systems deal with problems of classification in limited domains of knowledge where there are relatively few alternative outcomes and these possible outcomes are all known in advance. Expert systems are much less useful for dealing with unstructured problems typically encountered by managers.

Many expert systems require large, lengthy, and expensive development efforts. Hiring or training more experts may be less expensive than building an expert system. Typically, the environment in which an expert system operates is continually changing so that the expert system must also continually change. Some expert systems, especially large ones, are so complex that in a few years the maintenance costs equal the development costs.

ORGANIZATIONAL INTELLIGENCE: CASE-BASED REASONING

Expert systems primarily capture the tacit knowledge of individual experts, but organizations also have collective knowledge and expertise that they have built up over the years. This organizational knowledge can be captured and stored using case-based reasoning. In **case-based reasoning (CBR)**, descriptions of past experiences of human specialists, represented as cases, are stored in a database for later retrieval when the user encounters a new case with similar parameters. The system searches for stored cases with problem characteristics similar to the new one, finds the closest fit, and applies the solutions of the old case to the new case. Successful solutions are tagged to the new case and both are stored together with the other cases in the knowledge base. Unsuccessful solutions also are appended to the case database along with explanations as to why the solutions did not work (see Figure 11).

Expert systems work by applying a set of IF-THEN-ELSE rules extracted from human experts. Case-based reasoning, in contrast, represents knowledge as a series of cases, and this knowledge base is continuously expanded and refined by users. You will find case-based reasoning in diagnostic systems in medicine or customer support where users can retrieve past cases whose characteristics are similar to the new case. The system suggests a solution or diagnosis based on the best-matching retrieved case.

FUZZY LOGIC SYSTEMS

Most people do not think in terms of traditional IF-THEN rules or precise numbers. Humans tend to categorize things imprecisely using rules for making decisions that may have many shades of meaning. For example, a man or a woman can be *strong* or *intelligent*. A company can be *large*, *medium*, or *small* in size. Temperature can be *hot*, *cold*, *cool*, or *warm*. These categories represent a range of values.

Fuzzy logic is a rule-based technology that can represent such imprecision by creating rules that use approximate or subjective values. It can describe a particular phenomenon or process linguistically and then represent that description in a small number of flexible rules. Organizations can use fuzzy logic to create software systems that capture tacit knowledge where there is linguistic ambiguity.

Let's look at the way fuzzy logic would represent various temperatures in a computer application to control room temperature automatically. The terms (known as *membership functions*) are imprecisely defined so that, for example, in Figure 12, cool is between 50 degrees and 70 degrees, although the temperature is most clearly cool between about 60 degrees and 67 degrees. Note that cool is overlapped by *cold* or *norm*. To control the room environment using this logic, the programmer would develop similarly imprecise definitions for humidity and other factors, such as outdoor wind and temperature.

FIGURE 11   HOW CASE-BASED REASONING WORKS

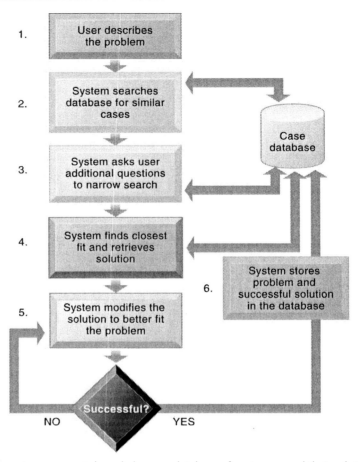

Case-based reasoning represents knowledge as a database of past cases and their solutions. The system uses a six-step process to generate solutions to new problems encountered by the user.

FIGURE 12   IMPLEMENTING FUZZY LOGIC RULES IN HARDWARE

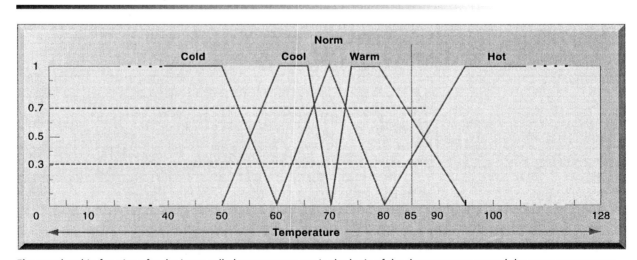

The membership functions for the input called temperature are in the logic of the thermostat to control the room temperature. Membership functions help translate linguistic expressions such as warm into numbers that the computer can manipulate.

Source: James M. Sibigtroth, "Implementing Fuzzy Expert Rules in Hardware," *AI Expert*, April 1992. © 1992 Miller Freeman, Inc. Reprinted with permission.

The rules might include one that says: "If the temperature is *cool* or *cold* and the humidity is low while the outdoor wind is high and the outdoor temperature is low, raise the heat and humidity in the room." The computer would combine the membership function readings in a weighted manner and, using all the rules, raise and lower the temperature and humidity.

Fuzzy logic provides solutions to problems requiring expertise that is difficult to represent in the form of crisp IF-THEN rules. In Japan, Sendai's subway system uses fuzzy logic controls to accelerate so smoothly that standing passengers need not hold on. Mitsubishi Heavy Industries in Tokyo has been able to reduce the power consumption of its air conditioners by 20 percent by implementing control programs in fuzzy logic. The autofocus device in cameras is only possible because of fuzzy logic. In these instances, fuzzy logic allows incremental changes in inputs to produce smooth changes in outputs instead of discontinuous ones, making it useful for consumer electronics and engineering applications.

Management also has found fuzzy logic useful for decision making and organizational control. A Wall Street firm created a system that selects companies for potential acquisition, using the language stock traders understand. A fuzzy logic system has been developed to detect possible fraud in medical claims submitted by health care providers anywhere in the United States.

NEURAL NETWORKS

Neural networks are used for solving complex, poorly understood problems for which large amounts of data have been collected. They find patterns and relationships in massive amounts of data that would be too complicated and difficult for a human being to analyze. Neural networks discover this knowledge by using hardware and software that parallel the processing patterns of the biological or human brain. Neural networks "learn" patterns from large quantities of data by sifting through data, searching for relationships, building models, and correcting over and over again the model's own mistakes.

A neural network has a large number of sensing and processing nodes that continuously interact with each other. Figure 13 represents one type of neural network comprising an input layer, an output layer, and a hidden processing layer. Humans "train" the network by feeding it a set of training data for which the inputs produce a known set of outputs or conclusions. This helps the computer learn the correct solution by example. As the computer is fed more data, each case is compared with the known outcome. If it differs, a correction is calculated and applied to the nodes in the hidden processing layer. These steps are repeated until a condition, such as corrections being less than a certain amount, is reached. The neural network in Figure 13 has learned how to identify a fraudulent credit card purchase. Also, self-organizing neural networks can be trained by exposing them to large amounts of data and allowing them to discover the patterns and relationships in the data.

Whereas expert systems seek to emulate or model a human expert's way of solving problems, neural network builders claim that they do not program solutions and do not aim to solve specific problems. Instead, neural network designers seek to put intelligence into the hardware in the form of a generalized capability to learn. In contrast, the expert system is highly specific to a given problem and cannot be retrained easily.

Neural network applications in medicine, science, and business address problems in pattern classification, prediction, financial analysis, and control and optimization. In medicine, neural network applications are used for

FIGURE 13   HOW A NEURAL NETWORK WORKS

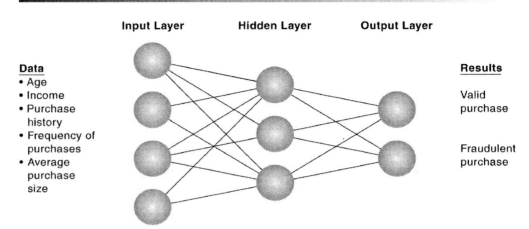

A neural network uses rules it "learns" from patterns in data to construct a hidden layer of logic. The hidden layer then processes inputs, classifying them based on the experience of the model. In this example, the neural network has been trained to distinguish between valid and fraudulent credit card purchases.

screening patients for coronary artery disease, for diagnosing patients with epilepsy and Alzheimer's disease, and for performing pattern recognition of pathology images. The financial industry uses neural networks to discern patterns in vast pools of data that might help predict the performance of equities, corporate bond ratings, or corporate bankruptcies. Visa International uses a neural network to help detect credit card fraud by monitoring all Visa transactions for sudden changes in the buying patterns of cardholders.

There are many puzzling aspects of neural networks. Unlike expert systems, which typically provide explanations for their solutions, neural networks cannot always explain why they arrived at a particular solution. Moreover, they cannot always guarantee a completely certain solution, arrive at the same solution again with the same input data, or always guarantee the best solution. They are very sensitive and may not perform well if their training covers too little or too much data. In most current applications, neural networks are best used as aids to human decision makers instead of substitutes for them.

GENETIC ALGORITHMS

Genetic algorithms are useful for finding the optimal solution for a specific problem by examining a very large number of possible solutions for that problem. Their problem-solving techniques are conceptually based on the method that living organisms use to adapt to their environments—the process of evolution. They are programmed to work the way populations solve problems—by changing and reorganizing their component parts using processes such as reproduction, mutation, and natural selection.

Thus, genetic algorithms promote the evolution of solutions to particular problems, controlling the generation, variation, adaptation, and selection of possible solutions using genetically based processes. As solutions alter and combine, the worst ones are discarded and the better ones survive to go on to produce even better solutions.

A genetic algorithm works by representing information as a string of 0s and 1s. A possible solution can be represented by a long string of these digits. The genetic algorithm provides methods of searching all possible combinations of digits to identify the right string representing the best possible structure for the problem.

In one method, the programmer first randomly generates a population of strings consisting of combinations of binary digits (see Figure 14). Each string corresponds to one of the variables in the problem. One applies a test for fitness, ranking the strings in the population according to their level of desirability as possible solutions. After the initial population is evaluated for fitness, the algorithm then produces the next generation of strings, consisting of strings that survived the fitness test plus offspring strings produced from mating pairs of strings, and tests their fitness. The process continues until a solution is reached.

Many business problems require optimization because they deal with issues such as minimization of costs, maximization of profits, efficient scheduling, and use of resources. If these situations are very dynamic and complex, involving hundreds or thousands of variables or formulas, genetic algorithms can expedite the solution because they can evaluate many different solution alternatives quickly to find the best one.

For example, General Electric engineers used genetic algorithms to help optimize the design for jet turbine aircraft engines, where each design change required changes in up to 100 variables. The supply chain management software from i2 Technologies uses genetic algorithms to optimize production-scheduling models incorporating hundreds of thousands of details about customer orders, material and resource availability, manufacturing and distribution capability, and delivery dates. International Truck and Engine used this software to iron out snags in production, reducing costly schedule disruptions by 90 percent in five of its plants. Genetic algorithms have helped market researchers performing market segmentation analysis (Kuo, Chang, and Chien, 2004; Burtka, 1993; Wakefield, 2001).

FIGURE 14   THE COMPONENTS OF A GENETIC ALGORITHM

		Color	Speed	Intelligence	Fitness
	1	White	Medium	Dumb	40
	2	Black	Slow	Dumb	43
	3	White	Slow	Very dumb	22
	4	Black	Fast	Dumb	71
	5	White	Medium	Very smart	53
A population of chromosomes			**Decoding of chromosomes**		**Evaluation of chromosomes**

This example illustrates an initial population of "chromosomes," each representing a different solution. The genetic algorithm uses an iterative process to refine the initial solutions so that the better ones, those with the higher fitness, are more likely to emerge as the best solution.

Source: Vasant Dhar and Roger Stein, *Seven Methods for Transforming Corporate Data into Business Intelligence*, p. 65, © 1997. Reprinted by permission of Prentice Hall, Upper Saddle River, New Jersey.

HYBRID AI SYSTEMS

Genetic algorithms, fuzzy logic, neural networks, and expert systems can be integrated into a single application to take advantage of the best features of these technologies. Such systems are called **hybrid AI systems**. Hybrid applications in business are growing. In Japan, Hitachi, Mitsubishi, Ricoh, Sanyo, and others are starting to incorporate hybrid AI systems in products such as home appliances, factory machinery, and office equipment. Matsushita has developed a "neurofuzzy" washing machine that combines fuzzy logic with neural networks. Nikko Securities has been working on a neurofuzzy system to forecast convertible-bond ratings.

INTELLIGENT AGENTS

Intelligent agent technology can help businesses navigate through large amounts of data to locate and act on information that is considered important. **Intelligent agents** are software programs that work in the background without direct human intervention to carry out specific, repetitive, and predictable tasks for an individual user, business process, or software application. The agent uses a limited built-in or learned knowledge base to accomplish tasks or make decisions on the user's behalf, such as deleting junk e-mail, scheduling appointments, or traveling over interconnected networks to find the cheapest airfare to California.

There are many intelligent agent applications today in operating systems, application software, e-mail systems, mobile computing software, and network tools. For example, the wizards found in Microsoft Office software tools have built-in capabilities to show users how to accomplish various tasks, such as formatting documents or creating graphs, and to anticipate when users need assistance.

Of special interest to business are intelligent agents for cruising networks, including the Internet, in search of information.

Many complex phenomena can be modeled as systems of autonomous agents that follow relatively simple rules for interaction. **Agent-based modeling** applications have been developed to model the behavior of consumers, stock markets, and supply chains and to predict the spread of epidemics (Samuelson and Macal, 2006).

Procter & Gamble (P&G) used agent-based modeling to improve coordination among different members of its supply chain in response to changing business conditions (Sadeh, Hildum, and Kjenstad 2003; Cavalieri, Cesarotti, and Introna 2003). Figure 15 illustrates the use of intelligent agents in Procter & Gamble's supply chain network. The network models a complex supply chain as a group of semiautonomous "agents" representing individual supply chain components, such as trucks, production facilities, distributors, or retail stores. The behavior of each agent is programmed to follow rules that mimic actual behavior, such as "dispatch a truck when it is full." Simulations using the agents enable the company to perform what-if analyses on inventory levels, in-store stockouts, and transportation costs.

Using intelligent agent models, P&G discovered that trucks should often be dispatched before being fully loaded. Although transportation costs would be higher using partially loaded trucks because of both driver time and fuel to deliver fewer goods, the simulation showed that retail store stockouts would

FIGURE 15   INTELLIGENT AGENTS IN P&G'S SUPPLY CHAIN NETWORK

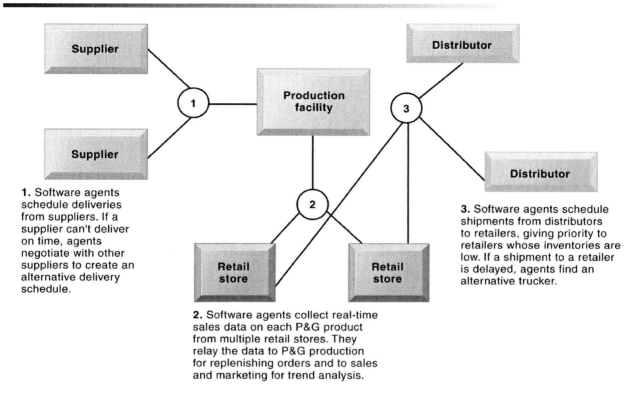

Intelligent agents are helping Procter & Gamble shorten the replenishment cycles for products such as a box of Tide.

occur less often, thus reducing the amount of lost sales, which would more than make up for the higher distribution costs. Agent-based modeling has saved P&G $300 million annually on an investment of less than 1 percent of that amount (Anthes, 2003).

5   HANDS-ON MIS

The projects in this section give you hands-on experience developing a knowledge management systems strategy for a real-world company, using expert system or spreadsheet tools to create a simple expert system, and using intelligent agents to research products for sale on the Web.

Achieving Operational Excellence: Identifying Opportunities for Knowledge Management

> Software skills: Web browser software, presentation software
> Business skills: Knowledge management strategy formulation

This project provides an opportunity for you to identify applications for knowledge management at a real-world business and to suggest value-adding knowledge management applications.

Senior management has started reading about knowledge management and has asked you to explore opportunities for improving knowledge management at Dirt Bikes. Write a report answering the following questions:

- What are the most important knowledge assets at Dirt Bikes? What functions and employee positions are responsible for creating, distributing, and using these knowledge assets? Are all of these assets explicit knowledge?

- What knowledge outside the organization is required by the company?

- How could the following employee groups benefit from knowledge management: designers and engineers, product development specialists, marketing specialists, sales department staff and representatives, and managers.

- Describe the kinds of knowledge management systems that would be most valuable for each of these groups. What information would each of these systems provide?

- Use the Web to research how the company could make better use of the Internet for knowledge management. What Internet information resources (specific Web sites or Usenet groups) would be most useful to Dirt Bikes?

- Describe an enterprise portal for one of the employee groups listed above. To which knowledge resources would it link? What would the home page of this portal look like?

- (Optional) Use electronic presentation software to summarize your findings for management.

Improving Decision Making: Building a Simple Expert System for Retirement Planning

Software skills: Spreadsheet formulas and IF function or expert system tool
Business skills: Benefits eligibility determination

Expert systems typically use a large number of rules. This project has been simplified to reduce the number of rules, but it will give you experience working with a series of rules to develop an application.

When employees at your company retire, they are given cash bonuses. These cash bonuses are based on the length of employment and the retiree's age. To receive a bonus, an employee must be at least 50 years of age and have worked for the company for five years. The following table summarizes the criteria for determining bonuses.

Using the information provided, build a simple expert system. Find a demonstration copy of an expert system software tool on the Web that you can download. Alternatively, use your spreadsheet software to build the expert system. (If you are using spreadsheet software, we suggest using the IF function so you can see how rules are created.)

LENGTH OF EMPLOYMENT	BONUS
< 5 years	No bonus
5–10 years	20 percent of current annual salary
11–15 years	30 percent of current annual salary
16–20 years	40 percent of current annual salary
21–25 years	50 percent of current annual salary
26 or more years	100 percent of current annual salary

Improving Decision Making: Using Intelligent Agents for Comparison Shopping

Software skills: Web browser and shopping bot software
Business skills: Product evaluation and selection

This project will give you experience using shopping bots to search online for products, find product information, and find the best prices and vendors.

You have decided to purchase a new digital camera. Select a digital camera you might want to purchase, such as the Canon PowerShot SD 700 or the Fuji FinePix E900. To purchase the camera as inexpensively as possible, try several of the shopping bot sites, which do the price comparisons for you. Visit My Simon (www.mysimon.com), BizRate.com (www.bizrate.com), and Froogle.com. Compare these shopping sites in terms of their ease of use, number of offerings, speed in obtaining information, thoroughness of information offered about the product and seller, and price selection. Which site or sites would you use and why? Which camera would you select and why? How helpful were these sites for making your decision?

LEARNING TRACK MODULE

Challenges of Knowledge Management Systems. If you want to learn more about the challenges of implementing and using knowledge management systems, you will find a Learning Track on this topic on the Laudon Web site for this chapter and on the Student CD-ROM.

Summary

1. *Assess the role of knowledge management and knowledge management programs in business.*

    Knowledge management is a set of processes to create, store, transfer, and apply knowledge in the organization. Businesses need knowledge management programs because knowledge has become a central productive and strategic asset in today's information economy and a potential source of competitive advantage. Much of a firm's value depends on its ability to create and manage knowledge. Knowledge management promotes organizational learning by increasing the ability of the organization to learn from its environment and to incorporate knowledge into its business processes. Effective knowledge management systems require organizational and management capital to promote a knowledge culture and programs for knowledge management, including the creation of a chief knowledge officer. There are three major types of knowledge management systems: enterprise-wide knowledge management systems, knowledge work systems, and intelligent techniques.

2. *Describe the types of systems used for enterprise-wide knowledge management and demonstrate how they provide value for organizations.*

    Enterprise-wide knowledge management systems are firmwide efforts to collect, store, distribute, and apply digital content and knowledge. Structured knowledge systems provide databases and tools for organizing and storing structured documents, whereas semistructured knowledge systems provide databases and tools for organizing and storing semistructured knowledge, such as e-mail or rich media. Knowledge network systems provide directories and tools for locating firm employees with special expertise who are important sources of tacit knowledge. Often these systems include group collaboration tools (including wikis and social bookmarking), portals to simplify information access, search tools, and tools for classifying information based on a taxonomy that is appropriate for the organization. Enterprise-wide knowledge management systems can provide considerable value if they are well designed and enable employees to locate, share, and use knowledge more efficiently.

3. *Describe the major types of knowledge work systems and assess how they provide value for firms.*

Knowledge work systems (KWS) support the creation of new knowledge and its integration into the organization. KWS require easy access to an external knowledge base; powerful computer hardware that can support software with intensive graphics, analysis, document management, and communications capabilities; and a user-friendly interface. These capabilities can increase the productivity of highly paid knowledge workers. KWS often run on workstations that are customized for the work they must perform. Computer-aided design (CAD) systems and virtual reality systems, which create interactive simulations that behave like the real world, require graphics and powerful modeling capabilities. KWS for financial professionals provide access to external databases and the ability to analyze massive amounts of financial data very quickly.

4. *Evaluate the business benefits of using intelligent techniques for knowledge management.*

Artificial intelligence lacks the flexibility, breadth, and generality of human intelligence, but it can be used to capture, codify, and extend organizational knowledge. Businesses can use artificial intelligence to help them capture and preserve tacit knowledge; for knowledge discovery; to generate solutions to specific problems that are too massive and complex to be analyzed by human beings on their own; and to help firms search for and filter information.

Expert systems capture tacit knowledge from a limited domain of human expertise and express that knowledge in the form of rules. The strategy to search through the knowledge base, called the inference engine, can use either forward or backward chaining. Expert systems are most useful for problems of classification or diagnosis. Case-based reasoning represents organizational knowledge as a database of cases that can be continually expanded and refined. When the user encounters a new case, the system searches for similar cases, finds the closest fit, and applies the solutions of the old case to the new case. The new case is stored with successful solutions in the case database.

Fuzzy logic is a software technology for expressing knowledge in the form of rules that use approximate or subjective values. Fuzzy logic has been used for controlling physical devices and is starting to be used for limited decision-making applications.

Neural networks consist of hardware and software that attempt to mimic the thought processes of the human brain. Neural networks are notable for their ability to learn and to recognize patterns that cannot be easily described by humans. They are being used in science, medicine, and business primarily to discriminate patterns in massive amounts of data.

Genetic algorithms develop solutions to particular problems using genetically based processes such as fitness, crossover, and mutation. Genetic algorithms are beginning to be applied to problems involving optimization, product design, and monitoring industrial systems where many alternatives or variables must be evaluated to generate an optimal solution.

Intelligent agents are software programs with built-in or learned knowledge bases that carry out specific, repetitive, and predictable tasks for an individual user, business process, or software application. Intelligent agents can be programmed to navigate through large amounts of data to locate useful information and in some cases act on that information on behalf of the user.

Key Terms

Agent-based modeling	*Intelligent agents*
Artificial intelligence (AI)	*Intelligent techniques*
Backward chaining	*Investment workstations*
Case-based reasoning (CBR)	*Knowledge*
Chief knowledge officer (CKO)	*Knowledge base*
Communities of practice (COPs)	*Knowledge discovery*
Computer-aided design (CAD)	*Knowledge engineer*
Data	*Knowledge management*
Expert systems	*Knowledge network systems*
Explicit knowledge	*Knowledge repository*
Forward chaining	*Knowledge work systems (KWS)*
Fuzzy logic	*Learning management systems (LMS)*
Genetic algorithms	*Neural networks*
Hybrid AI systems	*Organizational learning*
Inference engine	*Semistructured knowledge*

Semistructured knowledge systems
Social bookmarking
Structured knowledge
Structured knowledge systems
Tacit knowledge

Taxonomy
Virtual Reality Modeling Language (VRML)
Virtual reality systems
Wisdom

Review Questions

1. What is knowledge management? How does it promote organizational learning? Why is it of great interest to business?

2. Describe the important dimensions of knowledge. Distinguish between data, knowledge, and wisdom and between explicit and tacit knowledge.

3. Describe the stages in the knowledge management value chain that add value as data and information are transformed into useful knowledge.

4. Describe the role played by organizational and management capital in knowledge management.

5. What are structured knowledge systems? Describe their capabilities.

6. What are semistructured knowledge systems? Describe their capabilities.

7. How do taxonomies and tools for tagging facilitate knowledge management?

8. Describe the capabilities of knowledge network systems.

9. Describe the role of the following in facilitating knowledge management: portals, wikis, social bookmarking, and learning management systems.

10. What are knowledge work systems? What role do they play in knowledge management? What are the generic requirements of knowledge work systems?

11. Describe how the following systems support knowledge work: CAD, virtual reality, and investment workstations.

12. What are intelligent techniques? Why are they of interest to businesses for knowledge management? How does artificial intelligence differ from human intelligence?

13. Define an expert system, describe how it works, and explain how it can contribute to knowledge management.

14. What is case-based reasoning? How does it differ from an expert system? How does it support knowledge management?

15. What is a neural network? How can neural networks help companies with knowledge management?

16. Define and describe fuzzy logic. For what kinds of applications is it suited?

17. What are genetic algorithms? How can they help organizations solve problems? For what kinds of problems are they suited?

18. What are intelligent agents? How can they be used to benefit businesses?

Discussion Questions

1. Knowledge management is a business process, not a technology. Discuss.

2. Describe various ways that knowledge management systems could help firms with sales and marketing or with manufacturing and production.

Teamwork: Rating Knowledge Network Systems

With a group of classmates, select two knowledge network system products, such as AskMe Enterprise and Tacit ActiveNet™. Compare their features and capabilities. To prepare your analysis, use articles from computer magazines and the Web sites for the knowledge network software vendors. If possible, use electronic presentation software to present your findings to the class.

Video Case

You will find a video case illustrating some of the concepts in this chapter on the Laudon Web site and Student CD-ROM along with questions to help you analyze the case.

REFERENCES

Alavi, Maryam, Timothy R. Kayworth, and Dorothy E. Leidner. "An Empirical Investigation of the Influence of Organizational Culture on Knowledge Management Practices." *Journal of Management Information Systems* 22, No.3 (Winter 2006).

Alavi, Maryam and Dorothy Leidner. "Knowledge Management and Knowledge Management Systems: Conceptual Foundations and Research Issues," *MIS Quarterly* 25, No. 1 (March 2001).

Anandarajan, Murugan. "Profiling Web Usage in the Workplace: A Behavior-Based Artificial Intelligence Approach." *Journal of Management Information Systems* 19, no. 1 (Summer 2002).

Awad, Elias and Hassan M Ghaziri. Knowledge Management. Upper Saddle River, NJ: Prentice-Hall (2004).

Bargeron, David, Jonathan Grudin, Anoop Gupta, Elizabeth Sanocki, Francis Li, and Scott Le Tiernan. "Asynchronous Collaboration Around Multimedia Applied to On-Demand Education." *Journal of Management Information Systems* 18, No. 4 (Spring 2002).

Barker, Virginia E., and Dennis E. O'Connor. "Expert Systems for Configuration at Digital: XCON and Beyond." *Communications of the ACM* (March 1989).

Becerra-Fernandez, Irma, Avelino Gonzalez, and Rajiv Sabherwal. Knowledge Management. Upper Saddle River, NJ: Prentice-Hall (2004).

Birkinshaw, Julian and Tony Sheehan. "Managing the Knowledge Life Cycle." *MIT Sloan Management Review* 44, no. 1 (Fall 2002).

Blair, Margaret M. and Steven Wallman. "Unseen Wealth." Brookings Institution Press, 2001.

Booth, Corey and Shashi Buluswar. "The Return of Artificial Intelligence," *The McKinsey Quarterly* No. 2 (2002).

Burtka, Michael. "Generic Algorithms." *The Stern Information Systems Review* 1, no. 1 (Spring 1993).

Cannataro, Mario and Domenico Talia. "The Knowledge Grid" *Communications of the ACM* 46, no.1 (January 2003).

Cavalieri, Sergio, Vittorio Cesarotti, and Vito Introna. "A Multiagent Model for Coordinated Distribution Chain Planning." *Journal of Organizational Computing and Electronic Commerce* 13, no. 3 & 4 (2003)

Cole, R.E. "Introduction, Knowledge Management Special Issue." *California Management Review* (Spring 1998.)

Cross, Rob and Lloyd Baird. "Technology is Not Enough: Improving Performance by Building Organizational Memory." *Sloan Management Review* 41, no. 3 (Spring 2000).

Cross, Rob, Nitin Nohria, and Andrew Parker. "Six Myths about Informal Networks-and How to Overcome Them," *Sloan Management Review* 43, no. 3 (Spring 2002)

Davenport, Thomas H., Robert J. Thomas and Susan Cantrell. "The Mysterious Art and Science of Knowledge-Worker Performance." *MIT Sloan Management Review* 44, no. 1 (Fall 2002).

Desouza, Kevin C. "Facilitating Tacit Knowledge Exchange." *Communications of the ACM* 46, no. 6 (June 2003).

Desouza, Kevin C. and J. Roberto Evaristo. "Managing Knowledge in Distributed Projects." *Communications of the ACM* 47, No. 4 (April 2004).

Dhar, Vasant, and Roger Stein. *Intelligent Decision Support Methods: The Science of Knowledge Work.* Upper Saddle River, NJ: Prentice Hall (1997).

Du, Timon C., Eldon Y. Li, and An-pin Chang. "Mobile Agents in Distributed Network Management." *Communications of the ACM* 46, no.7 (July 2003).

Earl, Michael. "Knowledge Management Strategies: Toward a Taxonomy." *Journal of Management Information Systems* 18, no. 1 (Summer 2001).

Easley, Robert F., Sarv Devaraj, and J. Michael Crant. "Relating Collaborative Technology Use to Teamwork Quality and Performance: An Empirical Analysis." *Journal of Management Information Systems* 19, no. 4 (Spring 2003)

eMarketer, "Portals and Content Management Solutions." (June 2003).June 2003; and author estimates.

Frangos, Alex." New Dimensions in Design." *The Wall Street Journal* (July 7, 2004).

Gelernter, David. "The Metamorphosis of Information Management." *Scientific American* (August 1989).

Goodnoe, Ezra. "How to Use Wikis for Business." *Information Week* (August 8, 2005).

Gregor, Shirley and Izak Benbasat. "Explanations from Intelligent Systems: Theoretical Foundations and Implications for Practice." *MIS Quarterly* 23, no. 4 (December 1999).

Grover, Varun and Thomas H. Davenport. "General Perspectives on Knowledge Management: Fostering a Research Agenda." *Journal of Management Information Systems* 18, no. 1 (Summer 2001).

Gu, Feng and Baruch Lev. "Intangible Assets. Measurements, Drivers, Usefulness." http://pages.stern.nyu.edu/ ~blev/.

Guerra, Anthony. "Goldman Sachs Embraces Rules-Based Solution." *Wall Street and Technology* (May 2001).

Hinton, Gregory. "How Neural Networks Learn from Experience." *Scientific American* (September 1992).

Holland, John H. "Genetic Algorithms." *Scientific American* (July 1992).

Hollis, Emily. "U.S. Navy: Smooth Sailing for Education." (2004). www.clomedia.com accessed November 1, 2006.

Housel Tom and Arthur A. Bell. *Measuring and Managing Knowledge.* New York: McGraw-Hill (2001).

Jarvenpaa, Sirkka L. and D. Sandy Staples. "Exploring Perceptions of Organizational Ownership of Information and Expertise."*Journal of Management Information Systems* 18, no. 1 (Summer 2001).

Jeong, Woo Seok, Sun Gwan Han, and Geun Sik Jo. "Intelligent Cyber Logistics Using Reverse Auction." *Journal of Organizational Computing and Electronic Commerce* 13, no. 3 & 4 (2003).

Jones, Quentin, Gilad Ravid, and Sheizaf Rafaeli. "Information Overload and the Message Dynamics of Online Interaction Spaces: A Theoretical Model and Empirical Exploration." Information Systems Research 15, no. 2 (June 2004).

Kankanhalli, Atreyi, Frasiska Tanudidjaja, Juliana Sutanto, and Bernard C.Y Tan. "The Role of IT in Successful Knowledge Management Initiatives." *Communications of the ACM* 46, no. 9 (September 2003).

King, William R., Peter V. Marks, Jr. and Scott McCoy. "The Most Important Issues in Knowledge Management." *Communications of the ACM* 45, no.9 (September 2002).

KPMG. "Insights from KPMG's European Knowledge Management Survey 2002/2003," KPMG, 2003a.

Kuo, R.J., K. Chang, and S.Y.Chien. "Integration and Self-Organizing Feature Maps and Genetic-Algorithm-Based Clustering Method for Market Segmentation." Journal of Organizational Computing and Electronic Commerce 14, no. 1 (2004).

Lamont, Judith. "Communities of Practice Leverage Knowledge." *KMWorld* (July/August 2006).

Lamont, Judith. "Compliance: The Hazards of E-Mail." *KMWorld* (October 2006).

Leonard, Dorothy and Walter Swap. 'Deep Smarts.' Harvard Business Review (September 1, 2004).

Lee, Kyoung Jun, Yong Sik Chang, Hyung Rim Choi, Hyun Soo Kim, Young Jae Park, and Byung Joo Park. "A Time-Bound Framework for Negotiation and Decision Making of Virtual Manufacturing Enterprise." *Journal of Organizational Computing and Electronic Commerce* 14, no. 1 (2004).

Lev, Baruch. "Sharpening the Intangibles Edge." *Harvard Business Review* (June 1, 2004).

Lev, Baruch, and Theodore Sougiannis. "Penetrating the Book-to-Market Black Box: The R&D Effect," *Journal of Business Finance and Accounting* (April/May 1999).

Maes, Patti. "Agents that Reduce Work and Information Overload." *Communications of the ACM* 38, no. 7 (July 1994).

Maglio, Paul P. and Christopher S. Campbell. "Attentive Agents." *Communications of the ACM* 46, no. 3 (March 2003).

Markus, M. Lynne, Ann Majchrzak, and Less Gasser." A Design Theory for Systems that Support Emergent Knowledge Processes." *MIS Quarterly* 26, no. 3 (September 2002).

Markus, M. Lynne. "Toward a Theory of Knowledge Reuse: Types of Knowledge Reuse Situations and Factors in Reuse Success." *Journal of Management Information Systems* 18, no. 1 (Summer 2001).

Maryam Alavi and Dorothy E. Leidner. "Knowledge Management and Knowledge Management Systems." *MIS Quarterly* 25, no. 1 (March 2001).

McCarthy, John. "Generality in Artificial Intelligence." *Communications of the ACM* (December 1987).

Moravec, Hans. "Robots, After All." Communications of the ACM 46, no. 10 (October 2003).

Munakata, Toshinori, and Yashvant Jani. "Fuzzy Systems: An Overview." *Communications of the ACM* 37, no. 3 (March 1994).

Orlikowski, Wanda J. "Knowing in Practice: Enacting a Collective Capability in Distributed Organizing." *Organization Science* 13, no. 3 (May–June 2002).

Pastore, Richard. "Cruise Control." *CIO Magazine* (February 1, 2003).

Perry, Andrew. "KM in Review: Tracing the Value of Knowledge Assets." *KM World* (October 2002).

Rumelhart, David E., Bernard Widrow, and Michael A. Lehr. "The Basic Ideas in Neural Networks." *Communications of the ACM* 37, no. 3 (March 1994).

Samuelson, Douglas A. and Charles M. Macal. "Agent-Based Simulation." OR/MS Today (August 2006).

Semio Corporation. "Case Study: Leveraging the World's Largest Repository of Life Science Research With Entrieva's Semio Technology," www.semio.com, accessed September 5, 2006.

Spangler, Scott, Jeffrey T. Kreulen, and Justin Lessler. "Generating and Browsing Multiple Taxonomies over a Document Collection." *Journal of Management Information Systems* 19, no. 4 (Spring 2003)

Starbuck, William H. "Learning by Knowledge-Intensive Firms." *Journal of Management Studies* 29, no. 6 (November 1992).

Tiwana, Amrit. "Affinity to Infinity in Peer-to-Peer Knowledge Platforms." *Communications of the ACM* 46, no. 5 (May 2003).

Totty, Michael. "Information Found-and-Shared." *The Wall Street Journal* (September 11, 2006).

Vara, Vauhini. "Offices Co-Opt Consumer Web Tools Like 'Wikis' and Social Networking." *The Wall Street Journal* (September 12, 2006).

Voekler, Michael. "Staying a Step Ahead of Fraud." *Intelligent Enterprise* (September 2006).

Wakefield, Julie. "Complexity's Business Model." *Scientific American* (January 2001).

Walczak, Steven. "Gaining Competitive Advantage for Trading in Emerging Capital Markets with Neural Networks. " *Journal of Management Information Systems* 16, no. 2 (Fall 1999).

Wang, Huaiqing, John Mylopoulos, and Stephen Liao. "Intelligent Agents and Financial Risk Monitoring Systems." *Communications of the ACM* 45, no. 3 (March 2002).

Zack, Michael H "Rethinking the Knowledge-Based Organization." *MIS Sloan Management Review* 44, no. 4 (Summer 2003).

Can Knowledge Systems Help Boeing Trounce Airbus?
CASE STUDY

With over 150,000 employees, the Boeing Company is a giant producer of passenger airplanes, business jets, military aircraft, helicopters, flight instruments, and satellites. Until recently it was the world's number one commercial jet aircraft producer. It is now in a head-to-head struggle with Airbus for this position.

Airbus is 80 percent owned by European Aeronautic Defence & Space Co. (EADS) and 20 percent by the United Kingdom's BAE Systems and receives subsidized loans from European governments. In 1996, Airbus decided to challenge Boeing for the jumbo jet market. Airbus management predicts air travel will expand rapidly, requiring many giant jumbo jets to carry the increased mass of passengers without hiking up operational costs. It envisions a hub-and-spoke model of air travel where jumbo jets transport passengers to a small number of hub cities, from which passengers transfer to smaller connecting flights to their ultimate destinations.

Boeing management has a very different vision. It believes that most travelers prefer to fly from their own city nonstop to their destination, for example, Detroit to Shanghai rather than Detroit to Tokyo-to-Shanghai. Such flights do not need jumbo jets. It foresees a turn to smaller airliners that will fly quickly and inexpensively, enabling passengers to fly nonstop from departure to destination, bypassing the overcrowded hubs. All in all, Boeing foresees a strong expansion of smaller jet sales rather than of jumbo jet sales. Both companies' business and product development strategies are based on these differing visions.

In addition to Airbus competition, Boeing faced difficult conditions because the market for commercial airplanes has been shrinking due to airline mergers and the downturn in air travel after the September 11, 2001, terrorist attacks. The company moved its global headquarters from Seattle to Chicago to focus on newer businesses based on information and communications technologies.

Boeing's management has been trying to lower costs by using technology to reform inefficient business processes. Boeing's airplane production process used to be highly paper-intensive, with a final design of the Boeing 747 consisting of approximately 75,000 paper engineering drawings. Boeing designers long ago realized they would save much production time if they reused existing designs rather than designing each aircraft from scratch. However, the process of design customization was manual and took more than 1,000 engineers a year of full-time work to complete. For every customization choice on every airplane built, hundreds of pages of detailed drawings needed to be drawn manually.

To reuse old paper aircraft configurations and parts designs, the engineers first needed to search through an immense number of paper drawings to find appropriate designs to reuse for the specific configuration. They then laboriously copied the old designs to use for the new plane. Inevitably, errors crept into the new designs—large numbers of errors, given the large numbers of design sheets—because of unavoidable copying mistakes.

It used to take 800 computers to manage the coordination of engineering and manufacturing and many of these did not communicate directly with each other. The list of parts produced by engineering for a given airplane was configured differently from the lists used by manufacturing and customer service. Ultimately, the parts list had to be broken down, converted, and recomputed up to 13 times during the production of a single plane.

Another problem with manual design was that the staff needed to create life-size mock-ups in plywood and plastic to ensure that everything fit and that the pipes and wires that run through the plane are placed properly and do not interfere with other necessary equipment. They were also needed to verify the accuracy of part specifications. Building mock-ups was a slow, expensive, laborious process. At production time, errors would again occur when part numbers of specifications were manually copied and at times miscopied onto order sheets, resulting in many wrong or mis-sized parts arriving.

Engineers worked in separate fiefdoms based on their field of specialization. Some engineers designed the plane's parts, others assembled them, and others designed the parts' packing crates. They rarely compared notes. If production engineers discovered a part that didn't fit, they sent a complaint back to

From *Management Information Systems: Managing the Digital Firm, 10/e.* Kenneth C. Laudon, Jane P. Laudon. Copyright © 2007 by Pearson Prentice Hall. All rights reserved.

the designers located in another plant. The designers then pulled out their drawings, reconfigured the part to make it match drawings of the surrounding parts, and sent the new design back to the plant. Warehouses were filled with paper.

In the early 1990s, Boeing began switching to a "paperless design" model which it used to computerize the design and production of its 777 aircraft. The 777 aircraft carries 300 to 440 passengers and lowers operating, maintenance, and fuel costs because it uses lighter materials and can fly with only two pilots and two engines. The "paperless design" system employs Dassault Systems' CATIA computer-aided design software, nine IBM mainframes, a Cray supercomputer, and 2,200 workstations, storing 3500 billion bits of information. It enabled engineers to call up any of the 777's millions of parts, modify them, fit them into the surrounding structure, and put them back into the plane's "electronic box" so that other engineers can make their own adjustments.

Boeing assembled a single parts list that can be used by every division without modification. In addition, management established design-production teams that brought together designers and fabricators from a range of specialties throughout the whole process. Ultimately, the airplane was designed entirely on the computer screen and was initially assembled without expensive mock-ups. The company cut overall engineering design errors by 50 percent while designing and building a 777 in 10 months.

Although Boeing's 777 was a marketplace hit, Airbus continued to take market share from Boeing. The 9/11 terrorist attacks depressed demand for air travel, and Boeing's profits dropped 80 percent between 2001 and 2002. In 2002, Boeing's military division surpassed its commercial aviation division in revenue, despite Boeing's historic devotion to aircraft development. In 2003, for the first time in history, Airbus delivered more planes than Boeing. Boeing's market share had plunged from nearly 70 percent in 1996 to roughly 50 percent and the company had to cut 60,000 employees.

Since then, Boeing has been on the rebound. Airbus stumbled in its launch of its giant A380 jumbo jet, which has two decks and is capable of flying 550 passengers. The A380 completed a successful maiden flight in April 2005, but Airbus announced that deliveries would be six months late due to complexity wiring the aircraft for sophisticated custom equipment such as in-flight entertainment

and communications units requested by some airlines. Since the A380's electronic systems are highly integrated, a small change in one area ripples throughout the design. In July 2006, Airbus announced another six-month delay in A380 deliveries, again because of wiring problems. Inability to easily solve these problems caused Airbus to announce further delays the following September. At that time, EADS said it was too early to say how long the latest delivery delay would last or how much it would cost.

Boeing, in the meantime, innovated again with its 787 "Dreamliner." The 787 is designed to carry 200 to 300 people on routes from North America to Europe and Asia. Boeing designed this plane to fly long distances economically while keeping passengers comfortable and economizing on fuel. About half of each plane will be made from carbon-fiber composite materials, which are lighter than aluminum and can be built in larger sections. The 787 offers more cabin pressure, humidity, headroom, and window space than comparable commercial planes. Its engines use about 20 percent less fuel per mile than similarly-sized twin-engine planes. One version of the 787 is capable of flying 8,300 nautical miles, long enough to fly nonstop from New York to Hong Kong. Boeing only took 4.5 years to bring the 787 to market, 16 to 18 months faster than most other models, and the 787 will enter service in 2008.

Boeing's 787 made all Airbus models on the market look outdated. To compete with the 787, Airbus, in the summer of 2004, offered the A350, a midsize plane for carrying 250 to 375 passengers that is basically a retooled version of its older A330 model. So far it has had little success, with a number of airlines stating that the A350's operating economies and comfort did not match those of the 787.

For Boeing, the 787 is a daring experiment because it is using a new production process. Instead of being produced under one roof, the 787 is being built in a modular assembly process. Boeing farmed out design and construction of about 80 percent of the aircraft to hundreds of other companies, many outside the United States. Mitsubishi is in charge of the wings, while Messier-Dowty of France is making the landing gear. Foreign suppliers have freedom to design the components, reducing Boeing's product development costs.

Boeing and its key suppliers are using software that lets designers around the world electronically collaborate in designing components and manufacturing processes. Dassault Systems added features to its planning and design software to cope with Boeing's global supply chain. Boeing expanded its use of Dassault's version 5 Product Life Cycle Management software from 1,000 to 6,000 licenses. This software suite includes CATIA design software, Enovia, a tool for managing design data, and Delmia, which simulates assembly and manufacturing processes. These software tools enable designers to use a single set of data and to simulate digitally the plane's life cycle from design through production, quickly modeling iterations in design to reduce errors and redundant work. CATIA V5 software makes it possible for Boeing's suppliers and subcontractors to have a bigger role in designing and developing the new jet. Boeing wants this technology to cut both recurring and non-recurring design and manufacturing costs in half compared with the 777.

Outsourcing the 787 required Dassault to improve integration of its CATIA, Enovia, and Delmia modules for Boeing. So Dassault created in Enovia a 3-D master file to serve as a single source for digital definitions across the software suite. Boeing also needed custom tools to handle designs with the carbon-fiber composite material.

As crucial deadlines loomed, Boeing engineers wrestled with several significant technical and production problems that could threaten delivery of the 787 in 2008. The fuselage section failed in company testing, forcing Boeing to make more sections than planned and to re-examine quality and safety. The overall weight of the plane was too high, especially the carbon-fiber wing. Suppliers struggled to meet Boeing's technical standards and ambitious production deadlines. Boeing would not accept the first two nose sections. Software programs designed by a variety of vendors had trouble "talking" to one another.

Airbus has also run into additional snags. In July 2006, Airbus announced further design changes to the A350 to widen its cabin and windows and provide adjustable cabin humidity. But it won't enter service until 2012, four years after the 787. Airbus's problems with its A380 jumbo jet made it more difficult to make the design changes to the A350 required to match Boeing. Airbus also announced a long-term overhaul of its operations. To further cut costs, boost efficiency, and improve planning, Airbus needs to

involve its suppliers more in the design process as Boeing has done. While Boeing started making the switch 10 years ago, Airbus was focused on merging its operations into a single company from its original structure as a diffuse consortium. According to Airbus Chairman Christian Streiff, "It will take about 10 years for us to get back to the level of Boeing in terms of development and efficiency."

The 787 has been central to Boeing's revival, racking up 350 orders in two years. It forced Airbus onto the defensive and to rethink its big plane strategy. Boeing calls the 787 its "game changer." Any major problems with the 787 would not only jeopardize sales, but Boeing's credibility and leading position in the passenger aircraft market.

Sources: Leslie Wayne, "Boeing Bets the House on Its 787 Dreamliner," *The New York Times*, May 7, 2006; Daniel Michaels and J. Lynn Lunsford, "Under Pressure, Airbus Redesigns a Troubled Plane," *The Wall Street Journal*, July 14, 2006; Simon Clow and Maeve Curtain, "EADS Sees Years of Work Ahead to Repair Airbus," *The Wall Street Journal*, October 5, 2006; Mark Landler, "Airbus Offers Up Redesigned A350 in a Challenge to Boeing," *The New York Times*, July 18, 2006; Stanley Holmes, "On a Wing and a Prayer at Boeing," *Business Week*, June 7, 2006; Daniel Michaels, "Airbus Opens Overhaul by Looking at Procurement," *The Wall Street Journal*, September 25, 2006; J. Lynn Lunsford and Daniel Michaels, "Bet on Huge Plane Trips Up Airbus," *The Wall Street Journal*, June 15, 2006 and "After Four Years in the Rear, Boeing is Set to Jet Past Airbus," *The Wall Street Journal*, June 10, 2005; Beth Bacheldor, "Boeing's Flight Plan," *Information Week*, February 16, 2004; and Edward Wong, "For Jet Rivals, Caution Here, Swagger There," *The New York Times*, July 28, 2002.

CASE STUDY QUESTIONS

1. Analyze Boeing and its business strategy using the value chain and competitive forces models.

2. What is the relationship of knowledge management to Boeing's business strategy? How is Boeing using knowledge management systems to execute its business model and business strategy?

3. Evaluate Boeing's new business strategy. What management, organization, and technology issues will Boeing face as it attempts to implement the strategy? What role will knowledge management play in this strategy? How successful will Boeing be in pursuing that strategy?

4. Using the facts presented in this case, what role has knowledge management played in Airbus's business strategy and business performance?

Enhancing Decision Making

Enhancing Decision Making

PROCTER & GAMBLE RESTRUCTURES ITS SUPPLY CHAIN

Procter & Gamble (P&G) is one of the world's largest consumer goods companies, with annual revenues of $51 billion and 80,000 employees in 140 countries. The company sells more than 300 brands worldwide, including Crest, Charmin, Tide, Pringles, and Pampers. Although P&G is known for innovation and marketing muscle, it is always looking for ways to lower its costs, in response both to competitors and to pressure from large customers, such as Wal-Mart.

In the early 1990s, P&G started looking at ways to reduce supply chain costs and improve efficiency throughout its entire North American manufacturing and distribution network. Management wanted answers to questions such as, "How many plants should there be for a new product?" "Where should they be located?" "Where should distribution centers be located?" and "How can we deliver these products faster and better to our major customers?"

Answers were not easy to obtain because P&G's supply chains are incredibly complex, with more than 100,000 suppliers. P&G's Global Beauty Care division alone has hundreds of combinations of suppliers, manufacturing facilities, and markets to deal with, compounded by 10 to 15 new product launches per year. Each of the company's dozens of beauty care products has multiple sizes and package designs. A tiny change—and changes are constant—ripples through the supply chain, impacting inventory levels, service levels, and costs.

Jean Kinney, a P&G purchasing manager, recalls the launch of a new global healthcare product whose success depended on the choice of plant locations and sources of raw materials. The problem was very complicated and there were millions of possible solutions. If you asked the managers in the countries that would be marketing this product, they would all say the plants should be located in their countries. Corporate experts, however, would say that scale is important and P&G should build a single megaplant instead of distributing production. In between were millions of other options. What was the best approach?

P&G turned to its IT Global Analytics group for a solution. IT Global Analytics constructed some models using Microsoft Excel spreadsheet software enhanced by LINDO System's What'sBest! for more powerful optimization and Palisade's @RISK software for Monte Carlo simulation, which randomly generates values for uncertain variables. The models tried to maximize the value of the investment, considering manufacturing costs, freight costs, import/export duties, local wage rates, foreign exchange rates, taxes, and the cost of capital.

This model was one of a series of models developed by

Photo courtesy of AP Wide World Photos

IT Global Analytics for restructuring P&G's supply chain. P&G used optimization models to determine how best to allocate supply chain resources and simulation models to mathematically try out various options to see how they reacted to changes in important variables. In addition, the company used techniques, such as decision trees, that combined the possibilities of various outcomes with their financial results. Using these decision-support tools, IT Global Analytics found that the success of a supply chain is not necessarily based on the most optimal solution but rather a robust solution that would stand up under real-world conditions.

P&G uses a number of different software tools for implementing its models. In addition to Excel and add-on products, P&G also uses stand-alone software packages. These packages include Xpress-MP from Dash Optimization Inc. and Cplex from Ilog Inc. for building optimization models, and Extend from Imagine That Inc. for building simulation models. Most of the data for these decision-support systems come from a massive Oracle data warehouse with 36 months of data on supplier, manufacturing, customer, and consumer histories by region.

P&G's use of decision-support systems for restructuring its supply chain has paid off. The company consolidated North American plants by 20 percent and lowered supply chain costs by $200 million each year.

Sources: Gary H. Anthes, "Modeling Magic," *Computerworld*, February 7, 2005; "Procter & Gamble Uses @ RISK and PrecisionTree World-Wide," www.palisade.com, accessed August 6, 2005; and www.pg.com, accessed October 10, 2006.

Procter & Gamble's use of information systems to restructure its supply chain illustrates how information systems improve decision making. By improving decisions about how to restructure P&G's supply chain, information systems helped the company operate more efficiently, reduce its costs, and increase responsiveness to customers and to the marketplace.

The chapter-opening diagram calls attention to important points raised by this case and this chapter. P&G management was unable to make good decisions about where to locate plants and distribution centers for new products because P&G's supply chain was extremely large, complex, and affected by many different variables. Bad decisions about where to locate plants and distribution centers increased costs to procure, manufacture, warehouse, and ship P&G products because plants and distribution centers did not operate efficiently. P&G solved this problem by implementing new, model-based, decision-support systems capable of evaluating large quantities of data and thousands of variables. These systems helped decision makers find an optimal design for P&G's supply chain and improve the allocation of supply chain resources.

HEADS UP

This chapter focuses on how business firms use information systems to improve decision making. A wide variety of information systems directly improves decision making throughout the firm, from the executive suite to the customer service center and the factory floor. There are even systems to help customers make better decisions. It would not be an overstatement to say that a primary contribution of information systems to business firms has been to improve decision making at all levels.

- If your career is in finance and accounting, you will be working with decision-support systems that use financial models for break-even analysis, profitability analysis, capital budgeting, and financial forecasting, and executive support systems (ESS) providing overviews of firmwide financial performance.

- If your career is in human resources, you will use decision-support systems for analyzing the impact of employee compensation plans and for projecting the firm's long-term labor force requirements.

- If your career is in information systems, you will be developing databases, models, and reporting capabilities for systems to support decision making.

- If your career is in manufacturing, production, or operations management, you will be using decision-support systems to guide decisions about the optimization of sourcing, production, logistics, and maintenance that must evaluate many interrelated variables.

- If your career is in sales and marketing, you will be working with decision-support systems to guide decisions about product pricing, sales forecasting, advertising and promotional campaigns, and location of retail outlets.

---

1   DECISION MAKING AND INFORMATION SYSTEMS

Decision making in businesses used to be limited to management. Today, lower-level employees are responsible for some of these decisions, as information systems make information available to lower levels of the business. But what do we mean by better decision making? How does decision making take place in businesses and other organizations? Let's take a closer look.

BUSINESS VALUE OF IMPROVED DECISION MAKING

What is the monetary value to the business of better decision making? Table 1 attempts to measure the monetary value of improved decision making for a small U.S. manufacturing firm with $280 million in annual revenue and 140 employees. The firm has identified a number of key decisions where new system investments might improve the quality of decision making. The table provides selected estimates of annual value (in the form of cost savings or increased revenue) from improved decision making in selected areas of the business.

We can see from Table 1 that decisions are made at all levels of the firm and that some of these decisions are common, routine, and numerous. Although the value of improving any single decision may be small, improving hundreds of thousands of "small" decisions adds up to a large annual value for the business.

TYPES OF DECISIONS

There are different levels in an organization. Each of these levels has different information requirements for decision support and responsibility for different types of decisions (see Figure 1). Decisions are classified as structured, semi-structured, and unstructured.

Unstructured decisions are those in which the decision maker must provide judgment, evaluation, and insight to solve the problem. Each of these decisions is novel, important, and nonroutine, and there is no well-understood or agreed-on procedure for making them.

Structured decisions, by contrast, are repetitive and routine, and they involve a definite procedure for handling them so that they do not have to be treated each time as if they were new. Many decisions have elements of both types of decisions and are **semistructured**, where only part of the problem has a clear-cut answer provided by an accepted procedure. In general, structured decisions are more prevalent at lower organizational levels, whereas unstructured problems are more common at higher levels of the firm.

Senior executives face many unstructured decision situations, such as establishing the firm's five- or ten-year goals or deciding new markets to enter.

TABLE 1 BUSINESS VALUE OF ENHANCED DECISION MAKING

EXAMPLE DECISION	DECISION MAKER	NUMBER OF ANNUAL DECISIONS	ESTIMATED VALUE TO FIRM OF A SINGLE IMPROVED DECISION	ANNUAL VAUE
Allocate support to most valuable customers	Accounts manager	12	$ 100,000	$1,200,000
Predict call center daily demand	Call Center management	4	150,000	600,000
Decide parts inventory levels daily	Inventory manager	365	5,000	1,825,000
Identify competitive bids from major suppliers	Senior management	1	2,000,000	2,000,000
Schedule production to fill orders	Manufacturing manager	150	10,000	1,500,000
Allocate labor to complete a job	Production floor manager	100	4,000	400,000

498

FIGURE 1   **INFORMATION REQUIREMENTS OF KEY DECISION-MAKING GROUPS IN A FIRM**

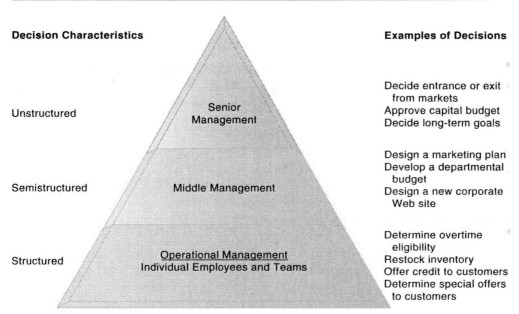

Senior managers, middle managers, operational managers, and employees have different types of decisions and information requirements.

Answering the question "Should we enter a new market?" would require access to news, government reports, and industry views as well as high-level summaries of firm performance. However, the answer would also require senior managers to use their own best judgment and poll other managers for their opinions.

Middle management faces more structured decision scenarios but their decisions may include unstructured components. A typical middle-level management decision might be "Why is the reported order fulfillment report showing a decline over the past six months at a distribution center in Minneapolis?" This middle manager could obtain a report from the firm's enterprise system or distribution management system on order activity and operational efficiency at the Minneapolis distribution center. This is the structured part of the decision. But before arriving at an answer, this middle manager will have to interview employees and gather more unstructured information from external sources about local economic conditions or sales trends.

Operational management and rank-and-file employees tend to make more structured decisions. For example, a supervisor on an assembly line has to decide whether an hourly paid worker is entitled to overtime pay. If the employee worked more than eight hours on a particular day, the supervisor would routinely grant overtime pay for any time beyond eight hours that was clocked on that day.

A sales account representative often has to make decisions about extending credit to customers by consulting the firm's customer database that contains credit information. If the customer met the firm's prespecified criteria for granting credit, the account representative would grant that customer credit to make a purchase. In both instances, the decisions are highly structured and are

499

routinely made thousands of times each day in most large firms. The answer has been preprogrammed into the firm's payroll and accounts receivable systems.

THE DECISION-MAKING PROCESS

Making a decision is a multistep process. Simon (1960) described four different stages in decision making: intelligence, design, choice, and implementation (see Figure 2). These stages correspond to the four steps in problem-solving used throughout this text.

Intelligence consists of discovering, identifying, and understanding the problems occurring in the organization—why there is a problem, where, and what effects it is having on the firm.

Design involves identifying and exploring various solutions to the problem.

Choice consists of choosing among solution alternatives.

Implementation involves making the chosen alternative work and continuing to monitor how well the solution is working.

What happens if the solution you have chosen doesn't work? Figure 2 shows that you can return to an earlier stage in the decision-making process and

FIGURE 2   STAGES IN DECISION MAKING

Problem discovery:
What is the problem?   Intelligence

Solution discovery:
What are the possible solutions?   Design

Choosing solutions:
What is the best solution?   Choice

Solution testing:
Is the solution working?
Can we make it work better?   Implementation

The decision-making process can be broken down into four stages.

repeat it if necessary. For instance, in the face of declining sales, a sales management team may decide to pay the sales force a higher commission for making more sales to spur on the sales effort. If this does not produce sales increases, managers would need to investigate whether the problem stems from poor product design, inadequate customer support, or a host of other causes that call for a different solution.

MANAGERS AND DECISION MAKING IN THE REAL WORLD

The premise of this chapter is that systems to support decision making produce better decision making by managers and employees, above average returns on investment for the firm, and ultimately higher profitability. However, information systems cannot improve all the different kinds of decisions taking place in an organization. Let's examine the role of managers and decision making in organizations to see why this is so.

Managerial Roles

Managers play key roles in organizations. Their responsibilities range from making decisions, to writing reports, to attending meetings, to arranging birthday parties. We can better understand managerial functions and roles by examining classical and contemporary models of managerial behavior.

The **classical model of management**, which describes what managers do, was largely unquestioned from its inception in the 1920s until recent years. Henri Fayol and other early writers first described the five classical functions of managers as planning, organizing, coordinating, deciding, and controlling. This description of management activities dominated management thought for a long time, and it is still popular today.

The classical model describes formal managerial functions but does not address what exactly managers do when they plan, decide things, and control the work of others. For this, we must turn to the work of contemporary behavioral scientists who have studied managers in daily action. **Behavioral models** state that the actual behavior of managers appears to be less systematic, more informal, less reflective, more reactive, and less well organized than the classical model would have us believe.

Observers find that managerial behavior actually has five attributes that differ greatly from the classical description: First, managers perform a great deal of work at an unrelenting pace—studies have found that managers engage in more than 600 different activities each day, with no break in their pace. Second, managerial activities are fragmented; most activities last for less than nine minutes, and only 10 percent of the activities exceed one hour in duration. Third, managers prefer current, specific, and ad hoc information (printed information often will be too old). Fourth, they prefer oral forms of communication to written forms because oral media provide greater flexibility, require less effort, and bring a faster response. Fifth, managers give high priority to maintaining a diverse and complex web of contacts that acts as an informal information system and helps them execute their personal agendas and short- and long-term goals.

Analyzing managers' day-to-day behavior, Mintzberg found that it could be classified into 10 managerial roles. **Managerial roles** are expectations of the activities that managers should perform in an organization. Mintzberg found that these managerial roles fell into three categories: interpersonal, informational, and decisional.

Interpersonal Roles. Managers act as figureheads for the organization when they represent their companies to the outside world and perform symbolic duties, such as giving out employee awards, in their **interpersonal role**. Managers act as leaders, attempting to motivate, counsel, and support subordinates. Managers also act as liaisons between various organizational levels; within each of these levels, they serve as liaisons among the members of the management team. Managers provide time and favors, which they expect to be returned.

Informational Roles. In their **informational role**, managers act as the nerve centers of their organizations, receiving the most concrete, up-to-date information and redistributing it to those who need to be aware of it. Managers are therefore information disseminators and spokespersons for their organizations.

Decisional Roles. Managers make decisions. In their **decisional role**, they act as entrepreneurs by initiating new kinds of activities; they handle disturbances arising in the organization; they allocate resources to staff members who need them; and they negotiate conflicts and mediate between conflicting groups.

Table 2, based on Mintzberg's role classifications, is one look at where systems can and cannot help managers. The table shows that information systems do not yet contribute to some important areas of management life.

Real-World Decision Making

We now can see that information systems are not helpful for all managerial roles. And in those managerial roles where information systems can improve decisions, investments in information technology do not always produce positive results. There are three main reasons: information quality, management filters, and organizational culture.

Information Quality. High-quality decisions require high-quality information. Table 3 describes information quality dimensions that can affect the quality of decisions.

TABLE 2 MANAGERIAL ROLES AND SUPPORTING INFORMATION SYSTEMS

ROLE	BEHAVIOR	SUPPORT SYSTEMS
Interpersonal Roles		
Figurehead		None exist
Leader	Interpersonal	None exist
Liaison		Electronic communication systems
Informational Roles		
Nerve center		Management information systems, ESS
Disseminator	Information	Mail, office systems
Spokesperson	processing	Office and professional systems, workstations
Decisional Roles		
Entrepreneur	Decision	None exist
Disturbance handler	making	None exist
Resource allocator		DSS systems
Negotiator		None exist

Sources: Kenneth C. Laudon and Jane P. Laudon; and Mintzberg, 1971.

TABLE 3 INFORMATION QUALITY DIMENSIONS

QUALITY DIMENSION	DESCRIPTION
Accuracy	Do the data represent reality?
Integrity	Are the structure of data and relationships among the entities and attributes consistent?
Consistency	Are data elements consistently defined?
Completeness	Are all the necessary data present?
Validity	Do data values fall within defined ranges?
Timeliness	Area data available when needed?
Accessibility	Are the data accessible, comprehensible, and usable?

If the output of information systems does not meet these quality criteria, decision-making will suffer. Corporate databases and files have varying levels of inaccuracy and incompleteness, which in turn can degrade the quality of decision making.

Management Filters. Even with timely, accurate information, some managers make bad decisions. Managers (like all human beings) absorb information through a series of filters to make sense of the world around them. Managers have selective attention, focus on certain kinds of problems and solutions, and have a variety of biases that reject information that does not conform to their prior conceptions.

For instance, Cisco Systems Corporation, one of the most advanced users of online decision-support systems, nevertheless was forced to write off as a loss $3.4 billion in excess inventory in 2001 because management had not interpreted the information from systems correctly. The company's online sales order entry system throughout 1999 and 2000 showed exceptionally strong orders. However, customers, perceiving a shortage of routers and other networking equipment, were placing orders with multiple manufacturers, awarding the business to the first one who could deliver, and canceling other orders. Cisco's systems were also recording high levels of order cancellation, but management ignored this "bad news" and emphasized the "good news": new orders were piling up (Laudon and Laudon, 2003).

Organizational Inertia and Politics. Organizations are bureaucracies with limited capabilities and competencies for acting decisively. When environments change and businesses need to adopt new business models to survive, strong forces within organizations resist making decisions calling for major change. Decisions taken by a firm often represent a balancing of the firm's various interest groups rather than the best solution to the problem.

Studies of business restructuring find that firms tend to ignore poor performance until threatened by outside takeovers, and they systematically blame poor performance on external forces beyond their control such as economic conditions (the economy), foreign competition, and rising prices, rather than blaming senior or middle management for poor business judgment (John, Lang, Netter, et al., 1992).

2   SYSTEMS FOR DECISION SUPPORT

There are four kinds of systems for supporting the different levels and types of decisions we have just described. *Management information systems (MIS)* provide routine reports and summaries of transaction-level data to middle and operational level managers to provide answers to structured and semistructured decision problems. *Decision-support systems (DSS)* provide analytical models or tools for analyzing large quantities of data for middle managers who face semistructured decision situations. *Executive support systems (ESS)* are systems that provide senior management, making primarily unstructured decisions, with external information (news, stock analyses, and industry trends) and high-level summaries of firm performance.

In this chapter, you will also learn about systems for supporting decision-makers working as a group. **Group decision-support systems (GDSS)** are specialized systems that provide a group electronic environment in which managers and teams can collectively make decisions and design solutions for unstructured and semistructured problems.

MANAGEMENT INFORMATION SYSTEMS (MIS)

Management information systems (MIS) help managers monitor and control the business by providing information on the firm's performance. They typically produce fixed, regularly scheduled reports based on data extracted and summarized from the firm's underlying transaction processing systems (TPS). Sometimes, MIS reports are exception reports, highlighting only exceptional conditions, such as when the sales quotas for a specific territory fall below an anticipated level or employees have exceeded their spending limits in a dental care plan. Today, many of these reports are available online through an intranet, and more MIS reports can be generated on demand. Table 4 provides some examples of MIS applications.

DECISION-SUPPORT SYSTEMS (DSS)

Whereas MIS primarily address structured problems, DSS support semistructured and unstructured problem analysis. The earliest DSS were heavily

TABLE 4   EXAMPLES OF MIS APPLICATIONS

COMPANY	MIS APPLICATION
California Pizza Kitchen	Inventory Express application "remembers" each restaurant's ordering patterns and compares the amount of ingredients used per menu item to predefined portion measurements established by management. The system identifies restaurants with out-of-line portions and notifies their managers so that corrective actions can be taken.
PharMark	Extranet MIS identifies patients with drug-use patterns that place them at risk for adverse outcomes.
Black & Veatch	Intranet MIS tracks construction costs for various projects across the United States.
Taco Bell	Total Automation of Company Operations (TACO) system provides information on food, labor, and period-to-date costs for each restaurant.

model-driven, using some type of model to perform "what-if" and other kinds of analyses. Their analysis capabilities were based on a strong theory or model combined with a good user interface that made the system easy to use. P&G's system for supply chain restructuring in the chapter-opening case is an example of model-driven DSS.

Some contemporary DSS are data-driven, using online analytical processing (OLAP), and data mining to analyze large pools of data. The spreadsheet pivot table applications we describe in this section are examples of these data-driven DSS. Data-driven DSS support decision making by enabling users to extract useful information that was previously buried in large quantities of data.

Components of DSS

Figure 3 illustrates the components of a DSS. They include a database of data used for query and analysis; a software system with models, data mining, and other analytical tools; and a user interface.

The **DSS database** is a collection of current or historical data from a number of applications or groups. It may be a small database residing on a PC that contains a subset of corporate data that has been downloaded and possibly combined with external data. Alternatively, the DSS database may be a massive data warehouse that is continuously updated by major corporate TPS (including enterprise applications) and data generated by Web site transactions). The data in DSS databases are generally extracts or copies of production databases so that using the DSS does not interfere with critical operational systems.

FIGURE 3   OVERVIEW OF A DECISION-SUPPORT SYSTEM

The main components of the DSS are the DSS database, the user interface, and the DSS software system. The DSS database may be a small database residing on a PC or a large data warehouse.

The DSS user interface permits easy interaction between users of the system and the DSS software tools. Many DSS today have Web interfaces to take advantage of graphic displays, interactivity, and ease of use.

The **DSS software system** contains the software tools that are used for data analysis. It may contain various OLAP tools, data mining tools, or a collection of mathematical and analytical models that easily can be made accessible to the DSS user. A **model** is an abstract representation that illustrates the components or relationships of a phenomenon. A model can be a physical model (such as a model plane), a mathematical model (such as an equation), or a verbal model (such as a description of a procedure for writing an order).

Statistical modeling helps establish relationships, such as relating product sales to differences in age, income, or other factors between communities. Optimization models determine optimal resource allocation to maximize or minimize specified variables, such as cost or time. A classic use of optimization models is to determine the proper mix of products within a given market to maximize profits. The chapter-opening case illustrates P&G's use of optimization models to determine how to maximize its return on investment in its supply chain.

Forecasting models often are used to forecast sales. The user of this type of model might supply a range of historical data to project future conditions and the sales that might result from those conditions. The decision maker could vary those future conditions (entering, for example, a rise in raw materials costs or the entry of a new, low-priced competitor in the market) to determine how new conditions might affect sales.

Sensitivity analysis models ask "what-if" questions repeatedly to determine the impact on outcomes of changes in one or more factors. *What-if analysis*—working forward from known or assumed conditions—allows the user to vary certain values to test results to better predict outcomes if changes occur in those values. What happens if we raise product price by 5 percent or increase the advertising budget by $100,000? What happens if we keep the price and advertising budgets the same? Desktop spreadsheet software, such as Microsoft Excel, is often used for this purpose (see Figure 4). Backward-sensitivity analysis software helps decision makers with goal seeking: If I want to sell 1 million product units next year, how much must I reduce the price of the product?

Using Spreadsheet Pivot Tables to Support Decision Making

Spreadsheet software is also useful for helping managers detect and understand patterns in data. For instance, let's a take a look at one day's worth of transactions at an online firm, Online Management Training Inc. (OMT Inc.), that sells online management training books and streaming online videos to corporations and individuals who want to improve their management techniques. On this day, the firm experienced 517 order transactions. Figure 5 shows the first 15 transaction records produced at the firm's Web site that day. The names of customers and other identifiers have been removed from this list.

You can think of this list as a database composed of transaction records (the rows). The fields for each customer record are: customer ID, region of purchase, payment method, source of contact (e-mail versus Web banner ad), amount of purchase, the product purchased (either online training or a book), and time of day (in 24-hour time).

FIGURE 4   SENSITIVITY ANALYSIS

Total fixed costs	19000						
Variable cost per unit	3						
Average sales price	17						
Contribution margin	14						
Break-even point	1357						

			Variable Cost per Unit				
Sales	1357	2	3	4	5	6	
Price	14	1583	1727	1900	2111	2375	
	15	1462	1583	1727	1900	2111	
	16	1357	1462	1583	1727	1900	
	17	1267	1357	1462	1583	1727	
	18	1188	1267	1357	1462	1583	

This table displays the results of a sensitivity analysis of the effect of changing the sales price of a necktie and the cost per unit on the product's break-even point. It answers the question, "What happens to the break-even point if the sales price and the cost to make each unit increase or decrease?"

There's a great deal of valuable information in this transaction list that could help managers answer important questions and make important decisions:

- Where do most of our customers come from? The answer might tell managers where to spend more marketing resources, or to initiate new marketing efforts.
- Where are the average purchases higher? The answer might tell managers where to focus marketing and sales resources, or pitch different messages to different regions.

FIGURE 5   SAMPLE LIST OF TRANSACTIONS FOR ONLINE MANAGEMENT TRAINING INC.

Cust ID	Region	Payment	Source	Amount	Product	Time Of Day
10001	East	Paypal	Web	$20.19	Online	22:19
10002	West	Credit	Web	$17.85	Online	13:27
10003	North	Credit	Web	$23.98	Online	14:27
10004	West	Paypal	Email	$23.51	Book	15:38
10005	South	Credit	Web	$15.33	Book	15:21
10006	West	Paypal	Email	$17.30	Online	13:11
10007	East	Credit	Web	$177.72	Book	21:59
10008	West	Credit	Web	$21.76	Book	4:04
10009	West	Paypal	Web	$15.92	Online	19:35
10010	South	Paypal	Web	$23.39	Online	13:26
10011	South	Paypal	Email	$24.45	Book	14:17
10012	East	Credit	Web	$20.39	Book	1:01
10013	North	Paypal	Web	$19.54	Online	10:04
10014	East	Credit	Web	$151.67	Book	9:09
10015	West	Credit	Web	$21.01	Online	5:05

This list shows a portion of the order transactions for Online Management Training Inc. (OMT Inc.) on October 28, 2006.

- What form of payment is the most common? The answer could be used to emphasize in advertising the most preferred means of payment.

- Are there any times of day when purchases are most common? Do people buy products while at work (likely during the day) or at home (likely in the evening)?

- Are there regional differences in the average purchase? If one region is much more lucrative, managers could focus their marketing and advertising resources on that region.

- Are there regional differences in the sources of our customers? Perhaps in some regions, e-mail is the most effective marketing tool, whereas in other regions, Web banner ads are more effective? The answer to this more complicated question could help managers develop a regional marketing strategy.

Microsoft Excel spreadsheet software offers many tools that are helpful in answering these kinds of questions. If the list was small, you could simply inspect the list and try to get a sense of patterns in the data. But this is impossible when you have a list of over 500 transactions. Notice that these questions often involve two dimensions: region and average purchase, time of day and average purchase, payment type and average purchase. But the last question is more complex because it has three dimensions: region, source of customer, and purchase.

You could use Excel's charting capabilities, such as a bar chart, to answer some of these questions, but this would require you to sort the transactions on one dimension, calculate an average purchase price for each value of that dimension, manually create a new worksheet, and then create a bar chart. This would take a lot of time and be very inefficient.

Fortunately, spreadsheet software has a very powerful tool called a pivot table that categorizes and summarizes data very quickly. A **pivot table** is simply a table that displays two or more dimensions of data in a convenient format. Excel's PivotTable Wizard creates a pivot table for you. It is located in the drop-down Data menu. When you click on **PivotTable and PivotChart Report** in the Excel Data menu and tell Excel where your data are, and what type of report your want (select PivotTable), the PivotTable and PivotChart Wizard screen appears (Figure 6). [For precise instructions on how to create PivotTable reports, refer to the Student CD-ROM Learning Track chapter on PivotTables.]

The PivotTable Wizard has three elements: an empty PivotTable with labels for rows, columns, and data areas; a PivotTable Field List which lists the fields in your list or database; and a PivotTable Toolbar. By dragging and dropping the fields you want to look at in your pivot table, you can analyze this list quickly, and arrive at decisions quickly.

For instance, let's take the first question: "Where do our customers come from?" There's several answers to this question, but let's start with region and ask the question: "How many customers come from each region?" To find the answer, simply drag the Region field to the "Drop Row Fields Here" area of the empty pivot table, and drag Cust ID to the "Drop Data Items Here" areas of the empty pivot table. Figure 7 shows the results.

The PivotTable shows most of our customers come from the Western region. So far we've looked at a single dimension, region, in understanding where our customers come from. Now let's take a more complicated question that involves two dimensions: Does the source of the customer make a difference in addition to region? We have two sources of customers: some customers respond to e-mail campaigns, and others respond to online banner advertising. In a few

FIGURE 6   THE EXCEL PIVOTTABLE WIZARD

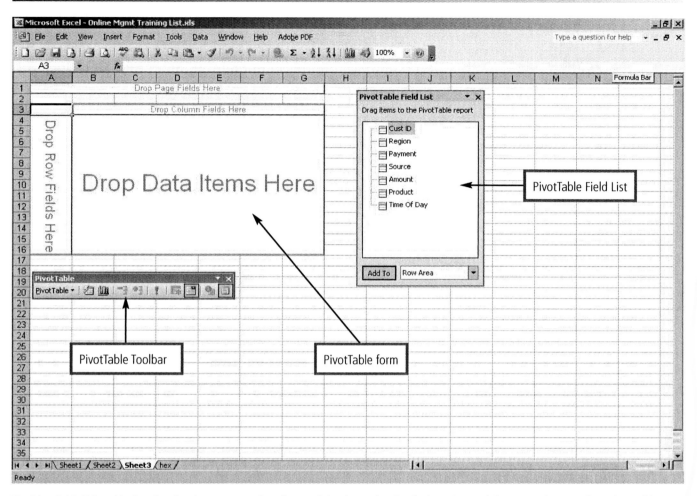

The PivotTable Wizard in Excel makes it easy to analyze lists and databases by simply dragging and dropping elements from the Field List to the PivotTable area.

seconds you can find the answer shown in Figure 8. This pivot table shows that Web banner advertising produces most of the customers, and this is true of all the regions.

Could we analyze the average amount of the purchase to the table in Figure 8? The answer is yes, very easily: just drag the Amount field to the data area of the pivot table. If you do this, you will find that while the average purchase on this day was $38, the customers who responded to e-mail from the Western region had an average sale of nearly $49! As a manager you might want to use this knowledge and expand your e-mail campaigns to Western audiences, and perhaps enlarge your banner advertising in other regions.

The complete Excel file for these examples is available on the Student CD ROM and Web site for this text (click on the appropriate chapter materials in the CD Bullet Text Study Guide, and look in the Learning Supplements section for the file named OMT List.xls). The Hands On MIS section at the end of this chapter asks you to find answers to a number of other questions regarding

FIGURE 7   A PIVOT TABLE THAT QUICKLY DETERMINES THE REGIONAL DISTRIBUTION OF CUSTOMERS

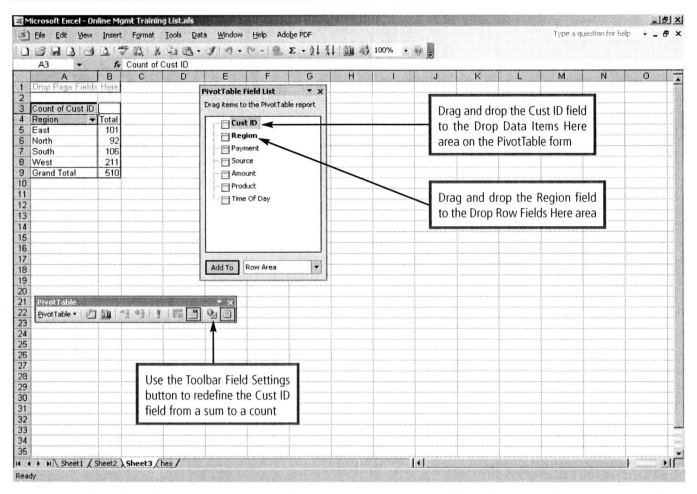

By dragging and dropping fields to row and data areas of the pivot table form, you can quickly produce a table showing the relationship between region and number of customers. You will need to use the Field Settings button on the Toolbar to produce this table in order to redefine the Cust ID field as a count rather than a sum so Excel reports the number of customers, not the sum of their customer IDs, which would be meaningless.

this data file. The Learning Track Chapter "Building and Using Pivot Tables" on the Student CD-ROM gives you in-depth instructions on how to work with Excel PivotTables.

BUSINESS VALUE OF DSS

DSS have become very powerful and sophisticated, providing fine-grained information for decisions that enable the firm to coordinate both internal and external business processes precisely. Some of these DSS are helping companies with decisions in customer relationship management or supply chain management (such as P&G's supply chain restructuring applications described in the chapter-opening case or Renault's DSS for supply chain planning described in the Interactive Session on Technology). Some DSS take advantage

FIGURE 8   A PIVOT TABLE THAT EXAMINES TWO DIMENSIONS

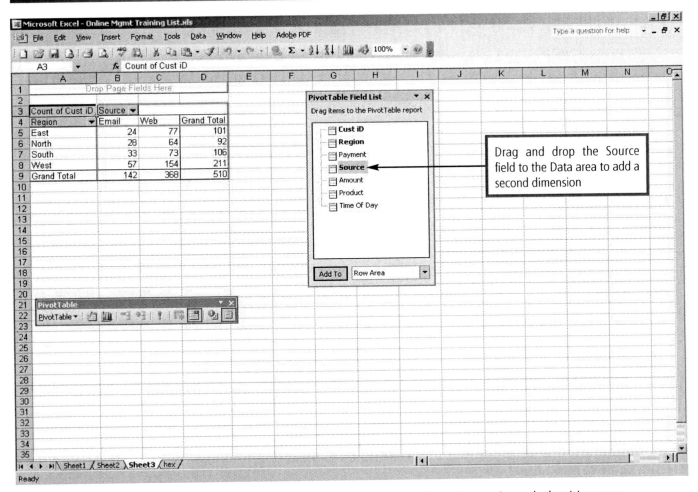

In this pivot table, we can examine where our customers come from in terms of two dimensions: region and advertising source. It appears nearly 40 percent of the customers respond to e-mail campaigns, and there are some regional variations in this theme.

of the company-wide data provided by enterprise systems. DSS today can also harness the interactive capabilities of the Web to provide decision-support tools to both employees and customers. Here are some examples that illustrate the range of DSS capabilities.

Burlington Coat Factory: DSS for Pricing Decisions. Many large retailers lose millions of dollars because their prices are "best guesses." If they wait too long to discount an item that isn't selling well, they will be stuck with excess. If they discount too early, or discount too heavily, they lose profits because people buy goods they might have bought at a higher price. Burlington Coat Factory Warehouse has solved this problem by implementing price optimization software.

Burlington Coat Factory uses ProfitLogic's Markdown Optimization Solution to manage pricing and inventory at all of its stores nationwide. ProfitLogic considers complex interdependencies between initial prices set for merchandise, prices for promotions, and prices for markdowns, including cross-item pricing effects and

INTERACTIVE SESSION: TECHNOLOGY

RENAULT SPEEDS UP DELIVERY WITH A NEW DSS

French auto maker Renault has been facing very intense competition in the Western European auto market. The time it takes to deliver a car after placing an order is a decisive factor in customer satisfaction. Renault wanted to turn it into a competitive weapon. The company decided to shorten the lead time between placement of the customer order and arrival in dealerships from six to two weeks.

This meant that Renault would have to transform its supply chain from a push to a pull model, in which cars were built to order. New information systems were required speed up the entire planning and production process.

In Renault's old system, Renault's national sales companies throughout Europe predicted monthly sales for each model for the current and following year. The headquarter sales department reviews the figures with industrial planners to make sure there is sufficient plant capacity to handle orders. This part of the planning process lasted nearly a month and took place each month.

In addition to planning data, customer orders taken at dealerships are transmitted daily to corporate headquarters, which dispatches them once a week to Renault's vehicle assembly plants. The plants then use these data to plan and schedule production. Except for this last step, the whole planning process was hampered by legacy mainframe systems, which could no longer handle all of Renault's widening number of models and options available to customers. The old system took hours to perform all the computations in nightly batches. Simulations were impossible.

Renault's operations research (OR) team was charged with overhauling the company's supply chain planning systems and processes. The company had tried to use ERP software, but its generic tools could not handle the complex data describing Renault products. Consequently, the OR team had to develop the system in-house using goal-seeking software that seeks to optimize the mix of models, critical options (engine, gearbox), and secondary options that can meet sales forecasts within the constraints of the company's production capacity and product range. "Feasible" sales forecasts are sent to headquarters where industrial planners use goal-seeking software again to determine the optimal weekly output of car factories that meet the sales targets.

On the assembly plant floor, software directs production sequencing. The car sequence is built to smooth the workload on the assembly line and to minimize production costs when colors are changed during sequencing, which requires painting tubes to be washed.

The team worked with groups of users in Renault's sales and industrial department to define the planning problem, its constraints, the decision variables, the objectives to be optimized, and business rules to be followed. Each department selected the information it needed to meet its goals. For example, the sales department focused on the ability to produce the right mix of models, engines, equipment levels, colors, and options every month while industrial planners focused on weekly production volumes for each plant.

The team created a proof-of-concept prototype system for validation by end users before moving into full-scale software development. All the software tools for the New Delivery Project were rolled out between 1999 and 2003. Plant operators asked for some modifications to the software because it was not handling car sequencing well. (There were too many color changeovers for assembly lines to handle.) Renault research teams from Europe, Canada, and Brazil competed to provide a solution. The software now performs more than 140 million evaluations in ten minutes.

The changes introduced by the new system were accompanied by changes in related systems and business processes. Customer orders flow directly from dealers to assembly plants, bypassing corporate headquarters.

Renault's OR team is now working on new software to optimize the time for routing vehicles from plants to dealerships via intermediate dispatching centers. This requires building an extensive collection of paths through Renault's worldwide transportation network and assigning departure and arrival dates for every vehicle leaving the assembly line each day.

In addition to shortening delivery times and reducing inventory, Renault's New Delivery system helps ensure that each customer obtains exactly the car he or she wants. Under the old commitment model, customers were encouraged to buy what dealers had ordered and maintained in inventory. Dealers had to reduce prices to sell vehicles that remained in inventory too long. Additionally, the ability to sell customers the model and options they

want and within a short delivery time gives Renault a more profitable product mix.

Sources: Alain Nguyen, "Renault Speeds Up Delivery," *OR/MS Today*, April, 2006, and www.renault.com, accessed October 2, 2006.

CASE STUDY QUESTIONS

1. How did this DSS improve decision making at Renault? Describe some of the decisions that were improved by using this system.
2. How much of an impact did this DSS have on business performance? Explain your answer.
3. What management, organization, and technology factors had to be addressed in order to make this system successful?

MIS IN ACTION

Visit the Renault Web site, select Buy a Renault, and then select a country of your choice. Review the Renault passenger cars available for sale in that country.

1. How many models are available for sale in the country you have chosen?
2. Select one model and explore its versions and prices. List the various options and accessories available for that vehicle.
3. If a customer were ordering a Renault car, what are some of the data that would have to be transmitted to suppliers?

item seasonality. It enables Burlington to gain earlier visibility into the performance of merchandise in order to clear out underperforming items and free up inventory to stock fresher merchandise that is more in demand (Murphy, 2005; ProfitLogic, 2005.)

DSS for Profitability Analysis. Although a company has a high level of sales revenue, not all of these sales may contribute to profits. A large customer with many requests for service or high-speed delivery of low-margin items may actually be costing the company money. The Brazilian unit of agricultural chemical maker Syngenta AG discovered in 2003 that it was losing money on some of its fastest-growing products. Syngenta's 200 salespeople were paid on how much they sold, and they had no way of calculating important cost components, such as expenditures for deliveries, rebates, and extended credit terms or the impact of currency shifts.

Syngenta built a DSS that estimates freight charges, employee commissions, currency shifts, and other costs to calculate a "pocket price" for a proposed sale. If the software determines the transaction is not profitable, the salesperson can't enter the order unless that person has special permission from a manager. Company executives changed the incentive plan for the sales team to encourage sales that genuinely contributed to profits. In Mato Grosso state in western Brazil, the software helped managers learn that shipping costs were too high to sell low-margin products such as copper-based fungicide. Syngenta Brazil stopped selling such products to farmers in that area. In 2004, when Syngenta started using this DSS, profit margins climbed by four percentage points (Badal, 2006).

Compass Bank: DSS for Customer Relationship Management. Some of the analytical CRM applications you may have seen earlier in this text are DSS for customer relationship management, using data mining to guide decisions about pricing, customer retention, market share, and new revenue streams. These systems typically consolidate customer data from a variety of systems, including data captured from Web site transactions, into massive data warehouses and use various analytical tools to slice it into tiny segments for one-to-one marketing and predictive analysis.

Compass Bank, a leading financial holding company with 376 banking centers and more than $28 billion in assets, uses a DSS to help it minimize default risk in its credit card business. Although credit cards generate considerable revenue and help the bank cross-sell its other financial products, credit card debt also represents a significant risk. (Compass had written off $34 million in bad credit card debt in 2003.) About 80 percent of Compass credit card accounts are opened by customers who already have checking and savings accounts. Compass uses Siebel Business Analytics to analyze the relationship between checking and savings account activity and default risk. The system is able to pull together and analyze 13 months of detailed data from multiple databases to flag customer accounts in danger of defaulting. Operational since the spring of 2004, the system helped Compass reduce credit card losses by 7 percent during its first year of operation (Siebel, 2005).

DATA VISUALIZATION AND GEOGRAPHIC INFORMATION SYSTEMS (GIS)

Data from information systems can be made easier for users to digest and act on by using graphics, charts, tables, maps, digital images, three-dimensional presentations, animations, and other data visualization technologies. By presenting data in graphical form, **data visualization** tools help users see patterns and relationships in large amounts of data that would be difficult to discern if the data were presented as traditional lists of text. Some data visualization tools are interactive, enabling users to manipulate data and see the graphical displays change in response to the changes they make.

Geographic information systems (GIS) are a special category of DSS that use data visualization technology to analyze and display data for planning and decision making in the form of digitized maps. The software assembles, stores, manipulates, and displays geographically referenced information, tying data to points, lines, and areas on a map. GIS have modeling capabilities, enabling managers to change data and automatically revise business scenarios to find better solutions.

GIS support decisions that require knowledge about the geographic distribution of people or other resources. For example, GIS might be used to help state and local governments calculate emergency response times to natural disasters, to help retail chains identify profitable new store locations, or to help banks identify the best locations for installing new branches or automatic teller machine (ATM) terminals.

The Interactive Session on Management describes an application of GIS for controlling crime. CompStat was created by the New York City Police Department to capture data about crime incidents and enforcement activities at each of the city's precincts. CompStat uses GIS software to display data about where crimes are occurring, and is credited with reducing crime rates in New York and other cities.

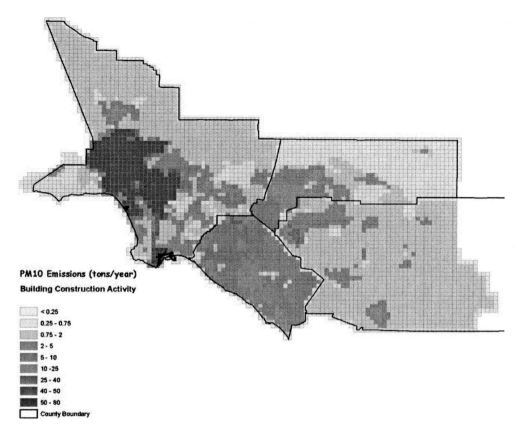

PM10 Emissions (tons/year)
Building Construction Activity

- < 0.25
- 0.25 - 0.75
- 0.75 - 2
- 2 - 5
- 5 - 10
- 10 - 25
- 25 - 40
- 40 - 50
- 50 - 80
- County Boundary

California's South Coast Air Quality Management District (AQMD) is responsible for monitoring and controlling emissions in all of Orange County and the urban portions of Los Angeles, Riverside, and San Bernardino counties. Displayed is a map produced with ESRI GIS software tracking particulate matter emissions from building construction activity in a two-by-two kilometer area.

Courtesy of South Coast AQMD

WEB-BASED CUSTOMER DECISION-SUPPORT SYSTEMS

The growth of electronic commerce has encouraged many companies to develop DSS for customers that use Web information resources and capabilities for interactivity and personalization to help users select products and services. People are now using more information from multiple sources to make purchasing decisions (such as purchasing a car or computer) before they interact with the product or sales staff. For instance, nearly all automobile companies use customer decision-support systems that allow Web site visitors to configure their desired car. **Customer decision-support systems (CDSS)** support the decision-making process of an existing or potential customer.

People interested in purchasing a product or service can use Internet search engines, intelligent agents, online catalogs, Web directories, newsgroup discussions, e-mail, and other tools to help them locate the information they need to help with their decision. Companies have developed specific customer Web sites where all the information, models, or other analytical tools for evaluating alternatives are concentrated in one location.

Web-based DSS have become especially popular in financial services because so many people are trying to manage their own assets and retirement savings. For example, RiskGrades.com, a Web site run by RiskMetrics Group lets users input all their stock, bond and mutual fund holdings to determine how much their portfolios might decline under various conditions. Users can see how the addition or subtraction of a holding might affect overall portfolio volatility and risk.

INTERACTIVE SESSION: MANAGEMENT

DOES COMPSTAT REDUCE CRIME?

CompStat or COMPSTAT (short for COMPuter STATistics or COMParative STATistics) originated in the New York City Police Department (NYPD) in 1994 when William Bratton was police commissioner. At that time, the prevailing belief was that crime could not be prevented by better information and analytical tools. Bratton and his associates believed that police could be effective in reducing crime if more operational decisions took place at the precinct level and if decision-makers had better information. Precinct commanders were in a better position than police headquarters to understand the specific needs of the communities they served and to direct the work of the 200 to 400 police officers they managed. CompStat gave precinct commanders more authority and responsibility but also more accountability.

At weekly meetings, representatives from each of the NYPD's precincts, service areas, and transit districts are required to provide a statistical summary of the week's crime complaint, arrest, and summons activity, as well as significant cases, crime patterns, and police activities. The data, which include specific times and locations where crimes and enforcement activities took place, are forwarded to the NYPD's CompStat Unit where they are loaded into a citywide database. A computer analyzes the data and produces a weekly CompStat report on crime complaint and arrest activity at the precinct, patrol borough, and citywide levels. The data are summarized by week, prior 30 days, and year-to-date for comparison with the previous year's activity and for establishing trends.

Using MAPINFO GIS software, the CompStat data can be displayed on maps showing crime and arrest locations, crime "hot spots," and other relevant information. Comparative charts, tables, and graphs can also be projected simultaneously. These visual presentations help precinct commanders and members of the NYPD's Executive Staff to quickly identify patterns and trends. Depending on the intelligence gleaned from the system, police chiefs and captains develop a targeted strategy for fighting crime, such as dispatching more foot patrols to high-crime neighborhoods, or issuing warnings to the public when a particular model of vehicle is susceptible to theft.

The CompStat Unit also issues weekly Commander Profile reports to measure the performance of precinct commanders. The reports include information on the commander's date of appointment, years in rank, education and specialized training, most recent performance evaluation rating, the units that person previously commanded, the amount of overtime generated by police under that commander, absence rates, community demographics, and civilian complaints.

All precinct commanders and other operational unit commanders are required to attend Crime Strategy Meetings twice weekly at police headquarters. Each commander makes a presentation at these meetings once a month and is questioned by members of the Executive Staff about initiatives they have undertaken to reduce crime.

During Bratton's 27-month tenure, serious crime in New York dropped by 25 percent and homicides went down by 44 percent. Crime in New York City has dropped by 69 percent in the last 12 years. Some skeptics do not believe that CompStat was responsible for these results. They point to demographic shifts, an improved economy, and programs that reduced welfare roles while giving poor people access to better housing, as well as increasing the size of the NYC police force and giving precinct commanders more decision-making responsibility and accountability.

Nevertheless, Bratton is convinced that CompStat was the catalyst for New York's drop in crime, and he is now trying to prove its worth in Los Angeles. Since the introduction of CompStat in that city three years ago, combined violent and property crimes have dropped by more than 26 percent. Yet the ratio of police officers to residents is only half that of New York and Chicago.

The Vancouver, British Columbia police department has also adopted CompStat . Every morning, the commander of each district receives a crime map that highlights all the criminal activity in his or her district over the past 24 hours. The commanders deploy their officers based on the information on the updated maps.

Every two months, each Vancouver district commander is put on the "hot seat" at police headquarters to explain what has been done to reduce crime in the district under his or her command. Crime statistics for the past month are displayed on a big screen alongside statistics from the previous month. If crime has gone up, the commander has to explain why. Commanders are held directly accountable for reducing crime in their area of command. In the past, they were evaluated

primarily on administrative skills, such as staying within budget or deploying resources efficiently.

Sources: Elizabeth Bennett, "Los Angeles Police Department: Safety in Numbers," *Baseline*, Febuary, 2006; New York City Police Department, "COMPSTAT Process," www.nyc.gov/html/nypd/html, accessed October 9, 2006; and Chad Skelton, "Software and a 'Hot Seat' are New Tools for Fighting Crime," *Vancouver Sun*, October 3, 2006.

CASE STUDY QUESTIONS

1. What management, organization, and technology factors make CompStat effective?
2. Can police departments effectively combat crime without the CompStat system? Explain your answer.

MIS IN ACTION

Use Google, Yahoo!, or another search tool to find a street address and zip code for a Los Angeles business. Then visit the Los Angeles Police Department Web site and click on Crime Maps. On the Crime Maps and COMPSTAT Web page, explore the crime statistics and trends.

1. Click on Current Crime Statistics for each of the city's police districts. What information is displayed? How is it organized? What can you learn about the commanding officer in that precinct? Does displaying this information help fight crime? Explain your answer.
2. Go to the LAPD crime maps. Enter the Los Angeles street address and zip code you located, click on Go, and observe the map of the area that is produced. Experiment with different date ranges and area ranges. What kinds of crimes took place in the area you selected? How helpful is it to see this information on a map?

3   EXECUTIVE SUPPORT SYSTEMS (ESS)

Executive support systems (ESS) help managers with unstructured and semistructured problems by focusing on the information needs of senior management. Combining data from internal and external sources, ESS help senior executives monitor organizational performance, track activities of competitors, spot problems, identify opportunities, and forecast trends.

THE ROLE OF EXECUTIVE SUPPORT SYSTEMS IN THE FIRM

Use of ESS has migrated down several organizational levels so that the executive and subordinates are able to look at the same data in the same way. Today's systems try to avoid the problem of data overload because the data can be filtered or viewed in graphic format (if the user so chooses). ESS have the ability to **drill down**, moving from a piece of summary data to lower and lower levels of detail. The ability to drill down is useful not only to senior executives but also to employees at lower levels of the firm who need to analyze data. OLAP tools for analyzing large databases provide this capability.

A major challenge of executive support systems has been to integrate data from systems designed for very different purposes so that senior executives can review organizational performance from a firm-wide perspective. Today, enterprise systems are able to provide managers with timely, comprehensive, and accurate firm-wide information. ESS based on such data can be considered logical extensions of enterprise system functionality.

Executives need a wide range of external data, from current stock market news to competitor information, industry trends, and even projected legislative action. Through their ESS, many managers have access to news services, financial market databases, economic information, and whatever other public data they may require.

Contemporary ESS include tools for modeling and analysis. With only a minimum of experience, most managers find they can use these tools to create graphic comparisons of data by time, region, product, price range, and so on. (Whereas DSS use such tools primarily for modeling and analysis in a fairly narrow range of decision situations, ESS use them primarily to provide status information about organizational performance.)

ESS need to have some facility for environmental scanning. A key information requirement of managers at the strategic level is the ability to detect signals of problems in the organizational environment that indicate strategic threats and opportunities (Walls et al., 1992). The ESS need to be designed so that both external and internal sources of information can be used for environmental scanning purposes.

BUSINESS VALUE OF EXECUTIVE SUPPORT SYSTEMS

Much of the value of ESS is found in their flexibility and their ability to analyze, compare, and highlight trends. The easy use of graphics enables the user to look at more data in less time with greater clarity and insight than paper-based systems provide. Executives are using ESS to monitor key performance indicators for the entire firm and to measure firm performance against changes in the external environment. The timeliness and availability of the data result in needed actions being identified and carried out earlier than previously could have been done. Problems can be handled before they become too damaging; opportunities can also be identified earlier. These systems can thus help businesses move toward a "sense-and-respond" strategy.

A well-designed ESS could dramatically improve management performance and increase upper management's span of control. Immediate access to so much data increases executives' ability to monitor activities of lower units reporting to them. That very monitoring ability could enable decision making to be decentralized and to take place at lower operating levels. Executives are often willing to push decision making further down into the organization as long as they can be assured that all is going well. Alternatively, executive support systems based on enterprise-wide data could potentially increase management centralization, enabling senior executives to monitor the performance of subordinates across the company and to take appropriate action when conditions change.

EXECUTIVE SUPPORT SYSTEMS AND THE DIGITAL FIRM

To illustrate the different ways in which an ESS can enhance decision making, we now describe important types of ESS applications for gathering business intelligence and monitoring corporate performance.

National Life: ESS for Business Intelligence

Headquartered in Toronto, Canada, National Life markets life insurance, health insurance, and retirement/investment products to individuals and groups. The company has more than 370 employees in Toronto and its regional offices. National Life uses an executive information system based on Information Builders' WebFOCUS, which allows senior managers to access information from corporate databases through a Web interface. The system provides statistical reporting and the ability to drill down into current sales information, which is organized to show premium dollars by salesperson. Authorized users can drill down into these data to see the product, agent, and client for each sale. They can examine the data many different ways—by region, by product, and by broker, accessing data for monthly, quarterly, and annual time periods (Information Builders, 2005).

Bonita Bay Properties and Pharmacia Corporation: Monitoring Corporate Performance with Digital Dashboards and Balanced Scorecard Systems

ESS can be configured to summarize and report on key performance indicators for senior management in the form of a **digital dashboard** or "executive dashboard." The dashboard displays on a single screen all of the critical measurements for piloting a company, similar to the cockpit of an airplane or an automobile dashboard. The dashboard presents key performance indicators as graphs and charts in a Web browser format, providing a one-page overview of all the critical measurements necessary to make key executive decisions.

Bonita Bay Properties Inc., which develops planned communities centered around golf courses and fitness centers in southwest Florida, uses a digital dashboard to monitor daily business performance. Bonita Bay's managers are responsible for running the golf courses, clubhouses, restaurants, and fitness centers in these communities. Analytical tools from QlikTech International pull data from many different systems to populate dashboards with key performance indicators for senior executives and high-level operational managers. The dashboards display summaries from point-of-sale systems and general-ledger accounts to show how the business is performing on a daily basis and whether staffing levels are appropriate for the areas where the company is making its profits. Senior managers also drill down to compare the performance of fitness centers or to see whether activity on a golf course experiencing a slowdown has been picking up (Babcock, 2005).

Companies have traditionally measured value using financial metrics, such as return on investment (ROI). Many firms have implemented a **balanced scorecard** model that supplements traditional financial measures with measurements from additional perspectives, such as customers, internal business processes, and learning and growth. The goals and measures for the balanced scorecard vary from company to company. Companies are setting up information systems to populate the scorecard for management.

Pharmacia Corporation, a global pharmaceutical firm based in Peapack, New Jersey, uses Oracle's Balanced Scorecard software and a data warehouse to ensure the entire organization is operating in a coordinated manner. Pharmacia spends about $2 billion annually on research and development, and the company wanted to make more effective use of the funds allocated for research. The balanced scorecard reports show, for example, how Pharmacia's U.S. or European clinical operations are performing in relation to corporate objectives and other parts of the company. Pharmacia can use the scorecard system to track the attrition rate of new compounds under study, to monitor the number of patents in clinical trials, and to see how funds allocated for research are being spent (Oracle, 2003).

Caesar's Entertainment: Enterprise-Wide Performance Analysis

Caesar's Entertainment, one the world's leading gaming companies recently acquired by Harrah's Entertainment Inc., has an integrated reporting structure to help management determine how well it is performing against forecasts on a daily basis. The system uses software from Cognos and SSA Global to integrate data from internal transaction processing systems with data from other internal and external sources. It gathers financial data from the general ledger system, personnel data, and weather pattern and real estate data to deliver daily cost, effect, impact analysis, and profit-and-loss reports to Caesar's executives. These reports predict the combined effect of all of these factors on the company's business performance. The system lets Caesar's executives adjust plans as required online (Cognos, 2005).

4 GROUP DECISION-SUPPORT SYSTEMS (GDSS)

The DSS we have just described focus primarily on individual decision making. However, so much work is accomplished in groups within firms that a special category of systems called group decision-support systems (GDSS) has been developed to support group and organizational decision making.

WHAT IS A GDSS?

A group decision-support system (GDSS) is an interactive, computer-based system used to facilitate the solution of unstructured problems by a set of decision makers working together as a group. Tools for collaboration and Web-based conferencing described earlier in this text support some group decision processes, but their focus is primarily on communication. GDSS, however, provide tools and technologies geared explicitly toward group decision making and were developed in response to a growing concern over the quality and effectiveness of meetings. The underlying problems in group decision making have been the explosion of decision-maker meetings, the growing length of those meetings, and the increased number of attendees. Estimates on the amount of a manager's time spent in meetings range from 35 to 70 percent.

Components of GDSS

GDSS make meetings more productive by providing tools to facilitate planning, generating, organizing, and evaluating ideas; establishing priorities; and documenting meeting proceedings for others in the firm. GDSS consist of three basic elements: hardware, software tools, and people. *Hardware* refers to the conference facility itself, including the room, the tables, and the chairs. Such a facility must be physically laid out in a manner that supports group collaboration. It also must include some electronic hardware, such as electronic display boards, as well as audiovisual, computer, and networking equipment.

GDSS *software tools* were originally developed for meetings in which all participants are in the same room, but they also can be used for networked meetings in which participants are in different locations. Specific GDSS software tools include the following:

- *Electronic questionnaire*s aid the organizers in premeeting planning by identifying issues of concern and by helping to ensure that key planning information is not overlooked.
- *Electronic brainstorming* tools enable individuals, simultaneously and anonymously, to contribute ideas on the topics of the meeting.
- *Idea organizers* facilitate the organized integration and synthesis of ideas generated during brainstorming.
- *Questionnaire tools* support the facilitators and group leaders as they gather information before and during the process of setting priorities.
- *Tools for voting or setting priorities* make available a range of methods from simple voting, to ranking in order, to a range of weighted techniques for setting priorities or voting.
- *Stakeholder identification and analysis tools* use structured approaches to evaluate the impact of an emerging proposal on the organization and to identify stakeholders and evaluate the potential impact of those stakeholders on the proposed project.
- *Policy formation tools* provide structured support for developing agreement on the wording of policy statements.
- *Group dictionaries* document group agreement on definitions of words and terms central to the project.

People refers not only to the participants but also to a trained facilitator and often to a staff that supports the hardware and software. Together, these elements have led to the creation of a range of different kinds of GDSS, from simple electronic boardrooms to elaborate collaboration laboratories.

OVERVIEW OF A GDSS MEETING

In a GDSS electronic meeting, each attendee has a workstation. The workstations are networked and connected to the facilitator's workstation and to the meeting's file server. All data that the attendees forward from their workstations to the group are collected and saved on the file server. Whiteboards are visible on either side of the projection screen. Many electronic meeting rooms have seating arrangements in semicircles and are tiered in legislative style to accommodate a large number of attendees. The facilitator controls the use of tools during the meeting.

Attendees have full control of their own desktop computers. During the meeting, all input to the integrated screens is saved on the file server and participants' work is kept confidential. When the meeting is completed, a full record of the meeting (both raw material and resultant output) is available to the attendees and can be made available to anyone else with a need for access. Figure 9 illustrates the sequence of activities at a typical electronic meeting along with the types of tools used and the output of those tools.

FIGURE 9   GROUP SYSTEM TOOLS

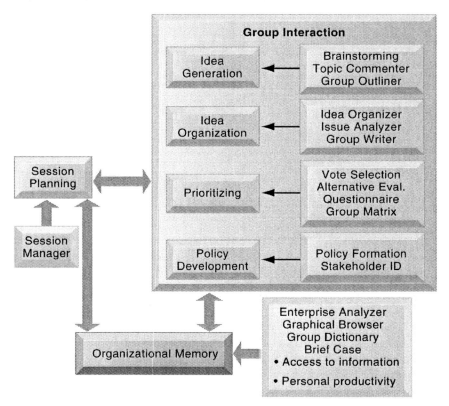

The sequence of activities and collaborative support tools used in an electronic meeting system facilitate communication among attendees and generate a full record of the meeting.

Source: From Nunamaker et al., "Electronic Meeting Systems to Support Group Work," *Communications of the ACM,* July 1991. Reprinted by permission.

BUSINESS VALUE OF GDSS

Studies show that in traditional decision-making meetings without GDSS support, the optimal meeting size is three to five attendees. Beyond that size, the meeting process begins to break down. Using GDSS software, studies show the number of attendees at a meeting can increase while productivity also increases. One reason for this is that attendees contribute simultaneously rather than one at a time, which makes more efficient use of meeting time.

A GDSS contributes to a more collaborative atmosphere by guaranteeing contributors' anonymity. Attendees can contribute without fear of personally being criticized or of having their ideas rejected because of the identity of the contributor. GDSS software tools follow structured methods for organizing and evaluating ideas and for preserving the results of meetings, enabling nonattendees to locate needed information after the meeting. The documentation of a meeting by one group at one site can also be used as input to another meeting on the same project at another site.

If properly designed and supported, GDSS meetings can increase the number of ideas generated and the quality of decisions while producing the desired results in fewer meetings in both face-to-face and distributed meeting environments (Anson and Munkvold, 2004). However, GDSS outcomes are not necessarily better than face-to-face meetings, and electronic brainstorming has not been widely adopted (Dennis and Reinicke, 2004). GDSS seem most useful for tasks involving idea generation, complex problems, and large groups (Fjermestad and Hiltz, 2000–2001, 1998–1999).

A GDSS can be configured in an almost infinite variety of ways, and the nature of electronic meeting technology is only one of a number of factors that affect meeting processes and output. The outcome of group meetings depends on the composition of the group, the manner in which the problem is presented to the group, the facilitator's effectiveness, the organization's culture and environment, the quality of the planning, the cooperation of the attendees, and the appropriateness of tools selected for different types of meetings and decision problems (Dennis and Wixom, 2001-2002; Dennis, Wixom, and Vandenberg, 2001; Hender, Dean, Rodgers, and Nunamaker, 2002).

5   HANDS-ON MIS

The projects in this section give you hands-on experience using spreadsheet software to analyze the impact of changes in prices of component parts on production costs for a real-world company, using a spreadsheet pivot table to analyze sales data, and using online retirement planning tools for financial planning.

Improving Decision Making: Analyzing the Impact of Component Price Changes

Software skills: Spreadsheet formulas, two-variable data table
Business skills: Manufacturing bill of materials sensitivity analysis

A bill of materials is used in manufacturing and production to show all of the parts and materials required to manufacture a specific item or for the subassembly of a finished product, such as a motorcycle. The information in the bill of materials is useful for determining product costs, coordinating orders, and managing inventory. It can also show how product costs will be affected by price changes in components or raw materials. This project provides you with an opportunity to use spreadsheet software to perform a sensitivity analysis showing the impact of various prices for component parts on the total costs of a dirt bike. The bill of materials for this project has been simplified for instructional purposes.

Dirt Bikes's management has asked you to explore the impact of changes in some of its parts components on production costs. Review the following bill of materials information for the brake system for Dirt Bikes's Moto 300 model.

The completed bill of materials contains the description of the component, the identification number of each component, the supplier (source) of the component, the unit cost of each component, the quantity of each component needed to make each finished brake system, the extended cost of each component, and the total materials cost. The extended cost is calculated by multiplying the quantity of each component needed to produce the finished brake system by the unit cost. The prices of components are constantly changing, and you will need to develop a spreadsheet application that can show management the impact of such price changes on the cost to produce each brake system and on total production costs for the Moto 300 model.

BILL OF MATERIALS: MOTO 300

BRAKE SYSTEM

COMPONENT	COMPONENT NO.	SOURCE	UNIT COST	QUANTITY	EXTENDED COST
Brake cable	M0593	Nissin	$27.81	1	
Brake pedal	M0546	Harrison Billet	$6.03	2	
Brake pad	M3203	Russell	$27.05	2	
Front brake pump	M0959	Brembo	$66.05	1	
Rear brake pump	M4739	Brembo	$54.00	1	
Front brake caliper	M5930	Nissin	$105.20	1	
Rear brake caliper	M7942	Nissin	$106.78	1	
Front brake disc	M3920	Russell	$143.80	1	
Rear brake disc	M0588	Russell	$56.42	1	
Brake pipe	M0943	Harrison Billet	$28.52	1	
Brake lever cover	M1059	Brembo	$2.62	1	

- Complete the bill of materials by calculating the extended cost of each component and the total materials cost for each brake system.
- Develop a sensitivity analysis to show the impact on total brake system materials costs if the front brake calipers unit cost ranges from $103 to $107 and if the brake pipe unit cost ranges from $27 to $30.
- The brake system represents 30 percent of the total materials cost for one Moto 300 motorcycle. Use sensitivity analysis again to show the impact of the changes in front brake caliper unit costs and brake pipe unit costs described previously on total materials costs for this motorcycle model.

Improving Decision Making: Using Pivot Tables to Analyze Sales Data

Software skills: Pivot tables
Business skills: Analyzing sales data

This project gives you an opportunity to learn how to use Excel's PivotTable functionality to analyze a database or data list.

Use the data list for Online Management Training Inc. described earlier in the chapter (OMT List.xls). This is a list of the sales transactions at OMT for one day. You can find this list in the Student CD-ROM data files folder. You can also find this spreadsheet file at the Laudon Web site for this chapter.

Use Excel's PivotTable to help you answer the following questions:

- Where are the average purchases higher? The answer might tell managers where to focus marketing and sales resources, or pitch different messages to different regions.
- What form of payment is the most common? The answer could be used to emphasize in advertising the most preferred means of payment.

- Are there any times of day when purchases are most common? Do people buy products while at work (likely during the day) or at home (likely in the evening)?
- What's the relationship between region, type of product purchased, and average sales price?

If you need instruction on how to use Excel PivotTables, read the Learning Track Chapter "Building and Using Pivot Tables" in the chapter on the Student CD-ROM.

Improving Decision Making: Using a Web-Based DSS for Retirement Planning

Software skills: Internet-based software
Business skills: Financial planning

This project will help develop your skills in using Web-based DSS for financial planning.

The Web sites for CNN Money and SmartMoney Magazine provide Web-based DSS for financial planning and decision making. Select either site to plan for retirement. Use your chosen site to determine how much you need to save to have enough income for your retirement. Assume that you are 50 years old and plan to retire in 16 years. You have one dependant and $100,000 in savings. Your current annual income is $85,000. Your goal is to be able to generate an annual retirement income of $60,000, including social security benefit payments.

- To calculate your estimated social security benefit, use the Quick Calculator at the Social Security Administration Web site.
- Use the Web site you have selected to determine how much money you need to save to help you achieve your retirement goal.
- Critique the site—its ease of use, its clarity, the value of any conclusions reached, and the extent to which the site helps investors understand their financial needs and the financial markets.

LEARNING TRACK MODULE

Building and Using Pivot Tables. This module is a full chapter with complete instructions on how to build and use Excel PivotTables. You can find it on the Student CD-ROM and Laudon Web site for this chapter.

Summary

1. *Describe different types of decisions and the decision-making process.*

   The different levels in an organization (strategic, management, operational) have different decision-making requirements. Decisions can be structured, semistructured, or unstructured, with structured decisions clustering at the operational level of the organization and unstructured decisions at the strategic level. Decision making can be performed by individuals or groups and includes employees as well as operational, middle, and senior managers. There are four stages in decision making: intelligence, design, choice, and implementation. Systems to support decision making do not always produce better manager and employee decisions that improve firm performance because of problems with information quality, management filters, and organizational inertia.

2. *Assess how information systems support the activities of managers and management decision making.*

   Several different models of what managers actually do in organizations show how information systems can be used for managerial support. Early classical models of managerial activities stress the functions of planning, organizing, coordinating, deciding, and controlling. Contemporary research looking at the actual behavior of managers has found that managers' real activities are highly fragmented, variegated, and brief in duration, with managers moving rapidly and intensely from one issue to another. Managers spend considerable time pursuing personal agendas and goals, and contemporary managers shy away from making grand, sweeping policy decisions.

   Information technology provides new tools for managers to carry out both their traditional and newer roles, enabling them to monitor, plan, and forecast with more precision and speed than ever before and to respond more rapidly to the changing business environment. Information systems have been most helpful to managers by providing support for their roles in disseminating information, providing liaisons between organizational levels, and allocating resources. However, some managerial roles cannot be supported by information systems, and information systems are less successful at supporting unstructured decisions.

3. *Demonstrate how decision-support systems (DSS) differ from MIS and how they provide value to the business.*

   Management information systems (MIS) provide information on firm performance to help managers monitor and control the business, often in the form of fixed regularly scheduled reports based on data summarized from the firm's transaction processing systems. MIS support structured decisions and some semistructured decisions.

   Decision-support systems (DSS) combine data, sophisticated analytical models and tools, and user-friendly software into a single powerful system that can support semistructured or unstructured decision making. The components of a DSS are the DSS database, the user interface, and the DSS software system. There are two kinds of DSS: model-driven DSS and data-driven DSS. DSS can help support decisions for pricing, supply chain management, and customer relationship management as well as model alternative business scenarios. DSS targeted toward customers as well as managers are becoming available on the Web. A special category of DSS called geographic information systems (GIS) uses data visualization technology to analyze and display data for planning and decision making with digitized maps.

4. *Demonstrate how executive support systems (ESS) help senior managers make better decisions.*

   Executive support systems (ESS) help senior managers with unstructured problems that occur at the strategic level of the firm. ESS provide data from both internal and external sources and provide a generalized computing and communications environment that can be focused and applied to a changing array of problems. ESS help senior executives monitor firm performance, spot problems, identify opportunities, and forecast trends. These systems can filter out extraneous details for high-level overviews, or they can drill down to provide senior managers with detailed transaction data if required. ESS take advantage of firmwide data provided by enterprise systems.

   ESS help senior managers analyze, compare, and highlight trends so that the managers may more easily monitor organizational performance or identify strategic problems and opportunities. They

are very useful for environmental scanning, providing business intelligen
strategic threats or opportunities from the organization's environment. ESS (
of senior management, allowing them to oversee more people with fewer res

5. *Evaluate the role of information systems in helping people working in a g
ciently.*

People working together in a group can use group decision-support systen
arriving at a decision. Group decision-support systems (GDSS) have hardwa
nents. Hardware components consist of the conference room facilities, incl
computer and other electronic hardware. Software components include tool
information, ranking and setting priorities, and documenting meeting sessi...
participants, a trained facilitator, and staff to support the hardware and software.

A GDSS helps decision makers meeting together to arrive at a decision more efficiently and is especially useful for increasing the productivity of meetings of more than four or five people. However, the effectiveness of a GDSS is contingent on the composition of the group, the task, appropriate tool selection and meeting support, and the organizational context of the meeting.

Key Terms

Balanced scorecard
Behavioral models
Choice
Classical model of management
Customer decision-support systems (CDSS)
Data visualization
Decisional role
Design
Digital dashboard
Drill down
DSS database
DSS software system
Geographic information systems (GIS)

Group decision-support systems (GDSS)
Implementation
Informational role
Intelligence
Interpersonal role
Managerial roles
Model
Pivot table
PivotTable and PivotChart Report
Sensitivity analysis
Semistructured decisions
Structured decisions
Unstructured decisions

Review Questions

1. What are the different decision-making levels and decision-making constituencies in organizations? How do their decision-making requirements differ?

2. What is the difference between an unstructured, semistructured, and structured decision?

3. List and describe the stages in decision making.

4. Compare the descriptions of managerial behavior in the classical and behavioral models.

5. Which specific managerial roles can information systems support? Where are information systems particularly strong in supporting managers, and where are they weak?

6. What is the difference between a decision-support system (DSS) and a management information system (MIS)?

7. What is the difference between a data-driven DSS and a model-driven DSS? Give examples.

8. What are the three basic components of a DSS? Briefly describe each.

9. How can DSS help firms with supply chain management and customer relationship management? How do DSS provide value for a business?

10. What is a geographic information system (GIS)? How does it use data visualization technology? How can it support decision making?

11. What is a customer decision-support system? How can the Internet be used for this purpose?

12. Define and describe the capabilities of an executive support system (ESS).

...nance managerial decision mak-
...ney provide value for a business?

...roup decision-support system (GDSS)?
...es it differ from a DSS? What underlying
...ems in group decision making led to the
...velopment of GDSS?

15. Describe the three elements of a GDSS and five GDSS software tools.

16. How can GDSS provide value for a business?

Discussion Questions

1. As a manager or user of information systems, what would you need to know to participate in the design and use of a DSS or an ESS? Why?

2. If businesses used DSS, GDSS, and ESS more widely, would managers and employees make better decisions? Why or why not?

Video Case

You will find a video case illustrating some of the concepts in this chapter on the Laudon Web site and Student CD-ROM along with questions to help you analyze the case.

Teamwork: Designing a University GDSS

With three or four of your classmates, identify several groups in your university that could benefit from a GDSS. Design a GDSS for one of those groups, describing its hardware, software, and people elements. If possible, use electronic presentation software to present your findings to the class.

REFERENCES

Anson, Rob and Bjorn Erik Munkvold. "Beyond Face-to-Face: A Field Study of Electronic Meetings in Different Time and Place Modes." Journal of Organizational Computing and Electronic Commerce 14, no. 2 (2004).

Apte, Chidanand, Bing Liu, Edwin P.D. Pednault, and Padhraic Smith." Business Applications of Data Mining." *Communications of the ACM* 45, no. 8 (August 2002).

Babcock, Charles. "Smaller Businesses Try Analytics." *Information Week* (May 9, 2005).

Bacheldor, Beth. "Beating Down Inventory Costs," *Information Week* (April 21, 2003).

———. "Nimble, Quick Supply Chains In Demand." *Information Week* (March 24, 2003).

Badal, Jaclyne. "A Reality Check for the Sales Staff." *The Wall Street Journal* (October 16, 2006).

Bannan, Karen J. "Smart Selling." *Profit Magazine* (May 2006).

Barkhi, Reza."The Effects of Decision Guidance and Problem Modeling on Group Decision-Making. "*Journal of Management Information Systems* 18, no. 3 (Winter 2001–2002).

Bazerman, Max H. and Dolly Chugh. "Decisions Without Blinders." *Harvard Business Review* (January 2006).

Briggs, Robert O., Gert-Jan de Vreede, and Jay. F. Nunamaker Jr.: "Collaboration Engineering with ThinkLets to Pursue Sustained Success with Group Support Systems."
Journal of Management Information Systems 19, no. 4 (Spring 2003).

Cognos Incorporated. "Integrated CPM Solution from Cognos and SSA Global Drives Performance at Caesars Entertainment." (May 15, 2005).

Cone, Edward and David F. Carr. "Unloading on the Competition." *Baseline Magazine* (October 2002).

De Vreede, Gert-Jan, Robert M. Daviso, and Robert O., Briggs. "How a Silvery Bullet May Lose Its Shine." *Communications of the ACM* 46, no. 8 (August 2003).

Dennis, Alan R. and Bryan A. Reinicke. "Beta Versus VHS and the Acceptance of Electronic Brainstorming Technology." MIS Quarterly 28, no. 1 (March 2004).

Dennis, Alan R. and Barbara H. Wixom, "Investigating the Moderators of the Group Support Systems Use with Meta-Analysis." *Journal of Management Information Systems* 18, no. 3 (Winter 2001–2002).

Dennis, Alan R. and Monica J. Garfield. "The Adoption and Use of GSS in Project Teams: Toward More Participative Processes and Outcomes." *MIS Quarterly* 27, no. 2 (June 2003).

Dennis, Alan R., Craig K. Tyran, Douglas R. Vogel, and Jay Nunamaker, Jr. "Group Support Systems for Strategic Planning." *Journal of Management Information Systems* 14, no. 1 (Summer 1997).

Few. Stephen. "Dashboard Confusion." *Intelligent Enterprise* (March 20, 2004).

Fjermestad, Jerry. "An Integrated Framework for Group Support Systems." Journal of Organizational Computing and Electronic Commerce 8, no. 2 (1998).

George, Joey. "*Organizational Decision Support Systems*." *Journal of Management Information Systems* 8, no. 3 (Winter 1991–1992).

Gorry, G. Anthony, and Michael S. Scott Morton. "A Framework for Management Information Systems." *Sloan Management Review* 13, no. 1 (Fall 1971).

Information Builders Inc. "Information Builders Underwrites New Enterprise Reporting System for National Life." www.informationbuilders.com, accessed August 7, 2005.

Kohavi, Ron, Neal J. Rothleder, and Evangelos Simoudis. "Emerging Trends in Business Analytics." *Communications of the ACM* 45, no. 8 (August 2002).

Kose John, Larry Lang, and Jeffry Netter. "The Voluntary Restructuring of Large Firms in Response to Performance Decline" The Journal of Finance (July 1992).

Kwok, Ron Chi-Wai, Jian Ma, and Douglas R. Vogel. "Effects of Group Support Systems and Content Facilitation on Knowledge Acquisition." *Journal of Management Information Systems* 19, no. 3 (Winter 2002–2003).

LaCroix, Benoit and Jacques Desrosiers. "Altitude Manpower Plannig." OR/MS Today (April 2004).

Latour, Almar. "After 20 Years, Baby Bells Face Some Grown-Up Competition," The Wall Street Journal (May 28, 2004).

Laudon , Kenneth C. and Jane P. *Management Information Systems: Managing the Digital Firm* 8th edition. Upper Saddle River, NJ: Prentice-Hall (2004).

Lilien, Gary L., Arvind Rangaswamy, Gerrit H. Van Bruggen, and Katrin Starke. "DSS Effectiveness in Marketing Resource Allocation Decisions: Reality vs. Perception." Information Systems Research 15, no. 3 (September 2004).

Oracle Corporation. "Pharmacia Gains Discipline and Improves Corporate Performance Management Thanks to a Comprehensive, Strategic View of Research Operations," www.oracle.com, accessed August 31, 2003.

Parlin, Kara with Jennifer Hawthorne. "Coaxing Additional Sales from Clients." *Internet World* (April 2003).

PeopleSoft. "Spotlight on Performance at Detroit Edison." www.peoplesoft.com, accessed November 3, 2002.

Pinsonneault, Alain, Henri Barki, R. Brent Gallupe, and Norberto Hoppen. "Electronic Brainstorming: The Illusion of Productivity." *Information Systems Research* 10, no. 2 (July 1999).

Siebel Systems. "Compass Bank Reduces Loan Write-Offs by 7 Percent Using Siebel Business Analytics." www.siebel.com/business-intelligence/success-stories.shtm, accessed August 14, 2005.

Simon, H. A. *The New Science of Management Decision*. New York: Harper & Row (1960).

Stodder, David. "True Tales of Performance Management," Intelligent Enterprise (June 1, 2004).

Wrazen, Ed. "UK Forces Cut Supply Chain Costs by $30 Million," Trillium Software, www.trillium.com, accessed May 26, 2004

Yoo, Youngjin and Maryam Alavi. "Media and Group Cohesion: Relative Influences on Social Presence, Task Participation, and Group Consensus." *MIS Quarterly* 25, no. 3 (September 2001).

Can Information Systems Make Your Doctor Better?
CASE STUDY

I magine that you have just been admitted to the hospital with a blood clot in your leg. You are already taking Tagament for treating ulcers. The hospital prescribes Coumadin to dissolve the clot. You refuse to take the medicine until someone double-checks the prescription to make sure there will be no adverse interaction with your other medication. In the end, you learn that you were correct. The Tagament interacts adversely with the Coumadin, leading to excess blood thinning and bleeding, and you must stop taking the Tagament until your blood clot has dissolved.

In the preceding scenario, the mistake probably would not have produced negative consequences because the error was caught in time. However, such errors do occur, and they are not always so innocuous. According to the National Academy of Sciences's Institute of Medicine, more than 1.5 million Americans are injured each year by drug errors in hospitals, nursing homes, and doctor's offices. Other reports estimate that more than 7,000 Americans are killed each year because of inappropriate prescriptions. A preventable drug error adds more than $5,800 to the hospital bill of a single patient, and preventable drug errors occurring in hospitals may amount to $3.5 billion annually.

Many of these errors are the results of human factors: poor handwriting, memory lapses, fatigue, and distractions, compounded by the sheer volume and complexity of available medications. There are more than 10,000 prescription drugs on the market and 300,000 over-the-counter products. Many have vastly different dosage and usage instructions depending on the patient's age, weight, and risk factors.

To prevent these factors from negatively impacting patients, some health care facilities are using information systems to help doctors and nurses make better prescription decisions. A computerized physician order entry, or CPOE, system tries to reduce prescription and dosage errors for medications, keep physicians updated on treatment guidelines, and prevent physicians from ordering superfluous tests or drugs that are not part of the standard formularies.

Physicians must be willing to incorporate the use of these systems into their workflow. Many doctors resist changing their ways because a system is complex or takes more time to use than the procedures to which they are accustomed. Therefore, any organization that plans to implement a CPOE must do so carefully. According to Asif Ahmad, vice president and chief information officer (CIO) of Duke University Health System, "CPOE is one system that no hospital can just deploy. What you buy from a vendor is just a shell." He likens the system to a blank notebook in which you have to fill the pages.

A study of errors at the Veterans Administration (VA) Medical Center in Salt Lake City, Utah, published in the American Medical Association's *Archives of Internal Medicine*, found that the use of simple systems that eliminate handwriting mistakes and offer only basic decision support, such as drug allergy and interaction alerts, do not significantly reduce high rates of adverse drug events. A similar study at the hospital of the University of Pennsylvania found numerous potential glitches in its hospital system. That system actually created new ways of making errors because of its design. It scattered patient data and drug-ordering forms over many different computer windows, increasing the likelihood that physicians would order the wrong medications. To impact the rate of adverse drug events, CPOE systems must support sophisticated decisions, such as drug choice, dosages, and patient-monitoring strategies, and they must be well designed.

Carolyn Clancy, director of the federal Agency for Healthcare Research and Quality, believes that the discovery of weaknesses in decision-support systems does not negate their worth; they simply need to be improved. Dr. Clancy states, "We can't improve safety until we see what the problems are, and these studies are showing us that we still have a lot to learn." However, hospitals may use the studies as justification for not investing the $8 million to $12 million that a CPOE system costs. The initial cost overshadows the return on investment, which they would likely see in a few years. Only 5 to 10 percent of all hospitals have CPOE systems.

From *Management Information Systems: Managing the Digital Firm, 10/e.* Kenneth C. Laudon, Jane P. Laudon.

Supporters of CPOE systems, such as Dr. Jonathan Teich of Harvard University and the medical IT company Healthvision, do not expect computers to replace the human expertise behind a doctor's diagnosis or course of treatment. Teich says that the value of decision support lies in its ability to remember thousands of details and bring the right ones to the attention of doctors at the right times. These are details that doctors know very well, but they may lose sight of small facts or rules among the myriad of tasks they need to perform. One pertinent example from the VA study involved doctors forgetting to prescribe laxatives or stool softeners for patients being treated for pain with narcotics. The secondary prescription would have prevented constipation caused by the narcotics. Instead, patients suffered from bowel impaction and some required emergency surgery.

Sophisticated CPOE systems, such as the one at the University of Pittsburgh Medical Center Children's Hospital, aim to reduce such mistakes. Here, the system calculates drug doses based on a patient's age and weight in addition to raising allergy and drug interaction issues. Even though a physician may be aware of these factors, the system acts as insurance. The extra check is particularly important for patients whose health is already compromised, such as those who have suffered kidney failure. Doctors must adjust drug dosages for these patients based on their precise conditions.

Assistant Duke University CIO Michael Russell says that mapping workflow "is a tedious process and requires the ability to translate physician-speak into computerese." To ensure that all critical processes are covered, his department makes rounds with physicians, sifts through stacks of orders, and holds committee meetings with members of the various hospital teams. One of the pitfalls to avoid is gearing the system too much toward physicians and not enough toward nurses, who may feel the greater impact on their daily tasks when a CPOE system is installed.

One side effect of a CPOE system is that it can be more rigid than traditional paperwork. For instance, under a paper system, a doctor might be able to write orders for a patient before that patient is formally admitted to the hospital. A stringent CPOE system might flag an attempt to enter orders for a patient who has not been admitted yet. To solve this problem, Duke added a new unit to its CPOE system that permits virtual admissions of cardiac patients. Hospital administrators determined that the practice would not violate regulations.

However, this same rigidity can provide benefits. It enables the Duke University hospital to identify sets of related activities that the CPOE system can automate. Then, when a physician enters a cardiac admission into the system, the system pulls out all of the necessary procedures, which serve as prompts for the course of treatment.

With a uniform architecture in place, communications between doctors and nurses run much more smoothly. The hospital staff members can avoid literally running back and forth to consult each other because the system contains all of the pertinent information. Doctors save time on their rounds by visiting patients with laptops in tow. They can enter orders for drugs and labs, as well as view lab results, without having to return to their offices midround. The orders are less likely to contain errors or be misread by labs or pharmacies because they are not handwritten. Some studies have shown that CPOE systems can prevent one-fourth of all adverse drug effects.

Doctors and nurses still must communicate effectively and they must trust the system. If they do not trust the system, they are more likely to ignore the automated prompts. Using decision-support software can be a difficult sell for doctors because they prefer to trust their experience and training. Some doctors resist the idea that they need help remembering procedures and treatments.

Jason Maude is a father who believes that the usefulness of decision-support software extends to diagnostics. In 1999, Maude's three-year-old daughter nearly died when doctors struggled to identify her malady over a period of months. The experience prompted Maude to leave his job as an investment manager to co-found an enterprise that makes diagnostic decision-support (DDS) software. The software tries to reduce misdiagnoses by presenting doctors with a comprehensive list of possible conditions. DDS systems also direct doctors to helpful information, such as medical journal articles with the latest research.

Maude's software, named after his daughter, Isabel, was tested in a study published by the United Kingdom's Medical Protection Society. In the study, Isabel Healthcare considered 88 cases of doctors' misdiagnoses or delayed diagnoses. The software made correct diagnoses in 69 percent of the cases using its pattern-matching technique, as opposed to keyword searches.

Proponents of DDS systems believe that DDS will make healthcare more efficient and save money for patients and insurance companies. However, many physicians argue that diagnosing medical conditions is as much an art as it is a science, and DDS systems have not proved to be more successful than human diagnostics. As a result, estimates place the percentage of doctors in the United States who use such systems at no higher than 2 percent. Doctors balk at the cost of systems such as Isabel ($750 per year), as well as the time it would take to enter the necessary patient data into the systems. "If your HMO allows you 10.5 minutes to see a patient, how are you going to do this?" notes Dr. David Goldmann, vice president and editor-in-chief of the Physicians' Information and Education Resource.

Isabel Healthcare's Web site offers a return on investment (ROI) calculator and notes that the system can help prevent costly malpractice cases. The company reminds users that its software is a "diagnosis reminder" and that the final decision is up to the doctor. As the technology improves and doctors become more involved in the development of DDS systems, the systems may become more desirable. Isabel is available for personal digital assistants, which many doctors are now using.

Both types of DSS systems will benefit from hospitals and physicians adopting digital patient record systems. For example, Hackensack University Medical Center in Hackensack, New Jersey, uses networked software that forms a central nervous system for the hospital. Using laptops, doctors and nurses can record symptoms; order prescriptions, X-rays, and labs; and keep track of patients'

schedules. Because the system contains all of the patient and treatment data, the staff does not need to engage in frequent communications that take time and could lead to errors. Doctors can even visit patients remotely using a robot equipped with two-way video named Mr. Rounder. In the past four years, overall patient mortality at the hospital is down 16 percent. Hackensack uses a CPOE system, and it spent many hours refining the software to eliminate many of the problems described in the University of Pennsylvania study. However, only one-tenth of tests and orders at that hospital are currently placed electronically.

Sources: Lauren Neergaard, "Report Finds Drug Errors Hurt 1.5 Million," Associated Press, July 20, 2006; Marianne Kolbasuk McGee, "A Pill, A Scalpel, A Database," *Information Week*, February 13, 2006; Laura Landro, "Tech Glitches Can Slow Patient Care," *The Wall Street Journal*, December 28, 2005 and "Drug Errors Show Need for Tech Aid," *The Wall Street Journal*, June 1, 2005; Jeannette Borzo, "Software for Symptoms," *The Wall Street Journal*, May 23, 2005; and M. L. Baker, "Duke Health Uses IT to Get Beyond Doctors' Handwriting," *CIO Insight*, March 23, 2005.

CASE STUDY QUESTIONS

1. What problems are hospitals and physicians encountering in diagnosing diseases and prescribing medications? What management, organization, and technology factors are responsible for these problems?

2. Are CPOE and DDS systems appropriate solutions? Why or why not? What management, technology, and organization issues are involved in the use of these systems?

3. What obstacles prevent computer systems from improving the medical industry? How can these obstacles be removed?

534

Building Systems

Building Systems

LEARNING OBJECTIVES

After reading this chapter, you will be able to:

1. Demonstrate how building new systems produces organizational change.

2. Identify and describe the core activities in the systems development process.

3. Evaluate alternative methods for building information systems.

4. Compare alternative methodologies for modeling systems.

5. Identify and describe new approaches for system-building in the digital firm era.

Interactive Sessions:

Business Process Redesign at the Small Business Administration

How to Get Outsourcing Right: Avoid Getting It Wrong

CHAPTER OUTLINE

1 **SYSTEMS AS PLANNED ORGANIZATIONAL CHANGE**
Systems Development and Organizational Change
Business Process Reengineering
Process Improvement: Business Process Management, Total Quality Management, and Six Sigma

2 **OVERVIEW OF SYSTEMS DEVELOPMENT**
Systems Analysis
Systems Design
Completing the Systems Development Process
Modeling and Designing Systems: Structured and Object-Oriented Methodologies

3 **ALTERNATIVE SYSTEMS-BUILDING APPROACHES**
Traditional Systems Life Cycle
Prototyping
End-User Development
Application Software Packages and Outsourcing

4 **APPLICATION DEVELOPMENT FOR THE DIGITAL FIRM**
Rapid Application Development (RAD)
Component- Based Development and Web Services

5 **HANDS-ON MIS**
Achieving Operational Excellence: Designing an Employee Training and Skills Tracking System and Database: Dirt Bikes USA
Improving Decision Making: Using Database Software to Design a Customer System for Auto Sales
Achieving Operational Excellence: Redesigning Business Processes for Web Procurement

LEARNING TRACK MODULES
Unified Modeling Language (UML)
Primer on Business Process Design and Documentation

Peanut Butter Petites, Caramel DeLites, Thin Mints—Girl Scout Cookies have been American favorites since the organization's first cookie drive in 1917. The Girl Scouts have been so successful selling cookies that cookie sales are a major source of funding for this organization. The Girl Scouts sell so many cookies that collecting, counting, and organizing the annual avalanche of orders has become a tremendous challenge.

The Girl Scouts' traditional cookie-ordering process depends on mountains of paperwork. During the peak sales period in January, each Girl Scout marked her sales on an individual order card and turned the card into the troop leader when she was finished. The troop leader would transfer the information onto a five-part form and give this form to a community volunteer who tabulated the orders. From there, the orders data passed to a regional council headquarters, where they would be batched into final orders for the manufacturer, ABC Cookies. In addition to ordering, Girl Scout volunteers and troop members had to coordinate cookie deliveries, from the manufacturer to regional warehouses, to local drop-off sites, to each scout, and to the customers themselves.

The Patriots' Trail Girl Scout Council, representing 65 communities and 18,000 Girl Scouts in the greater Boston area, sold more than 1.6 million boxes of eight different cookie varieties in 2004 alone. According to its associate executive director Deborah Deacetis, the paperwork had become "overwhelming." "It changed hands too many times. There was a lot of opportunity for error, because of all the added columns, multiple prices per box, and calculations that had to be made by different people, all on deadline."

The Patriots' Trail Council first looked into building a computerized system using Microsoft Access database management and application development tools. But this alternative would have cost $25,000 to develop and would have taken at least three to four months to get the system up and running. It was too time-consuming, complex, and expensive for the Girl Scouts. In addition to Microsoft Access software, the Girl Scouts would have to purchase a server to run the system plus pay for networking and Web site maintenance services so the system could be made available on the Web.

After consulting with management consultants Dovetail Associates, the council selected Intuit's QuickBase for Corporate Workgroups. QuickBase is a hosted Web-based software service for small businesses and corporate workgroups. It is especially well suited for building simple database applications very quickly and does not require a great deal of training to use. QuickBase is customizable and designed to collect, organize, and share data among teams in many different locations.

A Dovetail consultant created a working QuickBase prototype with some basic functions for the Girl Scouts

Photo courtesy of David Young Wolff/PhotoEdit Inc.

within a few hours. It only took two months to build, test, and implement the entire system using this software. The cost for developing the entire system was a fraction of the Microsoft Access solution. The Girl Scouts do not have to pay for any hardware, software, or networking services because QuickBase runs everything for them on its servers. QuickBase costs $500 per month for organizations with 100 users and $1,500 per month for organizations with up to 500 users.

The QuickBase solution eliminates paperwork and calculation errors by providing a clear central source of data for the entire council and easy online entry of cookie orders over the Web. Troop leaders collect the Girl Scouts' order cards and enter them directly into the QuickBase system using their home computers linked to the Web. With a few mouse clicks, the council office consolidates the unit totals and transmits the orders electronically to ABC Cookies.

In the past, the council relied on volunteers to handle their paperwork, dropping it off at the council office or mailing it in. "Now we have a way to actually watch the orders coming in," Deacetis notes. As local orders come in, local section leaders can track the data in real time.

The Patriots' Trail Council Girl Scouts also uses the QuickBase system to manage the Cookie Cupboard warehouse, where volunteers pick up their cookie orders. Volunteers use the system to make reservations so that the warehouse can prepare the orders in advance, saving time and inventory management costs. The trucking companies that deliver cookie shipments now receive their instructions electronically through QuickBase so that they can create efficient delivery schedules.

Since its implementation, the QuickBase system has cut paperwork by more than 90 percent, reduced errors to 1 percent, and reduced the time spent by volunteers by 50 percent. The old system used to take two months to tally the orders and determine which Scouts should be rewarded for selling the most cookies. Now that time has been cut to 48 hours.

Sources: "Girl Scouts Unite Behind Order Tracking," *Customer Relationship Management*, May 2005; and Intuit Inc., "QuickBase Customer Stories: Patriots' Trail Girl Scouts and Dovetail Associates," www.quickbase.com, accessed July 11, 2005.

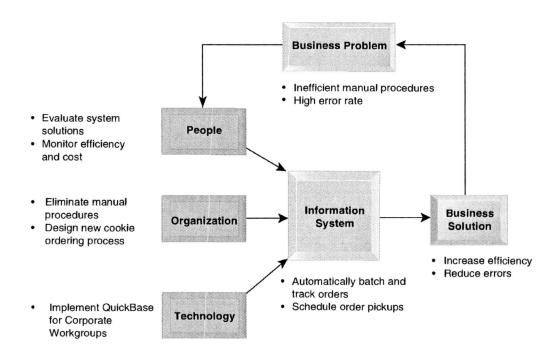

The experience of the Patriots' Trail Girl Scout Council illustrates some of the steps required to design and build new information systems. Building the new system entailed analyzing the organization's problems with existing information systems, assessing people's information needs, selecting appropriate technology, and redesigning business processes and jobs. Management had to monitor the system-building effort and to evaluate its benefits and costs. The new information system represented a process of planned organizational change.

The chapter-opening diagram calls attention to important points raised by this case and this chapter. The Girl Scout ordering process was heavily manual and could not support the large number of volunteers and cookie orders that must be coordinated. Consequently, cookie ordering was extremely inefficient with high error rates. The Girl Scouts have almost no financial resources, and volunteers are strapped for time. The Girl Scout cookie-ordering process required many steps and coordination of multiple groups and organizations. Given the constraints of the problem, the best solution was to rapidly create a system using an application service provider and QuickBase rapid application development tools. The new system reduces the amount of time, effort, and errors in the cookie-ordering process. The Girl Scout leadership had to design a new cookie-ordering process and manage the transition from the old manual cookie-ordering processes to the new system.

HEADS UP

During your career, you will undoubtedly be asked to work on the development of a new system to solve an important challenge for your firm. In the process of building new systems, you will face many choices about hardware and software, and you will have to think about how to redesign business processes and jobs in order to maximize the value derived from the new system. You will also have to decide whether to build your own software solution, or purchase packaged software or online Web services. But the most important decisions you will face involve understanding just exactly what it is you want the software to do and what value it will bring to your firm.

- If your career is in finance and accounting, you will help systems builders analyze the costs and benefits of new information system projects and assess their economic feasibility.

- If your career is in human resources, you will be analyzing changes in workflows and job responsibilities resulting from the new information systems and arranging for employee training in the new systems.

- If your career is in information systems, you will be working with end users to design new systems, choose appropriate hardware and software, and test these systems.

- If your career is in manufacturing, production, or operations management, you will work on process improvements and information systems that increase the quality of products or services.

- If your career is in sales and marketing, you will be helping to design and test new Web-based systems for online sales or a new customer relationship management system because these systems often receive high priority in many firms' information system plans.

1 SYSTEMS AS PLANNED ORGANIZATIONAL CHANGE

Building a new information system is one kind of planned organizational change. The introduction of a new information system involves much more than new hardware and software. It also includes changes in jobs, skills, management, and organization. When we design a new information system, we are redesigning the organization. System builders must understand how a system will affect specific business processes and the organization as a whole.

SYSTEMS DEVELOPMENT AND ORGANIZATIONAL CHANGE

Information technology can promote various degrees of organizational change, ranging from incremental to far-reaching. Figure 1 shows four kinds of structural organizational change that are enabled by information technology: (1) automation, (2) rationalization, (3) reengineering, and (4) paradigm shifts. Each carries different rewards and risks.

The most common form of IT-enabled organizational change is **automation**. The first applications of information technology involved assisting employees with performing their tasks more efficiently and effectively. Calculating paychecks and payroll registers, giving bank tellers instant access to customer deposit records, and developing a nationwide network of airline reservation terminals for airline reservation agents are all examples of early automation.

FIGURE 1   ORGANIZATIONAL CHANGE CARRIES RISKS AND REWARDS

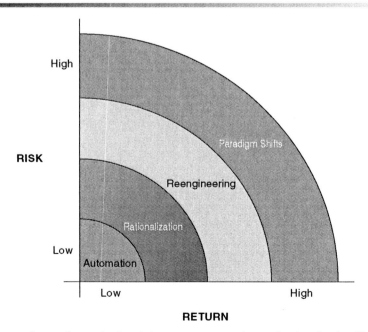

The most common forms of organizational change are automation and rationalization. These relatively slow-moving and slow-changing strategies present modest returns but little risk. Faster and more comprehensive change—such as reengineering and paradigm shifts—carries high rewards but offers substantial chances of failure.

A deeper form of organizational change—one that follows quickly from early automation—is **rationalization of procedures**. Automation frequently reveals new bottlenecks in production and makes the existing arrangement of procedures and structures painfully cumbersome. Rationalization of procedures is the streamlining of standard operating procedures. For example, the Girl Scouts' new cookie-ordering system described in the chapter-opening case is effective not only because it uses computer technology but also because its design enables the organization to operate more efficiently. The Girl Scouts had to have standard identification codes for each type of cookie and each troop, and standard rules for entering orders online. Without a certain amount of rationalization in the Girl Scouts' organization, its computer technology would have been useless.

A more powerful type of organizational change is **business process reengineering**, in which business processes are analyzed, simplified, and redesigned. Using information technology, organizations can rethink and streamline their business processes to improve speed, service, and quality. Business reengineering reorganizes work flows, combining steps to cut waste and eliminating repetitive, paper-intensive tasks (sometimes the new design eliminates jobs as well). It is much more ambitious than rationalization of procedures, requiring a new vision of how the process is to be organized.

A widely cited example of business reengineering is Ford Motor Company's invoiceless processing, which reduced headcount in Ford's North American Accounts Payable organization of 500 people by 75 percent. Accounts payable clerks used to spend most of their time resolving discrepancies between purchase orders, receiving documents, and invoices. Ford reengineered its accounts payable process so that the purchasing department enters a purchase order into an online database that can be checked by the receiving department when the ordered items arrive. If the received goods match the purchase order, the system automatically generates a check for accounts payable to send to the vendor. There is no need for vendors to send invoices.

Rationalizing procedures and redesigning business processes are limited to specific parts of a business. New information systems can ultimately affect the design of the entire organization by transforming how the organization carries out its business or even the nature of the business. For instance, the long-haul trucking and transportation firm Schneider National used new information systems to change its business model. Schneider created a new business managing the logistics for other companies. This more radical form of business change is called a **paradigm shift**. A paradigm shift involves rethinking the nature of the business, defining a new business model, and often changing the very nature of the organization.

Paradigm shifts and reengineering often fail because extensive organizational change is so difficult to orchestrate. Why, then, do so many corporations contemplate such radical change? Because the rewards are equally high (see Figure 1). In many instances, firms seeking paradigm shifts and pursuing reengineering strategies achieve stunning, order-of-magnitude increases in their returns on investment (or productivity). Some of these success stories, and some failure stories, are included throughout this book.

BUSINESS PROCESS REENGINEERING

Many companies today are focusing on building new information systems that will improve their business processes. Some of these system projects represent radical restructuring of business processes, whereas others entail more incremental process change.

If organizations rethink and redesign their business processes before building information systems, they can potentially obtain very large payoffs from their investments in information technology. Let's look at how the home mortgage industry in the United States accomplished this.

The application process for a home mortgage used to take about six to eight weeks and cost about $3,000. Leading mortgage banks, such as Wells Fargo, Washington Mutual, and JPMorgan Chase, have redesigned the mortgage application process to reduce the cost to $1,000 and the time to obtain a mortgage to about one week (see Figure 2).

In the past, a mortgage applicant filled out a paper loan application. The bank entered the application into its computer system. Specialists, such as credit analysts and underwriters from perhaps eight different departments, accessed and evaluated the application individually. If the loan application was approved, the closing was scheduled. After the closing, bank specialists dealing with insurance or funds in escrow serviced the loan. This "desk-to-desk" assembly-line approach might take up to 17 days.

The banks replaced the sequential desk-to-desk approach with a speedier "work cell" or team approach. Now, loan originators in the field enter the mortgage application directly into laptop computers. Software checks the application transaction to make sure that all of the information is correct and complete. The loan originators transmit the loan applications over a network to regional production centers. Instead of working on the application individually, the credit analysts, loan underwriters, and other specialists convene electronically, working as a team to approve the mortgage.

After closing, another team of specialists sets up the loan for servicing. The entire loan application process can take as little as two days. Loan information is easier to access than before, when the loan application could be in eight or nine different departments. Loan originators also can dial into the bank's network to obtain information on mortgage loan costs or to check the status of a loan for the customer.

By rethinking their approaches to mortgage processing, mortgage banks have achieved remarkable efficiencies. They have not focused on redesigning a single business process, but instead they have reexamined the entire set of logically connected processes required to obtain a mortgage.

To support the new mortgage application process, the banks have implemented work flow and document management software. **Work flow management** is the process of streamlining business procedures so that documents can be moved easily and efficiently. Work flow and document management software automates processes such as routing documents to different locations, securing approvals, scheduling, and generating reports. Two or more people can work simultaneously on the same document, allowing much quicker completion time. Work need not be delayed because a file is out or a document is in transit. And with a properly designed indexing system, users will be able to retrieve files in many different ways, based on the content of the document.

The Interactive Session on Organizations describes how the U.S. Small Business Administration (SBA) reengineered its processes for providing low-interest loans to disaster victims. When Hurricanes Katrina, Rita, and Wilma hit the southeastern United States in 2005, they crushed entire communities and parts of states. Besides horrendous loss of life, thousands lost businesses and homes. This in turn led to an onslaught of applications to SBA for disaster assistance. Fortunately, SBA was ready with a new system that could handle the load: the Disaster Credit Management System (DCMS), a Web-enabled electronic loan processing system responsible for all federal government loans to those affected by disasters.

FIGURE 2   REDESIGNING MORTGAGE PROCESSING IN THE UNITED STATES

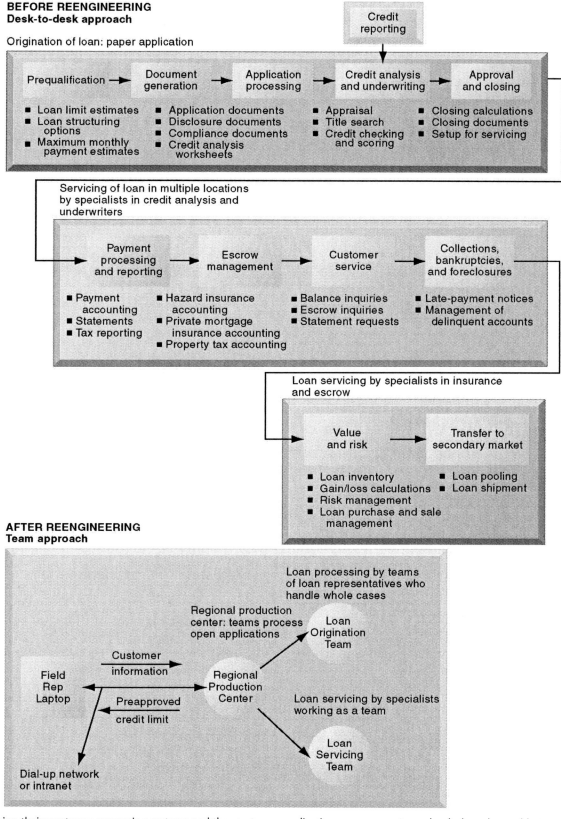

By redesigning their mortgage processing systems and the mortgage application process, mortgage banks have been able to reduce the costs of processing the average mortgage from $3,000 to $1,000 and reduce the time of approval from six weeks to one week or less. Some banks are even preapproving mortgages and locking interest rates on the same day the customer applies.

INTERACTIVE SESSION: ORGANIZATIONS

BUSINESS PROCESS REDESIGN AT THE SMALL BUSINESS ADMINISTRATION

The Small Business Administration (SBA) is a government-funded organization that assists business people and property owners in the United States with funding and advice. Following a disaster or economic disruption, the agency provides low-interest, taxpayer-subsidized loans to businesses and homeowners. Businesses can qualify for loans of up to $1.5 million, which cover repairs, inventory, machinery, and working capital. Homeowners can borrow $200,000 for real estate losses and $40,000 for replacing personal property.

SBA administers loans through its Office of Disaster Assistance (ODA). Prior to 2004, ODA was organized like many federal agencies into regional centers located in Atlanta, New York, Fort Worth, and Sacramento. At some point in history this probably made sense, but no one could say today why this was necessary. Each of these centers was a duplicate of the others, except that each had its own IT infrastructure. Each center had a small permanent crew that handled paperwork and routing, while others were field workers who were needed to inspect properties.

Until November 2004, the SBA loan application process was almost totally paper-based. The only computerized system was an Automated Loan Control System (ALCS), which was outdated, cumbersome, unreliable, and not compliant with the current IT security requirements. ALCS was not really a loan control system that handled all the details of a loan, but just a tracking system that interfaced with the agency's mainframe that ran a program that actually funded and dispersed loans.

Here's how the old system worked. Once the Federal Emergency Management Agency (FEMA) declared a disaster, SBA officials mailed out applications to victims who requested them. Then they set up temporary centers in the affected areas to advise applicants and receive applications.

The applications were taken to the regional office where the data was entered into ALCS, and a paper file was created. Then a manual credit report would be prepared. A Dun & Bradstreet report would be obtained for businesses, and other internal SBA systems were checked. These reports were stuffed into the file.

Once the physical file was prepared, it was shipped to the Loss Verification department, and by overnight mail to a property inspector, who would inspect the property. Stuffed with reports and photos, the physical file would be sent back to a loan officer, who then made the final decision about granting a loan. In the process, files were lost, duplicate entries made, calculations were mistaken, and this all caused further delay. Prior to redesigning its business processes, the agency required 200 people just to control the files, and over 3,000 people on staff to feed the paper monster.

In November 2004, SBA consolidated the four centers into a single center that created a single point of contact and base of command for IT support. This left the old offices free for other SBA tasks. For example, the agency created a call center at the former Buffalo, New York, location. All calls now go through one place rather than being routed based on geography. The Fort Worth office became a processing and disbursement center where the loan and legal staffs actually make and disburse loans. SBA contracted with SuperSolutions Corporation and Oracle to install SuperSolutions's Daybreak Lending Suite, which automates the lending process. The software runs on an Oracle9i database.

To help speed up the data collection process, and reduce errors and labor, SBA purchased Toshiba's Protégé M200 tablet PCs and a Java-based custom application that helped inspectors do their jobs. The process is simple: A loan request is created and keyed into the Oracle database. These requests are turned into assignments that are pushed out electronically to the inspectors' tablet PCs. They can enter data and inspection details directly into the tablet, and that data is then uploaded back to the database at the end of the day.

Rather than send reports by mail or FedEx, the inspectors enter their work and connect to the same Oracle database that they receive their assignments from. "They can go out independently without being connected to anything, perform their work, then go back to their hotel room, or anywhere with a Wi-Fi connection, and sync with the database. This process cuts days if not weeks out of the loan process.

Launched in November 2004, in the fall of 2005 DCMS underwent its first critical test: three large continental hurricanes in a year, including Katrina, the storm of the century. SBA working in the hurricane-ravaged Gulf Coast were hampered by a damaged regional IT infrastructure. The new system worked, but not as fast as victims arrived asking for help. The system had some setbacks and received some Congressional criticism, but it survived.

By 2006, the new system was working extremely well. Before Hurricane Katrina hit in 2005, ODA handled about 100 applications per day. Today it handles about 7,000 or 8,000 daily. So far the system has processed well over 400,000 loan applications. The largest savings have come from salary and daily expense reductions. You don't need as many people if you can pull up a record electronically whenever and wherever you need it. Postage savings are huge,

too, says Sorrento, considering each file often made its way back and forth across the country several times.

In the future, SBA envisages reducing costs further by implementing self-service applications. Instead of having disaster victims go to a center to fill out paper forms, they will go to the Internet and apply online. This would eliminate the need to key in from a paper-based application. Other applications include a staff management tool that can keep track of more than 5,000 emergency workers who come on board in a crisis. In the past, it was impossible to keep track of their hours, and paper vouchers were used.

Sources: Karen J. Bannan, "A Helping Hand," *Profit Magazine*, February, 2006; Thormeyer, "SBA weathers storm of criticism over loan processing," Government Computing News, October 5, 2006; and SRA, Inc., "Small Business Administration Disaster Credit Management System Support," October 2006.

CASE STUDY QUESTIONS

1. What was wrong with the existing computer system (ALCS) and why did SBA decide to replace it?

2. What was the purpose of re-organizing the ODA and centralizing IT in a single office, and centralizing other functions like the call center in a single office?

3. In what other ways could the agency use information systems to improve the process of loan application, approval, and maintenance?

MIS IN ACTION

1. Using any graphic tool available, diagram both the old and the new business process for loan applications at SBA. Try to identify the key decision-making points and persons, the amount of time they spend on their part of the process, and the cost of their labor. (You will have to estimate the time and labor cost elements because the case does not have enough detail.) When you are done, calculate the time it takes to make a decision about a loan, the number of people involved, and the cost of the labor involved. Compare the old and the new processes on the dimensions of time and resources required to process a single loan application.

2. Go to the SuperSolutions Web site (http://www.supersolution.com) and identify the features of the company's Daylight Lending Suite used by SBA. How were these features illustrated in the SBA case? What other features should SBA think about using?

3. At the SuperSolutions Web site, identify a success story, and describe how the firm using the Daylight Lending Suite redesigned its business processes in order to benefit from the new technology.

Steps in Effective Reengineering

One of the most important strategic decisions that a firm can make is not deciding how to use information systems to improve business processes but rather understanding what business processes need improvement. Businesses are composed of hundreds, sometimes thousands of business processes. How can you decide which need to be changed and which could really benefit from information systems? When systems are used to strengthen the wrong business model or business processes, the business can become more efficient at doing what it should not do (Hammer, 2002). As a result, the firm becomes vulnerable to competitors who may have discovered the right business model. Considerable time and cost can also be spent improving business processes that have little impact on overall firm performance and revenue.

You will need to determine what business processes are the most important to focus on when applying new information technology and how improving these processes will help the firm execute its strategy. It is typically senior management that determines which business processes need improvement and have the highest priority. This decision results from two considerations:

- Strategic analysis: senior managers identify the business processes that are most important for the firm's success and focus efforts on these processes.
- Pain points: senior managers identify the processes which produce the most complaints from vendors, customers, or employees and fix those first.

Once the proper business process has been selected, firms engage in the following activities:

- Identify the inputs and outputs to a business process.

    Inputs refer to tangible and intangible items that flow from the environment into the process, including customer requests for products, or services from vendors. Outputs flow back into the environment, and can include task orders, satisfied customers, cash, or materials.

- Identify the flow of products and/or services

    All processes are composed of a flow of goods or services.

- Identify the network of activities and buffers in the process

    Processes are collections of related business activities such as receiving requests from customers, filling orders, filing papers, and talking with vendors. Buffers are delay times built into the process to facilitate review and monitoring. All business processes consume time, as well as other resources.

- Identify all resources

    All processes consume capital, labor, and time. Because cost reduction is a major objective of business process design, it is imperative that baseline costs be established. Baseline costs refers to the cost of the original business process in time and resources before any improvements are made.

- Identify the information structure and flow

    Business processes are informed and supported by a flow of information required to make decisions.

- Identify the process owners

    Processes are "owned" by decision makers who have primary responsibility for the process and decisions. In some cases, ownership is shared.

- Identify process actors and decision makers

    Processes involve a network of activities and decisions.

There is a Learning Track for this chapter on the Student CD-ROM and Laudon Web site that explains in greater detail how to conduct a business process analysis.

Once firms are able to identify and describe the existing process, the next step is understanding how much the process costs and how long it takes to perform. Business processes are typically measured along the following dimensions:

- Process cost: the total cost of the business process for a "typical" transaction
- Process time: the total decision and activity time of all actors
- Process quality: the amount of time and money spent reworking defective parts and services
- Process flexibility: the ability of the process to produce a variety of outputs, or change in the face of environmental pressures. "Flexibility" translates directly into better utilization of plants and equipment, and lower labor costs.

Once the existing business process has been thoroughly understood, the next step is to think about how to improve it. New information systems and technologies offer many opportunities for greatly reducing costs, increasing efficiency, and enhancing effectiveness and revenues. Here are some common principles that business process designers use:

- Replace sequential steps in the process with parallel steps
- Enrich jobs by enhancing decision authority and concentrating information
- Enable information sharing throughout to all participants
- Eliminate buffers (decision delays and inventories)
- Transform batch processing and decision making into continuous flow processes
- Automate decision tasks where possible

While it is difficult to separate the contributions of new information technology from the new business processes enabled by that new technology, it is widely believed that over 50 percent of the improvements in organizational efficiency and business value occur because of improvements in business design, while the remainder results from the new technology, largely because it increases transparency, enables collaboration across the enterprise, and drastically reduces the cost of communication, information management, and business intelligence.

One result is that, today, a modern business organization would not attempt to install a new procurement system or other major enterprise system without doing a thorough documentation and analysis of its existing procurement processes.

As an example of the power of business process redesign, consider the case of Cemex, the international provider of cement and ready-mix concrete. Prior to reengineering its delivery process, Cemex required an average time of three hours to make a delivery. After Cemex's processes were reengineered, average delivery time dropped to 20 minutes. Without measuring the baseline original process, you will have no way to judge improvements.

Following the steps described previously does not automatically guarantee that reengineering will always be successful for you and your firm. Many reengineering projects do not achieve breakthrough gains in business performance because the organizational changes are often very difficult to manage. Managing change is neither simple nor intuitive, and companies committed to reengineering need a good change management strategy.

Interorganizational processes, such as those for supply chain management, not only need to be streamlined but also coordinated and integrated with those of customers and suppliers. In such cases, reengineering will involve multiple companies working together to jointly redesign their shared processes. Reengineering expert James Champy calls the joint redesign of interorganizational business processes X-engineering, and it is even more challenging to implement successfully than reengineering processes for a single company (Champy, 2002).

PROCESS IMPROVEMENT: BUSINESS PROCESS MANAGEMENT, TOTAL QUALITY MANAGEMENT, AND SIX SIGMA

Business process reengineering (BPR) is primarily a one-time effort, focusing on identifying one or two strategic business processes that need radical change. But organizations have many business processes and support processes that must be constantly revised to keep the business competitive. Business processes are not static, but continually change as employees adjust to changes in the markets. Business process management and quality improvement programs provide opportunities for more incremental and ongoing types of business process change.

Business Process Management

Mergers and acquisitions, changes in business models, new industry requirements, and changing customer expectations all pose multiple process-related problems that continually confront organizations. **Business process management (BPM)** is an effort to help firms manage process changes that are required in many areas of the business. There are a variety of methods and tools that are intended to help a firm revise and optimize its business processes on an ongoing basis. The goal of BPM is to enable organizations to make continual improvements to many business processes and to use processes as the fundamental building blocks of corporate information systems.

BPM includes work flow management, business process modeling notation, quality measurement and management, change management, and tools for recasting the firm's business processes into a standardized form where they can be continually manipulated. Companies practicing business process management use process-mapping tools to identify and document existing processes and to create models of improved processes that can then be translated into software systems. The process models might require entirely new systems or could be based on existing systems and data. Ideally, a business process can be expressed entirely in software, and be accomplished with little or no human intervention. For instance, the process of clearing credit card transactions is entirely automated in online businesses. But obviously there are many business processes that are not as mechanistic as credit card transactions. For instance, identifying and securing a new customer can be supported by software, but in most cases still requires a human sales person.

BPM also includes process monitoring and analytics. Firms need to verify that process performance has been improved and measure the impact of process changes on key business performance indicators. A number of commercial software vendors, including IBM, BEA Systems, Vitria, FileNet, Tibco, and Fuego, supply business process management products.

National Grid, a distributor of electricity and gas in the northeast United States, used the Ultimus BPM Suite to improve its process for selling items it no longer uses, such as office equipment, vehicles, and materials. The company's investment recovery process had not been well documented or efficiently executed. National Grid used the software to simplify its workflow to track these sales, increasing efficiency and reducing errors (Lamont, 2006).

Total Quality Management and Six Sigma

Quality management is another area of continuous process improvement. In addition to increasing organizational efficiency, companies must fine-tune their business processes to improve the quality in their products, services, and operations. Many are using the concept of **total quality management (TQM)** to make quality the responsibility of all people and functions within an organization. TQM holds that the achievement of quality control is an end in itself. Everyone is expected to contribute to the overall improvement of quality—the engineer who avoids design errors, the production worker who spots defects, the sales representative who presents the product properly to potential customers, and even the secretary who avoids typing mistakes. TQM derives from quality management concepts developed by American quality experts such as W. Edwards Deming and Joseph Juran, but it was popularized by the Japanese.

Another quality concept that is being widely implemented today is six sigma. **Six sigma** is a specific measure of quality, representing 3.4 defects per million opportunities. Most companies cannot achieve this level of quality but use six sigma as a goal to implement a set of methodologies and techniques for improving quality and reducing costs. Studies have repeatedly shown that the earlier in the business cycle a problem is eliminated, the less it costs the company. Thus, quality improvements not only raise the level of product and service quality, but they can also lower costs.

How Information Systems Support Quality Improvements

TQM and six sigma are considered to be more incremental than business process reengineering. TQM typically focuses on making a series of continuous improvements rather than dramatic bursts of change. Six sigma uses statistical analysis tools to detect flaws in the execution of an existing process and make minor adjustments. Sometimes, however, processes may have to be fully reengineered to achieve a specified level of quality. Information systems can help firms achieve their quality goals by helping them simplify products or processes, make improvements based on customer demands, reduce cycle time, improve the quality and precision of design and production, and meet benchmarking standards.

Benchmarking consists of setting strict standards for products, services, and other activities, and then measuring performance against those standards. Companies may use external industry standards, standards set by other companies, internally developed high standards, or some combination of the three. L.L.Bean, the Freeport, Maine, outdoor clothing company, used bench-marking to achieve an order-shipping accuracy of 99.9 percent. Its old batch order fulfillment system could not handle the surging volume and variety of items to be shipped. After studying German and Scandinavian companies with leading-edge order fulfillment operations, L.L.Bean carefully redesigned its order fulfillment process and information systems so that orders could be processed as soon as they were received and shipped within 24 hours. You can find other examples of systems promoting quality improvements throughout this text.

2 OVERVIEW OF SYSTEMS DEVELOPMENT

New information systems are an outgrowth of a process of organizational problem solving. A new information system is built as a solution to some type of problem or set of problems the organization perceives it is facing. The problem may be one in which managers and employees realize that the organization is not performing as well as expected, or it may come from the realization that the organization should take advantage of new opportunities to perform more successfully.

The activities that go into producing an information system solution to an organizational problem or opportunity are called **systems development**. Systems development is a structured kind of problem solving with distinct activities. These activities consist of systems analysis, systems design, programming, testing, conversion, and production and maintenance.

Figure 3 illustrates the systems development process. The systems development activities depicted here usually take place in sequential order. But some of the activities may need to be repeated or some may take place simultaneously, depending on the approach to system building that is being employed (see section 3).

SYSTEMS ANALYSIS

Systems analysis is the analysis of a problem that an organization will try to solve with an information system. It consists of defining the problem, identifying its causes, specifying the solution, and identifying the information requirements that must be met by a system solution.

The systems analyst creates a road map of the existing organization and systems, identifying the primary owners and users of data along with existing hardware and software. The systems analyst then details the problems of existing systems. By examining documents, work papers, and procedures; observing system operations; and interviewing key users of the systems, the analyst can identify the problem areas and objectives a solution would achieve.

FIGURE 3   THE SYSTEMS DEVELOPMENT PROCESS

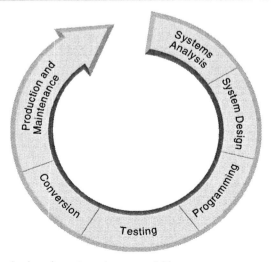

Building a system can be broken down into six core activities.

Often the solution requires building a new information system or improving an existing one.

The systems analysis would include a **feasibility study** to determine whether that solution was feasible, or achievable, from a financial, technical, and organizational standpoint. The feasibility study would determine whether the proposed system was a good investment, whether the technology needed for the system was available and could be handled by the firm's information systems specialists, and whether the organization could handle the changes introduced by the system.

Normally, the systems analysis process identifies several alternative solutions that the organization can pursue. The process then assesses the feasibility of each. A written systems proposal report describes the costs and benefits, advantages, and disadvantages of each alternative. It is up to management to determine which mix of costs, benefits, technical features, and organizational impacts represents the most desirable alternative.

Establishing Information Requirements

Perhaps the most challenging task of the systems analyst is to define the specific information requirements that must be met by the system solution selected. At the most basic level, the **information requirements** of a new system involve identifying who needs what information where, when, and how. Requirements analysis carefully defines the objectives of the new or modified system and develops a detailed description of the functions that the new system must perform. Faulty requirements analysis is a leading cause of systems failure and high systems development costs. A system designed around the wrong set of requirements will either have to be discarded because of poor performance or will need to undergo major modifications. Section 3 describes alternative approaches to eliciting requirements that help minimize this problem.

Some problems do not require an information system solution but instead need an adjustment in management, additional training, or refinement of existing organizational procedures. If the problem is information related, systems analysis still may be required to diagnose the problem and arrive at the proper solution.

SYSTEMS DESIGN

Systems analysis describes what a system should do to meet information requirements, and **systems design** shows how the system will fulfill this objective. The design of an information system is the overall plan or model for that system. Like the blueprint of a building or house, it consists of all the specifications that give the system its form and structure.

The systems designer details the system specifications that will deliver the functions identified during systems analysis. These specifications should address all of the managerial, organizational, and technological components of the system solution. Table 1 lists the types of specifications that would be produced during systems design.

Like houses or buildings, information systems may have many possible designs. Each design represents a unique blend of all technical and organizational components. What makes one design superior to others is the ease and efficiency with which it fulfills user requirements within a specific set of technical, organizational, financial, and time constraints.

TABLE 1   DESIGN SPECIFICATIONS

OUTPUT	PROCESSING	DOCUMENTATION
Medium	Computations	Operations documentation
Content	Program modules	Systems documents
Timing	Required reports	User documentation
	Timing of outputs	
INPUT		CONVERSION
Origins	MANUAL PROCEDURES	Transfer files
Flow	What activities	Initiate new procedures
Data entry	Who performs them	Select testing method
	When	Cut over to new system
USER INTERFACE	How	
Simplicity	Where	TRAINING
Efficiency		Select training techniques
Logic	CONTROLS	Develop training modules
Feedback	Input controls (characters, limit,	Identify training facilities
Errors	reasonableness)	
	Processing controls (consistency, record counts)	ORGANIZATIONAL CHANGES
DATABASE DESIGN	Output controls (totals, samples of output)	Task redesign
Logical data model	Procedural controls (passwords, special forms)	Job design
Volume and speed requirements		Process design
File organization and design	SECURITY	Organization structure design
Record specifications	Access controls	Reporting relationships
	Catastrophe plans	
	Audit trails	

The Role of End Users

User information requirements drive the entire system-building effort. Users must have sufficient control over the design process to ensure that the system reflects their business priorities and information needs, not the biases of the technical staff. Working on design increases users' understanding and acceptance of the system. Insufficient user involvement in the design effort is a major cause of system failure. However, some systems require more user participation in design than others, and section 3 shows how alternative systems development methods address the user participation issue.

COMPLETING THE SYSTEMS DEVELOPMENT PROCESS

The remaining steps in the systems development process translate the solution specifications established during systems analysis and design into a fully operational information system. These concluding steps consist of programming, testing, conversion, production, and maintenance.

Programming

During the **programming** stage, system specifications that were prepared during the design stage are translated into software program code. Today, many organizations no longer do their own programming for new systems. Instead, they purchase the software that meets the requirements for a new system from external sources such as software packages from a commercial software vendor, software services from an application service provider, or outsourcing firms that develop custom application software for their clients (see section 3).

Testing

Exhaustive and thorough **testing** must be conducted to ascertain whether the system produces the right results. Testing answers the question, "Will the system produce the desired results under known conditions?"

The amount of time needed to answer this question has been traditionally underrated in systems project planning. Testing is time-consuming: Test data must be carefully prepared, results reviewed, and corrections made in the system. In some instances, parts of the system may have to be redesigned. The risks resulting from glossing over this step are enormous.

Testing an information system can be broken down into three types of activities: unit testing, system testing, and acceptance testing. **Unit testing**, or program testing, consists of testing each program separately in the system. It is widely believed that the purpose of such testing is to guarantee that programs are error free, but this goal is realistically impossible. Testing should be viewed instead as a means of locating errors in programs, focusing on finding all the ways to make a program fail. Once they are pinpointed, problems can be corrected.

System testing tests the functioning of the information system as a whole. It tries to determine whether discrete modules will function together as planned and whether discrepancies exist between the way the system actually works and the way it was conceived. Among the areas examined are performance time, capacity for file storage and handling peak loads, recovery and restart capabilities, and manual procedures.

Acceptance testing provides the final certification that the system is ready to be used in a production setting. Systems tests are evaluated by users and reviewed by management. When all parties are satisfied that the new system meets their standards, the system is formally accepted for installation.

The systems development team works with users to devise a systematic test plan. The **test plan** includes all of the preparations for the series of tests we have just described.

Figure 4 shows an example of a test plan. The general condition being tested is a record change. The documentation consists of a series of test-plan screens maintained on a database (perhaps a microcomputer database) that is ideally suited to this kind of application.

Conversion

Conversion is the process of changing from the old system to the new system. Four main conversion strategies can be employed: the parallel strategy, the direct cutover strategy, the pilot study strategy, and the phased approach strategy.

In a **parallel strategy**, both the old system and its potential replacement are run together for a time until everyone is assured that the new one functions correctly. This is the safest conversion approach because, in the event of errors or processing disruptions, the old system can still be used as a backup. However, this approach is very expensive, and additional staff or resources may be required to run the extra system.

The **direct cutover** strategy replaces the old system entirely with the new system on an appointed day. It is a very risky approach that can potentially be more costly than running two systems in parallel if serious problems with the new system are found. There is no other system to fall back on. Dislocations, disruptions, and the cost of corrections may be enormous.

FIGURE 4   A SAMPLE TEST PLAN TO TEST A RECORD CHANGE

Procedure	Address and Maintenance "Record Change Series"		Test Series 2		
Prepared By:		Date:	Version:		
Test Ref.	Condition Tested	Special Requirements	Expected Results	Output On	Next Screen
2.0	Change records				
2.1	Change existing record	Key field	Not allowed		
2.2	Change nonexistent record	Other fields	"Invalid key" message		
2.3	Change deleted record	Deleted record must be available	"Deleted" message		
2.4	Make second record	Change 2.1 above	OK if valid	Transaction file	V45
2.5	Insert record		OK if valid	Transaction file	V45
2.6	Abort during change	Abort 2.5	No change	Transaction file	V45

When developing a test plan, it is imperative to include the various conditions to be tested, the requirements for each condition tested, and the expected results. Test plans require input from both end users and information systems specialists.

The **pilot study** strategy introduces the new system to only a limited area of the organization, such as a single department or operating unit. When this pilot version is complete and working smoothly, it is installed throughout the rest of the organization, either simultaneously or in stages.

The **phased approach** strategy introduces the new system in stages, either by functions or by organizational units. If, for example, the system is introduced by functions, a new payroll system might begin with hourly workers who are paid weekly, followed six months later by adding salaried employees (who are paid monthly) to the system. If the system is introduced by organizational units, corporate headquarters might be converted first, followed by outlying operating units four months later.

Moving from an old system to a new one requires that end users be trained to use the new system. Detailed **documentation** showing how the system works from both a technical and end-user standpoint is finalized during conversion time for use in training and everyday operations. Lack of proper training and documentation contributes to system failure, so this portion of the systems development process is very important.

Production and Maintenance

After the new system is installed and conversion is complete, the system is said to be in **production**. During this stage, the system will be reviewed by both users and technical specialists to determine how well it has met its original objectives and to decide whether any revisions or modifications are in order. In some instances, a formal **postimplementation audit** document is prepared. After the system has been fine-tuned, it must be maintained while it is in production to correct errors, meet requirements, or improve processing efficiency. Changes in hardware, software, documentation, or procedures to a production system to correct errors, meet new requirements, or improve processing efficiency are termed **maintenance**.

Studies of maintenance have examined the amount of time required for various maintenance tasks (Lientz and Swanson, 1980). Approximately 20 percent of the time is devoted to debugging or correcting emergency production problems; another 20 percent is concerned with changes in data, files, reports, hardware, or system software. But 60 percent of all maintenance work consists of making user enhancements, improving documentation, and recoding system components for greater processing efficiency. The amount of work in the third category of maintenance problems could be reduced significantly through better systems analysis and design practices. Table 2 summarizes the systems development activities.

MODELING AND DESIGNING SYSTEMS: STRUCTURED AND OBJECT-ORIENTED METHODOLOGIES

There are alternative methodologies for modeling and designing systems. Structured methodologies and object-oriented development are the most prominent.

Structured Methodologies

Structured methodologies have been used to document, analyze, and design information systems since the 1970s. **Structured** refers to the fact that the techniques are step by step, with each step building on the previous one. Structured methodologies are top-down, progressing from the highest, most abstract level to the lowest level of detail—from the general to the specific.

Structured development methods are process-oriented, focusing primarily on modeling the processes, or actions that capture, store, manipulate, and distribute data as the data flow through a system. These methods separate data from processes. A separate programming procedure must be written every time someone wants to take an action on a particular piece of data. The procedures act on data that the program passes to them.

The primary tool for representing a system's component processes and the flow of data between them is the **data flow diagram (DFD)**. The data flow diagram offers a logical graphic model of information flow, partitioning a system

TABLE 2   SYSTEMS DEVELOPMENT

CORE ACTIVITY	DESCRIPTION
Systems analysis	Identify problem(s) Specify solutions Establish information requirements
Systems design	Create design specifications
Programming	Translate design specifications into program code
Testing	Unit test Systems test Acceptance test
Conversion	Plan conversion Prepare documentation Train users and technical staff
Production and maintenance	Operate the system Evaluate the system Modify the system

into modules that show manageable levels of detail. It rigorously specifies the processes or transformations that occur within each module and the interfaces that exist between them.

Figure 5 shows a simple data flow diagram for a mail-in university course registration system. The rounded boxes represent processes, which portray the transformation of data. The square box represents an external entity, which is an originator or receiver of information located outside the boundaries of the system being modeled. The open rectangles represent data stores, which are either manual or automated inventories of data. The arrows represent data flows, which show the movement between processes, external entities, and data stores. They always contain packets of data with the name or content of each data flow listed beside the arrow.

This data flow diagram shows that students submit registration forms with their name, identification number, and the numbers of the courses they wish to take. In process 1.0, the system verifies that each course selected is still open by referencing the university's course file. The file distinguishes courses that are open from those that have been canceled or filled. Process 1.0 then determines which of the student's selections can be accepted or rejected. Process 2.0 enrolls the student in the courses for which he or she has been accepted. It updates the university's course file with the student's name and identification number and recalculates the class size. If maximum enrollment has been reached, the course number is flagged as closed. Process 2.0 also updates the university's student master file with information about new students or changes in address. Process 3.0 then sends each student applicant a confirmation-of-registration letter listing the courses for which he or she is registered, noting the course selections that could not be fulfilled.

FIGURE 5   DATA FLOW DIAGRAM FOR MAIL-IN UNIVERSITY REGISTRATION SYSTEM

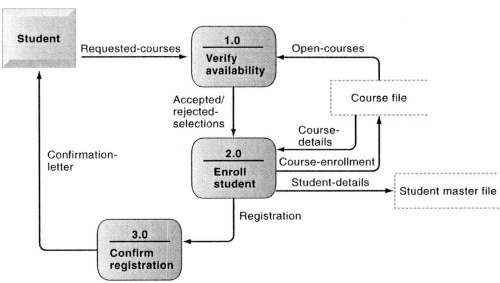

The system has three processes: Verify availability (1.0), Enroll student (2.0), and Confirm registration (3.0). The name and content of each of the data flows appear adjacent to each arrow. There is one external entity in this system: the student. There are two data stores: the student master file and the course file.

The diagrams can be used to depict higher-level processes as well as lower-level details. Through leveled data flow diagrams, a complex process can be broken down into successive levels of detail. An entire system can be divided into subsystems with a high-level data flow diagram. Each subsystem, in turn, can be divided into additional subsystems with second-level data flow diagrams, and the lower-level subsystems can be broken down again until the lowest level of detail has been reached.

Another tool for structured analysis is a data dictionary, which contains information about individual pieces of data and data groupings within a system. The data dictionary defines the contents of data flows and data stores so that systems builders understand exactly what pieces of data they contain. **Process specifications** describe the transformation occurring within the lowest level of the data flow diagrams. They express the logic for each process.

In structured methodology, software design is modeled using hierarchical structure charts. The **structure chart** is a top-down chart, showing each level of design, its relationship to other levels, and its place in the overall design structure. The design first considers the main function of a program or system, then breaks this function into subfunctions, and decomposes each subfunction until the lowest level of detail has been reached. Figure 6 shows a high-level structure chart for a payroll system. If a design has too many levels to fit onto one structure chart, it can be broken down further on more detailed structure charts. A structure chart may document one program, one system (a set of programs), or part of one program.

Object-Oriented Development

Structured methods are useful for modeling processes but do not handle the modeling of data well. They also treat data and processes as logically separate entities, whereas in the real world such separation seems unnatural. Different modeling conventions are used for analysis (the data flow diagram) and for design (the structure chart).

Object-oriented development addresses these issues. Object-oriented development uses the **object** as the basic unit of systems analysis and design. An object combines data and the specific processes that operate on those data. Data encapsulated in an object can be accessed and modified only by the operations, or methods, associated with that object. Instead of passing data to procedures, programs send a message for an object to perform an operation

FIGURE 6   HIGH-LEVEL STRUCTURE CHART FOR A PAYROLL SYSTEM

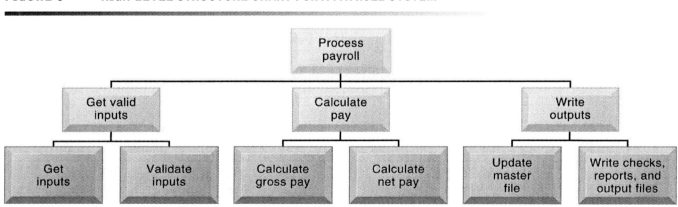

This structure chart shows the highest or most abstract level of design for a payroll system, providing an overview of the entire system.

557

that is already embedded in it. The system is modeled as a collection of objects and the relationships among them. Because processing logic resides within objects rather than in separate software programs, objects must collaborate with each other to make the system work.

Object-oriented modeling is based on the concepts of class and inheritance. Objects belonging to a certain class, or general categories of similar objects, have the features of that class. Classes of objects in turn can inherit all the structure and behaviors of a more general class and then add variables and behaviors unique to each object. New classes of objects are created by choosing an existing class and specifying how the new class differs from the existing class, instead of starting from scratch each time.

We can see how class and inheritance work in Figure 7, which illustrates the relationships among classes concerning employees and how they are paid. Employee is the common ancestor, or superclass, for the other three classes. Salaried, Hourly, and Temporary are subclasses of Employee. The class name is in the top compartment, the attributes for each class are in the middle portion of each box, and the list of operations is in the bottom portion of each box. The features that are shared by all employees (ID, name, address, date hired, position, and pay) are stored in the Employee superclass, whereas each subclass stores features that are specific to that particular type of employee. Specific to Hourly employees, for example, are their hourly rates and overtime rates. A solid line from the subclass to the superclass is a generalization path showing that the subclasses Salaried, Hourly, and Temporary have common features that can be generalized into the superclass Employee.

Object-oriented development is more iterative and incremental than traditional structured development. During analysis, systems builders document the functional requirements of the system, specifying its most important properties and what the proposed system must do. Interactions between the system and its users are analyzed to identify objects, which include

FIGURE 7   CLASS AND INHERITANCE

This figure illustrates how classes inherit the common features of their superclass.

both data and processes. The object-oriented design phase describes how the objects will behave and how they will interact with one other. Similar objects are grouped together to form a class, and classes are grouped into hierarchies in which a subclass inherits the attributes and methods from its superclass.

The information system is implemented by translating the design into program code, reusing classes that are already available in a library of reusable software objects, and adding new ones created during the object-oriented design phase. Implementation may also involve the creation of an object-oriented database. The resulting system must be thoroughly tested and evaluated.

Because objects are reusable, object-oriented development could potentially reduce the time and cost of writing software because organizations can reuse software objects that have already been created as building blocks for other applications. New systems can be created by using some existing objects, changing others, and adding a few new objects. Object-oriented frameworks have been developed to provide reusable, semicomplete applications that the organization can further customize into finished applications.

Computer-Aided Software Engineering

Computer-aided software engineering (CASE)—*sometimes called computer-aided systems engineering*—provides software tools to automate the methodologies we have just described to reduce the amount of repetitive work the developer needs to do. CASE tools also facilitate the creation of clear documentation and the coordination of team development efforts. Team members can share their work easily by accessing each other's files to review or modify what has been done. Modest productivity benefits can also be achieved if the tools are used properly. Many CASE tools are PC-based, with powerful graphical capabilities.

CASE tools provide automated graphics facilities for producing charts and diagrams, screen and report generators, data dictionaries, extensive reporting facilities, analysis and checking tools, code generators, and documentation generators. In general, CASE tools try to increase productivity and quality by doing the following:

- Enforce a standard development methodology and design discipline
- Improve communication between users and technical specialists
- Organize and correlate design components and provide rapid access to them using a design repository
- Automate tedious and error-prone portions of analysis and design
- Automate code generation and testing and control rollout

Many CASE tools have been classified in terms of whether they support activities at the front end or the back end of the systems development process. Front-end CASE tools focus on capturing analysis and design information in the early stages of systems development, whereas back-end CASE tools address coding, testing, and maintenance activities. Back-end tools help convert specifications automatically into program code.

CASE tools automatically tie data elements to the processes where they are used. If a data flow diagram is changed from one process to another, the elements in the data dictionary would be altered automatically to reflect the change in the diagram. CASE tools also contain features for validating design diagrams and specifications. CASE tools thus support iterative design by automating revisions and changes and providing prototyping facilities. A CASE information repository stores all the information defined by the analysts during the project. The repository includes data flow diagrams, structure charts, entity-relationship diagrams, data definitions, process specifications, screen and report formats, notes and comments, and test results.

To be used effectively, CASE tools require organizational discipline. Every member of a development project must adhere to a common set of naming conventions and standards as well as to a development methodology. The best CASE tools enforce common methods and standards, which may discourage their use in situations where organizational discipline is lacking.

3   ALTERNATIVE SYSTEMS-BUILDING APPROACHES

Systems differ in terms of their size and technological complexity and in terms of the organizational problems they are meant to solve. A number of systems-building approaches have been developed to deal with these differences. This section describes these alternative methods: the traditional systems life cycle, prototyping, application software packages, end-user development, and outsourcing.

TRADITIONAL SYSTEMS LIFE CYCLE

The **systems life cycle** is the oldest method for building information systems. The life cycle methodology is a phased approach to building a system, dividing systems development into formal stages. Systems development specialists have different opinions on how to partition the systems-building stages, but they roughly correspond to the stages of systems development that we have just described.

The systems life cycle methodology maintains a very formal division of labor between end users and information systems specialists. Technical specialists, such as system analysts and programmers, are responsible for much of the systems analysis, design, and implementation work; end users are limited to providing information requirements and reviewing the technical staff's work. The life cycle also emphasizes formal specifications and paperwork, so many documents are generated during the course of a systems project.

The systems life cycle is still used for building large complex systems that require a rigorous and formal requirements analysis, predefined specifications, and tight controls over the systems-building process. However, the systems life cycle approach can be costly, time-consuming, and inflexible. Although systems builders can go back and forth among stages in the life cycle, the systems life cycle is predominantly a "waterfall" approach in which tasks in one stage are completed before work for the next stage begins. Activities can be repeated, but volumes of new documents must be generated and steps retraced if requirements and specifications need to be revised. This encourages freezing of specifications relatively early in the development process. The life cycle approach is also not suitable for many small desktop systems, which tend to be less structured and more individualized.

PROTOTYPING

Prototyping consists of building an experimental system rapidly and inexpensively for end users to evaluate. By interacting with the prototype, users can get a better idea of their information requirements. The prototype endorsed by the users can be used as a template to create the final system.

The **prototype** is a working version of an information system or part of the system, but it is meant to be only a preliminary model. Once operational, the prototype will be further refined until it conforms precisely to users' requirements. Once the design has been finalized, the prototype can be converted to a polished production system.

The process of building a preliminary design, trying it out, refining it, and trying again has been called an **iterative** process of systems development because the steps required to build a system can be repeated over and over again. Prototyping is more explicitly iterative than the conventional life cycle, and it actively promotes system design changes. It has been said that prototyping replaces unplanned rework with planned iteration, with each version more accurately reflecting users' requirements.

Steps in Prototyping

Figure 8 shows a four-step model of the prototyping process, which consists of the following:

Step 1: *Identify the user's basic requirements.* The system designer (usually an information systems specialist) works with the user only long enough to capture the user's basic information needs.

Step 2: *Develop an initial prototype.* The system designer creates a working prototype quickly, using tools for rapidly generating software.

Step 3: *Use the prototype.* The user is encouraged to work with the system to determine how well the prototype meets his or her needs and to make suggestions for improving the prototype.

FIGURE 8   THE PROTOTYPING PROCESS

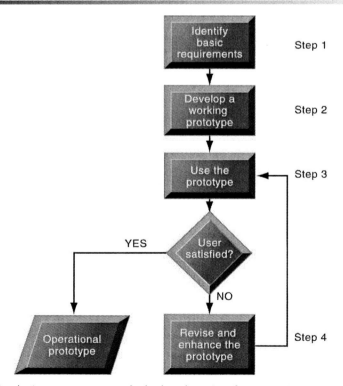

The process of developing a prototype can be broken down into four steps. Because a prototype can be developed quickly and inexpensively, systems builders can go through several iterations, repeating steps 3 and 4, to refine and enhance the prototype before arriving at the final operational one.

Step 4: *Revise and enhance the prototype.* The system builder notes all changes the user requests and refines the prototype accordingly. After the prototype has been revised, the cycle returns to step 3. Steps 3 and 4 are repeated until the user is satisfied.

When no more iterations are required, the approved prototype then becomes an operational prototype that furnishes the final specifications for the application. Sometimes the prototype is adopted as the production version of the system.

Advantages and Disadvantages of Prototyping

Prototyping is most useful when there is some uncertainty about requirements or design solutions and often used for designing an information system's **end-user interface** (the part of the system with which end users interact, such as online display and data-entry screens, reports, or Web pages). Because prototyping encourages intense end-user involvement throughout the systems development life cycle, it is more likely to produce systems that fulfill user requirements.

However, rapid prototyping can gloss over essential steps in systems development. If the completed prototype works reasonably well, management may not see the need for reprogramming, redesign, or full documentation and testing to build a polished production system. Some of these hastily constructed systems may not easily accommodate large quantities of data or a large number of users in a production environment.

END-USER DEVELOPMENT

Some types of information systems can be developed by end users with little or no formal assistance from technical specialists. This phenomenon is called **end-user development**. A series of software tools categorized as fourth-generation languages makes this possible. **Fourth-generation languages** are software tools that enable end users to create reports or develop software applications with minimal or no technical assistance. Some of these fourth-generation tools also enhance professional programmers' productivity.

Fourth-generation languages tend to be nonprocedural, or less procedural, than conventional programming languages. Procedural languages require specification of the sequence of steps, or procedures, that tell the computer what to do and how to do it. Nonprocedural languages need only specify what has to be accomplished rather than provide details about how to carry out the task.

Table 3 shows that there are seven categories of fourth-generation languages: PC software tools, query languages, report generators, graphics languages, application generators, application software packages, and very high-level programming languages. The table shows the tools ordered in terms of ease of use by nonprogramming end users. End users are most likely to work with PC software tools and query languages. **Query languages** are software tools that provide immediate online answers to requests for information that are not predefined, such as "Who are the highest-performing sales representatives?" Query languages are often tied to data management software and to database management systems.

On the whole, end-user-developed systems can be completed more rapidly than those developed through the conventional systems life cycle. Allowing users to specify their own business needs improves requirements gathering and often leads to a higher level of user involvement and satisfaction with the system. However, fourth-generation tools still cannot replace conventional tools for some business applications because they cannot easily handle the

TABLE 3   CATEGORIES OF FOURTH-GENERATION LANGUAGES

FOURTH-GENERATION TOOL	DESCRIPTION	EXAMPLE	
PC software tools	General-purpose application software packages for PCs.	WordPerfect Microsoft Access	**Oriented toward end users**
Query language	Languages for retrieving data stored in databases or files. Capable of supporting requests for information that are not predefined.	SQL	↑
Report generator	Extract data from files or databases to create customized reports in a wide range of formats not routinely produced by an information system. Generally provide more control over the way data are formatted, organized, and displayed than query languages.	Crystal Reports	
Graphics language	Retrieve data from files or databases and display them in graphic format. Some graphics software can perform arithmetic or logical operations on data as well.	SAS Graph Systat	
Application generator	Contain preprogrammed modules that can generate entire applications, including Web sites, greatly speeding development. A user can specify what needs to be done, and the application generator will create the appropriate program code for input, validation, update, processing, and reporting.	FOCUS Microsoft FrontPage	
Application software package	Software programs sold or leased by commercial vendors that eliminate the need for custom-written, in-house software.	Oracle PeopleSoft HCM mySAP ERP	
Very high-level programming language	Generate program code with fewer instructions than conventional languages, such as COBOL or FORTRAN. Designed primarily as productivity tools for professional programmers.	APL Nomad2	↓ **Oriented toward IS professionals**

processing of large numbers of transactions or applications with extensive procedural logic and updating requirements.

End-user computing also poses organizational risks because it occurs outside of traditional mechanisms for information systems management and control. When systems are created rapidly, without a formal development methodology, testing and documentation may be inadequate. Control over data can be lost in systems outside the traditional information systems department. To help organizations maximize the benefits of end-user applications development, management should control the development of end-user applications by requiring cost justification of end-user information system projects and by establishing hardware, software, and quality standards for user-developed applications.

APPLICATION SOFTWARE PACKAGES AND OUTSOURCING

The software for most systems today is not developed in-house but is purchased from external sources. Firms can rent the software from an application service provider, they can purchase a software package from a commercial vendor, or they can have a custom application developed by an outside outsourcing firm.

Application Software Packages

During the past several decades, many systems have been built on an application software package foundation. Many applications are common to all business organizations—for example, payroll, accounts receivable, general ledger, or inventory control. For such universal functions with standard processes that do not change a great deal over time, a generalized system will fulfill the requirements of many organizations.

If a software package can fulfill most of an organization's requirements, the company does not have to write its own software. The company can save time and money by using the prewritten, predesigned, pretested software programs from the package. Package vendors supply much of the ongoing maintenance and support for the system, including enhancements to keep the system in line with ongoing technical and business developments.

If an organization has unique requirements that the package does not address, many packages include capabilities for customization. **Customization** features allow a software package to be modified to meet an organization's unique requirements without destroying the integrity of the package software. If a great deal of customization is required, additional programming and customization work may become so expensive and time-consuming that they negate many of the advantages of software packages.

When a system is developed using an application software package, systems analysis will include a package evaluation effort. The most important evaluation criteria are the functions provided by the package, flexibility, user friendliness, hardware and software resources, database requirements, installation and maintenance efforts, documentation, vendor quality, and cost. The package evaluation process often is based on a **Request for Proposal (RFP)**, which is a detailed list of questions submitted to packaged-software vendors.

When a software package solution is selected, the organization no longer has total control over the system design process. Instead of tailoring the system design specifications directly to user requirements, the design effort will consist of trying to mold user requirements to conform to the features of the package. If the organization's requirements conflict with the way the package works and the package cannot be customized, the organization will have to adapt to the package and change its procedures.

Outsourcing

If a firm does not want to use its internal resources to build or operate information systems, it can outsource the work to an external organization that specializes in providing these services. Application service providers (ASPs) are one form of outsourcing. Subscribing companies would use the software and computer hardware provided by the ASP as the technical platform for their systems. In another form of outsourcing, a company could hire an external vendor to design and create the software for its system, but that company would operate the system on its own computers. The outsourcing vendor might be domestic or in another country.

Outsourcing has become popular because some organizations perceive it as providing more value than an in-house computer center or information systems staff. The provider of outsourcing services benefits from economies of scale and complementary core competencies that would be difficult for a firm that does not specialize in information technology services to replicate (Levina and Ross, 2003). The vendor's specialized knowledge and skills can be shared with many different customers, and the experience of working with so many information systems projects further enhances the vendor's expertise. Outsourcing enables a company with fluctuating needs for computer processing to pay for only what it uses rather than build its own computer center, which would be underutilized when there is no peak load. Some firms outsource because their internal information systems staff cannot keep pace with technological change or innovative business practices or because they want to free up scarce and costly talent for activities with higher paybacks.

Not all organizations benefit from outsourcing, and the disadvantages of outsourcing can create serious problems for organizations if they are not well understood and managed. Many firms underestimate costs for identifying and evaluating vendors of information technology services, for transitioning to a new vendor, and for monitoring vendors to make sure they are fulfilling their contractual obligations. These hidden costs can easily undercut anticipated benefits from outsourcing (Barthelemy, 2001). When a firm allocates the responsibility for developing and operating its information systems to another organization, it can lose control over its information systems function. If the organization lacks the expertise to negotiate a sound contract, the firm's dependency on the vendor could result in high costs or loss of control over technological direction. Firms should be especially cautious when using an outsourcer to develop or to operate applications that give it some type of competitive advantage.

A firm is most likely to benefit from outsourcing if it understands its own requirements, knows exactly how the outsourcing vendor will provide value, and identifies providers with capabilities and objectives that are best aligned with its specific needs. The firm must also be able to design an outsourcing contract that allows it to manage the vendor relationship. (Feeny, Lacity, and Willcocks, 2005 and 1996; Lee, Miranda, and Kim, 2004). The Interactive Session on Management provides more detail about these issues.

4   APPLICATION DEVELOPMENT FOR THE DIGITAL FIRM

In the digital firm environment, organizations need to be able to add, change, and retire their technology capabilities very rapidly to respond to new opportunities. Companies are adopting shorter, more informal development processes for many of their e-commerce and e-business applications, processes that provide fast solutions that do not disrupt their core transaction processing systems and organizational databases. They are also building more systems that tie the firm's business processes more closely to those of customers and suppliers. In addition to using software packages, application service providers, and other outsourcing services, businesses are relying more heavily on fast-cycle techniques such as joint application design, prototypes, and reusable standardized software components that can be assembled into a complete set of services for e-commerce and e-business.

RAPID APPLICATION DEVELOPMENT (RAD)

Object-oriented software tools, reusable software, prototyping, and fourth-generation language tools are helping systems builders create working systems much more rapidly than they could using traditional systems-building methods and software tools. The term **rapid application development (RAD)** is used

INTERACTIVE SESSION: MANAGEMENT

HOW TO GET OUTSOURCING RIGHT: AVOID GETTING IT WRONG

Among large corporations in the last decade there has been a stampede to turn technology management, system ownership, customer service, and back-office functions to third parties. The leading motivation for outsourcing is the belief that it will save money for the company, but there are other reasons as well: to gain access to technology expertise, to avoid capital expenditures on infrastructure the firm uses sporadically, to free up internal staff, to keep headcount down, and so on. Outsourcing vendor firms are in the business to make money. They claim they can do the job better, faster, and cheaper than your internal staff, and still make a profit. They claim to have the economies of scale to do the basic computing cheaper, and to have the complimentary assets in the form of people and expertise that your firm needs.

So it would seem we have a marriage of interests where both parties see advantage, and where both parties should benefit. But the reality of outsourcing is not so simple. A staggering 50 percent of all outsourcing deals fall apart, many ending in court proceedings. In a recent survey of 420 business IT professionals, only a third are neutral on outsourcing deals, and 17 percent called them complete disasters. Some recent bad outcomes include Sprint Nextel taking IBM (the outsourcing vendor) to court, claiming IBM failed to achieve productivity gains, and owes Sprint 119,000 hours of work. It was a $400 million deal. Sprint was shocked to learn that when it made the deal, it did not properly value the work of its own IT workers, and when its outsourcer IBM valued those services and sent a bill to Sprint management, it caused sticker shock. In another case, Sears Kmart tore up its $1.6 billion outsourcing contract with Computer Sciences Corporation (CSC) "for cause." CSC is suing Sears Kmart.

What's going on here? Why is it so difficult for large firms to get along with their outsourcing partners and cut a deal that makes sense for both parties? There are many sources of the problem but chief among them are the failure of firms to adequately value their internal staffs, and failure to understand their own cost structure. And when an outsourcer comes along and says "we can do it

cheaper, faster, and better," management of many firms really have no data to evaluate these claims. Once they sign the contract, they quickly learn that the vendors will charge for every hour of work, and they often find out it was cheaper to do the work in-house rather than pay market rates charged by vendors, plus a healthy profit margin.

But there are also lessons here from the successful outsourcing deals. Campbell Soup has had a successful outsourcing relationship with IBM since 1995, although the relationship has gone through periods of strain. Ontario Power Generation (OPG) has had a long-term $1 billion relationship with consulting firm Capgemini, which provides 80 percent of the power company's IT services. In this case, the firms did something quite unique: they set up a joint venture company to perform the work and share the risks and the rewards. In this way, both firms had an incentive to save OPG money, and to do the work properly.

In both the Campbell Soup and Ontario Power Generation cases, the firms have developed long-term strategic alliances with their vendors. Both parties have been able to take the other partner's interests into account as the relationship has evolved. Flexibility, trust, performance, and even self-sacrifice seem to be the key factors here. In these cases, it isn't just about money, it's also about continuing a mutually beneficial relationship even if, sometimes, in some cases, you pay a financial price. These deals are so big and so long term, it's impossible to write iron clad contracts. However, successful strategic alliances have a high failure rate. When they work, it's wonderful, and when they don't, it's awful.

Researchers at MIT Center for Information Systems Research (CISR) have identified two other outsourcing models: transaction relationships and co-sourcing alliances. In transaction relationships, the firm precisely understands its costs, and has a well-defined understanding of the functions it wants to outsource. In these cases, writing contracts for relatively small chunks of IT services is more straightforward, and less given to later surprises and misinterpretations. In co-sourcing alliances, both the vendor and the firm co-manage and co-own the outsourcing project. Here too there tends to be a more precise understanding of costs and benefits, and a greater transparency because both partners "own" the outcome. Over two-thirds of transaction relationships and co-sourcing alliances work out successfully.

Sources: Stephanie Overby, "Big Deals, Big Savings, Big Problems," *CIO Magazine*, February 1, 2006 and "Simple Successful Outsourcing," *CIO Magazine*, October 1, 2005; and Paul McDougall, "In Depth: When Outsourcing Goes Bad," *InformationWeek*, June 19, 2006.

CASE STUDY QUESTIONS

1. What is the basis for vendor firms claiming they can provide IT services more economically than a firm's own IT staff?

2. Why is it difficult to write iron-clad legal contracts specifying in detail strategic alliance outsourcing relationships?

3. Why do joint ventures and co-sourcing outsourcing relationships have a better chance of success?

MIS IN ACTION

1. Capgemini is one of the largest domestic IT service firms. Visit their Web site (http://www.capgemini.com). Identify and describe their outsourcing services. What are the benefits they promise to deliver?

2. At the Capgemini Web site, read one of the company's success stories of collaboration with a firm for providing IT services. Describe what is being outsourced and identify what type of outsourcing relationship is being used (strategic, transaction, or co-sourcing). Do you think this is the right model for the work being performed?

3. Review the article "In Depth: Customers Analyze Outsourcing Vendors and Strategies," by Paul McDougall, *InformationWeek*, June 19, 2006. This article is available at www.informationweek.com. What are the motivations for using outsourcing? Is outsourcing expected to grow, and why?

to describe this process of creating workable systems in a very short period of time. RAD can include the use of visual programming and other tools for building graphical user interfaces, iterative prototyping of key system elements, the automation of program code generation, and close teamwork among end users and information systems specialists. Simple systems often can be assembled from prebuilt components. The process does not have to be sequential, and key parts of development can occur simultaneously.

Sometimes a technique called **joint application design (JAD)** is used to accelerate the generation of information requirements and to develop the initial systems design. JAD brings end users and information systems specialists together in an interactive session to discuss the system's design. Properly prepared and facilitated, JAD sessions can significantly speed up the design phase and involve users at an intense level.

COMPONENT-BASED DEVELOPMENT AND WEB SERVICES

We have already described some of the benefits of object-oriented development for building systems that can respond to rapidly changing business environments, including Web applications. To further expedite software creation, groups of objects have been assembled to provide software components for common functions such as a graphical user interface or online ordering capability that can be combined to create large-scale business applications. This approach to software development is called **component-based development**, and it enables a system to be built by assembling and integrating existing software components. Businesses are using component-based development to create their e-commerce applications by combining commercially available components for shopping carts, user authentication, search engines, and catalogs with pieces of software for their own unique business requirements.

Web Services and Service-Oriented Computing

Web services are loosely coupled, reusable software components deliverable using Extensible Markup Language (XML) and other open protocols and standards that enable one application to communicate with another with no custom programming required to share data and services. In addition to supporting internal and external integration of systems, Web services can be used as tools for building new information system applications or enhancing existing systems. Web services can create software components that are deliverable over the Internet and provide new functions for an organization's existing systems or create new systems that link an organization's systems to those of other organizations. Because these software services use a universal set of standards, they promise to be less expensive and less difficult to weave together than proprietary components.

Web services can perform certain functions on their own, and they can also engage other Web services to complete more complex transactions, such as checking credit, procurement, or ordering products. By creating software components that can communicate and share data regardless of the operating system, programming language, or client device, Web services can provide significant cost savings in systems building while opening up new opportunities for collaboration with other companies (Ferris and Farrell, 2003; Hagel and Brown, 2001; Patel and Saigal, 2002).

5   HANDS-ON MIS

The projects in this section give you hands-on experience preparing systems analysis reports, designing and building an employee training and skills tracking system for a real-world company, designing and building a customer system for auto sales, and redesigning business processes for a company that wants to purchase goods over the Web.

Achieving Operational Excellence: Designing an Employee Training and Skills Tracking System and Database

Software skills: Database design, querying, and reporting
Business skills: Employee training and skills tracking

This project requires you to perform a systems analysis and then design a system solution using database software.

Dirt Bikes promotes itself as a "learning company." It pays for employees to take training courses or college courses to help them advance in their careers. As employees move on, their job positions become vacant and Dirt Bikes must quickly fill them to maintain its pace of production. Dirt Bikes's human resources staff would like to find a way to quickly identify qualified employees who have the training to fill vacant positions. Once the company knows who these employees are, it has a better chance of filling open positions internally rather than paying to recruit outsiders. Dirt Bikes would like to track each employee's years of education and the title and date completed of training classes that each employee has attended.

Dirt Bikes currently cannot identify such employees. Its existing employee database is limited to basic human resources data, such as employee name, identification number, birth date, address, telephone number, marital status, job position, and salary. A portion of this database is illustrated here. You can find some sample records from this database on the Laudon Web site for this chapter and on the Student CD-ROM. Dirt Bikes's human resources staff keeps skills and training data in paper folders.

Prepare a systems analysis report describing Dirt Bikes's problem and a system solution that can be implemented using PC database software. Then use the database software to develop a simple system solution. Your report should include the following:

- Description of the problem and its organizational and business impact.
- Proposed solution and solution objectives.
- Information requirements to be addressed by the solution.
- Management, organization, and technology issues to be addressed by the solution, including changes in business processes.

On the basis of the requirements you have identified, design the solution using database software and populate it with at least 10 records per table. Consider whether you can use or modify the existing employee database in your design. Print out the design for each table in your new application. Use the system you have created to create queries and reports that would be of most interest to management, such as which employees have college education or which employees have training in project management or advanced computer-aided design CAD tools.

If possible, use electronic presentation software to summarize your findings for management.

Improving Decision Making: Using Database Software to Design a Customer System for Auto Sales

Software skills: Database design, querying, reporting, and forms
Business skills: Sales lead and customer analysis

This project requires you to perform a systems analysis and then design a system solution using database software.

Ace Auto Dealers specializes in selling new vehicles from Subaru. The company advertises in local newspapers and also is listed as an authorized dealer on the Subaru Web site and other major Web sites for auto buyers. The company benefits from a good local word-of-mouth reputation and name recognition and is a leading source of information for Subaru vehicles in the Portland, Oregon, area.

When a prospective customer enters the showroom, he or she is greeted by an Ace sales representative. The sales representative manually fills out a form with information such as the prospective customer's name, address, telephone number, date of visit, and make and model of the vehicle in which the customer is interested. The representative also asks where the prospect heard about Ace—whether it was from a newspaper ad, the Web, or word of mouth—and this information is noted on the form also. If the customer decides to purchase an auto, the dealer fills out a bill of sale form.

Ace does not believe it has enough information about its customers. It cannot easily determine which prospects have made auto purchases, nor can it identify which customer touch points have produced the greatest number of sales leads or actual sales so it can focus advertising and marketing more on the channels that generate the most revenue. Are purchasers discovering Ace from newspaper ads, from word of mouth, or from the Web?

Prepare a systems analysis report detailing Ace's problem and a system solution that can be implemented using PC database management software. Then use database software to develop a simple system solution. Your systems analysis report should include the following:

- Description of the problem and its organizational and business impact.

- Proposed solution, solution objectives, and solution feasibility.

- Costs and benefits of the solution you have selected. The company has a PC with Internet access and the full suite of Microsoft Office desktop productivity tools.

- Information requirements to be addressed by the solution.

- Management, organization, and technology issues to be addressed by the solution, including changes in business processes.

On the basis of the requirements you have identified, design the database and populate it with at least 10 records per table. Consider whether you can use or modify the existing customer database in your design. Print out the database design. Then use the system you have created to generate queries and reports that would be of most interest to management. Create several prototype data input forms for the system and review them with your instructor. Then revise the prototypes.

Achieving Operational Excellence: Redesigning Business Processes for Web Procurement

Software skills: Web browser software
Business skills: Procurement

This project requires you to rethink how a business should be redesigned when it moves to the Web.

You are in charge of purchasing for your firm and would like to use the Grainger.com (www.grainger.com) B2B e-commerce site for this purpose. Find out how to place an order for painting supplies by exploring the Catalog, Order Form, and Repair Parts Order capabilities of this site. Do not register at the site. Describe all the steps your firm would need to take to use this system to place orders online for 30 gallons of paint thinner. Include a diagram of what you think your firm's business process for purchasing should be and the pieces of information required by this process.

In a traditional purchase process, whoever is responsible for making the purchase fills out a requisition form and submits it for approval based on the company's business rules. When the requisition is approved, a purchase order with a unique purchase order identification number is sent to the supplier. The purchaser might want to browse supplier catalogs to compare prices and features before placing the order. The purchaser might also want to determine whether the items to be purchased are available. If the purchasing firm were an approved customer, that company would be granted credit to make the purchase and would be billed for the total cost of the items purchased and shipped after the order was shipped. Alternatively, the purchasing company might have to pay for the order in advance or pay for the order using a credit card. Multiple payment options might be possible. How might this process have to change to make purchases electronically from the Grainger site?

LEARNING TRACK MODULES

Unified Modeling Language (UML). In this Learning Track Module, you will learn more about standards for representing object-oriented systems and Unified Modeling Language (UML). You can find this Learning Track on the Student CD-ROM and Laudon Web site for this chapter.

Primer on Business Process Design and Documentation. In this Learning Track Module, you can discover how to perform a business process analysis and apply this to a case study of ITC Corporation. You can find this Learning Track on the Student CD-ROM and Laudon Web site for this chapter.

Summary

1. **Demonstrate how building new systems produces organizational change.**

   Building a new information system is a form of planned organizational change that involves many different people in the organization. Because information systems are sociotechnical entities, a change in information systems involves changes in work, management, and the organization. Four kinds of technology-enabled change are (a) automation, (b) rationalization of procedures, (c) business reengineering, and (d) paradigm shift, with far-reaching changes carrying the greatest risks and rewards. Many organizations are attempting business reengineering to redesign work flows and business processes in the hope of achieving dramatic productivity breakthroughs. Information systems can also be used to support business process management, total quality management (TQM), six sigma, and other initiatives for incremental process improvement.

2. **Identify and describe the core activities in the systems development process.**

   The core activities in systems development are systems analysis, systems design, programming, testing, conversion, production, and maintenance. Systems analysis is the study and analysis of problems of existing systems and the identification of requirements for their solutions. Systems design provides the specifications for an information system solution, showing how its technical and organizational components fit together.

3. **Evaluate alternative methods for building information systems.**

   There are a number of alternative methods for building information systems, each suited to different types of problems. The oldest method for building systems is the systems life cycle, which requires that information systems be developed in formal stages. The stages must proceed sequentially and have defined outputs; each requires formal approval before the next stage can commence. The system life cycle is useful for large projects that need formal specifications and tight management control over each stage of systems building. However, this approach is very rigid and costly and is not well suited for unstructured, decision-oriented applications for which requirements cannot be immediately visualized.

   Prototyping consists of building an experimental system rapidly and inexpensively for end users to interact with and evaluate. The prototype is refined and enhanced until users are satisfied that it includes all of their requirements and can be used as a template to create the final system. Prototyping encourages end-user involvement in systems development and iteration of design until specifications are captured accurately. The rapid creation of prototypes can result in systems that have not been completely tested or documented or that are technically inadequate for a production environment.

   Developing an information system using an application software package eliminates the need for writing software programs when developing an information system. Using a software package reduces the amount of design, testing, installation, and maintenance work required to build a system. Application software packages are helpful if a firm does not have the internal information systems staff or financial resources to custom develop a system. To meet an organization's unique requirements, packages may require extensive modifications that can substantially raise development costs.

   End-user development is the development of information systems by end users, either alone or with minimal assistance from information systems specialists. End-user-developed systems can be created rapidly and informally using fourth-generation software tools. The primary benefits of end-user development are improved requirements determination; reduced application backlog; and increased end-user participation in, and control of, the systems development process. However, end-user development, in conjunction with distributed computing, has introduced new organizational risks by propagating information systems and data resources that do not necessarily meet quality assurance standards and that are not easily controlled by traditional means.

   Outsourcing consists of using an external vendor to build (or operate) a firm's information systems. The work is done by the vendor rather than by the organization's internal information systems staff. Outsourcing can save application development costs or enable firms to develop applications without an internal information systems staff. However, firms risk losing control over their information systems and becoming too dependent on external vendors.

Selection of a systems-building approach can have a big impact on the time, cost, and end product of systems development. Managers should be aware of the strengths and weaknesses of each systems-building approach and the types of problems for which each is best suited. The impact of application software packages and of outsourcing should be carefully evaluated before they are selected because these approaches give organizations less control over the systems-building process.

4. *Compare alternative methodologies for modeling systems.*

The two principal methodologies for modeling and designing information systems are structured methodologies and object-oriented development. Structured methodologies focus on modeling processes and data separately. The data flow diagram is the principal tool for structured analysis and the structure chart is the principal tool for representing structured software design. Object-oriented development models a system as a collection of objects that combine processes and data. Object-oriented modeling is based on the concepts of class and inheritance.

5. *Identify and describe new approaches for system-building in the digital firm era.*

Businesses today are often required to build e-commerce and e-business applications very rapidly to remain competitive. New systems are likely to have more interorganizational requirements and processes than in the past. Companies are turning to rapid application design, joint application design (JAD), and reusable software components to improve the systems development process. Rapid application development (RAD) uses object-oriented software, visual programming, prototyping, and fourth-generation tools for very rapid creation of systems. Component-based development expedites application development by grouping objects into suites of software components that can be combined to create large-scale business applications.

Web services enable firms to obtain software application components delivered over the Internet for building new systems or integrating existing systems. Web services provide a common set of standards that enable organizations to link their systems regardless of their technology platform through standard plug and play architecture.

Key Terms

Acceptance testing	Pilot study
Automation	Postimplementation audit
Benchmarking	Process specifications
Business process management (BPM)	Production
Business process reengineering	Programming
Component-based development	Prototype
Computer-aided software engineering (CASE)	Prototyping
Conversion	Query languages
Customization	Rapid application development (RAD)
Data flow diagram (DFD)	Rationalization of procedures
Direct cutover	Request for Proposal (RFP)
Documentation	Six sigma
End-user development	Structure chart
End-user interface	Structured
Feasibility study	Systems analysis
Fourth-generation languages	Systems design
Information requirements	Systems development
Iterative	Systems life cycle
Joint application design (JAD)	System testing
Maintenance	Test plan
Object	Testing
Object-oriented development	Total quality management (TQM)
Paradigm shift	Unit testing
Parallel strategy	Work flow management
Phased approach	

Review Questions

1. Describe each of the four kinds of organizational change that can be promoted with information technology.

2. What is business process reengineering? What steps are required to make it effective? How does it differ from business process management?

3. How do information systems support process changes that promote quality in an organization?

4. What is the difference between systems analysis and systems design? What activities does each process comprise?

5. What are information requirements? Why are they difficult to determine correctly?

6. Why is the testing stage of systems development so important? Name and describe the three types of testing for an information system.

7. What role do programming, conversion, production, and maintenance play in systems development?

8. Compare object-oriented and traditional structured approaches for modeling and designing systems.

9. What is the traditional systems life cycle? Describe each of its steps and its advantages and disadvantages for systems building.

10. What do we mean by information system prototyping? What are its benefits and limitations? List and describe the steps in the prototyping process.

11. What is an application software package? What are the advantages and disadvantages of developing information systems based on software packages?

12. What is meant by end-user development? What are its advantages and disadvantages? Name some policies and procedures for managing end-user development.

13. Under what circumstances should outsourcing be used for building information systems?

14. What is rapid application development (RAD)? How can it help system builders?

15. How can component-based development and Web services help firms build and enhance their information systems?

Discussion Questions

1. Why is selecting a systems development approach an important business decision? Who should participate in the selection process?

2. Some have said that the best way to reduce systems development costs is to use application software packages or fourth-generation tools. Do you agree? Why or why not?

Video Case

You will find a video case illustrating some of the concepts in this chapter on the Laudon Web site and Student CD-ROM along with questions to help you analyze the case.

Teamwork: Preparing Web Site Design Specifications

With three or four of your classmates, select a system described in this text that uses the Web. Review the Web site for the system you select. Use what you have learned from the Web site and the description in this book to prepare a report describing some of the design specifications for the system you select. If possible, use electronic presentation software to present your findings to the class.

REFERENCES

Agarwal, Ritu, Jayesh Prasad, Mohan Tanniru, and John Lynch. "Risks of Rapid Application Development." *Communications of the ACM* 43, no. 11 (November 2000).

Albert, Terri C., Paulo B. Goes, and Alok Gupta. "GIST: A Model for Design and Management of Content and Interactivity of Customer-Centric Web Sites." MIS Quarterly 28, no. 2 (June 2004).

Arinze, Bay and Murugan Anandarajan. "A Framework for Using OO Mapping Methods to Rapidly Configure ERP Systems." *Communications of the ACM 46*, no.2 (February 2003).

Barthelemy, Jerome. "The Hidden Costs of IT Outsourcing." *Sloan Management Review* (Spring 2001).

Boehm, Barry W. "Understanding and Controlling Software Costs." *IEEE Transactions on Software Engineering* 14, no. 10 (October 1988).

Champy, James A. *X-Engineering the Corporation: Reinventing Your Business in the Digital Age.* New York: Warner Books (2002).

Curbera, Francisco, Rania Khalaf, Nirmal Mukhi, Stefan Tai, and Sanjiva Weerawarana. "The Next Step in Web Services." *Communications of the ACM 46*, no 10 (October 2003).

Davenport, Thomas H., and James E. Short. "The New Industrial Engineering: Information Technology and Business Process Redesign." *Sloan Management Review* 31, no. 4 (Summer 1990).

Davidson, Elisabeth J. "Technology Frames and Framing: A Socio-Cognitive Investigation of Requirements Determination." *MIS Quarterly* 26, no. 4 (December 2002).

Den Hengst, Marielle and Gert-Jan DeVreede. "Collaborative Business Engineering: A Decade of Lessons from the Field." *Journal of Management Information Systems* 20, no. 4 (Spring 2004).

Earl, Michael and Bushra Khan. "E-Commerce Is Changing the Face of IT." *Sloan Management Review,*(Fall 2001)

El Sawy, Omar A. *Redesigning Enterprise Processes for E-Business.* McGraw-Hill (2001).

Feeny, David, Mary Lacity, and Leslie P. Willcocks. "Taking the Measure of Outsourcing Providers." *MIT Sloan Management Review* 46, No. 3 (Spring 2005).

Ferris, C. and J. Farrell. "What Are Web Services." *Communications of the ACM*, Vol. 46, No. 6 (2003).

Fingar, Peter. "Component-Based Frameworks for E-Commerce." *Communications of the ACM* 43, no. 10 (October 2000).

Gefen, David and Catherine M. Ridings. "Implementation Team Responsiveness and User Evaluation of Customer Relationship Management: A Quasi-Experimental Design Study of Social Exchange Theory." *Journal of Management Information Systems* 19, no. 1 (Summer 2002).

Gemino, Andrew and Yair Wand. "Evaluating Modeling Techniques Based on Models of Learning." *Communications of the ACM* 46, no. 10 (October 2003).

Grant, Delvin. "A Wider View of Business Process Engineering." *Communications of the ACM* 45, no. 2 (February 2002).

Grunbacher, Paul, Michael Halling, Stefan Biffl, Hasan Kitapci, and Barry W. Boehm. "Integrating Collaborative Processes and Quality Assurance Techniques: Experiences from Requirements Negotiation." *Journal of Management Information Systems* 20, no. 4 (Spring 2004).

Hammer, Michael, and James Champy. *Reengineering the Corporation.* New York: HarperCollins Publishers (1993).

Hammer, Michael. "Reengineering Work: Don't Automate, Obliterate." *Harvard Business Review* (July–August 1990).

Hammer, Michael. "Process Management and the Future of Six Sigma." *Sloan Management Review* 43, no.2 (Winter 2002)

Hickey, Ann M. and Alan M. Davis. "A Unified Model of Requirements Elicitation." *Journal of Management Information Systems* 20, no. 4 (Spring 2004)

Hirscheim, Rudy and Mary Lacity. "The Myths and Realities of Information Technology Insourcing." *Communications of the ACM* 43, no. 2 (February 2000).

Hoffer, Jeffrey, Joey George, and Joseph Valacich. *Modern Systems Analysis and Design*, 3rd ed. Upper Saddle River, NJ: Prentice-Hall (2002)

Ivari, Juhani, Rudy Hirscheim, and Heinz K. Klein. "A Dynamic Framework for Classifying Information Systems Development Methodologies and Approaches." *Journal of Management Information Systems* 17, no. 3 (Winter 2000–2001).

Iyer, Bala, Jim Freedman, Mark Gaynor, and George Wyner. "Web Services: Enabling Dynamic Business Networks." *Communications of the Association for Information Systems* 11 (2003).

Kendall, Kenneth E., and Julie E. Kendall. *Systems Analysis and Design*, 5th ed. Upper Saddle River, NJ: Prentice Hall (2002).

Klein, Gary, James J. Jiang, and Debbie B. Tesch. "Wanted: Project Teams with a Blend of IS Professional Orientations." *Communications of the ACM* 45, no. 6 (June 2002).

Lamont, Judith. "BPM: from the user's perspective." www.kmworld.com accessed November 1, 2006.

Lee, Jae Nam and Young-Gul Kim. "Effect of Partnership Quality on IS Outsourcing Success." *Journal of Management Information Systems* 15, no. 4 (Spring 1999).

Lee, Jae-Nam, Minh Q. Huynh, Ron Chi-wai Kwok, and Shih-Ming Pi. "IT Outsourcing Evolution-Past Present, and Future." *Communications of the ACM* 46, no. 5 (May 2003).

Lee, Jae Nam, Shaila M. Miranda, and Yong-Mi Kim. "IT Outsourcing Strategies: Universalistic, Contingency, and Configurational Explanations of Success." *Information Systems Research* 15, no. 2 (June 2004).

Levina, Natalia and Jeanne W. Ross. "From the Vendor's Perspective: Exploring the Value Proposition in Information Technology Outsourcing." *MIS Quarterly* 27, no. 3 (September 2003).

Limayem, Moez, Mohamed Khalifa, and Wynne W. Chin. "Case Tools Usage and Impact on System Development Performance." Journal of Organizational Computing and Electronic Commerce 14, no. 3 (2004).

Lunt, Penny. "Well-Oiled Machines. BPM Projects Point to Success." *Transform Magazine* (April 2003).

Martin, James. *Application Development without Programmers.* Englewood Cliffs, NJ: Prentice Hall (1982).

Mazzucchelli, Louis. "Structured Analysis Can Streamline Software Design." *Computerworld* (December 9, 1985).

Nerson, Jean-Marc. "Applying Object-Oriented Analysis and Design." *Communications of the ACM* 35, no. 9 (September 1992).

Nidumolu, Sarma R. and Mani Subramani. "The Matrix of Control: Combining Process and Structure Approaches to Managing Software Development." *Journal of Management Information Systems* 20, no. 4 (Winter 2004).

Peffers, Ken and Charles E. Gengler. "How to Identify New High-Payoff Information Systems for the Organization." *Communications of the ACM* 41, no.1 (January 2003).

Phillips, James and Dan Foody. "Building a Foundation for Web Services." *EAI Journal* (March 2002).

Pitts, Mitzi G. and Glenn J. Browne. "Stopping Behavior of Systems Analysts During Information Requirements Elicitation." *Journal of Management Information Systems* 21, no. 1 (Summer 2004).

Prahalad, C. K. and M.S.. Krishnan. "Synchronizing Strategy and Information Technology." *Sloan Management Review* 43, no. 4 (Summer 2002).

Ravichandran, T. and Marcus A. Rothenberger. "Software Reuse Strategies and Component Markets." *Communications of the ACM* 46, no. 8 (August 2003).

Sabherwahl, Rajiv. "The Role of Trust in IS Outsourcing Development Projects." *Communications of the ACM* 42, no. 2 (February 1999).

Scott, Louise, Levente Horvath, and Donald Day. "Characterizing CASE Constraints." *Communications of the ACM* 43, no. 11 (November 2000).

Shank, Michael E., Andrew C. Boynton, and Robert W. Zmud. "Critical Success Factor Analysis as a Methodology for MIS Planning." *MIS Quarterly* (June 1985).

Sharma, Srinarayan and Arun Rai. "CASE Deployment in IS Organizations." *Communications of the ACM* 43, no. 1 (January 2000).

Sircar, Sumit, Sridhar P. Nerur, and Radhakanta Mahapatra. "Revolution or Evolution? A Comparison of Object-Oriented and Structured Systems Development Methods." *MIS Quarterly* 25, no. 4 (December 2001).

Smith, Howard and Peter Fingar. *Business Process Management: The Third Wave* Tampa, Florida: Meghan-Kiffer Press (2002).

Sprott, David. "Componentizing the Enterprise Application Packages." *Communications of the ACM* 43, no. 3 (April 2000).

Swanson, E. Burton and Enrique Dans. "System Life Expectancy and the Maintenance Effort: Exploring their Equilibration." *MIS Quarterly* 24, no. 2 (June 2000).

Tam, Kar Yan and Kai Lung Hui. "A Choice Model for the Selection of Computer Vendors and Its Empirical Estimation" *Journal of Management Information Systems* 17, no. 4 (Spring 2001).

Turetken, Ozgur, David Schuff, Ramesh Sharda, and Terence T. Ow. "Supporting Systems Analysis and Design Through Fisheye Views." *Communications of the ACM* 47, no. 9 (September 2004).

Van Den Heuvel, Willem-Jan and Zakaria Maamar. "Moving Toward a Framework to Compose Intelligent Web Services." *Communications of the ACM* 46, no. 10 (October 2003).

Vitharana, Padmal. "Risks and Challenges of Component-Based Software Development." *Communications of the ACM* 46, no. 8 (August 2003).

Watad, Mahmoud M. and Frank J. DiSanzo. "Case Study: The Synergism of Telecommuting and Office Automation." *Sloan Management Review* 41, no. 2 (Winter 2000).

Weinberg Allen and William Forrest. "Infrastructure's Outer Limits." *Optimize Magazine* (April 2006).

Wulf, Volker and Matthias Jarke. "The Economics of End-User Development." *Communications of the ACM* 47, no. 9 (September 2004).

Yourdon, Edward, and L. L. Constantine. *Structured Design*. New York: Yourdon Press (1978).

Zachman, J. A. "Business Systems Planning and Business Information Control Study: A Comparison." *IBM Systems Journal* 21 (1982).

Can the U.S. Army Reserve Pay Soldiers Correctly?
CASE STUDY

When U.S. Army Reserve Staff Sergeant Ryan Kelly returned to Abilene, Texas, from Iraq, one of the things he had to do, aside from recovering from an amputated lower right leg, was pay the Army over $2,200. A notice on his pay stub stated that the Army had overpaid him for 22 days. Staff Sgt. Kelly learned that even though he earned a medical retirement at the beginning of August 2004, the Army continued to pay him as an active soldier, at a higher rate of pay, for the remainder of the month. The money, as always, was deposited into his bank account automatically. Now the Army wanted it back.

Staff Sgt. Kelly spent the better part of 18 months battling red tape in order to clarify what had happened and pay back the money he owed. Even if Staff Sgt. Kelly had been in a position to notice the change in his automatically deposited wages, he wouldn't have necessarily known that it was a mistake. Soldiers' pay could be adjusted frequently depending on where they were serving and what level of danger they were facing at a particular time.

The Army did not deny that its payroll systems were flawed. It conducted an audit in the fall of 2005 that showed payment irregularities for 14 percent of the 24,000 soldiers that had been wounded in Iraq and Afghanistan or evacuated for medical reasons. The population included soldiers from the Army, the Reserve, and the National Guard. Some had not received enough pay, some received too much, and in some cases there was simply an indication that more evidence was required to see if there was a problem. The Government Accountability Office (GAO) said that only some of the soldiers who were overpaid received notification; others simply stopped getting money. The GAO reported that at the time of the audit, the Army had logged $1.5 million worth of overpayments to 1,300 soldiers wounded or killed in Iraq and Afghanistan. In the case of Staff Sgt. Kelly, the pay systems were not up to date with the latest information regarding his status.

The GAO also found that non-injured soldiers were regularly receiving inaccurate paychecks, the result of reaching different stages of their deployments and redeployments. The GAO uncovered payroll and personnel system problems throughout the Army's operations, but it paid particular attention to those affecting the Reserves.

Before 2004, the Defense Finance and Accounting Service (DFAS) had been using a pay system called the Defense Joint Military Pay System (DJMS), which had been in place since the Vietnam War. DJMS actually consisted of separate systems for active duty soldiers and reserves. The two systems did not work together easily. The DJMS-Reserve Component was responsible for payroll management. Salaries, bonuses, and benefits for 200,000 reservists originated from this custom-built payroll application. But the payroll management system needed information from the personnel system, known as the Regional Level Application Software system, and the two systems were not well integrated.

Reservists normally received payment for performing weekend drills and for their two weeks of active duty per year. However, when a few hundred thousand of them were called up to active duty, the adjustments in their pay often necessitated manual updates to the system, which increased the chance of errors. A GAO study determined that over 90 percent of soldiers in units that were mobilized in 2002 and 2003 experienced some kind of pay error that was primarily due to the lack of compatibility between the payroll and personnel systems.

The Web-based Regional Level Application Software system tracked when reservists participated in their drills, which skills they learned, and where and how long they were called up for combat duty. The payroll system relied on the personnel system's data, including soldier deployment and marital status, to process pay transactions. The integration of the two systems improved over the years, but never really reached an acceptable level. The computer language used to write DJMS dated back almost 40 years.

Making changes was complicated by the age of the system, the number of patches that already had been applied, and a lack of documentation. The system contained millions of lines of programming code, and without proper documentation, changing any of them to perform a fix had the potential to damage the system elsewhere. Furthermore, in updating payroll software, DFAS had to account for over 1,000 different options in pay rate, entitlements, and allowances that were available to soldiers. Even after the update, these circumstances frequently called for manually updating records, which introduced more opportunities for data-entry errors. The software lacked even the flexibility to follow changes in state tax rates, which had to be programmed manually at a cost of 12 to 18 months. The lag time for such updates often forced soldiers to file corrected tax returns because their original W-2 forms were inaccurate.

In 2006, the Army was still waiting for a new, all-encompassing, integrated armed forces payment system called the Defense Integrated Military Human Resources System (DIMHRS). The system received over $300 million in funding from the Defense Department going back to 1998 but remained three years behind schedule. The delay was attributed to multiple agencies having influence on management of the project and inconsistent support from senior management. Paul Brinkley, deputy undersecretary of Defense for business transformation, noted that "The turnover in leadership created a lack of awareness and understanding of the goals of the program."

Once operational, DIMHRS would manage all personnel and pay processes and share its data with 500 defense applications. The architects of the system selected Oracle/PeopleSoft software to replace 79 different legacy systems in use throughout the U.S. military with one simplified and unified system. A simpler system decreased the number of opportunities for errors to be introduced.

The Army struggled to get DIMHRS up and running. The 150,000 reservists that were incrementally recalled first for domestic service following the 9/11 terrorist attacks and then for service abroad represented the largest Reserve mobilization since World War II. The systems at the disposal of DFAS were capable of handling changes to pay rates for an entire unit via a "mass update." However, changes in pay were not always so straightforward. Soldiers were eligible for certain entitlements, such as $100 per month for hazardous duty or $225 for hostile-fire proximity. Unfortunately, the system could only handle pay increases for periods of 30 days and deleted the entitlements at the end of each month.

DFAS relied on workarounds to solve these types of problems. For example, a finance office in Kuwait maintained the names of soldiers who were eligible for hazardous-duty pay in a Microsoft Access database. The office then uploaded the data to the payroll system in the United States monthly for a massive update. This type of fix proved to be unreliable because some soldiers received entitlement pay after they had been moved from hazardous duty. Unit commanders in the combat zone simply could not always report the changes in a timely manner. Even reservists who were just being mobilized sometimes had their new entitlements shipped to the domestic pay center as paper printouts. The approach encouraged multiple data entries, delays, and manual processing instead of automated processing, all of which created the potential for mistakes.

In 2004, the DFAS rolled out an interim solution called Forward Compatible Payroll (FCP) until a more comprehensive systems solution could be completed. The specific improvements of FCP included a clearer Leave and Earnings Statement for soldiers, instantaneous updating of pay records, and better capabilities for updating state tax rates. The FCP phased rollout was scheduled to begin in March 2005 with the Army Reserve and National Guard, and over the course of a year extend to the active duty Army, the Air Force, and then the Navy Department.

FCP provided more automation for the mobilization process for soldiers called up for active duty. A pay administrator could use a Web browser to review mobilization orders in the personnel system and access and update files in the personnel database without duplicating the data entry for the mobilized soldiers. The mobilization application requested additional information from the administrator, such as the beginning and ending dates of deployment for each soldier, before setting the pay rate for each and adding the appropriate entitlements.

After the pay rate was set, the process required a unit commander to approve and sign a hard copy of the mobilization order. Only then were the data transmitted in a nightly batch to a Microsoft SQL Server 2000 database at Reserve headquarters at Fort McPherson, Georgia. The SQL server formatted the data so that the Reserve payroll system could process them. The data were uploaded to a local server at a pay processing center, where staff members used Web browser software to review the pay records. Soldier tour of duty dates and pay data were then exported to the Reserve payroll system, which then paid the soldiers.

After building this system, the Army achieved a 97-percent success rate in paying soldiers properly within the first month of their deployment. Misfires occurred when soldiers already had an existing pay status or when order inputs lagged due to human error. Upgrading the personnel system progressed slowly because entitlements do not remain static, adding to the complexity of establishing rules for business during wartime.

Indeed, the changes built into the payroll and personnel systems were intended to be temporary. DIMHRS should be capable of replacing over 30 legacy applications in the Army branch of the Armed Forces alone. However, eight years after its conception, the integrated system has been halted while it undergoes a business requirements assessment. DIMHRS is only one segment of a large-scale business systems modernization effort at the Defense Department. Deployment is now scheduled for 2008. When DIMHRS finally rolls out, it will be the biggest deployment of human resources software on the globe. The Oracle/PeopleSoft application will manage the salaries of 3 million soldiers and civilians on the payrolls of the Armed Forces. Northrop Grumman received a $281 million contract to lead the systems integration project through 2013. If all goes according to plan, the integrated system will eliminate redundant data entries, simplify all processes related to personnel and payroll, and greatly reduce the number of mistakes that find their way through to pay stubs.

Sources: Elizabeth Bennett, "IT Integration: The Army's Pay Misstep," *Baseline Magazine*, May 6, 2006; John Moore, "BearingPoint Works DFAS Project," FCW.com, May 23, 2005; Tom Philpott, "New Military Pay System Being Readied for Phase-in," USAWOA Online, November 3, 2004.

CASE STUDY QUESTIONS

1. Write a systems analysis report about the U.S. Army pay system. What have been the problems with existing systems? What management, organization, and technology factors caused the problems? What was the impact of these problems? What are the objectives and information requirements of a new systems solution?

2. As part of your report, diagram the Forward Compatible Payroll business process for paying Army reservists. How should this process be improved?

3. Describe the role of end users and technical specialists in analyzing the problem and developing a solution.

Project Management: Establishing the Business Value of Systems and Managing Change

From *Management Information Systems: Managing the Digital Firm, 10/e*. Kenneth C. Laudon, Jane P. Laudon.

Project Management: Establishing the Business Value of Systems and Managing Change

A. G. Edwards is one of the oldest and largest full-service retail brokerages in the United States, offering securities and commodities brokerage, asset management, trust services, mutual funds, insurance, and investment banking through offices nationwide. It's in a very information-intensive and competitive industry where companies are expected to continually enhance existing systems and bring new systems on board to support new products and services.

When John Parker became A.G. Edwards's chief technology officer (CTO), the company's information technology costs were too high, and information systems projects dragged on for years. Most of these projects cost 54 percent more and took 54 percent longer than original estimates. One to two percent were never completed, and the cost of writing them off took a toll on the company's bottom line. In 2002 alone, the company wrote off $46 million in software investments.

Parker, who had experience with fast-track projects as Northwest Airlines vice president of information services from 1999 to 2001, was charged with turning A.G. Edwards's project management record around. Parker enlisted project management expert Ed Pilewski to implement a "standard plan framework" for monitoring, measuring, and reporting on project progress.

The framework lists 25 high-level activities for managers to track during the course of an information systems project, such as performing requirements analysis and constructing test plans. It also highlights interdependencies between systems, such as new interfaces that might be required for a new system that exchanges data with other systems. The framework also identifies the time each information systems group will work on a specific project each month. Managers have the flexibility to detail the tasks that must be performed within each activity and how they will be carried out.

Software from Primavera provides project managers, planners, and developers with dashboards and progress reports on each project. They can use this tool to compare original estimates with actual costs, determine if milestones have been met, list activities that require completion, or view all projects assigned to a specific information systems group.

But good project management methods and tools are not enough to guarantee success. To be used effectively, they require strong leadership and cooperative relationships between information systems and end user managers.

Parker worked with A.G. Edwards senior executives to identify the most important projects and to provide all IT managers with training to improve confidence and leadership skills. He staged a series of quarterly meetings to teach line managers how to work with budgets, provide vision,

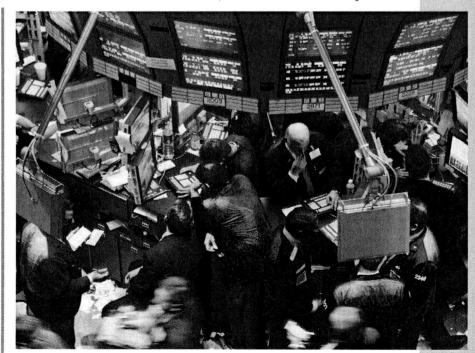

Photo courtesy of Getty Images, Inc.

and express opinions honestly yet diplomatically. He asked project managers receptive to new ideas to participate in pilot projects using the standard plan framework and then promote the methodology among their colleagues. He measured project success rates and published the results in quarterly reports to senior management.

It would appear that Parker has succeeded. In 2006, A.G. Edwards's project success rate (measured by the number of projects completed within time and budget that deliver the expected business value) soared to 88 percent. There are no longer any failed projects that must be written off. By managing its IT projects more effectively, the company reduced IT and telecom costs from $295 million in 2002 to $242 million in 2005.

Sources: Meridith Levinson, "When Failure Is Not an Option," CIO Magazine, June 1, 2006; "P.M.O. Success Story: A.G. Edwards Case Study," www. elounge.eproject.com, accessed June 14, 2006; and www.agedwards.com, accessed June 14, 2006.

One of the principal challenges posed by information systems is ensuring they can deliver genuine business benefits. There is a very high failure rate among information systems projects because organizations have incorrectly assessed their business value or because firms have failed to manage the organizational change surrounding the introduction of new technology.

John Parker and his team at A.G. Edwards realized this and took special pains to prepare managers and employees for the changes brought about by new systems.

The chapter-opening diagram calls attention to important points raised by this case and this chapter. A.G. Edwards is in an information-intensive industry where it must continually build new systems and enhance existing systems to remain competitive. Its inability to manage its information systems projects raised operating costs and prevented the company from realizing a good return on its IT investments. The company was able to reduce project costs and completion times by using better project management planning and monitoring methods, project management software tools, and by improving the project management skills of its managers. Strong management leadership and better communication between information systems specialists and end users were also essential.

HEADS UP

During your career, you will undoubtedly be asked to work on information systems projects to solve an important challenge for your firm. Whether the project entails building a new information system or enhancing an existing system, you will need to know how to measure the business benefits of these investments, and how to make sure that these systems work successfully in your organization. The success of your project will depend on how well it is managed.

- If your career is in finance and accounting, you will help systems builders use financial models to justify investments in information systems projects.

- If your career is in human resources, you will be working with employees to help them adjust to new job responsibilities, reporting relationships, and other changes associated with new systems.

- If your career is in information systems, you will be evaluating the technology for new system projects and working with project management tools and software to document and monitor project plans.

- If your career is in manufacturing, production or operations management, you will participate in projects to develop or enhance supply chain management systems and enterprise resource planning systems. These systems can provide significant benefits, but they are among the most difficult to implement successfully because they require major changes to the organization as well as new technology.

- If your career is in sales and marketing, you will be working on projects to develop or enhance customer relationship management (CRM) systems. CRM systems provide both tangible and intangible benefits, but are challenging to implement because they typically require extensive business process change.

---

1 THE IMPORTANCE OF PROJECT MANAGEMENT

There is a very high failure rate among information systems projects. In nearly every organization, information systems projects take much more time and money to implement than originally anticipated, or the completed system does not work properly. When an information system fails to work properly or costs too much to develop, companies may not realize any benefit from their information system investment, and the system may not be able to solve the problems for which it was intended. The development of a new system must be carefully managed and orchestrated, and the way a project is executed is likely to be the most important factor influencing its outcome (Wallace and Keil, 2004). That's why it's essential to have some knowledge about how to manage information systems projects and about how and why they succeed or fail.

RUNAWAY PROJECTS AND SYSTEM FAILURE

How badly are projects managed? On average, private sector projects are underestimated by one-half in terms of budget and time required to deliver the complete system promised in the system plan. A very large number of projects are delivered with missing functionality (promised for delivery in later versions). The Standish Group consultancy, which monitors IT project success rates, found that only 29 percent of all technology investments were completed on time, on budget, and with all features and functions originally specified (Levinson, 2006). Between 30 and 40 percent of all software projects are "runaway" projects that far exceed the original schedule and budget projections and fail to perform as originally specified (Keil, Mann, and Rai, 2000).

As illustrated in Figure 1, a systems development project without proper management will most likely suffer these consequences:

- Costs that greatly exceed budgets
- Unexpected time slippage
- Technical performance that is less than expected
- Failure to obtain anticipated benefits

The systems produced by failed information projects are often not used in the way they were intended, or they are not used at all. Users often have to develop parallel manual systems to make these systems work.

The actual design of the system may fail to capture essential business requirements or improve organizational performance. Information may not be provided quickly enough to be helpful; it may be in a format that is impossible to digest and use; or it may represent the wrong pieces of data.

The way in which nontechnical business users must interact with the system may be excessively complicated and discouraging. A system may be designed with a poor user interface. The **user interface** is the part of the system with which end users interact. For example, an online input form or data entry screen may be so poorly arranged that no one wants to submit data or request information. System outputs may be displayed in a format that is too difficult to comprehend (Spier and Morris, 2003).

Web sites may discourage visitors from exploring further if the Web pages are cluttered and poorly arranged, if users cannot easily find the information they are seeking, or if it takes too long to access and display the Web page on the user's computer.

Additionally, the data in the system may have a high level of inaccuracy or inconsistency. The information in certain fields may be erroneous or

FIGURE 1   CONSEQUENCES OF POOR PROJECT MANAGEMENT

Cost overruns
Time slippage
Technical shortfalls impairing performance
Failure to obtain anticipated benefits

Without proper management, a systems development project takes longer to complete and most often exceeds the allocated budget. The resulting information system most likely is technically inferior and may not be able to demonstrate any benefits to the organization. Great ideas for systems often flounder on the rocks of implementation.

ambiguous, or it may not be organized properly for business purposes. Information required for a specific business function may be inaccessible because the data are incomplete.

PROJECT MANAGEMENT OBJECTIVES

A **project** is a planned series of related activities for achieving a specific business objective. Information systems projects include the development of new information systems, enhancing existing systems, or projects for replacing or upgrading the firm's information technology (IT) infrastructure.

Project management refers to the application of knowledge, skills, tools, and techniques to achieve specific targets within specified budget and time constraints. Project management activities include planning the work, assessing risk, estimating resources required to accomplish the work, organizing the work, acquiring human and material resources, assigning tasks, directing activities, controlling project execution, reporting progress, and analyzing the results. As in other areas of business, project management for information systems must deal with five major variables: scope, time, cost, quality, and risk.

Scope defines what work is or is not included in a project. For example, the scope of project for a new order processing system might include new modules for inputting orders and transmitting them to production and accounting but not any changes to related accounts receivable, manufacturing, distribution, or inventory control systems. Project management defines all the work required to complete a project successfully, and should ensure that the scope of a project not expand beyond what was originally intended.

Time is the amount of time required to complete the project. Project management typically establishes the amount of time required to complete major components of a project. Each of these components is further broken down into activities and tasks. Project management tries to determine the time required to complete each task and establish a schedule for completing the work.

Cost is based on the time to complete a project multiplied by the cost of human resources required to complete the project. Information systems project costs also include the cost of hardware, software, and work space. Project management develops a budget for the project and monitors ongoing project expenses.

Quality is an indicator of how well the end result of a project satisfies the objectives specified by management. The quality of information systems projects usually boils down to improved organizational performance and decision making. Quality also considers the accuracy and timeliness of information produced by the new system and ease of use.

Risk refers to potential problems that would threaten the success of a project. These potential problems might prevent a project from achieving its objectives by increasing time and cost, lowering the quality of project outputs, or preventing the project from being completed altogether. Section 4 describes the most important risk factors for information systems.

2   SELECTING PROJECTS

Companies typically are presented with many different projects for solving problems and improving performance. There are far more ideas for systems projects than there are resources. Firms will need to select from this group the projects that promise the greatest benefit to the business. Obviously the firm's overall business strategy should drive project selection.

MANAGEMENT STRUCTURE FOR INFORMATION SYSTEMS PROJECTS

Figure 2 shows the elements of a management structure for information systems projects in a large corporation. It helps ensure that the most important systems projects are given priority.

At the apex of this structure is the corporate strategic planning group and the information system steering committee. The corporate strategic planning group is responsible for developing the firm's strategic plan, which may require the development of new systems.

The information systems steering committee is the senior management group with responsibility for systems development and operation. It is composed of department heads from both end-user and information systems areas. The steering committee reviews and approves plans for systems in all divisions, seeks to coordinate and integrate systems, and occasionally becomes involved in selecting specific information systems projects.

The project team is supervised by a project management group composed of information systems managers and end-user managers responsible for overseeing several specific information systems projects. The project team is directly responsible for the individual systems project. It consists of systems analysts, specialists from the relevant end-user business areas, application programmers, and perhaps database specialists. The mix of skills and the size of the project team depend on the specific nature of the system solution.

FIGURE 2   MANAGEMENT CONTROL OF SYSTEMS PROJECTS

Each level of management in the hierarchy is responsible for specific aspects of systems projects, and this structure helps give priority to the most important systems projects for the organization.

LINKING SYSTEMS PROJECTS TO THE BUSINESS PLAN

In order to identify the information systems projects that will deliver the most business value, organizations need to develop an **information systems plan** that supports their overall business plan and in which strategic systems are incorporated into top-level planning. The plan serves as a road map indicating the direction of systems development (the purpose of the plan), the rationale, the current systems/situation, new developments to consider, the management strategy, the implementation plan, and the budget (see Table 1).

The plan contains a statement of corporate goals and specifies how information technology will support the attainment of those goals. The report shows how general goals will be achieved by specific systems projects. It identifies specific target dates and milestones that can be used later to evaluate the plan's progress in terms of how many objectives were actually attained in the time frame specified in the plan. The plan indicates the key management decisions concerning hardware acquisition; telecommunications; centralization/decentralization of authority, data, and hardware; and required organizational change. Organizational changes are also usually described, including management and employee training requirements; recruiting efforts; changes in business processes; and changes in authority, structure, or management practice.

In order to plan effectively, firms need to inventory and document all of their information system applications and IT infrastructure components. For projects in which benefits involve improved decision making, managers should try to identify the decision improvements which would provide the greatest additional value to the firm. They should then develop a set of metrics to quantify the value of more timely and precise information on the outcome of the decision.

ENTERPRISE ANALYSIS AND CRITICAL SUCCESS FACTORS

To develop an effective information systems plan, the organization must have a clear understanding of both its long- and short-term information requirements. Two principal methodologies for establishing the essential information requirements of the organization as a whole are enterprise analysis and critical success factors.

Enterprise Analysis (Business Systems Planning)

Enterprise analysis (also called *business systems planning*) argues that the firm's information requirements can be understood only by examining the entire organization in terms of organizational units, functions, processes, and data elements. Enterprise analysis can help identify the key entities and attributes of the organization's data.

The central method used in the enterprise analysis approach is to take a large sample of managers and ask them how they use information, where they get their information, what their objectives are, how they make decisions, and what their data needs are. The results of this large survey of managers are aggregated into subunits, functions, processes, and data matrices. Data elements are organized into logical application groups—groups of data elements that support related sets of organizational processes.

TABLE 1 INFORMATION SYSTEMS PLAN

1. Purpose of the Plan
   Overview of plan contents
   Current business organization and future organization
   Key business processes
   Management strategy

2. Strategic Business Plan Rationale
   Current situation
   Current business organization
   Changing environments
   Major goals of the business plan
   Firm's strategic plan

3. Current Systems
   Major systems supporting business functions and processes
   Current infrastructure capabilities
      Hardware
      Software
      Database
      Telecommunications and Internet
   Difficulties meeting business requirements
   Anticipated future demands

4. New Developments
   New system projects
      Project descriptions
      Business rationale
      Applications' role in strategy
   New infrastructure capabilities required
      Hardware
      Software
      Database
      Telecommunications and Internet

5. Management Strategy
   Acquisition plans
   Milestones and timing
   Organizational realignment
   Internal reorganization
   Management controls
   Major training initiatives
   Personnel strategy

6. Implementation Plan
   Anticipated difficulties in implementation
   Progress reports

7. Budget Requirements
   Requirements
   Potential savings
   Financing
   Acquisition cycle

Figure 3 is an output of enterprise analysis conducted by the Social Security Administration as part of a massive systems redevelopment effort. It shows what information is required to support a particular process, which processes create the data, and which use them. The shaded boxes in the figure indicate a logical application group. In this case, actuarial estimates, agency plans, and budget data are created in the planning process, suggesting that an information system should be built to support planning.

The weakness of enterprise analysis is that it produces an enormous amount of data that is expensive to collect and difficult to analyze. The questions frequently focus not on management's critical objectives and where information is needed but rather on what existing information is used. The result is a tendency to automate whatever exists rather than developing entirely new approaches to conducting business.

FIGURE 3   PROCESS/DATA CLASS MATRIX

Data classes (columns, left to right): 1 Actuarial estimates, 2 Agency plans, 3 Budget, 4 Program regulations/policy, 5 Administrative regulations/policy, 6 Labor agreements, 7 Data standards, 8 Procedures, 9 Automated systems documentation, 10 Educational media, 11 Public agreements, 12 Intergovernmental agreements, 13 Grants, 14 External, 15 Exchange control, 16 Administrative accounts, 17 Program expenditures, 18 Audit reports, 19 Organization/position, 20 Employee identification, 21 Recruitment/placement, 22 Complaints/grievances, 23 Training resources, 24 Security, 25 Equipment utilization, 26 Space utilization, 27 Supplies utilization, 28 Workload schedules, 29 Work measurement, 30 Enumeration I.D., 31 Enumeration control, 32 Earnings, 33 Employer I.D., 34 Earnings control, 35 Claims characteristics, 36 Claims control, 37 Decisions, 38 Payment, 39 Collection/waiver, 40 Notice, 41 Inquiries control, 42 Quality appraisal.

Group	Process	1	2	3	4	5	6	7	8	9	10	11	12	13	14	15	16	17	18	19	20	21	22	23	24	25	26	27	28	29	30	31	32	33	34	35	36	37	38	39	40	41	42
PLANNING	Develop agency plans	C	C	C	U	U									U																												
	Administer agency budget	C	C	C	U	U					U	U	U			U	U	U		U	U					U	U	U			U		U			U		U			U	U	U
	Formulate program policies	U	U	C				U							U		U				U															U							U
	Formulate administrative policies		U		U	C	C	U							U		U	U			U																						
	Formulate data policies		U	U		U		C	U	U													U	U	U	U																	
	Design work processes		U		U	U				C	C	U	U							U																U							U
GENERAL MANAGEMENT	Manage public affairs		U		U	U		U		C	C	C																															
	Manage intrgovernment affairs	U	U		U	U		U				C	C	C												U	U		U	U			U		U								
	Exchange data			U				U				U	U	U	U	C	U	U									U																
	Maintain administrative accounts		U		U			U			U	U				C		U								U	U	U					U		U								
	Maintain program accounts		U	U				U			U	U						C													U			U		U	U	U	U		U		
	Conduct audits		U	U				U	U								U	U	C		U								U														
	Establish organizations		U		U			U												C	U					U	U																U
	Manage human resources		U		U	U		U												C	C	C	C	C																			
	Provide security				U	U			U	U	U														C	C	C	C			U												
	Manage equipment		U		U				U	U	U														C	C	C	C															
	Manage facilities		U		U			U																	U	U	C																
	Manage supplies		U		U			U																	C	U	U	C															
	Manage workloads	U	U	U	U			U							U											U	U	U	C	C	U			U		U		U				U	U
PROGRAM ADMINISTRATION	Issue Social Security numbers							U				U		U																	C	C											
	Maintain earnings							U			U	U	U																		U		C	C	C	C	U						
	Collect claims information				U	U		U					U																		U	U				C	C	U	U	U			
	Determine eligibility/entitlement							U																							U	U	U			U		C	U	U			
	Compute payments				U			U												U											U					U		U	C	C			
	Administer debt management				U			U												U																			U	C			
SUPPORT	Generate notices							U				U																			U					U		U	U	U	U	C	
	Respond to program inquiries				U			U			U	U																			U	U	U			U		U	U	U	U	C	
	Provide quality assessment				U	U		U	U																						U					U			U		U	U	C

KEY: C = creators of data   U = users of data

This chart depicts which data classes are required to support particular organizational processes and which processes are the creators and users of data.

591

Critical Success Factors

The strategic analysis, or critical success factors, approach argues that an organization's information requirements are determined by a small number of **critical success factors (CSFs)** of managers. If these goals can be attained, success of the firm or organization is assured (Rockart, 1979). CSFs are shaped by the industry, the firm, the manager, and the broader environment. For example, CSFs for the automobile industry might include styling, quality, and cost to meet the goals of increasing market share and raising profits. New information systems should focus on providing information that helps the firm meet these goals.

The principal method used in CSF analysis is personal interviews—three or four—with a number of top managers identifying their goals and the resulting CSFs. These personal CSFs are aggregated to develop a picture of the firm's CSFs. Then systems are built to deliver information on these CSFs. (For the method of developing CSFs in an organization, see Figure 4.)

The strength of the CSF method is that it produces less data to analyze than does enterprise analysis. Only top managers are interviewed, and the questions focus on a small number of CSFs rather than requiring a broad inquiry into what information is used in the organization. It is especially suitable for top management and for the development of decision-support systems (DSSs) and executive support systems (ESSs). Unlike enterprise analysis, the CSF method focuses organizational attention on how information should be handled.

The method's primary weakness is that there is no particularly rigorous way in which individual CSFs can be aggregated into a clear company pattern. In addition, interviewees (and interviewers) often become confused when

FIGURE 4   USING CSFs TO DEVELOP SYSTEMS

The CSF approach relies on interviews with key managers to identify their CSFs. Individual CSFs are aggregated to develop CSFs for the entire firm. Systems can then be built to deliver information on these CSFs.

distinguishing between *individual* and *organizational* CSFs. These types of CSFs are not necessarily the same. What may be considered critical to a manager may not be important for the organization as a whole. This method is clearly biased toward top managers, although it could be extended to elicit ideas for promising new systems from lower-level members of the organization (Peffers and Gengler, 2003).

PORTFOLIO ANALYSIS

Once strategic analyses have determined the overall direction of systems development, **portfolio analysis** can be used to evaluate alternative system projects. Portfolio analysis inventories all of the organization's information systems projects and assets, including infrastructure, outsourcing contracts, and licenses. This portfolio of information systems investments can be described as having a certain profile of risk and benefit to the firm (see Figure 5) similar to a financial portfolio.

Each information systems project carries its own set of risks and benefits. (Section 4 describes the factors that increase the risks of systems projects.) Firms would try to improve the return on their portfolios of IT assets by balancing the risk and return from their systems investments. Although there is no ideal profile for all firms, information-intensive industries (e.g., finance) should have a few high-risk, high-benefit projects to ensure that they stay current with technology. Firms in non-information-intensive industries should focus on high-benefit, low-risk projects.

Most desirable, of course, are systems with high benefit and low risk. These promise early returns and low risks. Second, high-benefit, high-risk systems should be examined; low-benefit, high-risk systems should be totally avoided; and low-benefit, low-risk systems should be reexamined for the possibility of rebuilding and replacing them with more desirable systems having higher benefits. By using portfolio analysis, management can determine the optimal mix of investment risk and reward for their firms, balancing riskier high-reward projects with safer lower-reward ones. Firms where portfolio analysis is aligned with business strategy have been found to have a superior return on their IT assets, better alignment of information technology investments with business objectives, and better organization-wide coordination of IT investments (Jeffrey and Leliveld, 2004).

FIGURE 5   A SYSTEM PORTFOLIO

Companies should examine their portfolio of projects in terms of potential benefits and likely risks. Certain kinds of projects should be avoided altogether and others developed rapidly. There is no ideal mix. Companies in different industries have different profiles.

SCORING MODELS

A **scoring model** is useful for selecting projects where many criteria must be considered. It assigns weights to various features of a system and then calculates the weighted totals. Using Table 2, the firm must decide among two alternative enterprise resource planning (ERP) systems. The first column lists the criteria that decision makers will use to evaluate the systems. These criteria are usually the result of lengthy discussions among the decision-making group. Often the most important outcome of a scoring model is not the score but agreement on the criteria used to judge a system.

Table 2 shows that this particular company attaches the most importance to capabilities for sales order processing, inventory management, and warehousing. The second column in Table 2 lists the weights that decision makers attached to the decision criteria. Columns 3 and 5 show the percentage of requirements for each function that each alternative ERP system can provide. Each vendor's score can be calculated by multiplying the percentage of requirements met for each function by the weight attached to that function. ERP System B has the highest total score.

As with all "objective" techniques, there are many qualitative judgments involved in using the scoring model. This model requires experts who understand the issues and the technology. It is appropriate to cycle through the

TABLE 2 EXAMPLE OF A SCORING MODEL FOR AN ERP SYSTEM

CRITERIA	WEIGHT	ERP SYSTEM A %	ERP SYSTEM A SCORE	ERP SYSTEM B %	ERP SYSTEM B SCORE
1.0 Order Processing					
1.1 Online order entry	4	67	268	73	292
1.2 Online pricing	4	81	324	87	348
1.3 Inventory check	4	72	288	81	324
1.4 Customer credit check	3	66	198	59	177
1.5 Invoicing	4	73	292	82	328
Total Order Processing			1,370		1,469
2.0 Inventory Management					
2.1 Production forecasting	3	72	216	76	228
2.2 Production planning	4	79	316	81	324
2.3 Inventory control	4	68	272	80	320
2.4 Reports	3	71	213	69	207
Total Inventory Management			1,017		1,079
3.0 Warehousing					
3.1 Receiving	2	71	142	75	150
3.2 Picking/packing	3	77	231	82	246
3.3 Shipping	4	92	368	89	356
Total Warehousing			741		752
Grand Total			3,128		3,300

scoring model several times, changing the criteria and weights, to see how sensitive the outcome is to reasonable changes in criteria. Scoring models are used most commonly to confirm, to rationalize, and to support decisions, rather than as the final arbiters of system selection.

3 ESTABLISHING THE BUSINESS VALUE OF INFORMATION SYSTEMS

Even if a system project supports a firm's strategic goals and meets user information requirements, it needs to be a good investment for the firm. The value of systems from a financial perspective essentially revolves around the issue of return on invested capital. Does a particular information system investment produce sufficient returns to justify its costs?

INFORMATION SYSTEM COSTS AND BENEFITS

Table 3 lists some of the more common costs and benefits of systems. **Tangible benefits** can be quantified and assigned a monetary value. **Intangible benefits**, such as more efficient customer service or enhanced decision making, cannot be immediately quantified but may lead to quantifiable gains in the long run. Transaction and clerical systems that displace labor and save space always produce more measurable, tangible benefits than management information systems, decision-support systems, and computer-supported collaborative work systems.

Total cost of ownership (TCO) is designed to identify and measure the components of information technology expenditures beyond the initial cost of purchasing and installing hardware and software. However, TCO analysis provides only part of the information needed to evaluate an information technology investment because it does not typically deal with benefits, cost categories such as complexity costs, and "soft" and strategic factors discussed later in this section.

CAPITAL BUDGETING FOR INFORMATION SYSTEMS

Capital budgeting models are one of several techniques used to measure the value of investing in long-term capital investment projects. Firms invest in capital projects to expand production to meet anticipated demand or to modernize production equipment to reduce costs. Firms also invest in capital projects for many noneconomic reasons, such as installing pollution control equipment, converting to a human resources database to meet some government regulations, or satisfying nonmarket public demands. Information systems are considered long-term capital investment projects.

The principal capital budgeting models for evaluating information technology projects are:

- The payback method
- The accounting rate of return on investment (ROI)
- The net present value
- The internal rate of return (IRR)

TABLE 3 COSTS AND BENEFITS OF INFORMATION SYSTEMS

COSTS

Hardware

Telecommunications

Software

Services

Personnel

TANGIBLE BENEFITS (COST SAVINGS)

Increased productivity

Lower operational costs

Reduced workforce

Lower computer expenses

Lower outside vendor costs

Lower clerical and professional costs

Reduced rate of growth in expenses

Reduced facility costs

INTANGIBLE BENEFITS

Improved asset utilization

Improved resource control

Improved organizational planning

Increased organizational flexibility

More timely information

More information

Increased organizational learning

Legal requirements attained

Enhanced employee goodwill

Increased job satisfaction

Improved decision making

Improved operations

Higher client satisfaction

Better corporate image

Capital budgeting methods rely on measures of cash flows into and out of the firm. Capital projects generate cash flows into and out of the firm. The investment cost for information systems projects is an immediate cash outflow caused by expenditures for hardware, software, and labor. In subsequent years, the investment may cause additional cash outflows that will be balanced by cash inflows resulting from the investment. Cash inflows take the form of increased sales of more products (for reasons such as new products, higher quality, or increasing market share) or reduced costs in production and operations. The difference between cash outflows and cash inflows is used for calculating the financial worth of an investment. Once the cash flows have been established, several alternative methods are available for comparing different projects and deciding about the investment.

CASE EXAMPLE: CAPITAL BUDGETING FOR A NEW SUPPLY CHAIN MANAGEMENT SYSTEM

Let's look at how financial models would work in a real-world business scenario. Heartland Stores is a general merchandise retail chain operating in eight Midwestern states. It has 5 regional distribution centers, 377 stores, and about 14,000 different products stocked in each store. The company is considering investing in new software and hardware modules to upgrade its existing supply chain management system to help it better manage the purchase and movement of goods from its suppliers to its retail outlets. Too many items in Heartland's stores are out of stock, even though many of these products are in the company's distribution center warehouses.

Management believes that the new system would help Heartland Stores reduce the amount of items that it must stock in inventory, and thus its inventory costs, because it would be able to track precisely the status of orders and the flow of items in and out of its distribution centers. The new system would reduce Heartland's labor costs because the company would not need so many people to manage inventory or to track shipments of goods from suppliers to distribution centers and from distribution centers to retail outlets. Telecommunications costs would be reduced because customer service representatives and shipping and receiving staff would not have to spend so much time on the telephone tracking shipments and orders. Heartland Stores expects the system to reduce transportation costs by providing information to help it consolidate shipments to retail stores and to create more efficient shipping schedules. If the new system project is approved, implementation would commence in January 2007 and the new system would become operational in early January 2008.

The solution builds the existing IT infrastructure at the Heartland Stores but requires the purchase of additional server computers, PCs, database software, and networking technology, along with new supply chain planning and execution software. The solution also calls for new radio-frequency identification technology to track items more easily as they move from suppliers to distribution centers to retail outlets.

Figure 6 shows the estimated costs and benefits of the system. The system had an actual investment cost of $11,467,350 in the first year (year 0) and a total cost over six years of $19,017,350. The estimated benefits total $32,500,000 after six years. Was the investment worthwhile? If so, in what sense? Financial models to evaluate the investment are depicted in Figure 7.

The Payback Method

The **payback method** is quite simple: It is a measure of the time required to pay back the initial investment of a project. The payback period is computed as follows:

$$\frac{\text{Original investment}}{\text{Annual net cash inflow}} = \text{Number of years to pay back}$$

In the case of Heartland Stores, it will take more than two years to pay back the initial investment. (Because cash flows are uneven, annual cash inflows are summed until they equal the original investment to arrive at this number.) The payback method is a popular method because of its simplicity and power as an initial screening method. It is especially good for high-risk projects in which the useful life of a project is difficult to determine. If a project pays for itself in two years, then it matters less how long after two years the system lasts.

FIGURE 6   COSTS AND BENEFITS OF THE NEW SUPPLY CHAIN MANAGEMENT SYSTEM

Estimated Costs and Benefits — New Supply Chain Management System

	A	B	C	D	E	F	G	H	I	J	K
1	Year :					0	1	2	3	4	5
2						2007	2008	2009	2010	2011	2012
3	**Costs: Hardware**										
4		Servers			7@ 80000	560,000					
5		Backup servers			4@ 80000	320,000					
6		PCs at loading dock			100@ 1250	125,000					
7		Radio-frequency devices			1000@ $1175	1,175,000					
8		Storage				800,000					
9											
10	**Network Infrastructure**										
11		Routers and hubs			300@ 4100	1,230,000					
12		Firewalls			2@ 6300	12,600					
13		Wireless RF network				1,750,000					
14		Backup network system				1,150,000					
15		Telecom links				74,250	225,000	225,000	225,000	225,000	225,000
16											
17	**Software**										
18		Database				475,000					
19		Web servers (Apache)				0					
20		Supply chain planning & execution modules				1,187,500					
21											
22	**Labor**										
23		Business staff				425,000	115,000	115,000	115,000	115,000	115,000
24		IS staff				1,225,000	525,000	525,000	525,000	525,000	525,000
25		External consultants				576,000	95,000	95,000	95,000	95,000	95,000
26		Training (end users)				382,000	35,000	35,000	35,000	35,000	35,000
27	**Subtotal**					11,467,350	995,000	995,000	995,000	995,000	995,000
28											
29	**Maintenance and Support**										
30		Hardware maintenance & upgrades					240,000	240,000	240,000	240,000	240,000
31		Software maintenance & upgrades					275,000	275,000	275,000	275,000	275,000
32		Subtotal					515,000	515,000	515,000	515,000	515,000
33	**Total by Year**					11,467,350	1,510,000	1,510,000	1,510,000	1,510,000	1,510,000
34											
35	**Total Costs**					19,017,350					
36	**Benefits**										
37		Reduced labor costs					1,650,000	1,400,000	1,400,000	1,400,000	1,400,000
38		Reduced inventory costs					3,500,000	3,500,000	3,500,000	3,500,000	3,500,000
39		Reduced transportation costs					1,300,000	1,300,000	1,300,000	1,300,000	1,300,000
40		Reduced telecommunications costs					250,000	250,000	250,000	250,000	250,000
41											
42	**Subtotal**					0	6,700,000	6,450,000	6,450,000	6,450,000	6,450,000
43											
44	**Net Cash Flow**					−11,467,350	5,190,000	4,940,000	4,940,000	4,940,000	4,940,000
45											
46	**Total Benefits**					32,500,000					

Sheet1 Sheet2 Sheet3

This spreadsheet analyzes the basic costs and benefits of implementing supply chain management system enhancements for a midsize midwestern U.S. retailer. The costs for hardware, telecommunications, software, services, and personnel are analyzed over a six-year period.

The weakness of this measure is its virtue: The method ignores the time value of money, the amount of cash flow after the payback period, the disposal value (usually zero with computer systems), and the profitability of the investment.

Accounting Rate of Return on Investment (ROI)

Firms make capital investments to earn a satisfactory rate of return. Determining a satisfactory rate of return depends on the cost of borrowing

FIGURE 7   FINANCIAL MODELS

	A	B	C	D	E	F	G	H	I	J	K	L	M
								Financial Models					
1	Year:							0	1	2	3	4	5
2	Net Cash Flow (not including original investment) for years 2007–2012								$5,190,000.00	$4,940,000.00	$4,940,000.00	$4,940,000.00	$4,940,000.00
3	Net Cash Flow (including original investment) for years 2007–2012							-$11,467,350.00	$5,190,000.00	$4,940,000.00	$4,940,000.00	$4,940,000.00	$4,940,000.00
4													
5	Payback Period = 2.5 years					Cumulative Cash Flow							
6	Initial Investment =			Year 0	-$11,467,350.00	-$11,467,350.00							
7				Year 1	$5,190,000.00	-$6,277,350.00							
8				Year 2	$4,940,000.00	_$1,337,350.00							
9				Year 3	$4,940,000.00	$3,602,650.00							
10				Year 4	$4,940,000.00	$8,542,650.00							
11				Year 5	$4,940,000.00	$13,482,650.00							
12													
13	Accounting Rate of Return												
14	(Total Benefits – Total Costs – Depreciation)/Useful Life						Total Benefits $32,500,000.00						
15							Total Costs $19,017,350.00						
16	Total Initial Investment						Depreciation $11,467,350.00						
17						Total Benefits–Total Costs–Deprec.	$2,015,300.00						
18													
19							Life 6 years						
20	Return on Investment (ROI) = 2.93%												
21													
22													
23													
24													
25													
26	Net Present Value =												
27			=NPV(0.05,H2:M2)−11,467,350				$10,158,359.99						
28													
29													
30													
31													
32	Internal Rate of Return												
33			= IRR(H3:M3)				33%						

Sheet1 / Sheet2 / Sheet3

To determine the financial basis for an information systems project, a series of financial models helps determine the return on invested capital. These calculations include the payback period, the accounting rate of return on investment (ROI), the net present value, and the internal rate of return (IRR).

money, but other factors can enter into the equation. Such factors include the historic rates of return expected by the firm. In the long run, the desired rate of return must equal or exceed the cost of capital in the marketplace. Otherwise, no one will lend the firm money.

The **accounting rate of return on investment (ROI)** calculates the rate of return from an investment by adjusting the cash inflows produced by the investment for depreciation. It gives an approximation of the accounting income earned by the project.

To find the ROI, first calculate the average net benefit. The formula for the average net benefit is as follows:

$$\frac{(\text{Total benefits} - \text{Total cost} - \text{Depreciation})}{\text{Useful life}} = \text{Net benefit}$$

This net benefit is divided by the total initial investment to arrive at ROI. The formula is as follows:

$$\frac{\text{Net benefit}}{\text{Total initial investment}} = \text{ROI}$$

In the case of Heartland Stores, the average rate of return on the investment is 2.93 percent.

The weakness of ROI is that it can ignore the time value of money. Future savings are simply not worth as much in today's dollars as are current savings. However, ROI can be modified (and usually is) so that future benefits and costs are calculated in today's dollars. (The present value function on most spreadsheets can perform this conversion.)

Net Present Value

Evaluating a capital project requires that the cost of an investment (a cash outflow usually in year 0) be compared with the net cash inflows that occur many years later. But these two kinds of cash flows are not directly comparable because of the time value of money. Money you have been promised to receive three, four, and five years from now is not worth as much as money received today. Money received in the future has to be discounted by some appropriate percentage rate—usually the prevailing interest rate, or sometimes the cost of capital. **Present value** is the value in current dollars of a payment or stream of payments to be received in the future. It can be calculated by using the following formula:

$$\text{Payment} \times \frac{1 - (1 + 1\ \text{interest})^n}{\text{Interest}} = \text{Present value}$$

Thus, to compare the investment (made in today's dollars) with future savings or earnings, you need to discount the earnings to their present value and then calculate the net present value of the investment. The **net present value** is the amount of money an investment is worth, taking into account its cost, earnings, and the time value of money. The formula for net present value is this:

Present value of expected cash flows – Initial investment cost = Net present value

In the case of Heartland Stores, the present value of the stream of benefits is $21,625,709, and the cost (in today's dollars) is $11,467,350, giving a net present value of $10,158,359. In other words, for a $21 million investment today, the firm will receive more than $10 million. This is a fairly good rate of return on an investment.

Internal Rate of Return (IRR)

Internal rate of return (IRR) is defined as the rate of return or profit that an investment is expected to earn, taking into account the time value of money. IRR is the discount (interest) rate that will equate the present value of the project's future cash flows to the initial cost of the project (defined here as negative cash flow in year 0 of $11,467,350). In other words, the value of R (discount rate) is such that Present value – Initial cost = 0. In the case of Heartland Stores, the IRR is 33 percent.

Results of the Capital Budgeting Analysis

Using methods that take into account the time value of money, the Heartland Stores project is cash-flow positive over the time period under consideration and returns more benefits than it costs. Against this analysis, you might ask what other investments would be better from an efficiency and effectiveness standpoint and if all the benefits have been calculated.

REAL OPTIONS PRICING MODELS

Some information systems projects are highly uncertain, especially investments in IT infrastructure. Their future revenue streams are unclear and their up-front costs are high. Suppose, for instance, that a firm is considering a $20 million investment to upgrade its information technology infrastructure—its hardware, software, data management tools, and networking technology. If this upgraded infrastructure were available, the organization would have the technology capabilities to respond more easily to future problems and opportunities. Although the costs of this investment can be calculated, not all of the benefits of making this investment can be established in advance. But if the firm waits a few years until the revenue potential becomes more obvious, it might be too late to make the infrastructure investment. In such cases, managers might benefit from using real options pricing models to evaluate information technology investments.

Real options pricing models (ROPMs) use the concept of options valuation borrowed from the financial industry. An option is essentially the right, but not the obligation, to act at some future date. A typical call option, for instance, is a financial option in which a person buys the right (but not the obligation) to purchase an underlying asset (usually a stock) at a fixed price (strike price) on or before a given date.

For instance, on June 5, 2006, for $8.70 you could purchase the right (a call option) maturing in January 2008 to buy a share of Procter & Gamble (P&G) common stock for $50 per share. If, by the end of January 2008, the price of P&G stock did not rise above $50 per share, you would not exercise the option, and the value of the option would fall to zero on the strike date. If, however, the price of Procter & Gamble common stock rose to, say, $100 per share, you could purchase the stock for the strike price of $50 and retain the profit of $50 per share minus the cost of the option. (Because the option is sold as a 100-share contract, the cost of the contract would be 100 ˘ $8.70 before commissions, or $870, and you would be purchasing and obtaining a profit from 100 shares of Procter & Gamble.) The stock option enables the owner to benefit from the upside potential of an opportunity while limiting the downside risk.

ROPMs value information systems projects similar to stock options, where an initial expenditure on technology creates the right, but not the obligation, to obtain the benefits associated with further development and deployment of the technology as long as management as the freedom to cancel, defer, restart, or expand the project. ROPMs give managers the flexibility to stage their IT investment or test the waters with small pilot projects or prototypes to gain more knowledge about the risks of a project before investing in the entire implementation. The disadvantages of this model are primarily in estimating all the key variables affecting option value, including anticipated cash flows from the underlying asset and changes in the cost of implementation. Models for determining option value of information technology platforms are being developed (Fichman, 2004; McGrath and MacMillan, 2000).

LIMITATIONS OF FINANCIAL MODELS

The traditional focus on the financial and technical aspects of an information system tends to overlook the social and organizational dimensions of information systems that may affect the true costs and benefits of the investment. Many companies' information systems investment decisions do not adequately consider costs from organizational disruptions created by a new system, such as the cost to train end users, the impact that users' learning curves for a new system have on productivity, or the time managers need to spend overseeing new system-related changes. Benefits, such as more timely decisions from a new system or enhanced employee learning and expertise, may also be overlooked in a traditional financial analysis (Ryan, Harrison, and Schkade, 2002).

4 MANAGING PROJECT RISK

In this section, we describe specific risks to information systems projects and show what can be done to manage them effectively.

DIMENSIONS OF PROJECT RISK

Systems differ dramatically in their size, scope, level of complexity, and organizational and technical components. Some systems development projects are more likely to create the problems we have described earlier or to suffer delays because they carry a much higher level of risk than others. The level of project risk is influenced by project size, project structure, and the level of technical expertise of the information systems staff and project team.

- *Project size.* The larger the project—as indicated by the dollars spent, the size of the implementation staff, the time allocated for implementation, and the number of organizational units affected—the greater the risk. Very large-scale systems projects have a failure rate that is 50 to 75 percent higher than that for other projects because such projects are complex and difficult to control. The organizational complexity of the system—how many units and groups use it and how much it influences business processes—contribute to the complexity of large-scale systems projects just as much as technical characteristics, such as the number of lines of program code, length of project, and budget (Xia and Lee, 2004; Concours Group, 2000; Laudon, 1989). In addition, there are few reliable techniques for estimating the time and cost to develop large-scale information systems.

- *Project structure.* Some projects are more highly structured than others. Their requirements are clear and straightforward so outputs and processes can be easily defined. Users know exactly what they want and what the system should do; there is almost no possibility of the users changing their minds. Such projects run a much lower risk than those with relatively undefined, fluid, and constantly changing requirements; with outputs that cannot be fixed easily because they are subject to users' changing ideas; or with users who cannot agree on what they want.

- *Experience with technology.* The project risk rises if the project team and the information system staff lack the required technical expertise. If the team is unfamiliar with the hardware, system software, application software, or database management system proposed for the project, it is highly likely that the project will experience technical problems or take more time to complete because of the need to master new skills.

Although the difficulty of the technology is one risk factor in information systems projects, the other factors are primarily organizational, dealing with the complexity of information requirements, the scope of the project, and how many parts of the organization will be affected by a new information system.

CHANGE MANAGEMENT AND THE CONCEPT OF IMPLEMENTATION

The introduction or alteration of an information system has a powerful behavioral and organizational impact. Changes in the way that information is defined, accessed, and used to manage the organization's resources often lead to new distributions of authority and power. This internal organizational change breeds resistance and opposition and can lead to the demise of an otherwise good system.

A very large percentage of information systems projects stumble because the process of organizational change surrounding system building was not properly addressed. Successful system building requires careful **change management**.

The Concept of Implementation

To manage the organizational change surrounding the introduction of a new information system effectively, you must examine the process of implementation. **Implementation** refers to all organizational activities working toward the adoption, management, and routinization of an innovation, such as a new information system. In the implementation process, the systems analyst is a **change agent**. The analyst not only develops technical solutions but also redefines the configurations, interactions, job activities, and power relationships of various organizational groups. The analyst is the catalyst for the entire change process and is responsible for ensuring that all parties involved accept the changes created by a new system. The change agent communicates with users, mediates between competing interest groups, and ensures that the organizational adjustment to such changes is complete.

The Role of End Users

System implementation generally benefits from high levels of user involvement and management support. User participation in the design and operation of information systems has several positive results. First, if users are heavily involved in systems design, they have more opportunities to mold the system according to their priorities and business requirements, and more opportunities to control the outcome. Second, they are more likely to react positively to the completed system because they have been active participants in the change process. Incorporating user knowledge and expertise leads to better solutions.

The relationship between users and information systems specialists has traditionally been a problem area for information systems implementation efforts. Users and information systems specialists tend to have different backgrounds, interests, and priorities. This is referred to as the **user-designer communications gap**. These differences lead to divergent organizational loyalties, approaches to problem solving, and vocabularies.

Information systems specialists, for example, often have a highly technical, or machine, orientation to problem solving. They look for elegant and sophisticated technical solutions in which hardware and software efficiency is optimized at the expense of ease of use or organizational effectiveness. Users prefer systems that are oriented toward solving business problems or facilitating organizational tasks. Often the orientations of both groups are so at odds that they appear to speak in different tongues.

These differences are illustrated in Table 4 which depicts the typical concerns of end users and technical specialists (information systems designers) regarding the development of a new information system. Communication problems between end users and designers are a major reason why user

603

TABLE 4 THE USER-DESIGNER COMMUNICATIONS GAP

USER CONCERNS	DESIGNER CONCERNS
Will the system deliver the information I need for my work?	How much disk storage space will the master file consume?
How quickly can I access the data?	How many lines of program code will it take to perform this function?
How easily can I retrieve the data?	How can we cut down on CPU time when we run the system?
How much clerical support will I need to enter data into the system?	What is the most efficient way of storing these data?
How will the operation of the system fit into my daily business schedule?	What database management system should we use?

requirements are not properly incorporated into information systems and why users are driven out of the implementation process.

Systems development projects run a very high risk of failure when there is a pronounced gap between users and technical specialists and when these groups continue to pursue different goals. Under such conditions, users are often driven out of the implementation process. Because they cannot comprehend what the technicians are saying, users conclude that the entire project is best left in the hands of the information specialists alone.

Management Support and Commitment

If an information systems project has the backing and commitment of management at various levels, it is more likely to be perceived positively by both users and the technical information services staff. Both groups will believe that their participation in the development process will receive higher-level attention and priority. They will be recognized and rewarded for the time and effort they devote to implementation. Management backing also ensures that a systems project receives sufficient funding and resources to be successful. Furthermore, to be enforced effectively, all the changes in work habits and procedures and any organizational realignments associated with a new system depend on management backing. If a manager considers a new system a priority, the system will more likely be treated that way by his or her subordinates.

Change Management Challenges for Business Process Reengineering, Enterprise Applications, and Mergers and Acquisitions

Given the challenges of innovation and implementation, it is not surprising to find a very high failure rate among enterprise application and business process reengineering (BPR) projects, which typically require extensive organizational change and which may require replacing old technologies and legacy systems that are deeply rooted in many interrelated business processes. A number of studies have indicated that 70 percent of all business process reengineering projects fail to deliver promised benefits. Likewise, a high percentage of enterprise applications fail to be fully implemented or to meet the goals of their users even after three years of work.

Many enterprise application and reengineering projects have been undermined by poor implementation and change management practices that failed to address employees' concerns about change. Dealing with fear and anxiety throughout the organization; overcoming resistance by key managers; changing job functions, career paths, and recruitment practices; and training have posed greater threats to reengineering than the difficulties companies faced visualizing and designing breakthrough changes to business processes. All of the enterprise applications require tighter coordination among different functional groups as well as extensive business process change.

Projects related to mergers and acquisitions have a similar failure rate. Mergers and acquisitions are deeply affected by the organizational characteristics of the merging companies as well as by their IT infrastructures. Combining the information systems of two different companies usually requires considerable organizational change and complex systems projects to manage. If the integration is not properly managed, firms can emerge with a tangled hodgepodge of inherited legacy systems built by aggregating the systems of one firm after another. Without a successful systems integration, the benefits anticipated from the merger cannot be realized, or, worse, the merged entity cannot execute its business processes and loses customers. The Interactive Session on Management on explores this topic.

CONTROLLING RISK FACTORS

Various project management, requirements gathering, and planning methodologies have been developed for specific categories of implementation problems. Strategies have also been devised for ensuring that users play appropriate roles throughout the implementation period and for managing the organizational change process. Not all aspects of the implementation process can be easily controlled or planned. However, anticipating potential implementation problems and applying appropriate corrective strategies can increase the chances for system project success.

The first step in managing project risk involves identifying the nature and level of risk confronting the project (Schmidt, Lyytinen, Keil, and Cule, 2001). Implementers can then handle each project with the tools and risk-management approaches geared to its level of risk (Iversen, Mathiassen, and Nielsen, 2004; Barki, Rivard, and Talbot, 2001; McFarlan, 1981).

Managing Technical Complexity

Projects with challenging and complex technology to master benefit from **internal integration tools**. The success of such projects depends on how well their technical complexity can be managed. Project leaders need both heavy technical and administrative experience. They must be able to anticipate problems and develop smooth working relationships among a predominantly technical team. The team should be under the leadership of a manager with a strong technical and project management background and team members should be highly experienced. Team meetings should take place frequently. Essential technical skills or expertise not available internally should be secured from outside the organization.

Formal Planning and Control Tools

Large projects benefit from appropriate use of **formal planning tools** and **formal control tools** for documenting and monitoring project plans. The two most commonly used methods for documenting project plans are Gantt charts and PERT charts. A **Gantt chart** lists project activities and their corresponding start and completion dates. The Gantt chart visually represents the timing and duration of different tasks in a development project as well as their human resource requirements (see Figure 8). It shows each task as a horizontal bar whose length is proportional to the time required to complete it.

INTERACTIVE SESSION: MANAGEMENT

MANAGING IT IN THE MERGER AND ACQUISITION GAME

In 2005, there were 7,736 mergers and acquisitions in the United States, and the average value of M&As has risen to a record $385.6 million in the first half of 2006. "Due diligence" is the concept used to describe what acquirers should perform before they make an acquisition. Technically, for public firms, due diligence is a legal requirement of senior management to ensure the financial and business statements of firms they are acquiring are accurate and complete.

In the past, acquiring firms have lost a great deal of money by ignoring a very important element of the acquired firm's business, namely, its information systems. Because M&As are typically entered into for financial reasons (greater market share, elimination of competitors, greater efficiency and profitability), and are led by financial managers, it is understandable that sizing up the target company's IT infrastructure is last on the list of due diligence activities.

But there is a price to pay for ignoring the IT/IS element in mergers. When Wells Fargo purchased its rival First Interstate, it created an IT nightmare. Wells Fargo closed down the First Interstate branches and ATMs, costing the bank over $100 million as 20 percent of First Interstate customers closed their accounts.

There are a number of systems-related risks in M&As. The target company may have stopped spending on maintenance years ago to decrease costs and increase profits. It may have fallen behind competitors in new applications. Its software licenses may not be transferable to the new company without significant new fees. The infrastructure may be outdated. The target company's systems may be totally incompatible with the acquirer's systems. One important reason Logicalis, an IT integration and consulting company, backed off acquiring a value-added reseller was that the company's CRM system was incompatible with its own.

So how do companies perform due diligence in the information systems area? What are some management tactics for dealing with the merger of two or more very different IT infrastructures? The first step is to classify the assets your firm is about to acquire, create an inventory of these assets, and establish the value of these systems to the newly merged firm. For instance, you could divide the target firm's IT assets into four categories:

transactional systems that perform the basic transactions of the firm; informational systems that inform management about the state of operations; strategic systems that differentiate the firm in the marketplace; and basic infrastructure that includes both the hardware and software installed, as well as the services provided by the IS group to the business.

Once you have created an inventory of the target firm's IT assets, you will need to value their potential contribution to the new firm. There are four options: keep the target company systems if they are better than your own; keep your own systems and retire the target company systems if yours are better; choose the best of both companies' systems; or use the M&A to build an entirely new infrastructure.

In general, firms rarely decided to build a new infrastructure completely. Most commonly, the acquiring firms shut down systems of the acquired company and extend the reach of their own systems. Target firms are usually smaller and less capitalized than acquiring firms and have systems that lag behind those of the acquiring firm. Moreover, the financial rationale for many mergers is scale economies. The argument is that the existing IT/IS infrastructure of the acquiring firm can be expanded with minimal cost, while the merged companies' revenues will increase many fold. The same fixed costs in infrastructure will be able to support a much larger and more profitable business.

But the evidence that managers at acquiring firms really understand the risks of mergers and acquisitions is not encouraging. Studies of M&A activity over the past 75 years show that about 60 percent actually destroy shareholder value and result in falling stock prices for the acquiring company. The reasons are that the acquiring firm overvalues the assets of the target firm and systematically underestimate the risks of the acquisition, especially the costs of merging the operational activities and information system infrastructures of two firms.

Sources: Eric Chabrow, "IT Plays Linchpin Role in High-Stakes M&As," *Information Week*, June 26, 2006; Spencer McIllmurray, "M&A Survival Kit: Relearning Enterprise Addition and Subtraction," *CIO Magazine*, October 24, 2006; Nick Moore, "The New Role of the CIO in M&A Due Diligence," *Software Mag.com*, July, 2006.

CASE STUDY QUESTIONS

1. What are some of the risks involved when one firm acquires another firm's IT infrastructure?

2. Why do firms often fail to take the target firm's information systems and IT infrastructure into account when purchasing other firms?

3. How would you go about assessing the value of another firm's IT infrastructure and operational capabilities? What questions would you ask?

MIS IN ACTION

1. Bain and Company is one of the premiere business consulting firms specializing in advice about mergers and acquisitions. Visit www.Bain.com and explore the advice on how to conduct a successful merger by clicking on the "Consulting Expertise" tab, and then selecting "Mergers & Acquisitions." Read this page, then click on "Deals Done Right." Why does Bain advise managers to stay close to their "core business?" Why might this advice ease the change in information systems infrastructure when mergers take place? What does Bain recommend about "integration" of the business and how would this affect IS/IT decisions?

2. On the Web, explore the IT/IS integration issues raised by one of these mega mergers of the past few years: Proctor & Gamble/Gillette; UJF/Mitsubishi Tokyo Financial, HEXAL/Novartis, or Kellog/Keebler. You can explore these mergers using Google searches such as "Kellogg Keebler merger."

This project team of professionals is using computing tools to enhance communication, analysis, and decision making.

Photo courtesy of Corbis Royalty Free

FIGURE 8   A GANTT CHART

HRIS COMBINED PLAN–HR

(Gantt chart spanning Oct 2006 – Mar 2008; task bars shown graphically.)

Task	Da	Who
DATA ADMINISTRATION SECURITY		
QMF security review/setup	20	EF TP
Security orientation	2	EF JA
QMF security maintenance	35	TP GL
Data entry sec. profiles	4	EF TP
Data entry sec. views est.	12	EF TP
Data entry security profiles	65	EF TP
DATA DICTIONARY		
Orientation sessions	1	EF
Data dictionary design	32	EFWV
DD prod. coordn-query	20	GL
DD prod. coordn-live	40	EF GL
Data dictionary cleanup	35	EF GL
Data dictionary maint.	35	EF GL
PROCEDURES REVISION		
DESIGN PREP		
Work flows (old)	10	PK JL
Payroll data flows	31	JL PK
HRIS P/R model	11	PK JL
P/R interface orient. mtg.	6	PK JL
P/R interface coordn. 1	15	PK
P/R interface coordn. 2	8	PK
Benefits interfaces (old)	5	JL
Benefits interfaces (new flow)	8	JL
Benefits communication strategy	3	PK JL
New work flow model	15	PK JL
Posn. data entry flows	14	WV JL

RESOURCE SUMMARY

Person		Who	Oct '06	Nov	Dec	Jan '07	Feb	Mar	Apr	May	Jun	Jul	Aug	Sep	Oct	Nov	Dec	Jan '08	Feb	Mar
Edith Farrell	5.0	EF	2	21	24	24	23	22	22	27	34	34	29	26	28	19	14			
Woody Vinton	5.0	WV	5	17	20	19	12	10	14	10	2								4	3
Charles Pierce	5.0	CP		5	11	20	13	9	10	7	6	8	4	4	4	4	4			
Ted Leurs	5.0	TL		12	17	17	19	17	14	12	15	16	2	1	1	1	1			
Toni Cox	5.0	TC	1	11	10	11	11	12	19	19	21	21	17	17	12	9				
Patricia Knopp	5.0	PC	7	23	30	34	27	25	15	24	25	16	11	13	17	10	3		3	2
Jane Lawton	5.0	JL	1	9	16	21	19	21	21	20	17	15	14	12	14	8	5			
David Holloway	5.0	DH	4	4	5	5	5	2	7	5	4	16	2							
Diane O'Neill	5.0	DO	6	14	17	16	13	11	9	4										
Joan Albert	5.0	JA	5	6			7	6	2	1				5	5	1				
Marie Marcus	5.0	MM	15	7	2	1	1													
Don Stevens	5.0	DS	4	4	5	4	5	1												
Casual	5.0	CASL		3	4	3			4	7	9	5	3	2						
Kathy Mendez	5.0	KM			1	5	16	20	19	22	19	20	18	20	11	2				
Anna Borden	5.0	AB						9	10	16	15	11	12	19	10	7	1			
Gail Loring	5.0	GL		3	6	5	9	10	17	18	17	10	13	10	10	7	17			
UNASSIGNED	0.0	X												9	236	225	230	14	13	
Co-op	5.0	CO		6	4				2	3	4	4	2	4	16			216	178	
Casual	5.0	CAUL										3	3	3						
TOTAL DAYS			49	147	176	196	194	174	193	195	190	181	140	125	358	288	284	237	196	12

The Gantt chart in this figure shows the task, person-days, and initials of each responsible person, as well as the start and finish dates for each task. The resource summary provides a manager with the total person-days for each month and for each person working on the project to manage the project successfully. The project described here is a data administration project.

Although Gantt charts show when project activities begin and end, they don't depict task dependencies, how one task is affected if another is behind schedule, or how tasks should be ordered. That is where **PERT charts** are useful. PERT stands for Program Evaluation and Review Technique, a methodology developed by the U.S. Navy during the 1950s to manage the Polaris submarine missile program. A PERT chart graphically depicts project tasks and their interrelationships. The PERT chart lists the specific activities that make up a project and the activities that must be completed before a specific activity can start, as illustrated in Figure 9.

The PERT chart portrays a project as a network diagram consisting of numbered nodes (either circles or rectangles) representing project tasks. Each node is numbered and shows the task, its duration, the starting date, and the completion date. The direction of the arrows on the lines indicates the sequence of tasks and shows which activities must be completed before the commencement of another activity. In Figure 9, the tasks in nodes 2, 3, and 4 are not dependent on each other and can be undertaken simultaneously, but each is dependent on completion of the first task. PERT charts for complex projects can be difficult to interpret, and project managers often use both techniques.

These project management techniques can help managers identify bottlenecks and determine the impact that problems will have on project completion times. They can also help systems developers partition projects

FIGURE 9   A PERT CHART

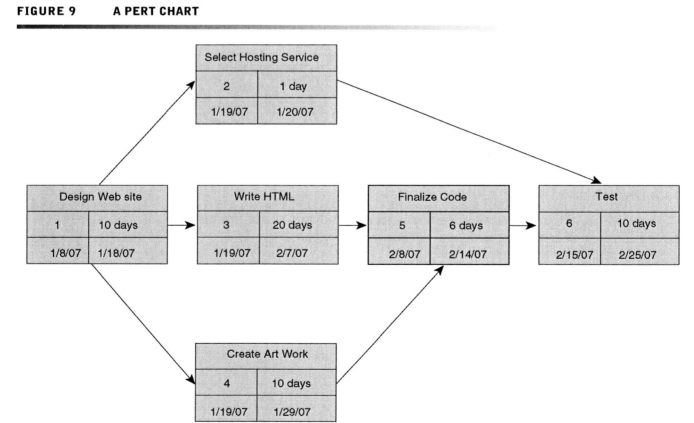

This is a simplified PERT chart for creating a small Web site. It shows the ordering of project tasks and the relationship of a task with preceding and succeeding tasks.

into smaller, more manageable segments with defined, measurable business results. Standard control techniques can successfully chart the progress of the project against budgets and target dates, so deviations from the plan can be spotted.

Increasing User Involvement and Overcoming User Resistance

Projects with relatively little structure and many undefined requirements must involve users fully at all stages. Users must be mobilized to support one of many possible design options and to remain committed to a single design. **External integration tools** consist of ways to link the work of the implementation team to users at all organizational levels. For instance, users can become active members of the project team, take on leadership roles, and take charge of installation and training. The implementation team can demonstrate its responsiveness to users, promptly answering questions, incorporating user feedback, and showing their willingness to help (Gefen and Ridings, 2002).

Participation in implementation activities may not be enough to overcome the problem of user resistance to organizational change. Different users may be affected by the system in different ways. Whereas some users may welcome a new system because it brings changes they perceive as beneficial to them, others may resist these changes because they believe the shifts are detrimental to their interests.

If the use of a system is voluntary, users may choose to avoid it; if use is mandatory, resistance will take the form of increased error rates, disruptions, turnover, and even sabotage. Therefore, the implementation strategy must not only encourage user participation and involvement, but it must also address the issue of counterimplementation (Keen, 1981). **Counterimplementation** is a deliberate strategy to thwart the implementation of an information system or an innovation in an organization.

Strategies to overcome user resistance include user participation (to elicit commitment as well as to improve design), user education and training, management edicts and policies, and better incentives for users who cooperate. The new system can be made more user friendly by improving the end-user interface. Users will be more cooperative if organizational problems are solved prior to introducing the new system.

The Interactive Session on Organizations illustrates how one company used these techniques to build user support for a new customer relationship management system (CRM). CRM system projects often encounter user resistance because they typically require marketing and sales staff to share information and change the way they work.

DESIGNING FOR THE ORGANIZATION

Because the purpose of a new system is to improve the organization's performance, information systems projects must explicitly address the ways in which the organization will change when the new system is installed, including installation of intranets, extranets, and Web applications. In addition to procedural changes, transformations in job functions, organizational structure, power relationships, and the work environment should be carefully planned.

Areas where users interface with the system require special attention, with sensitivity to ergonomics issues. **Ergonomics** refers to the interaction of people and machines in the work environment. It considers the design of jobs, health

INTERACTIVE SESSION: ORGANIZATIONS

GETTING BUY-IN AND ROI FOR CRM

The idea behind customer relationship management (CRM) seems simple enough: to centralize and share throughout the firm information about customers in order to maximize sales and profitability. For a variety of reasons—most having to do with implementation issues—achieving these objectives proves difficult.

Consider the case of Wallace, Welch & Willingham (WWW), a Florida-based insurance company. The firm decided to purchase a contemporary CRM system after its existing patchwork of file cards, rolodexes, and accounting packages failed to produce a coherent view of the customer. The job of implementing went to the IT Director, Kirstin Johnson. The firm has two lines of business: commercial and residential insurance, and a 20-person sales force. Each of the sales reps kept their own customer information on index cards, and sale information was stored on their personal spreadsheets and then uploaded to an accounting application when sales were finally booked and payments received. There was no ability to share information. Sales reps were paid on commission and received a percentage of the annual insurance revenue.

When sales people left the firm, they took the customer information with them, or just left it in their desks. The sales manager would assign a few sale reps to search through the empty desks of departed employees to find potential "workable leads."

In the search for a vendor, Johnson faced two barriers: finding the right vendor, and understanding the costs before committing to a single vendor. She spent several weeks interviewing CRM users in other firms to identify which vendors were most respected. Cost was another matter: it was painfully difficult to figure out how much licensing a system would really cost in day-to-day use. There were per-seat models, pay-for-use models, and hosted "on-demand" solutions where you paid by the month depending on how much your sales force used the system. She finally went with the "on demand" solution because it did not involve installing any new software or hardware at WWW, and seemed the least expensive way to go. The main vendors were Sage CRM SalesLogix and salesforce.com. Ultimately, she chose SalesLogix because it allowed her a choice: she could start with an on-demand, online model and

then later install the system on in-house servers if that became less expensive and more suitable.

Getting buy-in from the sales force was the most difficult barrier to implementation. For starters, she shut down the ability of sales people to use the accounting system for entering customer information, and forced them to enter customer data and establish files for all their customers on the SalesLogix system. If sales people did not file their customer prospecting information on the new system, it was assumed they were not doing their jobs, and this would show up in bi-annual performance reviews. Her logic was "if there's no driving force behind using the system, people can just ignore it."

Staff resistance sprung up immediately. Sales reps worried their information would be lost on another firm's Web site; they felt the system could not handle all the information they wanted to put in it; many felt the system would "blow up" someday if SalesLogix went out of business, or was purchased by another firm. The firm's largest revenue producing sales rep refused to use the new system. Instead, he printed out customer notes using a word processor and distributed them to other sales reps. He created his own manual paper-based CRM! When other reps saw this, they asked "Why should I use the new system?" Everyone wanted to continue doing their own thing.

Recognizing that sales reps don't like to take orders from the IT department, and that sales reps in many firms are the major producers of revenue that no one wants to disturb, Johnson called out to the sales manager for help. The sales manager was sympathetic, and told the recalcitrant user to either use the SalesLogix system or face severe consequences. After that, the leading revenue-producing sales rep started using the system, and in fact became its champion supporter.

After a year of training, educating, and cajoling, the implementation effort finally achieved its ambition of centralizing customer information, and creating a platform where the information could be shared, and where it was protected from high turnover in the sales force. Customer information was, for the first time, information that belonged to the firm, not the sales reps. This in itself was quite a revolution.

611

But other worries remain for Johnson and the firm. As system use goes up, so do costs, and it has been difficult to put a hard number on the benefits of information integration. How do you measure the benefits of CRM: the number of prospects contacted, sales made, customers retained, size of purchase, or some other metric? Not knowing ahead of time how you measure success often makes it difficult after the fact to claim success. How much is it worth for the firm to actually "own" the customer information and control it? Is this priceless, or is it just a nice thing?

For most enterprise implementations, the cost of implementing is typically two to three times the cost of the software and hardware. Once initial imple-

mentation is achieved, it does not end, but instead there needs to be an ongoing training and education effort to explain new features and to ensure real value is produced for the firm. There are also concerns about vendors: what if the chosen vendor is not financially stable and you need to switch to another? The switching costs of enterprise software can be quite high. Eventually, the firm would like to integrate the information in SalesLogix system with the sales information in the older financial accounting system, but there is no inexpensive way to do this.

Sources: Colin Beasty, "Barriers to CRM Success," *CRM Magazine*, May 1, 2006; Susannah Patton, "Customer Service: Answering the Call," *CIO Magazine*, June 1, 2006; and Bill Donlan, "Anatomy of a Successful CRM Implementation," CIOupdate.com, July 11, 2005.

CASE STUDY QUESTIONS

1. Why was the director of IT assigned the job of implementing a CRM system? Would this job be better performed by the sales manager?

2. Why were sales reps reluctant to share customer information with other sales reps? What strategies did Kirstin Johnson use to overcome user resistance? How would you recommend the firm overcome this problem?

3. What do you think the metrics for CRM success should be in a firm like this? How would you change the sales rep compensation plan to support more effective use of the CRM system?

MIS IN ACTION

1. Go to the Sage CRM SalesLogix Web site at www.saleslogix.com. Explore the product description for SalesLogix. What kinds of firms is this product aimed at? What kinds of functionality is provided in the suite of SalesLogix programs? What is the advantage of a hosted solution versus an on-demand solution?

2. At the SalesLogix Web site, explore the company's mobile solutions by playing the mobile solution Flash demo. How could firms take advantage of SalesLogix mobile solutions? What are some of the risks of a mobile solution?

3. On the SalesLogix Web site, identify and review a success case study (usually displayed on the home page). What are the major themes emphasized in the case?

issues, and the end-user interface of information systems. Table 5 lists the organizational dimensions that must be addressed when planning and implementing information systems.

Although systems analysis and design activities are supposed to include an organizational impact analysis, this area has traditionally been neglected. An **organizational impact analysis** explains how a proposed system will affect organizational structure, attitudes, decision making, and operations. To integrate information systems successfully with the organization, thorough and fully documented organizational impact assessments must be given more attention in the development effort.

TABLE 5 ORGANIZATIONAL FACTORS IN SYSTEMS PLANNING AND IMPLEMENTATION

Employee participation and involvement
Job design
Standards and performance monitoring
Ergonomics (including equipment, user interfaces, and the work environment)
Employee grievance resolution procedures
Health and safety
Government regulatory compliance

Sociotechnical Design

One way of addressing human and organizational issues is to incorporate **sociotechnical design** practices into information systems projects. Designers set forth separate sets of technical and social design solutions. The social design plans explore different workgroup structures, allocation of tasks, and the design of individual jobs. The proposed technical solutions are compared with the proposed social solutions. The solution that best meets both social and technical objectives is selected for the final design. The resulting sociotechnical design is expected to produce an information system that blends technical efficiency with sensitivity to organizational and human needs, leading to higher job satisfaction and productivity.

PROJECT MANAGEMENT SOFTWARE TOOLS

Commercial software tools that automate many aspects of project management facilitate the project management process. Project management software typically features capabilities for defining and ordering tasks, assigning resources to tasks, establishing starting and ending dates to tasks, tracking progress, and facilitating modifications to tasks and resources. Many automate the creation of Gantt and PERT charts.

Some of these tools are large, sophisticated programs for managing very large projects, dispersed work groups, and enterprise functions. These high-end tools can manage very large numbers of tasks and activities and complex relationships.

Microsoft Project has become the most widely used project management software today. It is PC-based, with capabilities for producing PERT and Gantt charts and for supporting critical path analysis, resource allocation, project tracking, and status reporting. Project Guide wizards are available to assist users in defining a project, listing tasks, setting deadlines, specifying workers and associated costs, choosing calendar templates, and saving a baseline version of the project plan. Project also tracks the way changes in one aspect of a project affect others.

Microsoft Project now has an Enterprise Project Management Solution version with a server component that helps large enterprises manage projects in many different locations. Project also provides a Web-based front end so that users can work with Web browser software to add project resources. Products such as EasyProjects.NET and Vertabase are also useful for firms that want Web-based project management tools.

5 ▐ HANDS-ON MIS

The projects in this section give you hands-on experience using spreadsheet software to perform capital budgeting analyses for new information systems investments and using Web tools to analyze the financing for a new home.

Improving Decision Making: Using Spreadsheet Software to Analyze the Return on a New System Investment

Software skills: Spreadsheet formulas and functions
Business skills: Capital budgeting

This project provides you with an opportunity to use spreadsheet software to use the capital budgeting models discussed in this chapter to analyze the return on a new information system investment for a real-world company.

Dirt Bikes's management would like to analyze the return on its investment in its employee training and skills tracking system. The system runs on the human resources specialists' PCs using PC database software. Because the entire corporate administrative staff recently received new desktop PC systems with database and other productivity software, there are no additional hardware and software purchase costs. The main costs include the initial cost of designing and implementing the database (business staff cost of $5,000; information systems staff cost of $15,000), gathering and adding employee skills and training data to the database ($5,500 initial data conversion cost plus $1,000 annual data entry costs), and ongoing maintenance and support ($3,000 annually). Human resources staff members believe the new application could save each of them two hours of work per week. (Their annual salaries are $37,000 and $42,000 each.) The company would also save about $11,000 annually in employee recruiting costs because it would be able to fill many vacant positions with existing employees, thereby reducing its costs for recruiting outside the company. The system would not be installed until the end of 2007 and would return benefits from 2008 to 2012.

- Prepare a report for management analyzing the return on the investment for this system over a five-year period using the following capital budgeting models: net present value, ROI, IRR, and payback method. Assume a 5 percent interest rate for your net present value calculations. Use spreadsheet software for your calculations.

- (Optional) Use electronic presentation software to summarize your findings for management.

Improving Decision Making: Using Spreadsheet Software for Capital Budgeting for a New CAD System

Software skills: Spreadsheet formulas and functions
Business skills: Capital budgeting

This project provides you with an opportunity to use spreadsheet software to use the capital budgeting models discussed in this chapter to analyze the return on an investment for a new computer-aided design (CAD) system.

Your company would like to invest in a new CAD system that requires purchasing hardware, software, and networking technology, as well as expenditures for installation, training, and support. The Laudon Web site for this chapter and Student CD-ROM contain tables showing each cost component for the new system as well as annual maintenance costs over a five-year period. You believe the new system will produce annual savings by reducing the amount of labor required to generate designs and design specifications, thus increasing your firm's annual cash flow.

- Using the data provided in these tables, create a worksheet that calculates the costs and benefits of the investment over a five-year period and analyzes the investment using the four capital budgeting models presented in this chapter.
- Is this investment worthwhile? Why or why not?

Improving Decision Making: Using Web Tools for Buying and Financing a Home

Software skills: Internet-based software
Business skills: Financial planning

This project will develop your skills using Web-based software for searching for a home and calculating mortgage financing for that home.

You have found a new job in Denver, Colorado, and would like to purchase a home in that area. Ideally, you would like to find a single-family house with at least three bedrooms and one bathroom that costs between $150,000 and $225,000 and finance it with a 30-year fixed rate mortgage. You can afford a down payment that is 20 percent of the value of the house. Before you purchase a house, you would like to find out what homes are available in your price range, find a mortgage, and determine the amount of your monthly payment. You would also like to see how much of your mortgage payment represents principal and how much represents interest. Use Yahoo!'s Real Estate site to help you with the following tasks:

- Locate homes in your price range in Denver, Colorado. Find out as much information as you can about the houses, including the real estate listing agent, condition of the house, number of rooms, and school district.
- Find a mortgage for 80 percent of the list price of the home. Compare rates from at least three sites. (Use search engines to find sites other than Yahoo!.)
- After selecting a mortgage, calculate your closing costs.
- Calculate the monthly payment for the mortgage you select.
- Calculate how much of your monthly mortgage payment represents principal and how much represents interest, assuming you do not plan to make any extra payments on the mortgage.
- When you are finished, assess the ease of use of the site and your ability to find information about houses and mortgages; the breadth of choice of homes and mortgages; and how helpful the whole process would have been for you if you were actually in the situation described in this project.

LEARNING TRACK MODULE

Information Technology Investments and Productivity. Increases in business productivity from information technology investments have been difficult to measure. The Learning Track module on this topic describes why this is so. You can find it on the Student CD-ROM and the Laudon Web site for this chapter.

Summary ▬▬▬▬▬▬▬▬▬▬▬▬▬▬▬▬▬▬▬

1. *Identify and describe the objectives of project management and why it is so essential in developing information systems.*

    A high percentage of information systems projects take more time and money to implement than originally anticipated or are delivered with missing functionality. Good project management is essential for ensuring that systems are delivered on time, on budget, and provide genuine business benefits. Project management activities include planning the work, assessing the risk, estimating and acquiring resources required to accomplish the work, organizing the work, directing execution, and analyzing the results. Project management must deal with five major variables: scope, time, cost, quality, and risk.

2. *Compare models for selecting and evaluating information systems projects and methods for aligning IS projects with the firm's business goals.*

    Organizations need to identify and select IS projects that best support their business goals. They need an information systems plan that describes how information technology supports the attainment of their business goals and documents all their system applications and IT infrastructure components. Large corporations will have a management structure to ensure the most important systems projects receive priority. Once strategic analyses have determined the overall direction of systems development, enterprise analysis, critical success factors, portfolio analysis, and scoring models can be used to identify and evaluate alternative information systems projects.

3. *Evaluate models for assessing the business value of information systems.*

    Information systems provide business value for a firm in many different ways, including increased profitability and productivity. Some, but not all, of these business benefits can be quantified and measured. Capital budgeting models are used to determine whether an investment in information technology produces sufficient returns to justify its costs. The principal capital budgeting models for evaluating systems projects are the payback method, accounting rate of return on investment (ROI), net present value, and internal rate of return (IRR). Real options pricing models, which apply the same techniques for valuing financial options to systems investments, can be useful when considering highly uncertain IT investments.

4. *Analyze the principal risk factors in information systems projects.*

    The level of risk in a systems development project is determined by three key dimensions: (1) project size, (2) project structure, and (3) experience with technology.

    A very large percentage of information systems fail to deliver benefits or solve the problems for which they were intended because the process of organizational change surrounding system building was not properly addressed. IS projects are more likely to fail when there is insufficient or improper user participation in the systems development process, lack of management support, and poor management of the implementation process. There is a very high failure rate among business process reengineering and enterprise application projects because they require extensive organizational change that is often resisted by members of the organization. System changes resulting from mergers and acquisitions are also difficult to implement successfully because they usually require far-reaching changes to business processes.

5. *Select appropriate strategies for managing project risk and system implementation.*

    Building an information system is a process of planned organizational change that must be carefully managed. The term implementation refers to the entire process of organizational change surrounding the introduction of a new information system. Especially important is the relationship between participants in the implementation process, notably the interactions between system designers and users. Eliciting user support and maintaining an appropriate level of user involvement at all stages of system building are essential.

    Management support and control of the implementation process are essential, as are mechanisms for dealing with the level of risk in each new systems project. Project risk factors can be brought under some control by a contingency approach to project management. The risk level of each project determines the appropriate mix of external integration tools, internal integration tools, formal planning tools, and formal control tools to be applied. Appropriate strategies can be applied to ensure the correct level of user participation in the systems development process and to minimize user resistance. Information systems design and the entire implementation process should be managed as planned organizational change. Sociotechnical design aims for an optimal blend of social and technical design solutions.

Key Terms

Accounting rate of return on investment (ROI)
Capital budgeting
Change agent
Change Management
Counterimplementation
Critical success factors
Enterprise analysis
Ergonomics
External integration tools
Formal control tools
Formal planning tools
Gantt chart
Implementation
Information systems plan
Intangible benefits
Internal integration tools

Internal rate of return (IRR)
Net present value
Organizational impact analysis
Payback method
PERT chart
Portfolio analysis
Present value
Project
Project management
Real options pricing models (ROPMs)
Scope
Scoring model
Sociotechnical design
Tangible benefits
User-designer communications gap
User interface

Review Questions

1. Why is project management so important for information systems projects?

2. What kinds of information systems problems result from poor project management?

3. What is project management? List and describe the project management activities and variables addressed by project management.

4. Name and describe the groups responsible for the management of information systems projects.

5. What are the major categories of an information systems plan?

6. How can enterprise analysis and critical success factors be used for selecting information systems projects?

7. Describe how portfolio analysis and scoring models can be used to select information systems projects.

8. List and describe the major costs and benefits of information systems. What is the difference between tangible and intangible benefits?

9. Name and describe the principal capital budgeting methods used to evaluate information system projects.

10. How can real options pricing models help evaluate information technology investments?

11. What are the limitations of financial models for establishing the value of information systems?

12. What dimensions influence the level of risk in each information systems project?

13. Why do builders of new information systems need to address change management?

14. What are implementation and counterimplementation?

15. Why are eliciting support of management and end users so essential for successful implementation of information systems projects? What is the user-designer communications gap?

16. Why is there such a high failure rate among enterprise application implementations and business process reengineering (BPR) projects? What role do information systems play in the success or failure of mergers and acquisitions?

17. What project management techniques can be used to control project risk?

18. What organizational considerations should be addressed by information systems planning and implementation?

19. How do project management software tools contribute to successful project managment?

Discussion Questions

1. How much does project management impact the success of a new information system?

2. It has been said that most systems fail because systems builders ignore organizational behavior problems. Why might this be so?

Video Case

You will find a video case illustrating some of the concepts in this chapter on the Laudon Web site and Student CD-ROM along with questions to help you analyze the case.

Teamwork: Identifying Implementation Problems

Form a group with two or three other students. Write a description of the implementation problems you might expect to encounter in one of the systems described in the Interactive Sessions or chapter-ending cases in this text. Write an analysis of the steps you would take to solve or prevent these problems. If possible, use electronic presentation software to present your findings to the class.

REFERENCES

Agarwal, Ritu and Viswanath Venkatesnh. "Assessing a Firm's Web Presence: A Heuristic Evaluation Procedure for the Measurement of Usability." *Information Systems Research* 13, no.3 (September 2002).

Aladwani, Adel M. "An Integrated Performance Model of Information Systems Projects." *Journal of Management Information Systems* 19, no.1 (Summer 2002).

Alleman, James. "Real Options Real Opportunities." *Optimize Magazine* (January 2002).

Andres, Howard P. and Robert W. Zmud. "A Contingency Approach to Software Project Coordination." *Journal of Management Information Systems* 18, no. 3 (Winter 2001–2002).

Attewell, Paul. "Technology Diffusion and Organizational Learning: The Case of Business Computing." *Organization Science*, no. 3 (1992).

Banker, Rajiv. "Value Implications of Relative Investments in Information Technology." Department of Information Systems and Center for Digital Economy Research, University of Texas at Dallas, January 23, 2001.

Barki, Henri and Jon Hartwick. "Interpersonal Conflict and Its Management in Information Systems Development." *MIS Quarterly* 25, no.2 (June 2001).

Barki, Henri, Suzanne Rivard, and Jean Talbot. "An Integrative Contingency Model of Software Project Risk Management." *Journal of Management Information Systems* 17, no. 4 (Spring 2001).

Baudisch, Patrick, Doug DeCarlo, Andrew T. Duchowski, and Wilson S. Geisler. "Focusing on the Essential: Considering Attention in Display Design." *Communications of the ACM* 46, no. 3 (March 2003).

Benaroch, Michel. "Managing Information Technology Investment Risk: A Real Options Perspective." *Journal of Management Information Systems* 19, no. 2 (Fall 2002).

Benaroch, Michel, Sandeep Shah, and Mark Jeffrey. "On the Valuation of Multistage Information Technology Investments Embedding Nested Real Options." *Journal of Management Information Systems* 23, No. 1 (Summer 2006).

Benaroch, Michel and Robert J. Kauffman. "Justifying Electronic Banking Network Expansion Using Real Options Analysis." *MIS Quarterly* 24, no. 2 (June 2000).

Bharadwaj, Anandhi. "A Resource-Based Perspective on Information Technology Capability and Firm Performance." *MIS Quarterly* 24, no. 1 (March 2000).

Bhattacherjee, Anol and G. Premkumar. "Understanding Changes In Belief and Attitude Toward Information Technology Usage: A Theoretical Model and Longitudinal Test." *MIS Quarterly* 28, no. 2 (June 2004).

Boer, F. Peter. "Real Options: The IT Investment Risk Buster." *Optimize Magazine* (July 2002).

Bostrom, R. P., and J. S. Heinen. "MIS Problems and Failures: A Socio-Technical Perspective. Part I: The Causes." *MIS Quarterly* 1 (September 1977); "Part II: The Application of Socio-Technical Theory." *MIS Quarterly* 1 (December 1977).

Brooks, Frederick P. "The Mythical Man-Month." *Datamation* (December 1974).

Brynjolfsson, Erik. "The Contribution of Information Technology to Consumer Welfare." *Information Systems Research* 7, no. 3 (September 1996).

———. "The IT Productivity GAP." *Optimize* 21 (July 2003).

———. "The Productivity Paradox of Information Technology." *Communications of the ACM* 36, no. 12 (December 1993).

Brynjolfsson, Erik, and Lorin M. Hitt. "Information Technology and Organizational Design: Evidence from Micro Data." (January 1998).

Brynjolfsson, Erik, and Lorin M. Hitt. "Beyond the Productivity Paradox." *Communications of the ACM* 41, no. 8 (August 1998)

Brynjolfsson, Erik and S. Yang. "Intangible Assets: How the Interaction of Computers and Organizational Structure Affects Stock Markets." MIT Sloan School of Management (2000).

Chatterjee, Debabroto, Carl Pacini, and V. Sambamurthy. "The Shareholder-Wealth and Trading Volume Effects of Information Technology Infrastructure Investments." *Journal of Management Information Systems* 19, no. 2 (Fall 2002).

Chatterjee, Debabroto, Rajdeep Grewal, and V. Sabamurthy. "Shaping Up for E-Commerce: Institutional Enablers of the Organizational Assimilation of Web Technologies." *MIS Quarterly* 26, no. 2 (June 2002).

Chau, PatrickY.K. and Vincent S. K. Lai. "An Empirical Investigtion of the Determinants of User Acceptance of Internet Banking." *Journal of Organizational Computing and Electronic Commerce* 13, no. 2 (2003).

Concours Group. "Delivering Large-Scale System Projects." (2000).

Cooper, Randolph B. "Information Technology Development Creativity: A Case Study of Attempted Radical Change." *MIS Quarterly* 24, no. 2 (June 2000).

Datz, Todd. "Portfolio Management: How to Do It Right," *CIO Magazine* (May 1, 2003).

Davern, Michael J. and Robert J. Kauffman. "Discovering Potential and Realizing Value from Information Technology Investments." *Journal of Management Information Systems* 16, no. 4 (Spring 2000).

Davis, Fred R. "Perceived Usefulness, Ease of Use, and User Acceptance of Information Technology." *MIS Quarterly* 13, no. 3 (September 1989).

De Meyer, Arnoud, Christoph H. Loch and Michael T. Pich. "Managing Project Uncertainty: From Variation to Chaos." *Sloan Management Review* 43, no.2 (Winter 2002).

Delone, William H. and Ephraim R. McLean. "The Delone and McLean Model of Information Systems Success: A Ten-Year Update." *Journal of Management Information Systems* 19, no. 4 (Spring 2003).

Doll, William J., Xiaodung Deng, T. S. Raghunathan, Gholamreza Torkzadeh, and Weidong Xia. "The Meaning and Measurement of User Satisfaction: A Multigroup Invariance Analysis of End-User Computing Satisfaction Instrument." Journal of Management Information Systems 21, no. 1 (Summer 2004).

Ein-Dor, Philip, and Eli Segev. "Organizational Context and the Success of Management Information Systems." Management Science 24 (June 1978).

Fichman, Robert G. "Real Options and IT Platforms Adoption: Implications for Theory and Practice." Information Systems Research 15, no. 2 (June 2004).

Frank, Robert and Robin Sidel. "Firms that Lived by the Deal in '90s Now Sink by the Dozens." *The Wall Street Journal* (June 6, 2002).

Gefen, David and Catherine M. Ridings. "Implementation Team Responsiveness and User Evaluation of Customer Relationship Management: A Quasi-Experimental Design Study of Social Exchange Theory." *Journal of Management Information Systems* 19, no. 1 (Summer 2002).

Hitt, Lorin, D.J. Wu, and Xiaoge Zhou. "Investment in Enterprise Resource Planning: Business Impact and Productivity Measures." *Journal of Management Information Systems* 19, no. 1 (Summer 2002).

Housel, Thomas J., Omar El Sawy, JianfangJ. Zhong, and Waymond Rodgers. "Measuring the Return on e-Business Initiatives at the Process Level: The Knowledge Value-Added Approach." *ICIS* (2001).

Iversen, Jakob H., Lars Mathiassen, and Peter Axel Nielsen. "Managing Risk in Software Process Improvement: An Action Research Approach." *MIS Quarterly* 28, no. 3 (September 2004).

Jeffrey, Mark and Ingmar Leliveld. "Best Practices in IT Portfolio Management." MIT Sloan Management Review 45, no. 3 (Spring 2004).

Kalin, Sari. "Making IT Portfolio Management a Reality." *CIO Magazine* (June 1, 2006).

Keen, Peter W. "Information Systems and Organizational Change." *Communications of the ACM* 24 (January 1981).

Keil, Mark and Daniel Robey. "Blowing the Whistle on Troubled Software Projects." *Communications of the ACM* 44, no. 4 (April 2001).

Keil, Mark and Ramiro Montealegre. "Cutting Your Losses: Extricating Your Organization When a Big Project Goes Awry." *Sloan Management Review* 41, no. 3 (Spring 2000).

Keil, Mark, Joan Mann, and Arun Rai. "Why Software Projects Escalate: An Empirical Analysis and Test of Four Theoretical Models." *MIS Quarterly* 24, no. 4 (December 2000).

Keil, Mark, Paul E. Cule, Kalle Lyytinen, and Roy C. Schmidt. "A Framework for Identifying Software Project Risks." *Communications of the ACM* 41, 11 (November 1998).

Keil, Mark, Richard Mixon, Timo Saarinen, and Virpi Tuunairen. "Understanding Runaway IT Projects." *Journal of Management Information Systems* 11, no. 3 (Winter 1994–95).

Kettinger, William J. and Choong C. Lee. "Understanding the IS-User Divide in IT Innovation." *Communications of the ACM* 45, no.2 (February 2002).

Klein, Gary, James J. Jiang, and Debbie B. Tesch. "Wanted: Project Teams with a Blend of IS Professional Orientations." *Communications of the ACM* 45, no. 6 (June 2002).

Kolb, D. A., and A. L. Frohman. "An Organization Development Approach to Consulting." *Sloan Management Review* 12 (Fall 1970).

Laudon, Kenneth C. "CIOs Beware: Very Large Scale Systems." Center for Research on Information Systems, New York University Stern School of Business, working paper (1989).

Levinson, Meridith. "When Failure Is Not an Option." *CIO Magazine* (June 1, 2006).

Lientz, Bennett P., and E. Burton Swanson. *Software Maintenance Management.* Reading, MA: Addison-Wesley (1980).

Lipin, Steven and Nikhil Deogun. "Big Mergers of 90s Prove Disappointing to Shareholders." *The Wall Street Journal* (October 30, 2000).

Mahmood, Mo Adam, Laura Hall, and Daniel Leonard Swanberg, "Factors Affecting Information Technology Usage: A Meta-Analysis of the Empirical Literature." *Journal of Organizational Computing and Electronic Commerce* 11, no. 2 (November 2, 2001)

Markus, M. Lynne, and Robert I. Benjamin. "The Magic Bullet Theory of IT-Enabled Transformation." *Sloan Management Review* (Winter 1997).

McFarlan, F. Warren. "Portfolio Approach to Information Systems." *Harvard Business Review* (September–October 1981).

McGrath, Rita Gunther and Ian C.McMillan. "Assessing Technology Projects Using Real Options Reasoning." *Industrial Research Institute* (2000)

Mumford, Enid, and Mary Weir. *Computer Systems in Work Design: The ETHICS Method.* New York: John Wiley (1979).

Nambisan, Satish and Yu-Ming Wang. "Web Technology Adoption and Knowledge Barriers." *Journal of Organizational Computing and Electronic Commerce* 10, no. 2 (2000).

Nedda Gabriela G. Olazabal. "Banking: The IT Paradox." *The McKinsey Quarterly.* (2002 Number 1).

Nidumolu, Sarma R. and Mani Subramani. "The Matrix of Control: Combining Process and Structure Approaches to Management Software Development." Journal of Management Informatin Systems 20, no. 3 (Winter 2004).

Palmer, Jonathan W. "Web Site Usability, Design and Performance Metrics." *Information Systems Research* 13, no.3 (September 2002).

Premkumar, G. "A Meta-Analysis of Research on Information Technology Implementation in Small Business." *Journal of Organizational Computing and Electronic Commerce* 13, no. 2 (2003).

Quan, Jin "Jim", Quing Hu, and Paul J. Hart. "Information Technology Investments and Firms' Performance—A Duopoly Perspective." Journal of Management Information Systems 20, no. 3 (Winter 2004).

Robey, Daniel, and M. Lynne Markus. "Rituals in Information System Design." *MIS Quarterly* (March 1984).

Robey, Daniel, Jeanne W. Ross, and Marie-Claude Boudreau. "Learning to Implement Enterprise Systems: An Exploratory Study of the Dialectics of Change." *Journal of Management Information Systems* 19, no. 1 (Summer 2002).

Rockart, John F. "Chief Executives Define Their Own Data Needs." *Harvard Business Review* (March–April 1979).

Ross, Jeanne W. and Cynthia M. Beath. "Beyond the Business Case: New Approaches to IT Investment." *Sloan Management Review* 43, no.2 (Winter 2002).

Ryan, Sherry D., David A. Harrison, and Lawrence L Schkade. "Information Technology Investment Decisions: When Do Cost and Benefits in the Social Subsystem Matter?" *Journal of Management Information Systems* 19, no. 2 (Fall 2002).

Sambamurthy, V., Anandhi Bharadwaj, and Varun Grover. "Shaping Agility Through Digital Options: Reconceptualizing the Role of Information Technology in Contemporary Firms." *MIS Quarterly* 27, no. 2 (June 2003).

Santhanam, Radhika and Edward Hartono. "Issues in Linking Information Technology Capability to Firm Performance." *MIS Quarterly* 27, no. 1 (March 2003).

Schmidt, Roy, Kalle Lyytinen, Mark Keil, and Paul Cule. "Identifying Software Project Risks: An International Delphi Study." *Journal of Management Information Systems* 17, no. 4 (Spring 2001)

Schwalbe, Kathy. *Information Technology Project Management*, 4/e. Course Technology (2005).

Siewiorek, Daniel P. "New Frontiers of Application Design." *Communications of the ACM* 45, no.12 (December 2002.)

Sircar, Sumit, Joe L. Turnbow, and Bijoy Bordoloi. "A Framework for Assessing the Relationship between Information Technology Investments and Firm Performance." *Journal of Management Information Systems* 16, no. 4 (Spring 2000).

Smith, H. Jeff, Mark Keil, and Gordon Depledge. "Keeping Mum as the Project Goes Under." *Journal of Management Information Systems* 18, no. 2 (Fall 2001)

Speier, Cheri and Michael. G. Morris. "The Influence of Query Interface Design on Decision-Making Performance." *MIS Quarterly* 27, no. 3 (September 2003).

Straub, Detmar W., Arun Rai and Richard Klein. "Measuring Firm Performance at the Network Level: A Nomology of the Business Impact of Digital Supply Networks." Journal of Management Information Systems 21, no 1 (Summer 2004).

Swanson, E. Burton. *Information System Implementation*. Homewood, IL: Richard D. Irwin (1988).

Tallon, Paul P, Kenneth L. Kraemer, and Vijay Gurbaxani. "Executives' Perceptions of the Business Value of Information Technology: A Process-Oriented Approach." *Journal of Management Information Systems* 16, no. 4 (Spring 2000).

Thatcher, Matt E. and Jim R. Oliver. "The Impact of Technology Investments on a Firm's Production Efficiency, Product Quality, and Productivity." *Journal of Management Information Systems* 18, no. 2 (Fall 2001).

Tornatsky, Louis G., J. D. Eveland, M. G. Boylan, W. A. Hetzner, E. C. Johnson, D. Roitman, and J. Schneider. *The Process of Technological Innovation: Reviewing the Literature*. Washington, DC: National Science Foundation (1983).

Venkatesh, Viswanath, Michael G. Morris, Gordon B Davis, and Fred D. Davis. "User Acceptance of Information Technology: Toward a Unified View." *MIS Quarterly* 27, No. 3 (September 2003).

Wallace, Linda and Mark Keil. "Software Project Risks and Their Effect on Outcomes." Communications of the ACM 47, no. 4 (April 2004).

Wang, Eric T.G., Gary Klein, and James J. Jiang. "ERP Misfit: Country of Origin and Organizational Factors." *Journal of Management Information Systems* 23, No. 1 (Summer 2006).

Xia, Weidong and Gwanhoo Lee. "Grasping the Complexity of IS Development Projects." Communications of the ACM 47, no. 5 (May 2004).

Zhu, Kevin. "The Complementarity of Information Technology Infrastructure and E-Commerce Capability: A Resource-Based Assessment of Their Business Value." Journal of Management Information Systems 21, no. 1 (Summer 2004).

Zhu, Kevin and Kenneth L. Kraemer. "E-Commerce Metrics for Net-Enhanced Organizations: Assessing the Value of e-Commerce to Firm Performance in the Manufacturing Sector." *Information Systems Research* 13, no.3 (September 2002).

Zhu, Kevin, Kenneth L. Kraemer, Sean Xu, and Jason Dedrick. "Information Technology Payoff in E-Business Environments: An International Perspective on Value Creation of E-business in the Financial Services Industry." Journal of Management Information Systems 21, no. 1 (Summer 2004).

620

What Went Wrong with Maine's New Medicaid System?
CASE STUDY

The state of Maine provides medical coverage for over 260,000 of its residents through its Medicaid program. Healthcare providers, including doctors, hospitals, clinics, and nursing homes, submit claims to Medicaid in order to be paid for the services they provide to Medicaid patients. As the 1990s drew to a close, Maine, like many other states, began planning for a complete overhaul of its Medicaid claims processing systems to comply with the Health Insurance Portability and Accountability Act of 1996 (HIPAA). HIPAA was enacted to standardize the management of patient health and records, and, most notably, the protection of patient privacy. HIPAA provided a deadline of October 1, 2002, to meet its patient privacy and security standards.

Maine had to consider a number of factors in addition to HIPAA in preparing for its systems overhaul. The Medicaid program, as outlined by the federal government, was becoming increasingly complex with new services added, each with codes and subcodes assigned to them. As a result, payments to providers were broken down into smaller and more numerous pieces. The state also wanted to offer providers access to patient eligibility and claim status data online in the hopes of reducing the volume of calls to the state Bureau of Medical Services, which ran Medicaid under the Department of Human Services (DHS).

At the time, Maine was processing over 100,000 Medicaid claims per week on a Honeywell mainframe that dated back to the 1970s. The system was not capable of supporting HIPAA requirements or the online access that the state wished to implement. The state's IT department decided that a completely new system would be more cost-effective and easier to maintain than an upgrade of the old system. This approach contrasted with what some other states had done. Nearby Massachusetts, for instance, chose to deploy a Web portal as an integrated front end to its existing legacy systems. However, the IT staff at the DHS believed a new custom-built system it would be more flexible because they could make it rule-based in order to accommodate frequent changes in Medicaid rules. The IT staff also rejected an option to outsource claims processing systems to a service provider such as Electronic Data Systems (EDS).

For such a large and significant project, the DHS enlisted a private contractor to work with its IT staff. The state put out a request for proposals in April 2001. In October 2001, CNSI, one of only two firms to bid, received the contract for its $15 million proposal. The deal called for CNSI to complete and deploy the new processing system by the HIPAA compliance deadline, which was 12 months away. In actuality, the system debuted on January 21, 2005, almost 27 months later. However, the badly missed deadline was hardly Maine's biggest problem. The new system failed on many levels.

Shortly after its rollout, the new system was rejecting claims much more frequently than the old system had. Most of the rejected claims were being held up as suspended, a designation usually applied to claim forms that contained errors. The suspended file grew quickly, causing millions of dollars in claims to be held back.

Within two months, 300,000 claims were frozen. The Bureau of Medical Services could keep up neither with the number of phone calls nor the processing of the suspended claims. The 65 members of the DHS/CNSI team worked feverishly to fix software glitches, but their efforts were accompanied by a lack of regard for critical management guidelines. Meanwhile, some providers who weren't getting paid were forced to turn away Medicaid patients or even shut down their operations. Others sought bank loans to keep their practices fluid. Even the state's finances were threatened due to the significant portion of the state budget that Medicaid regularly ate up. Charlene Kinnelly, executive director of Uplift Inc., a nonprofit service provider for the mentally handicapped and mentally ill, reported that the state owed her organization $250,000. Seven thousand other nonprofits and healthcare service providers had not been compensated properly. Maine began issuing interim payments to providers that were based on their average claims.

The claims system software was error-prone, even issuing checks to doctors for their total charges for a procedure instead of the amounts that were actually

From *Management Information Systems: Managing the Digital Firm*, 10/e. Kenneth C. Laudon, Jane P. Laudon. Copyright © 2007 by Pearson Prentice Hall. All rights reserved.

covered by Medicaid. Overpayments eventually recovered by Maine Medicaid totaled $9 million. Providers were having difficulty filling out the new claim forms correctly, which was not a big surprise since some of the forms required 30 to 40 fields of information. The incorrect forms were among those claims that were flagged for the suspended file.

CNSI recommended that all providers re-enroll so that their information would be complete according to the new system's requirements. The department chose, instead, to transfer existing information from the old system, which was considered incomplete by the new system. Adding to the chaos when the problems began was the fact that only 13 people were on staff to handle customer service calls from 7,000 providers. The disaster cost the state an additional $30 million. More than a year after rolling out the new system, Maine was the only state that still had not satisfied the HIPAA requirements.

CNSI had never before designed a Medicaid claims system. Furthermore, that the state received only two proposals, and the one from a firm named Keane asking twice as much money as CNSI's, should have been a cause for alarm. J. Davidson Frame, dean of the University of Management and Technology in Arlington, Virgina, described the weak response to the Request for Proposal (RFP) as a sign that its requirements were unreasonable. Had Maine's procurement department sensed this at the time, the RFP could have been revised and the state likely would have received more bids that were in line with Keane's $30 million initial proposal. After all, Keane had worked on similar systems, including Maine's Medicaid eligibility processing.

B. Chatterjee, president of CNSI, admitted that his company lacked the experience of working with Medicaid systems and described CNSI as "a no-name company" looking for an entry-way into claims processing system management. Chatterjee assumed that his Rockville, Maryland-based information technology firm could rely on end users' Medicaid background to form a successful team.

Citing the scalability requirements of the project, CNSI planned the programming based on J2EE (Java Platform Enterprise Edition), which was a mismatch with the legacy code from the old system. Dick Thompson, who was then head of procurement for the state of Maine, defended the decision to select CNSI by pointing out that the state was not in a position to overspend and the time constraints of the HIPAA deadline gave the state little time to delay its decision. Budget

concerns also prevented the project from being properly staffed, which slowed development during the design phase and hampered response time once the complaints started piling up.

The team had difficulty getting consulting time with the Medicaid experts on staff at the Bureau of Medical Services. The DHS IT staffers and CNSI contractors were forced to make judgments about Medicaid rules and requirements without the proper input. The team then had to reprogram parts of the system once the Medicaid experts became available. One break came when the federal body that runs Medicaid extended the HIPAA deadline by a full year to October 1, 2003. However, the DHS team continued to fight against the tide, fixing errors, writing new code to accommodate Medicaid rules changes, and adding storage capacity and processing power to support the new rules. Sensing that they would never catch up, the team began to take shortcuts. Comprehensive testing of the system was deemed impossible due to time constraints. Moreover, despite informing providers of the new system and new provider ID codes, the state did not offer training for providers on the new system; nor did the state properly train the staff that would be responsible for fielding calls from providers with problems.

When the DHS, now merged with the Department of Behavioral and Developmental Services as the Department of Health and Human Services (HHS), decided to launch the new claims processing system in January 2005, it did so with a clean break from the legacy system. There was no backup or parallel system to support the deployment because the legacy system was incompatible with the new code numbers (representing provider tax ID numbers and patient social security numbers) and electronic claim forms, and a parallel system was not feasible economically or technically. The one backup plan in place was a provision to pay providers for two to four weeks based on their average monthly claims payments in case of a failed deployment.

Within a few days of going live with the system, Craig Hitchings, director of information technology for DHS, noticed that the system was suspending an unusually high number of claims, around 50 percent or 24,000 claims in the very first week. The old system had rejected claims at a rate of 20 percent on average. And then the calls started coming in. Providers whose claims had been suspended were filing second claims, which were suspended automatically by the system because they were tagged as duplicates. The Bureau of Medical Services could not remedy the botched claims nearly as fast they were coming in. Soon there were 100,000 claims stuck in the system. Doctors were receiving statements in the mail for rejected claims over and over. Medicaid was behind on $50 million worth of payments. At the same time, Hitchings and CNSI discovered programming and design problems in the system that limited the size of claim files to an unreasonable 1,000 lines of code. Providers calling to complain were rarely able to get through and suffered through seemingly interminable waiting periods on hold when they did. Maine's healthcare system was in crisis, and the state budget was in danger of imploding.

In March 2005, Maine hired XWave, a project management consultant specializing in integration, for over $860,000 to right the ship. The problems persisted and as summer drew to a close, the backlog of suspended claims had reached 647,000 and providers were owed $310 million in payments. Rebecca Wyke, head of Maine's financing department, awarded a $7 million contract to the accounting firm Deloitte & Touche to make sure that the state would be able to pay its Medicaid obligations and to help sort out the mess of bills. Thompson, who by now had been named CIO by Wyke, brought in Jim Lopatosky, an Oracle database specialist, to fill the role of operations manager. Lopatosky and XWave both determined that the project suffered from ineffective project management and a dearth of communication among Maine's IT staff, CNSI, and the end users. Lopatosky worked to improve communications so that workers from the two branches of the team wouldn't work on the same parts of the system unaware of what the other was doing. He also prioritized the troubleshooting process so that suspended claims could be cleared before less critical work was done.

Thompson added another significant piece to the puzzle in October 2005 by appointing Dr. Laureen Biczak to be the organization's Medicaid expert. Thompson said, "It was something we should have done from the start: have someone who knew the business [of Medicaid] working full-time on the project." Beginning in January 2006, questions from providers were filtered to Medicaid specialists working under Biczak if they were business-process issues, or to the IT department if they were hardware or software issues. With this filtering system in

effect, Maine was able to reduce the claim suspension rate to about 15 percent with the remaining 85 percent of claims being processed properly as paid or denied. However, some providers still wondered why so much time and money was spent on a system that so far has not performed any better than the system it replaced, and, worse, caused harm to healthcare providers and their patients.

Chatterjee, whose company lost around $10 million on the project, believed that CNSI and the state bore responsibility for half of the problems, and providers who made mistakes on their claim forms could be blamed for the other half. He also insisted that Maine is better positioned to go forward than other states that updated their existing systems rather than building state-of-the-art new systems. In fact, CNSI has received additional state Medicaid contracts in the wake of its work with Maine. Maine was hopeful that its system would finally be fully functional sometime in 2006.

Sources: Allan Holmes, "Maine's Medicaid Mistakes," *CIO Magazine*, April 15, 2006; Victoria Wallack, "No One at the Helm: Maine Medicaid Struggles On," *Ellsworth American*, December 22, 2005; Susan M. Cover, "Stiffed by Software," *Kennebec Journal*, May 1, 2005; "Computer Debacle Could Cost Maine Medicaid Millions in Federal Matching Funds," www.freerepublic.com, September 28, 2005; Todd Benoit, "From a Medicaid Disaster, Hope," *Bangor Daily News*, June 25, 2005; "Maine Providers To Receive Payments Delayed by Medicaid Computer System," www.ihealthbeat.org, March 7, 2005; "Maine Addresses Medicaid Billing System Problems," www.ihealthbeat.org, April 6, 2005; and Victoria Wallack, "Computer Snafu Could Cost State $4 Million," *Boothbay Register*, July 21, 2005.

CASE STUDY QUESTIONS

1. How important are information systems for Maine's Department of Health and Human Services? Analyze the impact of its faulty Medicaid claims processing system.

2. Evaluate the risks of the Medicaid claims processing system project and key risk factors.

3. Classify and describe the problems the Maine Department of Human Services faced in implementing its new Medicaid claims processing system. What management, organization, and technology factors caused these problems?

4. Describe the steps you would have taken to control the risk in the IT modernization project.

5. If you were in charge of managing this project, what else would you have done differently to increase chances for success?

Managing Global Systems

Managing Global Systems

THINK GLOBAL, ACT LOCAL: DHL BUILDS A GLOBAL IT ORGANIZATION

Servicing over 140,000 destinations in over 220 countries with overnight and express package deliveries poses a unique problem: how do you work in very unique local environments, with different languages, cultures, and local knowledge, while at the same time deliver this service on a global, time-intense platform? This is the question facing DHL, a logistics and parcel delivery business with worldwide operations. Founded in 1969 by Adrian Dalsey, Larry Hillblom, and Robert Lynn (the source of **D**, **H**, and **L**), DHL began as a service shuttling bills of lading between San Francisco and Honolulu. Now owned by Deutsche Post World Net, DHL operates a global system of 4,400 local offices, 238 gateways, and more than 450 hubs, warehouses, and terminals. The company employs over 170,000 people. The company offers 4.2 million customers worldwide fast, reliable, and cost-efficient package delivery service around the world. More than 400 aircraft operate for or on behalf of DHL. Keeping track of its own operations, in addition to customer packages, is a major challenge for DHL.

For DHL, acting locally means that customers and employees would see on their computer screens information on their packages in their local language, databases would contain important country regulations, and local information would be current. Acting globally means that DHL computer systems around the world can check on the status and location of any DHL package, and have that information be current, and accurate within minutes of an event happening. If the information is delayed even more than a few seconds, or wrong, scanners can't operate, planes fly empty, and packages remain in warehouses.

Originally, DHL solved this problem by building over 50 different data centers in each of the major countries where it operated and coordinating these loosely with a common set of core database applications that were installed in each of the countries. The core applications sat on top of a messaging and communications network so information could transfer from one country to another. The core applications included a master common shipment database that kept the tracking information, as well as e-mail programs, customer shipment, transit times, and billing details. The global databases allowed local countries' units to see only the data needed locally, and required them to store only local data.

This arrangement of common global core systems that could be customized to local needs was adequate until traffic volume expanded rapidly in the last decade as global trade pushed the existing system to the limits. With 50 decentralized data centers running supposedly common programs, the risks that any one center or several centers would fail might jeopardize shipments in several countries. Through painful experience, DHL learned that maintaining 50 different IS centers to a single global standard was diffi-

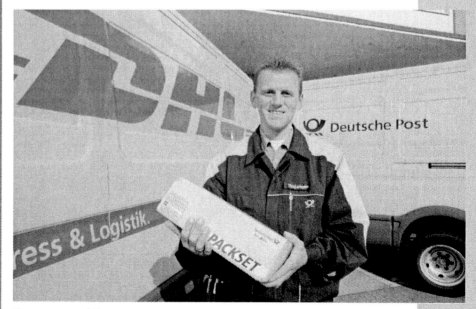

Photo courtesy of Alamy.com

cult in many countries. The company also learned that "the information is more important than the package." Customers might understand and be sympathetic when hurricanes or tsunamis lead to lost packages, but they are intolerant to the idea that the DHL system failed and cannot tell them where their package is—even if it's at the bottom of the ocean.

In addition, the highly decentralized IS structure raised costs and slowed down change. Upgrades to software programs would have to be deployed in 50 different countries, taking over 18 months. Costs rose because instead of maintaining the computers and programmers in one location, they had to be maintained in 50 locations.

When Managing Director of IT services, Stephen McGuckin, took over the Asian and Middle Eastern operation beginning in the late 1990s, management was increasingly strained by the existing organization of IT. Country managers were flying far too often to regional meetings with one another trying to coordinate policies, and McGuckin estimated that managers lost 20 percent of their productivity. The IT coordinating centers were headquartered in four different, expensive locations: London, Singapore, Hong Kong, and Bahrain. The software was all being developed in the United States which also was very costly. A new set of management processes needed to be built.

McGuckin started moving DHL toward a more centralized arrangement of systems to reduce its risks, decrease its costs, increase the speed with which it could deploy new applications, and raise the reliability of its systems. Beginning in 2000, DHL began concentrating its global computing infrastructure into three low-cost, regional global centers: Cyberjaya (Malaysia), Prague, and Scottsdale, Arizona, in the United States. Each of these regional centers handles the information processing for a group of countries in the region.

In the process of consolidating, McGuckin also changed the management of software production. Initially outsourcing all software development to InfoSys, a large Indian-based outsourcing firm, DHL learned how to separate the design work (now done in the U.S.) from the implementation and execution work (now done in India). Costs declined, and quality was enhanced despite an early period of misunderstandings with their outsourcing firm.

By 2006, the consolidation was completed. So far the move seems to have been a success. Costs of maintaining the IT infrastructure have fallen by 40 percent; the time to deploy new applications has fallen to a matter of hours from months. New applications are built in Arizona, deployed to the other two global centers, and in a matter of hours can be deployed to customers and employees who access these centers for all their information needs.

Sources: Laurie Sullivan, "DHL Taps Several Vendors For RFID Project," *TechWeb News*, March 8, 2006; Michael Bloch and Marcus Schaper, "Building a Global IT Organization: An Interview with DPWN's Managing Director of IT," *The McKinsley Quarterly*, May 2006; www.DHL-usa.com/company/history.htm.

DHL's transition from a highly decentralized global logistics company towards a more regional global structure illustrates how global firms are adjusting their systems to support the rapid growth in world trade. This case also illustrates the tensions between the need to be locally responsive, and achieve a seamless flow of information across national boundaries in a truly global system.

The chapter-opening diagram calls attention to important points raised by this case and this chapter. DHL's original solution to building a global logistics support system including package delivery was costly, slow, and difficult to manage. The solution consisted of three parts. DHL changed the organization of its systems by consolidating into three low-cost centers. It changed the management of its systems by also centralizing management in three centers, simplifying management communication, and changed how it managed software development by outsourcing implementation of software designs built in the United States. The technology change involved moving core applications from 50 local servers onto three regional server centers, and strengthening communication links with the local offices to ensure connectivity.

HEADS UP

During your career, you may work in a company that operates internationally. To be effective, you will need a global perspective on business and an understanding of the information systems needed to conduct business on an international scale. Special issues must be addressed when developing and managing global information systems. This chapter shows you how to organize, manage, and control the development of global systems.

- If your career is in finance or accounting, you will be using international systems to enable the flow of funds between corporate headquarters and operating units and to facilitate purchases in different countries.
- If your career is in human resources, you will be advising system builders about how to deal with language and cultural differences affecting implementation and use of international systems.
- If your career is in information systems, you will be developing connectivity solutions to link disparate local systems with different technology platforms and working with management to develop standard data definitions and business processes to integrate these systems.
- If your career is in manufacturing, production, or operations management, you will be helping to implement standard supply chain management software or enterprise software to coordinate global manufacturing processes and supply chains.
- If your career is in sales and marketing, you will be setting up Web sites designed for global sales and marketing.

1 THE GROWTH OF INTERNATIONAL INFORMATION SYSTEMS

I n earlier chapters, we describe the emergence of a global economic system and global world order driven by advanced networks and information systems. The new world order is sweeping away many national corporations, national industries, and national economies controlled by domestic politicians. Many localized firms will be replaced by fast-moving networked corporations that transcend national boundaries. The growth of international trade has radically altered domestic economies around the globe. Today, the combined value of imports and exports from all nations is about $20 trillion dollars annually, a little less than one-third of the world's total GDP (Gross Domestic Product) of $67 trillion. The United States exports about $1 trillion annually, while importing $1.7 trillion, for a combined $2.7 trillion in trade, or about 22 percent of the U.S. economy. While the world GDP is growing at about 4.7 percent a year, international trade is growing at about 5.6 percent annually (CIA, 2006).

Today, the production and design of many high-end electronic products is parceled out to a number of different countries. Consider the path to market for Hewlett-Packard's ProLiant ML150 server, which is illustrated in Figure 1. The idea for the product was hatched in Singapore, which did the initial design work. HP headquarters in Houston approved the concept. Contractors in Taiwan did the machine's engineering design and initial manufacture. Final assembly of the server takes place in Singapore, China, India, and Australia (Buckman, 2004). None of this would be possible without powerful international information and communication systems.

FIGURE 1   GLOBAL PRODUCT DEVELOPMENT AND PRODUCTION

A new HP server's path to market:
❶ Idea for product hatched in Singapore.
❷ Concept approved in Houston.
❸ Concept design done in Singapore.
❹ Engineering design in Taiwan, where many computer components are made;
   initial manufacture by a Taiwanese contractor.
❺ Final assembly in Singapore, Australia, China, and India. Products made in Australia,
   China, and India are primarily for those markets; machines made in Singapore go to all of Southeast Asia.

Hewlett-Packard and other electronics companies assign distribution and production of high-end products to a number of different countries.

Source: © *The New York Times.* Used with Permission.

630

DEVELOPING AN INTERNATIONAL INFORMATION SYSTEMS ARCHITECTURE

This chapter describes how to go about building an international information systems architecture suitable for your international strategy. An **international information systems architecture** consists of the basic information systems required by organizations to coordinate worldwide trade and other activities. Figure 2 illustrates the reasoning we follow throughout the chapter and depicts the major dimensions of an international information systems portfolio.

The basic strategy to follow when building an international system is to understand the global environment in which your firm is operating. This means understanding the overall market forces, or business drivers, that are pushing your industry toward global competition. A **business driver** is a force in the environment to which businesses must respond and that influences the direction of the business. Likewise, examine carefully the inhibitors or negative factors that create *management challenges*—factors that could scuttle the development of a global business. Once you have examined the global environment, you will need to consider a corporate strategy for competing in that environment. How will your firm respond? You could ignore the global market and focus on domestic competition only, sell to the globe from a domestic base, or organize production and distribution around the globe. There are many in-between choices.

After you have developed a strategy, it is time to consider how to structure your organization so it can pursue the strategy. How will you accomplish a division of labor across a global environment? Where will production, administration, accounting, marketing, and human resource functions be located? Who will handle the systems function?

Next, you must consider the management issues in implementing your strategy and making the organization design come alive. Key here will be the

FIGURE 2   INTERNATIONAL INFORMATION SYSTEMS ARCHITECTURE

The major dimensions for developing an international information systems architecture are the global environment, the corporate global strategies, the structure of the organization, the management and business processes, and the technology platform.

design of business procedures. How can you discover and manage user requirements? How can you induce change in local units to conform to international requirements? How can you reengineer on a global scale, and how can you coordinate systems development?

The last issue to consider is the technology platform. Although changing technology is a key driving factor leading toward global markets, you need to have a corporate strategy and structure before you can rationally choose the right technology.

After you have completed this process of reasoning, you will be well on your way toward an appropriate international information systems architecture capable of achieving your corporate goals. Let's begin by looking at the overall global environment.

THE GLOBAL ENVIRONMENT: BUSINESS DRIVERS AND CHALLENGES

Table 1 lists the business drivers in the global environment that are leading all industries toward global markets and competition.

The global business drivers can be divided into two groups: general cultural factors and specific business factors. Easily recognized general cultural factors have driven internationalization since World War II. Information, communication, and transportation technologies have created a *global village* in which communication (by telephone, television, radio, or computer network) around the globe is no more difficult and not much more expensive than communication down the block. The cost of moving goods and services to and from geographically dispersed locations has fallen dramatically.

The development of global communications has created a global village in a second sense: A **global culture** created by television, the Internet, and other globally shared media such as movies now permits different cultures and peoples to develop common expectations about right and wrong, desirable and undesirable, heroic and cowardly. The collapse of the Eastern bloc has speeded the growth of a world culture enormously, increased support for capitalism and business, and reduced the level of cultural conflict considerably.

A last factor to consider is the growth of a global knowledge base. At the end of World War II, knowledge, education, science, and industrial skills were highly concentrated in North America, Western Europe, and Japan, with the rest of the world euphemistically called the *Third World*. This is no longer true. Latin America, China, India, Southern Asia, and Eastern Europe have

TABLE 1 GLOBAL BUSINESS DRIVERS

GENERAL CULTURAL FACTORS	SPECIFIC BUSINESS FACTORS
Global communication and transportation technologies	Global markets
Development of global culture	Global production and operations
Emergence of global social norms	Global coordination
Political stability	Global workforce
Global knowledge base	Global economies of scale

developed powerful educational, industrial, and scientific centers, resulting in a much more democratically and widely dispersed knowledge base.

These general cultural factors leading toward internationalization result in specific business globalization factors that affect most industries. The growth of powerful communications technologies and the emergence of world cultures create the condition for *global markets*—global consumers interested in consuming similar products that are culturally approved. Coca-Cola, American sneakers (made in Korea but designed in Los Angeles), and Cable News Network (CNN) programming can now be sold in Latin America, Africa, and Asia.

Responding to this demand, global production and operations have emerged with precise online coordination between far-flung production facilities and central headquarters thousands of miles away. At Sealand Transportation, a major global shipping company based in Newark, New Jersey, shipping managers in Newark can watch the loading of ships in Rotterdam online, check trim and ballast, and trace packages to specific ship locations as the activity proceeds. This is all possible through an international satellite link.

The new global markets and pressure toward global production and operation have called forth whole new capabilities for global coordination of all factors of production. Not only production but also accounting, marketing and sales, human resources, and systems development (all the major business functions) can be coordinated on a global scale.

Frito-Lay, for instance, can develop a marketing sales-force automation system in the United States and, once provided, may try the same techniques and technologies in Spain. Micromarketing—marketing to very small geographic and social units—no longer means marketing to neighborhoods in the United States, but to neighborhoods throughout the world! These new levels of global coordination permit for the first time in history the location of business activity according to comparative advantage. Design should be located where it is best accomplished, as should marketing, production, and finance.

Finally, global markets, production, and administration create the conditions for powerful, sustained global economies of scale. Production driven by worldwide global demand can be concentrated where it can best be accomplished, fixed resources can be allocated over larger production runs, and production runs in larger plants can be scheduled more efficiently and precisely estimated. Lower cost factors of production can be exploited wherever they emerge. The result is a powerful strategic advantage to firms that can organize globally. These general and specific business drivers have greatly enlarged world trade and commerce.

Not all industries are similarly affected by these trends. Clearly, manufacturing has been much more affected than services that still tend to be domestic and highly inefficient. However, the localism of services is breaking down in telecommunications, entertainment, transportation, financial services, and general business services including law. Clearly, those firms within an industry that can understand the internationalization of the industry and respond appropriately will reap enormous gains in productivity and stability.

Business Challenges

Although the possibilities of globalization for business success are significant, fundamental forces are operating to inhibit a global economy and to disrupt international business. Table 2 lists the most common and powerful challenges to the development of global systems.

TABLE 2 CHALLENGES AND OBSTACLES TO GLOBAL BUSINESS SYSTEMS

GENERAL	SPECIFIC·
Cultural particularism: Regionalism, nationalism, language differences	Standards: Different Electronic Data Interchange (EDI), e-mail, telecommunications standards
Social expectations: Brand-name expectations, work hours	Reliability: Phone networks not uniformly reliable
Political laws: Transborder data and privacy laws, commercial regulations	Speed: Different data transfer speeds, many slower than United States
	Personnel: Shortages of skilled consultants

At a cultural level, **particularism**, making judgments and taking action on the basis of narrow or personal characteristics, in all its forms (religious, nationalistic, ethnic, regionalism, geopolitical position) rejects the very concept of a shared global culture and rejects the penetration of domestic markets by foreign goods and services. Differences among cultures produce differences in social expectations, politics, and ultimately legal rules. In certain countries, such as the United States, consumers expect domestic name-brand products to be built domestically and are disappointed to learn that much of what they thought of as domestically produced is in fact foreign made.

Different cultures produce different political regimes. Among the many different countries of the world are different laws governing the movement of information, information privacy of their citizens, origins of software and hardware in systems, and radio and satellite telecommunications. Even the hours of business and the terms of business trade vary greatly across political cultures. These different legal regimes complicate global business and must be considered when building global systems.

For instance, European countries have very strict laws concerning transborder data flow and privacy. **Transborder data flow** is defined as the movement of information across international boundaries in any form. Some European countries prohibit the processing of financial information outside their boundaries or the movement of personal information to foreign countries. The European Union Data Protection Directive, which went into effect in October 1998, restricts the flow of any information to countries (such as the United States) that do not meet strict European information laws on personal information. Financial services, travel, and health care companies could be directly affected. In response, most multinational firms develop information systems within each European country to avoid the cost and uncertainty of moving information across national boundaries.

Cultural and political differences profoundly affect organizations' business processes and applications of information technology. A host of specific barriers arise from the general cultural differences, everything from different reliability of phone networks to the shortage of skilled consultants.

National laws and traditions have created disparate accounting practices in various countries, which impact the ways profits and losses are analyzed. German companies generally do not recognize the profit from a venture until the project is completely finished and they have been paid. Conversely, British firms begin posting profits before a project is completed, when they are reasonably certain they will get the money.

These accounting practices are tightly intertwined with each country's legal system, business philosophy, and tax code. British, U.S., and Dutch firms share a predominantly Anglo-Saxon outlook that separates tax calculations from reports to shareholders to focus on showing shareholders how fast profits are growing. Continental European accounting practices are less oriented toward impressing investors, focusing rather on demonstrating compliance with strict rules and minimizing tax liabilities. These diverging accounting practices make it difficult for large international companies with units in different countries to evaluate their performance.

Language remains a significant barrier. Although English has become a kind of standard business language, this is truer at higher levels of companies and not throughout the middle and lower ranks. Software may have to be built with local language interfaces before a new information system can be successfully implemented.

Currency fluctuations can play havoc with planning models and projections. A product that appears profitable in Mexico or Japan may actually produce a loss because of changes in foreign exchange rates.

These inhibiting factors must be taken into account when you are designing and building international systems for your business. For example, companies trying to implement "lean production" systems spanning national boundaries typically underestimate the time, expense, and logistical difficulties of making goods and information flow freely across different countries.

STATE OF THE ART

One might think, given the opportunities for achieving competitive advantages as outlined previously and the interest in future applications, that most international companies have rationally developed marvelous international systems architectures. Nothing could be further from the truth. Most companies have inherited patchwork international systems from the distant past, often based on concepts of information processing developed in the 1960s—batch-oriented reporting from independent foreign divisions to corporate headquarters, manual entry of data from one legacy system to another, with little online control and communication. Corporations in this situation increasingly face powerful competitive challenges in the marketplace from firms that have rationally designed truly international systems. Still other companies have recently built technology platforms for international systems but have nowhere to go because they lack global strategy.

As it turns out, there are significant difficulties in building appropriate international architectures. The difficulties involve planning a system appropriate to the firm's global strategy, structuring the organization of systems and business units, solving implementation issues, and choosing the right technical platform. Let's examine these problems in greater detail.

2 ORGANIZING INTERNATIONAL INFORMATION SYSTEMS

Three organizational issues face corporations seeking a global position: choosing a strategy, organizing the business, and organizing the systems management area. The first two are closely connected, so we discuss them together.

TABLE 3 GLOBAL BUSINESS STRATEGY AND STRUCTURE

BUSINESS FUNCTION	DOMESTIC EXPORTER	MULTINATIONAL	FRANCHISER	TRANSNATIONAL
Production	Centralized	Dispersed	Coordinated	Coordinated
Finance/Accounting	Centralized	Centralized	Centralized	Coordinated
Sales/Marketing	Mixed	Dispersed	Coordinated	Coordinated
Human Resources	Centralized	Centralized	Coordinated	Coordinated
Strategic Management	Centralized	Centralized	Centralized	Coordinated

GLOBAL STRATEGIES AND BUSINESS ORGANIZATION

Four main global strategies form the basis for global firms' organizational structure. These are domestic exporter, multinational, franchiser, and transnational. Each of these strategies is pursued with a specific business organizational structure (see Table 3). For simplicity's sake, we describe three kinds of organizational structure or governance: centralized (in the home country), decentralized (to local foreign units), and coordinated (all units participate as equals). Other types of governance patterns can be observed in specific companies (e.g., authoritarian dominance by one unit, a confederacy of equals, a federal structure balancing power among strategic units, and so forth).

The **domestic exporter** strategy is characterized by heavy centralization of corporate activities in the home country of origin. Nearly all international companies begin this way, and some move on to other forms. Production, finance/accounting, sales/marketing, human resources, and strategic management are set up to optimize resources in the home country. International sales are sometimes dispersed using agency agreements or subsidiaries, but even here foreign marketing is totally reliant on the domestic home base for marketing themes and strategies. Caterpillar Corporation and other heavy capital-equipment manufacturers fall into this category of firm.

The **multinational** strategy concentrates financial management and control out of a central home base while decentralizing production, sales, and marketing operations to units in other countries. The products and services on sale in different countries are adapted to suit local market conditions. The organization becomes a far-flung confederation of production and marketing facilities in different countries. Many financial service firms, along with a host of manufacturers, such as General Motors, Chrysler, and Intel, fit this pattern.

Franchisers are an interesting mix of old and new. On the one hand, the product is created, designed, financed, and initially produced in the home country, but for product-specific reasons must rely heavily on foreign personnel for further production, marketing, and human resources. Food franchisers such as McDonald's, Mrs. Fields Cookies, and KFC fit this pattern. McDonald's created a new form of fast-food chain in the United States and continues to rely largely on the United States for inspiration of new products, strategic management, and financing. Nevertheless, because the product must be produced locally—it is perishable—extensive coordination and dispersal of production, local marketing, and local recruitment of personnel are required.

Generally, foreign franchisees are clones of the mother country units, but fully coordinated worldwide production that could optimize factors of production is not possible. For instance, potatoes and beef can generally not be bought where they are cheapest on world markets but must be produced reasonably close to the area of consumption.

Transnational firms are the stateless, truly globally managed firms that may represent a larger part of international business in the future. Transnational firms have no single national headquarters but instead have many regional headquarters and perhaps a world headquarters. In a **transnational** strategy, nearly all the value-adding activities are managed from a global perspective without reference to national borders, optimizing sources of supply and demand wherever they appear, and taking advantage of any local competitive advantages. Transnational firms take the globe, not the home country, as their management frame of reference. The governance of these firms has been likened to a federal structure in which there is a strong central management core of decision making, but considerable dispersal of power and financial muscle throughout the global divisions. Few companies have actually attained transnational status, but Citicorp, Sony, Ford, and others are attempting this transition.

Information technology and improvements in global telecommunications are giving international firms more flexibility to shape their global strategies. Protectionism and a need to serve local markets better encourage companies to disperse production facilities and at least become multinational. At the same time, the drive to achieve economies of scale and take advantage of short-term local advantage moves transnationals toward a global management perspective and a concentration of power and authority. Hence, there are forces of decentralization and dispersal, as well as forces of centralization and global coordination.

GLOBAL SYSTEMS TO FIT THE STRATEGY

Information technology and improvements in global telecommunications are giving international firms more flexibility to shape their global strategies. The configuration, management, and development of systems tend to follow the global strategy chosen (Ives, et al., 1993; Roche, 1992; Ives and Jarvenpaa, 1991). Figure 3 depicts the typical arrangements. By *systems* we mean the full

FIGURE 3   GLOBAL STRATEGY AND SYSTEMS CONFIGURATIONS

SYSTEM CONFIGURATION	Strategy			
	Domestic Exporter	Multinational	Franchiser	Transnational
Centralized	X			
Duplicated			X	
Decentralized	x	X	x	
Networked		x		X

The large Xs show the dominant patterns, and the small Xs show the emerging patterns. For instance, domestic exporters rely predominantly on centralized systems, but there is continual pressure and some development of decentralized systems in local marketing regions.

range of activities involved in building and operating information systems: conception and alignment with the strategic business plan, systems development, and ongoing operation and maintenance. For the sake of simplicity, we consider four types of systems configuration. *Centralized systems* are those in which systems development and operation occur totally at the domestic home base. Duplicated systems are those in which development occurs at the home base but operations are handed over to autonomous units in foreign locations. *Decentralized systems* are those in which each foreign unit designs its own unique solutions and systems. *Networked systems* are those in which systems development and operations occur in an integrated and coordinated fashion across all units.

As can be seen in Figure 3, domestic exporters tend to have highly centralized systems in which a single domestic systems development staff develops worldwide applications. Multinationals offer a direct and striking contrast: Here, foreign units devise their own systems solutions based on local needs with few if any applications in common with headquarters (the exceptions being financial reporting and some telecommunications applications). Franchisers have the simplest systems structure: Like the products they sell, franchisers develop a single system usually at the home base and then replicate it around the world. Each unit, no matter where it is located, has identical applications. Last, the most ambitious form of systems development is found in the transnational: Networked systems are those in which there is a solid, singular global environment for developing and operating systems. This usually presupposes a powerful telecommunications backbone, a culture of shared applications development, and a shared management culture that crosses cultural barriers. The networked systems structure is the most visible in financial services where the homogeneity of the product—money and money instruments—seems to overcome cultural barriers.

REORGANIZING THE BUSINESS

How should a firm organize itself for doing business on an international scale? To develop a global company and information systems support structure, a firm needs to follow these principles:

1. Organize value-adding activities along lines of comparative advantage.
   For instance, marketing/sales functions should be located where they can best be performed, for least cost and maximum impact; likewise with production, finance, human resources, and information systems.

2. Develop and operate systems units at each level of corporate activity—regional, national, and international. To serve local needs, there should be *host country systems* units of some magnitude. Regional systems units should handle telecommunications and systems development across national boundaries that take place within major geographic regions (European, Asian, American). *Transnational systems units* should be established to create the linkages across major regional areas and coordinate the development and operation of international telecommunications and systems development (Roche, 1992).

3. Establish at world headquarters a single office responsible for development of international systems, a global chief information officer (CIO) position.

INTERACTIVE SESSION: ORGANIZATIONS

AVNET: DEVELOPING SYSTEMS TO SUPPORT GLOBAL STRATEGY

You probably have not heard of Avnet Inc.—or its leading competitor Arrow Electronics—but chances are the computer you are using these days has components purchased from one of these distributors, if not the entire computer. Avnet is number 212 on the list of Fortune 500 firms, and number three on InformationWeek's list of most innovative users of information systems. Avnet and Arrow are two American-based firms that together dominate the world market for electronic parts, connectors, components, and computers, with a 60-percent global market share. While locked in competition for the remaining 40 percent of the world market, Avnet and Arrow have each adopted different business strategies for future growth, and each has a different idea about how to use information systems to support corporate growth.

Beginning as a radio-parts distributor started by Charles Avnet in 1921 in New York City, the company went public in 1959 and was managed by his sons. Since 1991, the company has been on a growth tear, purchasing 43 companies including British semiconductor distributor Access Group. About 60 percent of its business involves component distribution, and the rest distributing computers which it purchases from computer manufacturers and resells to corporations and large retail outlets. Avnet, like Arrow, is a middleman between manufacturers and ultimate end users. It's also a key supplier of industrial electronic components to the computer industries.

In 2001, Avnet had completed its expansion in Europe, and began moving into China and Asian markets by purchasing China's Sunrise Technology. In 2005, it purchased Memec Group Holdings, a $2 billion purchase of China's largest electronic components distributor.

Because it was so dependent on acquisitions and rapid integration of newly purchased companies, Avnet developed what it calls its "Cookbook" for acquisitions. Composed of more than 1,000 pages stored on Avnet servers, the Cookbook contains Avnet's accumulated wisdom on how to integrate new companies into Avnet's business process and information systems. It has chapters on human resources, finances, IT/IS, logistics, materials, sales, and marketing. You can think of the Cookbook as an encyclopedia of business processes for Avnet.

Rather than force all its acquisitions to adopt Avnet's American systems, Avnet has divided the world into three regions, each with its own regional enterprise resource planning (ERP) and related systems. The goal was—for the sake of speed of integration of newly acquired companies—to integrate new acquisitions tightly and smoothly within each region, and allow regional managers a certain degree of freedom in choosing how they organized their business within the region. When acquiring new companies, it tries to use the best systems from each company and not always its own. In the case of Memec, it chose to use the Avnet regional Asian system rather than Memec's own global system because it would lower the costs of training Avnet employees who otherwise would have to learn an entirely new system.

Avnet successfully integrated the Memec business and employees into its Asian system. Avnet now runs two regional ERP systems: SAP in Asia, and a custom-built mainframe system called Genesis in the United States. In Europe, Avnet runs 10 different SAP systems, nearly one for each European country where it does business, but it is attempting to consolidate them into a single European SAP system in the future.

The Cookbook has been very useful for ensuring commonality of business processes around the world despite different ERP systems in major regions and countries. The Cookbook goes into considerable detail on how to set up and process financial transactions, coordinate orders, pay accounts, and assign responsibility for transactions.

Arrow too has begun making acquisitions in Asia, most notably, purchasing a large Taiwanese distributor, Ultra Source Technology. Using a similar collection of best business practices it calls "the Playbook," Arrow once integrated a newly acquired company into the Arrow global systems in a single weekend. But Arrow, according to its executives, may rely less on acquisitions in Asia than on trading relationships with existing Asian distributors. They want to focus not just on revenue growth, but profit growth. They believe the costs of acquisitions may outweigh the profit benefits. Unlike Avnet, Arrow is pursuing a one-world, one system, strategy. In 2007, Arrow plans to be using a single Oracle financial system, and is working on plans for a single, global

ERP system to replace a hodgepodge of ERP systems that have sprung up around its global operations. "We want to move towards more conformity," explained one Arrow executive, "while trying to recognize the uniqueness of each market, we want to have a global view of the whole company when it makes sense for us." Without a single global system, they believe, it's difficult to view the company as a truly global entity.

Sources: Edward Cone, "Avnet Tries Buying Its Way to the Top," *CIO Insight*, February 1, 2006 and www.avnet.com, accessed October 15, 2006.

CASE STUDY QUESTIONS

1. Review Table 3 and then contrast and compare the global strategies of Avnet and Arrow. Are they the same or different?

2. Review Figure 3 and compare and contrast the Avnet system building strategy with that of Arrow. Has each company made the "correct" choice given their strategies?

3. Identify the risks which Avnet incurs by pursuing its regional strategy. What are the off-setting benefits?

4. Do you believe for this product and market that a multinational strategy is superior to a transnational strategy? Why or why not?

MIS IN ACTION

1. Go to the Avnet Web site (www.avnet.com) and identify (a) how many countries it operates in, and (b) how its revenues are divided among the major regions of North America, Europe, and Asia.

2. At the Avnet Web site, explore the sections on Avnet's Management Technologies and their logistics services. These are quite separate businesses from operating a global parts distribution system. Or are they? How is Avnet leveraging its investment in distribution systems?

3. Visit Avnet's largest competitor, Arrow Electronics Inc. (www.arrow.com). Compare Avnet's financial performance (revenue growth, operating margins, and net income) with that of Arrow over the last three years. Include their three-year stock price performance. Which of these companies has an edge in financial performance? How do their different global strategies, and systems, contribute to differences in their financial performance?

Many successful companies have devised organizational systems structures along these principles. The success of these companies relies not only on the proper organization of activities, but also on a key ingredient—a management team that can understand the risks and benefits of international systems and that can devise strategies for overcoming the risks. We turn to these management topics next.

3 MANAGING GLOBAL SYSTEMS

Table 4 lists the principal management problems posed by developing international systems. It is interesting to note that these problems are the chief difficulties managers experience in developing ordinary domestic systems as well. But these are enormously complicated in the international environment.

TABLE 4   MANAGEMENT CHALLENGES IN DEVELOPING GLOBAL SYSTEMS

Agreeing on common user requirements

Introducing changes in business processes

Coordinating applications development

Coordinating software releases

Encouraging local users to support global systems

A TYPICAL SCENARIO: DISORGANIZATION ON A GLOBAL SCALE

Let's look at a common scenario. A traditional multinational consumer-goods company based in the United States and operating in Europe would like to expand into Asian markets and knows that it must develop a transnational strategy and a supportive information systems structure. Like most multinationals, it has dispersed production and marketing to regional and national centers while maintaining a world headquarters and strategic management in the United States. Historically, it has allowed each of the subsidiary foreign divisions to develop its own systems. The only centrally coordinated system is financial controls and reporting. The central systems group in the United States focuses only on domestic functions and production.

The result is a hodgepodge of hardware, software, and telecommunications. The e-mail systems between Europe and the United States are incompatible. Each production facility uses a different manufacturing resources planning system (or a different version of the same ERP system), and different marketing, sales, and human resource systems. Hardware and database platforms are wildly different. Communications between different sites are poor, given the high-cost European intercountry communications. The central systems group at headquarters in the United States recently was decimated and dispersed to the U.S. local sites in the hope of serving local needs better and reducing costs.

What do you recommend to the senior management leaders of this company, who now want to pursue a transnational strategy and develop an information systems architecture to support a highly coordinated global systems environment? Consider the problems you face by reexamining Table 4. The foreign divisions will resist efforts to agree on common user requirements; they have never thought about much other than their own units' needs. The systems groups in American local sites, which have been enlarged recently and told to focus on local needs, will not easily accept guidance from anyone recommending a transnational strategy. It will be difficult to convince local managers anywhere in the world that they should change their business procedures to align with other units in the world, especially if this might interfere with their local performance. After all, local managers are rewarded in this company for meeting local objectives of their division or plant. Finally, it will be difficult to coordinate development of projects around the world in the absence of a powerful telecommunications network and, therefore, difficult to encourage local users to take on ownership in the systems developed.

FIGURE 4   LOCAL, REGIONAL, AND GLOBAL SYSTEMS

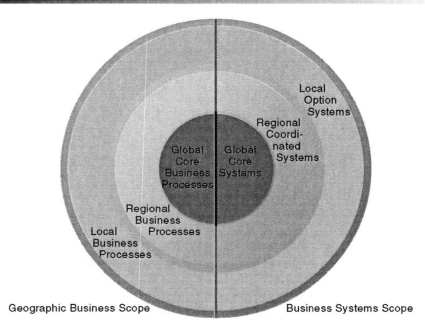

Agency and other coordination costs increase as the firm moves from local option systems toward regional and global systems. However, transaction costs of participating in global markets probably decrease as firms develop global systems. A sensible strategy is to reduce agency costs by developing only a few core global systems that are vital for global operations, leaving other systems in the hands of regional and local units.

Source: From *Managing Information Technology in Multinational Corporations* by Edward M. Roche, © 1993. Adapted by permission of Prentice Hall, Inc., Upper Saddle River, N.J.

GLOBAL SYSTEMS STRATEGY

Figure 4 lays out the main dimensions of a solution. First, consider that not all systems should be coordinated on a transnational basis; only some core systems are truly worth sharing from a cost and feasibility point of view. **Core systems** are systems that support functions that are absolutely critical to the organization. Other systems should be partially coordinated because they share key elements, but they do not have to be totally common across national boundaries. For such systems, a good deal of local variation is possible and desirable. A final group of systems is peripheral, truly provincial, and needed to suit local requirements only.

Define the Core Business Processes

How do you identify core systems? The first step is to define a short list of critical core business processes. Briefly, business processes are sets of logically related tasks to produce specific business results, such as shipping out correct orders to customers or delivering innovative products to the market. Each business process typically involves many functional areas, communicating and coordinating work, information, and knowledge.

The way to identify these core business processes is to conduct a business process analysis. How are customer orders taken, what happens to them once they are taken, who fills the orders, how are they shipped to the customers?

What about suppliers? Do they have access to manufacturing resource planning systems so that supply is automatic? You should be able to identify and set priorities in a short list of 10 business processes that are absolutely critical for the firm.

Next, can you identify centers of excellence for these processes? Is the customer order fulfillment superior in the United States, manufacturing process control superior in Germany, and human resources superior in Asia? You should be able to identify some areas of the company, for some lines of business, where a division or unit stands out in the performance of one or several business functions.

When you understand the business processes of a firm, you can rank-order them. You then can decide which processes should be core applications, centrally coordinated, designed, and implemented around the globe, and which should be regional and local. At the same time, by identifying the critical business processes, the really important ones, you have gone a long way to defining a vision of the future that you should be working toward.

Identify the Core Systems to Coordinate Centrally

By identifying the critical core business processes, you begin to see opportunities for transnational systems. The second strategic step is to conquer the core systems and define these systems as truly transnational. The financial and political costs of defining and implementing transnational systems are extremely high. Therefore, keep the list to an absolute minimum, letting experience be the guide and erring on the side of minimalism. By dividing off a small group of systems as absolutely critical, you divide opposition to a transnational strategy. At the same time, you can appease those who oppose the central worldwide coordination implied by transnational systems by permitting peripheral systems development to progress unabated, with the exception of some technical platform requirements.

Choose an Approach: Incremental, Grand Design, Evolutionary

A third step is to choose an approach. Avoid piecemeal approaches. These surely will fail for lack of visibility, opposition from all who stand to lose from transnational development, and lack of power to convince senior management that the transnational systems are worth it. Likewise, avoid grand design approaches that try to do everything at once. These also tend to fail, because of an inability to focus resources. Nothing gets done properly, and opposition to organizational change is needlessly strengthened because the effort requires huge resources. An alternative approach is to evolve transnational applications incrementally from existing applications with a precise and clear vision of the transnational capabilities the organization should have in five years. This is sometimes referred to as the "salami strategy," or one slice at a time.

Make the Benefits Clear

What is in it for the company? One of the worst situations to avoid is to build global systems for the sake of building global systems. From the beginning, it is crucial that senior management at headquarters and foreign division managers clearly understand the benefits that will come to the company as well as to individual units. Although each system offers unique benefits to a particular budget, the overall contribution of global systems lies in four areas.

Global systems—truly integrated, distributed, and transnational systems—contribute to superior management and coordination. A simple price tag cannot be put on the value of this contribution, and the benefit will not show up in any capital budgeting model. It is the ability to switch suppliers on a moment's notice from one region to another in a crisis, the ability to move production in response to natural disasters, and the ability to use excess capacity in one region to meet raging demand in another.

A second major contribution is vast improvement in production, operation, and supply and distribution. Imagine a global value chain, with global suppliers and a global distribution network. For the first time, senior managers can locate value-adding activities in regions where they are most economically performed.

Third, global systems mean global customers and global marketing. Fixed costs around the world can be amortized over a much larger customer base. This will unleash new economies of scale at production facilities.

Last, global systems mean the ability to optimize the use of corporate funds over a much larger capital base. This means, for instance, that capital in a surplus region can be moved efficiently to expand production of capital-starved regions; that cash can be managed more effectively within the company and put to use more effectively.

These strategies will not by themselves create global systems. You will have to implement what you strategize.

THE MANAGEMENT SOLUTION

We now can reconsider how to handle the most vexing problems facing managers developing the global information systems architectures that were described in Table 4.

Agreeing on Common User Requirements

Establishing a short list of the core business processes and core support systems will begin a process of rational comparison across the many divisions of the company, develop a common language for discussing the business, and naturally lead to an understanding of common elements (as well as the unique qualities that must remain local).

Introducing Changes in Business Processes

Your success as a change agent will depend on your legitimacy, your actual raw power, and your ability to involve users in the change design process. **Legitimacy** is defined as the extent to which your authority is accepted on grounds of competence, vision, or other qualities. The selection of a viable change strategy, which we have defined as evolutionary but with a vision, should assist you in convincing others that change is feasible and desirable. Involving people in change, and assuring them that change is in the best interests of the company and their local units, is a key tactic.

Coordinating Applications Development

Choice of change strategy is critical for this problem. At the global level, there is far too much complexity to attempt a grand design strategy of change. It is far easier to coordinate change by making small incremental steps toward a larger vision. Imagine a five-year plan of action rather than a two-year plan of action, and reduce the set of transnational systems to a bare minimum to reduce coordination costs.

Coordinating Software Releases

Firms can institute procedures to ensure that all operating units convert to new software updates at the same time so that everyone's software is compatible.

Encouraging Local Users to Support Global Systems

The key to this problem is to involve users in the creation of the design without giving up control over the development of the project to parochial interests. The overall tactic for dealing with resistant local units in a transnational company is cooptation. **Cooptation** is defined as bringing the opposition into the process of designing and implementing the solution without giving up control over the direction and nature of the change. As much as possible, raw power should be avoided. Minimally, however, local units must agree on a short list of transnational systems, and raw power may be required to solidify the idea that transnational systems of some sort are truly required.

How should cooptation proceed? Several alternatives are possible. One alternative is to permit each country unit the opportunity to develop one transnational application first in its home territory, and then throughout the world. In this manner, each major country systems group is given a piece of the action in developing a transnational system, and local units feel a sense of ownership in the transnational effort. On the downside, this assumes the ability to develop high-quality systems is widely distributed, and that, a German team, for example, can successfully implement systems in France and Italy. This will not always be the case.

A second tactic is to develop new transnational centers of excellence, or a single center of excellence. There may be several centers around the globe that focus on specific business processes. These centers draw heavily from local national units, are based on multinational teams, and must report to worldwide management. Centers of excellence perform the initial identification and specification of business processes, define the information requirements, perform the business and systems analysis, and accomplish all design and testing. Implementation, however, and pilot testing are rolled out to other parts of the globe. Recruiting a wide range of local groups to transnational centers of excellence helps send the message that all significant groups are involved in the design and will have an influence.

Even with the proper organizational structure and appropriate management choices, it is still possible to stumble over technology issues. Choices of technology platforms, networks, hardware, and software are the final element in building transnational information system architectures.

4   TECHNOLOGY ISSUES AND OPPORTUNITIES FOR GLOBAL VALUE CHAINS

Once firms have defined a global business model and systems strategy, they must select hardware, software, and networking standards along with key system applications to support global business processes. Many companies today are using teams in other countries to develop and run their software and hardware, so they'll need to address the challenges of managing global teams and global technology services as well.

645

TECHNOLOGY CHALLENGES OF GLOBAL SYSTEMS

Hardware, software, and networking pose special technical challenges in an international setting. One major challenge is finding some way to standardize a global computing platform when there is so much variation from operating unit to operating unit and from country to country. Another major challenge is finding specific software applications that are user friendly and that truly enhance the productivity of international work teams. The universal acceptance of the Internet around the globe has greatly reduced networking problems. But the mere presence of the Internet does not guarantee that information will flow seamlessly throughout the global organization because not all business units use the same applications, and the quality of Internet service can be highly variable (just as with the telephone service). For instance, German business units may use a Linux-based collaboration tool to share documents and communicate, which is incompatible with American headquarters teams which use Lotus Notes. Overcoming these challenges requires systems integration and connectivity on a global basis.

Computing Platforms and Systems Integration

The development of a transnational information systems architecture based on the concept of core systems raises questions about how the new core systems will fit in with the existing suite of applications developed around the globe by different divisions, different people, and for different kinds of computing hardware. The goal is to develop global, distributed, and integrated systems to support digital business processes spanning national boundaries. Briefly, these are the same problems faced by any large domestic systems development effort. However, the problems are magnified in an international environment. Just imagine the challenge of integrating systems based on the Windows, Linux, Unix, or proprietary operating systems running on IBM, Sun, Hewlett-Packard, and other hardware in many different operating units in many different countries!

Moreover, having all sites use the same hardware and operating system does not guarantee integration. Some central authority in the firm must establish data, as well as other technical standards, with which sites are to comply. For instance, technical accounting terms, such as the beginning and end of the fiscal year, must be standardized (review the earlier discussion of the cultural challenges to building global businesses), as well as the acceptable interfaces between systems, communication speeds and architectures, and network software.

Connectivity

Truly integrated global systems must have connectivity—the ability to link together the systems and people of a global firm into a single integrated network just like the phone system but capable of voice, data, and image transmissions. The Internet has provided an enormously powerful foundation for providing connectivity among the dispersed units of global firms. However, many issues remain. The public Internet does not guarantee any level of service (even in the U.S.) Few global corporations trust the security of the Internet and generally use private networks to communicate sensitive data, and Internet-based virtual private networks (VPNs) for communications that require less security. Not all countries support even basic Internet service, which requires obtaining reliable circuits, coordinating among different carriers and the regional telecommunications authority, obtaining bills in a common currency standard, and obtaining standard agreements for the level of telecommunications service provided. Table 5 lists the major challenges posed by international networks.

646

TABLE 5   PROBLEMS OF INTERNATIONAL NETWORKS

Quality of Service
Security
Costs and tariffs
Network management
Installation delays
Poor quality of international service
Regulatory constraints
Network capacity

An increasingly attractive alternative is to create global networks based on the Internet and Internet technology. Companies can create global intranets for internal communication or extranets to exchange information more rapidly with business partners in their supply chains. They can use the public Internet to create global networks using VPNs from Internet service providers, which provide many features of a private network using the public Internet. However, VPNs may not provide the same level of quick and predictable response as private networks, especially during times of the day when Internet traffic is very congested, and they may not be able to support large numbers of remote users.

Low penetration of PCs and widespread illiteracy limit demand for Internet service in many developing countries (see Figure 5). Where an infrastructure exists in less-developed countries, it is often outdated, lacks digital circuits, and has very noisy lines. The purchasing power of most people in developing countries makes access to Internet services very expensive. Many countries monitor transmissions. Governments in China, Singapore, Iran, and Saudi Arabia monitor

FIGURE 5   INTERNET POPULATION IN SELECTED COUNTRIES

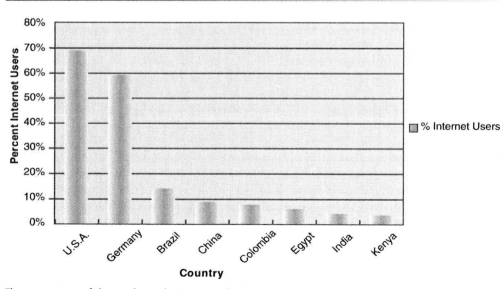

The percentage of the total population using the Internet in developing countries is much smaller than in the United States and Europe.

Source: CIA World Factbook, 2005.

Internet traffic and block access to Web sites considered morally or politically offensive.

Software

The development of core systems poses unique challenges for application software: How will the old systems interface with the new? Entirely new interfaces must be built and tested if old systems are kept in local areas (which is common). These interfaces can be costly and messy to build. If new software must be created, another challenge is to build software that can be realistically used by multiple business units from different countries given these business units are accustomed to their unique business processes and definitions of data.

Aside from integrating the new with the old systems, there are problems of human interface design and functionality of systems. For instance, to be truly useful for enhancing productivity of a global workforce, software interfaces must be easily understood and mastered quickly. Graphical user interfaces are ideal for this but presuppose a common language—often English. When international systems involve knowledge workers only, English may be the assumed international standard. But as international systems penetrate deeper into management and clerical groups, a common language may not be assumed and human interfaces must be built to accommodate different languages and even conventions.

What are the most important software applications? Many international systems focus on basic transaction and management reporting systems. Increasingly, firms are turning to supply chain management and enterprise systems to standardize their business processes on a global basis and to create coordinated global supply chains. However, these cross-functional systems are not always compatible with differences in languages, cultural heritages, and business processes in other countries (Martinons, 2004; Liang et al., 2004; Davison, 2002). Company units in countries that are not technically sophisticated may also encounter problems trying to manage the technical complexities of enterprise applications.

Electronic Data Interchange (EDI) systems and supply chain management systems are widely used by manufacturing and distribution firms to connect to suppliers on a global basis. Groupware systems, e-mail, and videoconferencing are especially important worldwide collaboration tools for knowledge- and data-based firms, such as advertising firms, research-based firms in medicine and engineering, and graphics and publishing firms. Internet-based tools will be increasingly employed for such purposes.

MANAGING GLOBAL SOFTWARE DEVELOPMENT

Both global and domestic firms increasingly are managing their hardware and software resources using global teams. Sometimes these teams work for the firm at offshore locations, and in some instances, these teams are working for external vendors in offshore locations. This practice is called **offshore software outsourcing** and it's becoming wildly popular. In 2007, Forrester Research Group predicts U.S. firms will spend $95 billion on offshore outsourcing to India (the largest recipient of outsourced jobs) of approximately 200,000 IT jobs. (Forrester Research, 2004; eMarketer, 2004). According to Gartner and other consulting groups, CIOs of major U.S. corporations are under considerable pressure to outsource as much of their non-strategic systems development work as feasible in order to reduce the cost of IS operations (McCue, 2006). The reasons for offshore outsourcing are very compelling: A skilled programmer in India or Russia earns about US$10,000 per year, compared to $70,000 per year for a comparable programmer in the United States. The Internet has drastically lowered the cost of communicating with and coordinating offshore development teams. In addition to cost savings, outsourcing provides firms with access to world-class complementary technology assets and skills.

There is a very strong chance that at some point in your career, you will be working with offshore outsourcers or global teams. Thus, it is very important to understand how offshore resources can best be managed. Not all work can be exported, special managerial and organizational issues must be addressed, and the savings are not as great as simple wage comparisons suggest (Krishna, Sahay and Walsham, 2004).

Your firm is most likely to benefit from outsourcing if it takes the time to evaluate all the risks and to make sure outsourcing is appropriate for its particular needs. Any company that outsources its applications must thoroughly understand the project, including requirements, method of implementation, source of expected benefits, cost components, and metrics for measuring performance.

Offshore outsourcing can reduce software development costs, but companies will not save as much as they initially think. There are hidden costs to offshore outsourcing, and these costs can increase the total cost of ownership (TCO) of offshore-developed software by over 50 percent. Here are the major cost components of offshore software development:

- *Contract cost.* Most of this cost is for labor required by the project—programmers, software engineers, systems analysts, network specialists, project team managers.

- *Vendor selection costs.* With any outsourced service, the expense of selecting a service provider can run from 0.1 percent to 10 percent in addition to the cost of the contract. Companies will need to allocate resources for documenting requirements, sending out requests for proposal (RFPs), travel expenses, negotiating contracts, legal fees, and project management. A project leader may be assigned to work full-time on this, with others contributing, and these are lost labor costs. The entire process can take three to six months to a year.

- *Transition management and knowledge transfer costs.* It takes from three months to a full year to completely transfer work to an offshore partner and make sure the vendor thoroughly understands your business. Users should be prepared to spend even more time with the offshore team than an in-house group to make sure the team fully understands their requirements. A certain number of outsourcer staff have to travel to the client company to analyze the client's technology and applications before they can begin the actual work. The client company's systems and specifications have to be thoroughly documented. The offshore employees have to work in parallel with costly in-house employees, and neither can produce very much during the training period. If not included in the outsourcing contract, additional travel costs and visa costs must be figured in. Companies should expect to spend an additional 2 to 3 percent of their contracts on transition costs.

- *Domestic human resources costs.* If your company has to lay off domestic employees as a result of the offshore outsourcing, you may have to pay laid-off workers severance pay and retention bonuses to keep them working long enough to share their knowledge with their offshore replacements. Layoffs can also adversely impact employee morale and productivity. The firm's staff may resist working with the outsourcer and resign, taking valuable knowledge with them. Layoffs and related costs can add an extra 3 to 5 percent.

649

Costs of improving software development processes. If a company doesn't have solid in-house processes for software development, it will take much longer to coordinate work with the vendor.

Both parties should agree on the processes to be used. If the outsourcer has to follow your standards, make sure the offshore team thoroughly understands them.

U.S. firms often use rather informal methods for documenting and analyzing software projects. They may need to formalize their software development processes and adopt the methodology used by the offshore vendor. (Many Indian companies use the Capability Maturity Model [CMM] developed by Carnegie-Mellon as their software development methodology, and their clients may need to come up to speed in CMM to work effectively with them.) Ability to write clear specifications is critical as well, and creating a good set of specifications is very time-consuming.

Quality assurance testing also must be beefed-up in an offshore arrangement. There must be a dedicated group of people in the client organization who are always available to develop test plans and review results as they are generated by the offshore team. Companies outsourcing software development to external vendors should anticipate spending an additional 1 to 10 percent on improving software development processes.

 Costs of adjusting to cultural differences. Cultural differences can drain productivity. A seasoned U.S. employee cannot automatically be replaced by an offshore worker. Their values and attitudes are different. American workers tend to feel much more comfortable about speaking up and making suggestions. If something doesn't make sense or does not appear workable, they'll voice concerns. But offshore programmers may keep these feelings to themselves, believing that their aim is to please and this is what the client wants. The work then may take more time and money to complete and require extensive rework. Likewise, an application that makes sense to a U.S. worker, such as automatically logging all customer calls, may be a foreign concept offshore. Lags in productivity caused by the need to adjust to cultural differences can add as much as 20 percent of additional costs to the offshore contract during the first two years. There will probably be a need for more face-to-face interaction, or more time spent on Internet teleconferencing, or Skyping at odd hours, than originally anticipated because offshore workers don't interpret things the same way.

Cost of managing an offshore contract. Managing the offshore relationship requires additional work—invoicing, auditing, additional telecommunications costs, ensuring work is billed correctly, making sure time is properly recorded. Maintaining security merits special attention. Offshoring partners must agree on common procedures for data security, data recovery, protection of intellectual property rights, network security, and access control. The EU Data Privacy Directive could prohibit an outsourcing agreement from transferring personal data to non-EU countries unless both parties satisfy EU data protection standards. Companies should expect to pay an additional 6 to 10 percent on managing the offshore contract.

Figure 6 shows best- and worst-case scenarios for the total cost of ownership of an outsourcing project. It shows how much hidden costs can affect the total cost of an outsourcing project. The best case reflects the lowest estimates for additional costs, and the worst case reflects the highest estimates for these costs. As you can see, hidden costs will increase the total cost of an outsourcing project by an extra 15 to 57 percent.

Even with these extra costs, many firms will benefit from offshore outsourcing if they manage the work well. The total cost of doing the software work in-house might run to $18 million, so even under the worse-case scenario, the firm would still save about 15 percent.

FIGURE 6   TOTAL COST OF OUTSOURCING

TOTAL COST OF OFFSHORE OUTSOURCING				
Cost of outsourcing contract			$10,000,000	
Hidden Costs	Best Case	Additional Cost ($)	Worst Case	Additional Cost ($)
1. Vendor selection	0%	20,000	2%	200,000
2. Transition costs	2%	200,000	3%	300,000
3. Layoffs & retention	3%	300,000	5%	500,000
4. Lost productivity/cultural issues	3%	300,000	27%	2,700,000
5. Improving development processes	1%	100,000	10%	1,000,000
6. Managing the contract	6%	600,000	10%	1,000,000
Total additional costs		1,520,000		5,700,000
	Outstanding Contract ($)	Additional Cost ($)	Total Cost ($)	Additional Cost
Total cost of outsourcing (TCO) best case	10,000,000	1,520,000	11,520,000	15.2%
Total cost of outsourcing (TCO) worst case	10,000,000	5,700,000	15,700,000	57.0%

If a firm spends $10 million on offshore outsourcing contracts, that company will actually spend 15.2 percent in extra costs even under the best-case scenario. In the worst-case scenario, where there is a dramatic drop in productivity along with exceptionally high transition and layoff costs, a firm can expect to pay up to 57 percent in extra costs on top of the $10 million outlay for an offshore contract.

Although offshore software outsourcing might benefit individual firms, its broader social impact is less clear and much more controversial in the countries that are shipping jobs to low-wage countries. Of course, in the countries which are the recipients of these outsourced jobs, the practice is celebrated not only as a powerful tool for economic development, but as a reflection of the natural order of international trade and comparative advantage. They argue that the United States benefits from outsourcing because the cost of building systems falls, and hence more systems can be built. The fear in developed countries like the United States, which are creating tens of thousands of IT jobs in India and other low-wage countries, is that this practice lowers wages paid to U.S. technical and managerial workers in the IS area, and worse, potentially permanently damages the system-building capabilities of American workers. The Interactive Session on Management looks at both sides of the debate.

5   HANDS-ON MIS

The projects in this section give you hands-on experience conducting international market research and in building a job posting database and Web page for an international company.

Achieving Operational Excellence: Expanding International Sales

In this project, you will use the Web to research international markets for a small manufacturing company.

    Software skills: Web browser and electronic presentation software
    Business skills: Identifying international markets

INTERACTIVE SESSION: MANAGEMENT

OFFSHORE OUTSOURCING: GOOD, BAD, OR DOES NOT MAKE A DIFFERENCE?

When truck rental giant Penske buys a new truck and leases it out to commercial trucking companies, its Indian vendor Genpact remotely arranges for state titles, registrations, and permits electronically from Hyderabad, India. When the truck is rented and returned, the driver's log and taxes, fuel, and toll documents are sent to Genpact. The paperwork is sent to Genpact's office in Juarez, Mexico, where the information is entered into Penske's computer system. Other workers in Hyderabad complete entering data for tax filings and accounting purposes. Penske's practice of componentizing its business processes, and sending out large chunks of business processes, including data entry and routine administration, is becoming standard practice in American service and manufacturing firms. It is part of a swelling movement toward *offshore outsourcing*, a term designating the movement of white-collar jobs abroad. Many other companies, including Delta Air Lines and American Express, have moved their call centers to India or the Philippines. The consulting firm Accenture doubled its staff in India to 10,000. Procter & Gamble has 7,000 workers handling payroll, travel, benefits administration, accounts payable, and invoice processing in offices in Costa Rica, the Philippines, and the United Kingdom. Mindcrest Incorporated of Chicago maintains a staff of 15 in Bombay to provide legal research for companies and law firms.

An estimated 1.4 million call center jobs, telemarketing jobs, financial analysts, and jobs in banking and insurance have been steadily moving offshore. Also threatened are jobs in medical transcription, insurance applications and claims processing, and typesetting, as well as some jobs in accounting and tax preparation. Low-cost telecommunications networks and the Internet make it possible to communicate and exchange documents with people many thousands of miles away as inexpensively as if they were in the next town. Estimates differ greatly, but arguably there are over 200,000 IT-related jobs from low-level programming to system administration, management, and design that used to be performed in the United States but are now performed in India.

Forrester Research estimated that 3.3 million white-collar jobs will be transferred from the United States abroad by 2015. The impact of offshore outsourcing in the information technology industry could be especially severe: According to the Gartner Group, one out of 10 jobs in U.S. computer services may have already shifted to lower-cost countries such as Russia or India.

In mid-July 2003, IBM set off a firestorm when news of its plans to move more white-collar and programming jobs overseas was leaked to the press. By 2006, IBM was employing over 40,000 people in India. Hewlett-Packard has 5,000 Indian employees in research, software development, and customer support. Many non-technology companies now use offshore programmers for much of their routine programming work, as well as low-level clerical jobs and some management jobs in human services, engineering, logistics, and procurement.

Critics claim that offshore outsourcing shifts jobs from high-wage countries to low-wage countries, taking jobs away from U.S. workers or pressuring them to take lower pay to remain working. These critics fear that highly trained and educated workers will be ground down by globalization, just as blue-collar workers were in the 1970s and 1980s. Several state legislatures in the United States are considering bills requiring state agencies and contractors to use employees based in the United States, and U.S. job losses to overseas companies became a hot button during the 2004 presidential campaign.

But other experts point out that offshore outsourcers often provide better quality work at lower costs. Domestic firms also have a better chance of long-term survival if they can keep their costs low, and prices more competitive. Companies can pass these saving from outsourcing on to consumers or use them to expand the business and create new jobs that provide more value than those replaced. A study by the McKinsey Global Institute estimated that every dollar of costs moved from the U.S. to offshore yields a benefit of $1.12 to $1.14 to the U.S. economy.

Another study by economics consulting firm Global Insight commissioned by the pro-outsourcing Information Technology Association of America found that the productivity generated by U.S. companies sending computer services work abroad boosted domestic employment by 257,000 new jobs in 2005. This study claimed that outsourcing created twice as many U.S. jobs as it displaced and would lead, by 2010, to the creation of 337,000 new jobs in construction, education, health care, and financial services (Global Insight, 2005). Other studies point out that while lower-level programming jobs are moving offshore to low-wage countries, higher-level design, managerial, and project management jobs are created in the United States.

But what gets lost in this debate often is that the U.S. labor force is now about 145 million people. Employment is growing as the labor force grows. About 2 million net new jobs are created each year just to keep unemployment from rising. About 14 million new jobs are created each year, and 12 million are destroyed. Given the huge labor market, the number of jobs being outsourced to India is a drop in the bucket with respect to overall levels of employment, even though certain occupations (generally those requiring less education and lower pay) are hit particularly hard.

In the IT sector, the bureau of labor statistics predicts that by 2012, the United States will need to employ 1.5 million technical IS workers, and over 400,000 managerial personnel. About 750,000 net new IT jobs will be added from 2005 to 2012. Without help from India in the form of outsourcing, there would be a severe IT labor shortage in the United States, the cost of systems would rise, and firms would reduce spending on systems. With outsourcing, the cost of system development and operation might just stabilize, and relative to other capital goods, fall in price. This could result in more system-building activity and growing demand for many higher-level IT employees.

Sources: Daniel Gross, "Why 'Outsourcing' May Lose Its Power as a Scare Word," *The New York Times*, August 13, 2006; Pete Engardio, "The Future of Outsourcing," *BusinessWeek*, January 30, 2006; Global Insight, "IT Outsourcing and the U.S. Economy," October, 2005; Charles Schultz, "Offshoring, Import Competition, and the Jobless Recovery," The Brookings Institute, Washington D.C., June 2004; Catherine Mann, "Globalization of IT Services and White Collar Jobs: the Next Wave of Productivity Growth," Institute for International Economics, December 2003; Stephen Baker and Manjeet Kripalani, "Software: Will Outsourcing Hurt America's Supremacy?" *BusinessWeek*, March 1, 2004; and Jesse Drucker and Ken Brown, "Press 1 for Delhi, 2 for Dallas," *Wall Street Journal*, March 9, 2004.

CASE STUDY QUESTIONS

1. Does offshore outsourcing create an ethical dilemma? Why or why not?

2. Should offshore outsourcing be restricted? How? Why or why not?

3. How could the outsourcing of jobs lead to the creation of new jobs in the United States? Explain.

MIS IN ACTION

1. WIPRO is one of India's largest outsourcing firms. Visit the www.wipro.com, click on "Investor," and read their current annual report. On a spreadsheet, chart their revenue, operating margin, and profit growth for the years reported. How fast did WIPRO grow in the last year? What are some of the limitations on this growth in the next five years?

2. There are many other countries where outsourcing is growing very rapidly. Why is this so? Read the article by Pete Engardio, "The Future of Outsourcing," *BusinessWeek*, January 30, 2006. Make a table containing two columns. In the left column, create a list of the top ten outsourcing countries, and in the right column, briefly explain the advantages of outsourcing to these countries. What are the risks?

3. *CIO Magazine* publishes an annual outsourcing guide. Go to the CIO.com Web site and read the "2006 Global Outsourcing Guide." You can search the site for this guide, or go to http://www.cio.com/archive/071506/global_outsourcing.html. What is the "cost versus risk" equation discussed in this report? After reading this report, describe how you would balance the cost versus risk when choosing an offshore outsourcing firm.

Management would like to expand international sales for Dirt Bikes. You have been asked to analyze opportunities for global business expansion of the company, using the Web to find the information you need. Prepare a report for management that answers the following questions:

- Which countries would provide the best markets for Dirt Bikes's products? Your analysis should consider factors such: in which countries are dirt bikes popular and the per capita income of these countries.
- How could Dirt Bikes use the Web to increase international sales? What features should it place on its Web site to attract buyers from the countries it targets?
- (Optional) If possible, use electronic presentation software to summarize your findings for management.

Achieving Operational Excellence: Building a Job Database and Web Page for an International Consulting Firm

Software skills: Database and Web page design
Business skills: Human resources internal job postings

Companies with many overseas locations need a way to inform employees about available job openings in these locations. In this project, you will use database software to design a database for posting internal job openings and a Web page for displaying this information.

KTP Consulting operates in various locations around the world. KTP specializes in designing, developing, and implementing enterprise systems for medium- to large-size companies. KTP offers its employees opportunities to travel, live, and work in various locations throughout the United States, Europe, and Asia. The firm's human resources department has a simple database that enables its staff to track job vacancies. When an employee is interested in relocating, she or he contacts the human resources department for a list of KTP job vacancies. KTP also posts its employment opportunities on the company Web site.

What type of data should be included in the KTP job vacancies database? What information should not be included in this database? Based on your answers to these questions, build a job vacancies database for KTP. Populate the database with at least 20 records. You should also build a simple Web page that incorporates job vacancy data from your newly created database. Submit a copy of the KTP database and Web page to your professor.

Improving Decision Making: Conducting International Marketing and Pricing Research

Software skills: Internet-based software
Business skills: International pricing and marketing

When companies sell overseas, it is important to determine whether their products are priced properly for non-domestic markets. In this project, you will use the Web to research overseas distributors and customs regulations and use Internet-based software to calculate prices in foreign currencies.

You are in charge of marketing for a U.S. manufacturer of office furniture that has decided to enter the international market. You have been given the name of Sorin SRL, a major Italian office furniture retailer, but your source had no other information. You want to test the market by contacting this firm to offer it a specific desk chair that you have to sell at about $125. Using the Web, locate the information needed to contact this firm and to find out how many European euros you would need to get for the chair in the current market. One source for locating European companies is the Europages Business Directory (www.europages.com). In addition, consider using the Universal Currency Converter Web site (www.xe.net/ucc/), which determines the value of one currency expressed in other currencies. Obtain both the information needed to contact the firm and the price of your chair in their local currency. Then locate and obtain customs and legal restrictions on the products you will export from the United States and import into Italy. Finally, locate a company that will represent you as a customs agent and gather information on shipping costs.

▄ Summary ▄

1. *Identify the major factors driving the internationalization of business.*

There are general cultural factors and specific business factors to consider. The growth of cheap international communication and transportation has created a world culture with stable expectations or norms. Political stability and a growing global knowledge base that is widely shared contribute also to the world culture. These general factors create the conditions for global markets, global production, coordination, distribution, and global economies of scale.

2. *Compare strategies for developing global businesses.*

There are four basic international strategies: domestic exporter, multinational, franchiser, and transnational. In a transnational strategy, all factors of production are coordinated on a global scale. However, the choice of strategy is a function of the type of business and product.

3. *Demonstrate how information systems can support different global business strategies.*

There is a connection between firm strategy and information systems design. Transnational firms must develop networked system configurations and permit considerable decentralization of development and operations. Franchisers almost always duplicate systems across many countries and use centralized financial controls. Multinationals typically rely on decentralized independence among foreign units with some movement toward development of networks. Domestic exporters typically are centralized in domestic headquarters with some decentralized operations permitted.

4. *Identify the challenges posed by global information systems and management solutions.*

Global information systems pose challenges because cultural, political, and language diversity magnifies differences in organizational culture and business processes and encourages proliferation of disparate local information systems that are difficult to integrate. Typically, international systems have evolved without a conscious plan. The remedy is to define a small subset of core business processes and focus on building systems to support these processes. Tactically, managers will have to co-opt widely dispersed foreign units to participate in the development and operation of these systems, being careful to maintain overall control.

5. *Evaluate the issues and technical alternatives to be considered when developing international information systems.*

Implementing a global system requires an implementation strategy that considers both business design and technology platforms. Typically, global systems have evolved without a conscious plan. The remedy is to define a small subset of core business processes and focus on building systems that could support these processes. Tactically, you will have to co-opt widely dispersed foreign units to participate in the development and operation of these systems, being careful to maintain overall control.

The main hardware and telecommunications issues are systems integration and connectivity. The choices for integration are to go either with a proprietary architecture or with open systems technology. Global networks are extremely difficult to build and operate. Firms can build their own global networks or they can create global networks based on the Internet (intranets or virtual private networks). The main software issue concerns building interfaces to existing systems and selecting applications that can work with multiple cultural, language, and organizational frameworks.

Key Terms

Business driver
Cooptation
Core systems
Domestic exporter
Franchisers
Global culture
International information systems architecture

Legitimacy
Multinational
Offshore software outsourcing
Particularism
Transborder data flow
Transnational

Review Questions

1. What are the five major factors to consider when building an international information systems portfolio?

2. Describe the five general cultural factors leading toward growth in global business and the four specific business factors. Describe the interconnection among these factors.

3. What is meant by a *global culture*?

4. What are the major challenges to the development of global systems?

5. Why have firms not planned for the development of international systems?

6. Describe the four main strategies for global business and organizational structure.

7. Describe the four different system configurations that can be used to support different global strategies.

8. What are the major management issues in developing international systems?

9. What are three principles to follow when organizing the firm for global business?

10. What are three steps of a management strategy for developing and implementing global systems?

11. What is meant by *cooptation*, and how can it be used in building global systems?

12. Describe the main technical issues facing global systems.

13. Describe some new technologies to help firms develop global systems.

14. What is offshore software outsourcing? What challenges does it pose? What are the cost components of offshore software development?

Discussion Questions

1. If you were a manager in a company that operates in many countries, what criteria would you use to determine whether an application should be developed as a global application or as a local application?

2. Describe ways the Internet can be used in international information systems.

Video Case

You will find a video case illustrating some of the concepts in this chapter on the Student CD-ROM and the Laudon Web site along with questions to help you analyze the case.

Teamwork: Identifying Technologies for Global Business Strategies

With a group of students, identify an area of information technology and explore how this technology might be useful for supporting global business strategies. For instance, you might choose an area such as digital telecommunications (e.g., e-mail, wireless communications, value-added networks), enterprise systems, collaborative work group software, or the Internet. It will be necessary to choose a business scenario to discuss the technology.

You might choose, for instance, an automobile parts franchise or a clothing franchise, such as Limited Express, as example businesses. Which applications would you make global, which core business processes would you choose, and how would the technology be helpful? If possible, use electronic presentation software to present your findings to the class.

REFERENCES

Baily, Martin N. and Diana Farrell. "Exploding the Myths of Offshoring." The McKinsey Quarterly (July 2004).

Buckman, Rebecca. "H-P Outsourcing: Beyond China," The Wall Street Journal (February 23, 2004).

Central Intelligence Agency. *The World Fact Book.* ttps://www.cia.gov/cia/publications/factbook (2006).

Davison, Robert. "Cultural Complications of ERP." *Communications of the ACM* 45, no. 7 (July 2002).

Deans, Candace P., and Michael J. Kane. *International Dimensions of Information Systems and Technology.* Boston, MA: PWS-Kent (1992).

Ein-Dor, Philip, Seymour E. Goodman, and Peter Wolcott. "From Via Maris to Electronic Highway: The Internet in Canaan." *Communications of the ACM* 43, no. 7 (July 2000).

eMarketer, "Worldwide Sourcing IT Services Export Share, by Country/Region." (March 2004).

Farhoomand, Ali, Virpi Kristiina Tuunainen, and Lester W. Yee. "Barrier to Global Electronic Commerce: A Cross-Country Study of Hong Kong and Finland." *Journal of Organizational Computing and Electronic Commerce* 10, no. 1 (2000).

Forrester Research, "IT Outsourcing Shows Accelerating Growth." Forrester Research (December 2004)

Global Insight. "IT Outsourcing and the U.S. Economy." www.globalinsight.com (2006).

Ives, Blake, and Sirkka Jarvenpaa. "Applications of Global Information Technology: Key Issues for Management." *MIS Quarterly* 15, no. 1 (March 1991).

———. "Global Business Drivers: Aligning Information Technology to Global Business Strategy." *IBM Systems Journal* 32, no. 1 (1993).

Ives, Blake, S. L. Jarvenpaa, and R. O. Mason, "Global business drivers: Aligning Information Technology to Global Business Strategy," *IBM Systems Journal* Vol 32, No 1 (1993).

Ives, Blake. "Global Information Technology: Some Lessons from Practice." *International Information Systems* 1, no. 3 (July 1992).

Jarvenpaa, Sirkka L., Kathleen Knoll, and Dorothy Leidner. "Is Anybody Out There? Antecedents of Trust in Global Virtual Teams." *Journal of Management Information Systems* 14, no. 4 (Spring 1998).

Jarvenpaa, Sirkka L., Thomas R. Shaw, and D. Sandy Staples. "Toward Contextualized Theories of Trust: The Role of Trust in Global Virtual Teams." Information Systems Research 15, no. 3 (September 2004)

King, William R. and Vikram Sethi. "An Empirical Analysis of the Organization of Transnational Information Systems." *Journal of Management Information Systems* 15, no. 4 (Spring 1999).

Krishna, S., Sundeep Sahay, and Geoff Walsham. "Managing Cross-Cultural Issues in Global Software Outsourcing." Communications of the ACM 47, No. 4 (April 2004).

Lai, Vincent S. and Wingyan Chung. "Managing International Data Communication." *Communications of the ACM* 45, no.3 (March 2002).

Liang, Huigang, Yajiong Xue, William R. Boulton, and Terry Anthony Byrd. "Why Western Vendors Don't Dominate China's ERP Market." Communications of the ACM 47, no. 7 (July 2004).

MacFarquhar, Neil. "Tunisia's Tangled Web Is Sticking Point for Reform." The New York Times (June 25, 2004).

Mann, Catherine L. "What Global Sourcing Means for U.S. I.T. Workers and for the U.S. Economy." Communications of the ACM 47, no. 7 (July 2004).

Martinsons, Maris G. "ERP In China: One Package Two Profiles," Communications of the ACM 47, no. 7 (July 2004).

McCue, Andy. "Gartner: Outsourcing Costs More than In-House." *CNET News* (March 7, 2006).

Overby, Stephanie, "The Hidden Costs of Offshore Outsourcing," *CIO Magazine* (Sept.1, 2003).

Roche, Edward M. *Managing Information Technology in Multinational Corporations.* New York: Macmillan (1992).

Shore, Barry. "Enterprise Integration Across the Globally Dispersed Service Organization." *Communications of the ACM* 49, NO. 6 (June 2006).

Soh, Christina, Sia Siew Kien, and Joanne Tay-Yap. "Cultural Fits and Misfits: Is ERP a Universal Solution?" *Communications of the ACM* 43, no. 3 (April 2000).

Tan, Zixiang, William Foster, and Seymour Goodman. "China's State-Coordinated Internet Infrastructure." *Communications of the ACM* 42, no. 6 (June 1999).

Tractinsky, Noam, and Sirkka L. Jarvenpaa. "Information Systems Design Decisions in a Global Versus Domestic Context." *MIS Quarterly* 19, no. 4 (December 1995).

Watson, Richard T., Gigi G. Kelly, Robert D. Galliers, and James C. Brancheau. "Key Issues in Information Systems Management: An International Perspective." *Journal of Management Information Systems* 13, no. 4 (Spring 1997).

Nestlé Tries for an All-for-One Global Strategy
CASE STUDY

Nestlé is the largest food and beverage company in the world. Headquartered in Vevey, Switzerland, the company has annual revenues in excess of $70 billion and nearly 250,000 employees at 500 facilities in 200 countries. Best known for its chocolate, coffee (it invented instant coffee), and milk products, Nestlé sells hundreds of thousands of other items, most of which are adapted to fit local markets and cultures.

Traditionally, this huge firm allowed each local organization to conduct business as it saw fit, taking into account the local conditions and business cultures. To support this decentralized strategy, it had 80 different information technology units that ran nearly 900 IBM AS/400 midrange computers, 15 mainframes, and 200 Unix systems, enabling observers to describe its infrastructure as a veritable Tower of Babel.

However, Nestlé's management found that allowing these local differences created inefficiencies and extra costs that could prevent the company from competing effectively in electronic commerce. The lack of standard business processes prevented Nestlé from, for example, leveraging its worldwide buying power to obtain lower prices for its raw materials. Even though each factory used the same global suppliers, each negotiated its own deals and prices.

Several years ago, Nestlé embarked on a program to standardize and coordinate its information systems and business processes. The company initially installed SAP's R/3 enterprise resource planning (ERP) software to integrate material, distribution, and accounting applications in the United States, Europe, and Canada.

Nestlé then extended its enterprise systems strategy to all of its facilities to make them act as a single-minded e-business. Once this project is completed, Nestlé will able to use sales information from retailers on a global basis to measure the effectiveness of its promotional activities and reduce overstocking and spoilage caused by having products sit around too long on grocery shelves.

Achieving global standardization of operational processes has been a complex task. None of Nestlé's products is considered a truly global brand, with perhaps the exception of Nescafé, of which 100 million cups are served around the world each year. But even Nescafé is rebranded, repackaged, and reformulated to create over 200 product versions for different regional preferences. This is just a small representation of the complexity that CEO Peter Brabeck wanted to address when he decided to bring a sense of order to the company's business operations.

In 1995, Nestlé facilities in 14 countries were running their businesses on SAP R/2, an older version of its ERP software. They all ran the software differently and used different schemes for formatting data and managing forms. The system disparity resulted in increasing maintenance costs. Compiling financial reports to gain a company-wide view of performance became more laborious.

Between 1994 and 1999, Nestlé increased its spending on information systems from $575 million to $750 million. Brabeck arrived in 1997, and while the technology budget was growing, he was actually decreasing the size of the company by selling off Nestlé brands. The cost of tracking the sales chain, as a percentage of total sales, rose from 1.2 percent in 1994 to 1.6 percent in 1999.

By April 2000, Brabeck had had enough of a corporate philosophy that allowed for thousands of differently configured supply chains, multiple methods of forecasting demand, and innumerable practices for invoicing customers and collecting payments. The inconsistencies and inefficiencies across the enterprise were chipping away at Nestlé's profits. Brabeck, chief financial officer Mario Corti, and the entire executive board launched a $2.4 billion initiative to compel its market heads around the world to adopt a single set of business processes and systems for procurement, distribution, and sales management.

Chris Johnson, who was in charge of Nestlé's Taiwan market, was asked to lead the initiative that would come to be known as GLOBE (Global Business Excellence). Johnson was instructed to find a way to harmonize processes, standardize data, and standardize systems. All of Nestlé's worldwide business units were to use the same processes for making sales commitments, establishing factory production

From *Management Information Systems: Managing the Digital Firm, 10/e.* Kenneth C. Laudon, Jane P. Laudon.

659

schedules, billing customers, compiling management reports, and reporting financial results. The units would no longer be permitted to adhere to local customs for conducting business except in cases where the laws of a particular country required that they do so. Every Nestlé facility would format and store data identically, using the same set of information systems. Johnson would have to oversee the confluence of divergent processes into a "single source of truth." Johnson would have three and a half years to deploy the GLOBE strategy at 70 percent of the company's global markets.

Such an undertaking was unusual for Nestlé. Large projects, such as the construction of a coffee factory, generally cost the company in the range of $30 million to $40 million. Putting up billions of dollars to fund a project was risky, but for Brabeck, the potential benefits were too important. He could significantly curb IT spending, which was growing dangerously. In addition, he could gain an advantage over competitors like Unilever and Kraft Foods in improving operational efficiency while continuing to grow with new markets and new products. Nestlé would also be able to reduce its number of suppliers from 600,000 to 167,000, and save hundreds of millions of dollars in the process. The savings would be reinvested in innovation, pleasing its largest customers like Wal-Mart and Tesco, and further strengthening Nestlé's position among the other global food suppliers. It would be the first global enterprise to conduct business as though it were operating in a single country.

The goal was lofty, and previous attempts at cooperative standards had mixed results. Technology experts from headquarters had emphasized standards and best practices to the 14 countries that deployed SAP in the past. The pleas for a unified corporate culture were largely ignored. On the other hand, market managers in Asia had come together to develop a common system for managing their supply chains using software from SSA Global. The Business Excellence Common Application flourished in Indonesia, Malaysia, the Philippines, and Thailand, and even spread to South Africa. The American division of Nestlé also standardized its practices using SAP software in a project known as BEST (Business Excellence through Systems Technology). However, it was the Asian effort that would serve as the model due to its success in crossing cultures and satisfying multiple market managers.

GLOBE, under the leadership of Johnson, launched on July 4, 2000. Johnson had support from

Olivier Gouin, chief information officer for Nestlé in France, and a panel of 12 senior executives with various backgrounds who had been chosen specifically for the project. Even before beginning the likely difficult task of convincing market managers worldwide to adopt a centralized culture, the GLOBE team had a more pressing challenge to confront: Was it actually possible to convert 70 percent of the business to a common set of best practices and systems by the December 2003 deadline?

There were to be no shortcuts. Everything had to be standardized on the new mySAP Internet-based software. Moreover, the deadline had already appeared in a company newsletter, so changing the date could have damaged confidence in the project.

Johnson's team studied the experiences of competitors, and received feedback from consultants at PricewaterhouseCoopers and deployment experts at SAP. Johnson and Gouin were not surprised to determine that the parameters of the project would have to be adjusted. GLOBE required a larger staff, more funding, and a larger window of time than the executive board had allotted. The GLOBE team predicted that its staff would need to grow to a maximum of 3,500 workers.

The team's projections also gave rise to the $2.4 billion budget. Gouin softened the blow of the cost by pointing out that the status quo, individual markets managing their own systems, projected to cost $3.2 billion over five years. In the end, considering the scope of the project, Johnson's team also concluded that the schedule was too ambitious. The schedule was revised so that a "majority of the company's key markets," rather than 70 percent, would be GLOBE-enabled by the end of 2005, instead of 2003.

Instead of technology managers, Johnson tried to build his team from a diverse group of business managers who had experience in a variety of business sectors including manufacturing, finance, marketing, and human resources. He recruited from Nestlé offices all over the world. He went after the best of the best—managers that were considered "untouchables" because they were too valuable in their current capacities to be let go for new projects.

Johnson put his first team together in the fall of 2000. By the following winter, the team had added 400 executives with diverse career backgrounds at Nestlé covering 40 different countries. In February 2001, this core group began the critical process of compiling the GLOBE Best Practices Library. The 400 were knowledgeable in how the company actually conducted business. They would need to know the processes for everything from calculating product demand and managing the supply chain to generating an invoice and ordering office equipment. Many of these processes had never been documented and were simply passed down by word of mouth. Johnson described the task as converting Nestlé's oral history into decoding "the DNA of how Nestlé does business."

The 400 executives documented the best ways of performing each process. Then, the GLOBE team brought in experts in each area to challenge the processes, find their weaknesses, and pare the list down to the best practice for each process. In this way, the Best Practices Library evolved into an online database of step-by-step guides for 1,000 processes, divided into 45 solution sets that focused on disciplines such as demand planning or financial reporting.

Some best practices, such as getting a product to market, were afforded a degree of flexibility to account for the wide variety of Nestlé products and the breadth of markets in which they were sold. Other practices, such as financial reporting, were given no wiggle room. Salespeople were to enter orders with precision in a standard format and by a specific date every month. Financial terms and recording dates were standardized across the enterprise. Johnson later described the accounting software as being "kind of like handcuffs in a way to make you do the right thing."

It became apparent to Johnson that the greatest challenge of GLOBE might not be technical, but personal. Despite clear support for the project from the highest-ranking executives, including Brabeck, managers resisted the idea of giving up control over their business processes to participate in a centralized solution. They feared the loss of decision-making power. Many thought that making back-office operations identical in so many different countries was impractical. They might agree to standardization, but only if it was their particular practices that were made the GLOBE standard. The resistance was fortified by the fact that each country's operations would have to spend its own money to pay for the project.

In the fall of 2001, Johnson was on the defensive. He was given a full day of a three-day meeting to convince market managers that falling in step with GLOBE was in their best interest and in the best interest of the company. The managers peppered him with questions that were intended to

demonstrate how GLOBE would make their jobs more difficult and degrade the performance of their units. Johnson did the best he could to satisfy them, and then took a frank approach. The project was going to proceed. If they did not get behind GLOBE, he would be fired, and Brabeck would select one of them to head the massive undertaking. The other managers were not interested in that outcome.

Johnson did receive support that day from Jose Lopez, the head of the Malaysia and Singapore markets, which were being used to test GLOBE's back-office systems. It was too early to measure the benefits of the project, but Lopez expressed his belief in the premise and his willingness to cooperate.

A year and a half later in the spring of 2003, the market heads had another opportunity to question Johnson. While there were still plenty of questions, a number of them described the operational efficiencies they had achieved since implementing GLOBE standards. For example, their financial reports and demand forecasts were better and faster.

By a third meeting in May 2005, 20 market heads were able to endorse the benefits of GLOBE. In the interim, however, an unwelcome financial problem arose. GLOBE was not controlling information technology costs as expected. As a percentage of sales, costs were approaching 2 percent. Brabeck instituted a cap on information technology expenses at 1.9 percent. In order to meet the cap, Johnson and Gouin revised the schedule of the project again. They set a goal of 80 percent of Nestlé being on the GLOBE system by the end of 2006. The extended schedule allowed the GLOBE team to maintain Brabeck's spending cap and protect the company's profits. In the fall of 2005, the percentage of Nestlé units running GLOBE reached 25 percent and costs were within the limit.

To help the rollouts along, Johnson asked each country to name a GLOBE manager who would facilitate the adoption of the system. These managers also provided value to each other by exchanging their experiences with the system and the solutions they employed for specific challenges. Johnson also established a steering committee at company headquarters to schedule and manage the rollouts. The steering committee oversaw the reduction of company data centers from 100 to four, including the center in Vevey, which stored the GLOBE templates, Best Practices Library, and central functions.

One of Brabeck's biggest concerns was that the rollouts occur with no effect on customers. A rollout could only be a true success if no one outside the company noticed it. The initial test markets found this daunting because they would have to fix bugs and confront unanticipated problems during the deployment. Nestlé also had to implement the new business processes concurrently with the new systems. There was no opportunity to perfect the processes. And, finally, the managers and their workers had no time to train on the new systems before they deployed them and began using them. Despite these challenges, the test markets experienced few problems, and rollouts proceeded around the world. After the test markets, market managers had at least nine months to document their processes and perfect them until they conformed with the GLOBE templates.

Along the way, Nestlé did encounter some technical issues. For example, Canadian market managers used special promotions liberally to attract business from local and regional grocery chains. The mySAP software was not designed to accommodate the extra data points generated by so many promotions. Nestlé worked with SAP to develop a "multiple angles approach" to allow for such a difference. The approach enabled Nestlé to separate the storage of data by market. This way, a country like Canada could have the extra storage space in the central system that it needed for its promotion data.

By the end of 2005, Nestlé had converted 30 percent of its business to GLOBE, and had the capacity for one major rollout every month. The 80 percent number by the end of 2006 was still looming, but the company had learned how to operate as a single unit on a global scale. Johnson was not entirely satisfied with the results, citing delayed and flawed summary reports compromising the work of factory and country managers. He was also eager to see reports made available instantly on a 24/7 basis rather than having to wait for them to be completed overnight each day.

To make sure that the data entering GLOBE's streamlined data centers are accurate and complete, each country has a data manager. Johnson believes that the system will never achieve perfection as long as time constraints remain a factor. However, Nestlé is much closer to achieving its goal of standardizing all processes, data, and systems. The closer the company comes to developing the perfect system, the better the company can serve its customers.

Sources: Tom Steinert-Threlkeld, "Nestlé Pieces Together Its Global Supply Chain," *Baseline Magazine,* January 20, 2006; "Nestlé Group in 2005: Record Sales and Profits—Higher Dividend Proposed," www.nestle.com, February 23, 2006; and The Associated Press, "Nestle Reports 14 Percent Rise in Sales," MSNBC.com, April 25, 2006, accessed October 11, 2006.

CASE STUDY QUESTIONS

1. Analyze Nestlé using the competitive forces and value chain models. What challenges did Nestlé face?

2. What type of global business and systems strategy did Nestlé adopt? Was this strategy appropriate for Nestlé's business model?

3. What management, organization, and technology challenges did Nestlé have to deal with to standardize its business processes and systems?

4. What strategies did Nestlé management use to deal with these challenges? How successful were these strategies? Explain your answer.

CASE STUDY:

Mobile Customer Services at Deutsche Lufthansa

Walter Brenner, Lutz M. Kolbe, and Adrian Bueren
University of St. Gallen (Switzerland)

"Sorry, I have to catch my flight..."

With a quick wave of a hand, John Smith rushes out of the business meeting for the drive to the airport. He had forgotten to check in online and will now have to check in at the airport at least 45 minutes before departure. On arriving at the airport, he runs to the check-in machine. There is a short waiting line but after a few minutes' wait he has his boarding pass. He checks the boarding pass for his gate number and realizes that the flight has been delayed. He is now not only exhausted but also annoyed that he has an hour to kill and nothing to keep him occupied. So John makes a couple of phone calls and finally kills time by listening to music on his MP3-enabled cell phone. Shortly before the due departure time he walks to his gate, but notices that the gate has changed since his check-in. He runs to the new gate through the crowded terminal, barely making it in time to board. When he takes his seat, he notices some of the other passengers' annoyed looks; his neighbor on the plane tells him that he had been paged twice and the plane had been delayed further waiting for him.

LUFTHANSA—GROWTH IN A TOUGH COMPETITION

The airline industry has undergone dramatic changes in recent years. Reduced revenues after September 11, 2001, oil prices at a historical high, and the increasing number of no-frills airlines have resulted in a fierce price war. Nevertheless, it is still a growth market with forecasted annual growth rates of 5–7 percent (in the number of bookings, not in revenue). To retain their revenue streams and cut costs, airlines must manage their customer relations very carefully. The major challenges are to invest in relations with valuable customers and to reduce the costs of handling less valuable customers. Full service carriers have consequently adopted the no-frills carriers' low priced minimal service, while simultaneously still offering their traditional higher priced premium service. To ensure that this price differentiation will succeed in the long run, full service carriers aim at providing different service levels in their customer interaction channels.

Deutsche Lufthansa is an aviation corporation that was initially founded in 1926, closed in the aftermath of World War II, and refounded in 1951 as a government-owned German flag carrier. The first public listing on stock markets was 1966, and privatization was completed in 1997. Lufthansa's major business is the "Passage" business area (passenger aviation) that comprises 63 percent of Lufthansa's corporate sales. In total, Lufthansa realized €16,965 million revenue and serviced 50 million passengers in 2004[1]. Lufthansa therefore transported more passengers on international routes than any other IATA[2] airline and was the world's top cargo carrier. Lufthansa's image is that of a premium brand promising quality, reliability, safety, competence and innovation. Lufthansa was, for example, the first airline worldwide to use the Boeing 747 as a cargo aircraft; Lufthansa's maintenance, repair, and overhaul (MRO) unit "Lufthansa Technik" has been certified as the first aviation company authorized to install a wireless radio connection (such as WirelessLAN for Web access and Voice over IP services) inside an aircraft cabin. Lufthansa itself uses these capabilities for its own passenger fleet under the product name "FlyNet".

Many customers still perceive Lufthansa as a high-priced premium service brand, even though it also offers tariffs that compete with those of discount airlines. In order to attract these price-sensitive customers, Lufthansa wants to improve awareness of its competitive price offerings. The company consequently started e-mail campaigns to convey their newest special offers: extremely low prices for flights on which there is undercapacity. Each Friday these offers are communicated by e-mail to those customers who have given their permission (by opting in, a legal requirement to fight spam in most countries). The conditions pertaining to these low tariffs include a reservation no later than the following Monday and departure no later than the following Friday. Lufthansa's competitors are usually unable to respond quickly to such short notice, making Lufthansa's price the cheapest on the market for the specific flights.

Lufthansa positions itself as a full-service provider and aims at meeting the specific requirements of each customer segment in the market. Like most other airlines, Lufthansa differentiates three product lines that provide different service levels: first class, business class, and economy class. To increase customer loyalty, the company, similar to most other airlines, offers a frequent flyer program called "Miles & More" (M&M) that offers members bonus miles for each flight they take with Lufthansa or a partner. Within the M&M program, a customer is allocated one of four different statuses (see Table 1), depending on the customer's bonus miles balance. The statuses are associated with product lines, e.g., a Senator status customer receives first-class service, a Frequent Traveler status customer receives business-class service, even when flying economy class (with very few exceptions, such as the first-class terminal in Frankfurt). Table 1 provides an overview of the different M&M member statuses, their qualifying characteristics, and their association with Lufthansa product lines:

Customers' expectations and requirements of the service of these segments vary. The Non-members (NM) are mostly customers who only fly

TABLE 1 CUSTOMER SEGMENTATION AT LUFTHANSA

M&M MEMBER STATUSES	CHARACTERISTICS	LUFTHANSA PRODUCT LINES
Honorable Circle (HON)	600,000 miles within two year	First Class
Senator (SEN)	150,000 miles within one year	First Class
Frequent Traveller (FTL)	50,000 miles within one year	Business Class
Basic Members	M&M membership	Economy Class
Non-members	Not a M&M member, a prospective or non-customer	Economy Class

occasionally, or who are not very loyal to Lufthansa. In general, their primary requirement is a low flight price. They are, to a certain extent, even willing to accept delays as long as the fare is low. Lufthansa's profit margin from this customer segment is small and the cost pressure high. Cost-cutting through self-services is often not feasible, since many of these customers are inexperienced in standard handling procedures (e.g., the check-in process). The Basic members have the same requirements and consequences for Lufthansa as the non-members. However, this segment flies more frequently and is therefore

more familiar with standard handling procedures. Self-service is suitable for this customer segment.

The Frequent Travelers (FTL) and the Senators (SEN) expect fast and efficient handling procedures as well as a high flexibility in respect of the changing of bookings. They are less price-sensitive and Lufthansa meets their requirements by providing better levels of service than to Basic members or Non-members. Self-services are very appropriate for the FTL and SEN, since they know the handling procedures well and are very interested in self-services for the time-saving that these allow. The difference between the FTL and SEN is noticeable in the Senator's additional service features (e.g., access to the Senator Lounge). The Honorable Circle (HON) has the same requirements as the FTL and SEN. Furthermore, HONs pay a great deal of attention to individual service, such as that provided by the new first class terminal in Frankfurt for the exclusive use of first-class and HON customers. Self-services are therefore not suitable for this customer segment.

Lufthansa aims to reflect the different service levels for its customer segments in each interaction, such as in check-in procedures, in-flight service or other offerings. FTL, SEN, and HON will specifically be able to perceive better service than the Non-members and Basic members.

THERE'S NO BETTER WAY TO FLY

TRAVELING WITH LUFTHANSA— AN ONLINE EXPERIENCE

Since the late 1990s, Lufthansa has offered numerous information and transaction services online at www.lufthansa.com. These include a booking service with electronic tickets (etix®), check-in, redemption of bonus miles on bookings or other items from Lufthansa's online shop, information about M&M account balances, or simply up-to-date information on flight arrivals and departures that notes the most recent gate changes, delays, and cancellations. By providing these services as online self-services, Lufthansa was able to reduce the workload spent on standard requests in staffed channels, such as the call center, and dedicate more time and effort to more complex requests. The customers benefit from the check-in deadline being 35 minutes prior to departure for online check-in as opposed to 45 minutes prior to check-in at the counter.

The travel process, with the full use of Lufthansa's self-services (starting with the check-in), occurs as follows: Starting at 18:00 the day before the flight's departure (24 hours before departure at the earliest), flights are ready for check-in through the Lufthansa check-in system. Customers can then complete the check-in procedure online at www.lufthansa.com. This must be done at least 35 minutes prior to departure (at smaller airports 25 minutes). On the day of the flight, passengers must pick up a

boarding pass at the Quick-Check-In machines located in the airport terminal. For identification, passengers need their M&M membership card or the credit card used to pay for the flight. Check-in baggage must be checked in at the counters. However, there are ten airports throughout Germany where Quick-Check-In machines are already capable of handling the check-in of baggage. Based on a predefined set of rules, the check-in machine may suggest an upgrade in exchange for bonus miles[3]. If the customer accepts this offer, he or she will receive a boarding pass for the higher class. Bonus miles are automatically deducted from the customer's account. With the boarding pass, the customer proceeds through the security check to the departure gate, where his or her boarding pass and identity are again checked. Boarding should commence about 20 minutes prior to departure. Quick Boarding turnstiles, which allow the boarding of etix® passengers without Lufthansa staff's involvement, have been installed at six airports throughout Germany. On arrival at a final destination, the customer picks up his or her check-in baggage at the baggage claim.

Figure 1 depicts the travel process (starting with the check-in) for a customer who uses all online self-service options.

THERE'S NO BETTER WAY TO FLY— REALLY?

Prior to the flight, the customer can check online for possible gate changes, delays, or flight cancellations. Without Web access, this is obviously not possible. The customer is, however, notified about the newest departure time and gate when checking in. Nevertheless, Lufthansa does not actively communicate any changes that occur after the customer has checked the flight's status on the Web or after check-in (online or at the airport) to the customer. The customer must periodically check the terminal's displays that show the newest flight statuses.

To reduce the time customers spend waiting for connecting flights, Lufthansa has optimized its flight plans at its major hubs in Frankfurt and Munich. The effectiveness of this measure does depend, of course, on all flights being punctual as well as on customers receiving up-to-date information on departure times and gates. During

FIGURE 1   TRAVEL PROCESS WITH ONLINE SELF-SERVICE OPTIONS

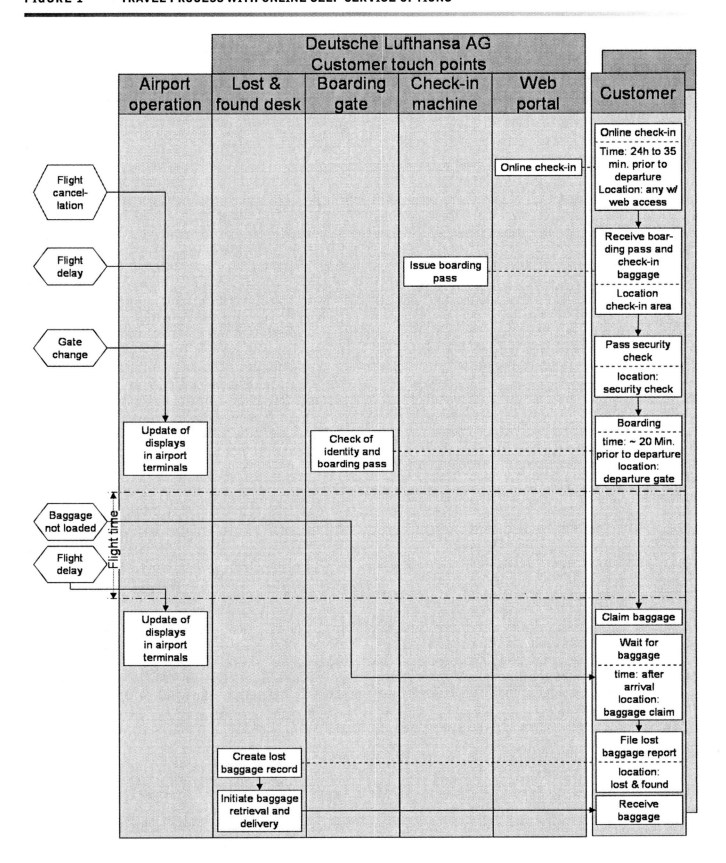

the flight, all communication has to be done personally, because the electronic channels are not accessible onboard. FlyNet, Lufthansa's in-flight Internet access via wireless LAN, should open this opportunity. However, it is not available on all flights and, secondly, it cannot be assumed that all customers carry the necessary laptop or wireless PDA with them.

After a flight, the customer collects his or her baggage at the baggage claim. If the baggage was not loaded onto the aircraft, the customer usually has to wait for the last baggage to arrive before he or she can file a lost baggage report at the Lost & Found desk. Lufthansa, however, has the information about the displaced baggage already, approximately 30 minutes after departure, in its baggage tracing systems. Once the baggage has been located and delivered to the destination, it is sent to the customer's address as given on the lost baggage record.

FACING COST PRESSURE

Lufthansa itself recognizes certain impediments that call for further improvement. Despite replacing staff involvement in some activities of the travel process with self-services, several cost drivers are still in place. On the one hand, the Quick-Check-In machines have replaced costly labor, but they are both costly to purchase as well as to maintain.

Another cost driver is balancing M&M members' bonus miles. Bonus miles are, in fact, Lufthansa's liabilities in respect of their customers, and are therefore reflected on the balance sheet as accrued liabilities. While the automatic upgrade offer at the Quick-Check-In machines was designed to encourage customers to use their bonus miles more frequently, it wasn't initially as successful as expected. The number of offers actually made was significantly lower, while the rate of acceptance of those offers was higher than initially expected. To counter this underachievement, Lufthansa adapted the set of rules, allowing more upgrade offers to be made.

THERE'S A BETTER WAY TO FLY— MOBILE CUSTOMERS, MOBILE INFORMATION

As described above, customers are cut off from access to information during large parts of their travel. Providing customers with information at the exact time when they need this information would improve the customer experience and the travel process's efficiency.

"Our customers are mobile by nature, so our service offerings should also be!" says Annette R., Manager CRM Strategy and Customer Processes.

In 2000, Lufthansa formed a strategic partnership with Vodafone, one of the largest European cellular network operators. The company began to analyze the existing processes and services for potential support by means of mobile technologies as well as to develop ideas for new processes and services based on mobile technologies. A new project, called Mobile Services, was initiated as part of a large CRM development project.

The project goals were diverse: First of all, the information supply to customers during a flight had to be improved. Secondly, the handling procedures had to be redesigned to improve efficiency in respect of both customers and Lufthansa. Thirdly, the project aimed at improving the exploitation of cross-selling potentials, particularly by encouraging customers to spend more of their bonus miles. Finally, Lufthansa's innovative image had to be stressed by demonstrating the company's capability to design new and innovative solutions for its customers and bringing them to market.

A typical business case was not calculated prior to project initialization. This was primarily due to the lack of experience with mobile services and the resulting uncertainty about customers' acceptance thereof. Potential savings through improved process efficiency are highly dependent on the number of transactions that the new processes carry out. But a reliable projection of such numbers is impossible without actual experience. Additional difficulties were encountered because the new procedures would mostly extend the service offerings, but would not replace previous procedures. Furthermore, much of the project's potential was seen as improving customer service and customer satisfaction, benefits which are hard to quantify in a business case. The management therefore accepted the project, without a proper business case due to the project's innovative nature and the plausible arguments for improved customer satisfaction.

The project was led by the Strategic CRM Development group, which is generally responsible for the development of Lufthansa's CRM strategy and processes. Since the targeted processes were primarily those associated with the handling procedures on the ground and not on board, the project was realized in close cooperation with the Global Passenger Processes department which is responsible for processes such as check-in and customer service outside aircrafts. The main project tasks were:

- *Development of business concepts:* The design of the ground stations (check-in areas, boarding gates etc.), design of the processes (check in, boarding, and lost & found).

- *Management of process-level problems:* During the project, several non-technical issues regarding the designed processes were raised and had to be addressed, e.g., the process to obtain customers' permission for Lufthansa to contact them on their cell phone had to be redesigned.

- *Identification of new potentials:* Throughout the course of the project, permanent monitoring of the affected processes and those connected to them were necessary to identify further potentials for future mobile services.

- *Management of relationships with other departments:* Even though the project mainly affected the ground processes, a number of other departments were affected, or had to be involved (e.g., Marketing, Call Centers, Lost & Found staff).

Lufthansa Systems, the company's IT service subsidiary, handled the technical aspects of the project. The main technical tasks were the following:

- *Operation, maintenance, and further development:* Development, operation, and maintenance of interfaces between Lufthansa's various systems and between Lufthansa's systems and those of the service providers.

- *Assessment of business concepts and transformation into IT concepts:* Business concepts' technical feasibility had to be assessed and estimates regarding implementation time and costs provided; IT concepts had to be designed and realized to implement the concepts; and a new business logic had to be implemented within the existing and new systems.

- *Selection and management of service providers:* External service providers had to be selected for certain services (e.g., SLAs[4] had to be developed and managed), after which the relationships with the chosen service providers had to be managed.

- *Documentation:* New systems as well as changes to existing systems had to be correctly documented, which was also required for the contracts and SLAs with service providers.

- *Bug fixing:* During the course of the projects, technical issues as well as bugs in the systems were identified which needed to be fixed.

Prior to the project's start, some content such as contact information was already available for mobile browsers using the Wireless Application Protocol (WAP). The entire project for the introduction of mobile services as described here took approximately one man-year (FTE[5]) (5 man-months in the business areas, and 7 man-months in the technical areas), and was partially done by service providers. Overall, the project budget, including software licenses and fees as well as other fixed costs, was more or less €200,000. Since most of the staff came from the Strategic CRM Development group, the daily business was unaffected. It was possible to handle the coordination with the Global Passenger Processes department besides the daily business.

> *"Almost all passengers have a mobile phone on them. The first thing most of them do after touch-down is to switch it on and check for messages. There simply had to be a way for Lufthansa to take advantage of this!" says Sylvia A., Senior Manager CRM Strategy and Customer Processes.*

In 2000, SMS[6] pull services were first introduced in addition to the existing WAP content. SMS pull services deliver information to users on request. The content of these services mainly comprised content already available on the Web, e.g., flight-related information such as departure and arrival times (see below for a detailed description). Initially the use of these services was below expectations. In 2002, SMS push services were added. These are services that Lufthansa uses to actively push communication to its customers. These services require prior permission from the user for compliance with most countries' anti-spam legislation. The content of these services comprises information about newest Lufthansa events, such as gate changes or flight delays (see below for a detailed description). With the advent of the SMS push service, all mobile services' frequency of use increased significantly.

The first project meetings already generated several ideas for mobile services. These had to be prioritized in order to build a mobile services portfolio to be implemented in the project. In alignment with the project goals, two dimensions were used for the prioritization: benefits for the customer (i.e., customer satisfaction) and benefits for Lufthansa (i.e., efficiency gains). The main criteria, against which the different services' customer benefits would be assessed, were:

- *Increased flexibility:* When customers are actively informed about irregular events that require them to react (e.g., a change of departure gate requires them to show up for boarding at a new gate).
- *Increased efficiency:* When the customer's process activities can be eliminated, or waiting times can at least be reduced.
- *Increased mobility:* When process activities can be carried out from anywhere and/or anytime.

Similarly, the benefits for Lufthansa were assessed in respect to the following criteria:

- *Implementation efforts:* The efforts and costs of the new service offerings' implementation.
- *Operation efforts:* The efforts and costs of running the new service in the operational environment.
- *Efficiency gains:* The savings in personal, transaction, and other costs which can be gained with the new service.

The result of the assessment is depicted in Figure 2. Before implementation, the suggested services (in the shaded area) were analyzed in more depth.

Prior to the selected services being designed in detail, they were classified according to the following task characteristics:

- *Intended use:* Why do customers use the service? This could be for purposes of transaction processing, access to information, or notification.
- *Task type:* What type of user task is supported by the service? Is it a routine, every-day task, or is there a need to respond to an irregularity?
- *Predictability:* How predictable in respect of the customer (either Lufthansa or the customer) is the service's relevance?

FIGURE 2   PRIORITY MATRIX OF SUGGESTIONS FOR MOBILE SERVICES

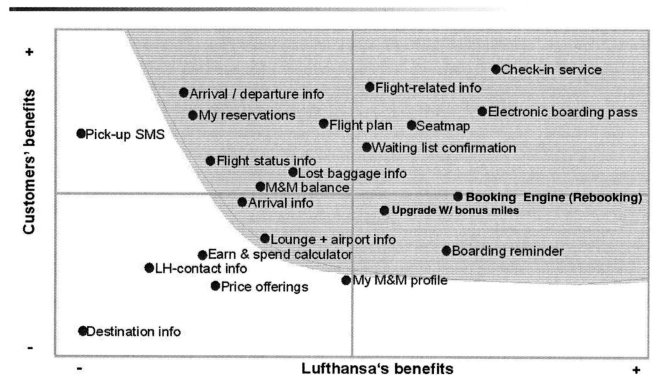

Finally, the service characteristics were determined. These were technical characteristics such as the type of application and communication as well as the target group for whom the services were intended, allowing for a service-level differentiation of mobile services as well. The choice of a type of application is between text messaging (the SMS service in the GSM networks that are common in Europe), or wireless Web (WAP services). The type of communication could be either push, i.e., Lufthansa automatically initiates the service's communication, or pull, i.e., the customer requests the service manually. In effect, the push type is only available if the text messaging type of application is chosen. There are technical standards available for WAP push services, but these are not widely accepted by users and are SMS-based anyway. In most countries, push services require the user's permission , they therefore only apply to registered users; in Lufthansa's case this means to members of the M&M program. Both the type of communication and application largely affect the chosen service's user friendliness. User-friendliness can, for example, be determined by how much text the customer needs to type, the number of steps, the difficulty and number of parameters to remember (e.g., username, password, and self-chosen vs. predefined usernames).

In order to allow for a manageable service level differentiation based on Lufthansa's customer segmentation (see Table 1), the following target groups were defined: Status customers (SC), comprising the Frequent Traveler, Senator, as well as Honorable Circle M&M members, Basic customers (BC) comprising the basic M&M members, and Non-members (NM) comprising other customers and non-customers (see Table 2). In this case, the product lines are not reflected in the segmentation; service level differentiation mostly happens within the M&M member groups. Partially this is a means to increase customer loyalty by giving another

incentive to become a member, partially this is also a technical requirement since push services can only be delivered to customers who have subscribed to the service. This subscription is handled within the M&M member profile.

Subject to the task and service characteristics, a matrix was developed mapping the mobile services' characteristics to target groups (see Table 3).

The project phase ended in November 2005 with the transferral of the operational responsibility for the services to the Global Passenger Processes department. In order to cope with the additional workload and to transfer knowledge of the mobile services to the department, a full-time employee from the Strategic CRM Development department was transferred to Global Passenger Processes.

In order to gain experience with the mobile services within a manageable environment, and due to budget and time restrictions, the mobile services are initially only available on Lufthansa-operated flights departing from Germany. The SMS services are currently also only available in Germany, i.e., for subscribers to German cellular networks. The following mobile services have been developed:

(1) *Mobile check-in service:* Using the mobile check-in service, customers can complete the check-in procedure *(data processing)*. The check-in procedure is a *routine task* that is *predictable* (within a limited time-frame prior to departure). The service differs in respect of Status and Basic customers. It is not provided to Non-members. Prior to departure, Status customers receive an invitation to check in via SMS (push). After the customer's confirmation, he or she receives a confirmation SMS with the flight information, or a rejection SMS (only if the deadline for check in has passed at the time of the customer's response). The customer simply needs to reply a "y" for yes followed by the flight number that was given in the invitation-to-check-in message.

TABLE 2 CUSTOMER SEGMENTATION IN RESPECT OF MOBILE SERVICES AT LUFTHANSA

M&M MEMBER STATUSES	TARGET GROUPS FOR MOBILE SERVICES
Honorable Circle (HON)	Status customers (SC)
Senator (SEN)	
Frequent Traveller (FTL)	
Miles & More Members	Basic customers (BC)
Non-members	Non-members (NM)

TABLE 3   LUFTHANSA'S MOBILE SERVICES—TASKS' AND MOBILE SERVICES' CHARACTERISTICS

	TASK CHARACTERISTICS			MOBILE SERVICE CHARACTERISTICS		
	Intended use	Task type	Predictability	Communication type	Application type	Target group
Mobile check-in	Data processing	Routine task	Predictable	Push Pull	SMS WAP	SC BC, NM
Flight-related information	Notification	needs to handle irregularity	Unpredictable	Push	SMS	SC, BC
Arrival/departure information	Information access	Routine task	Unpredictable	Pull	SMS/WAP	all
Flight plan	Information access	Routine task	Unpredictable	Pull	WAP	all
Miles &More balance	Information access	Routine task	Unpredictable	Pull	SMS/WAP	SC, BC
Lufthansa contact information	Information access	Routine task	Unpredictable	Pull	WAP	all
Price information	Notification	Routine task	Unpredictable	Push	SMS	all

In contrast to Status customers, *Basic customers* must initiate the check-in service themselves via WAP (pull). In a five-step process, they must enter the URL (which can be bookmarked), their Miles & More number or credit card number, as well as their surname. They can then select a flight. Both customer groups benefit from later check-in deadlines (25 minutes prior to departure in Frankfurt and Munich, 20 minutes at all other German airports), the reduced waiting time, and a check-in process that they can activate anywhere. Status customers benefit additionally from the convenience of not having to wait in any line at check-in and not having to remember their credit card or Miles & More membership number. For further convenience, no messages are sent between 22:00 until 04:00, while only urgent messages, i.e., those messages urging check-in for a flight departing within the next 90 minutes, are sent between 04:00 and 09:00.

(2) *Flight-related information service:* The flight-related information service notifies customers about events such as gate changes, flight delays, or flight cancellations *(notification)*. These events are *unpredictable* and create a *need to handle irregularity*, e.g., departing from a different gate. This service is the same for both Status and Basic customers, but is not provided to Non-members. As soon as one of the events listed above occurs, Status customers as well as Basic customers will receive an SMS alert *(push)* that does not require a reply (see Figure 3).

This service furthermore allows both customer groups to postpone their departure to the airport if their flight has been delayed. The waiting time at the airport and the associated discomfort are therefore reduced or eliminated. The customer can react directly to changes at the airport.

(3) *Arrival/departure information service:* The arrival/departure information service allows customers to access information on a specific flight (e.g., arrival and departure time, punctuality or gate number) *(information access)*. The service is a routine task, but is initiated by the customer and therefore unpredictable for Lufthansa. The service is the same for Status, Basic, and Non-members. One way of accessing this flight information is by sending an SMS with "d" (for departures) or "a" for arrivals, followed by the flight number *(pull)*. Another way is to apply the WAP service *(pull)* (see Figure 4). Four steps are necessary to receive such information using the WAP service: The customer must enter the URL (which can be bookmarked), select a departure or arrival location from a list of major airports or enter a city code, select the scheduled time (choices are "currently", "in 10 minutes", "10 minutes ago", "in 20 minutes" and "20 minutes ago"), and finally select the flight *(medium ease of use)*. The customer can use this service anytime and anywhere.

FIGURE 3   A SAMPLE SMS ALERT ABOUT A GATE CHANGE

FIGURE 4   A SAMPLE WALK-THROUGH OF THE ARRIVAL INFORMATION SERVICE[7]

(4) *Flight plan service:* The flight plan service allows any customer to request flight plans for specific dates and arrival or departure locations (*information access*). The service characteristics are similar to those of the previous service. The major difference is that it is not available via SMS pull, but only as WAP pull (see Figure 5). The customer must enter the URL, the departure and arrival locations, and select a date. The next step is to select a connecting flight from the list of connecting flights between the requested locations on the requested dates. The information the customer receives includes flight numbers, departure and arrival terminals as well as the make and type of aircraft used on the flights.

(5) *Miles & More balance service:* The Miles & More balance service allows the customer to access his or her Miles & More account's balance (*information access*). The service is a *routine* task initiated by the customer and therefore *unpredictable for Lufthansa*. It is the same for both Status and Basic customers, but does not apply to Non-members. The service is provided via SMS or WAP pull. Via WAP, the customer enters the URL and either a Miles & More number or username and password (*pull*). The customer sends the word "account" or "miles" to Lufthansa via SMS (*pull*).

(6) *Lufthansa contact information service:* The contact information service allows the customer to look up Lufthansa's contact phone numbers (*information access*). The service is a routine task, initiated by the customer and therefore *unpredictable for Lufthansa*. It is the same for Status and Basic customers as well as

FIGURE 5   A SAMPLE WALK-THROUGH OF THE FLIGHT PLAN SERVICE FOR FRANKFURT TO CHICAGO O'HARE

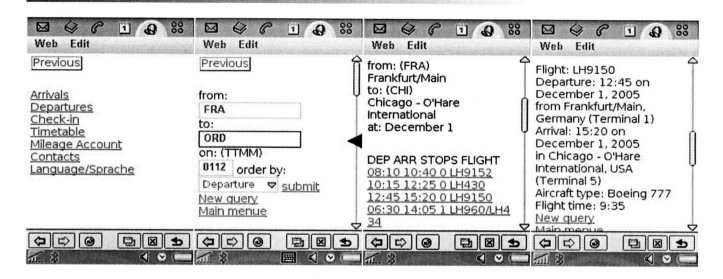

Non-members. The customer enters the URL via WAP and selects the Lufthansa contact information service (*pull*). The customer can then access Lufthansa's contact information regardless of the time or place without having to remember the phone numbers.

(7) *Price information service:* The price information service notifies the customer about the newest price offers (*notification*). The service is a *routine task* initiated by Lufthansa and is *unpredictable for the customer* since he or she can only make a decision regarding the offers after receiving them. It is the same for all target groups: M&M members can grant permission in their online profile, others can subscribe via SMS. Every Friday, Lufthansa sends an SMS (*push*) to draw the customer's attention to an e-mail (also *push*) with attractive price information. Customers benefit from this service because they do not need to do any research regarding this information themselves.

THERE'S NO BETTER WAY TO FLY— LUFTHANSA'S MOBILE SERVICES!

With the advent of its mobile services, Lufthansa aims to provide its customers with a higher quality of service and to live up to its reputation of being innovative. The quality of service can be increased through mobile services by saving customers' time or making it possible for them to use idle time resourcefully. Innovation is reflected in the perceived connotation of innovativeness associated with mobile services. In the following, the travel process is described once again and the support provided by mobile services is shown where applicable. Our customer is again an M&M member with a frequent traveler status. We furthermore assume that all the required permission has been obtained.

After the customer has booked a flight, he or she is notified about the gate changes that could occur, as well as any booked flights that have been rescheduled or cancelled. Every 15 minutes the mobile check-in service checks the availability of the flight in the check-in system. As soon as the flight is available, an SMS message is sent inviting the customer to check in, while respecting the telephone silence required between 22:00 and 09:00. The customer replies to the message by typing "y", followed by the flight number, which can be copied from the check-in notification. The reply must be sent only 20 minutes prior to departure (at Frankfurt and Munich airports 25 minutes). (Basic customers can complete the mobile check-in via WAP but must initiate the service themselves.) To receive a boarding pass and pass through security, the customer follows the same procedure as after the Web check-in as described above. An upgrade is offered following the same rules. If the flight's departure time or departure gate has changed, the customer is notified via SMS. No further notifications about delays or gate changes are sent 20 minutes before the expected departure, since boarding is supposed to be in process at this time. Cellular devices have to be switched off onboard anyway, so the customer is no longer able to receive messages. If the customer's connecting flight has been changed, an SMS message noting the new departure time and gate is sent to his or her cell phone. After arrival at the final destination, the customer picks up his or her check-in baggage at the baggage claim. Figure 6 depicts the process by means of mobile services.

FIGURE 6   TRAVEL PROCESS USING THE NEW MOBILE SERVICES

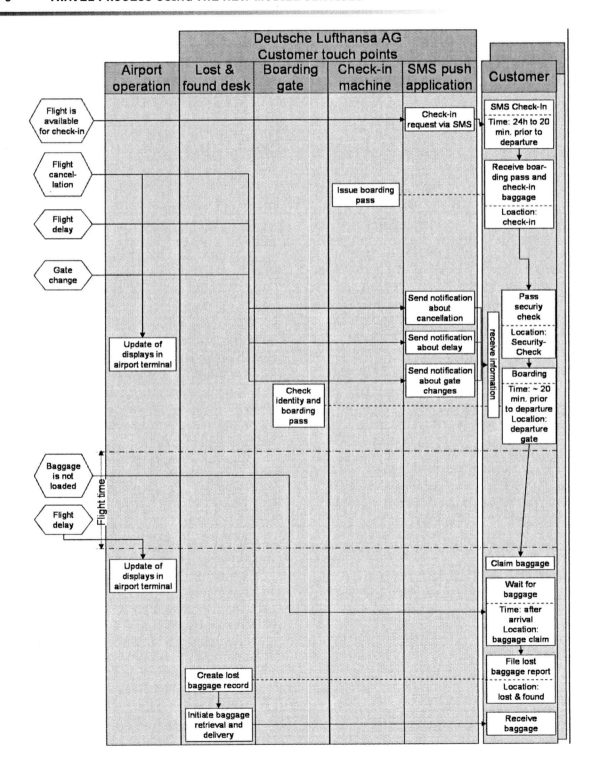

A LONG WAY

Although Lufthansa's mobile services were successfully implemented and customers' acceptance of them is at a satisfactory level and still growing, some issues did arise during the project, some of which are yet to be resolved.

One challenge was to obtain the customers' permission to contact them on their mobile phone. In most countries, anti-spam legislation requires permission to be obtained for commercial e-mail, but also for commercial SMS messages. Similar to other service providers, Lufthansa offers customers the choice to accept commercial communication appropriate to their member profile. This permission can be granted at the lufthansa.com Web portal. Initially, Lufthansa's obtained permission covered all of the company's commercial communications to the customer's mobile phone. Most customers had concerns about granting such a general permission and, consequently, the number of permissions granted was very low. After Lufthansa had changed the online forms in the member profile to allow for permission to be granted separately for each service (see Figure 7), the granting of permission grew significantly, since the customers felt they could better control the communications that they would receive.

Another challenge was caused by the dual-bill option offered by many cellular network operators. This feature is generally used to allow the seamless use of a single cellular device on both a corporate and a private bill. Dual-bill customers receive two phone numbers, s separate SIM[8] card and a separate bill for each number. Customers can have one card logged into the network at a time. Calls and messages to both numbers are forwarded to the currently logged-in SIM card, while outgoing messages and calls are placed with the active card's number as the sender ID. If such a dual-bill customer has registered his corporate cell phone number in his M&M profile, messages are sent to this number and he can receive them, no matter which SIM card is active. However, while his private SIM card is active, he will respond to received messages with a sender ID that Lufthansa's system does not recognize, thus the message cannot be properly processed. This problem could be handled by adding a second field to the M&M profile that will allow two cellular numbers and matching sender IDs to be stored in both fields when retrieving for the appropriate member profile.

The third challenge is based on the twin-card concept, which allows the seamless usage of two cellular devices with one phone number and one bill. Twin-card customers receive two SIM cards with identical subscriber information. Each SIM card can be inserted into a different cellular device, e.g., one phone installed in a car and a handset. All calls and messages will be received by whichever device is switched on at the time. The challenge arises because SMS messages are stored on the device rather than on the network. If a customer receives, for example, a check-in message while the first device is active (e.g., the car phone receives the message while the customer is driving to the airport), but switches to the other device and wishes to respond (e.g., from the hand set while in the shuttle from the parking lot to the terminal), the message is not available. This problem can be solved if the customer stores Lufthansa's response service number in her phones' address books (or the SIM card's). She would nevertheless have to remember her flight number to be able to send the proper response. Another solution would be if she could simply request the system to resend the last message by sending a message with a special keyword. At present this is, however, not yet available.

"DON'T WORRY, I'LL CATCH MY FLIGHT..."

John Smith is again at a business meeting. He had received a check-in invitation via SMS the evening before. Now he can check in until 20 minutes prior to departure and won't have to stand in line again. Already having checked in, he will only have to obtain his boarding pass before boarding. This means that he has a few precious minutes more with his clients! Almost simultaneously to realizing that the meeting would take longer than scheduled, he receives a second SMS saying that his flight has been delayed for an hour. This means that John can stay until the meeting is over. After the meeting, he answers the check-in invitation, drives to the airport at a leisurely speed and obtains his boarding pass. On his way to the gate, his cell phone beeps again, there's another SMS message from Lufthansa warning him that the departure gate has been changed. John changes direction to the new gate and boards the aircraft on time. In the plane, he sits down, relaxes, and looks back on his day: a successful business meeting, satisfied clients, no rush, and now a relaxed flight home.

CASE STUDY QUESTIONS

1. Describe the benefits that Lufthansa's mobile services provide for users. Compare the travel process before and after the introduction of the mobile services. Under which circumstances do the mobile services provide benefits to the customer? How does Lufthansa avoid contacting the customer with irrelevant information?

2. Extend Table 3 with two additional mobile service characteristics: "Ease of use" and "Benefits to the user". Assess the ease of use for each service and classify the benefits to users in each target group. Which services provide different service levels, and which do not? How do services with different service levels differ from those without?

3. Analyze the travel process using the mobile services. Where do you see further potential for mobile services? Describe the mobile services that you would add, and justify their benefits for either the user or Lufthansa. Do you see additional categories of benefits? Can service level differentiation be implemented in the services you suggest? If so, how?

4. Compare Lufthansa's mobile services to the service offering of your favorite airline or another public transport service (such as the railway, metropolitan trains etc.). What can these service providers learn from Lufthansa's services? In what aspects are they already ahead of Lufthansa?

ENDNOTES

[1] For further information about the company visit http://www.lufthansa.com/

[2] IATA: International Air Transport Association

[3] E.g., when a Status customer with a sufficient bonus mile balance checks in for economy class and enough seats are available in the higher classes.

[4] SLA: Service-level agreement

[5] FTE: Full-time equivalent

[6] SMS: Short message service, a text messaging service standard in GSM cellular networks.
GSM: Global system for mobile communications, a cellular network standard.

[7] These screenshots were taken on a device using the SymbianOS operating system with the UIQ user interface and the mobile edition of the Opera™ browser.

[8] Subscriber Identification Module, the chip card which identifies a cellular device for the network in GSM networks.

Congratulations! By completing your information systems course and using this text, you've made great strides in preparing for your future business career. Employers are actively seeking people who know how to use information technologies to work more efficiently and effectively, and who can use these tools to help them solve problems.

If you've worked through some or all of these projects, here are some of the skills and competencies you'll be able to demonstrate:

Business Application Skills

You've acquired software skills and business application knowledge. You know how to use spreadsheet, database, and Web page creation tools in business applications for finance and accounting, human resources, manufacturing and production, and sales and marketing.

Internet Skills

You know how to use Internet tools to access information, conduct research, or perform online calculations and analysis.

Analytical, Writing, and Presentation Skills

You know how to research a specific topic, analyze a problem, think creatively, suggest a solution, and prepare a clear written or oral presentation of the solution, working either individually or with others in a group.

MAKING THIS TEXT WORK FOR YOU AND YOUR CAREER

Keep your work for the Application Software Exercises, running case projects, Building Internet Skills projects, Teamwork projects, and case studies that you have personally completed. You'll definitely be able to use this material when you are job hunting.

We've created a special section of the Laudon student Web site (www.prenhall. com/laudon) devoted to career building. There you'll find instructions and templates to show you how to create a structured digital portfolio demonstrating your mastery of problem-solving and information systems skills for use in job hunting. The Web site includes instructions for the following:

- How to incorporate software, business, and problem-solving skills acquired from this course in resumes and cover letters, both paper-based and electronic. We provide sample resumes and cover letters tailored to jobs in finance, accounting, marketing, human resources, manufacturing/production/operations management, and information systems.
- How and when to highlight your problem-solving and information system skills and business application knowledge in interviews.
- How to organize your work completed for this course into a supplementary digital portfolio and personal Web page for employers requiring more detail about you.
- Tips on career opportunities and job hunting, including links to useful job-hunting sites.

Good luck in developing your career!

Glossary

2.5G networks Wireless cellular networks that are packet-switched and to provide higher-speed data transmission rates ranging from 50 to 144 Kbps using the existing cellular network infrastructure.

3G networks Cellular networks based on packet-switched technology with speeds ranging from 144 Kbps for mobile users to over 2 Mbps for stationary users, enabling users to transmit video, graphics, and other rich media, in addition to voice.

acceptable use policy (AUP) Defines acceptable uses of the firm's information resources and computing equipment, including desktop and laptop computers, wireless devices, telephones, and the Internet, and specifies consequences for noncompliance.

acceptance testing Provides the final certification that the system is ready to be used in a production setting.

access control Policies and procedures a company uses to prevent improper access to systems by unauthorized insiders and outsiders.

access point Box in a wireless LAN consisting of a radio receiver/transmitter and antennae that link to a wired network, router, or hub.

accountability The mechanisms for assessing responsibility for decisions made and actions taken.

accounting rate of return on investment (ROI) Calculation of the rate of return on an investment by adjusting cash inflows produced by the investment for depreciation. Approximates the accounting income earned by the investment.

accumulated balance digital payment systems Systems enabling users to make micropayments and purchases on the Web, accumulating a debit balance on their credit card or telephone bills.

agent-based modeling Modeling complex phenomena as systems of autonomous agents that follow relatively simple rules for interaction.

agency theory Economic theory that views the firm as a nexus of contracts among self-interested individuals who must be supervised and managed.

Ajax Development technique for creating interactive Web applications capable of updating the user interface without reloading the entire browser page.

analog signal A continuous waveform that passes through a communications medium; used for voice communications.

analytical CRM Customer relationship management applications dealing with the analysis of customer data to provide information for improving business performance.

antivirus software Software designed to detect, and often eliminate, computer viruses from an information system.

application proxy filtering Firewall screening technology that uses a proxy server to inspect and transmit data packets flowing into and out of the organization so that all the organization's internal applications communicate with the outside using a proxy application.

application server Software that handles all application operations between browser-based computers and a company's back-end business applications or databases.

application service provider (ASP) Company providing software that can be rented by other companies over the Web or a private network.

application software package A set of prewritten, precoded application software programs that are commercially available for sale or lease.

application software Programs written for a specific application to perform functions specified by end users.

artificial intelligence (AI) The effort to develop computer-based systems that can behave like humans, with the ability to learn languages, accomplish physical tasks, use a perceptual apparatus, and emulate human expertise and decision making.

asynchronous transfer mode (ATM) A networking technology that parcels information into 8-byte cells, allowing data to be transmitted between computers from different vendors at any speed.

attribute A piece of information describing a particular entity.

authentication The ability of each party in a transaction to ascertain the identity of the other party.

authorization management systems Systems for allowing each user access only to those portions of a system or the Web that person is permitted to enter, based on information established by a set of access rules.

authorization policies Determine differing levels of access to information assets for different levels of users in an organization.

automation Using the computer to speed up the performance of existing tasks.

autonomic computing Effort to develop systems that can manage themselves without user intervention.

backbone Part of a network handling the major traffic and providing the primary path for traffic flowing to or from other networks.

backward chaining A strategy for searching the rule base in an expert system that acts like a problem solver by beginning with a hypothesis and seeking out more information until the hypothesis is either proved or disproved.

balanced scorecard Model for analyzing firm performance which supplements traditional financial measures with measurements from additional business perspectives, such as customers, internal business processes, and learning and growth.

bandwidth The capacity of a communications channel as measured by the difference between the highest and lowest frequencies that can be transmitted by that channel.

banner ad A graphic display on a Web page used for advertising. The banner is linked to the advertiser's Web site so that a person clicking on it will be transported to the advertiser's Web site.

batch processing A method of collecting and processing data in which transactions are accumulated and stored until a specified time when it is convenient or necessary to process them as a group.

baud A change in signal from positive to negative or vice versa that is used as a measure of transmission speed.

behavioral models Descriptions of management based on behavioral scientists' observations of what managers actually do in their jobs.

benchmarking Setting strict standards for products, services, or activities and measuring organizational performance against those standards.

best practices The most successful solutions or problem-solving methods that have been developed by a specific organization or industry.

biometric authentication Technology for authenticating system users that compares a person's unique characteristics such as fingerprints, face, or retinal image, against a stored set profile of these characteristics.

bit A binary digit representing the smallest unit of data in a computer system. It can only have one of two states, representing 0 or 1.

blade server Entire computer that fits on a single, thin card (or blade) and that is plugged into a single chassis to save space, power and complexity.

blog Popular term for Weblog, designating an informal yet structured Web site where individuals can publish stories, opinions, and links to other Web sites of interest.

blogosphere Totality of blog-related Web sites.

Bluetooth Standard for wireless personal area networks that can transmit up to 722 Kbps within a 10-meter area.

botnet A group of computers that have been infected with bot malware without users' knowledge, enabling a hacker to use the amassed resources of the computers to launch distributed denial-of-service attacks, phishing campaigns or spam.

broadband High-speed transmission technology. Also designates a single communications medium that can transmit multiple channels of data simultaneously.

bullwhip effect Distortion of information about the demand for a product as it passes from one entity to the next across the supply chain.

bus network Network topology linking a number of computers by a single circuit with all messages broadcast to the entire network.

business continuity planning Planning that focuses on how the company can restore business operations after a disaster strikes.

business driver A force in the environment to which businesses must respond and that influences the direction of business.

business ecosystem Loosely coupled but interdependent networks of suppliers, distributors, outsourcing firms, transportation service firms, and technology manufacturers

business functions Specialized tasks performed in a business organization, including manufacturing and production, sales and marketing, finance and accounting, and human resources.

business intelligence Applications and technologies to help users make better business decisions.

business model An abstraction of what an enterprise is and how the enterprise delivers a product or service, showing how the enterprise creates wealth.

business process management Methodology for revising the organization's business processes to use business processes as fundamental building blocks of corporate information systems.

business process reengineering The radical redesign of business processes, combining steps to cut waste and eliminating repetitive, paper-intensive tasks in order to improve cost, quality, and service, and to maximize the benefits of information technology.

business processes The unique ways in which organizations coordinate and organize work activities, information, and knowledge to produce a product or service.

business-to-business (B2B) electronic commerce Electronic sales of goods and services among businesses.

business-to-consumer (B2C) electronic commerce Electronic retailing of products and services directly to individual consumers.

byte A string of bits, usually eight, used to store one number or character in a computer system.

cable Internet connections Internet connections that use digital cable lines to deliver high-speed Internet access to homes and businesses.

call center An organizational department responsible for handling customer service issues by telephone and other channels.

campus area network (CAN) an interconnected set of local area networks in a limited geographical area such as a college or corporate campus.

capacity planning The process of predicting when a computer hardware system becomes saturated to ensure that adequate computing resources are available for work of different priorities and that the firm has enough computing power for its current and future needs.

capital budgeting The process of analyzing and selecting various proposals for capital expenditures.

carpal tunnel syndrome (CTS) Type of RSI in which pressure on the median nerve through the wrist's bony carpal tunnel structure produces pain.

case-based reasoning (CBR) Artificial intelligence technology that represents knowledge as a database of cases and solutions.

cellular telephone A device that transmits voice or data, using radio waves to communicate with radio antennas placed within adjacent geographic areas called cells.

centralized processing Processing that is accomplished by one large central computer.

change agent In the context of implementation, the individual acting as the catalyst during the change process to ensure successful organizational adaptation to a new system or innovation.

change management Managing the impact of organizational change associated with an innovation, such as a new information system.

channel conflict Competition between two or more different distribution chains used to sell the products or services of the same company.

channel The link by which data or voice are transmitted between sending and receiving devices in a network.

chat Live, interactive conversations over a public network.

chief information officer (CIO) Senior manager in charge of the information systems function in the firm.

chief knowledge officer (CKO) Senior executive in charge of the organization's knowledge management program.

chief security officer (CSO) Heads a formal security function for the organization and is responsible for enforcing the firm's security policy.

choice Simon's third stage of decision making, when the individual selects among the various solution alternatives.

churn rate Measurement of the number of customers who stop using or purchasing products or services from a company. Used as an indicator of the growth or decline of a firm's customer base.

classical model of management Traditional description of management that focused on its formal functions of planning, organizing, coordinating, deciding, and controlling.

click fraud Fraudulently clicking on an online ad in pay per click advertising to generate an improper charge per click.

clicks-and-mortar Business model where the Web site is an extension of a traditional bricks-and-mortar business.

clickstream tracking Tracking data about customer activities at Web sites and storing them in a log.

client The user point-of-entry for the required function in client/server computing. Normally a desktop computer, workstation, or laptop computer.

client/server computing A model for computing that splits processing between clients and servers on a network, assigning functions to the machine most able to perform the function.

coaxial cable A transmission medium consisting of thickly insulated copper wire; can transmit large volumes of data quickly.

Code Division Multiple Access (CDMA) Major cellular transmission standard in the United States that transmits over several frequencies, occupies the entire spectrum, and randomly assigns users to a range of frequencies over time.

collaborative commerce The use of digital technologies to enable multiple organizations to collaboratively design, develop, build and manage products through their life cycles.

collaborative filtering Tracking users' movements on a Web site, comparing the information gleaned about a user's behavior against data about other customers with similar interests to predict what the user would like to see next.

collaborative planning, forecasting, and replenishment (CPFR) Firms collaborating with their suppliers and buyers to formulate demand forecasts, develop production plans, and coordinate shipping, warehousing, and stocking activities.

competitive forces model Model used to describe the interaction of external influences, specifically threats and opportunities, that affect an organization's strategy and ability to compete.

complementary assets Additional assets required to derive value from a primary investment.

component-based development Building large software systems by combining pre-existing software components.

computer Physical device that takes data as an input, transforms the data by executing stored instructions, and outputs information to a number of devices.

computer abuse The commission of acts involving a computer that may not be illegal but are considered unethical.

computer crime The commission of illegal acts through the use of a computer or against a computer system.

computer forensics The scientific collection, examination, authentication, preservation, and analysis of data held on or retrieved from computer storage media in such a way that the information can be used as evidence in a court of law.

computer hardware Physical equipment used for input, processing, and output activities in an information system.

computer literacy Knowledge about information technology, focusing on understanding of how computer-based technologies work.

computer software Detailed, preprogrammed instructions that control and coordinate the work of computer hardware components in an information system.

computer virus Rogue software program that attaches itself to other software programs or data files in order to be executed, often causing hardware and software malfunctions.

computer vision syndrome (CVS) Eyestrain condition related to computer display screen use; symptoms include headaches, blurred vision, and dry and irritated eyes.

computer-aided design (CAD) Information system that automates the creation and revision of designs using sophisticated graphics software.

computer-aided software engineering (CASE) Automation of step-by-step methodologies for software and systems development to reduce the amounts of repetitive work the developer needs to do.

computer-based information systems (CBIS) Information systems that rely on computer hardware and software for processing and disseminating information.

connectivity The ability of computers and computer-based devices to communicate with each other and share information in a meaningful way without human intervention..

consumer-to-consumer (C2C) electronic commerce Consumers selling goods and services electronically to other consumers.

controls All of the methods, policies, and procedures that ensure protection of the organization's assets, accuracy and reliability of its records, and operational adherence to management standards.

conversion The process of changing from the old system to the new system.

cookies Tiny file deposited on a computer hard drive when an individual visits certain Web sites. Used to identify the visitor and track visits to the Web site.

cooptation Bringing the opposition into the process of designing and implementing a solution without giving up control of the direction and nature of the change.

copyright A statutory grant that protects creators of intellectual property against copying by others for any purpose for a minimum of 70 years.

core competency Activity at which a firm excels as a world-class leader.

core systems Systems that support functions that are absolutely critical to the organization.

cost transparency the ability of consumers to discover the actual costs merchants pay for products.

counterimplementation A deliberate strategy to thwart the implementation of an information system or an innovation in an organization.

cracker Hacker with criminal intent.

critical success factors (CSFs) A small number of easily identifiable operational goals shaped by the industry, the firm, the manager, and the broader environment that are believed to assure the success of an organization. Used to determine the information requirements of an organization.

cross-selling Marketing complementary products to customers.

culture The set of fundamental assumptions about what products the organization should produce, how and where it should produce them, and for whom they should be produced.

customer-decision-support system (CDSS) System to support the decision-making process of an existing or potential customer.

customer lifetime value (CLTV) Difference between revenues produced by a specific customer and the expenses for acquiring and servicing that customer minus the cost of promotional marketing over the lifetime of the customer relationship, expressed in today's dollars.

customer relationship management (CRM) Business and technology discipline that uses information systems to coordinate all of the business processes surrounding the firm's interactions with its customers in sales, marketing, and service.

customer relationship management systems Information systems that track all the ways in which a company interacts with its customers and analyze these interactions to optimize revenue, profitability, customer satisfaction, and customer retention.

customization The modification of a software package to meet an organization's unique requirements without destroying the package software's integrity.

cybervandalism Intentional disruption, defacement, or destruction of a Web site or corporate information system.

data Streams of raw facts representing events occurring in organizations or the physical environment before they have been organized and arranged into a form that people can understand and use.

data administration A special organizational function for managing the organization's data resources, concerned with information policy, data planning, maintenance of data dictionaries, and data quality standards.

data cleansing Activities for detecting and correcting data in a database or file that are incorrect, incomplete, improperly formatted, or redundant. Also known as data scrubbing.

data definition DBMS capability that specifies the structure and content of the database.

data dictionary An automated or manual tool for storing and organizing information about the data maintained in a database.

data-driven DSS A system that supports decision making by allowing users to extract and analyze useful information that was previously buried in large databases.

data element A field.

data flow diagram (DFD) Primary tool for structured analysis that graphically illustrates a system's component process and the flow of data between them.

data governance Policies and processes for managing the availability, usability, integrity, and security of the firm's data.

data inconsistency The presence of different values for same attribute when the same data are stored in multiple locations.

data management software Software used for creating and manipulating lists, creating files and databases to store data, and combining information for reports.

data manipulation language A language associated with a database management system that end users and programmers use to manipulate data in the database.

data mart A small data warehouse containing only a portion of the organization's data for a specified function or population of users.

data mining Analysis of large pools of data to find patterns and rules that can be used to guide decision making and predict future behavior.

data quality audit A survey and/or sample of files to determine accuracy and completeness of data in an information system.

data redundancy The presence of duplicate data in multiple data files.

data visualization Technology for helping users see patterns and relationships in large amounts of data by presenting the data in graphical form.

data warehouse A database, with reporting and query tools, that stores current and historical data extracted from various operational systems and consolidated for management reporting and analysis.

data workers People such as secretaries or bookkeepers who process the organization's paperwork.

database A group of related files.

database (rigorous definition) A collection of data organized to service many applications at the same time by storing and managing data so that they appear to be in one location.

database administration Refers to the more technical and operational aspects of managing data, including physical database design and maintenance.

database management system (DBMS) Special software to create and maintain a database and enable individual business applications to extract the data they need without having to create separate files or data definitions in their computer programs.

database server A computer in a client/server environment that is responsible for running a DBMS to process SQL statements and perform database management tasks.

dataconferencing Teleconferencing in which two or more users are able to edit and modify data files simultaneously.

decisional roles Mintzberg's classification for managerial roles where managers initiate activities, handle disturbances, allocate resources, and negotiate conflicts.

decision-support systems (DSS) Information systems at the organization's management level that combine data and sophisticated analytical models or data analysis tools to support semistructured and unstructured decision making.

dedicated lines Telephone lines that are continuously available for transmission by a lessee. Typically conditioned to transmit data at high speeds for high-volume applications.

demand planning Determining how much product a business needs to make to satisfy all its customers' demands.

denial of service (DoS) attack Flooding a network server or Web server with false communications or requests for services in order to crash the network.

dense wave division multiplexing (DWDM) Technology for boosting transmission capacity of optical fiber by using many different wavelengths to carry separate streams of data over the same fiber strand at the same time.

Descartes' rule of change A principle that states that if an action cannot be taken repeatedly, then it is not right to be taken at any time.

design Simon's second stage of decision making, when the individual conceives of possible alternative solutions to a problem.

digital cash Currency that is represented in electronic form that moves outside the normal network of money.

digital certificate An attachment to an electronic message to verify the identity of the sender and to provide the receiver with the means to encode a reply.

digital checking Systems that extend the functionality of existing checking accounts so they can be used for online shopping payments.

digital credit card payment system Secure services for credit card payments on the Internet that protect information transmitted among users, merchant sites, and processing banks.

digital dashboard Displays all of a firm's key performance indicators as graphs and charts on a single screen to provide one-page overview of all the critical measurements necessary to make key executive decisions

digital divide Large disparities in access to computers and the Internet among different social groups and different locations.

digital firm Organization where nearly all significant business processes and relationships with customers, suppliers, and employees are digitally enabled, and key corporate assets are managed through digital means.

digital goods Goods that can be delivered over a digital network.

digital market A marketplace that is created by computer and communication technologies that link many buyers and sellers.

Digital Millennium Copyright Act (DMCA) Adjusts copyright laws to the Internet Age by making it illegal to make, distribute, or use devices that circumvent technology-based protections of copy-righted materials.

digital signal A discrete waveform that transmits data coded into two discrete states as 1-bits and 0-bits, which are represented as on-off electrical pulses; used for data communications.

digital signature A digital code that can be attached to an electronically transmitted message to uniquely identify its contents and the sender.

digital subscriber line (DSL) A group of technologies providing high-capacity transmission over existing copper telephone lines.

digital wallet Software that stores credit card, electronic cash, owner identification, and address information and provides this data automatically during electronic commerce purchase transactions.

direct cutover A risky conversion approach where the new system completely replaces the old one on an appointed day.

disaster recovery planning Planning for the restoration of computing and communications services after they have been disrupted.

disintermediation The removal of organizations or business process layers responsible for certain intermediary steps in a value chain.

distance learning Education or training delivered over a distance to individuals in one or more locations.

distributed database A database that is stored in more than one physical location. Parts or copies of the database are physically stored in one location, and other parts or copies are stored and maintained in other locations.

distributed denial-of-service (DDoS) attack Numerous computers inundating and overwhelming a network from numerous launch points.

distributed processing The distribution of computer processing work among multiple computers linked by a communications network.

documentation Descriptions of how an information system works from either a technical or end-user standpoint.

domain name English-like name that corresponds to the unique 32-bit numeric Internet Protocol (IP) address for each computer connected to the Internet

Domain Name System (DNS) A hierarchical system of servers maintaining a database enabling the conversion of domain names to their numeric IP addresses.

domestic exporter Form of business organization characterized by heavy centralization of corporate activities in the home county of origin.

downsizing The process of transferring applications from large computers to smaller ones.

downtime Period of time in which an information system is not operational.

drill down The ability to move from summary data to lower and lower levels of detail.

DSS database A collection of current or historical data from a number of applications or groups. Can be a small PC database or a massive data warehouse.

DSS software system Collection of software tools that are used for data analysis, such as OLAP tools, datamining tools, or a collection of mathematical and analytical models.

due process A process in which laws are well-known and understood and there is an ability to appeal to higher authorities to ensure that laws are applied correctly.

dynamic pricing Pricing of items based on real-time interactions between buyers and sellers that determine what a item is worth at any particular moment.

e-government Use of the Internet and related technologies to digitally enable government and public sector agencies' relationships with citizens, businesses, and other arms of government.

e-learning Instruction delivered through purely digital technology, such as CD-ROMs, the Internet, or private networks.

edge computing Method for distributing the computing load (or work) across many layers of Internet computers in order to minimize response time.

efficient customer response system System that directly links consumer behavior back to distribution, production, and supply chains.

electronic billing and payment presentation system Systems used for paying routine monthly bills that allow users to view their bills electronically and pay them through electronic funds transfers from banks or credit card accounts.

electronic business (e-business) The use of the Internet and digital technology to execute all the business processes in the enterprise. Includes e-commerce as well as processes for the internal management of the firm and for coordination with suppliers and other business partners.

electronic commerce The process of buying and selling goods and services electronically involving transactions using the Internet, networks, and other digital technologies.

electronic data interchange (EDI) The direct computer-to-computer exchange between two organizations of standard business transactions, such as orders, shipment instructions, or payments.

electronic payment system The use of digital technologies, such as credit cards, smart cards and Internet-based payment systems, to pay for products and services electronically.

electronic records management (ERM) Policies, procedures, and tools for managing the retention, destruction, and storage of electronic records.

e-mail The computer-to-computer exchange of messages.

e-mail handheld Handheld device for wireless data transmission that includes small display screen and a keypad for typing short e-mail messages.

employee relationship management (ERM) Software dealing with employee issues that are closely related to CRM, such as setting objectives, employee performance management, performance-based compensation, and employee training.

encryption The coding and scrambling of messages to prevent their being read or accessed without authorization.

end-user development The development of information systems by end users with little or no formal assistance from technical specialists.

end-user interface The part of an information system through which the end user interacts with the system, such as on-line screens and commands.

end users Representatives of departments outside the information systems group for whom applications are developed.

enterprise analysis An analysis of organization-wide information requirements by looking at the entire organization in terms of organizational units, functions, processes, and data elements; helps identify the key entities and attributes in the organization's data.

enterprise applications Systems that can coordinate activities, decisions, and knowledge across many different functions, levels, and business units in a firm. Include enterprise systems, supply chain management systems, and knowledge management systems.

enterprise application integration (EAI) software Software that works with specific software platforms to tie together multiple applications to support enterprise integration.

enterprise portal Web interface providing a single entry point for accessing organizational information and services, including information from various enterprise applications and in-house legacy systems so that information appears to be coming from a single source.

enterprise software Set of integrated modules for applications such as sales and distribution, financial accounting, investment management, materials management, production planning, plant maintenance, and human resources that allow data to be used by multiple functions and business processes.

enterprise systems Integrated enterprise-wide information systems that coordinate key internal processes of the firm.

entity A person, place, thing, or event about which information must be kept.

entity-relationship diagram A methodology for documenting databases illustrating the relationship between various entities in the database.

ergonomics The interaction of people and machines in the work environment, including the design of jobs, health issues, and the end-user interface of information systems.

ethical "no free lunch" rule Assumption that all tangible and intangible objects are owned by someone else, unless there is a specific declaration otherwise, and that the creator wants compensation for this work.

ethics Principles of right and wrong that can be used by individuals acting as free moral agents to make choices to guide their behavior.

EV-DO Technology used in Verizon's cellular network service for providing anytime, anywhere broadband wireless Internet access for PCs and other devices at average speeds of 300 to 500 Kbps. Stands for Evolution Data Optimized.

evil twins Wireless networks that pretend to be legitimate to entice participants to log on and reveal passwords or credit card numbers.

exchange Third-party Net marketplace that is primarily transaction oriented and that connects many buyers and suppliers for spot purchasing.

executive support systems (ESS) Information systems at the organization's strategic level designed to address unstructured decision making through advanced graphics and communications.

expert system Knowledge-intensive computer program that captures the expertise of a human in limited domains of knowledge.

explicit knowledge Knowledge that has been documented.

external integration tools Project management technique that links the work of the implementation team to that of users at all organizational levels.

extranet Private intranet that is accessible to authorized outsiders.

Fair Information Practices (FIP) A set of principles originally set forth in 1973 that governs the collection and use of information about individuals and forms the basis of most U.S. and European privacy laws.

fault-tolerant computer systems Systems that contain extra hardware, software, and power supply components that can back a system up and keep it running to prevent system failure.

feasibility study As part of the systems analysis process, the way to determine whether the solution is achievable, given the organization's resources and constraints.

feedback Output that is returned to the appropriate members of the organization to help them evaluate or correct input.

fiber-optic cable A fast, light, and durable transmission medium consisting of thin strands of clear glass fiber bound into cables. Data are transmitted as light pulses.

field A grouping of characters into a word, a group of words, or a complete number, such as a person's name or age.

file transfer protocol (FTP) Tool for retrieving and transferring files from a remote computer.

file A group of records of the same type.

finance and accounting information systems Systems keep track of the firm's financial assets and fund flows.

firewall Hardware and software placed between an organization's internal network and an external network to prevent outsiders from invading private networks.

focused differentiation Competitive strategy for developing new market niches for specialized products or services where a business can compete in the target area better than its competitors.

foreign key Field in a database table that enables users find related information in another database table.

formal control tools Project management technique that helps monitor the progress toward completion of a task and fulfillment of goals.

formal planning tools Project management technique that structures and sequences tasks, budgeting time, money, and technical resources required to complete the tasks.

forward chaining A strategy for searching the rule base in an expert system that begins with the information entered by the user and searches the rule base to arrive at a conclusion.

fourth-generation language A programming language that can be employed directly by end users or less-skilled programmers to develop computer applications more rapidly than conventional programming languages.

frame relay A shared network service technology that packages data into bundles for transmission but does not use error-correction routines. Cheaper and faster than packet switching.

franchiser Form of business organization in which a product is created, designed, financed, and initially produced in the home country, but for product-specific reasons relies heavily on foreign personnel for further production, marketing, and human resources.

fuzzy logic Rule-based AI that tolerates imprecision by using nonspecific terms called membership functions to solve problems.

Gantt chart Visually representats the timing, duration, and resource requirements of project tasks.

genetic algorithms Problem-solving methods that promote the evolution of solutions to specified problems using the model of living organisms adapting to their environment.

geographic information system (GIS) System with software that can analyze and display data using digitized maps to enhance planning and decision-making.

global culture The development of common expectations, shared artifacts, and social norms among different cultures and peoples

Global System for Mobile Communication (GSM) Major cellular transmission standard outside the United States, with strong international roaming capability, operating primarily in the 900-MHz and 1.8-GHz frequency bands using time division multiple access (TDMA) in which each user is allocated a portion of time on the frequency.

global positioning system (GPS) Worldwide satellite navigational system.

graphical user interface (GUI) The part of an operating system users interact with that uses graphic icons and the computer mouse to issue commands and make selections.

Gramm-Leach-Bliley Act Requires financial institutions to ensure the security and confidentiality of customer data.

grid computing Applying the resources of many computers in a network to a single problem.

group decision-support system (GDSS) An interactive computer-based system to facilitate the solution to unstructured problems by a set of decision makers working together as a group.

groupware Software that provides functions and services that support the collaborative activities of work groups.

hacker A person who gains unauthorized access to a computer network for profit, criminal mischief, or personal pleasure.

hertz Measure of frequency of electrical impulses per second, with 1 Hertz equivalent to 1 cycle per second.

high-availability computing Tools and technologies ,including backup hardware resources, to enable a system to recover quickly from a crash.

HIPAA Law outlining rules for medical security, privacy, and the management of health care records.

home page A World Wide Web text and graphical screen display that welcomes the user and explains the organization that has established the page.

hotspot A specific geographic location in which an access point provides public Wi-Fi network service.

hubs Very simple devices that connect network components, sending a packet of data to all other connected devices.

human resources information systems Systems that maintain employee records, track employee skills, job performance and training, and support planning for employee compensation and career development.

hybrid AI systems Integration of multiple AI technologies into a single application to take advantage of the best features of these technologies.

hypertext markup language (HTML) Page description language for creating Web pages and other hypermedia documents.

hypertext transfer protocol (HTTP) The communications standard used to transfer pages on the Web. Defines how messages are formatted and transmitted.

identity theft Theft of key pieces of personal information, such as credit card or Social Security numbers, in order to obtain merchandise and services in the name of the victim or to obtain false credentials.

Immanuel Kant's Categorical Imperative A principle that states that if an action is not right for everyone to take it is not right for anyone.

I-mode Standard developed by Japan's NTT DoCoMo mobile phone network for enabling cell phones to received Web-based content and services.

implementation Simon's final stage of decision-making, when the individual puts the decision into effect and reports on the progress of the solution.

industry structure The nature of participants in an industry and their relative bargaining power. Derives from the competitive forces and establishes the general business environment in an industry and the overall profitability of doing business in that environment.

inference engine The strategy used to search through the rule base in an expert system; can be forward or backward chaining.

information Data that have been shaped into a form that is meaningful and useful to human beings.

information appliance Device that has been customized to perform a few specialized computing tasks well with minimal user effort.

information asymmetry Situation where the relative bargaining power of two parties in a transaction is determined by one party in the transaction possessing more information essential to the transaction than the other party.

information density The total amount and quality of information available to all market participants, consumers, and merchants.

information policy Formal rules governing the maintenance, distribution, and use of information in an organization.

information requirements A detailed statement of the information needs that a new system must satisfy; identifies who needs what information, and when, where, and how the information is needed.

information rights The rights that individuals and organizations have with respect to information that pertains to themselves.

information system Interrelated components working together to collect, process, store, and disseminate information to support decision making, coordination, control, analysis, and visualization in an organization.

information systems department The formal organizational unit that is responsible for the information systems function in the organization.

information systems literacy Broad-based understanding of information systems that includes behavioral knowledge about organizations and individuals using information systems as well as technical knowledge about computers.

information systems managers Leaders of the various specialists in the information systems department.

information systems plan A road map indicating the direction of systems development: the rationale, the current situation, the management strategy, the implementation plan, and the budget.

information technology (IT) All the hardware and software technologies a firm needs to achieve its business objectives.

information technology (IT) infrastructure Computer hardware, software, data, storage technology, and networks providing a portfolio of shared IT resources for the organization.

informational roles Mintzberg's classification for managerial roles where managers act as the nerve centers of their organizations, receiving and disseminating critical information.

informed consent Consent given with knowledge of all the facts needed to make a rational decision.

input The capture or collection of raw data from within the organization or from its external environment for processing in an information system.

instant messaging Chat service that allows participants to create their own private chat channels so that a person can be alerted whenever someone on his or her private list is on-line to initiate a chat session with that particular individual.

intangible benefits Benefits that are not easily quantified; they include more efficient customer service or enhanced decision making.

Integrated Services Digital Network (ISDN) International standard for transmitting voice, video, image, and data to support a wide range of service over the public telephone lines.

intellectual property Intangible property created by individuals or corporations that is subject to protections under trade secret, copyright, and patent law.

intelligence The first of Simon's four stages of decision making, when the individual collects information to identify problems occurring in the organization.

intelligent agent Software program that uses a built-in or learned knowledge base to carry out specific, repetitive, and predictable tasks for an individual user, business process, or software application.

internal integration tools Project management technique that ensures that the implementation team operates as a cohesive unit.

Internal Rate of Return (IRR) The rate of return or profit that an investment is expected to earn.

international information systems architecture The basic information systems required by organizations to coordinate worldwide trade and other activities.

Internet Global network of networks using universal standards to connect millions of different networks.

Internet Protocol (IP) address Four-part numeric address indicating a unique computer location on the Internet.

Internet Service Provider (ISP) A commercial organization with a permanent connection to the Internet that sells temporary connections to subscribers.

Internet telephony Technologies that use the Internet Protocol's packet-switched connections for voice service.

Internet2 Research network with new protocols and transmission speeds that provides an infrastructure for supporting high-bandwidth Internet applications.

internetworking The linking of separate networks, each of which retains its own identity, into an interconnected network.

interorganizational systems Information systems that automate the flow of information across organizational boundaries and link a company to its customers, distributors, or suppliers.

interpersonal roles Mintzberg's classification for managerial roles where managers act as figureheads and leaders for the organization.

intranet An internal network based on Internet and World Wide Web technology and standards.

intrusion detection system Tools to monitor the most vulnerable points in a network to detect and deter unauthorized intruders.

investment workstation Powerful desktop computer for financial specialists, which is optimized to access and manipulate massive amounts of financial data.

ISO 17799 International set of standards and best practices for security and control.

iterative A process of repeating over and over again the steps to build a system.

Java Programming language that can deliver only the software functionality needed for a particular task, such as a small applet downloaded from a network; can run on any computer and operating system.

Joint Application Design (JAD) Process to accelerate the generation of information requirements by having end users and information systems specialists work together in intensive interactive design sessions.

just-in-time Scheduling system for minimizing inventory by having components arrive exactly at the moment they are needed and finished goods shipped as soon as they leave the assembly line.

key field A field in a record that uniquely identifies instances of that record so that it can be retrieved, updated, or sorted.

key logger Spyware that records every keystroke made on a computer to steal personal information or passwords or to launch Internet attacks.

knowledge Concepts, experience, and insight that provide a framework for creating, evaluating, and using information.

knowledge–and information-intense products Products that require a great deal of learning and knowledge to produce.

knowledge base Model of human knowledge that is used by expert systems.

knowledge discovery Identification of novel and valuable patterns in large databases.

knowledge engineer A specialist who elicits information and expertise from other professionals and translates it into a set of rules, or frames, for an expert system.

knowledge management The set of processes developed in an organization to create, gather, store, maintain, and disseminate the firm's knowledge.

knowledge management systems Systems that support the creation, capture, storage, and dissemination of firm expertise and knowledge.

knowledge network system Online directory for locating corporate experts in well-defined knowledge domains.

knowledge repository Collection of documented internal and external knowledge in a single location for more efficient management and utilization by the organization.

knowledge workers People such as engineers or architects who design products or services and create knowledge for the organization.

learning management system (LMS) Tools for the management, delivery, tracking, and assessment of various types of employee learning.

legacy system A system that has been in existence for a long time and that continues to be used to avoid the high cost of replacing or redesigning it.

legitimacy The extent to which one's authority is accepted on grounds of competence, vision, or other qualities. Making judgments and taking actions on the basis of narrow or personal characteristics.

liability The existence of laws that permit individuals to recover the damages done to them by other actors, systems, or organizations.

Linux Reliable and compactly designed operating system that is an offshoot of UNIX and that can run on many different hardware platforms and is available free or at very low cost. Used as alternative to UNIX and Windows NT.

local area network (LAN) A telecommunications network that requires its own dedicated channels and that encompasses a limited distance, usually one building or several buildings in close proximity.

mainframe Largest category of computer, used for major business processing.

maintenance Changes in hardware, software, documentation, or procedures to a production system to correct errors, meet new requirements, or improve processing efficiency.

malware Malicious software programs such as computer viruses, worms, and Trojan horses.

managed security service provider (MSSP) Company that provides security management services for subscribing clients.

management information systems (MIS) The study of information systems focusing on their use in business and management..

management-level systems Information systems that support the monitoring, controlling, decision-making, and administrative activities of middle managers.

managerial roles Expectations of the activities that managers should perform in an organization.

man-month The traditional unit of measurement used by systems designers to estimate the length of time to complete a project. Refers to the amount of work a person can be expected to complete in a month.

manufacturing and production information systems Systems that deal with the planning, development, and production of products and services and with controlling the flow of production.

marketspace A marketplace extended beyond traditional boundaries and removed from a temporal and geographic location.

mashups Composite software applications that depend on high-speed networks, universal communication standards, and open-source code.

mass customization The capacity to offer individually tailored products or services using mass production resources..

megahertz A measure of cycle speed, or the pacing of events in a computer; one megahertz equals one million cycles per second.

menu costs Merchants' costs of changing prices.

metric A standard measurement of performance.

metropolitan area network (MAN) Network that spans a metropolitan area, usually a city and its major suburbs. Its geographic scope falls between a WAN and a LAN.

microbrowser Web browser software with a small file size that can work with low-memory constraints, tiny screens of handheld wireless devices, and low bandwidth of wireless networks.

micropayment Payment for a very small sum of money, often less than $10.

microprocessor Very large scale integrated circuit technology that integrates the computer's memory, logic, and control on a single chip.

microwave A high-volume, long-distance, point-to-point transmission in which high-frequency radio signals are transmitted through the atmosphere from one terrestrial transmission station to another.

middle management People in the middle of the organizational hierarchy who are responsible for carrying out the plans and goals of senior management.

middleware Software that connects two disparate applications, allowing them to communicate with each other and to exchange data.

midrange computer Middle-size computer that is capable of supporting the computing needs of smaller organizations or of managing networks of other computers.

minicomputer Middle-range computer used in systems for universities, factories, or research laboratories.

MIS audit Identifies all the controls that govern individual information systems and assesses their effectiveness.

mobile commerce (m-commerce) The use of wireless devices, such as cell phones or handheld digital information appliances, to conduct both business-to-consumer and business-to-business e-commerce transactions over the Internet.

mobile wallets (m-wallets) Store m-commerce shoppers' personal information and credit card numbers to expedite the purchase process.

moblog Specialized blog featuring photos with captions posted from mobile phones.

model An abstract representation that illustrates the components or relationships of a phenomenon.

model-driven DSS Primarily stand-alone system that uses some type of model to perform "what-if" and other kinds of analyses.

modem A device for translating a computer's digital signals into analog form for transmission over ordinary telephone lines, or for translating analog signals back into digital form for reception by a computer.

module A logical unit of a program that performs one or several functions.

Moore's Law Assertion that the number of components on a chip doubles each year

MP3 (MPEG3) Compression standard that can compress audio files for transfer over the Internet with virtually no loss in quality.

multicore processor Integrated circuit to which two or more processors have been attached for enhanced performance, reduced power consumption and more efficient simultaneous processing of multiple tasks.

multimedia The integration of two or more types of media such as text, graphics, sound, voice, full-motion video, or animation into a computer-based application.

multinational Form of business organization that concentrates financial management and control out of a central home base while decentralizing

multiplexing Ability of a single communications channel to carry data transmissions from multiple sources simultaneously.

multitiered (N-tier) client/server architecture Client/server network which the work of the entire network is balanced over several different levels of servers.

nanotechnology Technology that builds structures and processes based on the manipulation of individual atoms and molecules.

natural language Nonprocedural language that enables users to communicate with the computer using conversational commands resembling human speech.

net marketplace A single digital marketplace based on Internet technology linking many buyers to many sellers.

net present value (NPV) The amount of money an investment is worth, taking into account its cost, earnings, and the time value of money.

network The linking of two or more computers to share data or resources, such as a printer.

network address translation (NAT) Conceals the IP addresses of the organization's internal host computer(s) to prevent sniffer programs outside the firewall from ascertaining them and using that information to penetrate internal systems.

network economics Model of strategic systems at the industry level based on the concept of a network where adding another participant entails zero marginal costs but can create much larger marginal gains.

network interface card (NIC) Expansion card inserted into a computer to enable it to connect to a network.

network operating system (NOS) Special software that routes and manages communications on the network and coordinates network resources.

networking and telecommunications technology Physical devices and software that link various computer hardware components and transfer data from one physical location to another.

neural network Hardware or software that attempts to emulate the processing patterns of the biological brain.

nonobvious relationship awareness (NORA) Technology that can find obscure hidden connections between people or other entities by analyzing information from many different sources to correlate relationships.

normalization The process of creating small stable data structures from complex groups of data when designing a relational database.

object Software building block that combines data and the procedures acting on the data.

object-oriented DBMS An approach to data management that stores both data and the procedures acting on the data as objects that can be automatically retrieved and shared; the objects can contain multimedia.

object-oriented development Approach to systems development that uses the object as the basic unit of systems analysis and design. The system is modeled as a collection o objects and the relationship between them.

object-oriented programming An approach to software development that combines data and procedures into a single object.

object-relational DBMS A database management system that combines the capabilities of a relational DBMS for storing traditional information and the capabilities of an object-oriented DBMS for storing graphics and multimedia.

offshore software outsourcing Outsourcing systems development work or maintenance of existing systems to external vendors in another country.

on-demand computing Firms off-loading peak demand for computing power to remote, large-scale data processing centers, investing just enough to handle average processing loads and paying for only as much additional computing power as the market demands. Also called utility computing.

on-line analytical processing (OLAP) Capability for manipulating and analyzing large volumes of data from multiple perspectives.

online processing A method of collecting and processing data in which transactions are entered directly into the computer system and processed immediately.

online transaction processing Transaction processing mode in which transactions entered on-line are immediately processed by the computer.

open-source software Software that provides free access to its program code, allowing users to modify the program code to make improvements or fix errors.

operating system The system software that manages and controls the activities of the computer.

operational CRM Customer-facing applications, such as sales force automation, call center and customer service support, and marketing automation.

operational management People who monitor the day-to-day activities of the organization.

operational-level systems Information systems that monitor the elementary activities and transactions of the organization.

opt-in Model of informed consent permitting prohibiting an organization from collecting any personal information unless the individual specifically takes action to approve information collection and use.

opt-out Model of informed consent permitting the collection of personal information until the consumer specifically requests that the data not be collected.

optical network High-speed networking technologies for transmitting data in the form of light pulses.

organization (behavioral definition) A collection of rights, privileges, obligations, and responsibilities that are delicately balanced over a period of time through conflict and conflict resolution.

organization (technical definition) A stable, formal, social structure that takes resources from the environment and processes them to produce outputs.

organizational and management capital Investments in organization and management such as new business processes, management behavior, organizational culture, or training.

organizational impact analysis Study of the way a proposed system will affect organizational structure, attitudes, decision making, and operations.

organizational learning Creation of new standard operating procedures and business processes that reflect organizations' experience.

output The distribution of processed information to the people who will use it or to the activities for which it will be used.

outsourcing The practice of contracting computer center operations, telecommunications networks, or applications development to external vendors.

P3P Industry standard designed to give users more control over personal information gathered on Web sites they visit. Stands for Platform for Privacy Preferences Project.

packet filtering Examines selected fields in the headers of data packets flowing between a trusted network and the Internet.

packet switching Technology that breaks messages into small, fixed bundles of data and routes them in the most economical way through any available communications channel..

paradigm shift Radical reconceptualization of the nature of the business and the nature of the organization.

parallel strategy A safe and conservative conversion approach where both the old system and its potential replacement are run together for a time until everyone is assured that the new one functions correctly.

particularism Making judgments and taking action on the basis of narrow or personal characteristics, in all its forms (religious, nationalistic, ethnic, regionalism, geopolitical position).

partner relationship management (PRM) Automation of the firm's relationships with its selling partners using customer data and analytical tools to improve coordination and customer sales.

patch Small pieces of software to repair the software flaws without disturbing the proper operation of the software.

patent A legal document that grants the owner an exclusive monopoly on the ideas behind an invention for 17 years; designed to ensure that inventors of new machines or methods are rewarded for their labor while making widespread use of their inventions.

payback method A measure of the time required to pay back the initial investment on a project.

peer-to-peer Network architecture that gives equal power to all computers on the network; used primarily in small networks.

peer-to-peer payment system Electronic payment system for people who want to send money to vendors or individuals who are not set up to accept credit card payments.

personal area network (PAN) Computer network used for communication among digital devices (including telephones and PDAs) that are close to one person.

personal digital assistant (PDA) Small, pen-based, handheld computer with built-in wireless telecommunications capable of entirely digital communications transmission.

personalization Ability of merchants to target marketing messages to specific individuals by adjusting the message for a person's name, interests, and past purchases.

PERT chart Network diagram depicting project tasks and their interrelationships.

pharming Phishing technique that redirects users to a bogus Web page, even when an individual enters the correct Web page address.

phased approach Introduces the new system in stages either by functions or by organizational units.

phishing Form of spoofing involving setting up fake Web sites or sending e-mail messages that resemble those of legitimate businesses that ask users for confidential personal data.

pilot study A strategy to introduce the new system to a limited area of the organization until it is proven to be fully functional; only then can the conversion to the new system across the entire organization take place.

pivot table Spreadsheet tool for reorganizing and summarizing two or more dimensions of data in a tabular format.

podcasting Publishing audio broadcasts via the Internet so that subscribing users can download audio files onto their personal computers or portable music players.

pop-up ad Ad that opens automatically and does not disappear until the user clicks on it.

portal Web interface for presenting integrated personalized content from a variety of sources. Also refers to a Web site service that provides an initial point of entry to the Web.

portfolio analysis An analysis of the portfolio of potential applications within a firm to determine the risks and benefits, and to select among alternatives for information systems.

post-implementation audit Formal review process conducted after a system has been placed in production to determine how well the system has met its original objectives.

predictive analysis Use of datamining techniques, historical data, and assumptions about future conditions to predict outcomes of events.

present value The value, in current dollars, of a payment or stream of payments to be received in the future.

price discrimination Selling the same goods, or nearly the same goods, to different targeted groups at different prices.

price transparency The ease with which consumers can find out the variety of prices in a market.

primary activities Activities most directly related to the production and distribution of a firm's products or services.

primary key Unique identifier for all the information in any row of a database table.

privacy The claim of individuals to be left alone, free from surveillance or interference from other individuals, organizations, or the state.

private exchange Another term for a private industrial network.

private industrial networks Web-enabled networks linking systems of multiple firms in an industry for the coordination of trans-organizational business processes.

process specifications Describe the logic of the processes occurring within the lowest levels of a data flow diagram.

processing The conversion, manipulation, and analysis of raw input into a form that is more meaningful to humans.

✓ **procurement** Sourcing goods and materials, negotiating with suppliers, paying for goods, and making delivery arrangements.

✓ **product differentiation** Competitive strategy for creating brand loyalty by developing new and unique products and services that are not easily duplicated by competitors.

production The stage after the new system is installed and the conversion is complete; during this time the system is reviewed by users and technical specialists to determine how well it has met its original goals.

production or service workers People who actually produce the products or services of the organization.

profiling The use of computers to combine data from multiple sources and create electronic dossiers of detailed information on individuals.

program-data dependence The close relationship between data stored in files and the software programs that update and maintain those files. Any change in data organization or format requires a change in all the programs associated with those files.

programmers Highly trained technical specialists who write computer software instructions.

programming The process of translating the system specifications prepared during the design stage into program code.

project Planned series of related activities for achieving a specific business objective.

project management Application of knowledge, tools, and techniques to achieve specific targets within a specified budget and time period.

protocol A set of rules and procedures that govern transmission between the components in a network.

prototype The preliminary working version of an information system for demonstration and evaluation purposes.

prototyping The process of building an experimental system quickly and inexpensively for demonstration and evaluation so that users can better determine information requirements.

public key encryption Uses two keys: one shared (or public) and one private.

public key infrastructure(PKI) System for creating public and private keys using a certificate authority (CA) and digital certificates for authentication.

pull-based model Supply chain driven by actual customer orders or purchases so that members of the supply chain produce and deliver only what customers have ordered.

pure-play Business models based purely on the Internet.

push-based model Supply chain driven by production master schedules based on forecasts or best guesses of demand for products, and products are "pushed" to customers.

query language Software tool that provides immediate online answers to requests for information that are not predefined.

radio-frequency identification (RFID) Technology using tiny tags with embedded microchips containing data about an item and its location to transmit short-distance radio signals to special RFID readers that then pass the data on to a computer for processing.

Rapid Application Development (RAD) Process for developing systems in a very short time period by using prototyping, fourth-generation tools, and close teamwork among users and systems specialists.

rational model Model of human behavior based on the belief that people, organizations, and nations engage in basically consistent, value-maximizing calculations.

rationalization of procedures The streamlining of standard operating procedures, eliminating obvious bottlenecks, so that automation makes operating procedures more efficient.

real options pricing models Models for evaluating information technology investments with uncertain returns by using techniques for valuing financial options.

record A group of related fields.

recovery-oriented computing Computer systems designed to recover rapidly when mishaps occur.

relational DBMS A type of logical database model that treats data as if they were stored in two-dimensional tables. It can relate data stored in one table to data in another as long as the two tables share a common data element.

Repetitive Stress Injury (RSI) Occupational disease that occurs when muscle groups are forced through repetitive actions with high-impact loads or thousands of repetitions with low-impact loads.

Request for Proposal (RFP) A detailed list of questions submitted to vendors of software or other services to determine how well the vendor's product can meet the organization's specific requirements.

resource allocation The determination of how costs, time, and personnel are assigned to different phases of a systems development project.

responsibility Accepting the potential costs, duties, and obligations for the decisions one makes.

richness Measurement of the depth and detail of information that a business can supply to the customer as well as information the business collects about the customer.

ring network A network topology in which all computers are linked by a closed loop in a manner that passes data in one direction from one computer to another.

risk assessment Determining the potential frequency of the occurrence of a problem and the potential damage if the problem were to occur. Used to determine the cost/benefit of a control.

Risk Aversion Principle Principle that one should take the action that produces the least harm or incurs the least cost.

router Specialized communications processor that forwards packets of data from one network to another network.

routines Precise rules, procedures and practices that have been developed to cope with expected situations.

RSS Technology using aggregator software to pull content from Web sites and feed it automatically to subscribers' computers.

safe harbor Private self-regulating policy and enforcement mechanism that meets the objectives of government regulations but does not involve government regulation or enforcement.

Sales and marketing information systems Systems that help the firm identify customers for the firm's products or services, develop products and services to meet their needs, promote these products and services, sell the products and services, and provide ongoing customer support.

Glossary

Sarbanes-Oxley Act Law passed in 2002 that imposes responsibility on companies and their management to protect investors by safeguarding the accuracy and integrity of financial information that is used internally and released externally.

satellite The transmission of data using orbiting satellites that serve as relay stations for transmitting microwave signals over very long distances.

scalability The ability of a computer, product, or system to expand to serve a larger number of users without breaking down.

scope Defines what work is and is not included in a project.

scoring model A quick method for deciding among alternative systems based on a system of ratings for selected objectives.

search costs The time and money spent locating a suitable product and determining the best price for that product.

search engine A tool for locating specific sites or information on the Internet.

search engine marketing Use of search engines to deliver in their results sponsored links, for which advertisers have paid.

Secure Hypertext Transfer Protocol (S-HTTP) Protocol used for encrypting data flowing over the Internet; limited to individual messages.

Secure Sockets Layer (SSL) Enables client and server computers to manage encryption and decryption activities as they communicate with each other during a secure Web session.

security Policies, procedures, and technical measures used to prevent unauthorized access, alteration, theft, or physical damage to information systems.

security policy Statements ranking information risks, identifying acceptable security goals, and identifying the mechanisms for achieving these goals.

semistructured decisions Decisions in which only part of the problem has a clear-cut answer provided by an accepted procedure.

semistructured knowledge Information in the form of less structured objects, such as e-mail, chat room exchanges, videos, graphics, brochures, or bulletin boards.

semistructured knowledge system System for organizing and storing less structured information, such as e-mail, voice mail, videos, graphics, brochures, or bulleting boards. Also known as digital asset management system.

senior management People occupying the topmost hierarchy in an organization who are responsible for making long-range decisions.

sensitivity analysis Models that ask "what-if" questions repeatedly to determine the impact of changes in one or more factors on the outcomes.

server Computer specifically optimized to provide software and other resources to other computers over a network.

server farm Large group of servers maintained by a commercial vendor and made available to subscribers for electronic commerce and other activities requiring heavy use of servers.

service-oriented architecture Software architecture of a firm built on a collection of software programs that communicate with each other to perform assigned tasks to create a working software application.

service platform Integration of multiple applications from multiple business functions, business units, or business partners to deliver a seamless experience for the customer, employee, manager, or business partner.

shopping bot Software with varying levels of built-in intelligence to help electronic commerce shoppers locate and evaluate products or service they might wish to purchase.

short message service (SMS) Text message service used by digital cell phone systems to send and receive short alphanumeric messages less than 160 characters in length.

Simple Object Access Protocol (SOAP) Set of rules that allows Web services applications to pass data and instructions to one another.

six sigma A specific measure of quality, representing 3.4 defects per million opportunities; used to designate a set of methodologies and techniques for improving quality and reducing costs.

smart card A credit-card-size plastic card that stores digital information and that can be used for electronic payments in place of cash.

smart phone Wireless phone with voice, text, and Internet capabilities.

sniffer Type of eavesdropping program that monitors information traveling over a network.

social bookmarking Capability for users to save their bookmarks to Web pages on a public Web site and tag these bookmarks with keywords to organize documents and share information with others.

social engineering Tricking people into revealing their passwords by pretending to rrbe legitimate users or members of a company in need of information.

social networking sites Online community for expanding users' business or social contacts by making connections through their mutual business or personal connections.

social shopping Use of Web sites featuring user-created Web pages to share knowledge about items of interest to other shoppers.

sociotechnical design Design to produce information systems that blend technical efficiency with sensitivity to organizational and human needs.

sociotechnical view Seeing systems as composed of both technical and social elements.

software package A prewritten, precoded, commercially available set of programs that eliminates the need to write software programs for certain functions.

spam Unsolicited commercial e-mail.

spamming Form of abuse in which thousands and even hundreds of thousands of unsolicited e-mail and electronic messages are sent out, creating a nuisance for both businesses and individual users.

spyware Technology that aids in gathering information about a person or organization without their knowledge.

star network A network topology in which all computers and other devices are connected to a central host computer. All communications between network devices must pass through the host computer.

stateful inspection Determines whether network packets are part of an ongoing dialogue between a sender and receiver.

storage area network (SAN) A high-speed network dedicated to storage that connects different kinds of storage devices, such as tape libraries and disk arrays so they can be shared by multiple servers.

storage technology Physical media and software governing the storage and organization of data for use in an information system.

stored value payment systems Systems enabling consumers to make instant on-line payments to merchants and other individuals based on value stored in a digital account.

strategic information systems Computer systems at any level of the organization that change goals, operations, products, services, or environmental relationships to help the organization gain a competitive advantage.

strategic transitions A movement from one level of sociotechnical system to another. Often required when adopting strategic systems that demand changes in the social and technical elements of an organization.

structure chart System documentation showing each level of design, the relationship among the levels, and the overall place in the design structure; can document one program, one system, or part of one program.

structured Refers to the fact that techniques are carefully drawn up, step by step, with each step building on a previous one.

structured decisions Decisions that are repetitive, routine, and have a definite procedure for handling them.

structured knowledge Knowledge in the form of structured documents and reports.

structured knowledge system System for organizing structured knowledge in a repository where it can be accessed throughout the organization. Also known as content management system.

Structured Query Language (SQL) The standard data manipulation language for relational database management systems.

supply chain Network of organizations and business processes for procuring materials, transforming raw materials into intermediate and finished products, and distributing the finished products to customers.

supply chain execution systems Systems to manage the flow of products through distribution centers and warehouses to ensure that products are delivered to the right locations in the most efficient manner.

supply chain management Integration of supplier, distributor, and customer logistics requirements into one cohesive process.

supply chain management systems Information systems that automate the flow of information between a firm and its suppliers in order to optimize the planning, sourcing, manufacturing, and delivery of products and services.

supply chain planning systems Systems that enable a firm to generate demand forecasts for a product and to develop sourcing and manufacturing plans for that product.

support activities Activities that make the delivery of a firm's primary activities possible. Consist of the organization's infrastructure, human resources, technology, and procurement.

switch Device to connect network components that has more intelligence than a hub and can filter and forward data to a specified destination.

✓**switching costs** The expense a customer or company incurs in lost time and expenditure of resources when changing from one supplier or system to a competing supplier or system.

syndicator Business aggregating content or applications from multiple sources, packaging them for distribution, and reselling them to third-party Web sites.

system testing Tests the functioning of the information system as a whole in order to determine if discrete modules will function together as planned.

systems analysis The analysis of a problem that the organization will try to solve with an information system.

systems analysts Specialists who translate business problems and requirements into information requirements and systems, acting as liaison between the information systems department and the rest of the organization.

systems design Details how a system will meet the information requirements as determined by the systems analysis.

systems development The activities that go into producing an information systems solution to an organizational problem or opportunity.

systems life cycle A traditional methodology for developing an information system that partitions the systems development process into formal stages that must be completed sequentially with a very formal division of labor between end users and information systems specialists.

T lines High-speed data lines leased from communications providers, such as T-1 lines (with a transmission capacity of 1.544 Mbps).

tacit knowledge Expertise and experience of organizational members that has not been formally documented.

tangible benefits Benefits that can be quantified and assigned a monetary value; they include lower operational costs and increased cash flows.

taxonomy Method of classifying things according to a predetermined system.

teamware Group collaboration software that is customized for teamwork.

technology standards Specifications that establish the compatibility of products and the ability to communicate in a network.

technostress Stress induced by computer use; symptoms include aggravation, hostility toward humans, impatience, and enervation.

telecommunications system A collection of compatible hardware and software arranged to communicate information from one location to another.

teleconferencing The ability to confer with a group of people simultaneously using the telephone or electronic-mail group communication software.

Telnet Network tool that allows someone to log on to one computer system while doing work on another.

test plan Prepared by the development team in conjunction with the users; it includes all of the preparations for the series of tests to be performed on the system.

testing The exhaustive and thorough process that determines whether the system produces the desired results under known conditions.

token Physical device similar to an identification card that is designed to prove the identity of a single user.

touch point Method of firm interaction with a customer, such as telephone, e-mail, customer service desk, conventional mail, or point-of-purchase.

topology The way in which the components of a network are connected.

Total Cost of Ownership (TCO) Designates the total cost of owning technology resources, including initial purchase costs, the cost of hardware and software upgrades, maintenance, technical support, and training.

Total Quality Management (TQM) A concept that makes quality control a responsibility to be shared by all people in an organization.

trade secret Any intellectual work or product used for a business purpose that can be classified as belonging to that business, provided it is not based on information in the public domain.

✓**transaction cost theory** Economic theory stating that firms grow larger because they can conduct marketplace transactions internally more cheaply than they can with external firms in the marketplace.

transaction processing systems (TPS) Computerized systems that perform and record the daily routine transactions necessary to conduct the business; they serve the organization's operational level.

transborder data flow The movement of information across international boundaries in any form.

Transmission Control Protocol/Internet Protocol (TCP/IP) Dominant model for achieving connectivity among different networks. Provides a universally agree-on method for breaking up digital messages into packets, routing them to the proper addresses, and then reassembling them into coherent messages.

transnational Truly global form of business organization with no national headquarters; value-added activities are managed from a global perspective without reference to national borders, optimizing sources of supply and demand and local competitive advantage.

transport layer security (TLS) Successor to SSL, which enables client and server computers to manage encryption and decryption activities while communicating during a secure Web session.

Trojan horse A software program that appears legitimate but contains a second hidden function that may cause damage.

tuple A row or record in a relational database.

twisted wire A transmission medium consisting of pairs of twisted copper wires; used to transmit analog phone conversations but can be used for data transmission.

UDDI (Universal Description, Discovery, and Integration) Allows a Web service to be listed in a directory of Web services so that it can be easily located by other organizations and systems.

Unified Modeling Language (UML) Industry standard methodology for analysis and design of an object-oriented software system.

uniform resource locator (URL) The address of a specific resource on the Internet.

unit testing The process of testing each program separately in the system. Sometimes called program testing.

UNIX Operating system for all types of computers, which is machine independent and supports multiuser processing, multitasking, and networking. Used in high-end workstations and servers.

unstructured decisions Nonroutine decisions in which the decision maker must provide judgment, evaluation, and insights into the problem definition; there is no agreed-upon procedure for making such decisions.

Usenet Forums in which people share information and ideas on a defined topic through large electronic bulletin boards where anyone can post messages on the topic for others to see and to which others can respond.

user interface The part of the information system through which the end user interacts with the system; type of hardware and the series of on-screen commands and responses required for a user to work with the system.

user-designer communications gap The difference in backgrounds, interests, and priorities that impede communication and problem solving among end users and information systems specialists.

Utilitarian Principle Principle that assumes one can put values in rank order and understand the consequences of various courses of action.

utility computing Model of computing in which companies pay only for the information technology resources they actually use during a specified time period. Also called on-demand computing or usage-based pricing.

value chain model Model that highlights the primary or support activities that add a margin of value to a firm's products or services where information systems can best be applied to achieve a competitive advantage.

value web Customer-driven network of independent firms who use information technology to coordinate their value chains to collectively produce a product or service for a market.

Value-Added Network (VAN) Private, multipath, data-only, third-party-managed network that multiple organizations use on a subscription basis.

videoconferencing Teleconferencing in which participants see each other over video screens.

virtual company Organization using networks to link people, assets and ideas to create and distribute products and services without being limited to traditional organizational boundaries or physical location.

Virtual Private Network (VPN) A secure connection between two points across the Internet to transmit corporate data. Provides a low-cost alternative to a private network.

Virtual Reality Modeling Language (VRML) A set of specifications for interactive three-dimensional modeling on the World Wide Web.

virtual reality systems Interactive graphics software and hardware that create computer-generated simulations that provide sensations that emulate real-world activities.

virtualization Presenting a set of computing resources so that they can all be accessed in ways that are not restricted by physical configuration or geographic location.

Voice over IP (VoIP) Facilities for managing the delivery of voice information using the Internet Protocol (IP).

war driving Technique in which eavesdroppers drive by buildings or park outside and try to intercept wireless network traffic.

Web 2.0 Second-generation, interactive Internet-based services that enable people to collaborate, share information, and create new services online, including mashups, blogs, RSS, and wikis.

Web browser An easy-to-use software tool for accessing the World Wide Web and the Internet.

Web bugs Tiny graphic files embedded in e-mail messages and Web pages that are designed to monitor online Internet user behavior.

Web hosting service Company with large Web server computers to maintain the Web sites of fee-paying subscribers.

Web server Software that manages requests for Web pages on the computer where they are stored and that delivers the page to the user's computer.

Web services Set of universal standards using Internet technology for integrating different applications from different sources without time-consuming custom coding. Used for linking systems of different organizations or for linking disparate systems within the same organization.

Web Services Description Language (WSDL) Common framework for describing the tasks performed by a Web service so that it can be used by other applications.

Web site All of the World Wide Web pages maintained by an organization or an individual.

Webmaster The person in charge of an organization's Web site.

Wi-Fi Standards for Wireless Fidelity and refers to the 802.11 family of wireless networking standards.

Wide Area Network (WAN) Telecommunications network that spans a large geographical distance. May consist of a variety of cable, satellite, and microwave technologies.

wiki Collaborative Web site where visitors can add, delete, or modify content, including the work of previous authors.

WiMax Popular term for IEEE Standard 802.16 for wireless networking over a range of up to 31 miles with a data transfer rate of up to 75 Mbps. Stands for Worldwide Interoperability for Microwave Access.

Windows Microsoft family of operating systems for both network servers and client computers. The most recent version is Windows Vista.

Wintel PC Any computer that uses Intel microprocessors (or compatible processors) and a Windows operating system.

Wireless Application Protocol (WAP) System of protocols and technologies that lets cell phones and other wireless devices with tiny displays, low-bandwidth connections, and minimal memory access Web-based information and services.

wireless NIC add-in-card (network interface card) that has a built-in-radio and antenna.

wireless portals Portals with content and services optimized for mobile devices to steer users to the information they are most likely to need.

wireless sensor networks (WSNs) Networks of interconnected wireless devices with built-in processing, storage, and radio frequency sensors and antennas that are embedded into the physical environment to provide measurements of many points over large spaces.

wisdom The collective and individual experience of applying knowledge to the solution of problems.

WML (Wireless Markup Language) Markup language for Wireless Web sites; based on XML and optimized for tiny displays.

workflow management The process of streamlining business procedures so that documents can be moved easily and efficiently from one location to another.

World Wide Web A system with universally accepted standards for storing, retrieving, formatting, and displaying information in a networked environment.

worms Independent software programs that propagate themselves to disrupt the operation of computer networks or destroy data and other programs.

XML (eXtensible Markup Language) General-purpose language that describes the structure of a document and supports links to multiple documents, allowing data to be manipulated by the computer. Used for both Web and non-Web applications.

Index